PIERO DELLA FRANCESCA

CONTENTS

Marco Bussagli

On the cover:
Madonna del Parto (after 1459), detail; Cemetery chapel, Monterchi (Arezzo).

Opposite page:
Portrait of Sigismondo Pandolfo Malatesta (1450-1451); Louvre, Paris.

Right:
Sigismondo Malatesta before St. Sigismund (1451), detail; Tempio Malatestiano, Rimini.

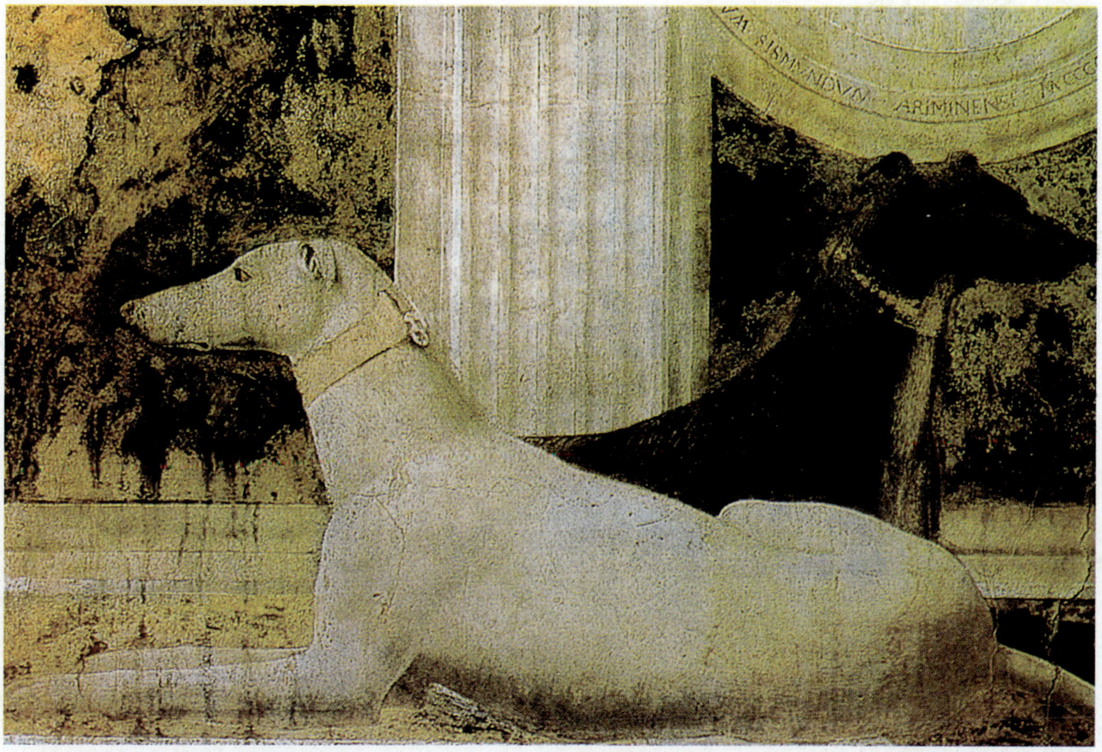

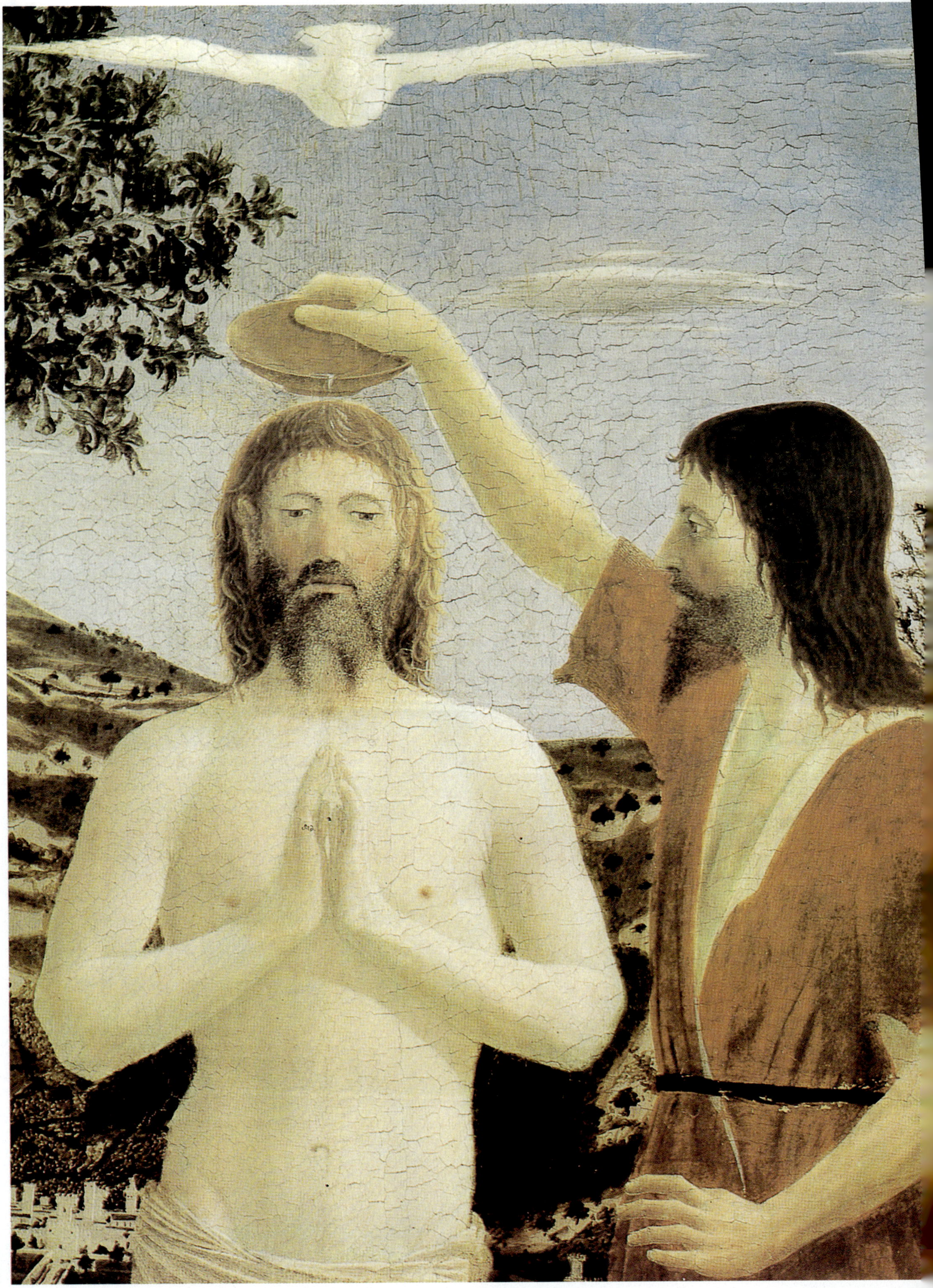

Piero the Mathematician

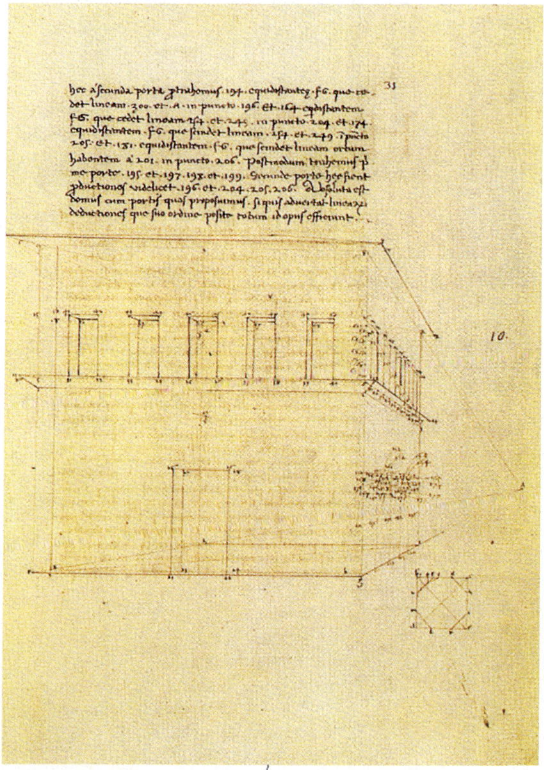

Above:
De prospectiva pingendi (before 1482), cod. S.P.6 bis, fol. 25 v; Biblioteca Ambrosiana, Milan.

Opposite page:
Baptism of Christ (1459-1460 circa), detail; National Gallery, London.

«**TIERRA, TIERRA!**», called the sailor Rodrigo de Triana aboard the Pinta on that 12 October 1492 that so radically changed the course of history. Oddly enough, the coincidence does not hide the realization of some designs of fate, rather it confirms the indisputable importance of an event that was entered on that same day more or less five hundred years ago in the *Libro III dei morti* (Registry of Deaths) of the Confraternita di San Bartolomeo in Borgo Sansepolcro with the following words: «On this 12th day of October 1492 Maestro Pier dei Franceschi famous painter [was] buried in Badia»[1].

No other date could have been more significant for Piero's death. In conventional historiographic chronology that day marks the end of the Middle Ages and the start of the Modern Age. It was an epoch-making turning point that equals the one marked by the works of the master from Borgo, for whom the mere definition of painter or artist is inadequate when describing the scope of this complex character who was, above all, an intellectual. It is proved by the fact that, in addition to painting, Piero felt the need to set down the methods and criteria for making art in theoretical writings. In his treatises he also dealt with mathematics, not unusual for a fifteenth century architect, but rare for a painter of the period.

Therefore, even though we generally speak of Piero's theoretical writings in footnotes to his paintings, as if they were a corpus of secondary importance, in reality his treatises make it possible to understand exactly what painting meant to him and to discover as Arrighi points out, that «mathematics was one of the components of Piero della Francesca's *forma mentis*, and one of the most important at that»[2]. Some may raise the objection that these writings date from the last decades of his work, so that *De prospectiva pingendi* and the mathematical description of regular solids and semi-regular polyhedrons in *De quinque corporibus regolaribus* could be the result of a senile passion. This is anything but true. As Vasari recounted, «In his youth Piero applied himself to mathematics, and although when he became fifteen it was decided that he should be a painter he nevertheless always kept up his earlier studies. Indeed, it was because of his accomplishments both as a mathematician and a painter...»[3].

That Piero was a real mathematician is also borne out *ad abundantiam* in the *Trattato d'abaco* of which, unfortunately, neither the date nor the name of the client are known. According to Salmi's hypothesis, it was commissioned around 1470 by a certain Bartolomeo Pichi, member of one of Borgo Sansepolcro's most important families. It seems that Pichi went to the artist so that he would write «some things about the abacus that are necessary for merchants»[4]. The treatise, which is arranged in chapters, not only reviews all arithmetic – like all late Medieval works of this type –, it deals with radicals and algebra resolving «equations above the second degree that cannot be reduced»[5]; there is another section dedicated to geometric solids which is nothing more than the Italian version of *De quinque corporibus regolaribus*.

If, among the uncertain chronology of Piero's writings the *Trattato d'abaco* was in all likelihood the first to see the light, the second theoretic text would seem to be *De prospectiva pingendi* (Perspective in painting). It was dedicated to Federico da Montefeltro and probably was a gift to him, and was therefore written before the Duke of Urbino died on 10 September 1482. The treatise, which is divided into three books was conceived as a manual for painters. Through mathematical proofs it gradually leads to a mastery of the laws of perspective. Thus, the first book is dedicated to plane geometry and teaches how to bring, first the points that are to be on the real plane, then the straight lines and then the plane geometric figures onto the sloping plane (that is a plane which is perspectively tilted according to a given viewpoint). The second book develops the procedure by applying it to solid geometry. The third, geometrically determines the perspective view of complex objects according to principles that are also applied to portrayals of the human body and the head in particular. The educational aims of *De prospectiva pingendi* risks limiting the treatise to a sort of "do it yourself" manual, carrying it in the direction of an evaluation incapable of understanding the scope of a text that begins to delve into fields of study such as projective and descriptive geometry[6]. And there is more: it is the spirit of the work itself that tends to be misunderstood only if we consider that in *De prospectiva pingendi* perspective becomes a statement of esthetics and perspective itself ends by being identified with painting which, «is nothing if not demonstrations of surfaces and bodies that are tilted and enlarged within the confines»[7].

Piero, wanted to proceed only through demonstrations and theorems. However, in this way he constructed space similar to reality and at the same time unreal since a pictorial universe, governed by the strict law of numbers and geometry, is only a mental space[8]. For this reason, in a two dimensional microcosm that extends like an optical illusion, *more geometrico demonstrata* (that is "demonstrated according to geometry", to use an expression of Spinoza's), for esthetic and symbolic purposes Piero used perspective aberrations that are only possible in a mental space and not in real space.

This is what we see in works such as the *Baptism of Christ* in London, the fresco in Monterchi or the *Polyptych of St. Anthony*

Bottom:
De prospectiva pingendi (before 1482), cod. S.P.6 bis, fol. 81r; Biblioteca Ambrosiana, Milan.

Below:
graphic reconstruction of the scene of the *Annunciation* from the *Polyptych of St. Anthony.*

As seen by the Archangel Gabriel, the double middle column of the loggia that protrudes from the portico is perspectively between the Virgin and the Archangel.

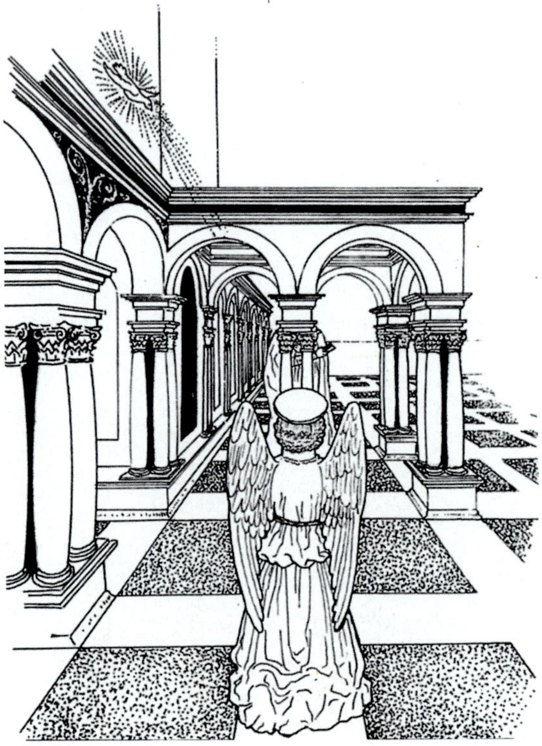

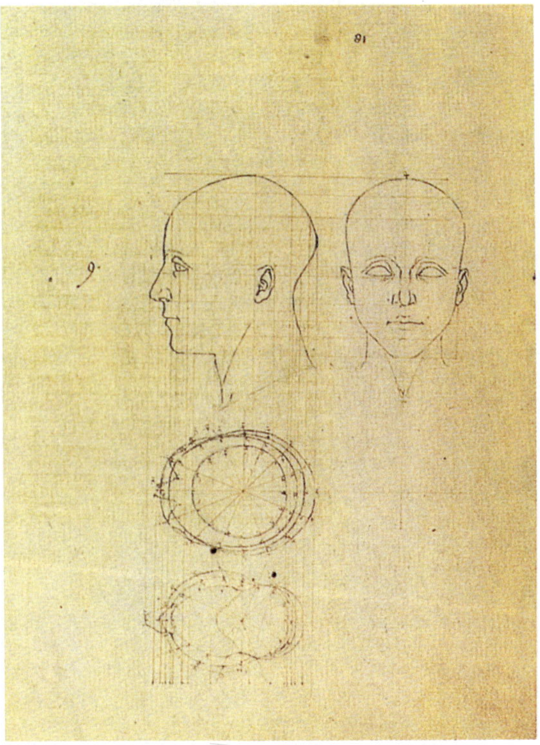

Polyptych of St. Anthony (1470, circa); Galleria Nazionale dell'Umbria, Perugia.

In the central register, to the left of the Virgin, saints Anthony of Padua and John the Baptist; to the right, Francis and Elizabeth; in the predella, miracles performed by some of the saints in the register above.

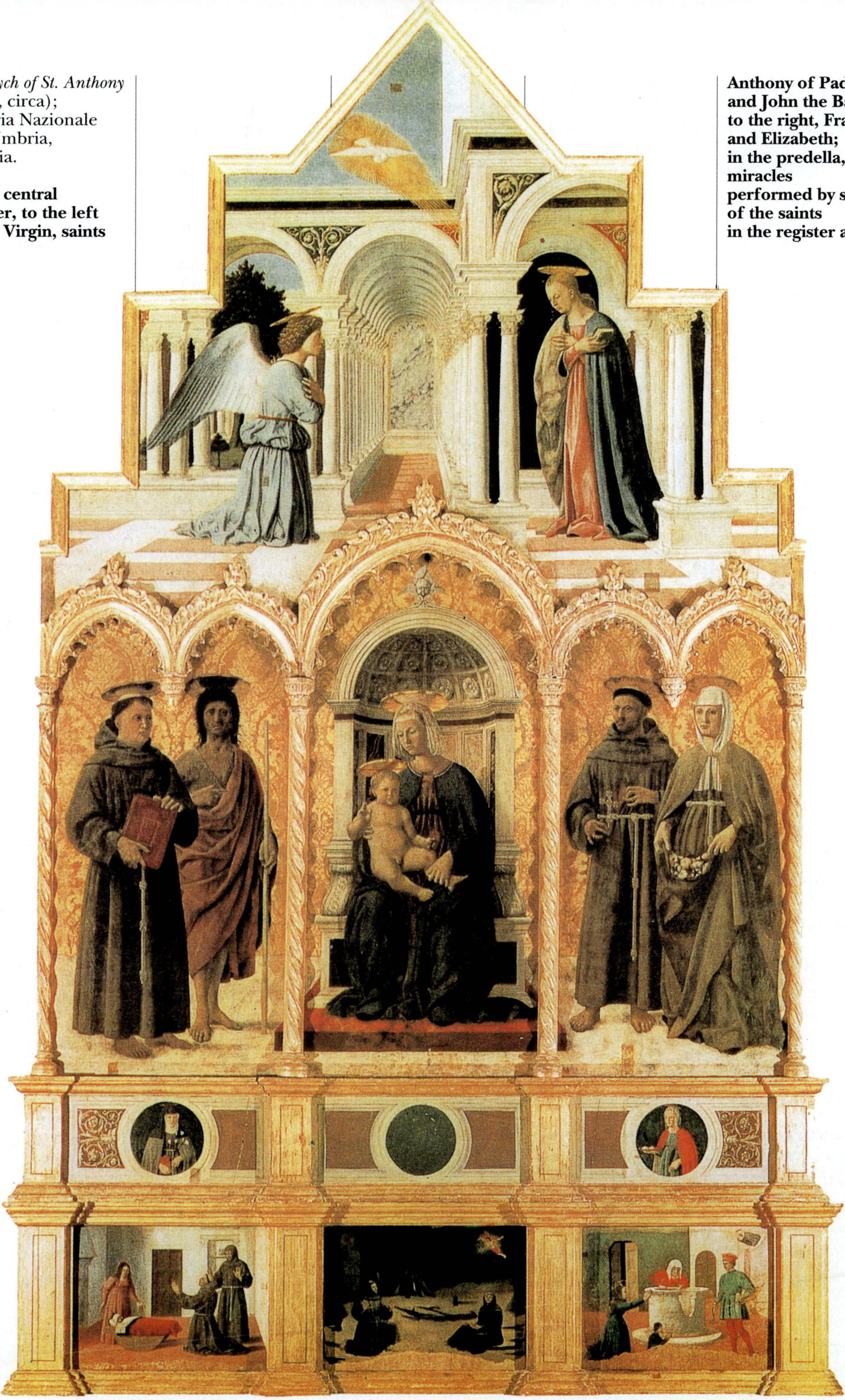

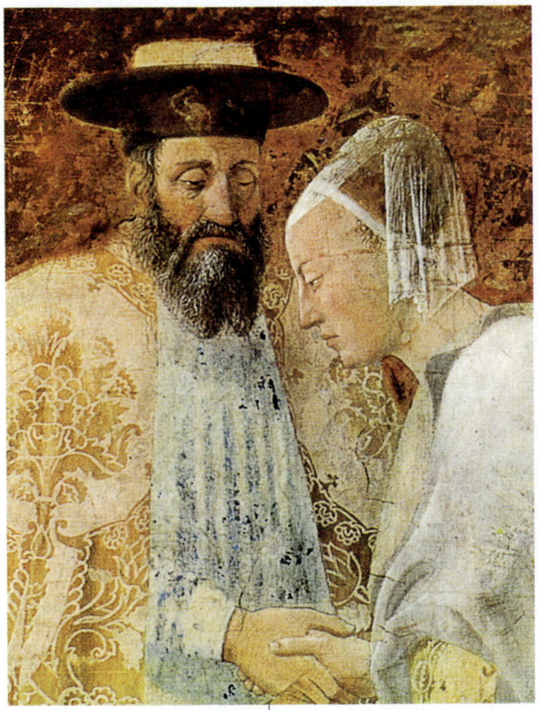

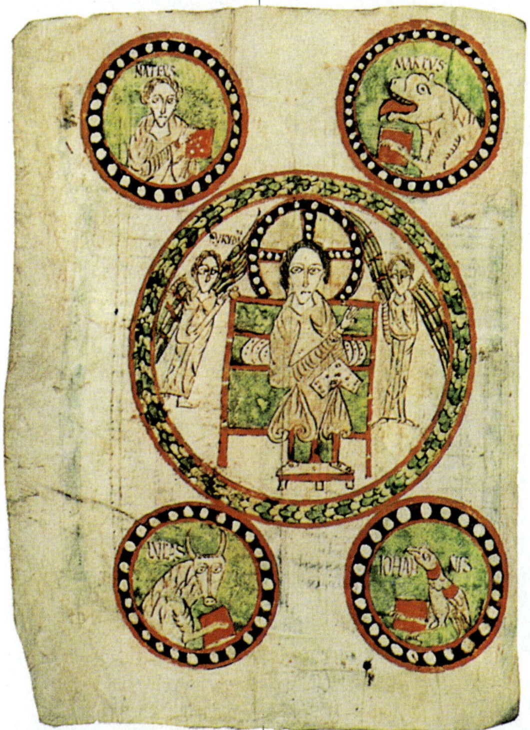

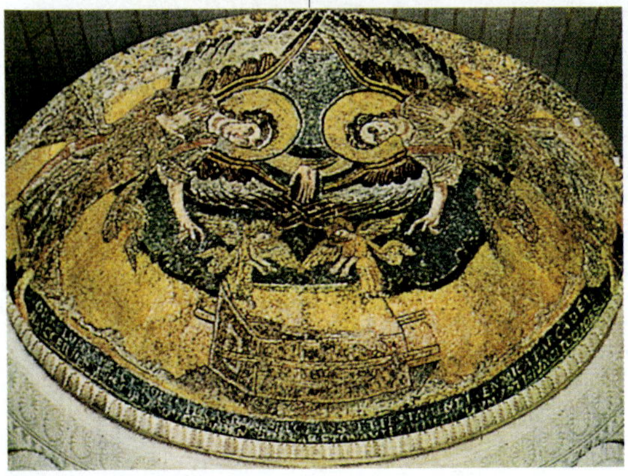

in Perugia. Here it is sufficient to recall that Thomas Martone so convincingly proved that in the *Annunciation* painted on the cornice of the Perugia polyptych, Piero created a subtle play of space (that the viewer must try to comprehend). Looking from where the angel stands, or rather kneels, the Virgin Mary is perspectively "divided" by the median column of the loggia that protrudes from the portico[9]. This is not difficult to realize if we note that the loggia consists of two bays on the long side (the side oriented in depth), so that the column between the two bays is right in front of the Madonna who stands on the same white tile on which the angel is kneeling. The exasperated perspective squeezing and the cornice that covers the base of the columns on the left create a deliberate ambiguity so that at first glance the Virgin seems to be standing outside the loggia. Similarly, at first glance the Virgin in Piero's fresco in the cemetery chapel in Monterchi (the famous *Madonna del Parto*) seems to be in the middle of the canopy that is over her. However, if we compare the circumference of the covering over the pavilion with the much bigger circumference of the floor, and consider the limits of the shadowy area, the angels are beyond it as is the Virgin ever so slightly, it is impossible not to realize that the Virgin is standing outside of the pavilion.

Quite rightly, Martone calls Piero's a «perspective of the mind» and compares it to Alberti's system in which the viewer's eye remains passive accepting the perspective illusion. In Piero's system, on the other hand, the mind becomes a "partner" of the illusory creation of space which for this reason become similar to reality but not like reality. In this sense the space created by the master from Borgo is, as Calvesi emphasizes, symbolic since it is equivalent to real space (that is, for Piero, with the same numerical and symbolic values)[10]. However, constructing space in perspective – according to proportions – also means visually recovering the Neoplatonic philosophical system that is closely related to the Bible (*Book of Wisdom* 11:20), and the Jewish cabala that sees harmoniously connected numbers as the cornerstone of the universe.

Now, in a spatial system conceived in this manner, Piero's choices cannot be ends unto themselves. Therefore, the fact that the Virgin in the Perugia polyptych is "marked" by the column must be related to the Medieval symbolism which postulates the equation: column = *turris eburnea* = Virgin, where clearly, the reference to the *turris eburnea,* that is the ivory tower implies the Virgin as the repository of divine knowledge, the *Sedes Sapientiae* of Medieval and Renaissance tradition[11]. Similarly, the spatial ambiguity that characterizes the Monterchi fresco must be tied to the interrelationship between the Old and New Testament, with the former considered as a prefiguration of the latter. It was no coincidence that Piero wanted to insist on the equivalence, as Martone points out, between the shape of the pavilion and the style of the Virgin's robe[12]. In fact, by deciding to dress the Virgin in the "maternity clothes" of the era, that could be loosened thanks to the inside pleats, Piero used those clothes to better highlight the analogy with the curtain.

Calvesi's careful iconological reconstruction refers to the Biblical passage (*Exodus* 26:1-14) in which God instructs Moses how to build His house, the Ark of the Covenant, so that Piero's pavilion can be identified with the house of Yahweh and the Vir-

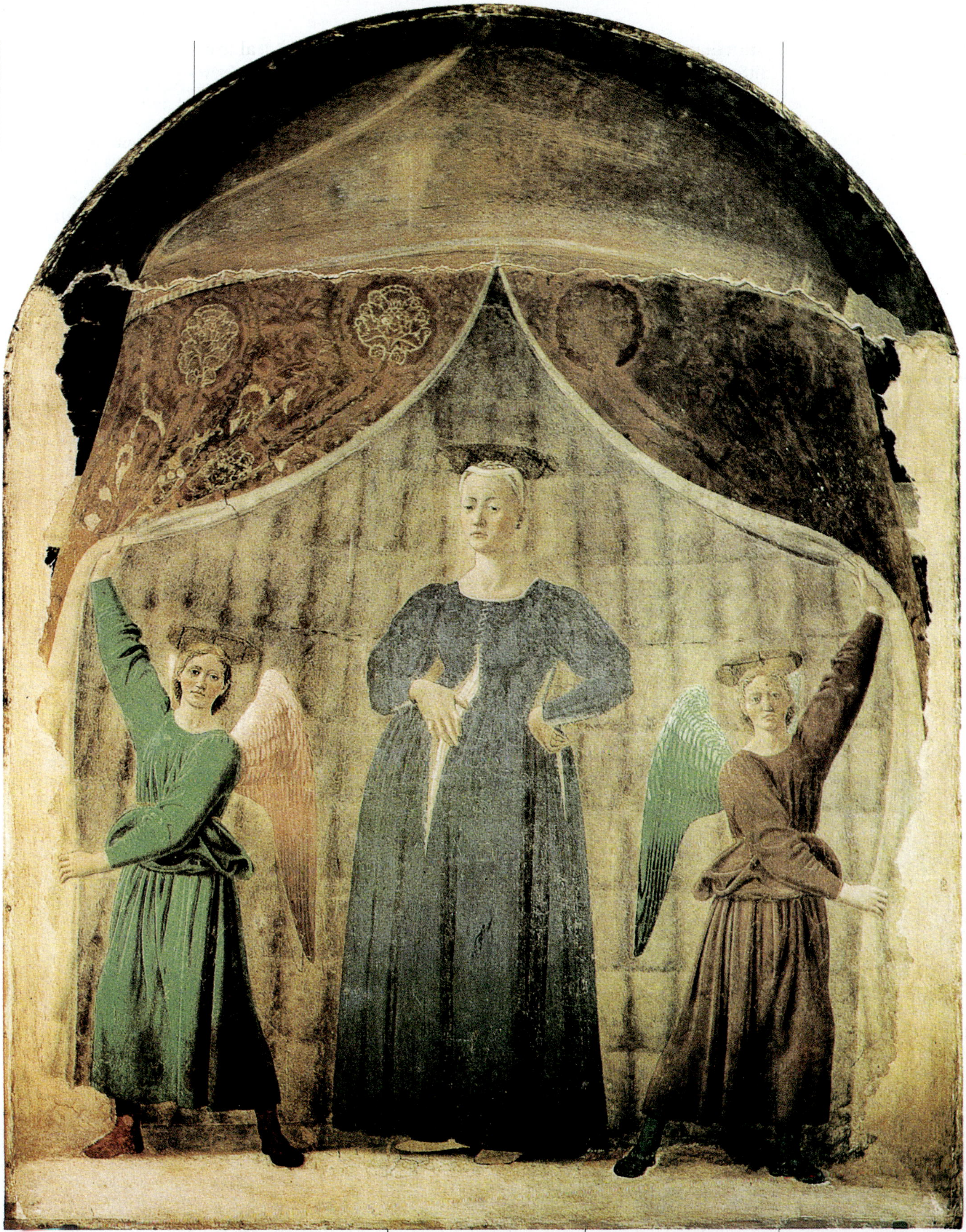

Above:
Madonna del Parto (after 1459); Cemetery chapel, Monterchi (Arezzo).

Opposite page, from the top:
The Queen of Sheba Worshipping the Wood of the True Cross and The meeting of Solomon and the Queen of Sheba, episode from the *Legend of the True Cross* (1452-1466 circa), detail; Bacci Chapel, Church of San Francesco, Arezzo.

Christ in Majesty, miniature from *Gospel of Gundohino* (754); ms. 3, f. 12 v; Bibliothèque Municipale, Autun.

The Ark of the Covenant, mosaic (806, circa); apse of the Church of Germigny-des-Prés.

gin (thanks to a series of textual references and mainly the tradition of the Holy House of Loreto that defines Mary as *foederis arca*) becomes the Ark of the Covenant[13]. By virtue of the last equivalence, the angels that open the curtain of the pavilion will be the cherubs, which as deduced from yet another passage in *Exodus* that tells that Bezaleel, the sculptor, «made the ark of acacia wood [...] and he made cherubim [...] on the two ends of the mercy seat» (*Exodus* 37:1-7).

Piero placed the two angels at the ends of the pavilion clearly relating them thanks to a correspondence, which, already close because of the fact that they are mirror images of each other, is strengthened by the inversion of the colors of the wings, hose and robes (green wings and hose with a red robe for the angel on the right, red wings and hose with a green robe for the angel on the left).

However, it is known that according to the traditional iconography based on Ezekiel's vision (*Ezekiel* 1:4-25; 10:1-22) the cherubs have four wings. There is also another tradition based on the above mentioned passages from *Exodus* that describes the cherubs as almost human figures with only two wings. This is shown in the IX century Carolingian mosaic that Theodulf bishop of Orléans had made for the apse of the church in Germigny-des-Prés which depicts the two Biblical cherubs on the Ark of the Covenant. The *Gospel of Gundohino*, written during the preceding century (Bibliothèque Municipale, Autun) contains the exact same iconography (that they are cherubs is confirmed by the word «Cyrubim») and offers yet another clue. The two angels have a wing raised towards Christ in accordance with the Biblical passage specifying that the «cherubs shall stretch forth their wings on high, covering the mercy seat» (*Exodus* 25:20). Thus, in the *Gospel of Gundohino* it is Christ who assumes the role of the ark, that role which, in the Loreto tradition, is transferred to the Virgin[14]. Therefore, it is no coincidence that in at least two examples (a medal in the Kunstgewerbe Museum in Cologne and an early sixteenth century woodcut) the cherubs flanking the Madonna of Loreto stretch their wings upwards.

We can, then, ask why Piero did not copy the same iconography. Probably he also wanted to make other references. We must recall that the episode in *Exodus* where God instructs Moses on how to build the Ark of the Covenant follows a narrative scheme that recurs in the passages concerning Solomon's construction of the Temple in Jerusalem. As opposed to the details in *Exodus*, in those passages the cherubs are not described as having their wings stretched upwards, but horizontally «over the place of the ark» (*I Kings* 6:27; 8:7). There is no doubt that Piero's image was influenced by both Biblical books, and that the artist also wanted to refer to the story in the *I Kings* is demonstrated by the fact that cloth, decorated with pomegranates, of the pavilion, (that can, as we have said, be interpreted as the house of Yahweh) in the Monterchi fresco varies only in color with respect to Solomon's cloak as portrayed in one of the frescoes in the church of San Francesco in Arezzo. The choice could not have casual.

A confirmation comes from the episode of Moses which, as we have said, seems linked to the passages describing the construction of the temple ordered by the King of Israel. In that

Baptism of Christ (1459-1460, circa), National Gallery, London.

The painting, which was put on sale in 1857, was acquired by the London museum in 1861. Previously, it was the central panel of a triptych of which the lateral panels, the predella and the two pillars can be dated around 1465 and were done by Matteo di Giovanni (1430 circa-1495), who, like Piero, was a native of Borgo Sansepolcro. In the portion of the cornice above the *Baptism* there was a tondo (that has also been lost) with *God the Father*, the only other part attributed to Piero. The only reliable document concerning the placement of the triptych is dated 1629, the year in which it was in the priory of San Giovanni Battista in Borgo Sansepolcro.

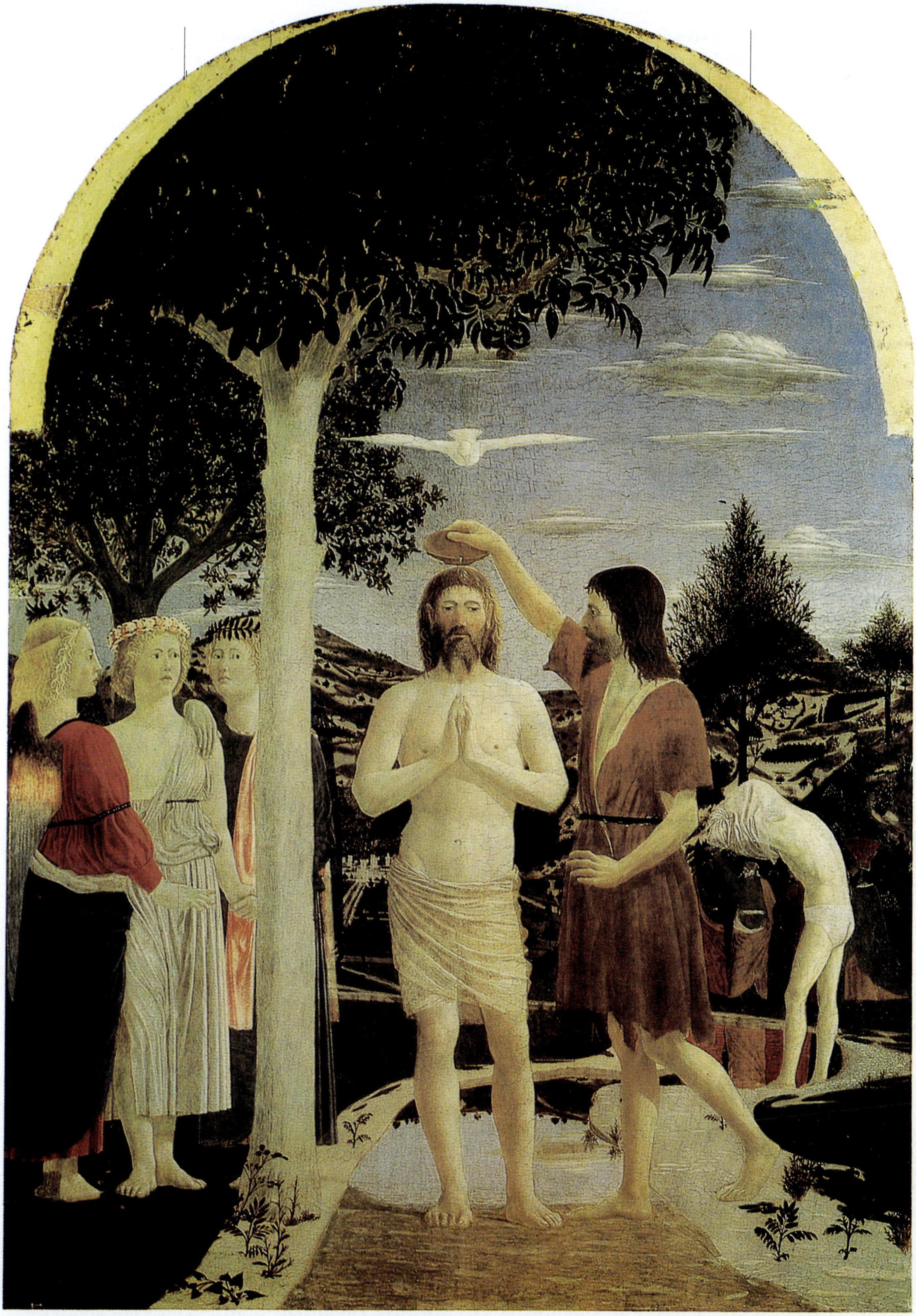

early account Aaron wears a robe with «pomegranates of blue and purple» (*Exodus* 28:33) and it is quite probable that Piero was inspired by that description when he decided to paint Solomon dressed in a robe which, in the artist's transposition modernly becomes a lovely brocade from Prato. Pomegranates are also mentioned in the verses concerning the construction of the temple in Jerusalem (*I Kings* 7:18-20) where they are described as decorative elements around the capitals of the columns. At this point, in view of the continuous symbolic references to the Old Testament in the Monterchi fresco, even the perspective structure and composition of the image take on a more profound symbolic meaning. The figure of the Virgin emerges from the background the way the word of Christ emerges from the Old Testament.

Even in the *Baptism of Christ* in the National Gallery (London) the co-presence of Old and New Testament themes emerges. The three angels on the left refer to the Biblical episode in which three angels appear before Abraham under the oak in the plains of Mamre (*Genesis* 18:1-3), and he tells them to rest under "the tree" which becomes the beautiful larch in the background of the upper Tiber valley[15].

This Old Testament episode has always been interpreted as a precise prefiguration of the Trinitarian dogma in which baptism, along with the transfiguration on Mount Tabor constitutes the manifestation of the Gospel[16]. Thus, the three angels dressed in the colors that allude to the Trinity (blue, red and white) represent the Father (the angel with the jewel on the forehead), the Holy Spirit (clothed in white) and the Son. The Father and Son, as we can see are both clothed in garments of red and blue (improper nineteenth century cleaning lightened the red garments of the latter too much), and the Son, appears to be perspectively "split" by the tree in the foreground (that plays a role similar to the column that perspectively frames the Virgin in the *Polyptych of St. Anthony*). The tree is a walnut, one of the symbols of Christ[17]. This is the angel which is closest to Jesus and bears a robe on his shoulders that Bertelli rightly identifies as the robe of the Savior[18].

As we can see, the arrangement of the figures repeats the same sequence that we find along the median axis of the composition where the Holy Spirit hovers above the head of Christ and hence between the Son and the Father that was in the now lost frame. However, the entire arrangement of the composition alludes to the Trinity. In fact, in the London *Baptism of Christ* there are two ideal axes that affect the entire composition: one is vertical, central and paradigmatic and the other is horizontal and perspectively oriented. The first coordinates the figures related to the Gospel episode and thus to the Trinitarian epiphany as the absolute revelation of the Christian truth. The second indicates the human dimension, where the Story takes place, and it, too, intersects with the divine as represented by the central figure of Christ. Therefore, Piero placed the angels that represent the Trinity, the catechumen about to receive the sacrament, and the Pharisees, mentioned in the Gospel according to St. Matthew (*Matthew* 3:7-11), on the perspectively directed horizontal axis, going from the foreground to the background (but the four figures in the background are characterized, as we shall see, by considerable semantic ambiguity).

Composite geometric diagram of the *Baptism of Christ*, National Gallery, London.

**The median GF axis is the paradigmatic axis on which the image of Christ is placed.
The oblique axis with the arrows at the ends comprises the human dimension that intersects with the divine and ideally joins the figures**

Segment OJ is the radius of the circle O, the upper semi-circumference of which corresponds to the frame of the panel.

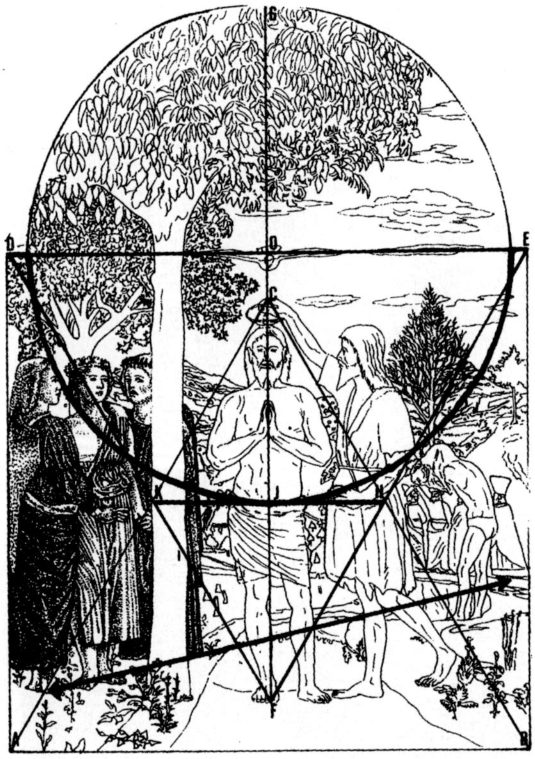

**of the angels with that of the catechumen and the Pharisees in the background.
The figure of Jesus is inscribed in two equilateral triangles, DFE and ABC.
The point of intersection of sides DF with AC and CB with EF identify the end points of segment KH that passes along the upper edge of the loincloth and intersects with axis GF at point J.**

Opposite page:
Baptism of Christ (1459-1460, circa) detail;
National Gallery, London.

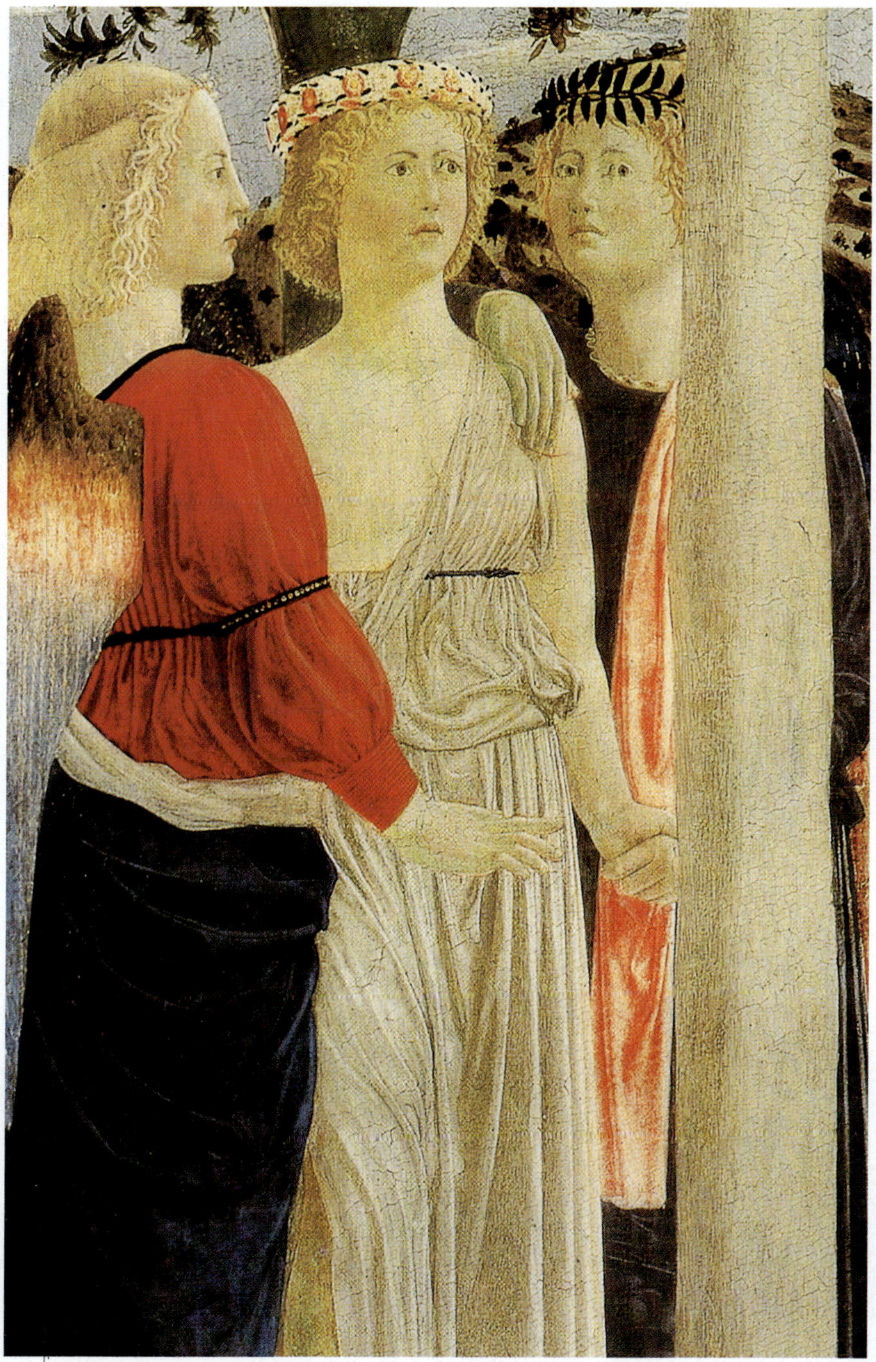

Furthermore, a geometric framework governs the composition, making yet another reference to the Trinitarian theme according to an idea in which simple geometric figures and mathematical aspects in general contained metaphors of the Absolute: «Since we can only accede to divine things through symbols, we shall use mathematical signs which are of incontrovertible certainty»[19].

These words were written by Cardinal Niccolò Cusano. Piero must have been working for him from 22 January 1459, when Pope Pius II left the pontifical seat to go to Mantua where he called a crusade (but without success) against the Turks to whom the Eastern Empire had fallen in 1453. Piero, who had been in Rome for six months doing the frescoes in the papal apartments and the chamber of Goro Lori Piccolomini, ended up working for the cardinal who had to govern during the pope's absence.

(1) *Published for the first time by F. Corazzini,* Appunti storici e filologici sulla Valle Tiberina superiore, *San Sepolcro, 1875, p. 60, has recently been reported in that goldmine of data and ideas, E. Battisti,* Piero della Francesca, *Milan, 1971, II, p. 242, doc. CCIX.*

(2) *P. Arrighi,* Piero matematico, *in* Piero teorico dell'arte, *edited by O. Calabrese, Bari, 1985, p. 52.*

(3) *G. Vasari,* Le vite dei più eccellenti pittori, scultori e architetti, *edited by M. Marini, Rome 1991, p. 377.*

(4) *Piero della Francesca,* Trattato d'abaco, *Pisa 1970, p. 39. For the hypothesis on dating and clients: M. Salmi,* Piero della Francesca, *Novara 1979, pp. 198-199. For the relationships between the mercantile mentality of the era and the fifteenth century artistic vision: M. Baxandall,* Pittura ed esperienze sociali nell'Italia del Quattrocento, *Turin 1979, pp. 85-95.*

(5) *P. Arrighi,* op. cit., *p. 52. Arrighi does not hesitate to define Piero as the greatest mathematician of his era.*

(6) *F. Ghione,* Breve introduzione sul contenuto matematico del "De prospectiva Pingendi" di Piero della Francesca, *in Piero della Francesca,* De prospectiva Pingendi, *edited by G. Nicco Fasola, Florence 1984, p. XXIX.*

(7) *Piero della Francesca,* De prospectiva Pingendi, *cit., III, p. 128. Two manuscript copies of Piero's work have come down to us. This is the handwritten manuscript in the Biblioteca Palatina in Parma (ms. par. 1576) that was later translated into Latin by Fra Matteo Cioni; the current codex S.P.6 bis in the Biblioteca Ambrosiana in Milan was also brought to light this way. Both works include a series of original drawings. For further information, see: L. Vagnetti,* Riflessioni sul "De prospectiva Pingendi", in *"Commentari", XXV, 1975, pp.14-55.*

(8) *We can recall the issue concerning the perspective rendering, on a plane, of a colonnade that is parallel to the plane itself. The lateral columns are deformed in a way that broadens them. According to Leonardo, the rule of perspective must be adjusted according to visual experience. According to Piero, the theory of perspective must be applied in full because it can be geometrically proved. Piero's space is mental, Leonardo's is likely. Cfr. G. Nicco Fasola,* La prospettiva nell'estetica del rinascimento, *introduzione a Piero della Francesca,* De prospectiva Pingendi,*cit., p. 26.*

(9) *T. Martone,* Piero della Francesca e la prospettiva dell'intelletto, *in* Piero teorico dell'arte, *cit., pp. 173-186.*

(10) *M. Calvesi,* Sistema degli equivalenti ed equivalenze del sistema in Piero della Francesca, *in "Storia dell'Arte", 24/25, pp. 83-110.*

(11) *The symbolism of the column in relation to the Virgin is analyzed by M. Fagiolo dell'Arco in relation to the* Madonna with the Long Neck *by Parmigianino. The primary source is a Medieval hymn that describes the Virgin so «Collum tuum ut columna, turris eburnea». Cfr. M. Fagiolo dell'Arco,* Il Parmigianino, *Rome 1970, p. 47.*

(12) *T. Martone,* L'affresco di Piero della Francesca in Monterchi. una pietra miliare della pittura rinascimentale, *in* Atti del Convegno Internazionale sulla "Madonna del Parto" di Piero della Francesca, *Città di Castello 1982, pp. 16-100.*

(13) *M. Calvesi,* Nel grembo dell'arca, *"Art e Dossier", 33, March 1989, pp. 16-20.*

(14) *On this issue see: M. Bussagli,* Storia degli Angeli, *Milan 1991, p. 304, n. 12; idem., s.v.* Angelo, *in* Enciclopedia dell'Arte Medievale, *I, Rome 1991, p. 630.*

(15) *The first scholar to consider the "archeological" matrix of the Three Graces was C. de Tolnay,* Conceptions religieuses dans la peinture de Piero della Francesca, *in "Arte Antica e Moderna", VI, 1963, p. 214. Bertelli emphasized the close similarity of the arrangement with the* Four Crowned Saints *by Nanni di Banco:* Piero della Francesca, *Milan 1991, p. 58. The link with the Old Testament episode was identified by M. Tanner,* Concordia in Piero della Francesca's Baptism of Christ, *in "The Art Quarterly", XXXV, 1972, pp. 1-20.*

(16) *Cfr. Saint Augustine,* De tribus viris qui beato Abrahae apparuerunt. Sermo V, *in J.P. Migne,* Patrologia latina, *XXXIX, coll. 1747-1749.*

(17) *M. Bussagli,* Il "Battesimo" di Londra di Piero della Francesca. Per una rilettura in chiave trinitaria, *in "Quaderni Medievali", 20, 1985, pp. 28-65.*

(18) *C. Bertelli,* op. cit., *p. 59.*

(19) *N. Cusano,* La dotta ignoranza, *I, XI, in* Opere filosofiche, *ed. by G. Federici Vescovini, Turin 1972, p. 74. On the geometric aspects of the* Baptism*: M. Bussagli,* Il "Battesimo" di Londra di Piero della Francesca, *cit., pp. 56-65. A different geometric interpretation is given by B.A.R. Carter,* A Mathematical interpretation of Piero della Francesca's *Baptism of Christ, in M. Aronberg Lavin,* Piero della Francesca's Baptism of Christ, *New Haven, 1981, pp. 149-163.*

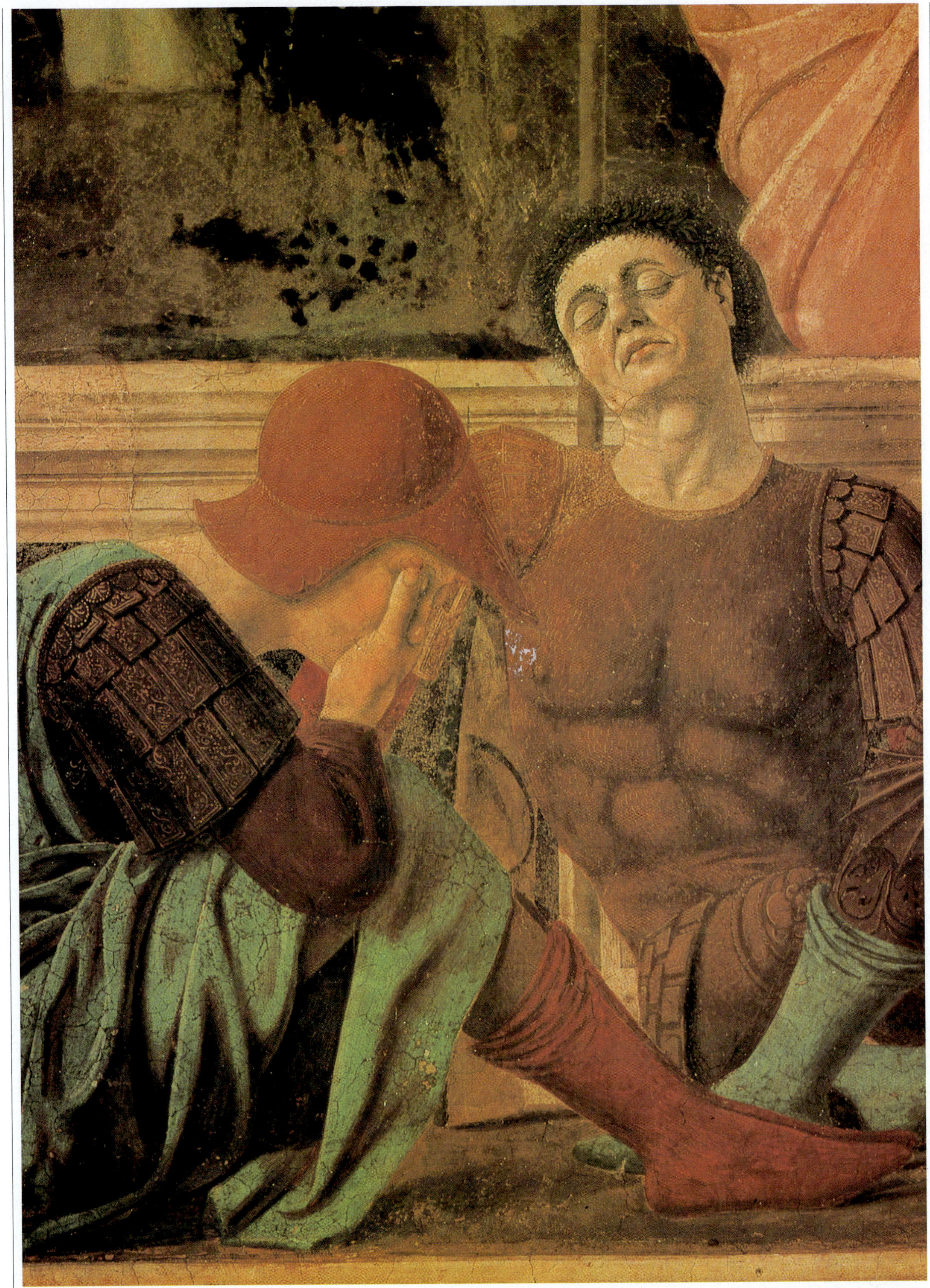

Piero the Platonic

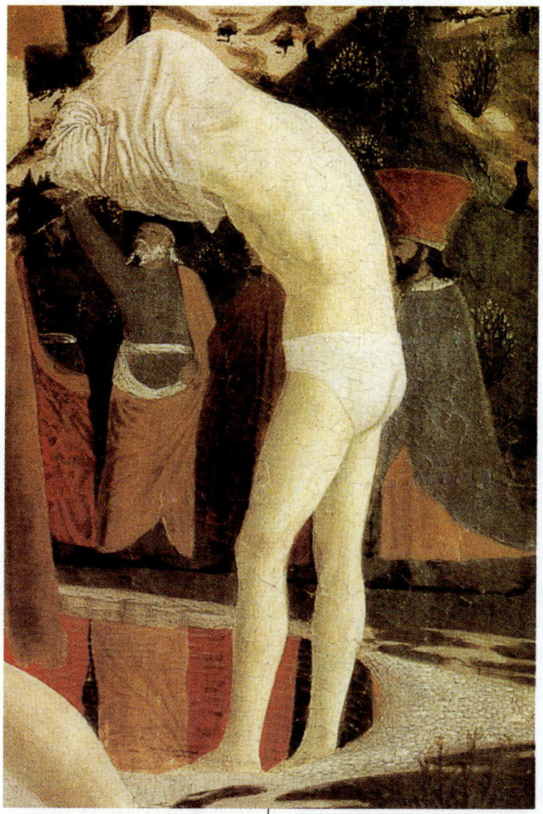

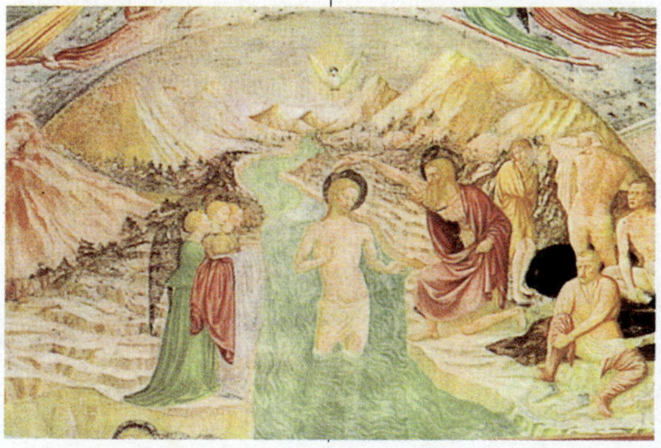

THE GEOMETRICAL ARrangement of the *Baptism of Christ* thus seems to have been inspired by the geometric-philosophical ideas expressed by Cusano in the *De docta ignorantia* written in 1440.

Furthermore, no one can have any doubts about the Platonic and Augustinian elements of Piero's thought. He revealed it, in the beginning of the *De prospectiva pingendi*, where he defined painting as an art which «... consists of three main parts [...] drawing, proportion and color...», so that this idea ends up by resembling St. Augustine's definition of corporeal beauty which consists of the «proportion of the parts with a certain softness of color»[20].

However, all this leads to further reflection. In a pictorial universe that was so lengthily pondered and scientifically constructed, where the geometric and perspective arrangements were nothing more than symbolic elements to present the dimension of the Absolute of which reality is a sensible mirror, even the characters that occupy and populate it must be consistent with it.

These, in fact, are the incarnations of the absolute values: they are mental figures that occupy a mental space, therefore they are contrary to the accidental and the occasional. In other words: in Piero's works we distinctly feel a sort of repulsion for the trivial anecdote, for the story as an end unto itself, for the banal narrative.

Thus, for example in the *Baptism of Christ*, there is only one catechumen, a definite antithesis to the Gospel text according to which crowds flocked to the Baptist «and were baptized of him in Jordan, confessing their sins» (*Matthew* 3:6). But that catechumen, precisely because he is alone, is so much for effective than, for example the three in Masolino's fresco of the same subject in the baptistry of Castiglione Olona. In Masolino's painting they undress and dry themselves as if they were bathers, Piero's, as curved as the bend of the Jordan – represents all humanity that is released from the weight of sin thanks to the sacrament of baptism.

Below:
The Queen of Sheba Worshipping the Wood of the True Cross and the Meeting of Solomon and the Queen of Sheba, episode from *The Legend of the True Cross* (1452-1466, circa) detail; Bacci Chapel, Church of San Francesco, Arezzo.

For the same reasons, the Master from Borgo not infrequently reused the same cartoons or drawings, sometimes reversing them (left/right) in the same composition. He did this with the angels in the *Madonna del Parto,* and there is a clear example, as Battisti justly showed on the basis of Kenneth Clark's findings, in *The Queen of Sheba Worshipping the Wood of the True Cross and the Meeting of Solomon and the Queen of Sheba,* the fresco in the Bacci Chapel in the church of San Francesco in Arezzo. In this case, the comparison between the two parts into which the scene is divided clearly shows the repetition of «at least three tracings»[21].

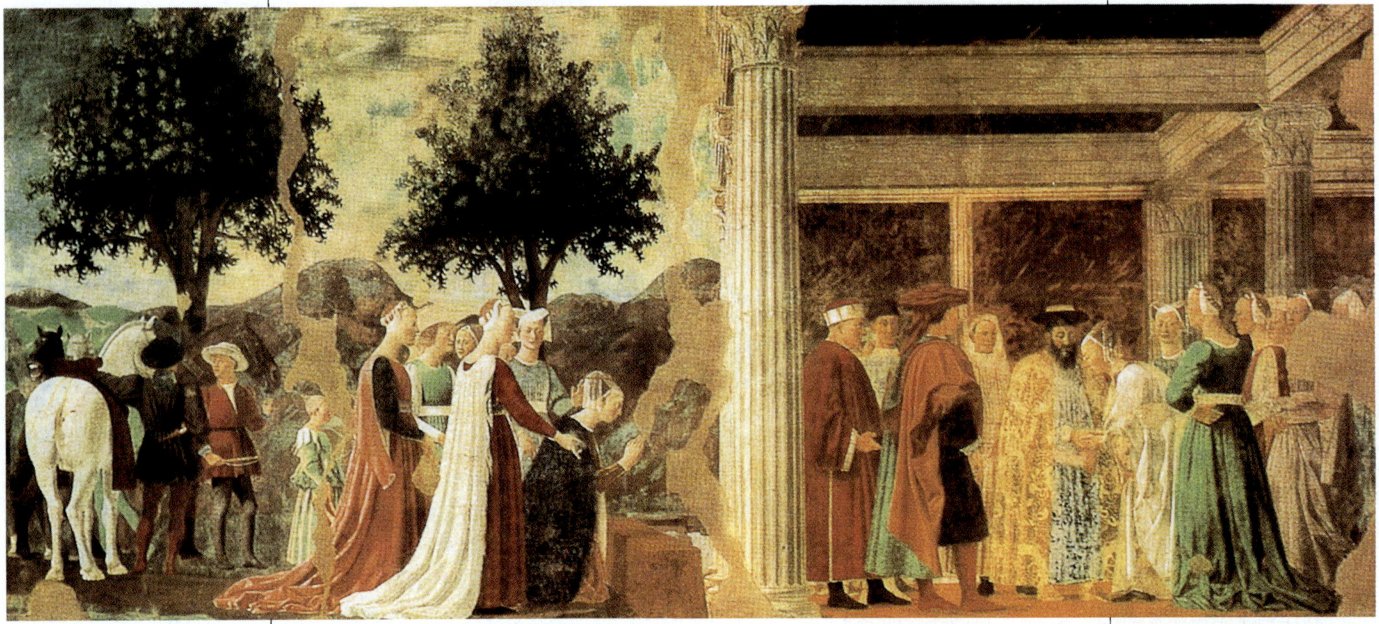

On page 14:
Resurrection (1468), detail; Museo Civico, Sansepolcro.

Page 15, from the top:
Baptism of Christ (1459-1460, circa), detail of the catechumen; National Gallery, London.

Masolino da Panicale *Baptism of Christ* (1435), detail; Baptistry, Castiglione Olona (Varese).

The one he used for the queen kneeling outside Solomon's palace before the bridge was reused for the bust of the queen at the moment of her meeting with the king inside the palace; the tracing of the two ladies in profile; and the one of the handmaid who is wedged between the queen and her retinue. That this was an expedient to hasten the completion of a painting which – as we shall see – according to the critics took fourteen years (1452-1466), is difficult to believe. Rather, it could have been once more a way of suspending the scene in a timeless immobility that pushes the episode into the transcendental dimension of Platonic world of ideas.

Sometimes Piero even used the same physical types to portray different characters and to highlight certain ideal similarities. It is certainly not a chance event that in the altarpiece painted for Federico da Montefeltro, Duke of Urbino (now in the Pinacoteca di Brera in Milan) there is a St. Jerome (third figure from the left) who is beardless, and this is contrary to Piero's custom, and who has the same face as the St. Bernardino of Siena who is behind him (see page 42). This may seem to be an oddity, but it is not if we think of the biographies of the two saints (furthermore, 14 May 1474, the day that the remains of St. Bernardino – who had died in Aquila on 20 May 1444 – were translated to the church built expressly for that purpose in the same city, is a date that is not entirely removed from the history of the altarpiece, which was, in all likelihood, completed in the

Opposite page, from the top:
Filippo Lippi *The Adoration of the Child* (1452, circa), detail; Gemäldegalerie, Berlin-Dahlem.

Maestro di Ocrida, *Baptism of Christ* (early XIV century), detail; Church of St. Clement, gallery of the icons, Ocrida (Macedonia).

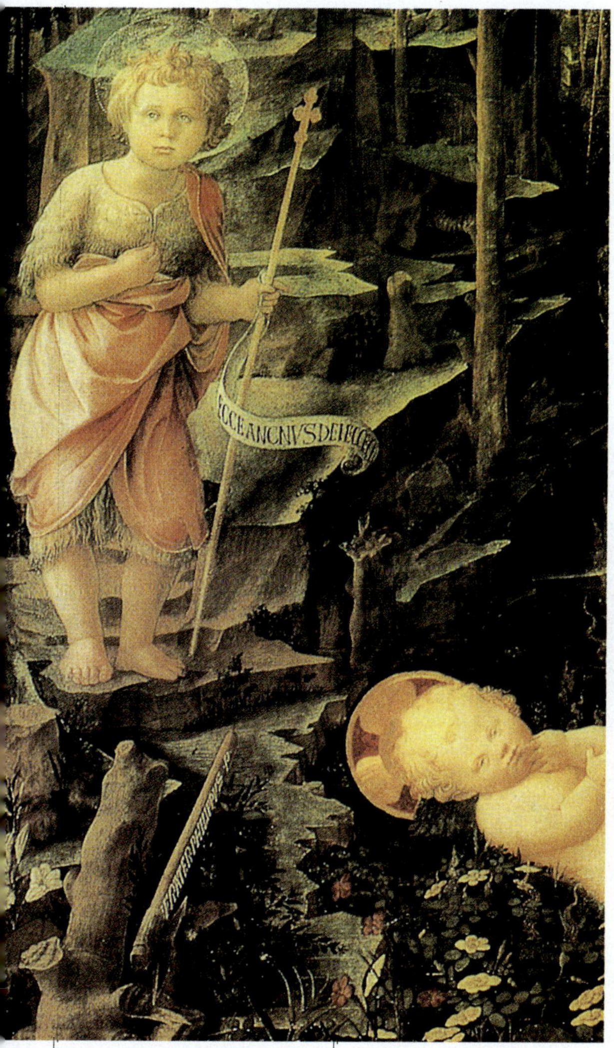

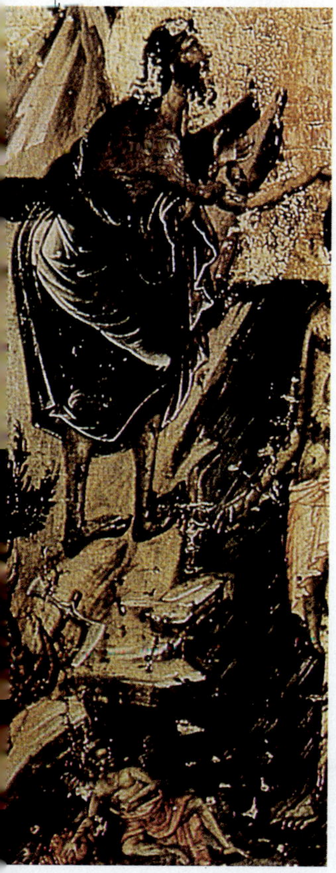

The axe, as an attribute of St. John the Baptist (whether or not used in conjunction with the other canonical element, the felled trees), does not belong solely to the Byzantine iconography of the saint, but it is also seen, albeit rarely, in the western iconography. One example is Lippi's painting, where there are the axe (at the saint's feet) and the cut trees, whereas in Piero's *Baptism of Christ* and other works there are only the tree trunks.

autumn of that year, while the church of San Gerolamo was being finished in Urbino at the same time).

First of all, St. Bernardino was a contemporary of Piero's and attributing the same features of the preacher from Siena to a champion of Christianity such as St. Jerome meant up-dating the figure of the latter. Furthermore, both men are recognized as Doctors of the Church, both were literati, both dealt with heresies, both were opposed during their lives and both had lived as hermits.

Thus, it is as if Piero had wanted to say that saintliness always bears the same face: a saintliness made of sacrifices and solitude. For this reason, the Baptist (the first figure on the left) is next to the two characters. On the other hand, Piero more than once highlighted the bond between St. Jerome and St. John the Baptist.

In the famous London altarpiece of the *Baptism of Christ* (see page 11), the grassy slopes that gradually merge with the background hills are scattered with the trunks of fallen trees. It is not difficult to see the connection, as Battisti rightly does, between them and that Gospel passage about the Pharisees and Sadducees which reads: «... every tree which bringeth not forth good fruit is hewn down and cast into the fire» (*Matthew* 3:10). What is not noted is that the presence of the trunks and the axe (mentioned by Matthew) is a constant, or nearly so, in the Byzantine iconography of John the Baptist. In western figurative traditions, these features are much less common and yet we unexpectedly find them in Filippo Lippi's three paintings of the *Adoration of the Child* (such as the one in the Gemäldegalerie in Berlin-Dahlem).

The landscape with the downed trunks, therefore, unequivocally qualifies itself as a precise reference to John the Baptist. Thus, when Piero painted cut trees in *St. Jerome Penitent* (Gemäldegalerie in Berlin-Dahlem), or placed the trunk exhibiting a crucifix in the foreground of the *St. Jerome and a Worshipper* (Gallerie dell'Accademia, Venice), it is obvious that he wanted to allude to the overlap of the two images of saints, just as proposed by Medieval and fifteenth century hagiographic culture. Therefore, we can understand why, in the *Brera Altarpiece*, John the Baptist appears next to St. Bernardino and St. Jerome who both have the same face.

It is as if it were a model of saintliness handed down through the centuries to Piero's generation, and besides Piero himself, in the *Polyptych of the Misericordia* (Museo Civico, Sansepolcro), had not hesitated in creating a relationship between St. John the Baptist and St. Bernardino (the second figure from the left and the last figure in the central register, respectively), linked by the same gesture: St. John points with his right hand, alluding to Christ (this pose was typical of the Forerunner in western iconography); while the saint from Siena points upwards, as Leonardo's St. John the Baptist, in the painting of the same name (Louvre, Paris), would do many years later, and with his hand turned.

As for the perspective, therefore, the characters that populated Piero's universe were almost intellectual "rhymes" of coherent "stanzas". It is not surprising, therefore, that decades later Piero repeated the poses of certain characters with few variations. Thus, the St. Francis in the *Brera Altarpiece* holds the cross in his right hand and with the left opens his habit to reveal the wounds on his ribs, exactly like the *Polyptych of the Misericordia* or the *Polyptych of St. Anthony* (see page 7).

In my opinion such close similarities justify questioning the differences. The fact that, in the Milan altarpiece, St. Francis is portrayed as beardless cannot be considered casual (just as the hairless face of St. Jerome in the same painting – as I believe I have clearly demonstrated – is not casual).

The St. Francis in the *Brera Altarpiece* (whose presence is fully justified by the fact that St. Bernardino titular saint of the church in Urbino where the altarpiece has been kept since 1491 was a member of the Franciscan order) has given rise to a series of hypotheses. The most banal is the one which identifies him with the prior of San Bernardino in Urbino, the most fascinating is the one that believes it to be a portrait of Samson of Brescia, the father general of the Franciscans in Urbino who was in touch with Leonardo da Vinci and Luca Pacioli[22]. It was precisely Pacioli who was considered for the figure of St. Peter Martyr, whose face is behind that of the saint's from Assisi.

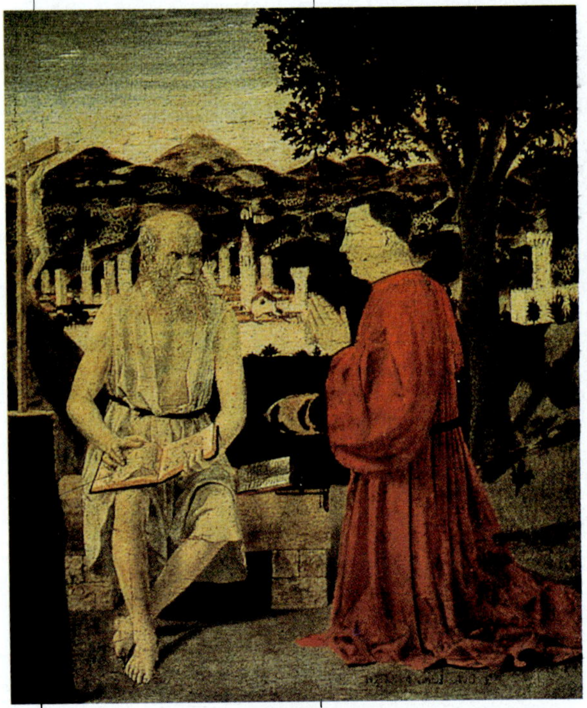

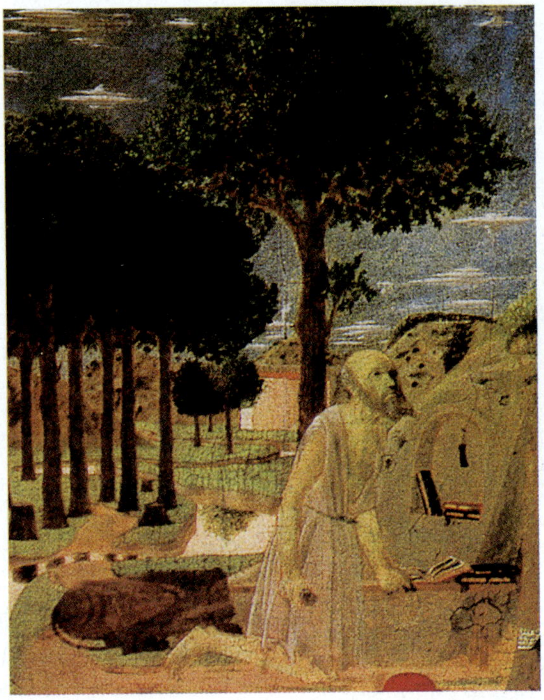

This page, from the left: *St. Jerome and a Worshipper* (after 1450); Gallerie dell'Accademia, Venice.

St. Jerome Penitent (1450); Gemäldegalerie, Berlin-Dahlem.

Both paintings are signed by the artist, at the base of the trunk on which the crucifix stands. In the *St. Jerome* in Venice, the inscription that simulates letters carved into the wood reads: «Petri de Bu[r]go S[an]c[t]i Sepulcri opus». In the Berlin *St. Jerome* a scroll bears the worlds «Petrii de Burgo opus MCCCCL». The *St. Jerome Penitent* offers yet further confirmation of a date, a precious bit of information in a panorama of works that are as difficult to date as Piero's.

Generally, it is a source of surprise to see the Veronese saint in this altarpiece which is so dominated by Franciscans. Peter was in fact a Dominican and it is well known that there has always been a certain amount of friction between the two orders. However, here his presence is justified by the fact that he is remembered as the founder of the Marian confraternities of Milan, Florence and Perugia where he was canonized in 1253. To this we must add his martyrdom which earned him having his portrait in the Bacci Chapel in the church of San Francesco in Arezzo.

It is more difficult to fully understand the reason for the identification with Pacioli that seems supported (bearing in mind the idealization of the physiognomy that is normal in Piero's paintings) by the similarity with the portrait of the fifteenth century mathematician attributed to Jacopo de' Barbari

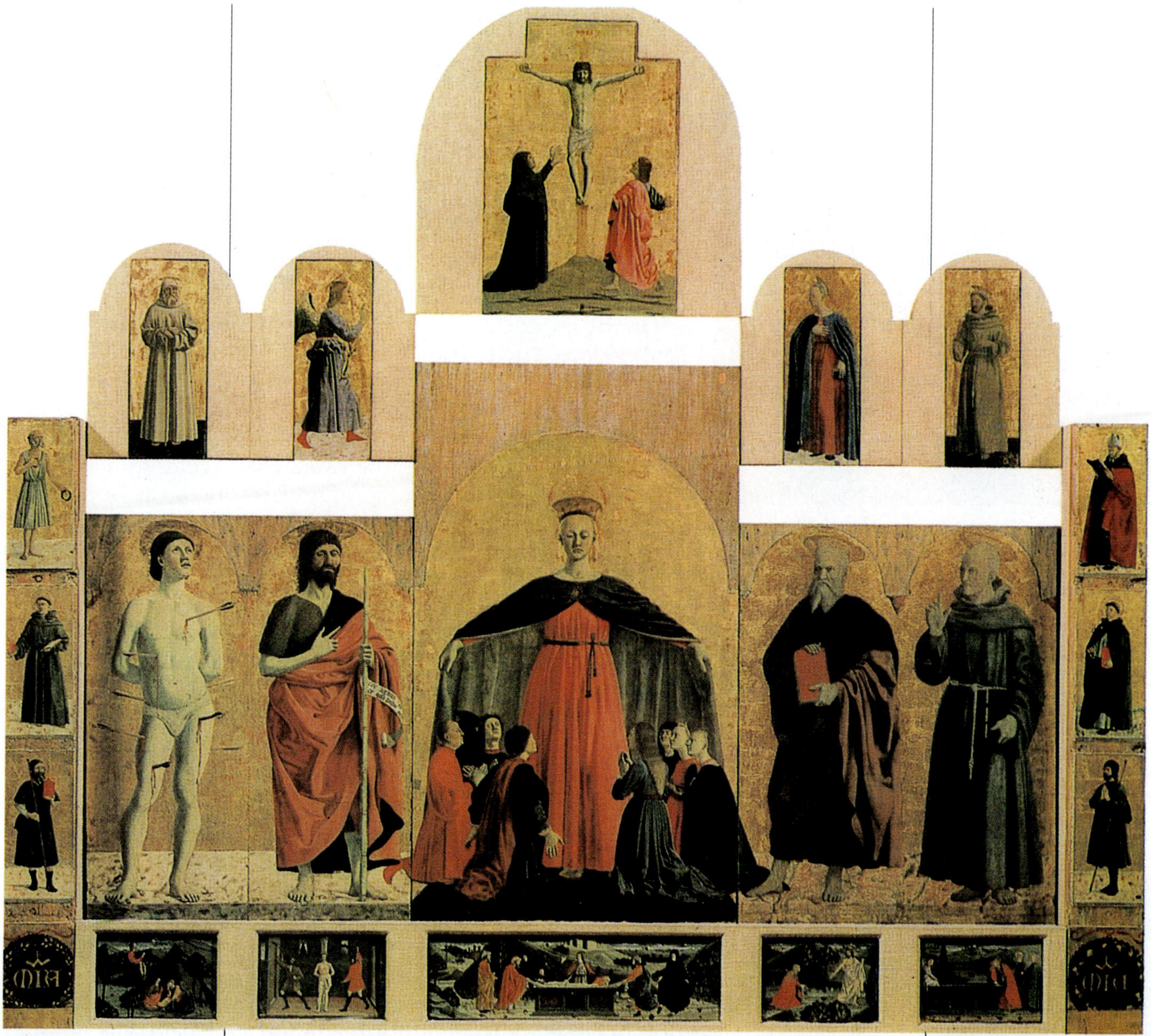

Above:
Polyptych of the Misericordia (1445-1462); Museo Civico, Sansepolcro.

Right:
Leonardo da Vinci, *St. John the Baptist* (1513-1516); Louvre, Paris.

which is in the Museo di Capodimonte in Naples. Perhaps a link may be found in the fact that Peter of Verona was a convinced supporter of the idea of the goodness of creation, against the heretic sects of Gnostic origin (from the Enriciani to the Catharists) that were swarming throughout northern Italy, just as – albeit for other reasons – Luca Pacioli sought the secret of the universe's harmony in mathematical rigor and geometric perfection. As we can see, we are in the field of conjecture.

Be that as it may, the bond between Piero della Francesca and Pacioli was quite close, as noted by Giorgio Vasari who recalled him as the «disciple» of the Master from Borgo[23]. The *De divina proportione* – the treatise, illustrated by Leonardo, that Pacioli wrote six years after Piero's death and dedicated to Ludovico il Moro, Duke of Milan – depends entirely on that Platonic culture with which his friend and master was imbued. It examines the symbolic aspects of the five regular solids (icosahedron, cube, tetrahedron, octahedron, dodecahedron) which, as in Plato's *Timeaus,* correspond to the four elements (water, earth, fire and air); a new one, the fifth essence, must be added to them.

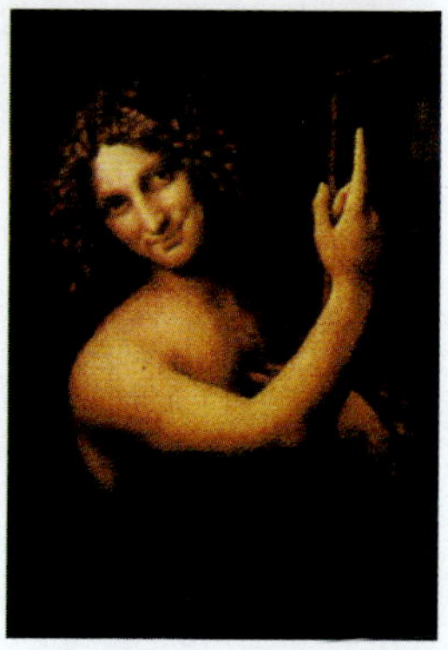

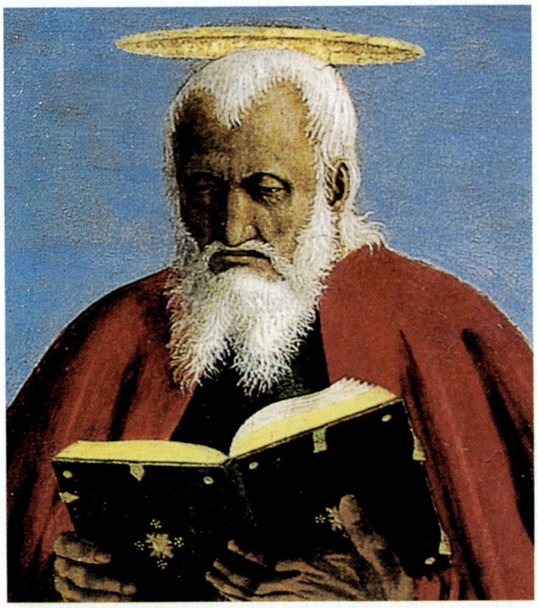

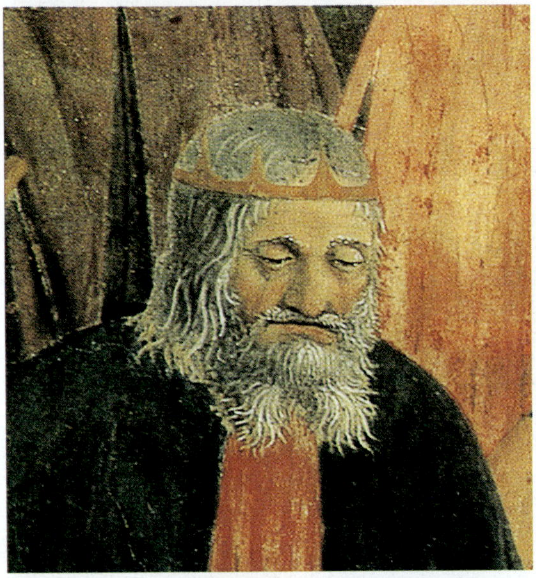

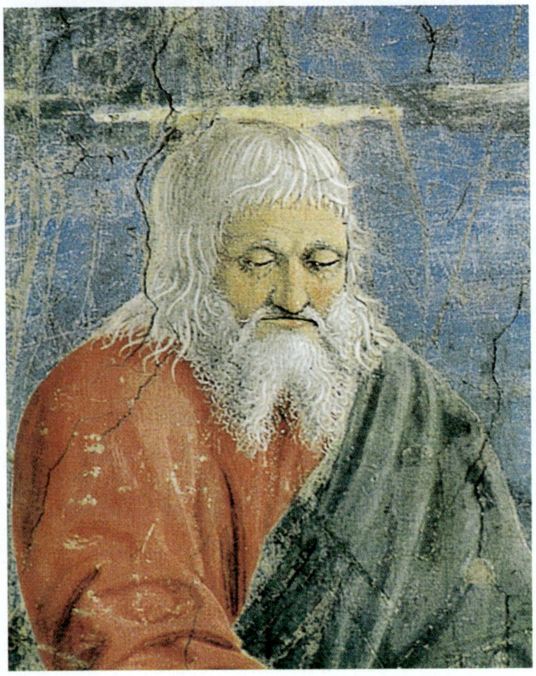

Returning to the *Brera altarpiece*, the third saint who closes the group on the right of the painting is John the Evangelist, who matches John the Baptist in the trio on the left, probably alluding, in this way, to the cycle of the solar year. It is well known that the Baptist was linked to the summer solstice while St. John the Evangelist symbolized the winter solstice[24]. But even in this case, the Evangelist, characterized by the attribute of the book (the Gospel), reproposes the usual system of the character repeated over the years with but few variations.

In fact, we find the same, and nearly identical saint, in the *Polyptych of the Misericordia* (the next to the last figure from the left in the middle register) and in the dismembered *Polyptych of St. Augustine*. The portion with the saint is currently in the Frick Collection in New York, however, here he is portrayed as having much more hair and holding the book open.

We must also mention that certain images of old people that Piero used (including the Evangelist) seem influenced by references to the Emperor Sigismund, whom the artist portrays as St. Sigismund in the fresco in the Tempio Malatestiano in Rimini. With more or less marked variations, Piero used the face of the emperor to give substance to the great old people in his pictorial epoch. Thus, God the Father in the *Annunciation* in the Bacci Chapel in the church of San Francesco in Arezzo has the same divided beard, the same white hair and the same expression as Sigismund[25].

Moreover, in the same painting cycle in Arezzo, the defeated Chosroes has the same suffering and preoccupied face that we saw characterizing the image of God. It is not the victorious Heraclius the one who has the face of God, but the deposed and conquered Sassanide sovereign. It is as if Piero wanted to say that the face of the Eternal can be seen in the sorrow of the others. As we can see, a rigorous geometric arrangement of the space influences the entire painting, including the choice of the characters and their respective portrayals which tend to create a series of coherent intellectual references.

It is in this sense that we must understand the use of the presumed self-portrait. A portrait of the artist has come down to us only through the engraving by Cristoforo Coriolano, in the second edition of Giorgio Vasari's *Lives* (1568). It was on the basis of this engraving that scholars have identified Piero in the praying figure immediately behind the man with the hood in the central part of the *Polyptych of the Misericordia*; or in one of the sleeping guards (the second from the left) in the *Resurrection* which is in the Museo Civico in Sansepolcro; or in a character in *The Queen of Sheba Worshipping the Wood of the True Cross and the Meeting of Solomon and the Queen of Sheba*, the man seen frontally who, inside the palace, emerges between the character wearing a red, fur-lined *oppelanda* (a typical ceremonial costume) and the other wearing the *mazzocchio* (a typical fifteenth century head covering).

If, in this last case, the mature figure of the painter serves to up-date the scene, and this also applies to the costumes of the various figures, in the *Polyptych of the Misericordia* his image serves the purpose of invoking protection upon himself, according to a custom that was widely documented, for example in Duccio's late Medieval art.

Finally, the *Resurrection* shows us the master in the garb of one of the sleeping guards: the detail recalls the other equally bold face of the sleeping guard in the *Resurrection,* frescoed earlier (1445-1450) by Andrea del Castagno in the Florentine Cenacle of St. Apollonia, which in turn cannot but recall the Giottesque prototype in the Scrovegni chapel in Padua.

However, the subtle symbolic plot that shapes Piero's work

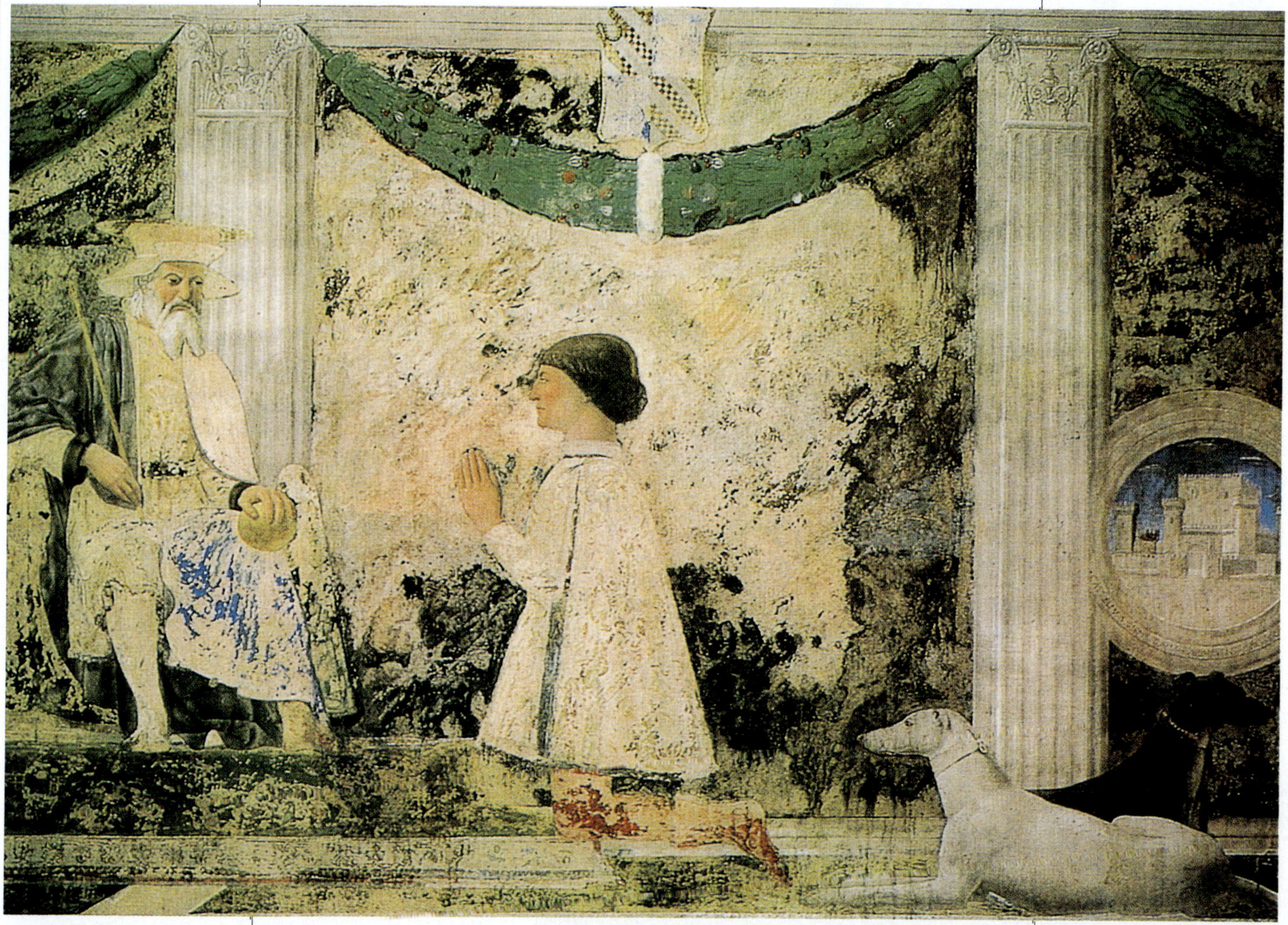

Above:
Sigismondo Malatesta before St. Sigismund (1451);
Tempio Malatestiano, Rimini.

Opposite page, from the top:
Polyptych of St. Augustine (1454-1469), detail of St. John the Evangelist; Frick Collection, New York.

The Battle of Heraclius and Chosroes, detail of Chosroes, episode from the *Legend of the True Cross* (1452-1466, circa); Bacci Chapel, Church of San Francesco, Arezzo.

Annunciation, detail of God the Father, episode from the *Legend of the True Cross* (1452-1466, circa); Bacci Chapel, Church of San Francesco, Arezzo.

makes the overlap, even in this case, a coincidence that can hardly be considered casual, even if we must say from the start that Salmi did not agree that the character in question was the artist because «we cannot understand how this figure, lacking any inner light, could be understood as a self-portrait of the master»[26]. The scholar's observation is, as we shall see, correct in a sense, even if his conclusion does not seem to be.

On the other hand, Salmi is decidedly right when he contests the interpretations of Clark and De Tolnay who, in the background landscape, saw the rebirth of nature at the end of winter[27]. It is not difficult to see that the landscape to the right of Christ (the left side of the fresco) is bleak with dry trees, while the one to the left of the Redeemer (the right side of the fresco) looks green and flourishing. The arrangement of contrasting landscapes on the background is indicative in itself, because it contains implications of a moral kind – signifying that the landscape on the right of Christ represents the ascetic and contemplative life, while the one on his left is the symbol of pleasure and lasciviousness[28].

This interpretation is confirmed by the fact that the light

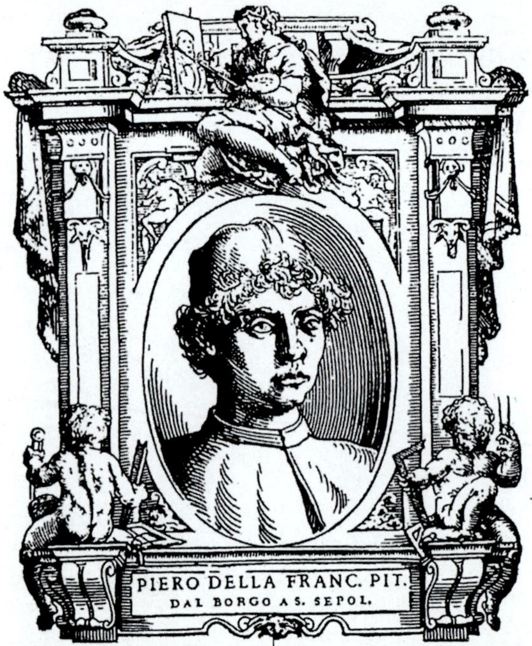

of the sun (which significantly is rising: it is dawn) comes from the barren area, and is "marked" by the presence of the standard of Christ. The spring landscape, on the other hand, includes a castle (which recalls the one in Borgo Sansepolcro, depicted in the *Baptism of Christ*). On this side the master painted the guards with military insignias. The guard in the foreground has a decorated helmet and sword; the other holds his lance and shield on which we can see the letters S.P., part of the S.P.Q.R. («Senatus Populusque Romanus») that refers to the Roman domination[29].

It is evident, therefore, that the flourishing landscape appears with the negative connotations that lead back to the concrete yet futile questions of this world. The standard and the wounds of the resurrected Christ (there are three including the one on his ribs) are on the side of the barren landscape and eloquently indicate the road to take so that the soul can rise again like its savior. Obviously, following the bitter and harsh road of salvation is difficult; one cannot sleep like the guards do (only the one in the foreground on the left appears to be waking up and rubs his eyes before the dazzling light of Truth); the sleep they are immersed in is not the blessed sleep of Jacob or Joseph prior to the flight into Egypt, but rather the tragic sleep of the drunken Noah (*Genesis* 9:21-27), of Samson on Delilah's lap (*Judges* 16; 19), of Holofernes decapitated by Judith (*Judith* 13:2 ff.): it is the sleep of the death of the soul.

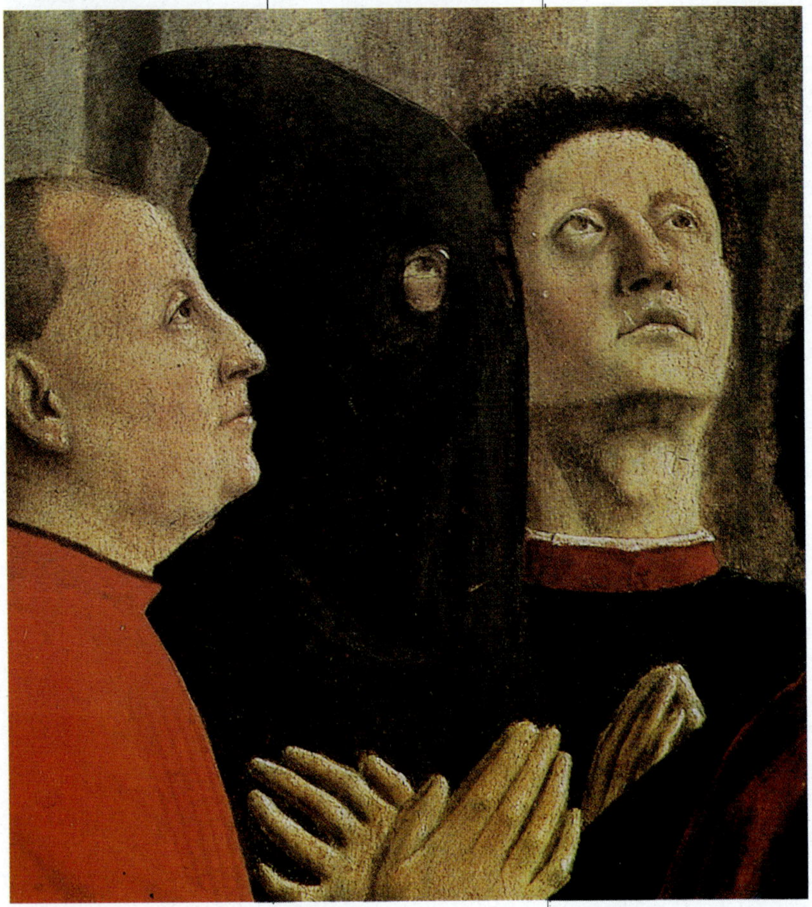

However, there is a sort of graduality in the guards' poses: the ones on the right, holding the insignias of power, sleep deeply like rocks, and the light of Truth cannot reach them, even though it is right there; on the left is the guard who is waking up while the other (the one which seems to be the artist's self-portrait) is still laying down, abandoned to this destiny of spiritual laziness. Thus, Salmi's observation seems to fit in part, since the characterizing feature of the presumed self-portrait is the guard's status of humble sinner who not by chance is seated on the ground.

Even in the *Resurrection*, perspective is used in the symbolic arrangement to the point that it forces a unitary vision of the scene which, as Nicco Fasola noted, consists of two viewpoints[30]: one is clearly frontal, characterizing the figure of Christ which is an atemporal and paradigmatic image, that «does not belong entirely to this world»; the other, from below, shows the guards as men caught in the flow of life. In this case the comparison with Masaccio's *Trinity* (Santa Maria Novella, Florence) is not out of place; Piero must certainly have seen it around 1439 during his sojourn in Florence.

Masaccio's fresco, which as a matter of fact reverses the situation with respect to Piero's version – as it shows from below

Top:
Cristoforo Coriolano, *Piero della Francesca,* woodcut from the second edition of *Lives* (1568) by Giorgo Vasari.

Above:
Polyptych of the Misericordia (1445-1462), detail;
Museo Civico, Sansepolcro.

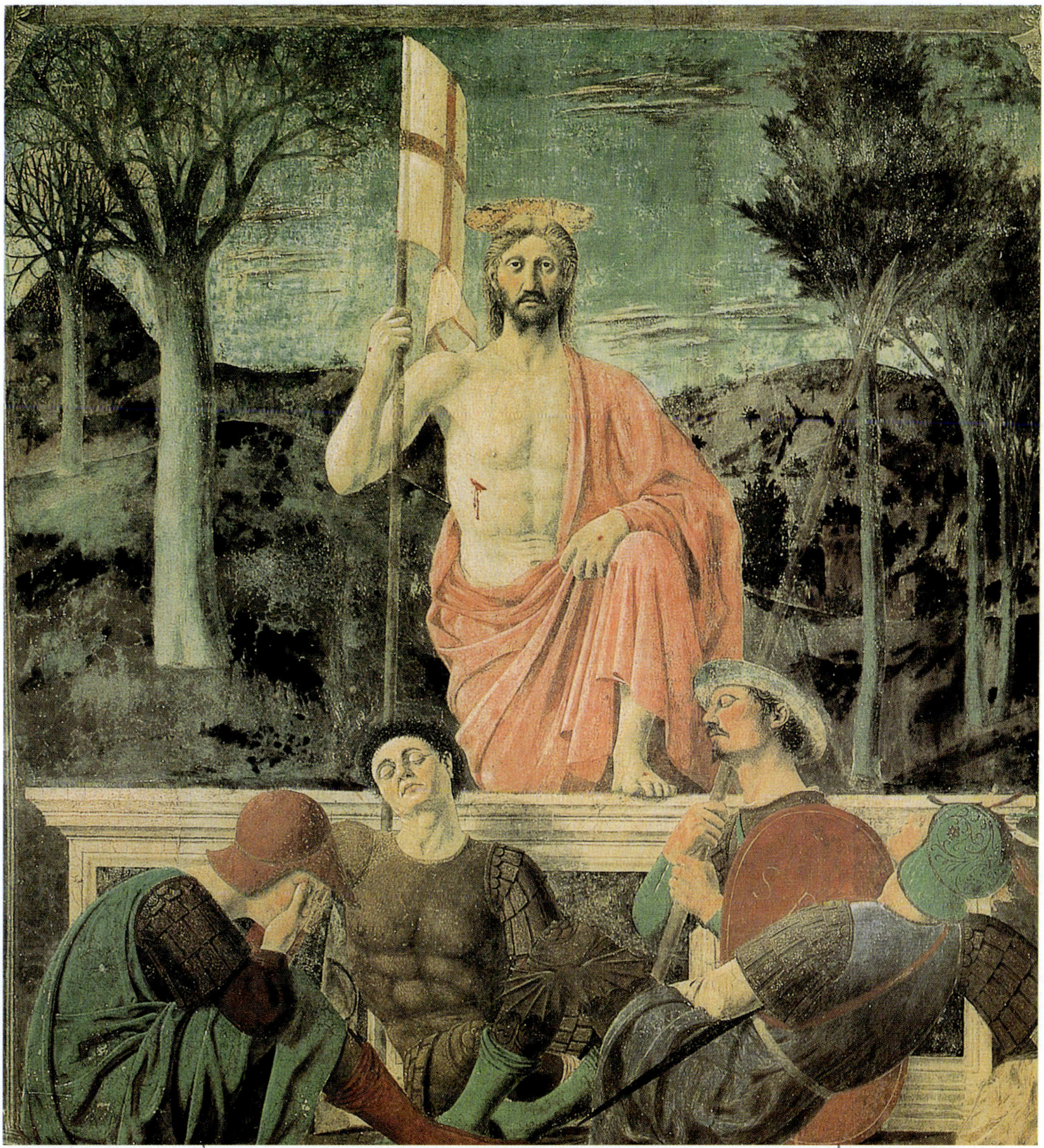

Resurrection (1468); Museo Civico, Sansepolcro.

the Trinity, the Virgin and St. John the Evangelist (the divine component in the painting) while the patrons (the human component) are seen from a mere frontal point of view –, like the *Resurrection* uses the new perspective tool to portray through an updated language the difference between the divine and the human, which Medieval painting syntax used to express in terms of different dimensions, by varying the sizes of the figures. One outstanding example of such a language is the *Maestà* by Segna di Bonaventura (Collegiata, Castiglion Fiorentino), a painting in which we have a full range of sizes: the Virgin takes up nearly the entire height of the painting, the angels and saints (Gregory

From left:
Segna di Bonaventura, *Maestà* (after 1302); Collegiata, Castiglion Fiorentino

Niccolò di Segna, *Madonna of the Misericordia* (1331-1332); Pinacoteca nazionale, Siena

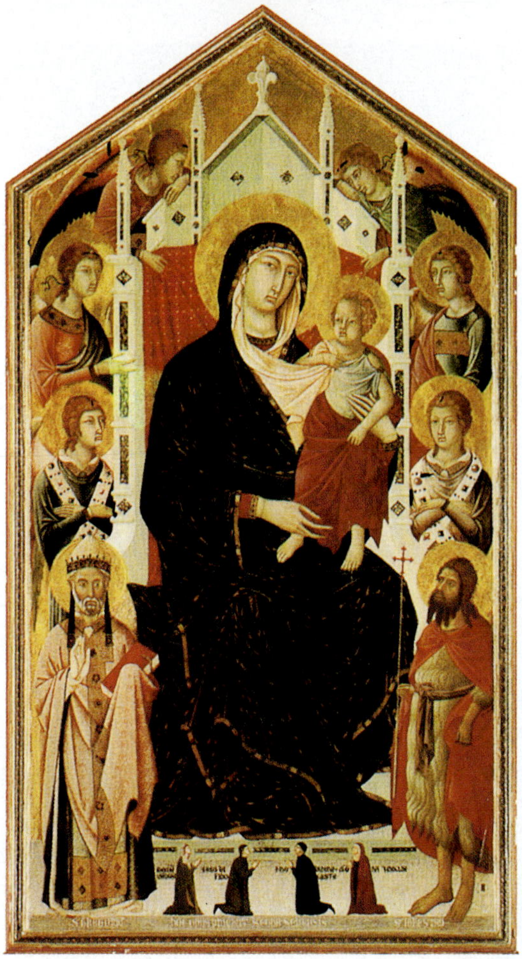

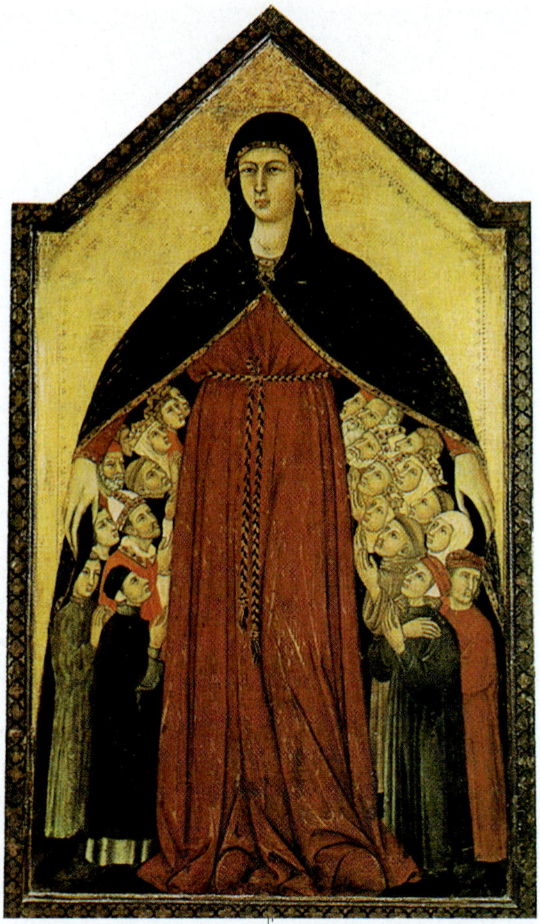

Below, right:
Andrea del Castagno, *Resurrection* (1445-1450), detail; Cenacle of St. Apollonia, Florence.

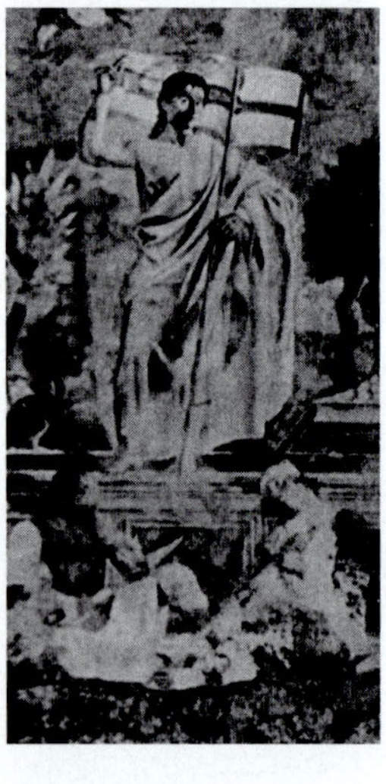

In Piero's work the relationship between divinity and humanity is expressed with figurative solutions which are related either to a still Medieval type or portrayal, or to a "modus operandi" open to the new trends. In the central panel of the *Polyptych of the Misericordia* (see page 19), the figure of the Virgin is much bigger than the figures of the donors beneath her cloak. This is entirely in keeping with the Medieval model that resolved the divine-human relationship in dimensional terms, as we can see in the two fourteenth century paintings shown here. In the *Resurrection*, via Andrea del Castagno and Giotto – obviously – the determining model is Masaccio's *Trinity*. Here the relationship between divine and human is not resolved in terms of size, but rather by perspective. They can no longer be "framed" the same way. It is of little importance that Piero overturned Masaccio's perspective solutions. In the *Resurrection* it is the guards who are seen from below and Christ from the front; in the *Trinity* Christ and the saints are seen from below, and the patron from the front.

and John the Baptist) are of intermediate size and the worshippers are almost microscopic.

Piero, too, used the same Medieval language in the *Polyptych of the Misericordia*, where the worshippers are smaller. However, we must note that in this case he was conditioned by a rigid and specific iconographic arrangement for the subject: Our Lady of Mercy.

The confraternity of Misericordia that commissioned the painting asked that it "match" (albeit with possible variations) the model of the panel – which has since been lost – that was previously on the same altar for which Piero's painting was destined[31]. As a matter of fact, the image had been codified and used for years, so it is not possible to identify a definite source of it, especially since we do not have the altarpiece that is mentioned in the contract.

However, it seems to me that no attention has ever been dedicated to the unusual similarity between the arrangement of Piero's work and the *Madonna of the Misericordia* painted by Niccolò di Segna which is currently in the Pinacoteca Nazionale in Siena. Comparisons have been made with the fresco of Santa Maria delle Grazie in Arezzo. However, because of the red robe, and the deep blue cloak, the same type of girdle for the Virgin and the gold background, Niccolò's painting is very similar to the panel by Piero[32].

Niccolò, son of Segna di Bonaventura to whom the *Christ Resurrected* (cathedral, Sansepolcro) – in which Piero saw the iconographic model of the *Resurrection*[33] –, is attributed was linked to the house of Santa Maria della Misericordia by a lease for a workshop that belonged to the confraternity. It is therefore

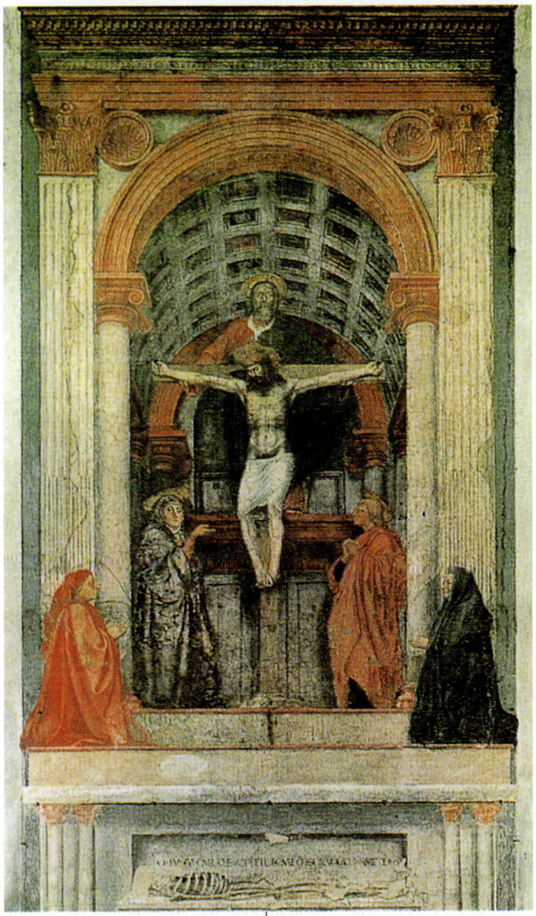

Left:
Masaccio,
Trinity
(1427);
Santa Maria Novella,
Florence.

Below:
Giotto,
Noli me tangere,
episode from
Scenes from the Lives of the Virgin and Christ
(1305-1310),
detail;
Scrovegni Chapel,
Padua.

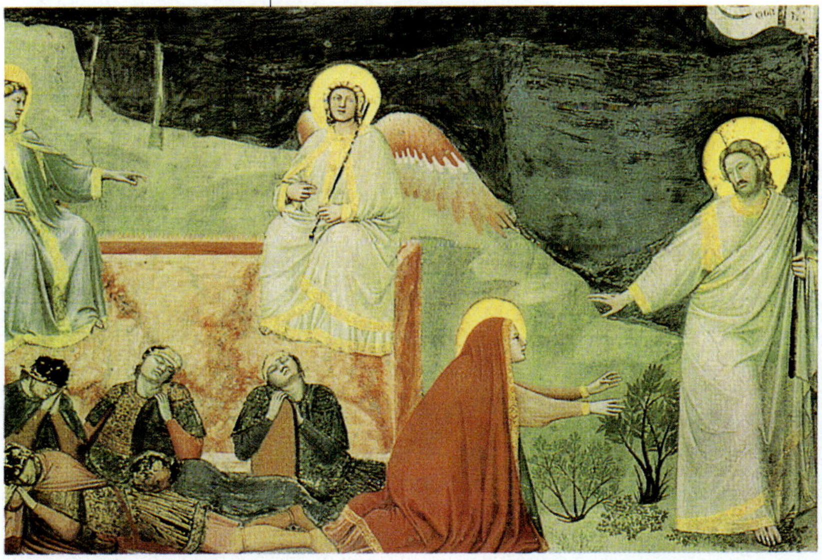

possible, as Carli suggests, that the painting destined for the church of San Bartolomeo in Vertine in Chianti was done at around that time (1331-1332). Be that as it may, it is one of the oldest portrayals of this popular iconography so that it is possible that Niccolò's painting could have been considered a prototype and the basis for Piero's, and it may well have been done by Niccolò himself.

It is obvious that we are dealing with hypotheses, however the reference does not seem arbitrary. What is even more likely, however, is that – precisely because of what we have said, a tribute to a Medieval prototype and for the use of appropriate language – the *Polyptych of the Misericordia* is the first important work by Piero della Francesca.

(20) *Piero della Francesca,* De prospectiva pingendi, *cit. I, p. 63. Saint Augustine,* Epistola III, *in* Ordine, musica, bellezza, *ed. by. M. Bettetini, Milan 1992, p. 275.*
(21) *E. Battisti,* op. cit. *I, p. 170.*
(22) Ivi, *p. 512, n. 445.*
(23) *G. Vasari,* op. cit., *p. 379. We cannot remain silent about Vasari's insult to Pacioli, accusing him of having published Piero's theoretical works under his own name. The accusation was specifically about* De divina proportione *that contains the* De quinque corporibus regolaribus.
(24) *M. Salmi,* op. cit., *p. 125. Actually, the figure of the saint has been identified, without any basis, with St. Ubaldo, St. Andrew and even cardinal Bessarione. What remain incontrovertible, as Battisti justly notes* (op. cit. , *I. p. 444*) *is that it is an evangelizing saint. However, to me it seems that the scholar's prudence could be reasonably superseded in favor of St. John, considering the fact that the same figure also appears in relation to the Baptist in the* Polyptych of the Misericordia.
(25) *According to a very old tradition, the door against which the announcing stands in the Arezzo fresco symbolizes the Virgin, as Donatello must certainly have known since he used the same motif in the* Annunciation *dated 1435 in Santa Croce in Florence, a work with which Piero must have been familiar. the relationship was noted for the first time by F. Hartt,* Order and Meaning in Piero's True Cross Cycle (*paper presented at the College Art Association of America, Boston, 1969*) *and then by Battisti,* op. cit., *II, p. 31.*
(26) *M. Salmi.* op. cit., *p. 104.*
(27) *For Clark* (Piero della Francesca, *New York 1969, p. 57*) *the Christ in the* Resurrection, *in line with Longhi, is almost a rural divinity, symbol of life. For De Tolnay* (La Résurrection du Christ par Piero della Francesca. Essai d'interpretation, *in "Gazette des Beaux-Arts", XCVI, 1954, pp. 35-40; 62-63*) *the image of Christ rising from the tomb coincides with the cosmic renewal of nature. Subsequently, De Tolnay flanked this concept with that of* "Sol novus".
(28) *The theme developed during the Renaissance* (*Cfr. A. Gentili,* Da Tiziano a Tiziano, *Milan 1980, pp. 49-53*), *but its roots are in Medieval and fifteenth century culture with the juxtaposition of the tree of knowledge (dry) and the tree of life (green), both of which are attributes of the figure of Justice: Cfr. Battisti,* op. cit., *I, n. 308. The scholar mentions* Pèlerinage de l'ame *which, reproposing this concept had a certain influence on the era's culture. See also: R. Wittkower,* Transformation of Minerva in Renaissance Imagery, *in "Journal of the Warburg Institute", 2, 1938-1939, pp. 194-205.*
(29) *Battisti interprets the missing letters Q and R* (op. cit., *I, p. 284*) *as a sign that Borgo Sansepolcro had attained a certain dignity as a city, and the creation of its diocese* (ivi, *II, p. 36*). *This consideration shifts the date of the fresco to 1464. We must mention that the painting also took on a political value in relation to the town which is linked by its name to the Gospel episode (Sansepolcro, Holy Sepulchre).*
(30) *G. Nicco Fasola, introduction to Piero della Francesca,* De prospectiva Pingendi, *cit. pp. 51-52.*
(31) *The contract, dated 11 June 1445 is conserved in the State Archives in Florence and is mentioned by E. Battisti,* op. cit. , *II, p. 220.*
(32) *P. Torriti,* La Pinacoteca Nazionale di Siena, *I, Genoa, 1977, pp. 76-77. For the iconography of the Polyptych of the Misericordia: L. Silvy,* L'origine de la Vierge de la Miséricordie, *in "Gazette des beaux-arts", XXXIV, 1905, pp. 401-410.*
(33) *A. Paolucci,* Piero della Francesca. Catalogo completo, *Florence 1990, p. 102; on Niccolò di Segna: E. Carli,* La pittura senese del Trecento, *Milan 1981, p. 74.*

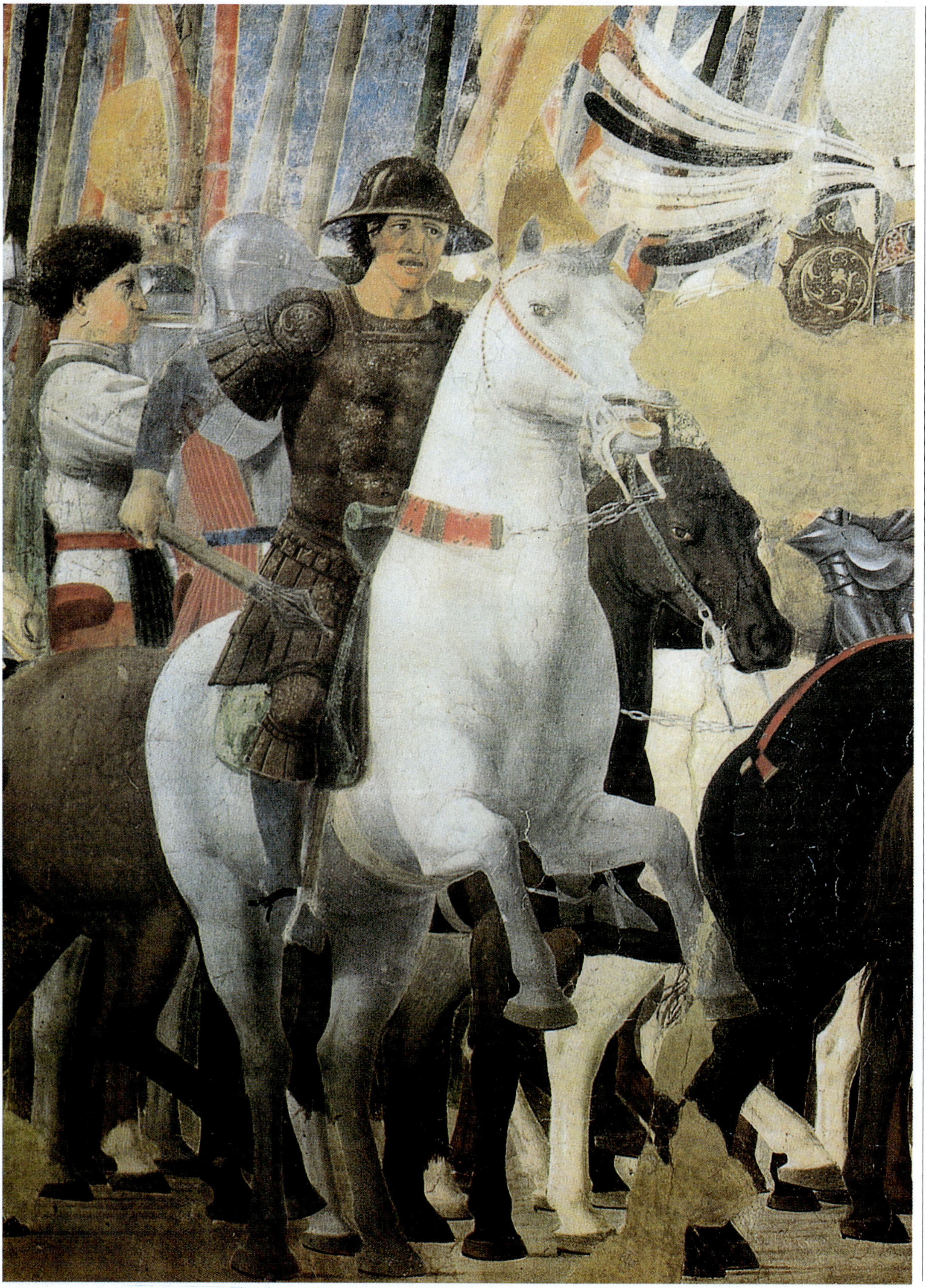

The chronological problem

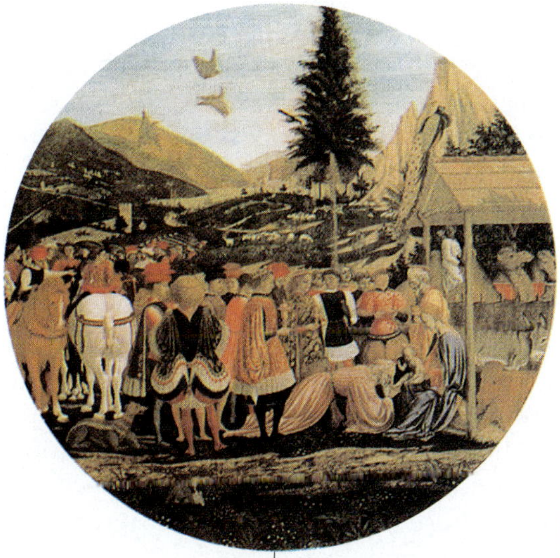

Above:
Domenico Veneziano, *Adoration of the Magi,* (1439-1441, circa); Gemäldegalerie, Berlin-Dahlem.

Opposite page:
Constantine Defeats Maxentius, episode from the *Legend of the True Cross* (1452-1466, circa); Bacci Chapel, Church of San Francesco, Arezzo.

T**HE PROBLEM REGARD**ing the chronology of Piero's works has been compared to climbing sheer rock. We are dealing with an artist who displayed not insignificant stylistic variations when it comes to dating the single works, and this is aggravated by a lack of historical documentation. Not even Vasari's biography offers any adequate guarantees of reliability from this standpoint. In fact, the writer from Arezzo notes that Piero «lived to be 86 years old». Since we know the year of his death we can establish that he was born around 1406.

If Vasari's information were exact, however, at the time he signed the contract for the *Polyptych of the Misericordia,* that is 11 June 1445, Piero would have been more or less forty-one years old. Therefore, he would have been a grown, established man, who enjoyed civil rights and would have assumed the respective legal responsibilities. Thus, we cannot explain why Benedetto, Piero's father had to act as his guarantor. The only plausible reason could be that Piero had not yet reached majority, that is the age of twenty-five that would have allowed him to sign a document without his father. In light of this consideration it is probable that Piero was born after 1420, which seems to be confirmed by the fact that in 1445 he could not have been an established artist if he had to comply with a predetermined form: «ad foggiam eius que nunc est» (according to the form that exists now), as the contract reads[34].

In any event, Piero had for some time been pursuing his artistic career by that date. In September 1439 he was in Florence, helping Domenico Veneziano who was doing the frescoes in the chapel of the main altar in the church of Sant'Egidio, a project that was interrupted in 1445 and of which just a few fragments remain[35]. Domenico's art was already mature as we can see in the *Adoration of the Magi* that preceded the fresco cycle, in fact we can easily trace the stylistic codes that would soon become part of Piero's language. However, 1439 was an important year for Florence and for Christianity, the ecumenical council that had begun in Ferrara had moved to the city of the lily. It

Below:
Piero di Domenico,
Nativity
(1510);
Pinacoteca
Nazionale,
Siena.

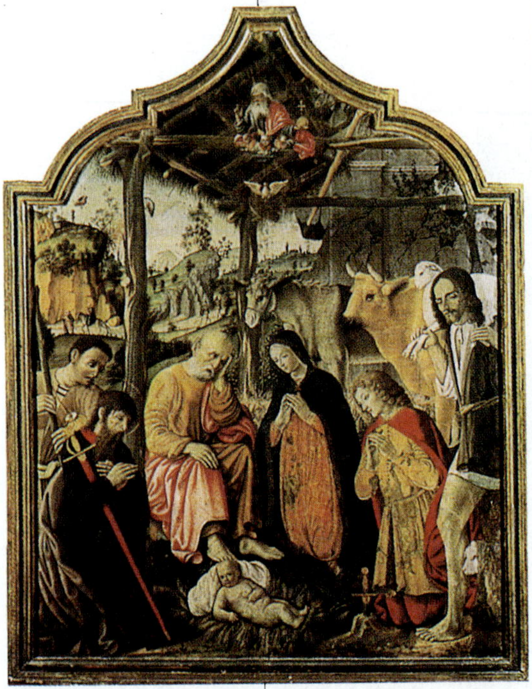

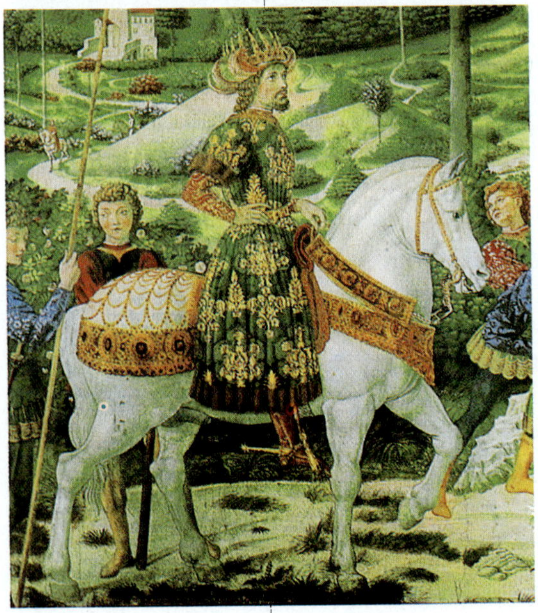

Above:
Benozzo Gozzoli,
Procession of the Magi
(1459-1463),
detail of the king
identified as
John VIII Paleologus;
Palazzo
Medici-Riccardi,
Florence.

was this council that launched the renewed unification (that would last but a short time) between the churches of Rome and Constantinople. At that time Florence was the center of the Christian world and the young Piero certainly would have been amazed by the lavish dress and exotic nature of the delegations from Constantinople, and excited by the fact that the Byzantine Emperor, John VIII Paleologus, himself was in the city. All of this became part of his pictorial world.

Of the subjects discussed during the council, the Trinity problems and the formula for the sacrament of baptism were among the key issues. This is the reason that prompted more than one scholar to consider the *Baptism of Christ* of London as belonging to Piero's Florentine period[36]. If that were the case, this would be Piero's first great achievement. However, the stylistic and geometrical arrangement that we have already reviewed would speak for a much later date. What is more, the archeological references are related to knowledge and experiences that Piero could only have acquired in Rome[37]. Furthermore, the references to the council and the issues of the Trinity are so precise that it would not have been possible for the artist to conceive of them in Florence since, with regard to those subtle theological arguments the eighteen year old Piero della Francesca, like many of his contemporaries was merely amateur. The Roman sojourn, therefore, between 1459 and 1460 seems the probable date for the painting.

In this case, however, we must ask why Piero would have created an altarpiece based on events that took place twenty years earlier. The reason is the same one that dominates Benozzo Gozzoli's *Procession of the Magi*: the crusade called by Pius II to reconquer Byzantium that had fallen to Mehmed II in 1453. Benozzo drew his inspiration from the joust of 1459, a sort of tournament held to honor Pius II who had passed through Florence, and albeit for different purposes, makes references to the Council of 1439 and John VIII Paleologus's stay in Florence since he is portrayed in the fresco[38]. The fall of Constantinople made the reference to "better times", that is the days of the Council, quite logical since there was strong hope for a reconciliation of the two churches.

In Rome Piero must have had the same theme in mind since the Pope had left his seat to try to seek a solution to that unfortunate situation. Thus, the four figures in Eastern dress already identified as the Pharisees mentioned in the Gospel of St. Matthew (on page 15 see the figures behind the catechumen), allude also to the Byzantine bishops who attended the council. Marie Tanner has identified them with the magi since one of them points to the Holy Spirit as if it were the falling star of the Gospel story. The American scholar's hypothesis is all but negligible, however matters are not than simple.

The problem is that in the iconography of the period the magi had already been three for a long time; furthermore, for her identification between the star and the dove, Ms. Tanner only refers to the Roman liturgy and the catacomb of saints Peter and Marcellinus[39]. In reality, a passage from St. Thomas seems more explicit and accessible to Piero: «As the Holy Spirit descended on the Lord who was to be baptized in the form of a dove, thus it appeared to the three Kings as a star», but the philosopher Roccasecca hastens to add: «others truly say that

Below:
Andrea di Niccolò, *Adoration of the Shepherds* (1470-1480); Pinacoteca Nazionale, Siena.

The paintings shown here offer interesting points for understanding one of Piero's masterpieces, *The Baptism of Christ* (shown on page 11). The *Procession of the Magi* by Benozzo Gozzoli, with its definite references to the Council of Florence held in 1489 (one example is the hypothetical portrait of the emperor John VIII Paleologus, who was in Florence on that occasion) and the doctrinaire question of baptism that was discussed in that meeting are valid helps not only in interpreting, but also in dating Piero's work, suggesting a nearly contemporary date for both works. The paintings from the Sienese school, on the other hand, portray a well-defined theme, the overlappability of the star that marks the road for the magi and the dove of the Holy Spirit, an iconographic tradition which even the *Baptism* seems to take into account.

the angel that appeared to the shepherds in human form appeared to the magi as a star»[40]. Most probably there was some sort of contamination between the two iconographies so that in several works from the Sienese school, albeit later than the *Baptism of Christ* in London, we see the dove of the Holy Spirit rather than the star over the hut or grotto in which the Child is portrayed. I refer, in particular, to the *Adoration of the Shepherds* by Andrea di Niccolò, to the *Nativity* by Gerolamo di Benvenuto and the *Nativity* by Piero di Domenico, all three of which are in the Pinacoteca nazionale in Siena. Then, we must also note that

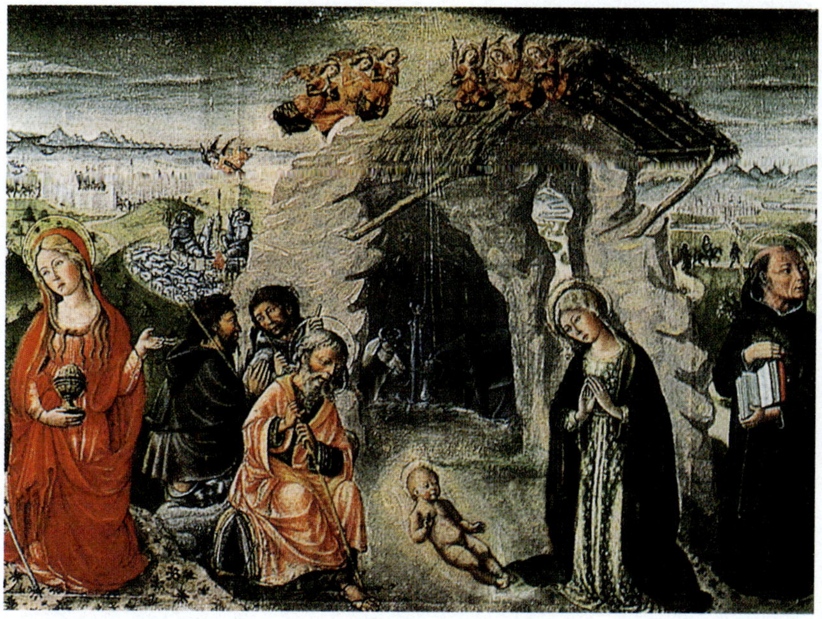

in Benozzo's fresco we see neither the star of the magi, nor the angel who appears to the shepherds frescoed in two separate groups on the western and eastern walls. Among the various hypotheses regarding the identification of the star, there is one that considers it the dove in Filippo Lippi's *Adoration of the Child* which is now in Berlin.

This painting was the altarpiece in the Medici palace chapel; today there is a copy in its place. Here the thematic similarities with Piero's *Baptism* are even closer. Lippi's *Adoration* is a Trinitarian epiphany and the reference to the sacrament of baptism is guaranteed by the figure of the young St. John wearing the camel skin of the Baptist and holding a scroll that reads: «Ecce Agnus Dei qui tollit peccata Mundi». The reference to the subject of baptism (and hence to the council) is further emphasized by the presence of the cut-down trees that are mentioned in the Gospel according to Matthew and by a river that alludes to the Jordan. If then, in Lippi's painting, the magi and the shepherds follow the dove of the Holy Spirit in compliance with Thomas' texts, in Piero's work the figures in the background should represent the shepherds who see in the dove the light that will lead them to the Truth. This fact does preclude Piero's having wanted to play on the ambiguities between the magi who came from the Orient like the Byzantine cardinals who attended the council and the fact that they, by definition, are shepherds of the soul. In any event, the identification of the four characters in the background of the *Baptism of Christ* is more complex than Ms. Tanner would maintain.

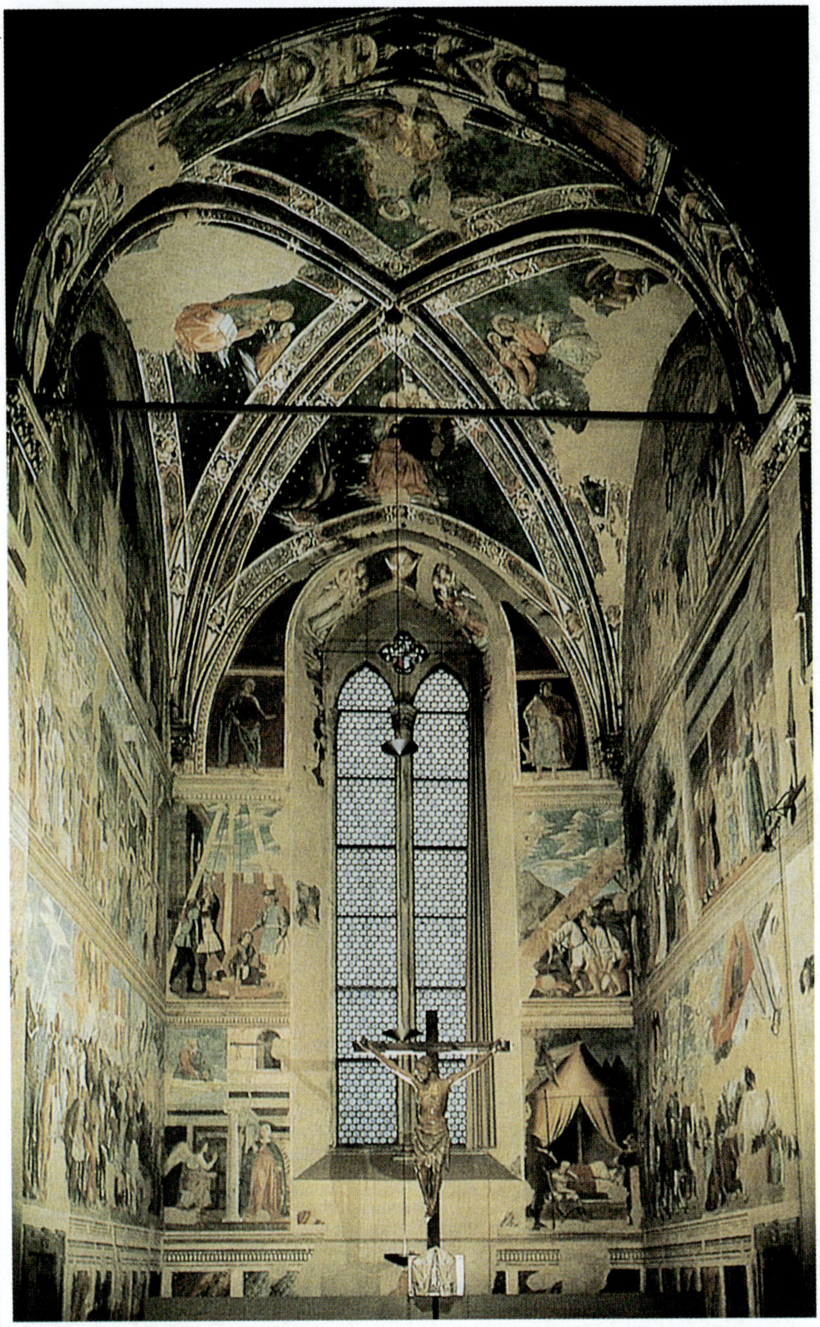

Left:
the Bacci Chapel
in the Church
of San Francesco,
Arezzo.

The ten frescoed scenes in the chapel comprise the cycle of the *Legend of the True Cross.* Piero drew his inspiration from a thirteenth century text, the *Golden Legend* by Jacopo da Varagine. The sequence begins at the top of the right wall, in accordance with the traditional order of the times and then continues; the development is not entirely linear and this may have been due to compositional requirements. As we can clearly see from the comparison between the *Exaltation of the Cross* by Agnolo Gaddi, shown here, Piero showed his knowledge of the fresco cycle on the same subject that the Florentine painter had done in the main chapel of the church of Santa Croce in the late fourteenth century.

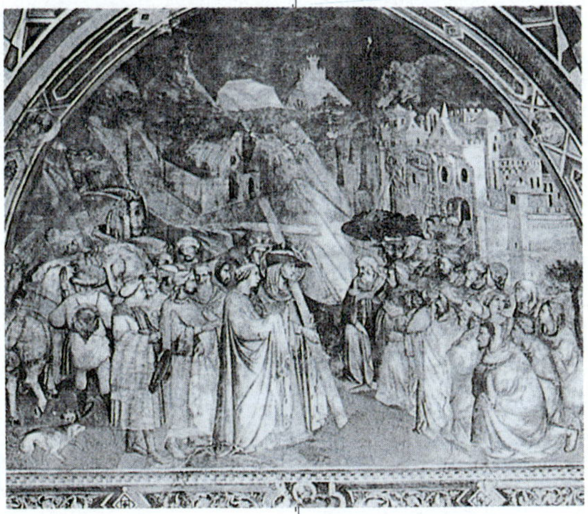

Above:
Agnolo Gaddi,
The Entrance of Constantine and St. Helena into Jerusalem,
(1385, circa),
Main Chapel,
Church
of Santa Croce,
Florence.

As it can be easily seen, the difficulty of dating Piero's works can be avoided only in part by attempting a reconstruction of the historic context within which the various paintings were produced. The fact remains that only very few works are dated or datable: the *St. Jerome Penitent* of Berlin (signed and dated 1450), the Rimini fresco (signed and dated 1451), the *Polyptych of the Misericordia* that was not yet completed in 1454. These are the only definitive points in Piero's painting; the rest is entirely hypothetical.

Today, the great achievement of the Master from Borgo seems to be the fresco cycle of Arezzo. However, we must remember that the majority of Piero's important works have been lost, starting from the fresco cycle in Ferrara for the Estense court where the duke Lionello summoned him to work (1449-1450, circa), to the frescoes in the Vatican commissioned by Pope Nicholas V (1454-1455, circa)[41]. The paintings in Arezzo belonged to that category of provincial commissions which provided the artists' income and were not scorned. The Bacci family, rich merchants from Arezzo called Piero to complete the decorations in the family chapel in the church of San Francesco that Bicci di Lorenzo had started in 1447. The most likely date for this switch seems to be 1452, the year of Bicci's death. The other chronological term comes from a document from the Compagnia della Nunziata of Arezzo concerning the commission from the gonfalonier of that confraternity. It is dated 20 December 1446 and Piero is mentioned in it as «the one who painted the main chapel in San Francesco of Arezzo»[42].

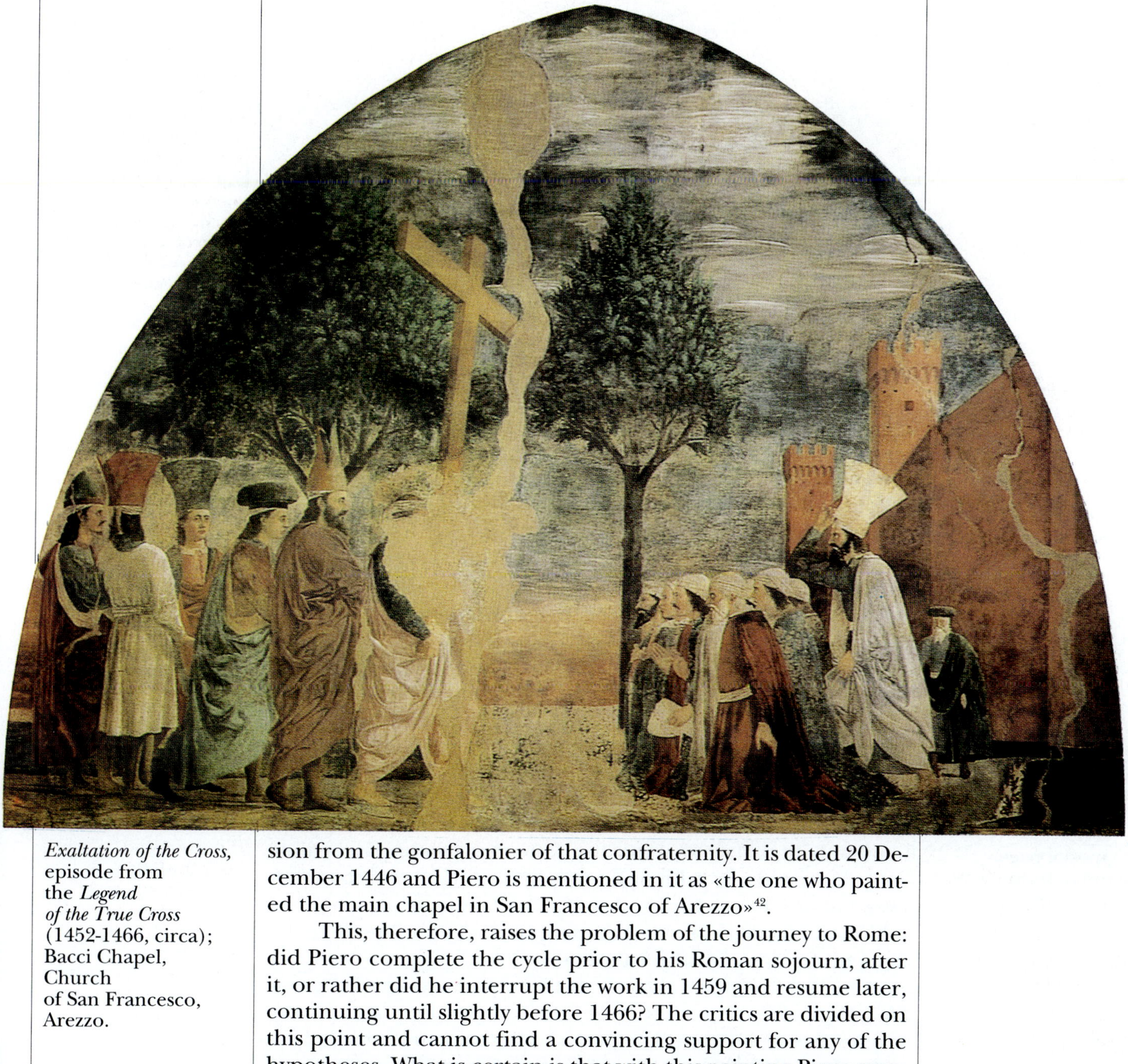

Exaltation of the Cross, episode from the *Legend of the True Cross* (1452-1466, circa); Bacci Chapel, Church of San Francesco, Arezzo.

This, therefore, raises the problem of the journey to Rome: did Piero complete the cycle prior to his Roman sojourn, after it, or rather did he interrupt the work in 1459 and resume later, continuing until slightly before 1466? The critics are divided on this point and cannot find a convincing support for any of the hypotheses. What is certain is that with this painting Piero revolutionized not only the narrative system of the story but also the internal organization of the cycle based, according to De Tolnay's observations, on principles of analogies of form and theme as well as contrast.

It is sufficient to compare the work of the Master from Borgo with the cycle that Agnolo Gaddi had frescoed earlier in the church of Santa Croce in Florence drawing his inspiration from the same subject that Piero treated in the Arezzo cycle (the Leg-

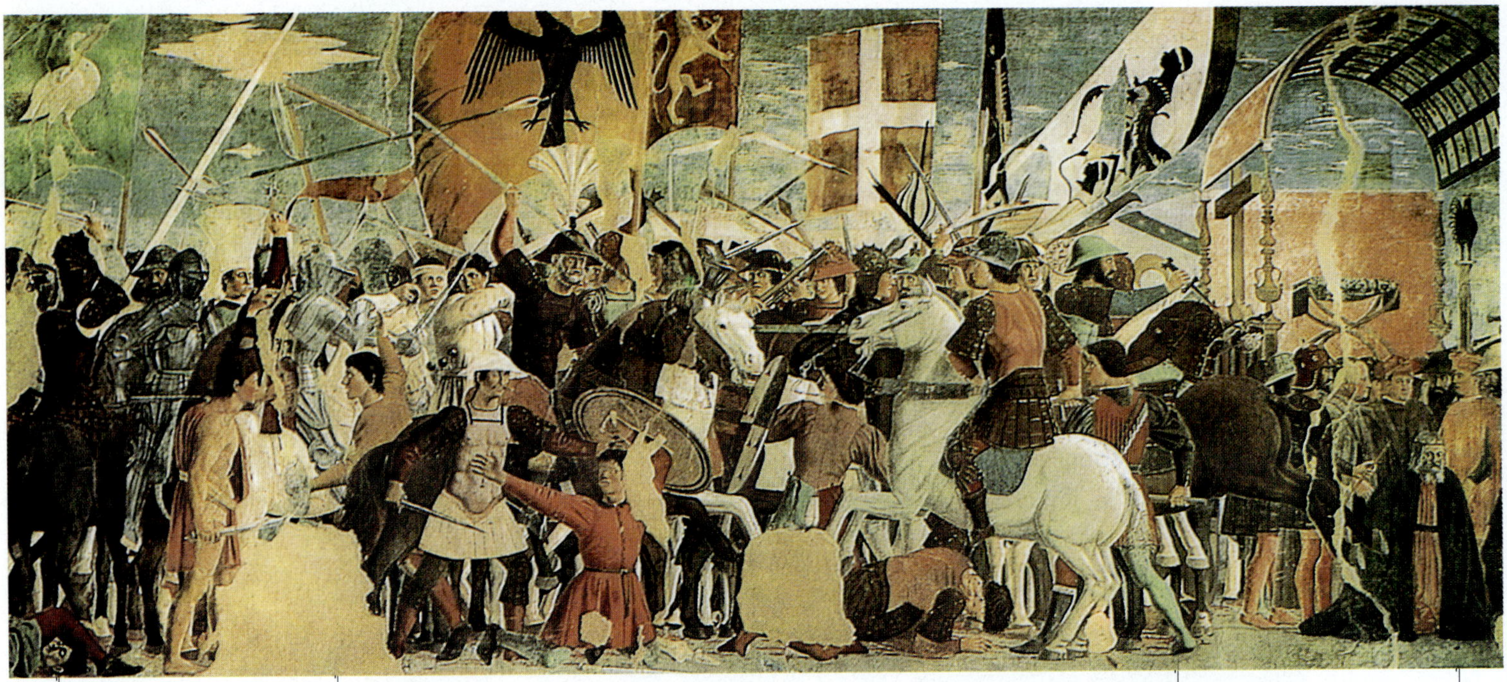

Above:
The Battle of Heraclius and Chosroes, episode from the *Legend of the True Cross* (1452-1466, circa); Bacci Chapel, Church of San Francesco, Arezzo.

Opposite page, top:
Constantine Defeats Maxentius, episode from the *Legend of the True Cross* (1452-1466, circa); Bacci Chapel, Church of San Francesco, Arezzo.

Opposite page, bottom, from the left:
Annunciation, episode from the *Legend of the True Cross* (1452-1466, circa); Bacci Chapel, Church of San Francesco, Arezzo.

Constantine's Dream, episode from the *Legend of the True Cross* (1452-1466, circa); Bacci Chapel, Church of San Francesco, Arezzo.

end of the true cross told by Jacopo da Varagine in the *Legenda Aurea*). Although explicitly cited in the scenes in the Bacci chapel (perhaps because the client wanted), Agnolo's frescoes have a narrative gait that is slavishly respectful of Jacopo da Varagine's text on which they are based. Piero, instead, carefully chose the scenes to portray so that we can feel the desire not to fall into a trivial retelling of the story, but to emphasize the salient and universally valid elements that the narrative provides. It is quite probable that Bacci participated in the drafting of the decorative plans, but what emerges, once again, is Piero's revulsion for the banal anecdote. This is revealed mainly by the inclusion of episodes such as the *Annunciation* (which does not appear in Gaddi's frescoes), and the *Dream of Constantine* on the same register[43]; in both cases the angel who brings the tidings changes the progress of the story of the men, the divine design interweaves with the flow of daily events.

In the *Annunciation*, the palm in Gabriel's hand, which led Salmi to interpret the episode as heralding the death of the Virgin Mary, rather than the birth of Christ, must be explained in another light. In fact we must specify that the palm plays the dual role of martyrdom/palm of victory. According to the first interpretation it refers to Christ's sacrifice on the cross (to which the entire cycle is dedicated), according to the latter it must be related to the victorious Constantine.

In the *Exaltation of the Cross* Piero portrays the Emperor Heraclius who returns the holy relic to Jerusalem after having taken it from Chosroes. The precise reference to Gaddi's pictorial text is apt for this scene; Gaddi portrays the entrance of Constantine and his mother St. Helena into Jerusalem. In the Florentine fresco the Roman emperor embraces the cross as Christ would have done; in the Arezzo episode, Heraclius carries it like a processional standard, but it is obvious that Piero also wanted to allude to Constantine's gesture in Agnolo's fresco[44]. Actually, Jacopo da Varagine's "narrative machine" was particularly suited to Piero's sensitivity: the legend of the cross shows the sequence of events and the unraveling of the thread of Prov-

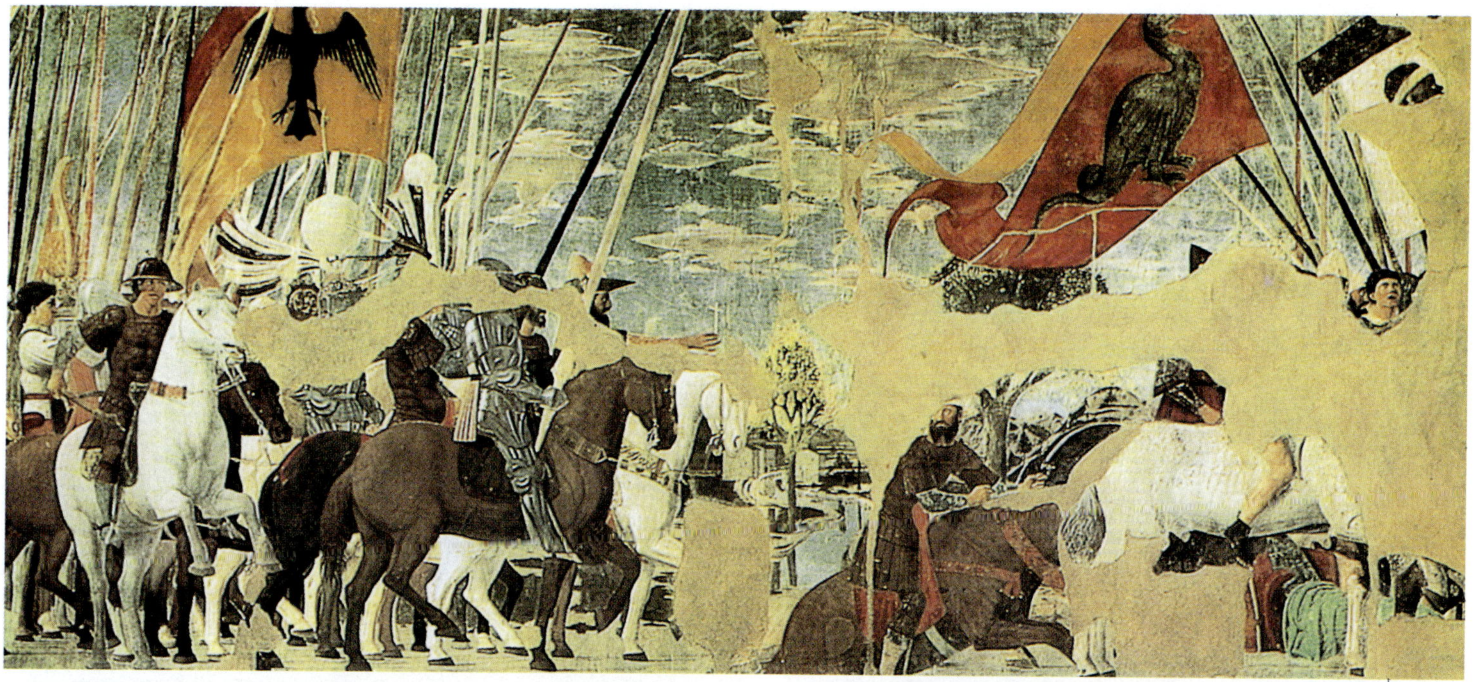

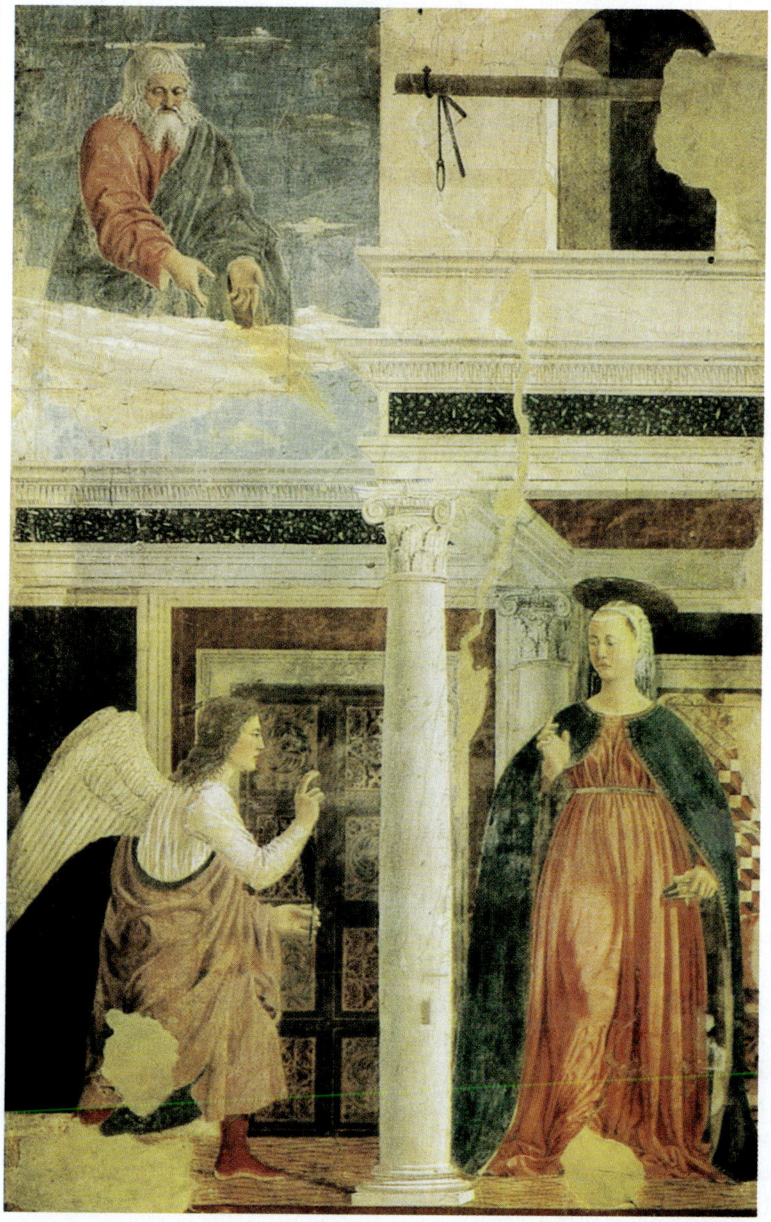

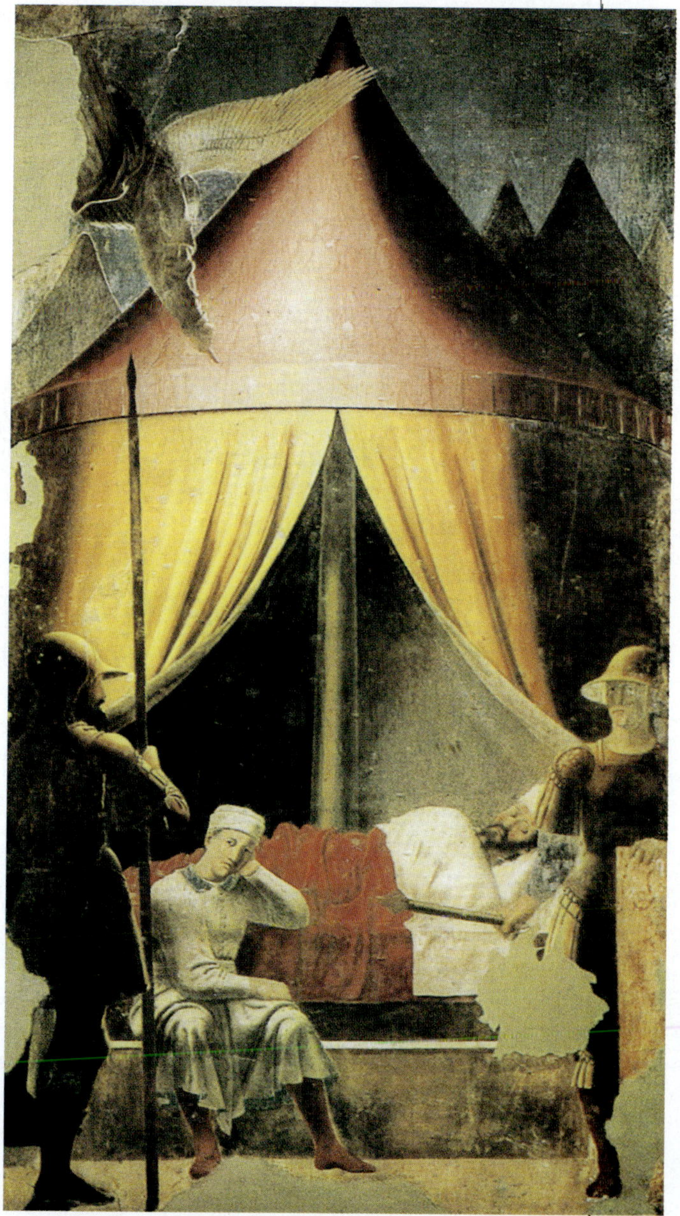

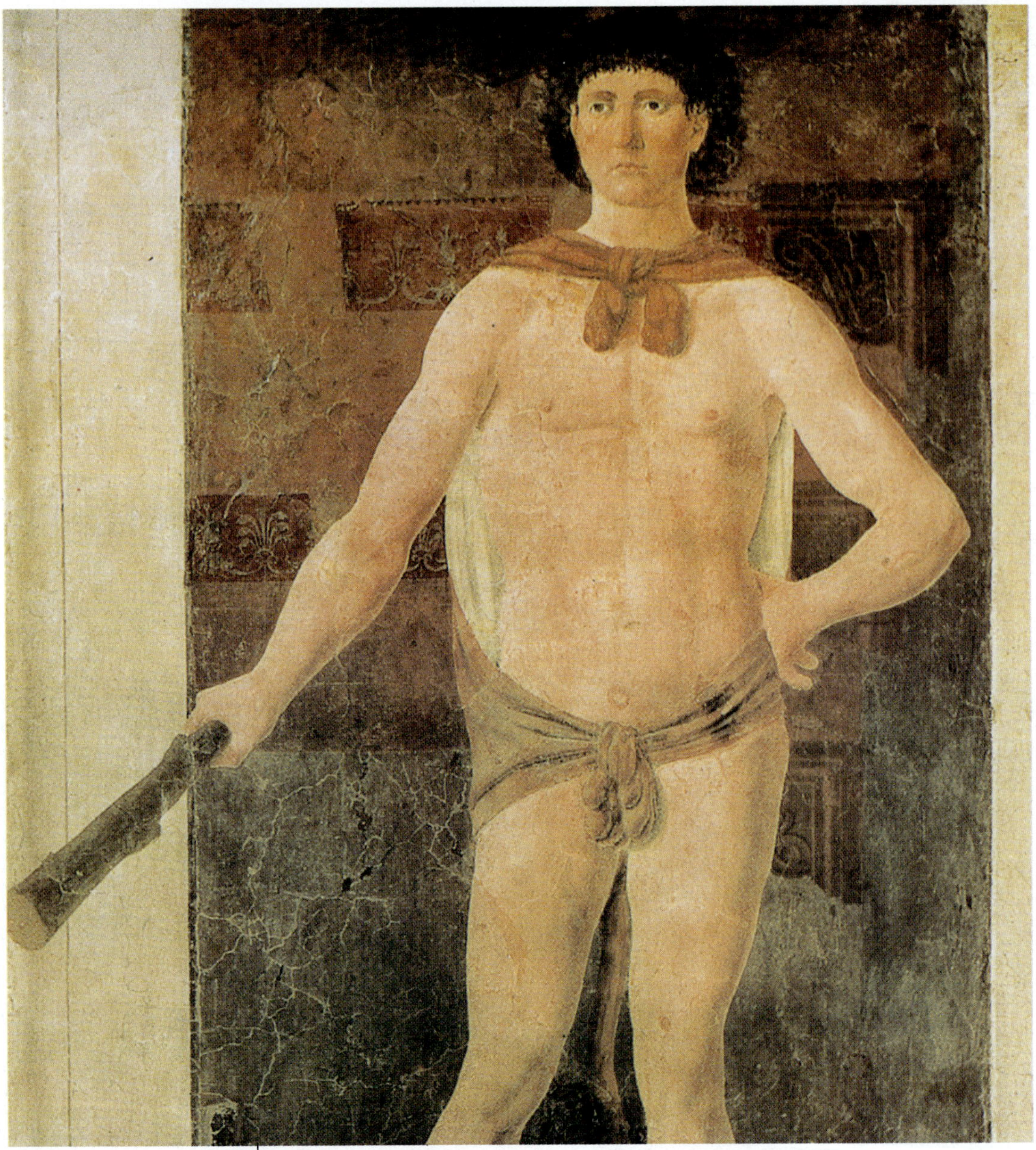

Hercules
(after 1465);
Isabella Stewart
Gardner Museum,
Boston.

The *Hercules* fresco was discovered in the artist's family home in Via delle Aggiunte in Borgo Sansepolcro during the latter half of the nineteenth century. It suffered considerable damage when it was detached and shipped to Boston in 1908. The hypothesis of a broader scope of work, and a theory about mythological characters where the young hero could have been properly situated is not unanimously accepted by the critics. This is, however, the only known instance in which Piero painted a pagan subject.

idence so that the painter can put together a series of references and overlappings that carry the story onto the level of the absolute and eternal. For this reason Heraclius (who is also Constantine) is surrounded by figures dressed as fathers of the Eastern Church, the ones whom Piero saw in Florence as a young man.

If Grohn exaggerates in affirming that the Arezzo cycle is closely related to the fall of Constantinople, we cannot but note Piero's attention to emphasizing the currentness of the scene, through the costumes and characters (the portrayal of the client, the presumed self-portrait and so forth), relating it to the contemporary events that would rock Christianity[45]. Perhaps, and once again, it is the desire to up-date the legendary episodes that prompted the artist to insert characters dressed in skins (perhaps lion skins) into the scene of the *Death of Adam* to allude, probably, to Hercules, and through him to Monterchi where Piero's mother was born, the place to which the mythical hero was traditionally linked (Hercules who killed the hydra, as Salmi noted, became the symbol of the Tuscan town in the XVI century)[46]. It is evident that in the Arezzo fresco Piero wanted to portray the descendants of the Adamites but the reference to

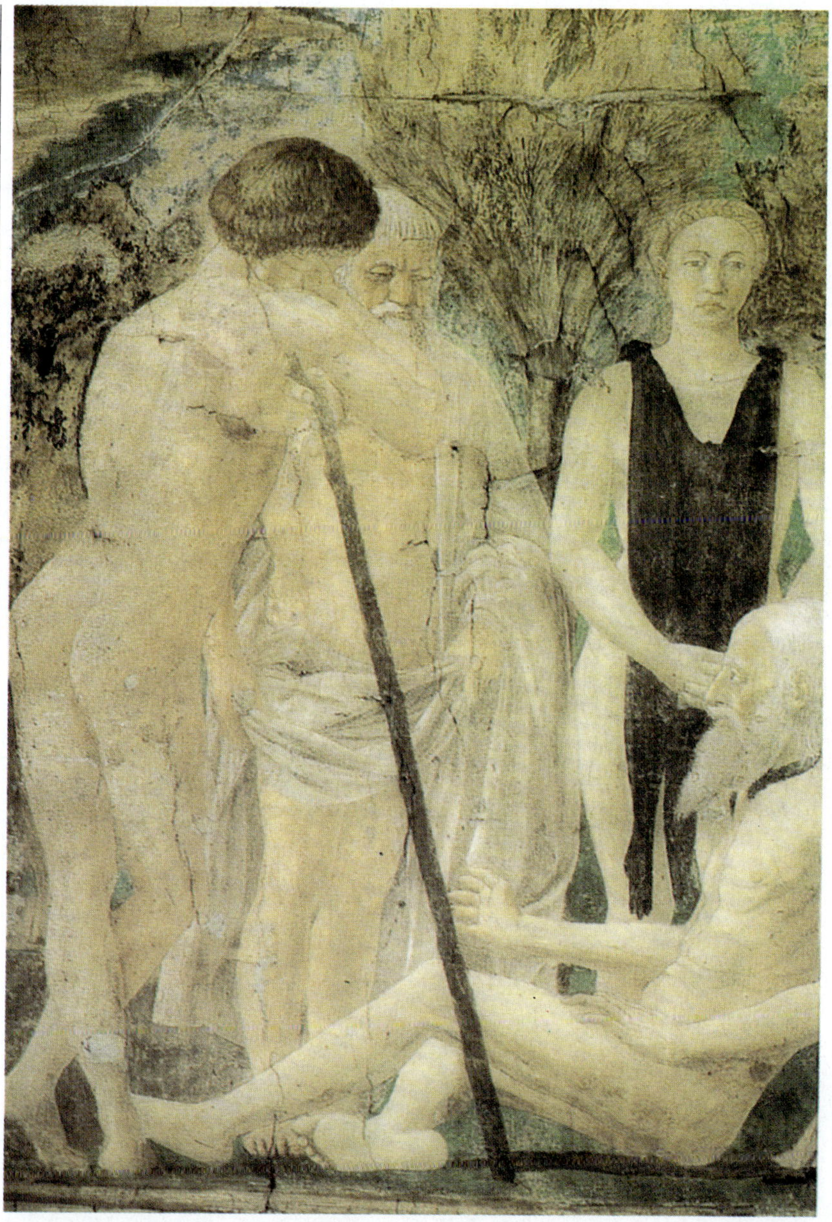

Death of Adam, episode from the *Legend of the True Cross* (1452-1466, circa), detail; Bacci Chapel, Church of San Francesco, Arezzo.

Hercules does not seem casual. It would also be confirmed by the fact that artist frescoed the subject in his own house in Borgo (today the painting is in the Isabella Stewart Gardner Museum in Boston), portraying him with the Monterchi coat of arms. The comparison between the *Hercules* in Boston and the first figure on the left in the ogive of the choir in Arezzo is significant. In the San Francesco fresco Adam dies in the "land of Arezzo": the story of the cross loses the vague and generic nature of a legend to become live and close to those who conceived of and admired it.

And then, a final consideration. Piero drew his inspiration from Jacopo da Varagine's text in two other paintings. One is the *Resurrection* where the closed tomb is based on Jacopo's account: «Christ rose on the third day after his death and miraculously because the sepulchre remained closed»[47]. The other is the obvious sleep of the guards, because it was in the *Golden Legend* that Piero found a specific reference to the following passage from the Pauline epistles (*I Corinthians* 15:20-21): «But now Christ is risen from the dead and become the firstfruits of them that slept. For since by man came death, by man came also the resurrection of the dead»[48].

(34) *E. Battisti,* op. cit., *II, p. 220.*
(35) *M. Salmi,* Ricerche intorno a un perduto ciclo pittorico del Rinascimento, *in "Atti e Memorie dell'Accademia Fiorentina di Scienze Morali La Colombaria", n.s. I, 1943-1946, pp. 421-432, where the painting is graphically reconstructed.*
(36) *This is the position held by M. Tanner* (op. cit., *p. 15*) *as well as by Longhi* (Piero della Francesca, *1927, repr. Florence 1975, p. 27*).
(37) *Battisti's observations* (op. cit., *I, p. 13 and n. 162) in this regard reflect those of Verneule* (European Art and Classical Past, *Cambridge, Mass. , 1964, pp. 39-42*). *We must also mention the similarity between Piero's catechumen and the one in the fresco by Gentile da Fabriano in San Giovanni in Laterano in Rome of which we have learned through a drawing by Pisanello. Recently Bertelli* (op. cit., *p. 61*) *proposed that the work be dated after the left panel of the* Polyptych of the Misericordia, *but before the right panel, that is between 1445 and 1450. See also, C. Pizzorusso,* Sul "Battesimo" di Piero della Francesca, *in "Artista. Critica dell'arte in Toscana", 1991, pp. 122-133.*
(38) *Cfr. M. Bussagli,* Identificazione di un imperatore, *in "Art e Dossier", 67, April 1992.*
(39) *M. Tanner,* op. cit., *pp. 13-14.*
(40) *Thomas Aquinas,* Summa Theologiae, *III, q. 36, a. 7.*
(41) *On the Ferrara frescoes: E. Battisti,* op. cit., *I, pp. 44-52, which includes copies from the National Gallery in London. Regarding the matter of the works in the Vatican under Nicholas V and the information from Vasari: ivi, pp. 106-112.*
(42) *The document is integrally edited by Battisti, op. cit., pp.226-227.*
(43) *C. de Tolnay,* Les conceptions religieuses dans la peinture de Piero della Francesca, *in "Arte Antica e Moderna", 23, 1963, pp. 205-241; and L. Marin,* La théorie narrative et Piero peintre d'histoire, *in* Piero teorico dell'arte, *cit., pp. 55-84, with bibliography.*
(44) *D. Arasse,* Piero della Francesca, peintre d'histoire, *in* Piero teorico dell'arte, *cit., pp. 90 and 100.*
(45) *H. W. Grohn,* Piero della Francesca, die Fresken in San Francesco zu Arezzo, *Munich, 1961.*
(46) *M. Salmi,* op. cit., *p. 109.*
(47) *Jacopo da Varagine,* Legenda aurea, *trans. by C. Lisi, Florence, 1984, I, p. 250.*
(48) *The passage from St. Paul appears in the complete Latin edition of Jacopo's book:* Jacobi a Varagine Legenda aurea, *ed. by Th. Graesse, repr. Osnabrück 1965, p. 239.*

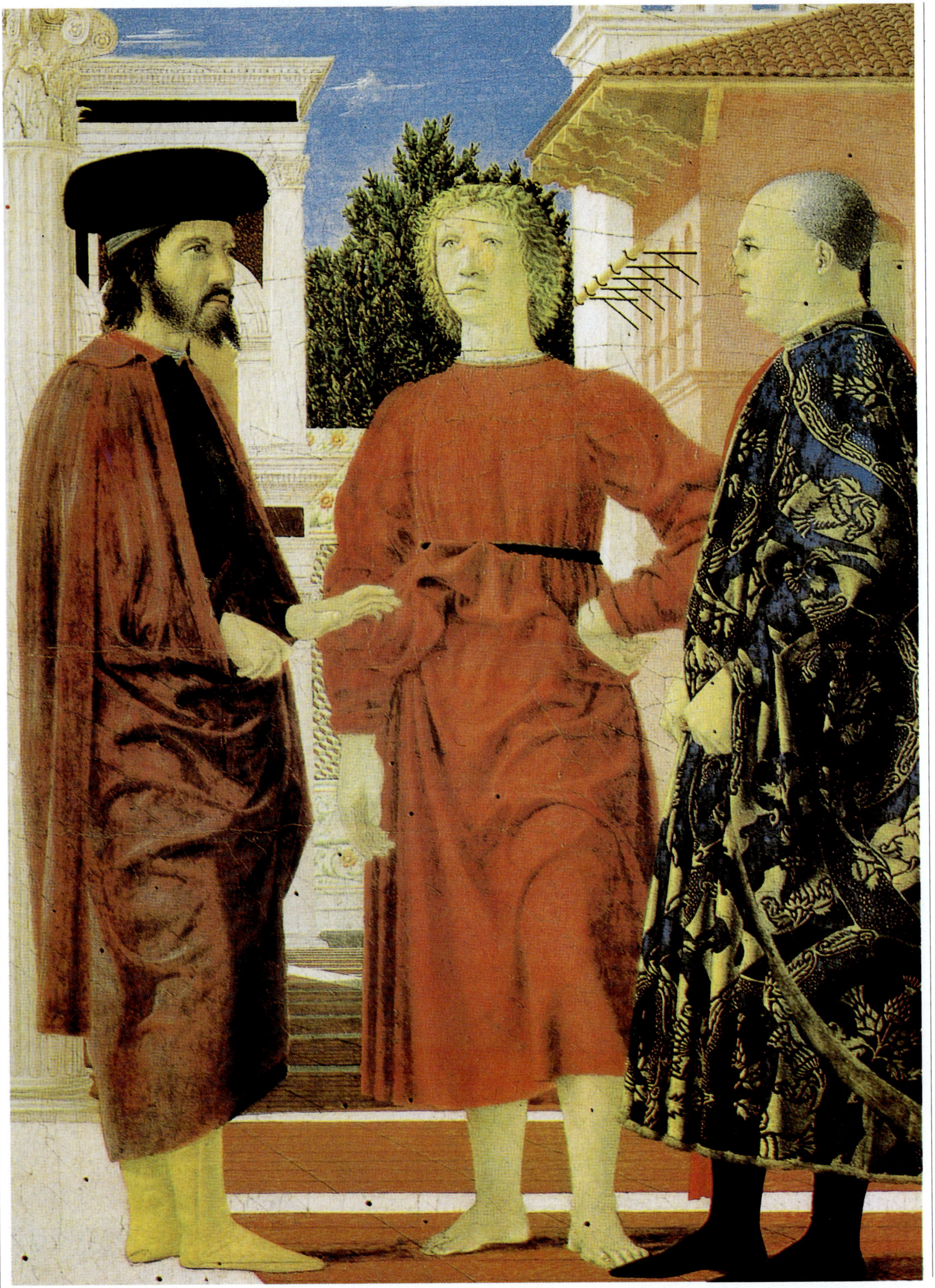

The *Flagellation*

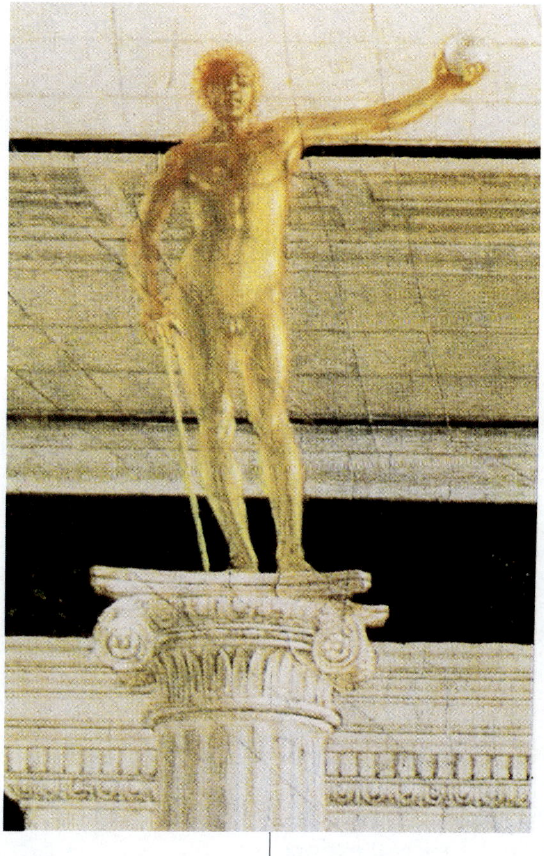

Opposite page:
Flagellation
(after 1459),
detail;
Galleria Nazionale
delle Marche,
Urbino.

Above:
Flagellation,
detail;
Galleria Nazionale
delle Marche,
Urbino.

THE ENIGMA OF PIERO'S painting can be summarized in a single work that caused proverbial rivers of ink to flow, the *Flagellation* which is in the Galleria Nazionale delle Marche in Urbino. Nothing is known about this small (59 x 81.5 cm) painting. The date and provenance are still the subjects of discussion and the only thing that is certain is that it was done by Piero's hand: *Opus Petri de Burgo S[an]c[t]i Sepulcri* can be clearly seen on the platform of the base of Pilate's throne. There are two main interpretative lines that the critics have followed up to now.

The first, sustained by Roberto Longhi, is based on a 1744 inventory in which, describing the painting that was then in the sacristy of the Urbino cathedral, three characters on the right were identified as «the dukes Oddo Ant[oni]o, Federico and Guid'Ub[ald]o»[49]. However, the identification of the two figures with Federico da Montefeltro and his son Guidobaldo, whose features are well known from other portraits seems most arbitrary. As to the identification of the young blond man as Oddantonio da Montefeltro, Federico's stepbrother, a comparison with a portrait in the Kunsthistorisches Museum of Vienna seems to support the eighteenth century theory. Further, the reference to Oddantonio, who died in a conspiracy in 1444 could seem to favor a "high" dating of the work that is accepted by Longhi and others. On the other hand, in this case a stylistic analysis seems to be a valid tool for dating the work as subsequent not only to the meeting with Leon Battista Alberti whose acquaintance Piero made in Rimini in 1451, but perhaps, given the similarity with the Arezzo frescoes, also to the San Francesco cycle. This would be confirmed by the architectural structure which hosts the event and is very similar to the building that hosts the meeting between Solomon and the Queen of Sheba in the Arezzo fresco, as well as the use of the decorative motif of perspective blocks that appear in another scene in the Arezzo cycle, *The Annunciation* and in the background of the *Flagellation* behind the supposed Oddantonio. Thus, the small painting in Urbino must have been done at least after 1459.

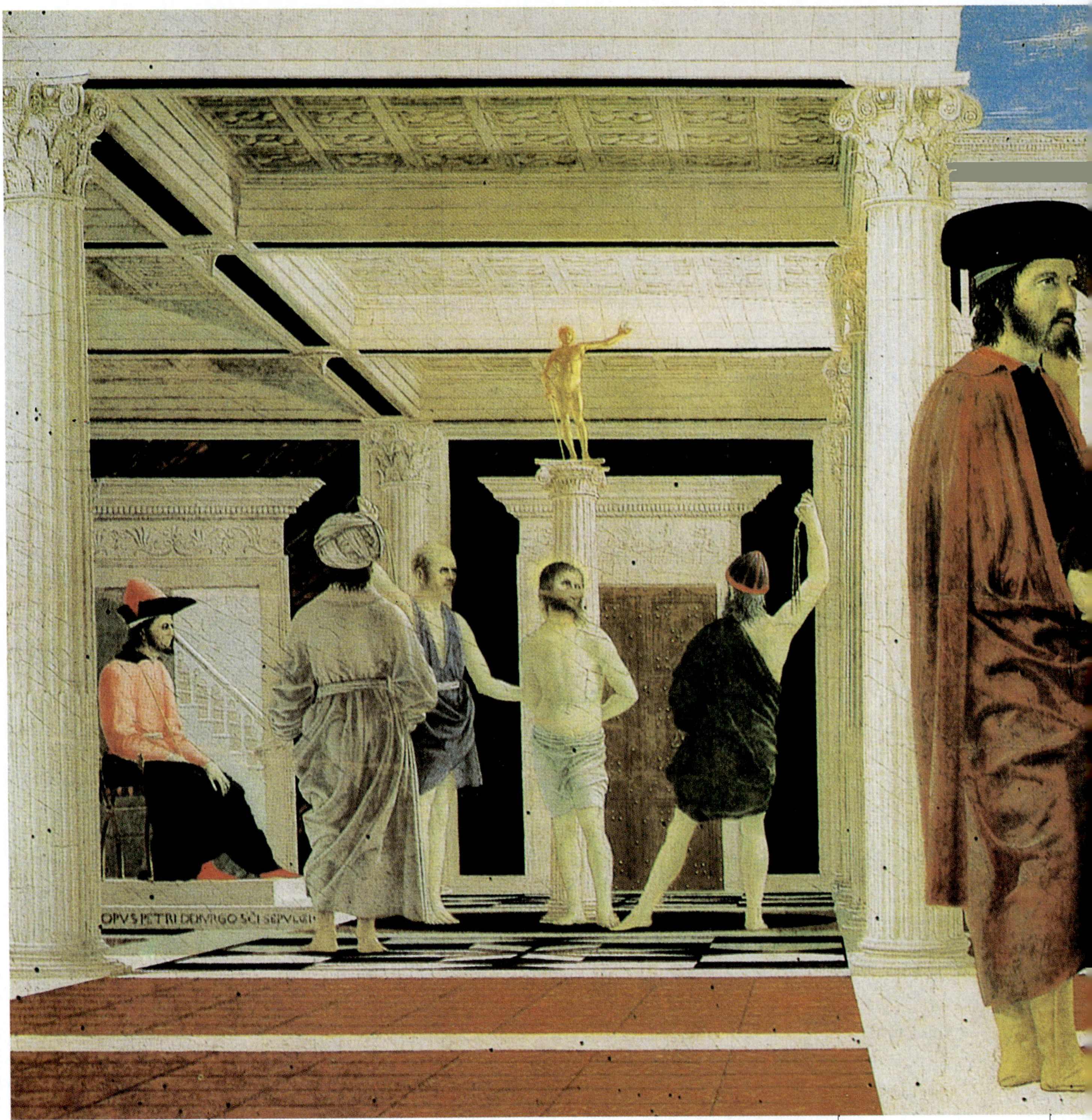

The other hypothesis is based on Clark who, taking into account the stylistic elements, links the painting to historical events of the time, maintaining that the three characters are meditating on the tribulations of the Church because of the fall of Constantinople. The scholar thus identifies Pilate with the Byzantine emperor, John VIII Paleologus and the bearded character in Byzantine clothes with the emperor's brother, Thomas Paleologus. The dates of the painting, therefore, become 1459 when Pius II went to Mantua to call the crusade, or 1461 when Thomas Paleologus went to Rome to offer a relic of the apostle Andrew[50]. Clark's thesis was picked up by Battisti who modified the interpretation basing it partly on Longhi's. For Battisti, therefore, the

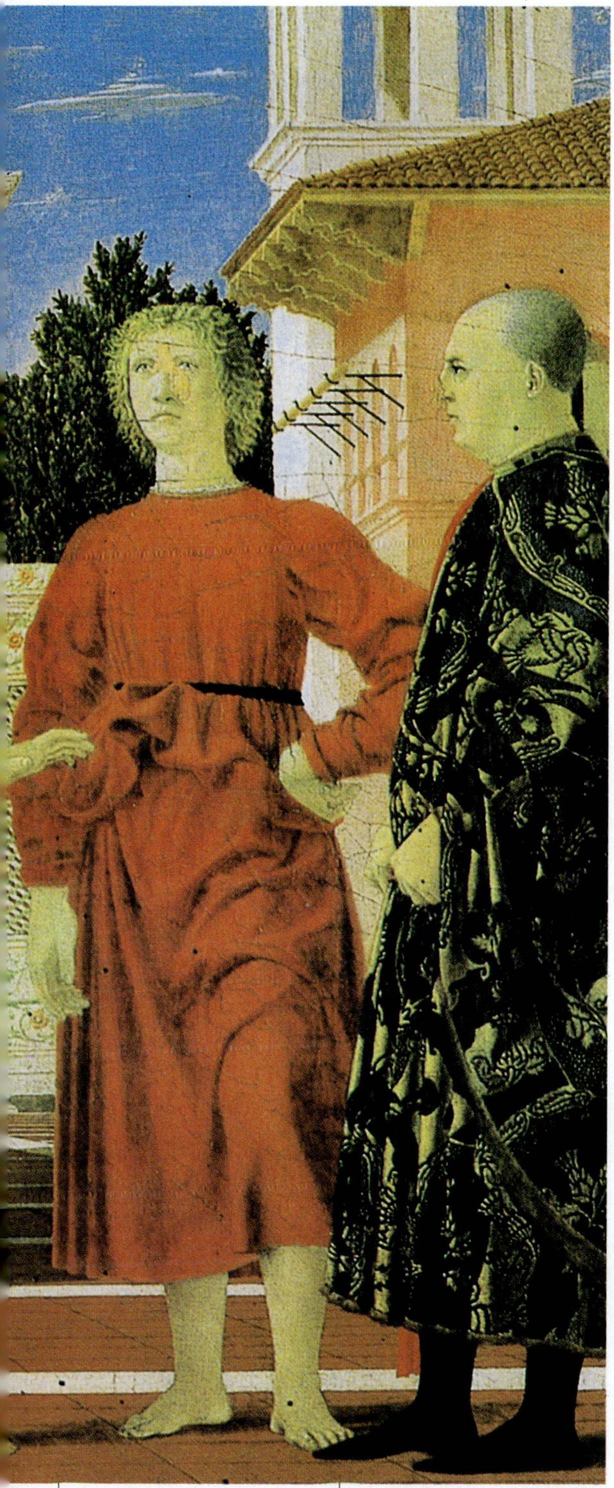

Flagellation (after 1459), detail; Galleria Nazionale delle Marche, Urbino.

central figure in the group would be Oddantonio, the one on the left a Byzantine ambassador, and the last, Filippo Maria Visconti or Francesco Sforza. Pilate, instead, would be Mehmed II the sultan who usurped the throne of the Paleologus. The purpose of the painting, according to Battisti, was to rehabilitate the memory of Oddantonio who did not participate in the anti-Turkish crusade of 1443[51].

Carlo Ginzburg's essay which carries Clark's thesis to the extreme did nothing more than feed the disputes by introducing new elements for the identification of the characters. Ginzburg notes that the figure in the brocade robes has the same face as the man in red kneeling below the Madonna's cloak in the *Polyptych of the Misericordia* (see page 19), who, in turn, resembles two other characters in the Bacci chapel frescoes: the first is the bareheaded man who, in the *Battle Between Heraclius and Chosroes* (see page 32) is to the left of the king who is about to be struck by the conqueror's sword; the other is the figure with the red *oppelanda* in the scene of the meeting of Solomon and the Queen of Sheba (see page 16). Since, in both cases they have been identified as Giovanni Bacci, one of the family that ordered the Arezzo frescoes, Ginzburg also believes that it is he wearing the brocaded robes in the Urbino painting and that he commissioned the *Flagellation* as well. The bearded figure on the left would be Cardinal Bessarione, friend of Federico da Montefeltro for whom the painting was supposedly done. The central figure, would not be Oddantonio but Buonconte da Montefeltro, the cardinal's godson and illegitimate child of Federico. The analysis continues by identifying Piero's setting (the stairs in the background are considered an allusion to the Sacred Steps in the Lateran Palace in Rome which, in that period were known as "Pilate's stairs") as the room of the relics in the Lateran Palace and the scene itself as a reference to the Good Friday celebrations[52].

Unfortunately, not even such sharp arguments are definitive. First of all, we must say that the resemblance between the figure that Ginzburg identified as Bessarione and the portraits of the cardinal leaves much to be desired, and the identification of the blond figure as Buonconte seems entirely arbitrary. As to the figure of the presumed Giovanni Bacci, there is indeed a resemblance to the person who ordered the Arezzo frescoes, but in the *Flagellation* did Piero really want to portray Bacci or did he just borrow the face to impersonate someone else? The fact is that in the Urbino painting the link between the scene of the flagellation and the three characters in the foreground seems to slip away. In 1986, Pope-Hennessy proposed a totally new interpretation which, though it cannot be shared, fits perfectly into the logic of Piero's art. The comparison with a painting by Matteo di Giovanni in the Art Institute of Chicago leads the American scholar to see the episode of St. Jerome's dream, as described by the saint himself in a letter to Eustachius (*Epistle XII*), and as retold by Jacopo da Varagine in the *Golden Legend*, in the *Flagellation*. In brief, in the delirium of the desert Jerome consoled himself by reading Cicero rather than the *Psalms*. One night the saint dream that he had been called before a judge who condemned him to be beaten until bloody because of his passion for classical culture. Jerome asked for mercy and «tunc qui astabant precabantur judicem, ut veniam tribueret adolescenti», that is, «those present (for Pope-Hennessy the three figures on the right) begged the judge to pardon that adolescent»[53]. The weak points in this interpretation are, first of all, the fact that in Sano di Pietro's painting Jerome is not – as it may seem – tied to the column behind him; it is part of the architectural background and creates that sensation because of its position, but the saint's hands are absolutely free. Secondly, if in the Chicago painting Jerome is really an adolescent, in the Urbino painting the only possible adolescent is the pseudo-Oddantonio and certainly not the figure tied to the column of punishment.

In spite of this, however, to me it seems that Pope-Hennessy's interpretation that breaks with the traditional line of criticism is salutary. To resolve the enigma of the *Flagellation* we must, without a doubt, find a codified scene that justifies the presence of the figures in the foreground. This does not mean to say that it is incorrect to see a precise reference to the crusade against the Turks and advance new hypotheses for the identification of the characters as Calvesi has recently done. He sees the

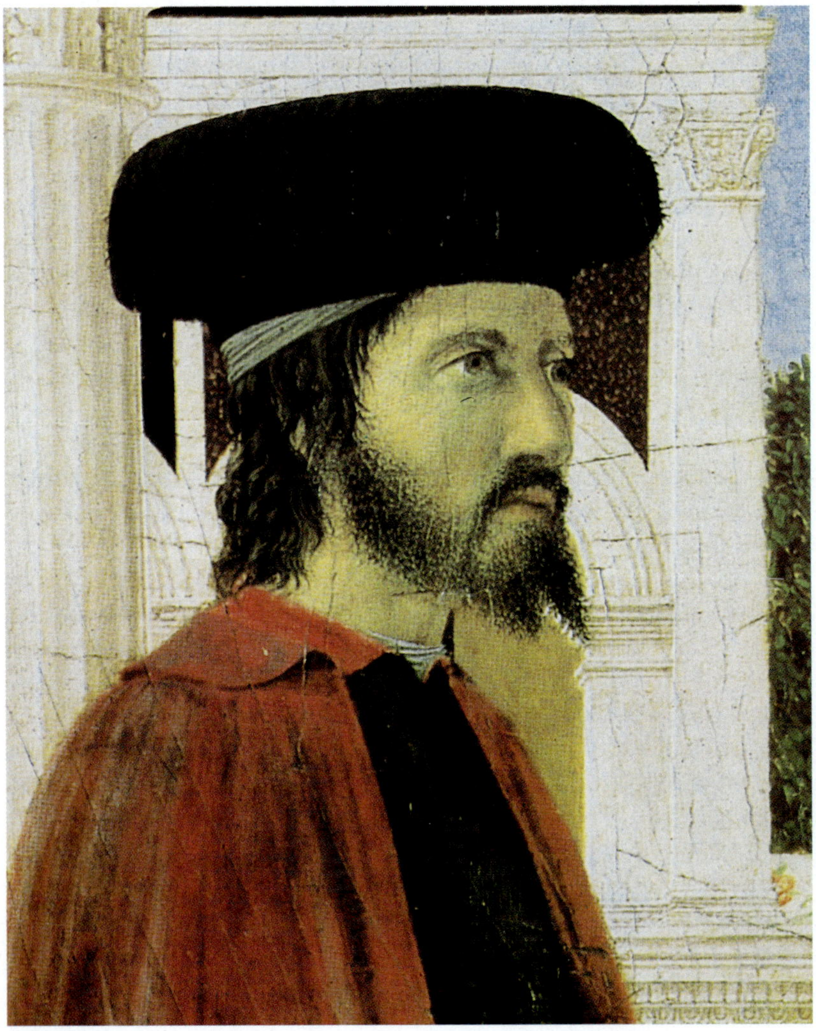

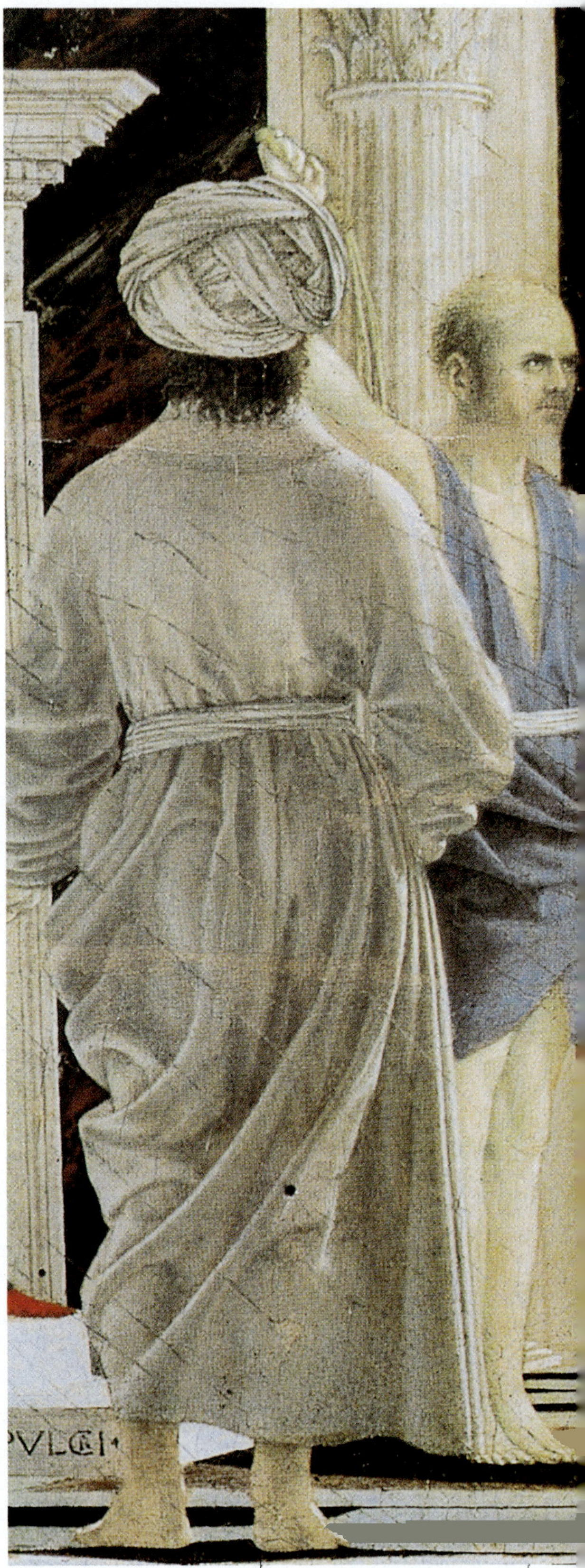

young blonde man as the Hungarian king Matthias Corvinus, one of the few who joined the crusade launched by Pius II[54].

Finally, it seems certain that in the *Flagellation* Piero wanted to refer to events before 1453 and that the painting contains definite allusions to the crusade and to the Paleologus. What is missing is the understanding of a subject that certainly is not, or is not only, a mere flagellation of Christ.

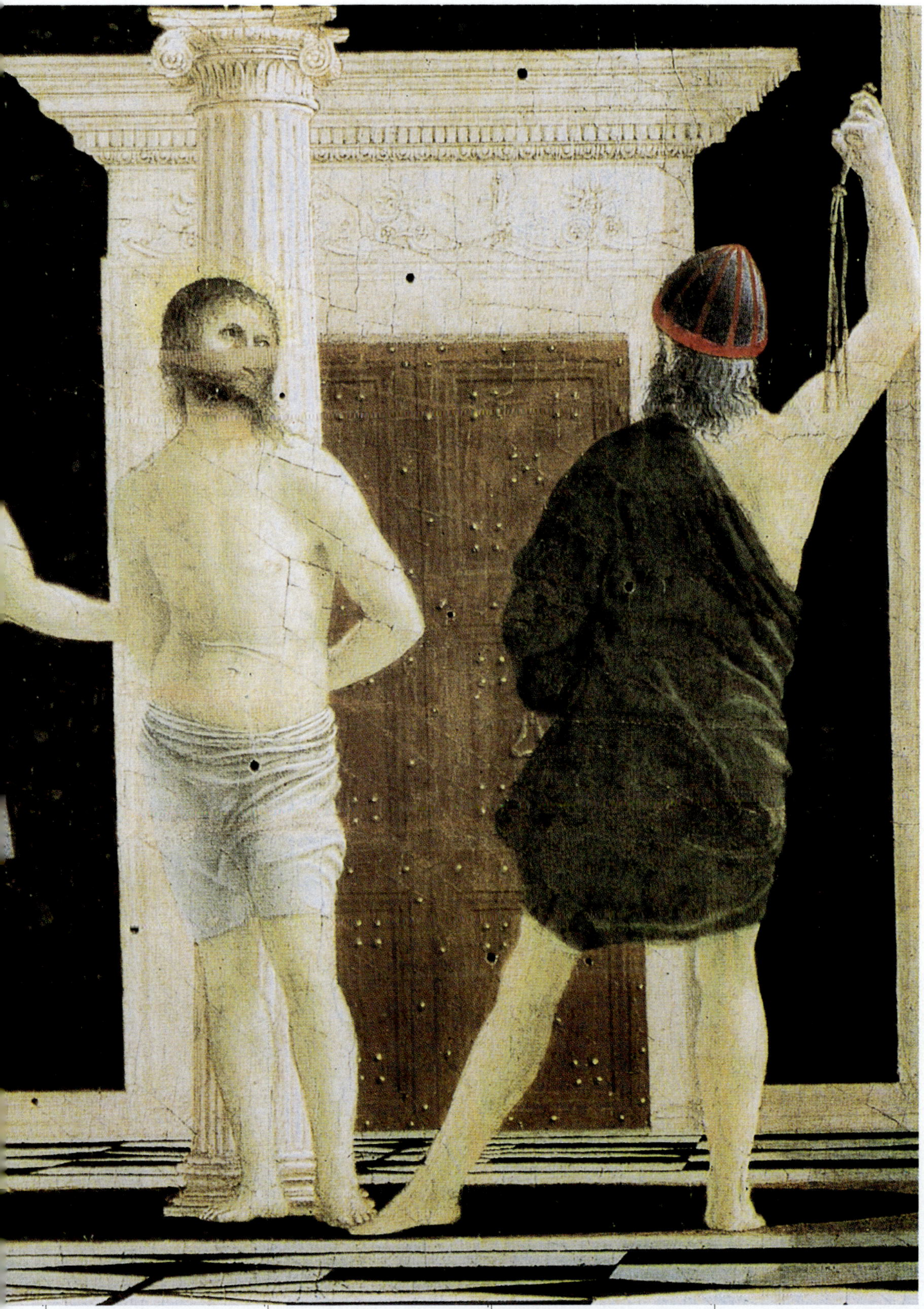

Above and left:
Flagellation
(after 1459),
details;
Galleria Nazionale
delle Marche,
Urbino.

(49) *R. Longhi,* op. cit., *p. 39. The description comes from a manuscript by P.G. Vernacchia, see Battisti,* op. cit., *II, p. 50.*
(50) *K. Clark,* op. cit., *pp. 19-21.*
(51) *E. Battisti,* op. cit., *I, p. 325.*
(52) *C. Ginzburg,* Indagini su Piero, *Turin 1981, pp. 64-66. On the basis of the studies by Wittkower and Carter* (The Perspective of Piero della Francesca's Flagellation, *in "Journal of the Warburg and Courtauld Institutes", 16, 1953, pp. 292-302), Ginzburg considers the column as the structural module for the entire composition and notes the proportional relationship between the "mensura Christi" in the Lateran Palace and the figure of Christ* (op. cit., *pp. 72-73).*
(53) *J. Pope Hennessy,* Whose Flagellation?, *in "Apollo", CXXIV, 1986, pp. 162-165. For the quotation cfr.* Jacobi a Varagine Legenda aurea, *cit., p. 654.*
(54) *M. Calvesi,* Identikit di un enigma, *in "Art e Dossier", n. 70, July 1992, pp. 27-30.*
(55) *In the history of the interpretation of the painting, we must remember the "Jewish trail" beginning with Gombrich* (The repentance of Judas in Piero della Francesca's Flagellation of Christ, *in "Journal of the Warburg and Courtauld Institutes", XXII, 1/2, 1959, p. 172), according to which the bearded man in the trio would be Judas; it continues with Borgo* (New Questions for Piero's Flagellation, *in "The Burlington Magazine", CXXI, 1979, pp. 546-553) which cites a IX century Jewish text mentioning 3 opponents of Christ (but we don't know if this text was known during Piero's era), and then, with greater emphasis, with Lollini* (Una possibile connotazione antiebraica nella Flagellazione di Piero della Francesca, *in "Bollettino d'Arte", 65, 1991, pp. 1-28).*

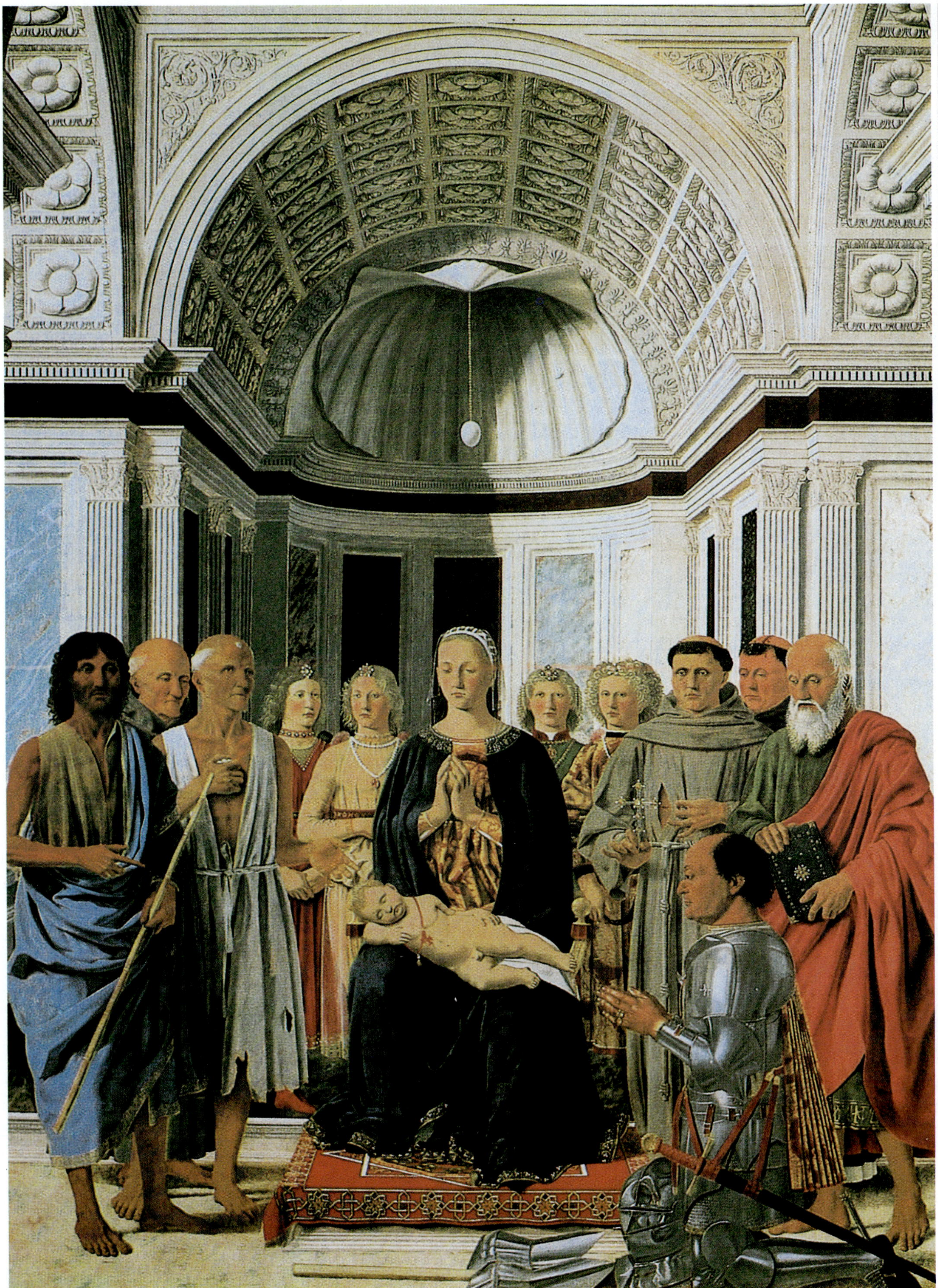

Piero and Urbino

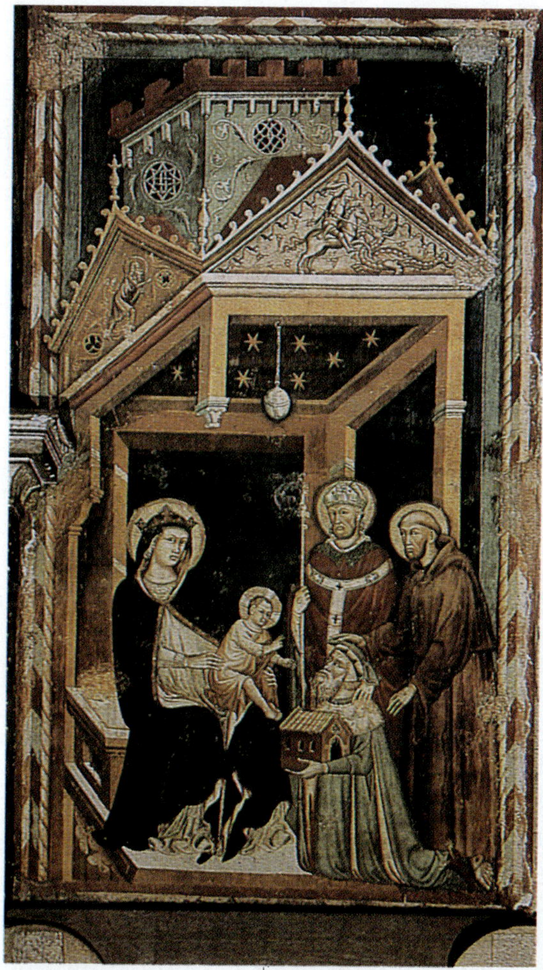

Opposite page:
Brera Altarpiece
(*The Madonna with Child, Angels, Saints and Federico da Montefeltro, Duke of Urbino*)
(1472-1474);
Brera, Milan.

Above:
Maestro della Tomba Fissiraga,
The Madonna with Child, Saints and Antonio Fissiraga
(1327);
San Francesco,
Lodi (Milan).

IT DOES EMERGE FROM THE succinct critical survey of the *Flagellation* that Piero had a connection with Urbino and Federico da Montefeltro. Any related documents, it is superfluous to say, are scarce: the master's presence in the city (he was the guest of Giovanni Santi, Raphael's father) is only mentioned in the registries of the local Corpus Domini confraternity which, on 8 April 1469, report on the «master Piero del Borgo [...] who came here to see the *taula* in order to do it for the fraternity»[56].

Piero was to have finished the altarpiece for the confraternity of which the by now seventy-year old Paolo Uccello had only completed the predella. But not even Piero did the painting, that was completed by Giusto di Gand. Probably Piero was relieved of such an assignment so that he could take care of another commitment, that is, to paint the large altarpiece which is now in Brera. In any event, the lack of documentation leaves room for any hypothesis. In fact, neither the portraits in the Uffizi, nor the *Brera Altarpiece* are registered or documented in any way whatsoever, therefore the problem of dating arises for these works as well.

In July 1472 Battista Sforza, wife of Federico, died after giving birth to Guidobaldo, the heir they had awaited for so long. The circumstances thus led life and death to intertwine in the pictorial fabric of the *Brera Altarpiece*, which is enriched by the significance of being at the same time an *ex voto* of thanks for the birth of Guidobaldo, a commemorative monument to Battista who had just perished and a celebrative work to glorify the power of the Montefeltro family, a meaning that does not exclude a reference to the conquest of Volterra that took place on 18 June 1472.

The egg that almost seems to be a pearl, in line with the Child, and put inside the shell of the apse, alludes without a doubt to the first event[57]. However, it is likely that the egg – the use of which in architectural decoration is widely documented – also alludes to the concept of resurrection and eternal life, as we can also affirm for the fresco on Fissiraga tomb in the

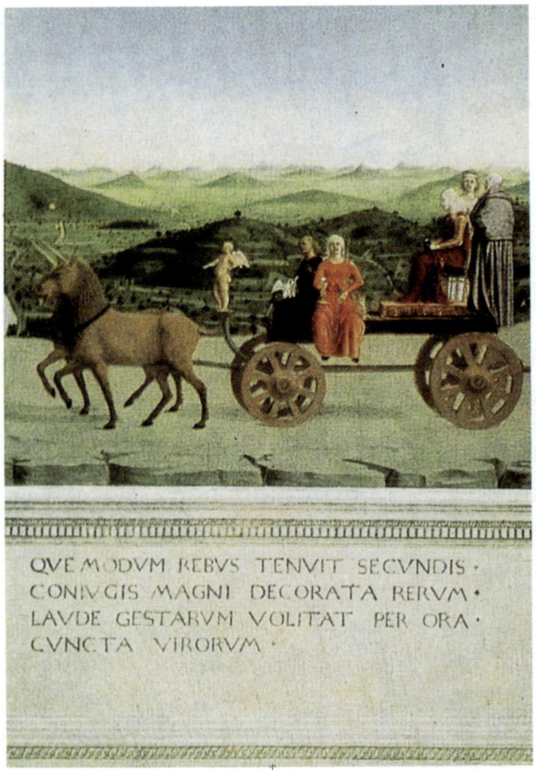

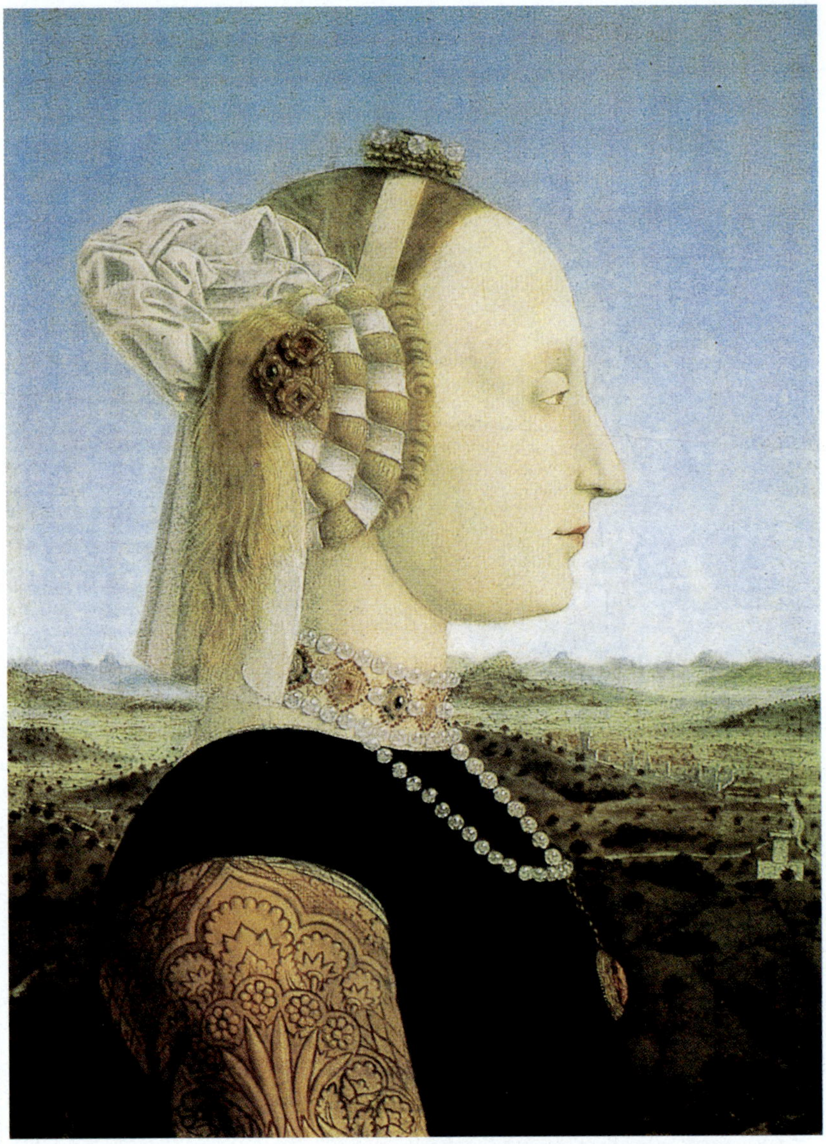

Above:
Triumph of Battista Sforza (after 1472), on the back of the portrait of *Battista Sforza*; Uffizi Gallery, Florence.

Right:
Battista Sforza (after 1472); Uffizi Gallery, Florence.

Opposite page, left:
Federico da Montefeltro (before 1476); Uffizi Gallery, Florence.

Right:
Triumph of Federico da Montefeltro (before 1467) on the back of the portrait of *Federico da Montefeltro*; Uffizi Gallery, Florence.

church of San Francesco in Lodi[58]. A reference to the duchess is certainly made by St. John the Baptist, due to their respective names. For what concerns the glorification of the house, the presence of Federico in armor, kneeling before the Virgin, is too explicit an image to warrant further comment.

However, the altarpiece has another peculiarity: it is an unfinished work, because Federico's hands were not painted by Piero. According to some critics such as Longhi and Lavin, they were done by Pedro Berruguete, according to Meiss they were painted by Giusto di Gand. Why? Vasari's words come to mind as he described Piero as sick and blind in the latter part of his life. Are those unfinished hands the tragic sign of his illness? May it be that the *Brera Altarpiece* was is very last work? In this case, too, all we can do is fumble in the dark.

The fact that the master used the same cartoon as the one he used to portray Federico in the Uffizi diptych, instead of making a new portrait, has been interpreted as proof that the entire painting was done after the duke's death (it occurred in 1482) and that Piero had drawn out the work until 1488, when his blindness would have forced him to stop painting it[59]. But, have we got any right to suppose that an artist such as Piero – who in more than one painting, as we have seen, reused trac-

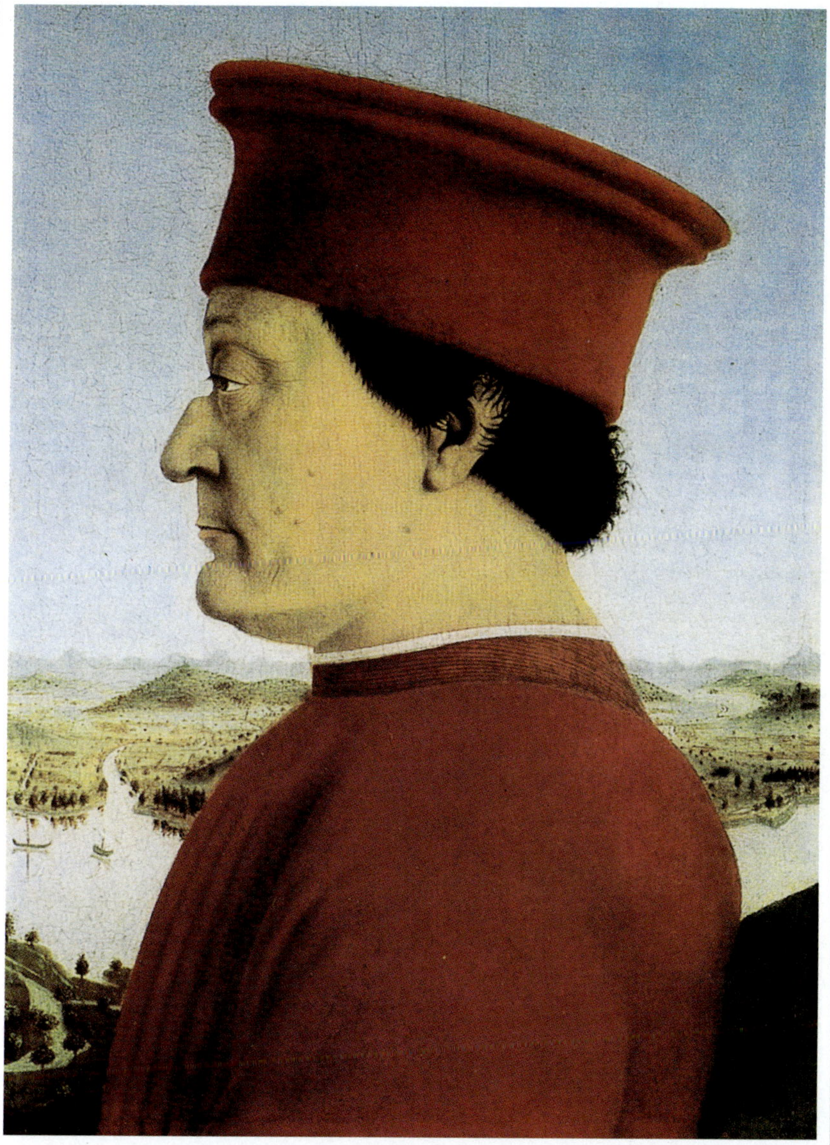

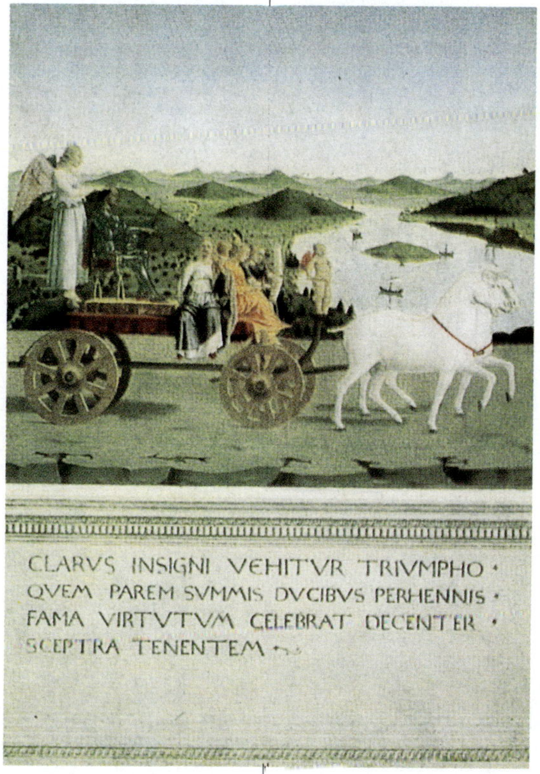

ings to create symmetrical plays – would use a similar expedient? Was it not more of a desire to portray the lord of Urbino in an identical manner?

The Uffizi diptych was conceived as a medal with the profiles of the duke and duchess on one side and the allegorical carts of their respective triumphs on the other. Federico's cart shows the duke on the sedia gestatoria in armor, helmet on his thigh, slightly raised, scepter in hand as the Latin lines that describe the scene. Behind him Victory, who looks almost entirely like an angel, crowns him. In the front of the cart, drawn by white steeds, are the four Virtues: from the left, Prudence, Temperance, Fortitude and Justice; in the background, the crystalline Lake Trasimeno. Battista's cart is drawn by two unicorns, symbolizing chastity and purity. The inscription celebrates the modesty of the duchess who seems intent on reading while Faith and Charity sit in front of her, and Hope and Modesty next to her. In the background is the fertile landscape of the Valdichiana[60].

The delicate *Senigallia Madonna* which is in the Galleria Nazionale delle Marche in Urbino should also be ascribed to the Urbino period. In this painting we can understand how the simplicity of everyday things could, in Piero's pictorial world,

The portraits of the Duke of Urbino and his wife were a hinged diptych that could be opened and closed like a book, showing the two *Triumphs* on the outside. The subjects have only recently been correctly identified. The old hypotheses, that they were Petrarch and Laura or Sigismondo Pandolfo Malatesta, lord of Rimini, and his wife Isotta degli Atti were abandoned in 1834. The Latin inscription beneath the *Triumph of Battista Sforza* can be translated as follows: «She who could maintain moderation in good times is on the lips of all men, [she] graces the undertakings of her great husband». The inscription on the *Triumph of Federico* reads: «He whom fame lord of the virtues proclaims worthy of holding the scepter, as an equal of the greatest *condottieri*, is carried in grandiose triumph». The attention to detail, the way the two profiles stand out against the carefully depicted distant landscape seem evidence of Piero's interest in Flemish art.

become an allegory of the mysteries of the faith. As Aronberg Lavin has shown, the box for the wafers high up on the shelf alludes to the sacrifice of the Eucharist, while the clean white linen in the wicker basket symbolizes the redeeming role of the Virgin and her assimilation with the Ark of the Covenant as well

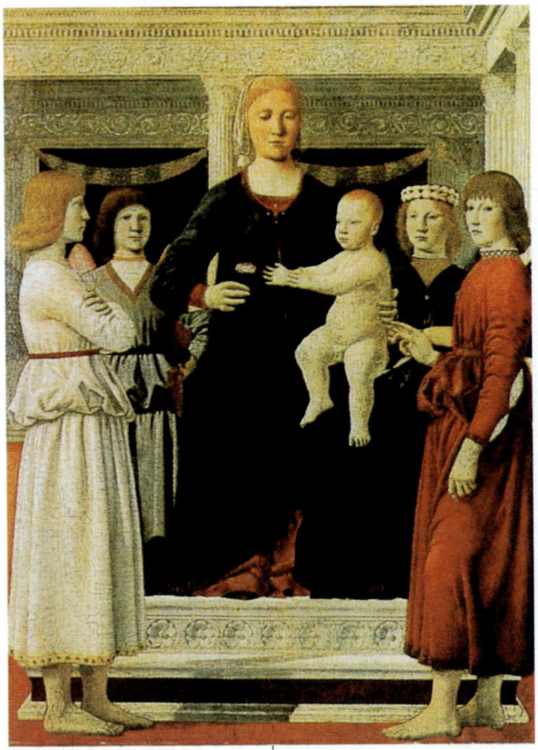

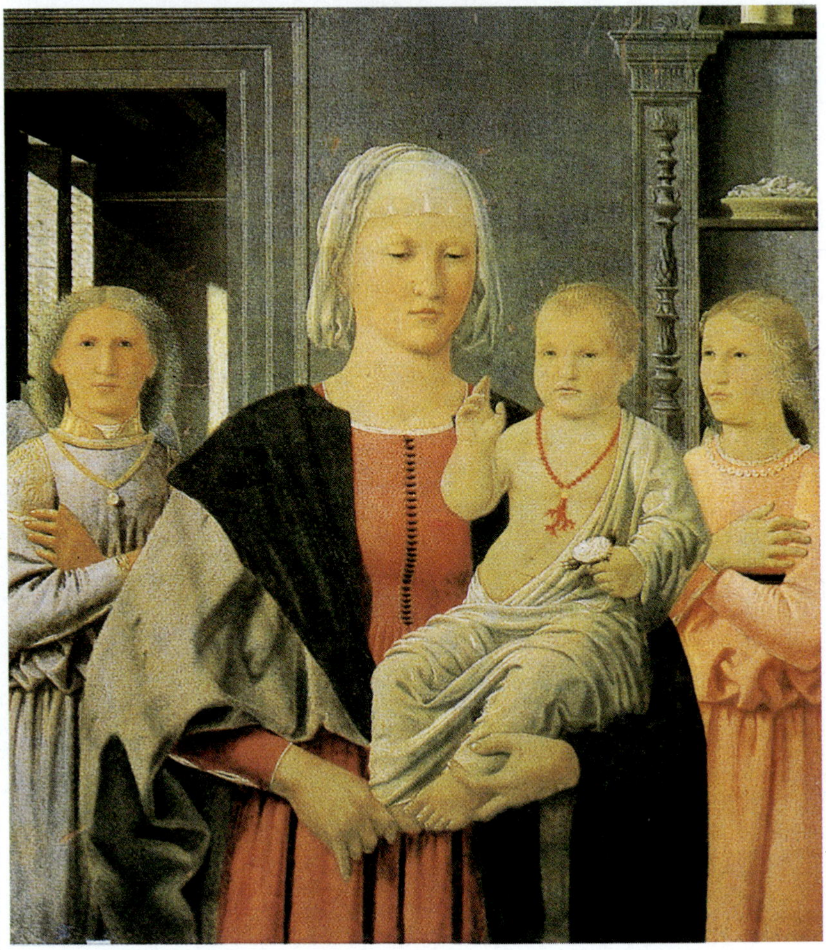

Above:
Madonna with Child and Four Angels (1478);
Sterling and Francine Clark Art Institute, Williamstown (Massachusetts).

Right:
Senigallia Madonna (1474, circa);
Galleria Nazionale delle Marche, Urbino.

This painting, from the church of Santa Maria delle Grazie in Senigallia (Ancona) was only attributed to Piero della Francesca at the end of the nineteenth century. The use of variations of the indirect light to highlight the spatial relationships is related to his experiences in Florence, in particular, the Santa Lucia dei Magnoli altarpiece (1445) by Domenico Veneziano which is in the Uffizi Gallery.

as a reference to the Old Testament episode of Moses – a sort of *ante litteram* Christ – saved from the waters of the Nile in a wicker basket. Finally, the light that shines in through the window is a metaphor for Mary's totally spiritual conception. In this scene, I believe that the angel's jewels should be interpreted as drops of light as they are mute sentinels for the divine pair: the stones, transparent as tourmalines are symbols of purity[62]. The rose in the Child's hand (the Virgin holds the same flower in the *Virgin and Child with Four Angels* which is in the Sterling and Francine Clark Art Institute in Williamstown) is a symbol of the rosary as well as a sign of divine love.

Piero della Francesca's last painting was perhaps the *Nativity* which is today in the National Gallery in London. It was definitely not completed, and could be identified as the painting which, according to a document dated 30 January 1500 listing the painter's properties, was described as a Nativity «manu magistri Petri» («by the hand of the master Pietro»)[63]. If its precarious condition cannot be ascribed to uncareful cleanings as Longhi and Clark have hypothesized, then – as Battista believes – it could well be Piero's last painting that remained in his home after his death.

For its dating at the 1483, reference has always been made

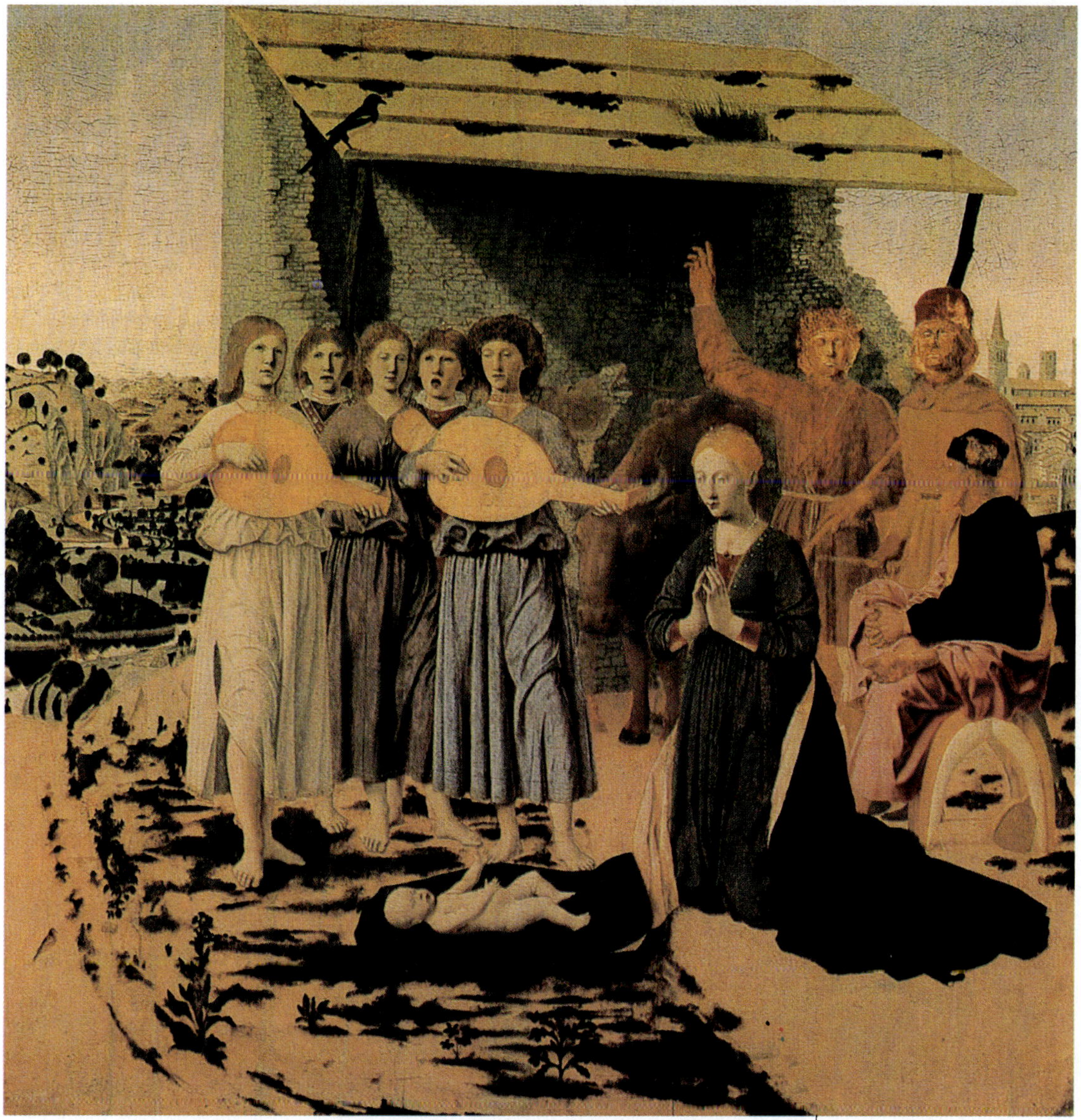

Nativity (before 1482); National Gallery, London.

to the Flemish plan of the *Nativity* by Hugo van der Goes which is also known as the *Portinari Triptych* (Uffizi Gallery, Florence), that can be dated around 1482. However, Piero could have been familiar with this type of arrangement after having seen the Filippo Lippi's *Adoration of the Child* (if not the original painting, then prints or reproductions of it, since it was already famous). And this goes without considering that, as Bertelli rightly notes, the musical angels in the London *Nativity* were badly used by Lorentino d'Andrea in a 1482 altarpiece which is in the Museo Statale in Arezzo. Therefore, the painting must already have been arranged and partly completed prior to the *Portinari Tryptych*[64].

Piero's painting is a fascinating work, whose theme is celestial harmonies sung by angels playing lutes and rebecks. Battisti has justly drawn attention to the tawny colored (hence demoniacal) donkey braying in the background, comprising the dissonant note that breaks up the harmony and heralds the Apocalypse[65]. One of the three shepherds on the right points to something on high: the angel, the dove or the star of the magi according to St. Thomas Aquinas? It is certain that the measured gesture of that figure, pointing to the sky is the most appropriate for representing the universal meaning of Piero's art.

(56) *Cfr. E. Battisti,* op. cit., *II, p. 228.*
(57) *C. Marinesco* (Echos byzantins dans l'oeuvre de Piero della Francesca, *in "Bulletin de la Société Nationale des Antiquaires de France", 1958, pp. 193-203) links Piero's painting to the symbolism of the pearl on the basis of the works of St. Ephrem of Syria, which seems pushing the issue (p. 201). However, Piero may indeed have juggled with the ambiguity between the egg and the pearl, symbols which he may have known through the Apocalyptic text of John which likens the pearl to the gate* (Apocalypse, *21:21). See also M. Meiss,* Ovum Struthionis, Symbol and Allusion in Piero della Francesca's Montefeltro altarpiece, *in* Studies in Art and Literature for Belle da Costa Green, *Princeton, 1954, pp. 92-101; for further Eastern implications see: R. Ettinghausen,* From Byzantium to Sassanian Iran and the Islamic World, *Leida, 1972, p. 34.*
(58) *The relationship with the fresco on the Fissiraga tomb was already proposed by Battisti,* op. cit., *I, p. 514, n. 450.*
(59) *P. Hendy,* Piero della Francesca and the Early Renaissance, *London-New York, 1968, p. 155.*
(60) *Salmi* (op. cit., *p. 120) identifies it this way with photographic support.*
(61) *M. Aronberg Lavin,* The Altar of Corpus Domini in Urbino: Paolo Uccello, Joos van Ghent, Piero della Francesca, *in "Art Bulletin", XLIX, 1967, p. 186, n. 115 and 116. For the other symbolic references, Battisti,* op. cit., *I, p. 378.*
(62) *For the symbolism of the stones in Piero's angels: M. Bussagli,* Storia degli angeli, *cit., pp. 252-258.*
(63) *E. Battisti,* op. cit., *vol. II, p. 244.*
(64) *C. Bertelli,* op. cit., *p. 218.*
(65) *E. Battisti,* op. cit., *I, p. 440. On the apocalyptic significance of the braying donkey: M. Schneider,* El origen musical de los animales simboles en la mitologia y la mitologia y la escultura anticuas, *Barcelona 1946, pp. 272-273.*

CHRONOLOGY

HISTORICAL AND ARTISTIC EVENTS		THE LIFE OF PIERO DELLA FRANCESCA
Charles V cedes Borgo Sansepolcro to the Malatestas of Rimini.	**1370**	
Pope Martin V solemnly enters Rome. Brunelleschi builds a masonry model of the dome of Santa Maria del Fiore in Florence.	**1420**	This date is the "post quem" term for the birth of Piero della Francesca in Borgo Sansepolcro near Arezzo, to Benedetto de' Franceschi, shoemaker and tanner, and Romana di Perino from Monterchi. The reasons for the change of the name to "della Francesca", made quite early, are unknown.
Borgo Sansepolcro is returned to Pope Martin V. A new war between Florence and Milan for the domination of Lucca, which is occupied by Francesco Sforza. Antonio d'Anghiari is commissioned to do the altarpiece, which he never did, for the church of San Francesco in Borgo Sansepolcro.	**1430**	
Niccolò da Tolentino is defeated by Niccolò Piccinino and dies as a prisoner of the Viscontis. Leon Battista Alberti published *De Pictura* in Latin.	**1435**	Perhaps Piero had already begun his Florentine internship at Domenico Veneziano's atelier. It is possible that the young Piero went to the Marches, and Umbria, with Domenico.
Niccolò Piccinino occupies Borgo Sansepolcro. The Ecumenical Council of Ferrara moves to Florence. Donatello completes the Cantoria of Santa Maria del Fiore in Florence.	**1439**	On 7 September he is mentioned as one of Domenico's helpers when the frescoes in the church of Sant'Egidio, commissioned by the Spedale di Santa Maria Nuova in Florence, are paid.
Masolino dies. Pope Eugenius IV reconquers Borgo Sansepolcro and cedes it to Florence.	**1440**	
Beato Angelico completes the frescoes in the Convent of San Marco.	**1442**	Piero returns to Borgo Sansepolcro where he is mentioned among the council members.
Domenico Veneziano stops work on the frescoes in the church of Sant'Egidio and completes the altarpiece of Santa Lucia dei Magnoli. Sandro Botticelli is born.	**1445**	He receives the commission for the polyptych for the altar of the church of the Confraternity of the Misericordia in Borgo Sansepolcro. He had probably already begun frequenting the court of Urbino.
Lorenzo de'Medici is born. In Ferrara Rogier van der Weyden paints a *Deposition.* Mantegna is in Ferrara.	**1449**	In Ferrara he does some fresco cycles (lost) for Lionello d'Este in the Estense castle and the church of Sant'Agostino.
Alberti begins work on the Tempio Malatestiano in Rimini.	**1450**	He paints *St. Jerome Penitent* (Gemäldegalerie, Berlin-Dahlem).
	1451	This date is inscribed on the fresco of *Sigismondo Malatesta before St. Sigismund* in the Tempio Malatestiano in Rimini. Piero meets Leon Battista Alberti. He works in Ancona, Pesaro and Bologna on paintings lost.
Frederick III is crowned Holy Roman Emperor. Ghiberti completes the *Door of Paradise.* Bicci di Lorenzo dies. Leonardo da Vinci is born.	**1452**	He takes over from Bicci di Lorenzo, dead in this same year, decorating the choir of the church of San Francesco in Arezzo (*The Legend of the True Cross*) commissioned by the powerful Bacci family of Arezzo.
The Turks conquer Constantinople on 29 May. Poggio Bracciolini is the Chancellor of the Florentine Republic.	**1453**	He is back in Borgo Sansepolcro, where he is given a crossbow to participate in a military review, in view of a coming war between Florence and Aragon.
The Peace of Lodi opens a period of political stability. Agnolo Poliziano is born.	**1454**	On 4 October he signs a contract with the Augustinian monks of his home town for the polyptych to be placed on the main altar of their church. Shortly afterwards, summoned by Pope Nicholas V, he probably goes to Rome, where he paints frescoes for the church of Santa Maria Maggiore (only some fragments of these remain).
Enea Silvio Piccolomini is elected pope and takes the name of Pius II. Alfonso I dies and is succeeded by Ferdinando I as king of Naples. Donatello is working on *Judith and Holofernes.*	**1458**	
Benozzo Gozzoli begins working on the fresco with the *Procession of the Magi* in the Medici palace on Via Larga in Florence. Mantegna completes the *Altarpiece di San Zeno.*	**1459**	He goes to Rome, where he is mentioned in a document in the pontifical archives as creditor of 150 "filoni" «as part of his work on certain paintings [...] in the chambers of His Holiness...» commissioned by Pius II. This is presumably the date he began working on the *Baptism of Christ* (London).
Alberti begins the construction of San Sebastiano in Mantua.	**1460**	"Post quem" date for the *Flagellation* of Urbino. On 30 October, in Borgo Sansepolcro he is appointed one of the twelve members of the college created to reform the public administration.
	1462	The artist's brother, Marco di Benedetto, receives 15 *scudi* as an advance payment for the *Polyptych of the Misericordia* commissioned to Piero in 1445 but only recently completed. Piero obviously is elsewhere, perhaps in Urbino or Arezzo. In Urbino he comes into contact with Luca Pacioli and Luciano Laurana.
Piero de' Medici succeeds his father Cosimo as the new lord of Florence. Feliciano published *Jubilatio.* Antonello da Messina paints the *Salvator mundi.* Luciano Laurana begins the transformation on the Ducal Palace in Urbino.	**1465**	

HISTORICAL AND ARTISTIC EVENTS		THE LIFE OF PIERO DELLA FRANCESCA
Francesco Sforza dies. Donatello dies in Florence. Luca della Robbia decorates the vault of the chapel of the Portuguese Cardinal in the church of San Miniato al Monte in Florence.	**1466**	On 20 December he is commissioned to paint a banner for the Compagnia dell'Annunziata of Arezzo; by that date the frescoes in the church of San Francesco had been completed.
	1467	"Ante quem" date for the panel of the diptych in the Uffizi that portrays *Federico da Montefeltro* and his triumph. In Borgo he holds public office.
	1468	He is at Bastia, near Borgo Sansepolcro, to escape the plague. He paints the now lost gonfalon for the Compagnia dell'Annunziata of Arezzo that was picked up by Benedetto della Valle on 7 November. The *Resurrection* dates from this year.
Piero de'Medici dies and is succeeded by his son Lorenzo who soon marries Clarice Orsini. Niccolò Machiavelli is born. Francesco del Cossa decorates the Schifanoia palace in Florence.	**1469**	On 8 April the Confraternita del Corpus Domini of Urbino reimburses the painter Giovanni Santi 10 *bolognini* spent on behalf of Piero della Francesca who had come to negotiate the commission for a painting he never did. On 14 November, in his home town, he is paid by the Augustinians in money and land for having completed the panel commissioned in 1454.
Sixtus IV becomes Pope. Albrecht Dürer is born in Nürenberg. Giusto of Gand paints the *Communion of the Apostles* for the Confraternita del Corpus Domini of Urbino. Cosmè Tura begins the *Roverella Polyptych.*	**1471**	He is listed as being arrears in payment of local taxes.
Federico da Montefeltro conquers Volterra. Leon Battista Alberti dies. Francesco di Giorgio Martini paints the altarpiece of the *Coronation of the Virgin.*	**1472**	The *Brera Altarpiece* can be hypothetically dated between 1472 and 1474.
	1473	Piero is again in Borgo Sansepolcro where he signs a power of attorney for his brother. Around this time he is mentioned in sonnet written by the Ferrarese Niccolò Testa Cilenio.
Antonello da Messina paints the *Portrait of a Gentleman.* Andrea Mantegna frescoes the Wedding chamber in the Ducal Palace in Mantua.	**1474**	On 12 April he is paid for the work he did in the church of Badia in Borgo Sansepolcro. He is not mentioned in any Borgo documents until 1478; he is probably in Urbino working on the *Senigallia Madonna.*
Savonarola enters the Dominican order. Paolo Uccello dies. Michelangelo is born in Caprese.	**1475**	Some documents, almost certainly forgeries, indicate Piero has having done the frescoes in the Vatican portraying *Sixtus IV and the Platina Librarian,* actually painted by Melozzo da Forlì.

HISTORICAL AND ARTISTIC EVENTS		THE LIFE OF PIERO DELLA FRANCESCA
In Florence the Pazzi conspiracy against the Medicis fails: Giuliano is assassinated, but Lorenzo maintains and consolidates his power. Melozzo da Forlì frescoes the Vatican Library in Rome. Giorgione is born.	**1478**	The Confraternita della Misericordia commissions Piero to fresco a Madonna on a wall «between the Church and the Hospital». There is no trace of this painting.
Verrocchio receives the commission for the equestrian monument to Colleoni in Venice.	**1479**	The *Resurrection* is moved to the Palazzo dei Conservatori in Borgo (this building is currently the Museo Civico) and the painting is still kept there.
In Milan, Ludovico Sforza (the "Moro") orders Simonetta killing and illegitimately attains power. Ghirlandaio paints the *Last Supper* and *St. Jerome in his Study* in the Church of Ognissanti in Florence.	**1480**	The city allocates money for the restoration of the wall where Piero had painted the Resurrection. Until 1482 he is the head of the priors of the Confraternita of San Bartolomeo.
Sixtus IV summons Rosselli, Botticelli, Ghirlandaio, Perugino, Pinturicchio to fresco the Sistine Chapel. Leonardo commissioned the *Adoration of the Magi.*	**1481**	
In Milan, Leonardo is at the court of Ludovico il Moro, and Bramante begins work on San Satiro. Botticelli paints the *Allegory of Spring.* The *Portinari Triptych* by Hugo van der Goes can be dated 1482.	**1482**	Piero is in Rimini, where he rents a house, with use of the vegetable garden and the well, from Giacosa, the widow of Ganimede Borelli.
Raphael Sanzio is born in Urbino. Leonardo receives the commission to paint the *Virgin of the Rocks.* Botticelli paints the *Birth of Venus* between 1483 and 1485.	**1483**	
In Milan Leonardo prepares some plans for the cathedral lantern. This is the presumed date for Giovanni Bellini's *St. Job Altarpiece.* Filippino Lippi works on the frescoes in the Carafa Chapel in the church of Santa Maria sopra Minerva in Rome.	**1487**	On 5 July, elderly yet «sound of mind and body», Piero appears before the notary Ser Lionardo di ser Mario Fedeli and entrusts him to change some notes written on a bit of paper into his last will and testament. This paper was found by Mancini and is now in the State Archives in Florence. He asked in the note to be buried in the church of the Badia. There is moving testimony of this, final period of his life in words of a certain Marco di Longaro «who when little, led by the hand *Mastro Piero di la Francesca,* excellent painter, who was blind».
On 12 October Christopher Columbus lands at San Salvador, discovering the new continent that would be called America. Lorenzo the Magnificent dies in Florence and Savonarola comes to power. The system of alliances sanctioned by the Peace of Lodi crumbles.	**1492**	In February, along with members of his family Piero divided his property. On 12 October, the burial of «Maestro Pier dei Franceschi, famous painter», is recorded in the *Libro III dei morti* (registry of deaths) of the Confraternita di San Bartolomeo in Borgo Sansepolcro.

BIBLIOGRAPHY

Perspective of the ideal city, attributed to Piero della Francesca (1460, circa); Galleria Nazionale delle Marche, Urbino.

The bibliography on Piero della Francesca is endless; the titles up to 1971 are listed in E. Battisti, *Piero della Francesca,* Milan 1971, 2 vols., which we suggest you see for works published prior to that date. We must mentioned the two versions, published in 1927 and 1950 of Roberto Longhi's book which were later combined in R. Longhi, *Piero della Francesca,* Florence 1975. Short, but important for the horizons they open are the two papers that C. Marinesco presented to the Société Nationale des Antiquaires de France: *Deux empereurs byzantins, Manuel II e Jean VIII Paléologue, vus par des artistes parisiens et italiens,* February 1958; *Echos byzantins des l'oeuvre de Piero della Francesca,* December 1958, in "Bulletin de la Société Nationale des Antiquaires de France", pp. 38-41 and 192-203. Another equally important source is K. Clark's *Piero della Francesca* in the 1951 and 1969 editions. The geometric implications came from the study by R. Wittkower and B.A.R. Carter, *The Perspective of Piero della Francesca's Flagellation,* in "Journal of the Warburg and Courtauld Institutes", 16, 1953, pp. 292-302, which can be considered the first in a series of studies that followed the same research scheme. Finally, we must mention O. del Buono and P. de Vecchi, *L'opera completa di Piero della Francesca,* Milan 1967. Battisti's study led to a blossoming of new critical contributions concerning the painter from Borgo starting with: M.A. Lavin, *Piero della Francesca, The Flagellation,* London 1972; M. Tanner, *Concordia in Piero della Francesca's Baptism of Christ,* in "The Art Quarterly", XXXV, 1972, pp. 1-20; P. d'Ancona, *Piero della Francesca. Il ciclo affrescato della Santa Croce nella chiesa di San Francesco ad Arezzo,* Milan 1973; F. Sangiorgi, *Ipotesi sulla collocazione originaria della pala di Brera,* in "Commentari", XXIV, 1973, pp. 211-216; C. Maltese, *Architectura ficta 1472 circa,* in *Studi Bramanteschi,* Congress Proceedings (Milan, Urbino, Rome 1970), Rome 1974, pp. 283-292; M. Calvesi, *Sistema degli equivalenti ed equivalenze del sistema in Piero della Francesca,* in "Storia dell'Arte", XXIV-XXV, 1975, pp. 83-100; M. Salmi, *La casa di Piero della Francesca,* in "Commentari", XXVI, 1975, pp. 276-296; G. Arrighi, *Arte e matematica in Piero della Francesca,* in "Commentari", XXVII, 1976, p. 24; M. Salmi, *Perché Piero della Francesca,* in "Commentari", XXVII, 1976, pp. 121-126; T. Gouma Peterson, *Piero della Francesca's Flagellation: an Historical interpretation,* in "Storia dell'Arte", XXVIII, 1976, pp. 217-233; M. Daly Davis, *Piero della Francesca's Mathematical Treatises: a Study of his Trattato d'abaco and Libellus de quinque corporibus regolaribus,* Ravenna 1977; C. Verga, *Un pavimento di Piero?,* in "Critica d'Arte", XLII, 1977, pp. 151-153 and 100-155; M. Salmi, *Piero della Francesca,* Novara 1979; L. Borgo, *New Questions for Piero's Flagellation,* in "The Burlington Magazine", CXI, 1979, pp. 546-553; M. Apa, *La Resurrezione di Cristo. Itinerario sull'affresco di Piero a Sansepolcro.* Sansepolcro 1980; M.A. Lavin, *Piero della Francesca's Baptism of Christ,* New Haven, 1981; C. Ginzburg, *Indagini su Piero,* Turin 1981; AA.VV., *Atti del Convegno Internazionale sulla "Madonna del Parto"* (Monterchi, 1980), Città di Castello 1982; F. Gualdoni, *Piero della Francesca. La leggenda della Vera Croce,* Novara 1982; A. Turchini, *Un'ipotesi sulla Flagellazione di Piero della Francesca,* in "Quaderni Medievali", XIV, 1982; M. A. Lavin, *Piero della Francesca a Rimini,* Bologna 1984; *Piero teorico dell'arte,* ed. O. Calabrese, Bari 1985; A. Angelini, *Piero della Francesca,* Florence 1985; M. Bussagli, *Il "Battesimo" di Londra di Piero della Francesca. Per una rilettura in chiave trinitaria,* in "Quaderni Medievali", 20, 1985, pp. 28-65; G. Ugolini, *La pala di Montefeltro. Una porta per il mausoleo dinastico di Federico,* Pesaro 1985; R. Black, *The Uses and Abuses of Iconology: Piero della Francesca and Carlo Ginzburg,* in "The Oxford Art Journal", IX, 2, 1986, pp. 67-71; J. Aiken, *Renaissance Perspective: Its Mathematical Source and Sanction,* Ann Arbor 1986; J. Pope-Hennessy, *Whose Flagellation?* in "Apollo", CXXIV, 1986, pp. 162-165; L. Bellosi, *Giovanni di Piamonte e gli affreschi di Piero ad Arezzo,* in "Prospettiva", 50, 1987, pp. 15-35; J. and M. Guillaud, *Piero della Francesca Poet of Form. The Frescoes of San Francesco in Arezzo,* Paris – New York 1988; *Ricerche su Piero,* ed. M.G. Paolini, Arezzo 1989; A. Paolucci, *Piero della Francesca,* Florence, 1989; idem, *Piero della Francesca. Catalogo Completo,* Florence, 1990; G. Renzi, *Piero della Francesca, pittore teologo nella basilica di San Francesco di Arezzo,* Arezzo 1990; L. Vayer, *Problemi iconologici nel ciclo di affreschi di Piero della Francesca ad Arezzo,* in "Arte Cristiana", LXXX-VII, 1990, pp. 161-168; C. Bertelli, *Piero della Francesca,* Milan 1991; F. Collini, *Una possibile connotazione antiebraica della Flagellazione di Piero della Francesca,* in "Bollettino d'Arte", 65, 1991, pp. 1-28; C. Pizzorusso, *Sul "Battesimo" di Piero della Francesca,* in "Artista. Critica dell'arte in Toscana", 1991, pp. 122-133.

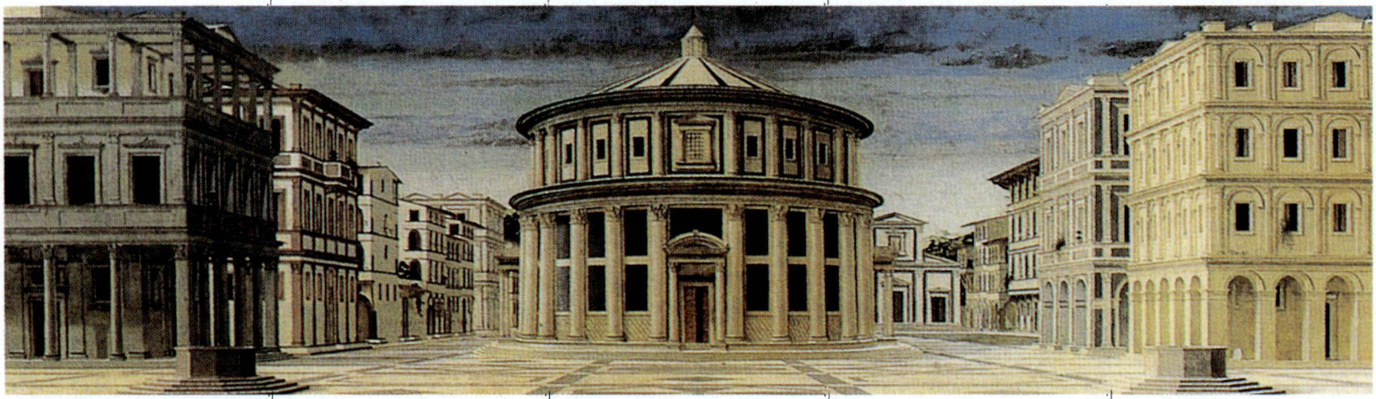

PHOTOGRAPHS

All photographs belong to the Giunti Archive.

English translation by:
Julia Weiss for Traduco snc di Bovone e Bulckaen

Art e Dossier
Supplement
to issue n. 71,
September 1992.

Chief Editor:
Bruno Piazzesi

Periodical press:
Reg. Cancell. Trib. Firenze
no. 3384 of 22.11.1985.

Printed in Italy
Printed by Giunti,
Industrie Grafiche S.p.A.
Printing-factory of Prato

VAT paid by the publisher
as laid down in Art. 74
let.c - DPR 633 of 26.10.72

ISBN 88-09- 21559-1

BENJAMIN WEST

AND THE STRUGGLE TO BE MODERN

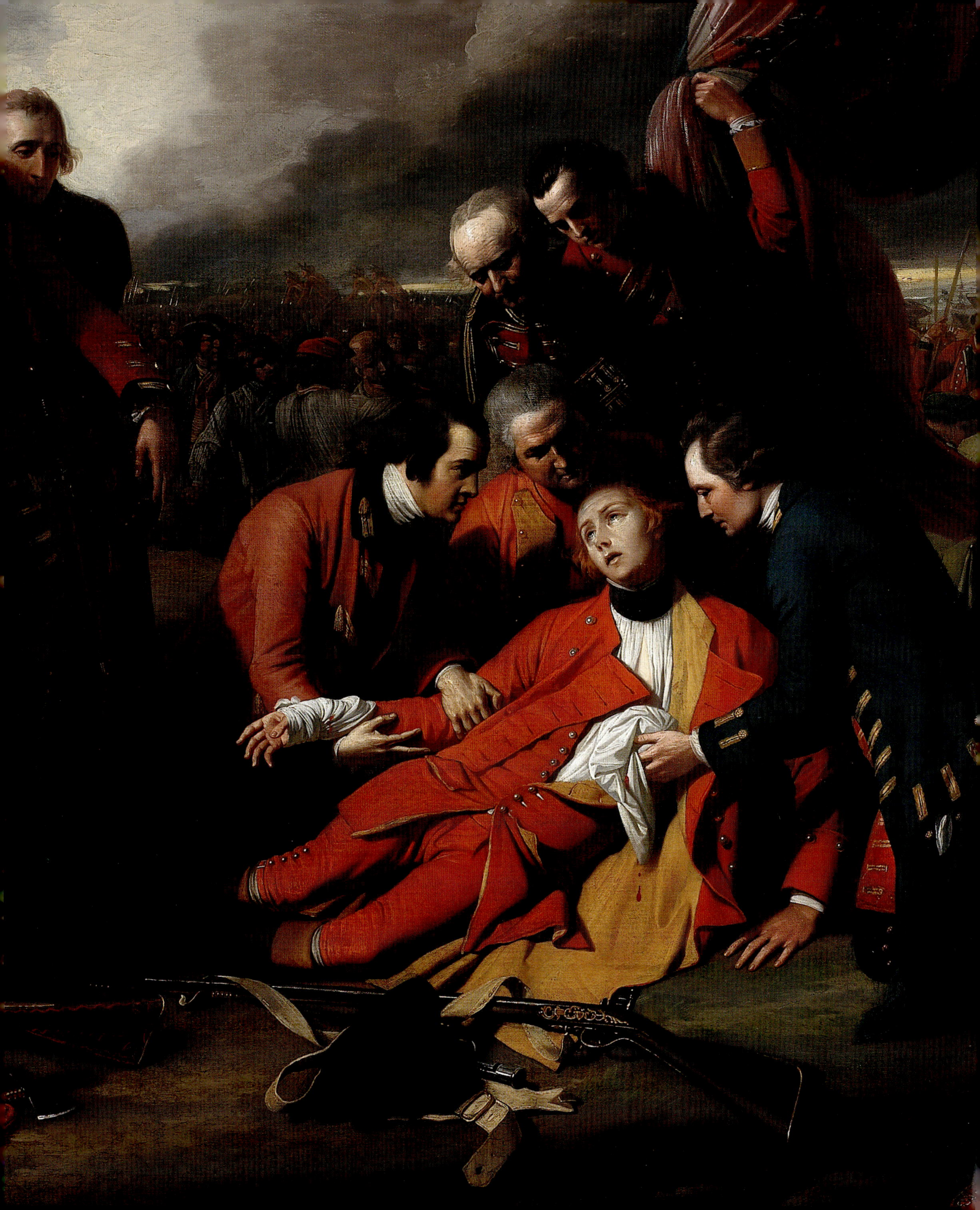

BENJAMIN WEST

AND THE STRUGGLE TO BE MODERN

Loyd Grossman

MERRELL
LONDON • NEW YORK

For Gracie and Connie:
lovely, loving, beloved

CONTENTS

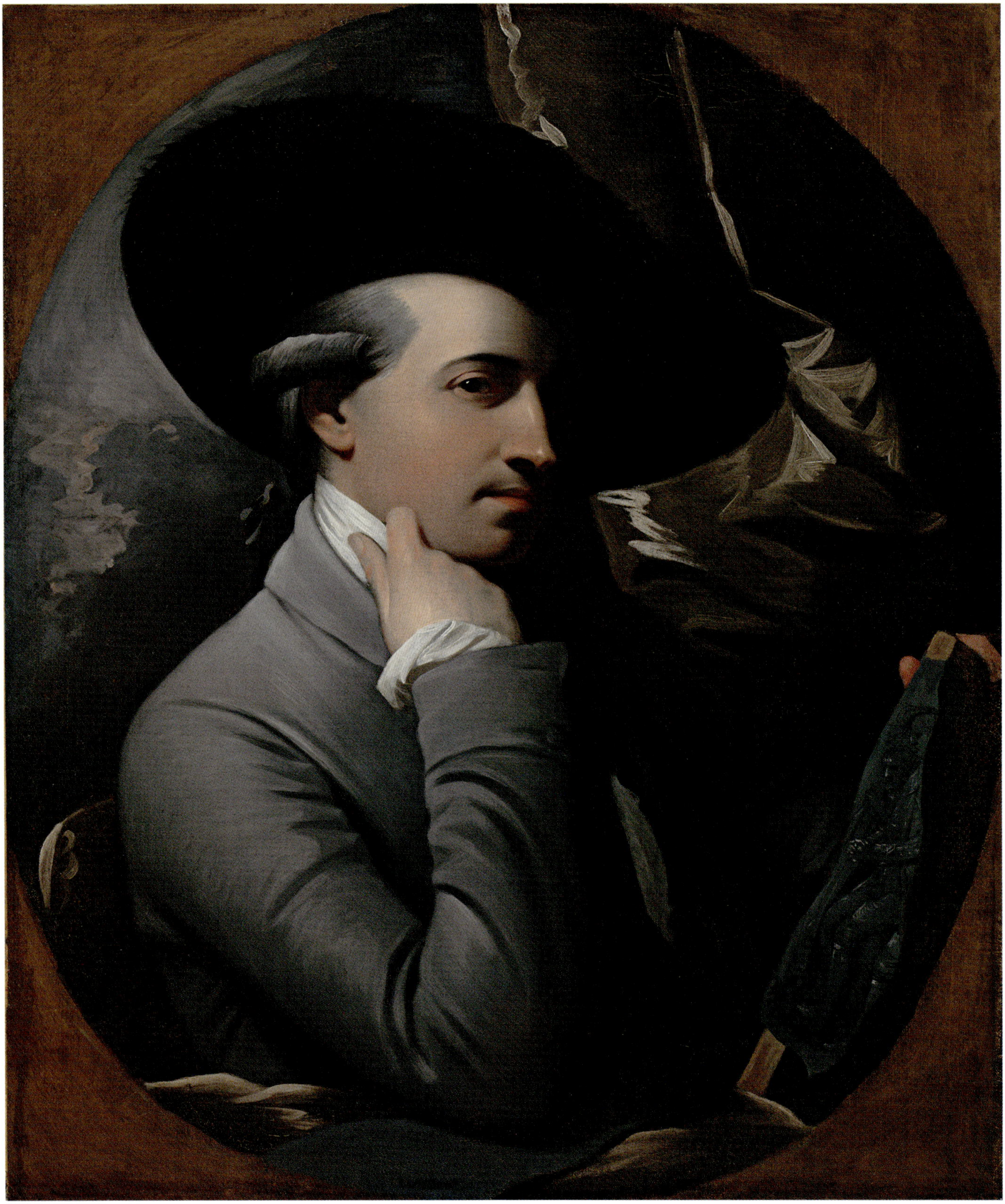

PREFACE

Growing up in New England, I was familiar with Benjamin West's work long before I was familiar with Benjamin West and the context in which he worked. Nearly two hundred years after it was painted, West's *Death of General Wolfe* remained the iconic image of a time when eastern North America – including my native Massachusetts – was a battlefield during the protracted Anglo-French conflict that Americans call the French and Indian War. General James Wolfe's victory at the Battle of Quebec in 1759 was, among other things, the reason why we did not speak French. No matter how it was reproduced, whether on a book jacket or as a postcard or black-and-white engraving, *Wolfe* powerfully conveyed the drama and romance of history. I first saw the real thing, the version that West painted for George III, in the early 1980s. It was no longer on public view, so my encounter took place in the cold and gloomy surroundings of a Hampton Court storeroom. Even so far removed from the damask-covered walls where the King had given it a privileged position among all his pictures, *Wolfe* was a magnetic and thrilling work of art.

A work of art that represents a key moment: a moment when Enlightenment ideas about history and progress were given visual expression. To contemporary eyes, West looks like anything but a modern artist. His work is literal, figurative, narrative. Yet *Wolfe* was a disruptive, even revolutionary picture that, I believe, helped to change the course of art. Being modern is not a style, but a way of thinking and an attitude that believes in the value of the present. It was a struggle for artists and writers to find a language that, while respecting the value of the classical past, was confident of the present. Just before and during West's lifetime, men and women of letters, philosophers, artists and historians were increasingly convinced that they could equal and maybe even surpass the achievements of the ancient Greeks and Romans. Their newfound confidence and ability to look forward to a progressive future are very much the foundations of the 'modern' attitude that has

1
Benjamin West (1738–1820)
Self-Portrait
1770–76
Oil on canvas
76.8 × 63.8 cm
(30¼ × 25⅛ in.), oval
BALTIMORE MUSEUM OF ART

affected the way we live and think ever since. It was West's triumph to create an image that instantly and unforgettably conveyed the heroic nature of the contemporary.

At the time of his death in 1820, Benjamin West was the most famous artist in the English-speaking world, and much honoured and admired in France, Italy and Germany. In his lifetime, his rapid rise to prominence and the pleasure he took in his success had attracted opprobrium – Lord Byron damningly referred to him as 'England's best artist and Europe's worst' – and his posthumous reputation took a savage mauling from such Victorian critics as Walter Thornbury, who dubbed him 'The Monarch of Mediocrity'. But even at his critical nadir, West's most celebrated work, *Wolfe*, continued to fascinate. In a sign of declining royal favour, the picture was moved from Buckingham Palace to Hampton Court, where the author of a late nineteenth-century guidebook praised it as 'a triumph of its kind ... the scene is told with sober sincerity, honesty and with a genuine pathos', before going on to remark that it was 'easy enough to sneer at, but in historical interest, in sympathy, in composition, and in colour, it is a work which is worthy of a full and respectful attention'.[1]

West remains among the most neglected and misunderstood of Britain's great eighteenth-century artists, lacking the social bite of Hogarth, the bravura of Reynolds or the easy elegance of Gainsborough. Unlike Hogarth and Reynolds in particular, West was not an especially articulate or forceful writer, and seemed to lack the intellectual credentials to which so many of his fellow artists aspired. And yet, he was extraordinarily in tune with the artistic and intellectual currents that swirled through his turbulent times. He was in the vanguard that created Neoclassicism and Romanticism, and among the very first artists to represent the exciting and inspirational qualities of contemporary events, as opposed to episodes dredged up from the biblical, classical or mythological past, which had long enjoyed the highest artistic status.

West's reputation has slowly recovered following a rise in interest in the late 1930s around the bicentenary of his birth and the publication in 1986 of Helmut von Erffa and Allen Staley's monumental catalogue raisonné. In more recent years a growing number of art historians – including most prominently Jules Prown and David Solkin – have contributed to the reassessment of West's accomplishments.

It has not been my explicit intention to contribute further to the rehabilitation of West's still-precarious reputation, although I am happy to do so. I have mostly wanted to understand and consequently explain why *Wolfe* was such an instant success, and why it has exercised such a strong grip on our imaginations ever since it was first shown to the public in 1771. In order to do so, I have situated West in the midst of Enlightenment thinking and, I hope, demolished some of the prejudices about the talent and intentions of the young man from the Pennsylvania frontier who attained such eminence at the court of George III.

A NOTE ON CITATIONS, SPELLING AND TITLES OF WORKS

All newspapers are published in London unless otherwise indicated.

When modern editions of historic works have been used, the original publication date is noted in brackets after the title.

Original spelling, capitalization and punctuation have been used for all quotations, and to avoid cluttering the text I have not used [*sic*] to indicate such peculiarities as may be found.

The titles of works by West are those used by Helmut von Erffa and Allen Staley in their catalogue raisonné (see note 2 on page 204), except when otherwise titled because of copyright requirements. All other works are as titled by their holders.

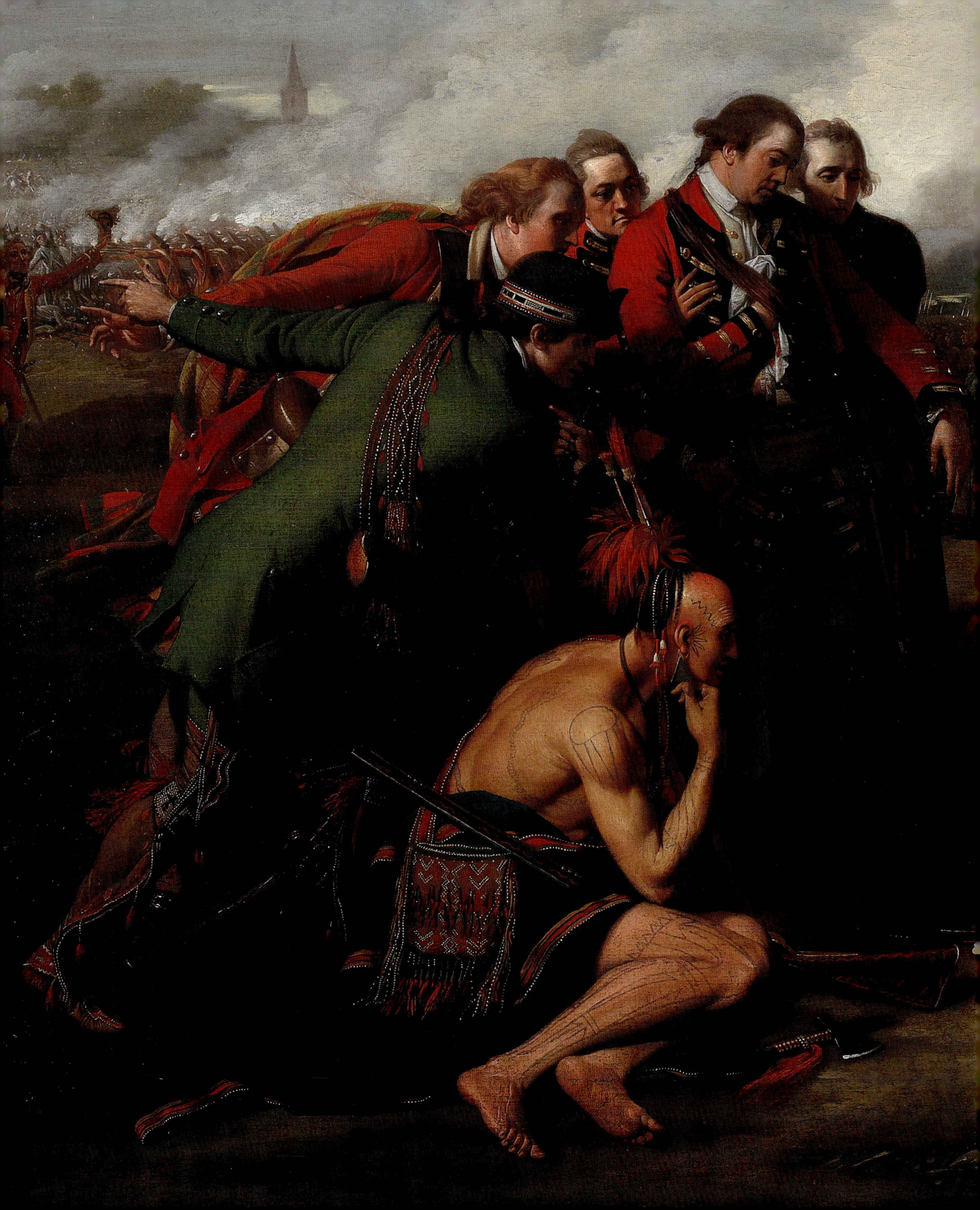

A COSTUME DRAMA

Detail of Benjamin West, *The Death of General Wolfe*, 1770 (see fig. 2)

From his retreat at Mount Vernon in 1786, George Washington pondered how Jean-Antoine Houdon should represent him in a new statue commissioned for the Virginia State Capitol. Would the legislators of the newly independent commonwealth wish to see their former Commander-in-Chief as Washington *togata* or as Washington the modern man? 'Perhaps a servile adherence to the garb of antiquity might not be altogether so expedient, as some little deviation in favor of the modern costume', Washington wrote to Thomas Jefferson, the American Minister in Paris. 'This was a circumstance hinted in conversation by Mr. West to Mr. Houdon. This taste, which has been introduced in painting by Mr. West, I understand is received with applause, and prevails extensively.'[1] In spite of being praised as a new Cincinnatus, Washington chose to be portrayed in modern dress as a hero of his time.

'This taste' for 'the modern costume' about which Washington wrote so thoughtfully to Jefferson was the result of Benjamin West's decision to paint a heroic contemporary event – the death of General James Wolfe at the Battle of Quebec in 1759 – in modern costume, rather than in the classicizing mode thought to be appropriate for such a subject. By doing so, West had aroused at worst hostility, at best puzzlement from many of his colleagues and patrons. But he struck a chord with the exhibition-going public that resonated far beyond London. *The Death of General Wolfe* (fig. 2)[2] was the popular hit of the Royal Academy exhibition of 1771, and William Woollett's subsequent engraving (fig. 3) was a huge commercial success. Whether in the original or in the many pirated versions that quickly appeared, *Wolfe* could be found hanging on walls from Königsberg to the Carolinas. Although West and his contemporaries, like Washington, discussed the innovatory nature of *Wolfe* in terms of costume, such language was a mere metaphor for the triumph of the modern, and *Wolfe* was the first great visual expression of that triumph. Through a deft combination of baroque pictorial rhetoric, religious imagery and protoromantic sensibility, West elevated a contemporary event to the highest realms of classical history. If modernity is, in Michel Foucault's phrase, 'the will to "heroize" the present',[3] then *Wolfe* is among the first great modern pictures. And it was perceived as such by West's contemporaries, even if many of them expressed themselves in somewhat opaque language. Writing in 1802, the visionary American poet and radical ideologue Joel Barlow more straightforwardly, and enthusiastically, described 'the revolution which has been brought about in art within the last thirty years by [West] having broken the ancient shackles and modernized the art'.[4]

In his old age, West recalled the events around the painting of *Wolfe*, nearly half a century earlier, to his biographer John Galt. According to West, his most important patron, George III, had remarked 'that it was thought very ridiculous to exhibit heroes in coats, breeches, and cock'd hats'. Undaunted, the artist told the King 'that he was quite aware of the objection, but that it was founded in prejudice'.

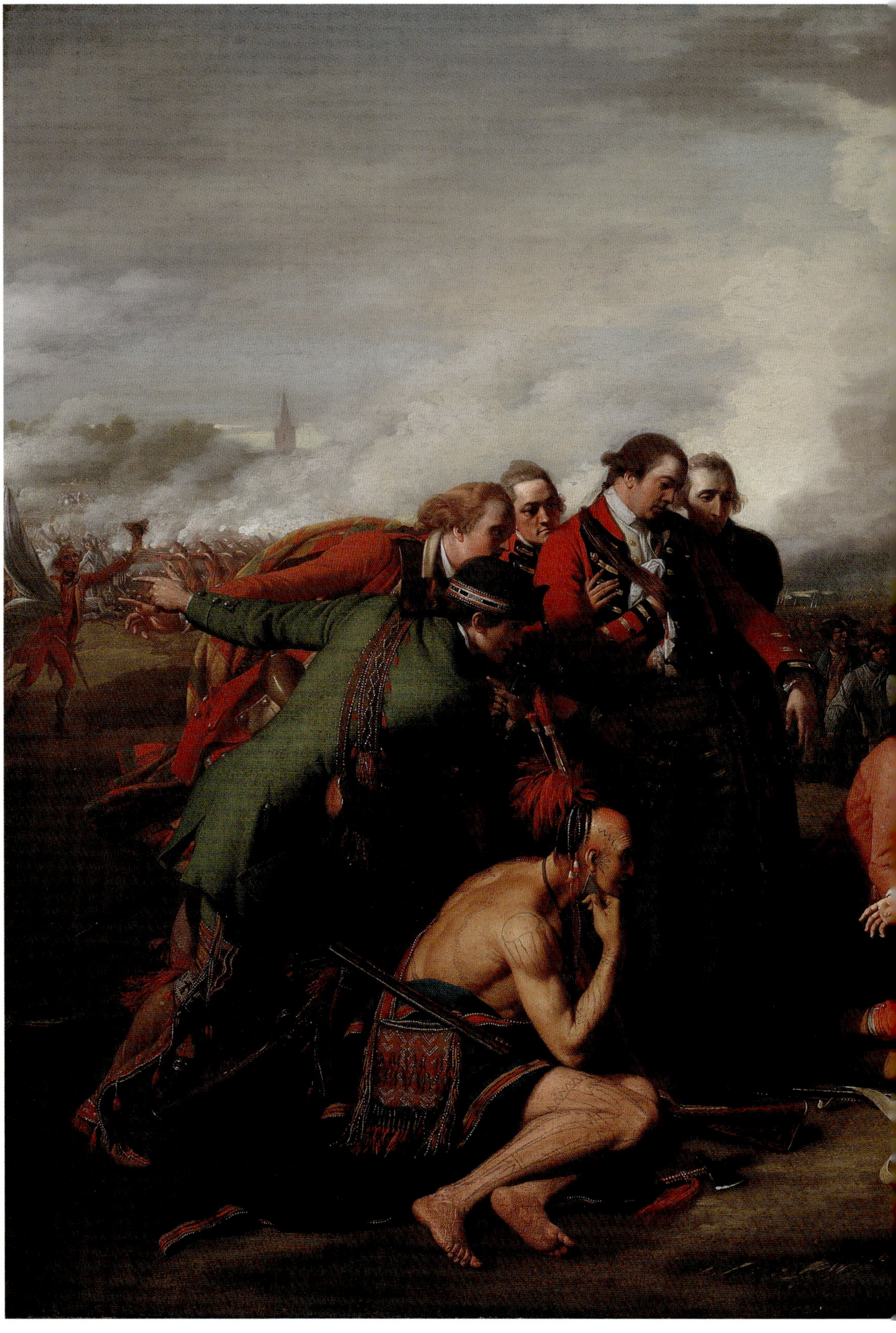

2
Benjamin West
The Death of General Wolfe
1770
Oil on canvas
152.6 × 214.5 cm (60 × 84½ in.)
NATIONAL GALLERY OF CANADA, OTTAWA

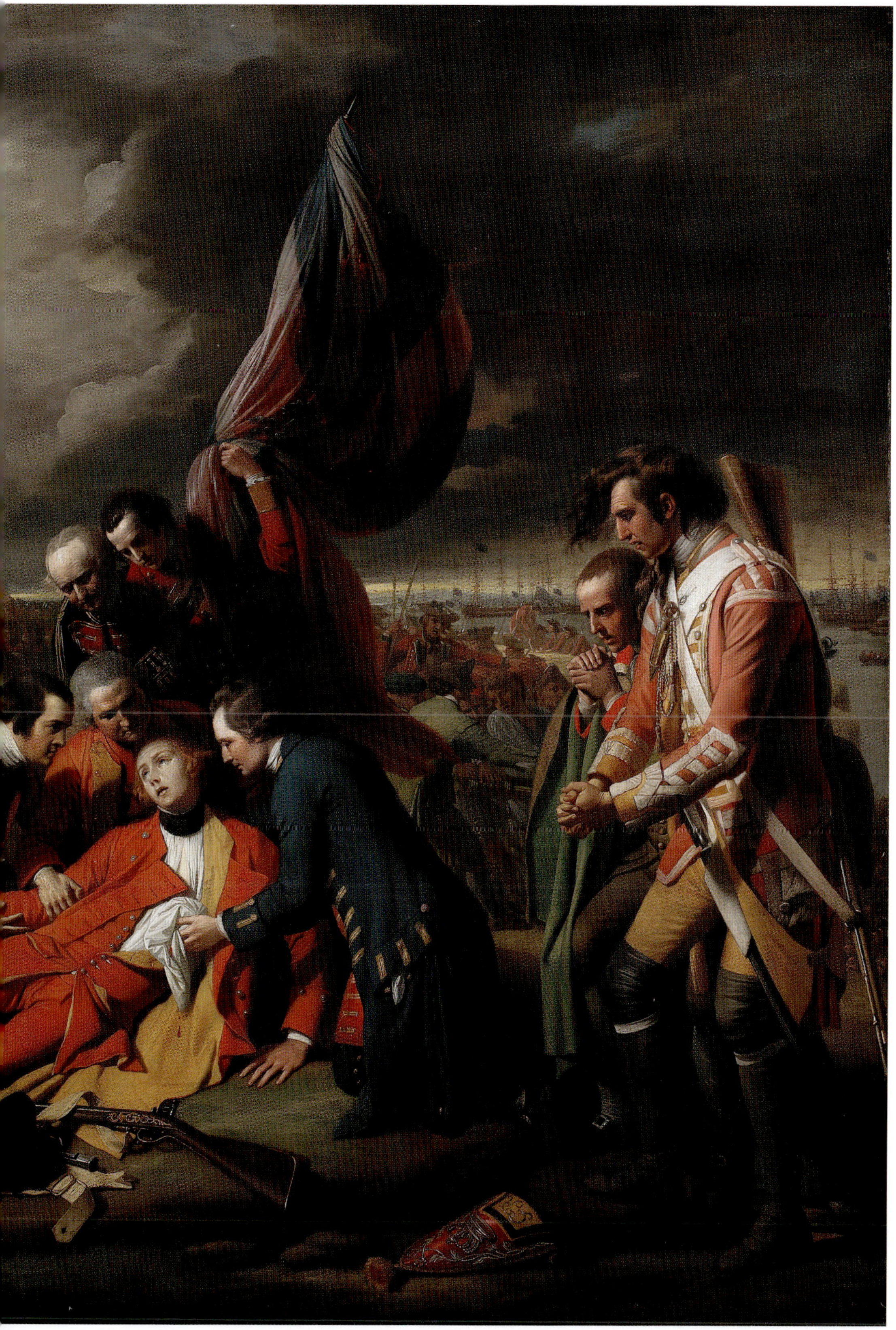

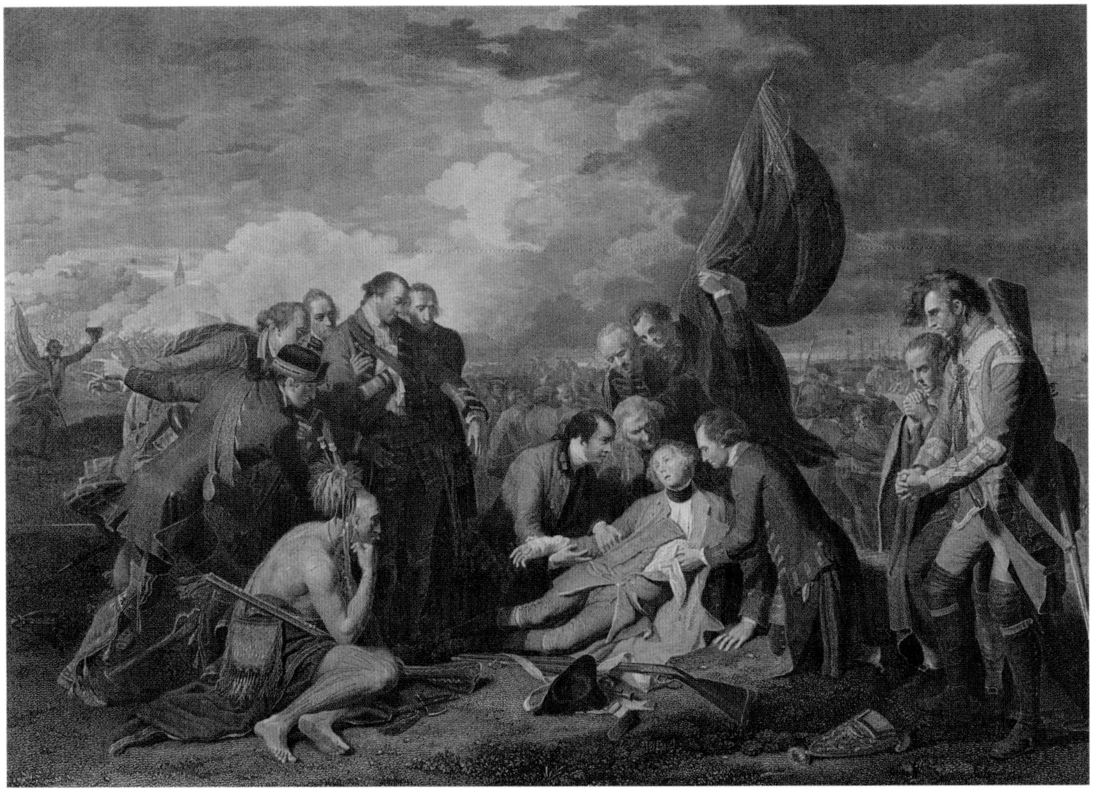

3
William Woollett (1735–1785), after Benjamin West
The Death of General Wolfe
1776
Engraving with etching
42.5 × 59.1 cm
(16¾ × 23¼ in.)
PAUL MELLON COLLECTION, YALE CENTER FOR BRITISH ART, NEW HAVEN, CONNECTICUT

And to make the point to his royal critic, West related how Robert Hay Drummond, Archbishop of York, and Sir Joshua Reynolds had come to his studio in Castle Street, Westminster, to 'dissuade me from running so great a risk'. Reynolds and Drummond were a formidable delegation. As President of the Royal Academy, Reynolds was the de facto head of the artistic profession in England, as well as chief propagandist and would-be enforcer of academic orthodoxy. The worldly, aesthetic and politically influential Drummond had been West's protector and mentor, shepherding him into the royal circle. The opinions and influence of such men mattered a great deal to Benjamin West, still carefully climbing the ladder towards artistic, social and financial eminence in 1770 when Reynolds and Drummond came to call.

As West told the story:

> Reynolds then began a very ingenious and elegant dissertation on the state of the public taste in this country, and the danger which every attempt at innovation necessarily incurred of repulse or ridicule; and he concluded with urging me earnestly to adopt the classic costume of antiquity, as much more becoming the inherent greatness of my subject than the modern garb of war.

West must have been as taut as a bowstring as he took in Reynolds's objections: 'I listened to him with the utmost attention in my power to give, but could perceive no principle in what he had delivered; only a strain of persuasion to induce me to comply with an existing prejudice, – a prejudice which I thought could not be too soon removed.' As West recollected, this was a scene of the highest drama as the urbane and intellectual Reynolds and the opulent Archbishop faced off against the principled young artist. Answering Reynolds's objections, West remarked

> that the event intended to be commemorated took place on the 13th of September, 1758, in a region of the world unknown to the Greeks and Romans, and at a period of time when no such nations, nor heroes in their costume, any longer existed. The subject I have to represent is the conquest of a great

> province of America by the British troops. It is a topic that history will proudly record, and the same truth that guides the pen of the historian should govern the pencil of the artist.[5]

West was not only looking for the approval of his contemporaries, no matter how eminent; he was also, rather grandly, thinking about his future reputation:

> I consider myself as undertaking to tell this great event to the eye of the world; but if, instead of the facts of the transaction, I represent classical fictions, how shall I be understood by posterity! The only reason for adopting the Greek and Roman dresses, is the picturesque forms of which their drapery is susceptible; but is this an advantage for which all the truth and propriety of the subject should be sacrificed?

By this time, perhaps the President and the Archbishop were shifting in their chairs. West then moved on to a masterful summing-up and a diplomatic conclusion:

> I want to mark the date, the place, and the parties engaged in the event; and if I am not able to dispose of the circumstances in a picturesque manner, no academical distribution of Greek or Roman costume will enable me to do justice to the subject. However, without insisting upon principles to which I intend to adhere, I feel myself so profoundly impressed with the friendship of this interference, that when the picture is finished, if you do not approve of it, I will consign it to the closet, whatever may be my own opinion of the execution.

When the painting was finished, West invited Drummond and Reynolds to return to his studio:

> They came accordingly, and the latter [Reynolds] without speaking, after his first cursory glance, seated himself before the picture, and examined it with deep and minute attention for about half an hour. He then rose, and said to His Grace, Mr. West has conquered. He has treated his subject as it ought to be treated … I foresee that this picture will not only become one of the most popular, but occasion a revolution in art.[6]

So the collective authority of the Academy and the Establishment elegantly bowed to the power of individual genius; the past stepped aside to give centre stage to the present; the Old World retired gracefully to make room for the New. As retold by Galt in 1820 and subsequent editions, and recycled by others, beginning with *The Progress of Genius … Abridged for the use of young persons by a Lady* in 1831,[7] the story of West's clash with the titans rapidly acquired mythic status. But did these events, so vividly described, happen as West recounted them? Indeed, did they happened at all?

West, for all his post hoc bravado, was not a person to endanger his career for the sake of an intellectual principle. He was by 1770 one of the most successful artists in London: at thirty-two, already a founder-member of the Royal Academy and a recipient of two commissions from King George – *The Departure of Regulus from Rome* (fig. 4) and *The Oath of Hannibal* (fig. 5). His house and studio in Castle Street, hard by the new and socially desirable church of St Martin-in-the-Fields, were more than respectable; but bigger and better beckoned. By the end of 1772, West and family would be installed in grand premises in Newman Street, and West would be honoured by appointment as Historical Painter to the King, an appointment that from 1780 brought with it a generous £1000 a year. The early 1770s were, for Benjamin West, *anni mirabiles*. And *Wolfe* was the threshold over which West stepped to lifelong fame, success and status. *Wolfe* was so stunning a triumph that West after *Wolfe* was a different man. West knew it and his contemporaries knew it. As James Northcote so beautifully sniped: 'With West it was always "My Wolfe, my Wolfe" … He thought Wolfe owed all his fame to the picture: it was he who immortalized Wolfe, not Wolfe who had immortalized him.'[8]

From his youth in Pennsylvania to his maturity in London, West advanced his art and his career relentlessly but cautiously. So it is worth considering whether, at such a critical point in that career, West would really have challenged Reynolds so

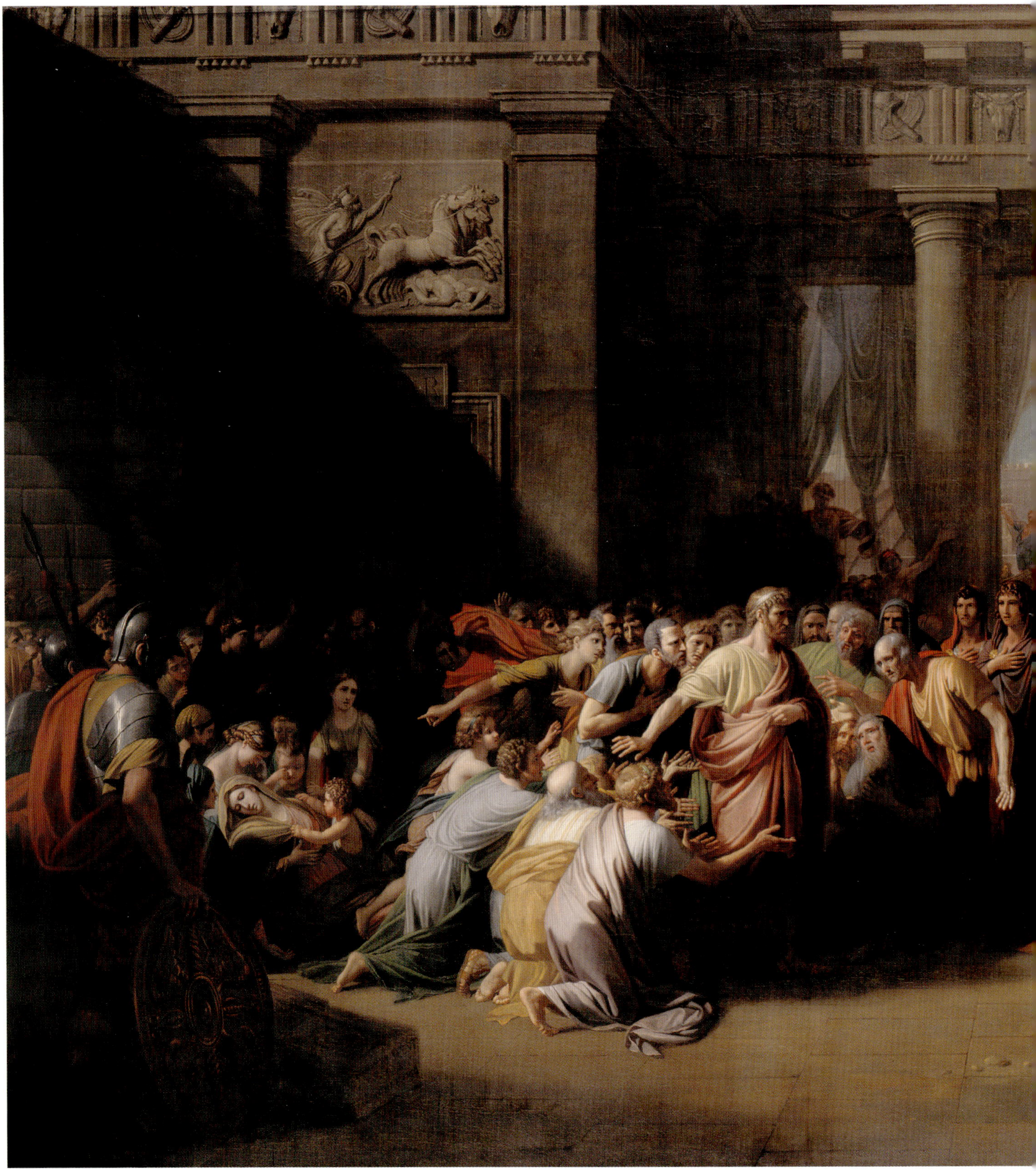

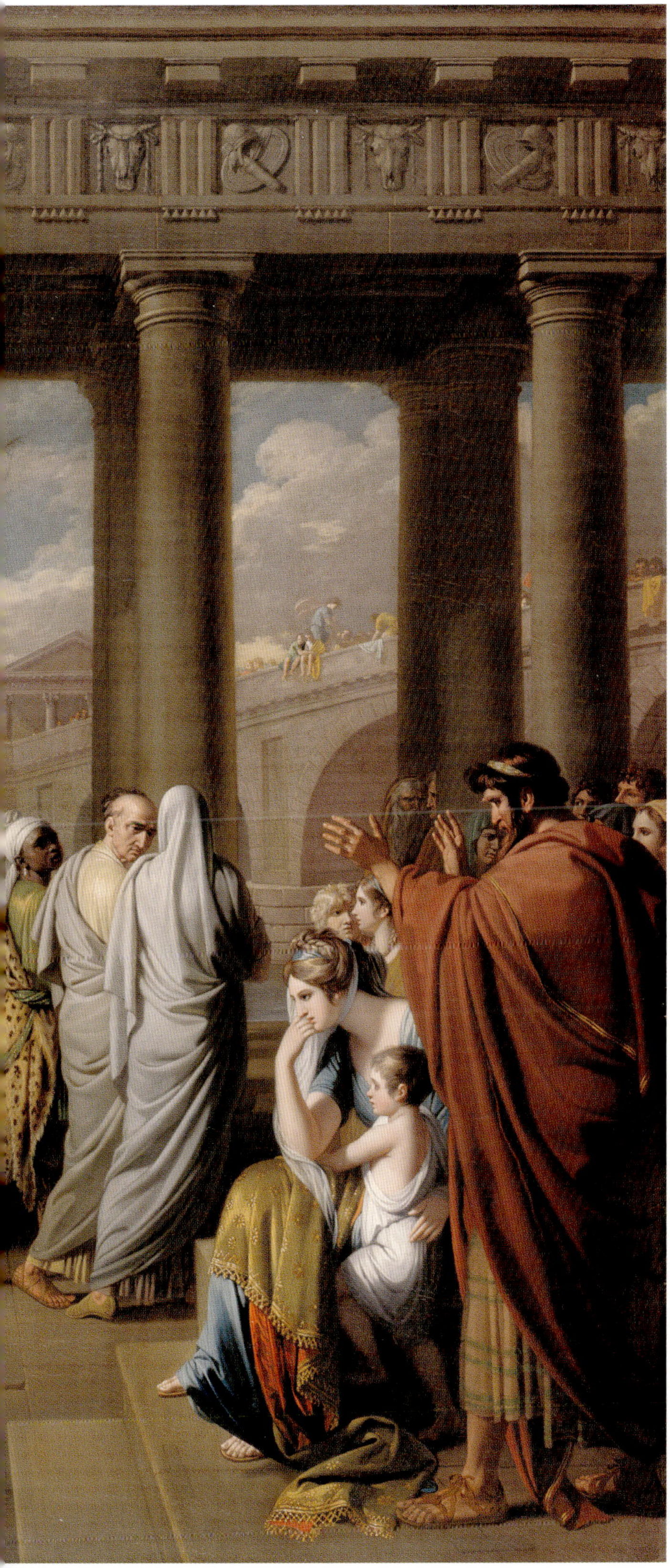

4
Benjamin West
The Departure of Regulus from Rome
1769
Oil on canvas
225.4 × 307.2 cm
(88¾ × 121 in.)
ROYAL COLLECTION, LONDON

5
Benjamin West
The Oath of Hannibal
1770
Oil on canvas
224.9 × 307.7 cm
(88½ × 121⅛ in.)
ROYAL COLLECTION, LONDON

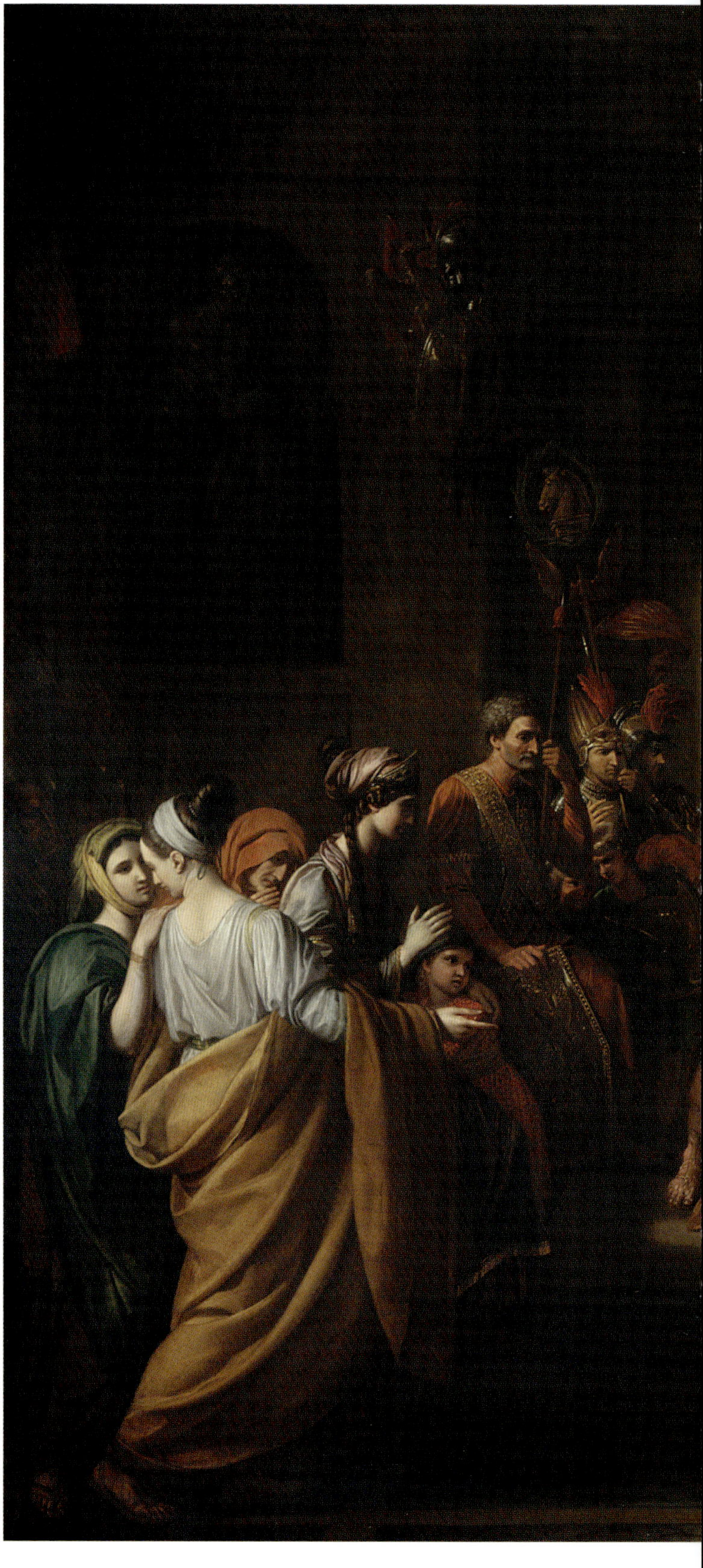

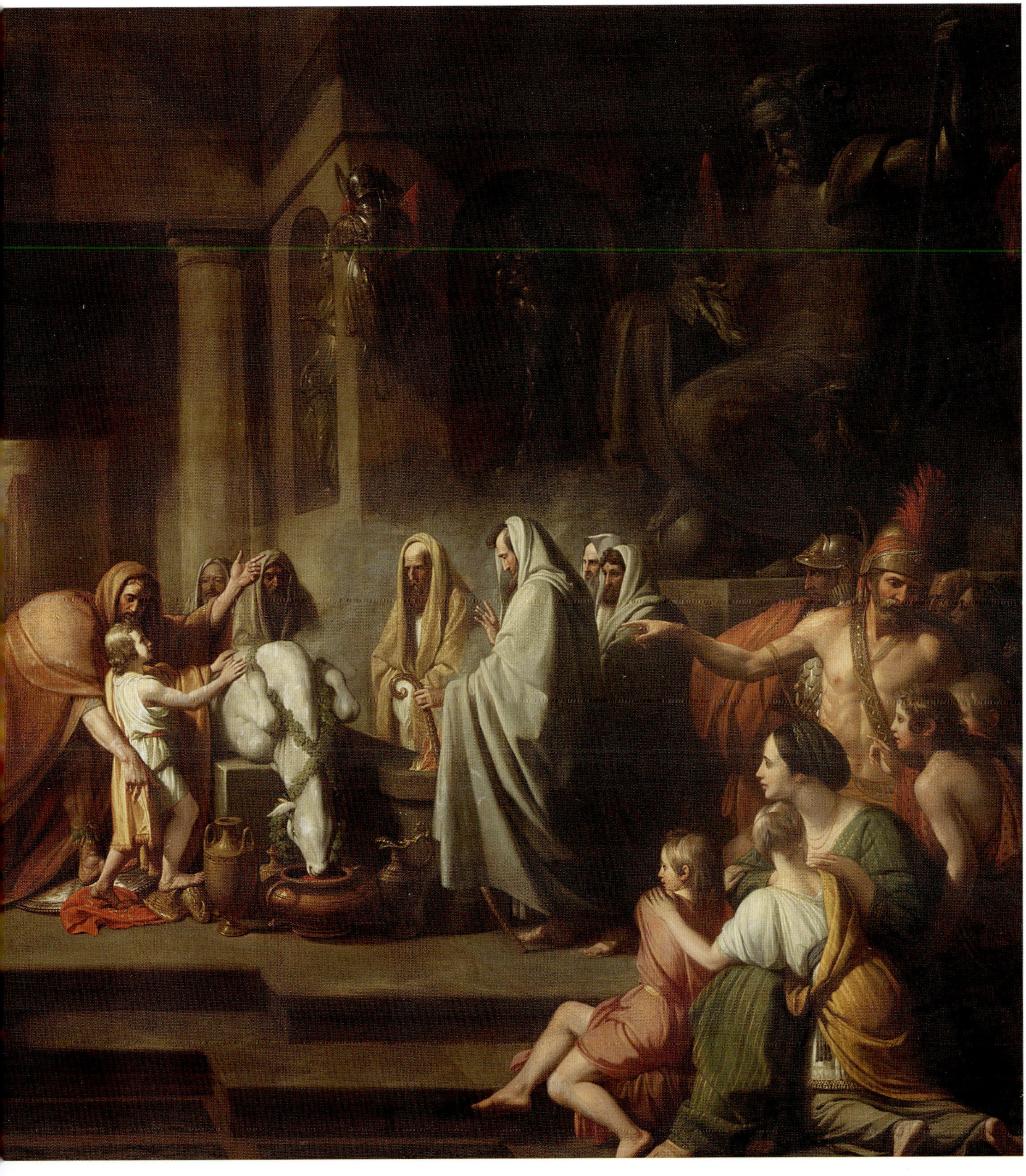

boldly; similarly, whether it is likely that Reynolds would have proclaimed the triumph of a picture so obviously contrary to the academic canon, particularly when we consider his *Discourses* both before and after the painting of *Wolfe*. Yet there is something remarkably truthful about the story.

There is no evidence so far discovered that even hints that Reynolds and Drummond came to call on West – no evidence, that is, other than West's version. And almost since it was published, West's version, as polished and presented by Galt, has been questioned and criticized. As early as 1834, West's former student William Dunlap referred to the Galt biography as 'injudicious'[9] even while repeating much of its material. Subsequent biographers and art historians have done likewise. Only in recent years has the Galt biography been examined more closely, and while found wanting in certain aspects – the 'hard facts' of West's life – Galt has been revealed as more illuminating than previously thought. For all its invented dialogue, fabulism and fictionalizing, it is the life of the artist as he chose to tell it.[10] While West's story of the creation of *Wolfe* may have been – almost certainly was – factually inaccurate, it is essentially truthful. This sometimes slippery, or at the very least malleable, notion of what was truthful in the eighteenth century was a significant factor in the way that West chose both to portray an event from contemporary history – the death of James Wolfe – and to fashion his own life story as a romantic adventure that took him from the forests of Pennsylvania to the state rooms of Windsor Castle.

In one of his most memorable phrases, West remarked that 'the same truth that guides the pen of the historian should guide the pencil of the artist'.[11] But for West and his contemporaries there was a clear distinction between 'literal' truth and what could be characterized as a deeper 'essential' truth. Indeed, it could be said that such 'essential' truth was more highly regarded by contemporaries than the mere accuracy of reportage. With its Aristotelian roots, this long-lived contest between the universal and the particular continued to exercise artists and thinkers throughout the eighteenth century.

One such thinker was the Reverend Robert Bromley, Rector of St Mildred, Poultry, in the City of London. Bromley is a minor figure, even in the history of the eighteenth-century Anglican clergy, but a minor figure with literary and artistic ambitions who stepped briefly into the spotlight in the 1790s with his *Philosophical and Critical History of the Fine Arts*. Bromley so fervently promoted West's status as the principal history painter of the age that the Royal Academy was – and this was not uncommon – thrown into chaos as bitter dissent broke out between West's supporters and opponents, including his one-time protégé John Singleton Copley. Bromley was further attacked in the most violent terms by those such as Henry Fuseli, who felt that the clergyman had no business at all writing about either the history or the theory of art. Consequently, attempts were made to remove his book from the Academy's library. Bromley was, though, an erudite man and if not exactly a mouthpiece for West, certainly very close to the artist.[12] It is reasonable to believe that his views on truth were near to West's. Defending West's *Wolfe* against charges that it was not an accurate portrayal of the event, Bromley said:

> The historic painter must therefore lay down to himself the first duty, TO KEEP NEAR TO THE TRUTH OF THE HISTORY HE REPRESENTS. This however is no slavish tie; it admits of some latitude, reasonably restrained. It is not necessary that he confine himself to the precise order in which the event took place, the precise situation of circumstances, or the precise point of time. In these several respects he may exercise a discretionary selection for the purpose of giving the best effect to the story: he may even indulge invention so far as to introduce other circumstances which might well be supposed to have happened, although they did not, but which shall all in their measure contribute to give a more precise elucidation to the piece.[13]

'A discretionary selection for the purpose of giving the best effect' and 'other circumstances which might well be supposed to have happened, although they did not' are phrases to keep in mind when viewing *Wolfe*, when interpreting West's celebrated encounter with Drummond and Reynolds, or when reading any part of the Galt biography: a biography that was very much in the tradition of such canonical but imaginative biographers as Vasari, whose status as the paramount writer on the history of art was unquestioned in the eighteenth century, and Plutarch, whose *Parallel Lives* were read by all educated people at the time, including the scantily educated West.

In spite of the ruthless commitment to fact that Rousseau brought to the biographical genre with his *Confessions* – 'I have told the good and the bad with equal frankness. I have neither omitted anything bad, nor interpolated anything good … I have shown myself as I was: mean and contemptible, good, high-minded and sublime'[14] – the moralizing, mythologizing, hagiographic biography continued to flourish well into the nineteenth century: *A History of the Life and Death, Virtues and Exploits of General George Washington* by Parson Mason Weems, published in 1800, sixteen years before Galt, being a prime example. Galt's book is quite clearly an autobiography in all but name, and to that extent can also be considered as a sort of literary analogue to the many self-portraits and family portraits that West painted (one of which is studied in detail in the next chapter).

Discussing the famous incident, as recounted by Vasari, in which Leonardo frightened his own father with the terrifying realism of a monster's face that he had painted, Paul Barolsky wrote:

> Walter Pater sensed that this story was a fiction, 'perhaps an invention,' as he said, but he also recognized its 'air of truth,' by which he meant its historical verisimilitude. Although for a long time art historians often misread Vasari, either misconstruing his fictions as facts or misidentifying them as errors, in recent years they have returned increasingly to Pater's point of view, recognizing the deeper truths of Vasari's poetic fabrications.[15]

What are 'the deeper truths' of West's 'poetic fabrications', and how do they fit into the contradictions and complexities of personal identity in the eighteenth century, a period in which self-fashioning or even self-invention was a tool to be used by those like West who were determined to survive and thrive in the social and economic rough and tumble of the time? As James Boswell, another ambitious outsider whose goal was to make it in London, excitedly confided to his diary on 21 November 1762: 'I have discovered that we may be in some degree whatever character we choose … practice forms a man to anything.'[16]

The character that West chose for himself in this instance was the brave young artist, ready to risk 'repulse or ridicule' in his ambitious quest for a new type of history painting. And to highlight this, West condensed what was a lengthy and sometimes difficult process of thought and consultation around the creation of *Wolfe* into a brief and unforgettable story that could be immediately grasped by the readers of the Galt biography.

West must have been aware that his portrayal of Wolfe's death would attract a great deal of attention. As we shall see, Wolfe remained the pre-eminent British hero even eleven years after his death. Both Edward Penny and George Romney had already exhibited their versions of the death of Wolfe (figs. 6 and 7) to some public acclaim, and Joseph Wilton was still at work on his substantial and long-awaited monument to Wolfe for Westminster Abbey (fig. 8). So there were a number of yardsticks against which West's *Wolfe* could be judged. The upward trajectory of West's career was sharp: his work was fetching good prices and, importantly, the King was buying. There was everything to play for and everything to lose. *Wolfe* had to be a success, and West would do everything he had to in order to make it one. First there would have been the process of understanding and meeting any theoretical objections that might have come from artists or patrons. And this was not the work of a mere few house calls. West thus far in his career had shown

6
Edward Penny (1714–1791)
The Death of General Wolfe
1763
Oil on canvas
102 × 127 cm (40⅛ × 50 in.)
ASHMOLEAN MUSEUM OF ART AND ARCHAEOLOGY, OXFORD

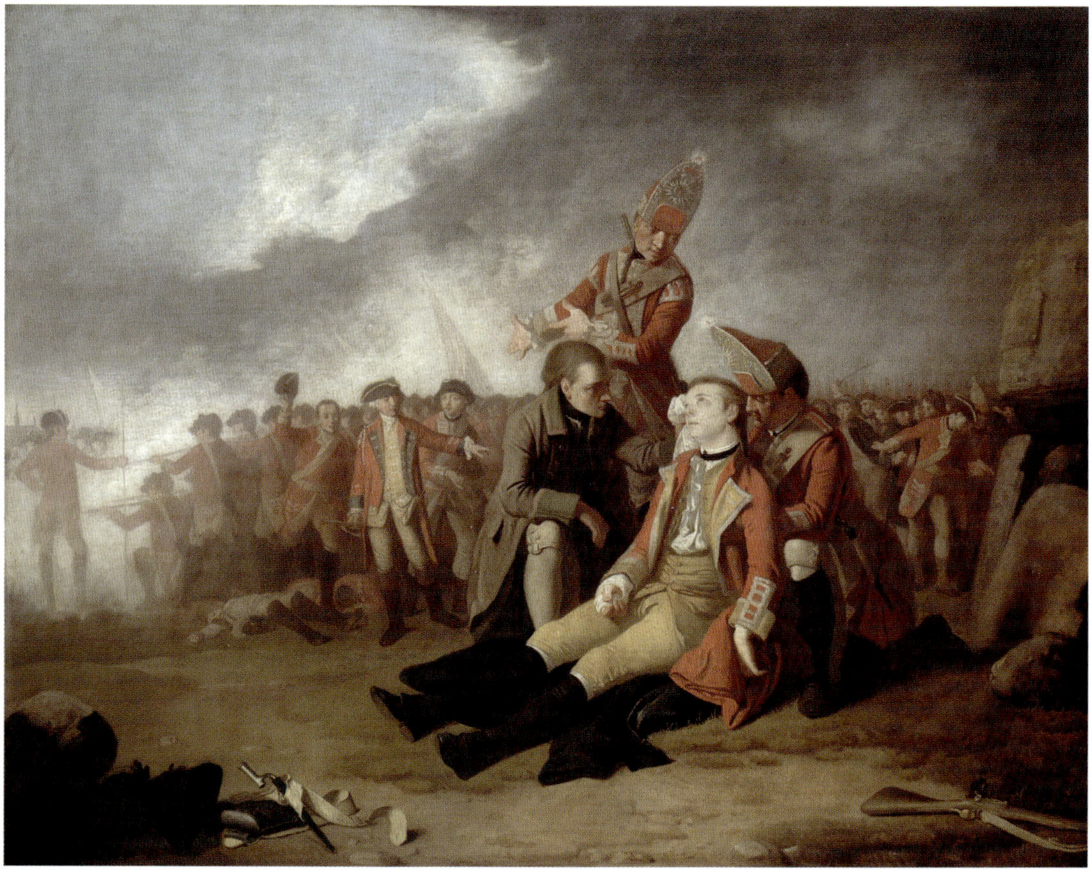

7
George Romney (1734–1802)
Study: The Death of General Wolfe at Quebec in 1759
c. 1762–63
Oil on canvas
36.8 × 46.4 cm
(14½ × 18¼ in.)
ABBOT HALL ART GALLERY, KENDAL, CUMBRIA

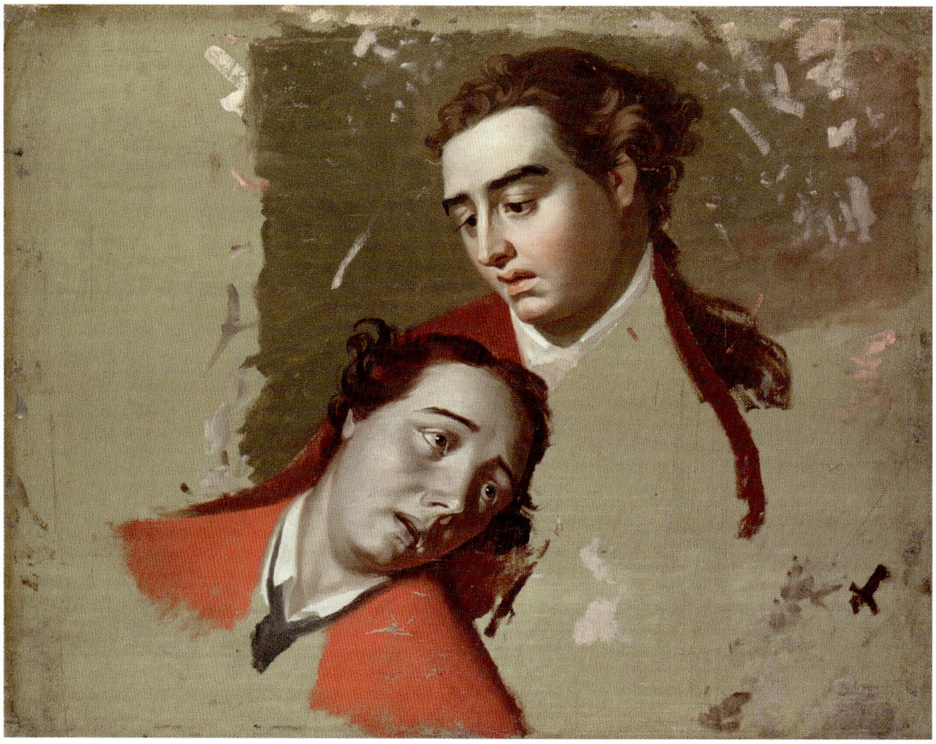

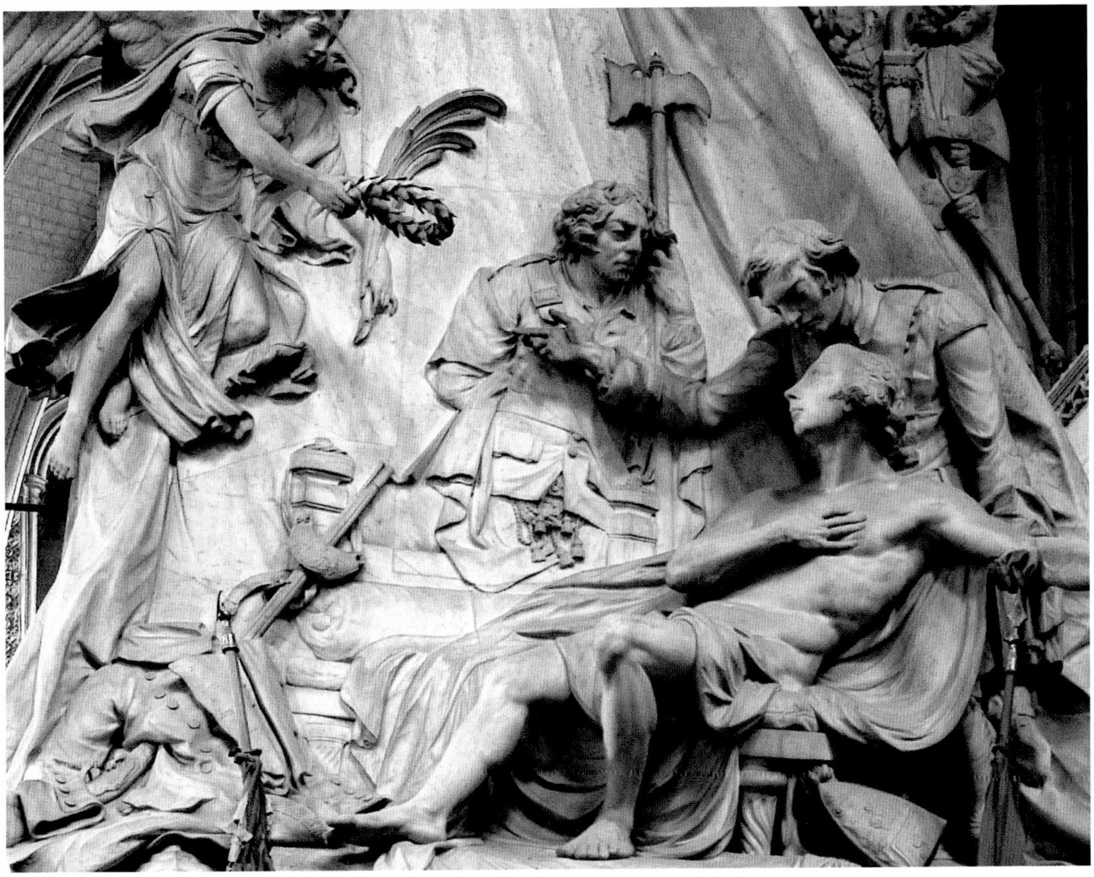

a great talent for listening to and flourishing under the protection of the more skilful or powerful. It is almost certain that West would have discussed *Wolfe* in detail with Drummond, who played such a major role both in the creation of one of West's most important works, *Agrippina Landing at Brundisium with the Ashes of Germanicus* (fig. 9), and in the promotion of Benjamin West himself. Certainly, West would also have solicited the views of Reynolds, his most eminent professional colleague. But such discussions may well have been discursive and iterative. West's account of his debate with Reynolds was therefore shorthand for a longer, subtler and less dramatic series of events.

Overshadowing all would have been West's considerations of the King's sensitivities. The triumphant end of the Seven Years War (1756–63) had been a glorious beginning to the new King's reign, and Wolfe had been hero-in-chief and imperial martyr to boot. Although *Wolfe* was not commissioned by George III, the King's opinion was of paramount importance as West wanted to consolidate his position as the King's favourite history painter. A picture of Wolfe that displeased the King would have been a disaster for West.

West proceeded with great care with *Wolfe*. There was, for example, the long, actually uncommonly long, period of time that passed between the painting of the picture and its exhibition to the public. In a letter of 21 June 1770, West wrote, with barely restrained excitement, to his friend and former student Charles Willson Peale:

> Am at work on the second picture for His Majesty, the approbation of the picture of Regulus met with from him produced a commission for two more of the same size. The one I am painting on at present is the subject of Hamilcar swearing his son Hannibal when a boy of nine years old. I have painted a picture of the death of

8
Joseph Wilton (1722–1803)
Monument to General James Wolfe
1772 (unveiled 1773)
Marble and bronze
WESTMINSTER ABBEY, LONDON

9
Benjamin West
Agrippina Landing at Brundisium with the Ashes of Germanicus
1768
Oil on canvas
163.8 × 240 cm (64½ × 94½ in.)
YALE UNIVERSITY ART GALLERY, NEW HAVEN, CONNECTICUT

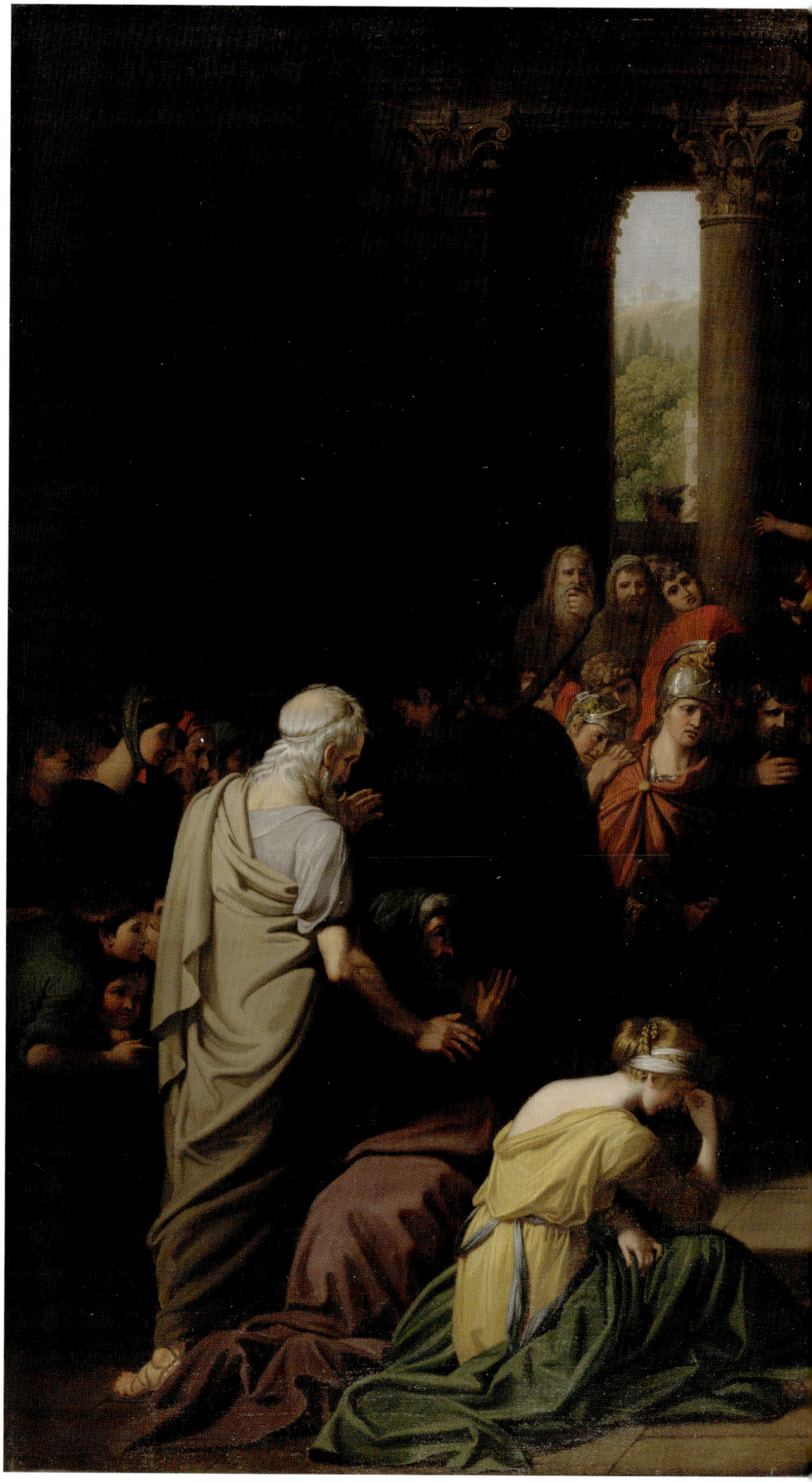

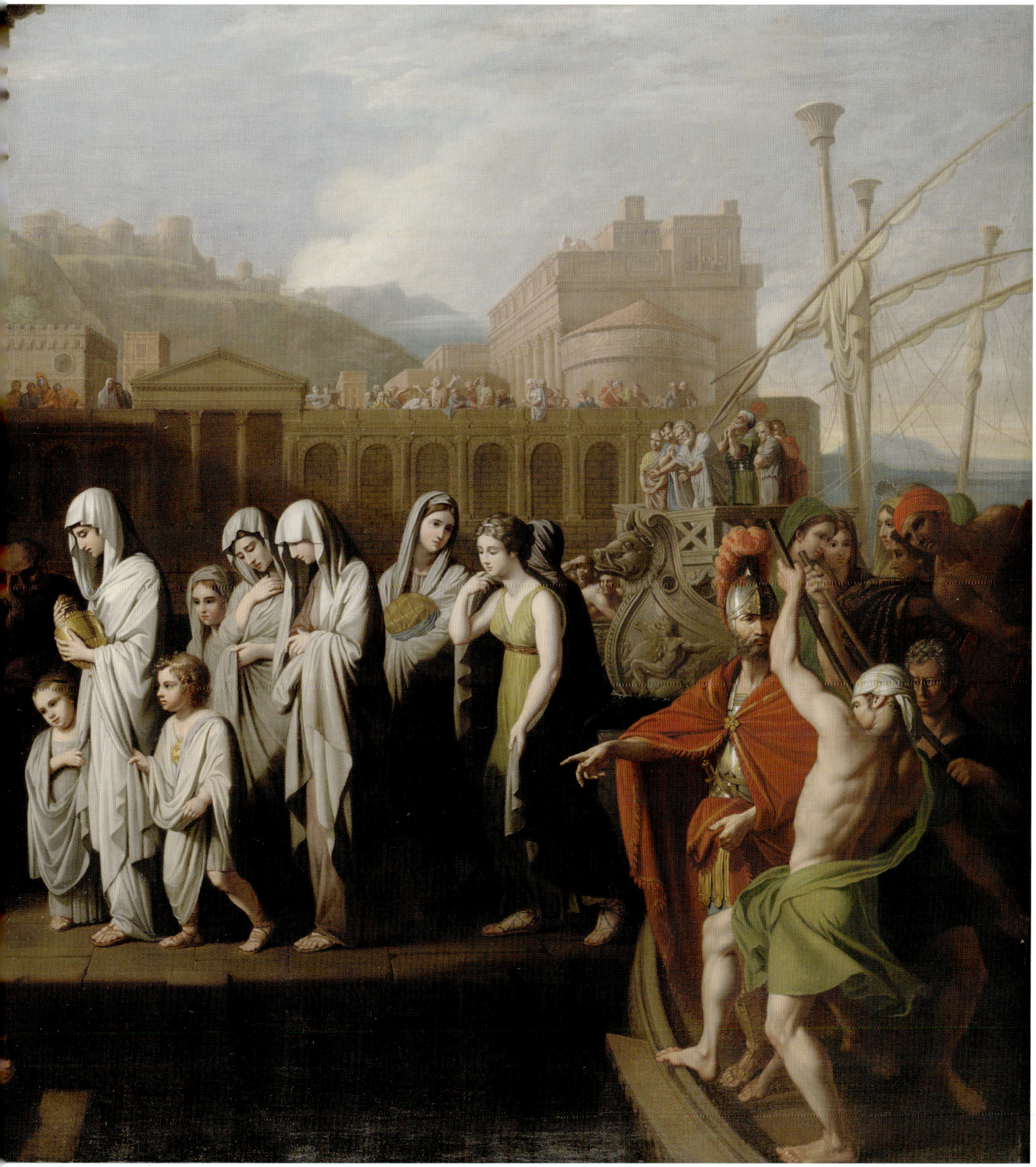

> Genl Wolfe that has procured me great honour. The Hannibal and the Wolfe are the two pictures of the most consequence I have painted since you left here.[17]

Peale had left London to return home to Baltimore in March 1769,[18] so West began work on *Wolfe* sometime after that date and finished the picture before June 1770, when he was already engaged in painting *Hannibal*. In the same letter West tells Peale that he has had 'much sickness' and as a result has not painted for six months, which would give us a completion date for *Wolfe* no later than December 1769 or January 1770. Douglas Fordham has uncovered a newspaper report – 'Extract of a Letter from London', which is undated, but appears from the letters published on either side of it to have been written between 23 March and 25 March 1770 – that informs us 'Our friend Mr. West has just given the finishing Stroke to a most excellent Piece of Painting. The Subject is the Death of General Wolfe, in the Moment of Victory. It is a masterly Performance, and is strongly expressive of the Delicacy and Purity of his Genius.'[19] Now this is quite compelling because it not only reinforces the evidence that *Wolfe* had been completed by early 1770, but also tells us that its existence was known and discussed beyond West's circle of patrons, connoisseurs and fellow professionals. So it was hardly a secret. Yet the painting was not displayed to the wider public until it appeared at the third Royal Academy Exhibition, which opened on 24 April 1771.

Fordham proposes the intrusion of political events as the reason for West's hesitation:

> According to our new timeline, West may have completed The Death of General Wolfe in the same month that Boston witnessed a 'massacre,' March 1770. The London public would have just been coming to terms with this event when the Royal Academy opened its exhibition in April of that year. As an American, and as the king's preferred historical painter, did West hesitate to introduce The Death of Wolfe at this uncertain moment?[20]

The Boston Massacre, in which five civilians were killed by British troops, was a defining moment in the breakdown of relations between Britain and her American colonies. While West's star was ascending in London, Boston was turning into the most unruly of British settlements. The refusal of Bostonians to pay new taxes imposed on glass, paper and tea by the Townshend Acts of 1767 led to the virtual occupation of their city by British troops, beginning in October 1768. Tensions between soldiers and civilians rose steadily until the fatal events of 5 March 1770, when a highly charged mob taunted and threw snowballs at British sentries and were then – either intentionally or accidentally – fired upon. The death of five of those civilians – the 'massacre' – was quickly exploited by political agitators and future rebels. Almost immediately the silversmith Paul Revere and the engraver Henry Pelham, stepfather of John Singleton Copley, were at work on prints commemorating the scene (fig. 10).[21]

Fordham's suggestion that West was reluctant to display *Wolfe* at such a tense and troubling time is plausible, but may not stand up to scrutiny. In 1770, even following the Boston Massacre, there was little hostility towards Americans in Britain. The timing of when the news from Boston reached London is an important issue here, in terms of Fordham's proposal that West may have decided not to display *Wolfe* because of the political climate.

News of the massacre first appeared in the London newspapers during the third week in April, as a report from the *Boston Gazette* was widely reprinted. Because that report was reprinted from an American source, the initial account was coloured more by sympathy than outrage: 'The town of Boston affords a recent and melancholy demonstration of the destructive consequences of quartering troops among Citizens in a time of peace'.[22] The Council of the Royal Academy had already met three days earlier, on Wednesday 18 April, to approve the pictures that would be hung at the forthcoming exhibition.[23] So West could not have decided not to submit *Wolfe* in response to the

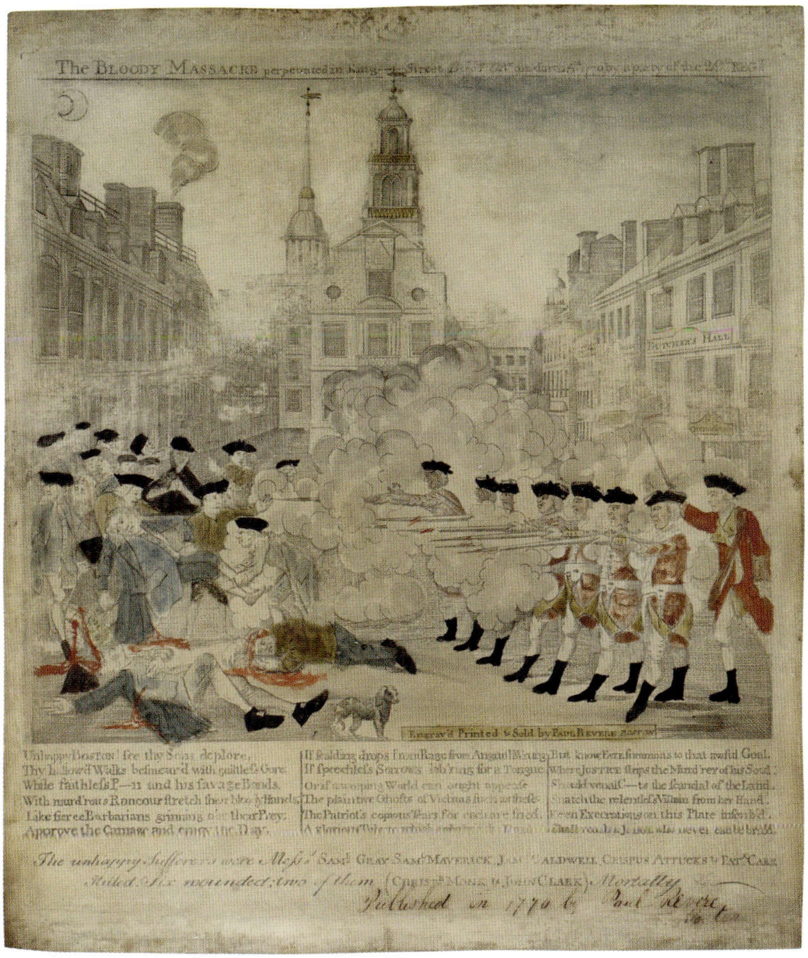

10
Paul Revere (1735–1818)
The bloody massacre perpetrated in King Street Boston on March 5th 1770 by a party of the 29th Regt.
1770
Engraving with watercolour
33.4 × 25.8 cm (13⅛ × 10⅛ in.)
LIBRARY OF CONGRESS, WASHINGTON, D.C.

political situation created by the Boston Massacre. And, if he had decided to withdraw the picture from the exhibition following the news from Boston, such an unprecedented action would have occasioned comment.

Horace Walpole discussed West in the very same letter to Sir Horace Mann, dated 6 May 1770, in which he considered the impact of the Boston Massacre and did not even mention West's American origins. 'You have seen the accounts from Boston. The tocsin appears to be sounded to America', Walpole wrote to Mann. 'I have many visions about that country, and fancy I see twenty empires and republics forming on vast scales over all that continent, which is growing too mighty to be kept in subjection to half a dozen exhausted nations in Europe.' Fewer than a dozen sentences later, Walpole reported on the new London exhibition season: 'There are at present three exhibitions. One West, who paints history in the taste of Poussin, gets £300 for a piece not too large to hang over a chimney.'[24] If the events in America had in any way influenced West's decision regarding what to show or not to show to the British public in 1770, surely Walpole, with his acuity and his finely tuned ear for gossip, would have noticed the connection.

So we have to search for another answer to the question of why West kept *Wolfe* out of the public eye for more than a year, perhaps for even as long as eighteen months, after it was finished. It is possible that ill health may have delayed West's submission of *Wolfe*: his letter to Peale refers to 'much sickness'. Although remarkably long-lived for his era – he died aged eighty-one – West was often incapacitated by chronic rheumatism, gout

11
Benjamin West
Angelica and Medoro
c. 1763–64
Oil on canvas
92.1 × 71.8 cm (36¼ × 28¼ in.)
BINGHAMTON UNIVERSITY ART MUSEUM, NEW YORK

and the after-effects of a life-threatening bout of osteomyelitis (a bone infection), which had tormented him during his stay in Italy in 1760–63. But West was proud to claim that sickness had never interfered with his professional duties. Indeed, while bedridden for six months in Florence, 'he had a frame so constructed as to enable him to paint when obliged to be in bed – and in that situation painted several Ideal pictures as well as Portraits'.[25]

West was a member of the first generation of British artists to mature and flourish in the age of exhibitions. In April 1764, eight months after his arrival in London, he took part in the Society of Artists exhibition at Spring Gardens, encouraged to do so by Reynolds and Richard Wilson. West showed two history paintings there – *Cymon and Iphigenia* and *Angelica and Medoro* (fig. 11) – as well as his freshly painted full-length portrait *General Robert Monckton* (fig. 12), one of Wolfe's brigadiers at the Battle of Quebec. As West later wrote, speaking of himself in the third person: 'the favourable reception those pictures met with from the artists and the public: with the advice of his friends induced him to rest in England'.[26] West also boasted that 'from the Exhibition at Spring Gardens in 1764 to the Exhibition of last year 1804 a space of fourty years, Mr. West has not one year omited giving his works for the entertainment of the public'.[27]

West's success at the Society of Artists convinced him that he would have a career in England, and his pride in forty years of exhibiting tells us that he knew the value of constantly being in front of the public.

For West, the exhibition was no casual undertaking. The number of pictures and the choice and combination of subjects all seem to have been carefully worked out. The sensational nature of *Wolfe* made it absolutely imperative to place it within a context of more academically acceptable history painting. West submitted two pictures to both the Academy's inaugural exhibition of 1769 and second exhibition of 1770, but the 1771 exhibition was a bumper year for the artist. *Wolfe* was one of eight history paintings West displayed that year, neatly covering all the bases of sacred – *The Compassion of Pharaoh's Daughter for the Infant Moses* (fig. 13), *The Prodigal Son Received by His Father*, *Tobias Curing His Father's Blindness* – and mythological – *Hector Taking Leave of Andromache*, *The Death of Procris* (fig. 14) – subject matter, as well as scenes from ancient – *The Continence of Scipio*, *Hannibal* – and modern – *Wolfe* – history.[28] West's presence at the 1771 exhibition was both a tour de force of sheer productivity and a powerful statement of his ability to master the whole range of history painting.

West was also as keen to flaunt his royal patronage as the audience was to see the fruits of it. Part of the spectacle of the exhibition was the chance to see what the grandees were buying, and the grandest of the grand was George III. When West showed *Regulus* at the 1769 exhibition, it was admired not only for its subject matter and execution but also for its regal provenance. It was well known that George III had pointed out the relevant passage in Livy as an inspiration for West, and as Charles Robert Leslie and Tom Taylor remarked in their biography of Reynolds, 'hence the picture which was one of the attractions of the first Academy exhibition; and we may be sure the story of the King's reading of Livy was not forgotten in the room'.[29] It was important for West's reputation not just that George III supported his work, but that others should know about that support.

It seems that West intended to use the 1771 exhibition to proclaim and reinforce his rapid ascent to the top of the greasy pole of British art. No artist displayed more pictures at the 1771 exhibition than West, and only Nathaniel Hone and William Pars exhibited as many, none of which was a history painting. Even the earnest Angelica Kauffmann submitted only four history paintings to the show. So at the most successful exhibition yet staged in Britain, West was able to display unequivocally his dominance of the

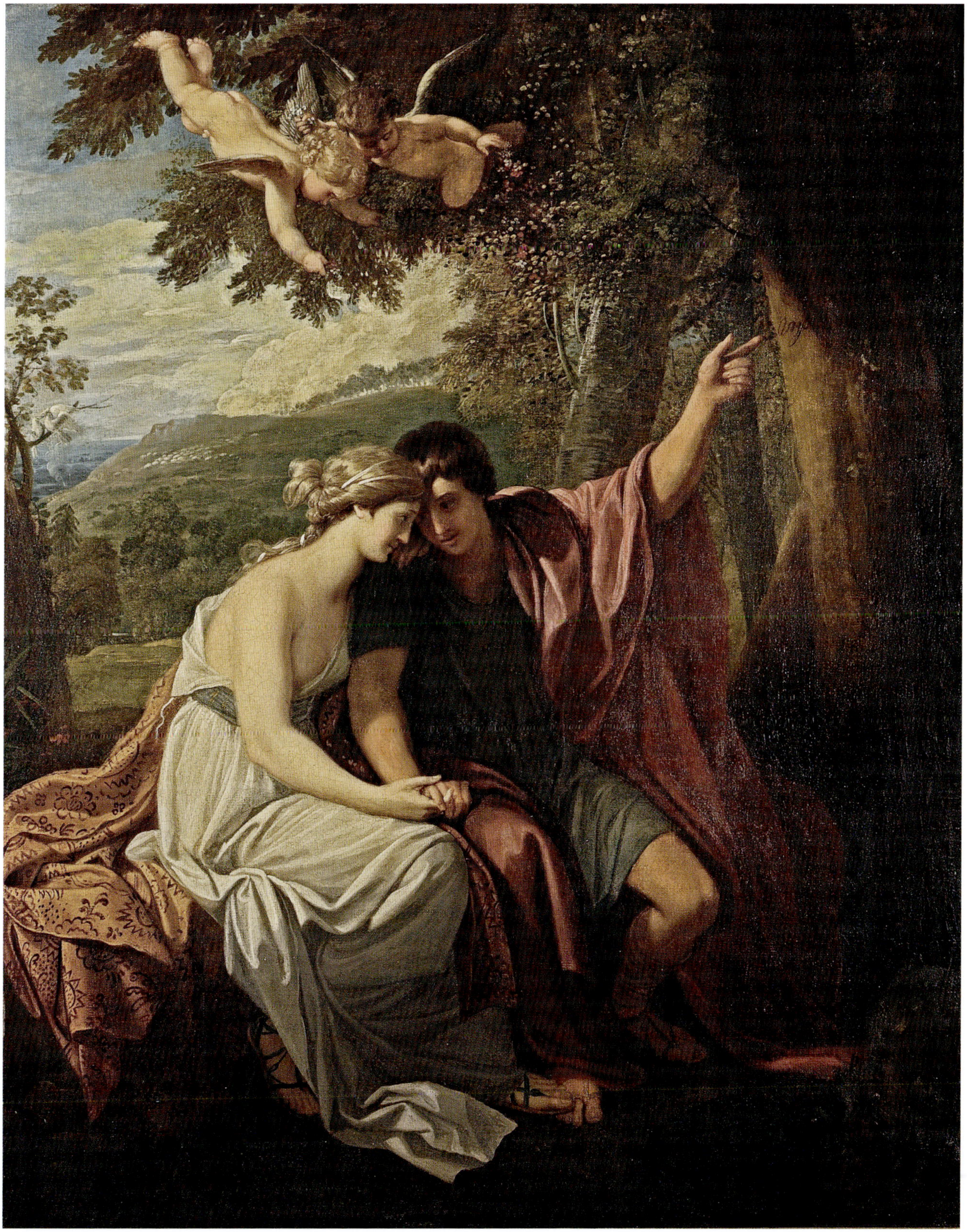

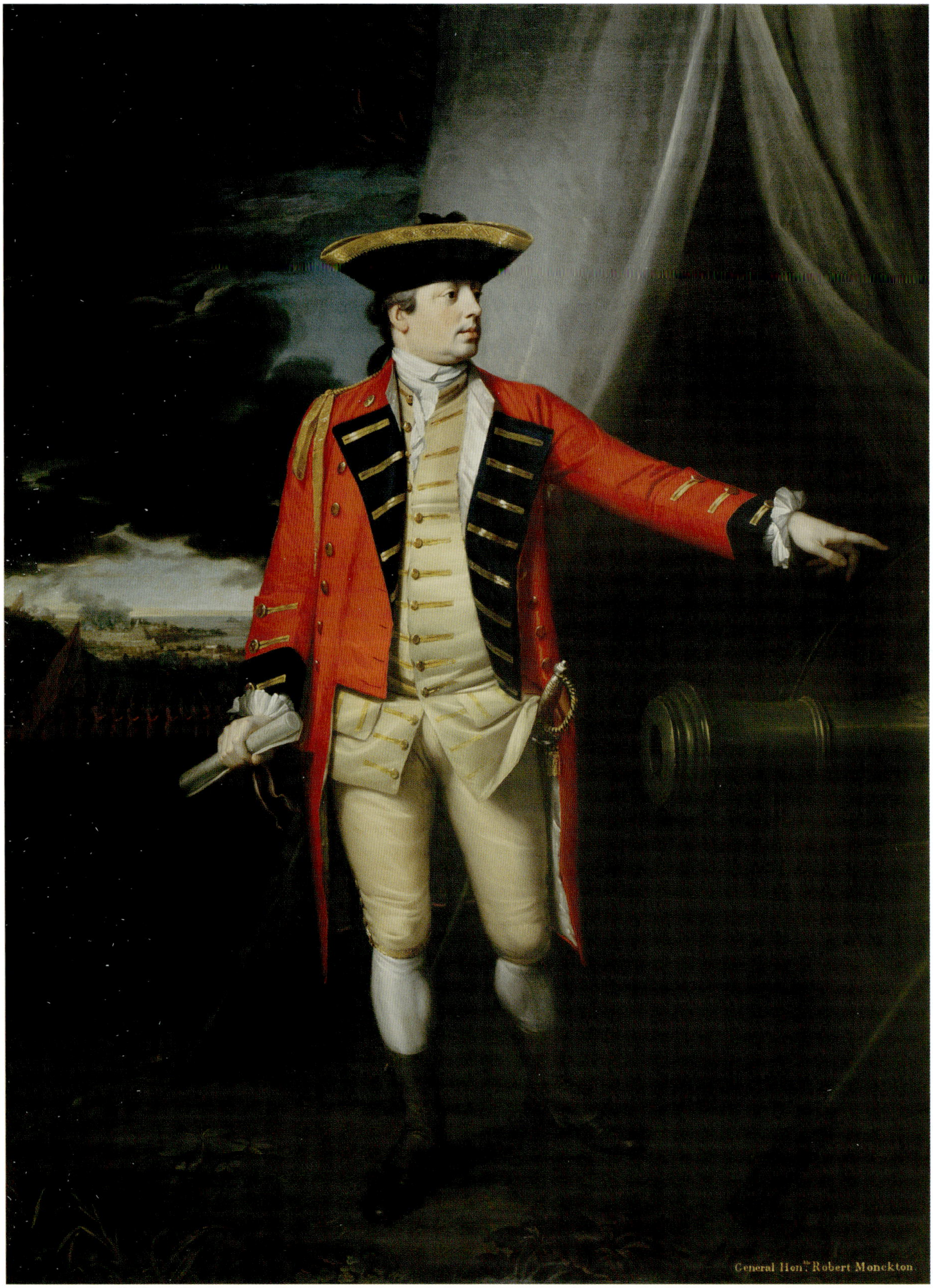
General Hon.ble Robert Monckton.

highest artistic genre. He clearly recognized the competitive nature of exhibitionary culture; many would display, but few would triumph. He not only relished the combat, but also believed that it was good for art and artists. Describing the 1770 exhibition to Peale, West told him that

> The last exhibition at the Royal Academy was the superior one that has been in London every artist here endeavouring to outdo his competitors. I hope your wanting one in Maryland will not let you lose that great desire for improvement that you carried from here.[30]

These two sentences reveal so much about the young West: his competitiveness, his optimism, his concern for his students. They reveal much, too, about those expansive decades when the belief in progress dictated that each exhibition must be more successful than the last. After all, the title page of the 1770 exhibition catalogue bore a quote from Virgil: *Et vires acquirit eundo*, 'It gains strength as it goes.'

Throughout his long career, West prided himself on his capacity for hard work. William Carey exhorted others to follow West's example: 'Artists, you who talk and write and dream of becoming eminent painters, in busy idleness and querulous abstraction, go and take a lesson in industry, from West, from the founder of historical painting in England, and in the spirit of noble ambition, do likewise.'[31] When the American diplomat Nicholas Biddle visited the 69-year-old West in 1807, he was astonished by the stamina of the 'good old man' who, he observed, 'paints by candlelight – immense industry'.[32] West's industry was not just about working hard at making pictures; it was also about working hard at making his pictures successful.

The Third Exhibition of the Royal Academy was displayed in rented rooms in Pall Mall from 24 April to 28 May 1771. As in previous years, admission was by catalogue, price one shilling, and over the course of the exhibition 22,485 catalogues were sold. This contrasts with a sale of 14,008 catalogues for the inaugural exhibition and 19,428 sold for the 1770 exhibition. On busy days more than a thousand people would attend.[33]

And the Royal Academy's was by no means the only show in town. Spring was the exhibition season. The Society of Artists was showing at the auctioneer James Christie's Great Room, also in Pall Mall, and the Royal Incorporated Society of Artists was on display around the corner in Spring Gardens. Private individuals were busy as well: a Mr Goodall of Marsham Street was exhibiting his collection, which included 'fifty fine Pictures from Abroad, never before publicly exposed … several rich and well finished pictures by Rembrandt, Titian … and a most striking and very capital picture by Coreggio'.[34] In London there was much to look at, and there were many who wanted to look. Exhibition-going had become a well-recognized fashion in the decade since the first Society of Artists exhibition in 1761. With the 1771 exhibition season at its height, it was reported that 'At present the whole town is running helter skelter after exhibitions; and as they are staring all day at Paintings, Sculptures and Drawings; it is not surprising that they should dream of them all night.'[35] As an anonymous poet observed, 'Now feels Pall Mall a gen'ral bustle,/ And coaches – chairs, each other justle;/ Fashion lends wings to expedition;/ For now a glorious Exhibition/ Opens indeed!'[36]

David Garrick was one of the many thousands who visited the Royal Academy exhibition, and in some ways was like other members of this new exhibition-mad public. A middle-class provincial, he grew up in a household with neither ancestral portraits nor old masters on the walls. Like many, as he became more prosperous he learned to appreciate art. But Garrick was no typical man. The friend and protégé of Samuel Johnson, Garrick had brought a new energy and naturalism to the stage, as well as a degree of respectability to his hitherto disreputable profession. In the spring of 1771 Garrick was among the most famous men in Britain, an intimate of the great and one of the first modern celebrities created by the

12
Benjamin West
General Robert Monckton
c. 1763–64
Oil on canvas
240 × 173.5 cm
(94½ × 68⅜ in.)
NATIONAL ARMY MUSEUM, LONDON

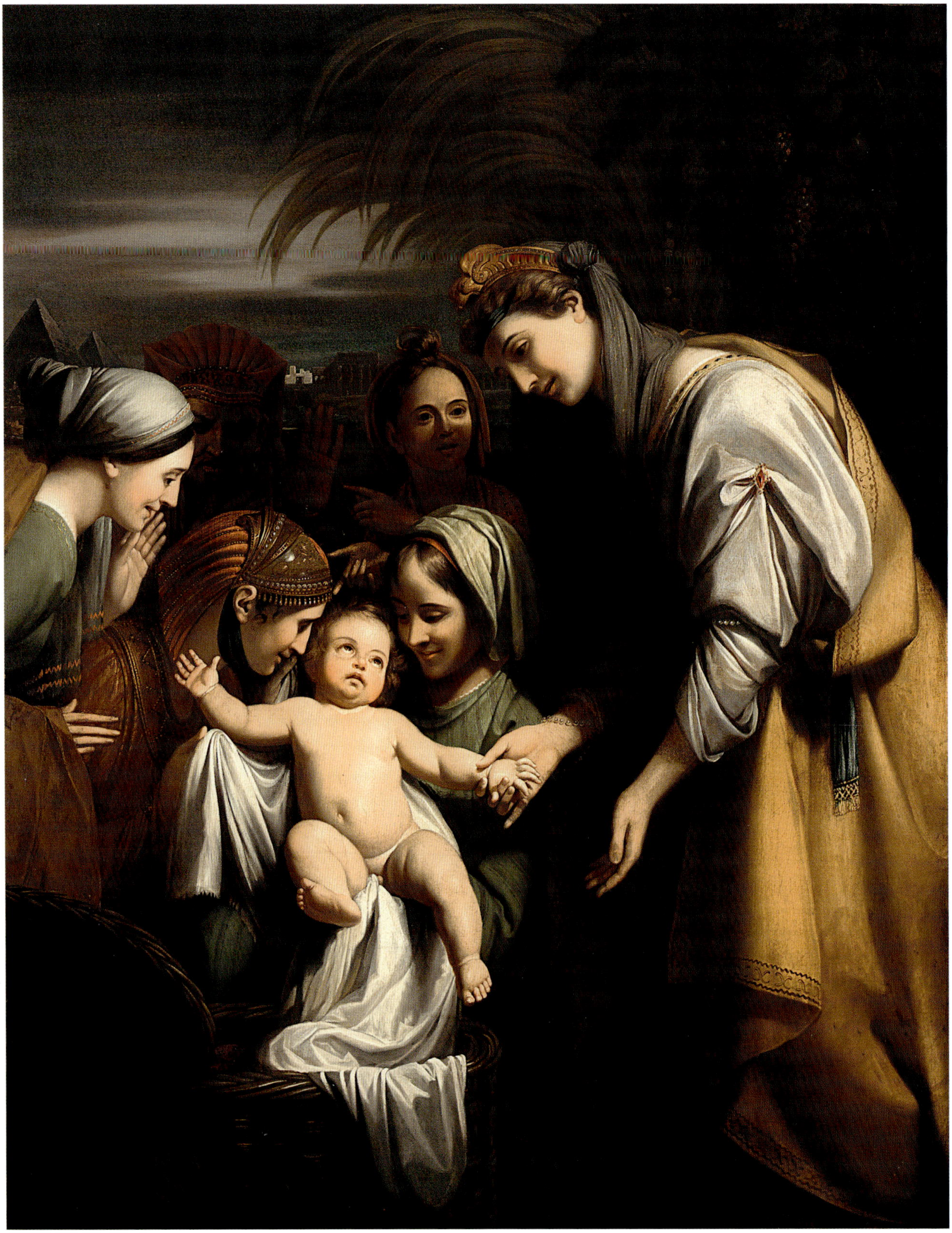

13 OPPOSITE
Benjamin West
The Compassion of Pharaoh's Daughter for the Infant Moses
c. 1771
Oil on canvas
150 × 115.5 cm (59 × 45½ in.)
SNITE MUSEUM OF ART, UNIVERSITY OF NOTRE DAME, INDIANA

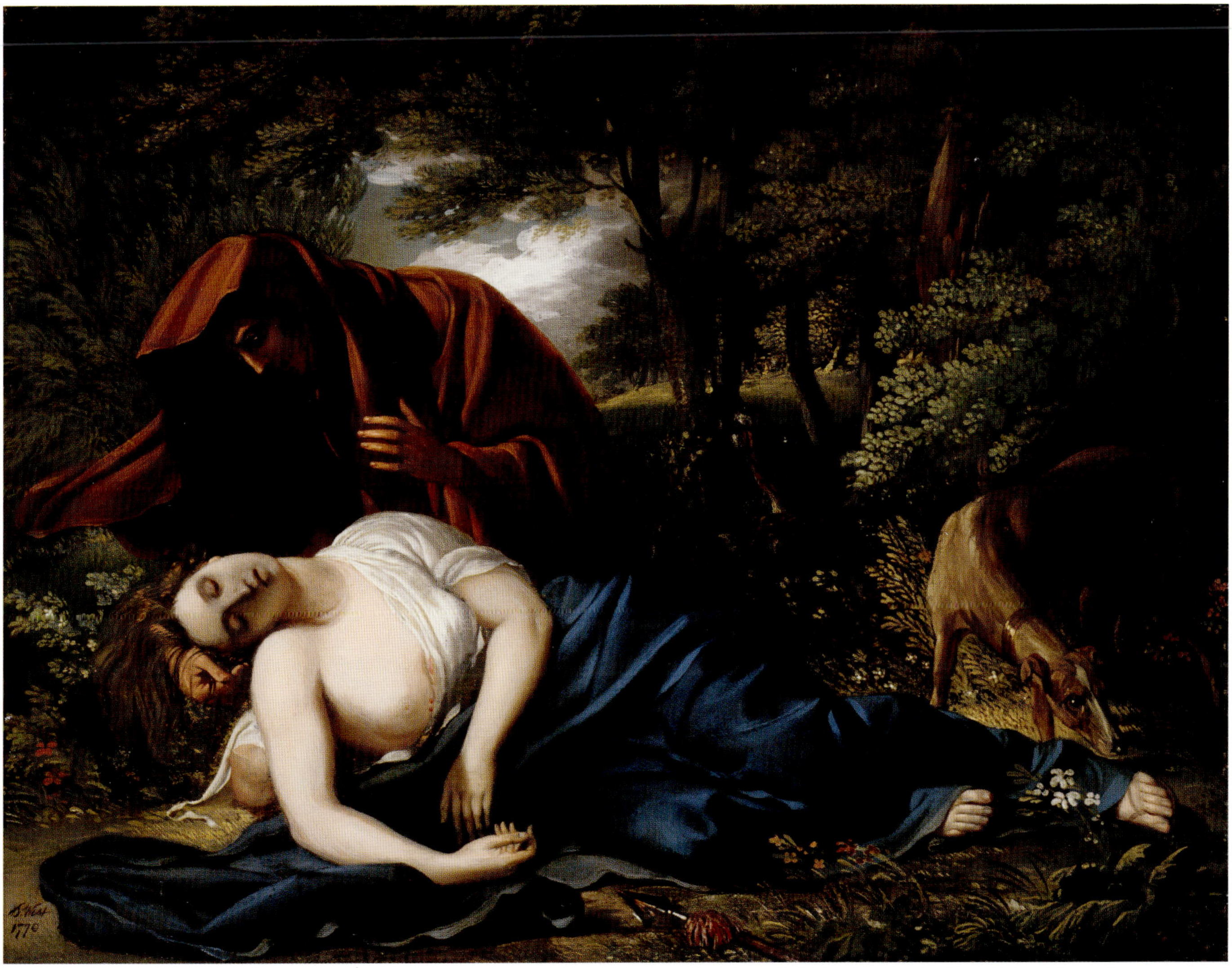

14
Benjamin West
The Death of Procris
1770
Oil on panel
32.4 × 41.2 cm
(12¾ × 16¼ in.)
THE ART INSTITUTE OF CHICAGO

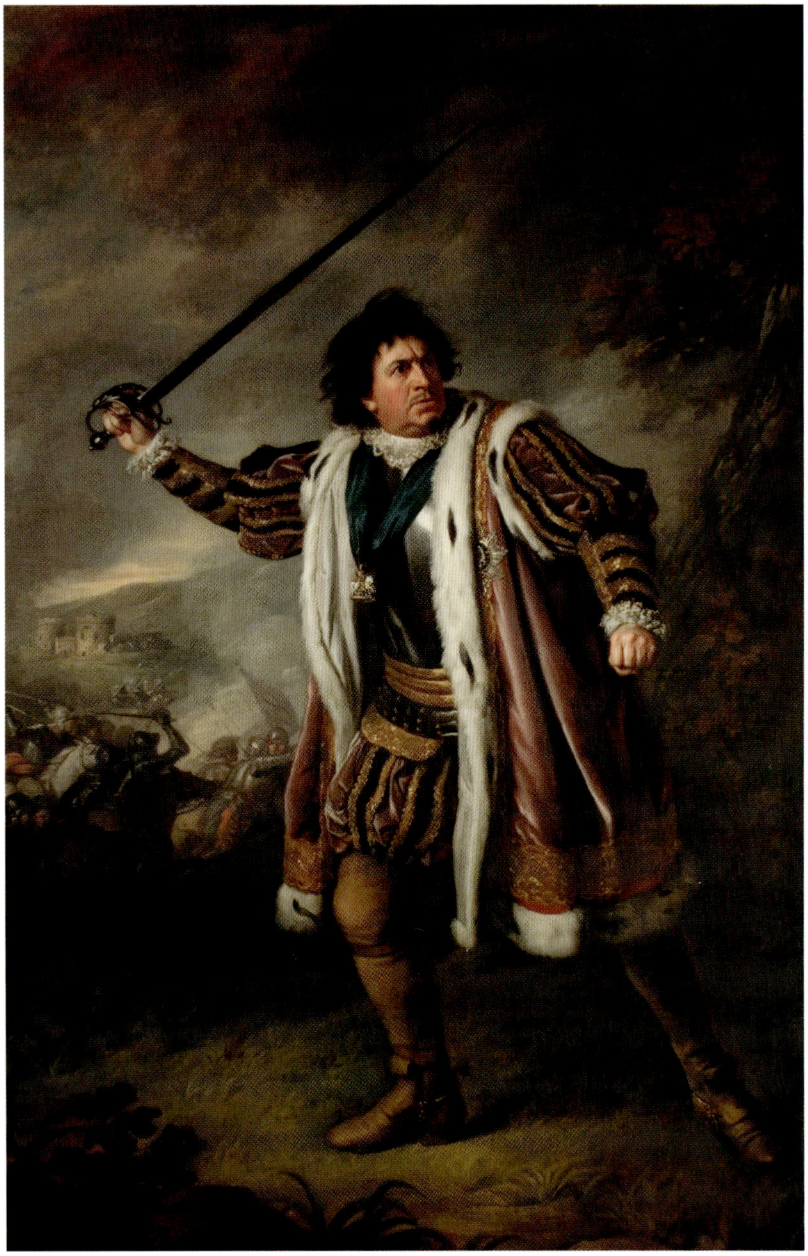

15
Nathaniel Dance (1735–1811)
David Garrick as Richard III
1771
Oil on canvas
236 × 144 cm (92⅞ × 56¾ in.)
STRATFORD-UPON-AVON TOWN HALL

growth of the mass media and the birth of public patronage of the arts. He had been painted by Hogarth and Zoffany, Batoni and Gainsborough, Hayman and Reynolds. As a testimony to Garrick's towering fame, he featured in three pictures at the Royal Academy exhibition that year. The young watercolourist John James Barralet showed two views of Garrick's 'seat' by the Thames at Hampton: there was growing popular interest in the domestic lives of the famous. More spectacular was Nathaniel Dance's full-length portrait of Garrick in the role of Richard III bursting with malign energy on the field at Bosworth (fig. 15). Even before the exhibition opened, the Dance portrait was sold to Sir Watkin Williams Wynn for £150.[37] Garrick himself was pleased with the picture. One morning as he was leaving the exhibition, the actor met an acquaintance who enquired after his health – Garrick had been very ill with gout for much of the year – and received the reply: 'so so this morning; but if your Lordship will but walk up stairs, you'll see me as well as ever I was in my life'.[38]

As an exhibition-goer, as the subject of art, as a collector and as someone whose career was based on an ability to grasp and satisfy the demands of the public, Garrick was acutely aware that he was part of a phenomenon that he could both analyse and satirize. Writing his prologue to Samuel Foote's play of 1752, *Taste*, Garrick observed: 'Before you buy, be sure to understand/ Oh! think on us what various ills will flow/ When great ones only purchase what they know./ Why laugh at Taste? It is a harmless fashion,/ And quite subdues each detrimental passion.'[39]

While Garrick's latest portrait was much admired, a greater deal of attention was being paid to West's *Wolfe*. Perhaps to Garrick's chagrin, a dead Wolfe was more attractive than a live actor. On an early-morning visit – the exhibition opened at 8 am – Garrick was surprised to find a number of people already there to admire *Wolfe,* including, in William T. Whitley's words, 'a young woman of singular beauty whose comments on the picture

… were so apt and well expressed that Garrick ventured to compliment her upon them. She admired West's picture extremely but objected to the expression of the dying commander.' Garrick shared her reservations and suggested that he show the crowd how West should have painted Wolfe: 'Supported by two gentlemen he placed himself in the attitude of Wolfe and "displayed in his features the exact countenance depicted by the artist." He then assumed the expression of the transient rapture felt by the dying general when he heard the cry "They run, they run!" Garrick's feat was loudly applauded'.[40]

Another eminent visitor to the exhibition also demanded his time with *Wolfe*. William Pitt, 1st Earl of Chatham, was the Prime Minister who had given the young general command of the expedition against Quebec. Now, ageing and unwell, the great war leader came to see the much-talked-about picture of the greatest victory in Britain's global struggle with France. As *The Gazetteer* reported:

> Lord Chatham lately went to the exhibition … on purpose to see Mr. West's celebrated picture of General Wolfe's death; his Lordship placed himself before the piece for a considerable time and examined it with great attention: upon retiring he pronounced it well executed upon the whole, but thought there was too much dejection not only in the dying hero's face, but in the faces of the surrounding officers, who, he said, as Englishmen should forget all traces of private misfortunes, when they had so gloriously conquered for their country.[41]

Garrick's performance was no doubt entertaining and a fine example of theatrical egotism. Having had his own portrait over-shadowed by *Wolfe*, he himself played to the gallery and upstaged West's picture. It is certainly an amusing anecdote but, together with the account of Pitt's visit, it also reveals a central conflict of history painting in the late eighteenth century. In one corner, the 'young woman of singular beauty', who stands for the new, bourgeois 'modern' audience, demanded that the dying Wolfe should have an expression of 'transient rapture'; in the other corner, Chatham, part of the classically educated elite, demanded Spartan heroism. It was the sentimental versus the instrumental. Should a history painting move the audience or instruct them? Chatham and the young woman may be seen as exemplars of typical eighteenth-century debates about the purpose of art, whom it was for, and who was competent to judge it. Garrick's satirical verses in *Taste* revealed his real anxieties about the growing public of culture consumers, the breakdown of the classical canon and the ever-increasing role of novelty. As usual, Reynolds was conflicted by the new phenomenon in which he played such a prominent part, torn between his strong commercial instinct and his anxieties about vulgarization:

> Be as select in those whom you endeavor to please, as in those whom you endeavor to imitate. Without the love of fame you can never do anything excellent; but by an excessive and undistinguishing thirst after it, you will come to have vulgar views … our Exhibitions, while they produce such admirable effects by nourishing emulation and calling out genius, have also a mischievous tendency, by seducing the Painter to an ambition of pleasing indiscriminately the mixed multitude of people who resort to them.[42]

To Reynolds's concern, his friend Oliver Goldsmith added fears of social subversion, writing that 'Painting is now become the sole object of fashionable care; the title of connoisseur in that art is at present the safest passport into every fashionable society; a well timed shrug, an admiring attitude, and one or two exotic tones of exclamation are sufficient qualifications for men of low circumstances to curry favour'.[43]

Even though constrained by the aegis of a Royal Academy, the exhibition presented a challenge to the established order. There is an element of distaste in Walpole's explanation of the exhibition phenomenon to Sir Horace Mann: 'The rage to see these exhibitions is so great, that sometimes one cannot pass through the streets where they are. But it is incredible what sums are raised by mere exhibitions of anything; a new fashion, and to enter at which you pay a shilling or half a crown.'[44] The one-shilling cost of the catalogue, which it was hoped would stop 'inferior people crowding the exhibition-room',[45] had little effect on the numbers who wished to see and be seen at the exhibition. For the sensitive and conservative Walpole the popularity of the exhibition was an assault on the idea that art should be for the learned, the landed and the gentlemanly.

The exhibition was poised in so many ways between an old world and a new. It was an agora at which many of Britain's most celebrated artists displayed their wares in front of a large and eager public who could not afford what was on display, but who wished to be seen and who might be encouraged to buy reproductions of some of the pictures they had viewed. It was an opportunity for a select bunch of connoisseurs and aristocrats to buy what the public could not afford and to study it in tranquillity before the crowds arrived. The *Middlesex Journal* reported that on Tuesday 23 April 1771 – the day before the exhibition opened – the members of the Academy dined with a select group, including 'the Earls of Buckinghamshire, Hardwick and Besborough, Lords Grantham, Palmerston, Kerry, Sir Watkin Williams Wynn Bart. Sir James Grey, the Hon. Mr. Horace Walpole … And many of the pictures which were to be disposed of were either bought or bespoke by the company present.'[46] And finally the exhibition was an occasion for the display of royal authority and beneficence: the day before the Academicians and connoisseurs dined, King George and Queen Charlotte, with a retinue that included the Prince of Wales; the Queen's brother, Prince Ernest of Mecklenburg-Strelitz; and the Bishop of Osnabrück, visited the exhibition.[47]

This pattern of previews and 'VIP' visits followed by an opening to the public, all enthusiastically reported by the press, has a rather contemporary feel. Certainly, the exhibition was a tense compromise between the demands and requirements of grandee patronage and the clamour of the emerging marketplace. And from this tension, as well as cultural and economic changes in the wider society, arose the mix of mass communications, mechanical reproduction, professional criticism and public involvement that characterizes a modern way of buying, selling and looking at art. As David Solkin puts it: 'It seems beyond dispute that London can be identified as one of the first metropolitan art centres where the various commercial, cultural and institutional mechanisms characteristic of a distinctively modern art world came into being.'[48]

Charles Brandoin's acerbic view of the 1771 exhibition (fig. 16) captures well the motley and somewhat hectic atmosphere of the public exhibition. 'Brandoin presents us with a range of individuals possessing dramatically varied aesthetic backgrounds and expectations (as their dress, posture and pantomimic responses to art suggest),' C.S. Matheson observes, 'but it is not entirely clear if a narrative or satirical account of their public conjunction is on offer here.'[49] It is less a documentary snapshot of a particular moment than a vivid illustration of what the audience for art was becoming: a salmagundi of learned connoisseurs, imperious members of the sword-wearing class, earnest self-improvers, public figures – the unmistakable John Wilkes is prominent in the middle ground right of centre – and, that perennial feature of exhibitions, bored and tired children.

This human comedy of spectators contrasts all too vividly with the languid aristocrats, idealized landscapes and biblical figures on the walls around them. The gawky and squint-eyed Wilkes and his squat woman companion are an almost cruel counterpoint to the physical perfection of James Barry's prelapsarian *Temptation of Adam* hanging above them. To me, Brandoin's work is above all a pointed comment on the new irony of the art-loving public: how could such a varied, transient and often unlovely crowd judge the eternal truths and beauties of art?

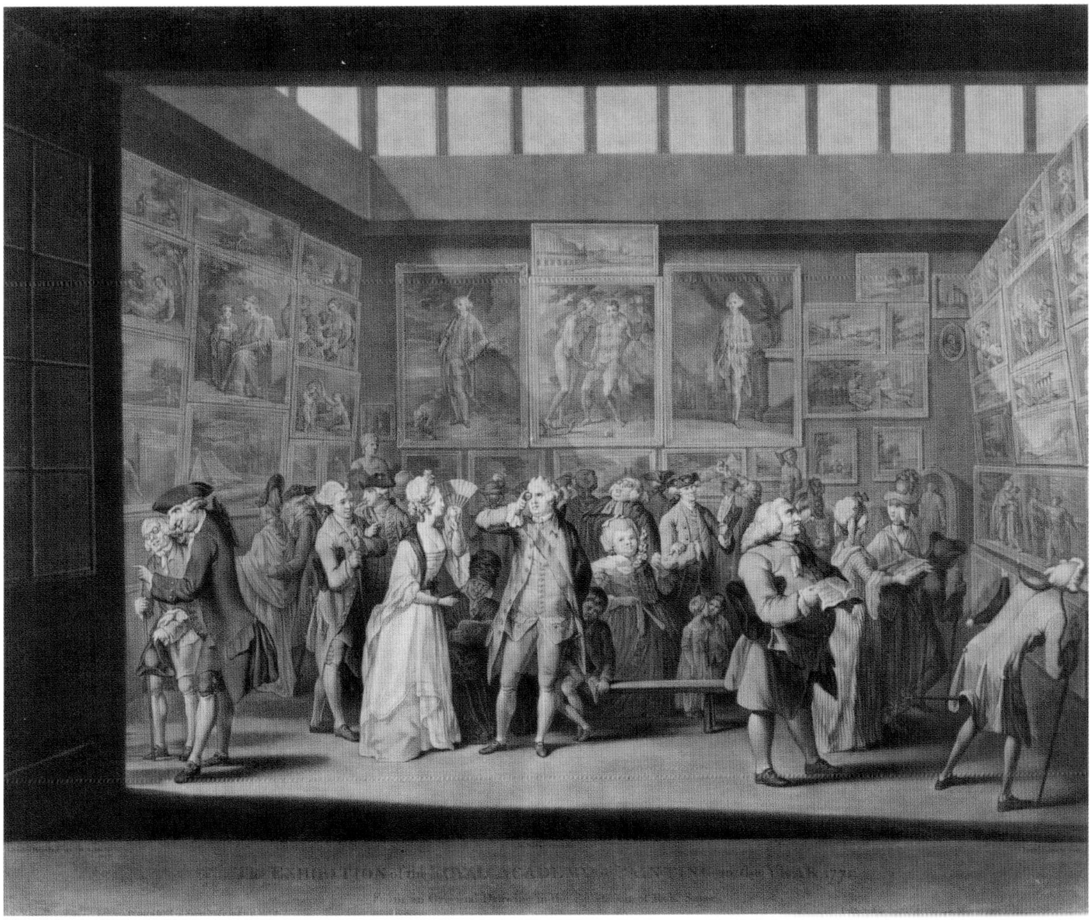

16
Richard Earlom (1743–1822), after Charles Brandoin (1733–1807)
The Exhibition of the Royal Academy of Painting 1771
1772
Mezzotint
47 × 55.9 cm ($18\frac{1}{2}$ × 22 in.)
PAUL MELLON COLLECTION, YALE CENTER FOR BRITISH ART, NEW HAVEN, CONNECTICUT

As a subject, Wolfe had an almost unique power to unite that disparate exhibition-going public. Wolfe was a new type of hero: physically frail, middle class, rather ordinary-looking, provincial and with a grieving mother and heart-broken fiancée left behind in Kent to boot. As Francis Parkman wrote, 'never was the soul of a hero cased in a frame so incongruous'.[50] It was this incongruity, this ordinariness that stoked the flame of Wolfe's fame. He could be both the object of adulation and for the rapidly expanding bourgeois audience 'one of us'. 'It was Wolfe's very lack of specialness', David Solkin notes, 'which caused his loss to be so widely mourned ... In the burgeoning Wolfe mythology, his humble origins and lack of ambition were highlighted over and over again.'[51]

The death of Wolfe happened quickly on the morning of 13 September 1759, when a British expeditionary force under his command fought and defeated a French army defending Quebec, the citadel and capital of New France. Although the French put more men on to the field of battle, British professionalism and discipline prevailed. The redcoats' first lethal volley, delivered at a mere 40 yards' distance, had broken the French line almost as soon as the battle started. The eighteenth-century battlefield was crowded, chaotic and harrowing. Officers led from the front and died with their troops. The 32-year-old Wolfe was shot successively in the wrist, the stomach and through the chest. Carried from the field, he died before noon, but not before being told of the victory and remarking, 'Now God be praised, I die contented.'[52]

The British victory at Quebec was immediately recognized as a turning point in the Seven Years

War, another triumph in a year that had already seen Britain defeat the French on land at Minden in Germany and at sea at Lagos, off the coast of Portugal. With the fall of Quebec, an existential threat to Britain's American colonies was removed, and soon all of eastern North America would be in British hands.

News of Quebec reached London on 16 October 1759 and was in the press the following day as the *London Gazette* published an extraordinary issue carrying a letter to William Pitt from Wolfe's second-in-command, the badly wounded General Robert Monckton: 'I have the pleasure to acquaint you, that, on the 13th Instant, His Majesty's troops gained a very signal Victory over the French, a little above the town of Quebec. General Wolfe, exerting himself on the Right of our Line, received a Wound pretty early, of which he died soon after'.[53]

From the moment the news arrived, public jubilation was mingled with extravagant mourning for the young, dead hero of Quebec. Indeed, as soon as the day after the news was published in London, Wolfe was already being compared to great heroes of the classical (Epaminondas) and recent past (Gustavus Adolphus): 'The virtuous Theban and the mighty Swede/ For Freedom fought and conquer'd as they bled;/ England shall claim her Wolfe, and mourn his Fate,/ In Life as Virtuous and in Death as Great.'[54]

It took nearly as long for the news to reach New York, where the 21-year-old West was nearing the end of a profitable but unhappy time in that city as a portrait painter, honing his skills and filling his purse in preparation for a trip to Italy the following spring. West might have read the report in the *New York Gazette*: 'General Wolfe landed on the North-Side above the Town … a most bloody Engagement commenced, in which poor General Wolfe was killed, much lamented, but he died gloriously, and I think rather to be envied than pitied'.[55] Within a week the pseudonymous poet Massachutensis was asking, 'What honours, WOLFE, should thy brows adorn?'[56] It was a question that was repeated on both sides of the Atlantic as an absolute frenzy of Wolfe commemoration was unleashed.

The Wolfe cult began as soon as the ink was dry on the first newspaper reports of his death and was still going strong more than a decade after his death, as Wolfe's charisma and popularity remained undimmed. On Sunday 18 April 1770, the Reverend Judah Champion climbed into the pulpit of the First Church of Litchfield, Connecticut, to preach, and reminded his parishioners of the Battle of Quebec. Referring to Wolfe, he declaimed:

> Let us drop a tear over the renowned warrior, who died in the bloom of life, at the head of his troops, commanding, as with angelic wisdom and noble ardor, forgetting that he was mortal. O glorious instrument of God for our deliverance. Let him live in all succeeding annals and shine in a full blaze of glory; with a monument erected over his grave, more durable than statues of brass and marble.[57]

Such highly charged language, full of religious reference, had immediately become the vocabulary of the Wolfe cult. When the first biography of Wolfe was rushed out in 1760, its author, John Pringle, told his readers how

> God, glorious in Holiness, fearful in Praises, doing Wonders, has lately manifested his Power and stretched-out Arm, in Defence of this Nation; his Munificence has showered down upon us all the Blessings of Peace, whilst his Justice makes other Nations feel all the Calamities of War; he has crowned our Arms with signal Successes both by Sea and Land … so Sweet a Source of Pleasure for Britons, is soon marred with Bitterness. Britons see, with Sorrow painted on their down-cast Faces, their General breathing his last; they count over, with Regret, his honourable Wounds; and while they bathe them with their Tears, they cannot help thinking, that, that Victory must be inestimable, which required for its Purchase the Blood of so great and so good a General.[58]

Wolfe was also presented as an exemplar of the sacrifices demanded by the constant threat of French aggression. In the final act of George Cockings's popular play of 1766, *The Conquest of*

Canada; or, The Siege of Quebec, the heroine exhorted her audience: 'Nobly to save wives, children, lands and laws/ To glory's goal what Briton would not fly!/ To fall like Wolfe, who would not wish to die!/ Who would not fight the treaty breaking Gaul!/ When George, and liberty, and martial honour call!'[59]

The commemorative poetry inspired by Wolfe's death frequently invoked Britannia's mourning for her dead son General Wolfe. In his 'Elegy on the Death of General Wolfe', published in 1760, the otherwise unknown Reverend Mr Blacklock of Edinburgh described Britannia: 'O'er her fallen son,/ Dissolv'd in grief, the lovely mourner stands;/ Forgets the glory by the hero won,/ And with vain sighs his precious life demands.'[60] When Myles Cooper of Queen's College, Oxford, published the poem 'Britannia's Tears' the following year, his Britannia too was grief-stricken: 'All on a rock the beauteous mourner lies,/ The martial spear neglected by her side:/ The briny tears roll copious from her eyes,/ While thus she harps her sorrows to the tide.' In spite of much praise for triumphs in war and commerce, his Britannia is inconsolable, declaring: 'Such soothing sounds, alas! can charm no more,/ Nor aught avail my sorrows to becalm,/ Since death, unpitying, from this bosom tore/ My son ...'[61]

The image of a tearful Britannia mourning Wolfe was quite clearly in the air, and it is easy to see that image as a secular analogue to the Virgin Mary's grief at Christ's death. The chapter 'How Beautiful is Death' returns to this issue, analysing in detail how West chose to depict the death of Wolfe, but first we should consider Wolfe's importance as a subject.

Writing as his scurrilous alter ego Anthony Pasquin, the satirist John Williams, hardly an unqualified fan of West, commented that *Wolfe* 'was produced at a time when the national pulse of gratitude had not ceased to vibrate; but, in my opinion, the choice of subject was more advantageous to Mr. West than the execution.' Williams went on to say that

> the theme was so popular that it laid the foundation of a celebrity for the performancer, before the matter was exhibited. Every lover of his country surveyed with eagerness what operated to perpetuate the memory of their gallant countryman and in the moments of high admiration and retrospective gratitude, the judgment permitted those encomiums to pass muster, which on subjects less interesting would have been coolly questioned.[62]

Williams's assumption that Wolfe's continued popularity with the public contributed a great deal to the picture's success underlines the importance of choosing the right subject and the particular difficulty that history painters faced in making that choice. One of West's most enthusiastic supporters, William Carey, noted that familiar subjects 'have a variety of powerful interests in them *before they are executed*, founded in our affection, esteem, or reverence for the Persons and events, which they represent; altogether distinct from the merits of their execution'.[63] Here the tug for any artist was between what was recognizable and resonant yet at the same time appealed to the public thirst for the new. As Walpole scoffed, 'We live in a country where so many novelties or follies start forth every day, that we have not time to try a general's capacity by the rules of Polybius.'[64] The public – becoming ever broader and consequently less well educated – demanded easily identifiable, understandable subjects, but they were also quickly bored. The most well-known biblical and classical subjects were becoming exhausted. After all, there were a finite number of versions of the *Continence of Scipio* or *David and Goliath* that the market could bear.

The critical importance of subject matter had been crystallized two decades earlier, in France in 1747, when Lenormand de Tournehem, the Directeur Général des Bâtiments du Roi, commissioned eleven members of the Académie Royale de Peinture et de Sculpture to create a series of paintings for the Galerie d'Apollon in the Louvre. The results were a disaster, with one

17
Jean-Baptiste Greuze
(1725–1805)
The Village Bride
1761
Oil on canvas
92 × 117 cm (36¼ × 46 in.)
MUSÉE DU LOUVRE, PARIS

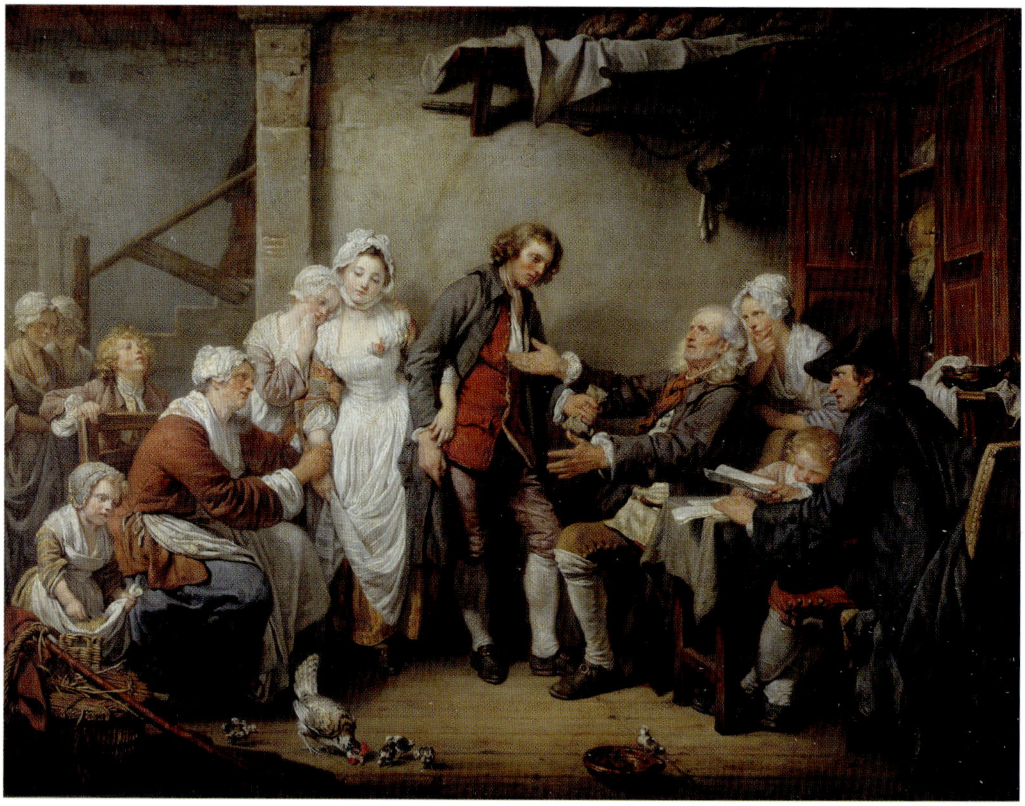

18
Jean-Baptiste Greuze
(1725–1805)
Filial Piety (The Paralytic)
1763
Oil on canvas
115 × 146 cm (45¼ × 57½ in.)
THE STATE HERMITAGE MUSEUM, ST PETERSBURG

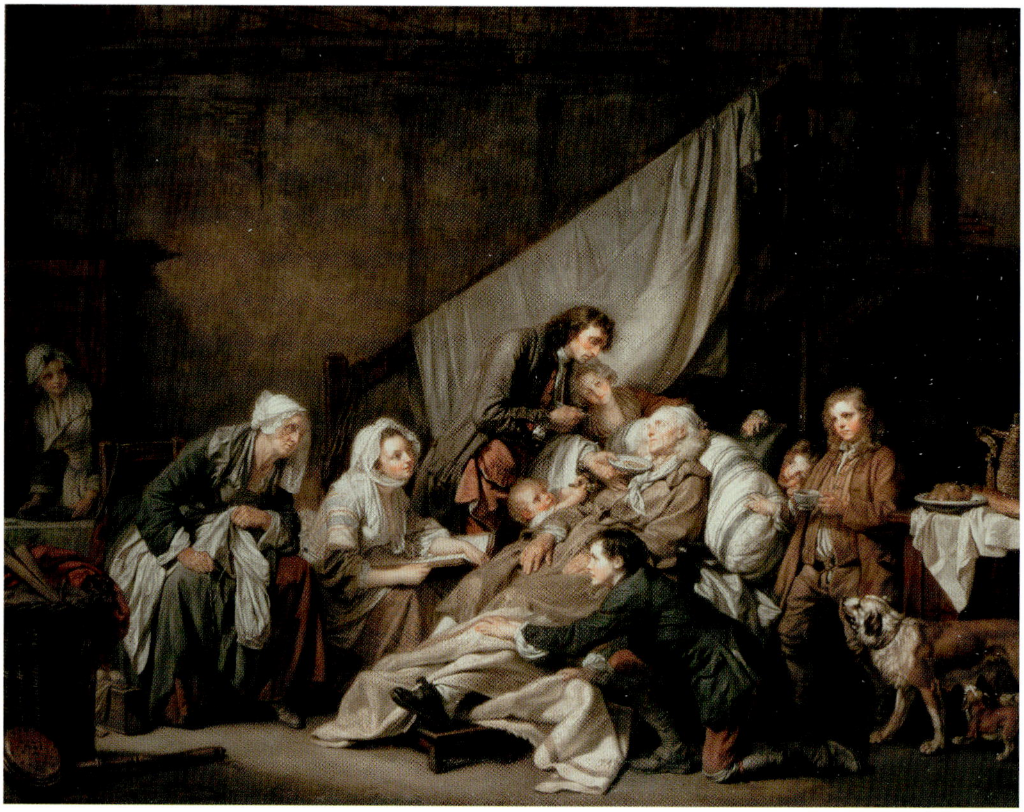

mocking critic writing: '"Pyrrhus at the Court of Glaucius" is a subject which is little known and even less interesting. And what a lovely gift to offer a king in need of a *tableau d'histoire*, this "Diogenes Drinking from his Hand after breaking his Cup".'[65] This crisis of subject matter in history painting opened the door to new approaches to the genre. Such a situation was ideal for the emergence of Jean-Baptiste Greuze, who was in some way able to bring the earnestness of academic history painting to the depiction of familiar petit-bourgeois dramas. As history painters trawled the bottom for increasingly weak and obscure episodes from sacred and classical literature, Greuze's paintings such as *The Village Bride* (fig. 17) and *Filial Piety* (fig. 18) had a fresh and immediate appeal to the public and connoisseurs alike. Writing in 1765, Diderot speculated that the time might come when 'We'd no longer see Juno, or Jupiter, or Mars, or Venus, or the Graces, or ancient mythologies, or modern mythologies treated on canvas; we'd be reduced to historical subjects and public or domestic scenes drawn from life, and perhaps this wouldn't be such a bad thing. I'm not embarrassed to say that Greuze's *Village Bride* interests me more than any *Judgment of Paris*.'[66]

Things in Britain in the early 1770s were different. There was no long tradition of state support for history painting as there had been in France, and in Britain the public, while largely indifferent to history painting, was, at least, less jaded. William Hogarth was hardly Greuze *avant la lettre*, but he too had tried to combine recognizable contemporary subjects with the highest aspirations of history painting. This is not the place to discuss whether he failed or succeeded. But although West and the other history men of the Royal Academy were in high-minded mood when it came to subject matter, their struggle was to find subjects that were understandable, appealing and, they hoped, even profitable, yet with the didactic moral purpose they felt their mission required.

'The greatest imprudence a poet or painter can commit,' the Abbé Dubos had warned some decades earlier, 'is to choose for a principal object of imitation, such things as we would look upon with an eye of indifference in nature ... How is it possible for us to be touched with the copy of an original, when the original itself is incapable of moving us?'[67]

As expressed by Dubos, recognition of and respect for the hierarchy of subject matter was essential to the dignity of painting. But by 1770 that hierarchy was beginning to crumble, an issue to which I shall return. Fundamental to the birth of modern painting is the liberation of the artist in terms of subject matter: the need to descend from Olympus. Within a hundred years the greatest artists would be painting apples and peasants – but not yet.

For such an artist as West, who wanted to be both great and popular, the choice of subject matter was as important as the execution of the picture. The death of Wolfe was a risky choice. Wolfe's popularity was immense and would guarantee a great deal of attention. The gamble for West was how to paint Wolfe in a way that commanded the approval of the King, the respect of his fellow Academicians and the enthusiasm of the public. Before we look in greater detail at how West played that great gamble, it is time to know more about the man he was.

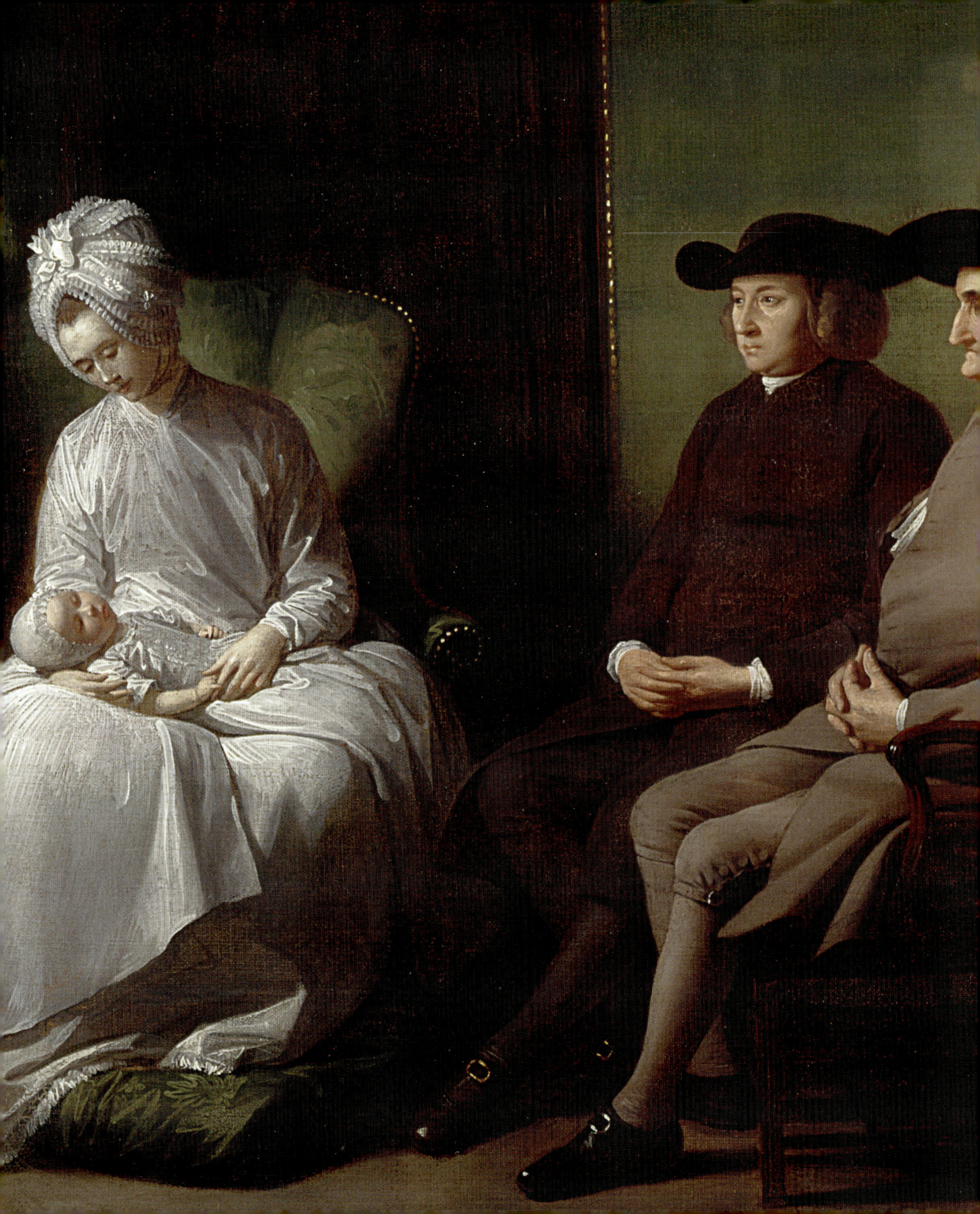

'THE MAN I WAS YESTERDAY'

Detail of Benjamin West, *The West Family*, c. 1772 (see fig. 21)

West painted around twenty self-portraits and portraits of family members. *The West Family* (fig. 21) is the most unusual of these and an exceptional picture in the artist's vast body of work. It is one of only two conversation pieces painted by West[1] and, at a modest 52.1 by 66.7 centimetres (20½ × 26¼ in.), among the smallest works he showed at the Royal Academy. West liked big pictures; big in drama and big in size. Physically big pictures, guaranteed to grab attention, were favoured by exhibitionary culture. Such pictures were expensive and laborious to make and frame. They required grand rooms in which to be displayed. A big picture signalled an artist who could command high prices and the most elevated patronage, or one who was willing to take risks. It is surprising that so little consideration has been given to the size of pictures displayed at the Royal Academy: these works were also *objets de luxe* and status symbols; as such, size mattered a great deal.

Although painted in about 1772, *The West Family* was displayed to the public at the 1777 exhibition of the Royal Academy, as was *The Copley Family* (fig. 19) by John Singleton Copley. Resident in London for less than three years at the time, Copley was determined to make a splash, and *The Copley Family* is a magnificent, swaggering group portrait of the artist; his father-in-law, Richard Clarke; Copley's wife, Elizabeth; and their four children. And it is big: almost twelve times bigger than *The West Family*. 'Mr. Copley,' the critic of the *Morning Chronicle* observed, 'from the size of his family piece, is likely to be as much the subject of observation in the rooms as any artist who has exhibited'.[2] *The Copley Family* was 'the subject of observation', but disappointingly little praised. Copley had to wait another year for his breakthrough picture *Watson and the Shark* (fig. 103), the sensational hit of the 1778 exhibition.

In spite of its small size and reticence, *The West Family* was 'the subject of observation' too, thanks to West's ever-rising celebrity. 'The small picture of a family', it was reported, 'representing Mr. West's father, friend, lady, and son, is a neat

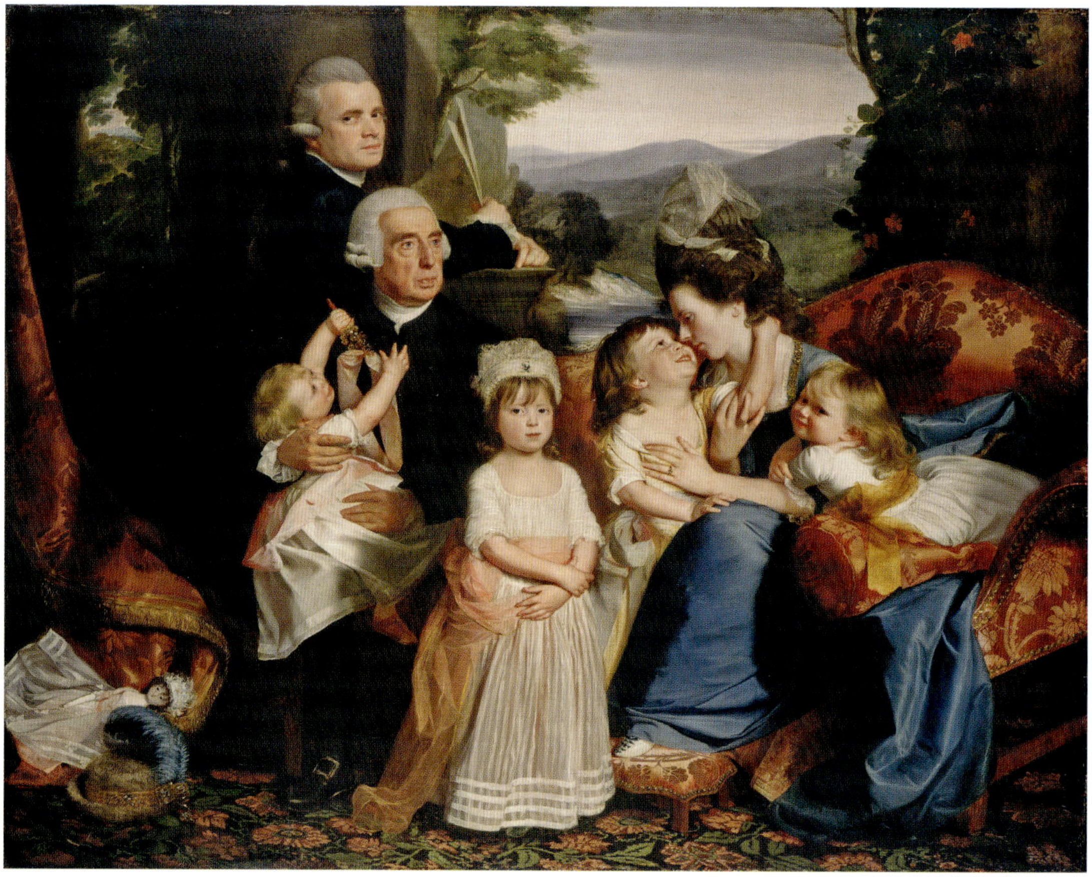

19
John Singleton Copley
(1738–1815)
The Copley Family
1776/77
Oil on canvas
184.1 × 229.2 cm
(72½ × 90¼ in.)
NATIONAL GALLERY OF ART, WASHINGTON, D.C.

little scene of domestic happiness, and does the artist credit on the score of his feelings.'[3] Perhaps because of the speed and enthusiasm with which West had succeeded, another critic regarded it as a mere piece of self-promotion:

> We do not, however, pretend to say, that the painter was not stimulated by one of the noblest motives in the world, the love of his family, to exhibit so pleasing and rational view of them; but he should no more publish this to the world, than the poet should a commendatory poem on his own family; for however the shallow loungers of the Royal Academy may apostrophize to the dear, good-natured man! The thinkers will call it a pitiful scene-trap for applause.[4]

Such carping invited response from the pseudonymous Phlalethes, who retorted that 'West's superior merits, as a Man, and as a Painter, and his known modesty, have placed him so far beyond the reach of disappointed malice, that I hope he will treat the pitiful insinuations of an assuming pedant with the silent contempt they deserve.'[5] As Kate Retford sees it:

> The attack on West reveals the fundamental tension at the heart of the elevation and sentimentalisation of domestic virtues … one had to be seen as a loving father and kind husband to receive approbation and applause. However to advertise one's domestic credentials could be seen to seek that applause actively and to make it appear that all was being done for show.[6]

The West Family is, on the surface, precisely such an advertisement for West's 'domestic credentials'. Charles Robert Leslie, looking more deeply, regarded it as an allegory, writing, 'I know not a more original illustration of the oft painted subject, the ages of man. Infancy, childhood, youth, middle life and extreme age are beautifully brought together … he has here succeeded in making a picture, which, being intended only for himself, is for that reason a picture for the whole world'.[7]

Jules Prown pushed the allegorical even further when he described the picture as 'An intimate family scene ... informed not only with the larger general theme of the Ages of Man but the specifically Christian themes of the Holy Family and of the Nativity, of birth as the immanent manifestation of the Divine in the affairs of men.' In this domestic scene, as Prown sees it, 'the quotidian is made universal'.[8]

The West Family can be viewed as a secularized nativity, as a variation on the theme of the ages of man or merely as a group portrait of an eighteenth-century happy family. West was neither a Rousseau in his writing nor a Rembrandt in his self-portraiture. Intense, painful self-scrutiny never stopped him in his tracks nor informed his work; self-doubt – if there was ever any – was not articulated. In the Galt biography, just as in his self-portraits, West saw himself, and wanted us to see him, as the personification of the rags-to-riches story in which natural ability, hard work and morality provided a replicable recipe for worldly success. We can, however, discern the tensions and struggles beneath this encouraging tale. *The West Family* reveals, more than any other document or work of art, just how conflicted an individual West was, even in the context of his conflicted century.

The West Family was painted in the high summer – August or early September – of 1772, when three generations of the West family – West's children, the artist and his wife, West's father, John, and West's half-brother by his father's first marriage, Thomas – were gathered to celebrate the birth of West's second son, Benjamin Jr. The place was probably the house in Hammersmith that the increasingly affluent artist was renting so the family could spend the hot months away from the noise, smell and crowds of the West End.[9]

The six figures in the picture are arranged in two distinct groups. On the left, the mother and her two sons form a tight compositional triangle; and, on the right, the artist, his father and half-brother form another, rather looser triangle. A complex rhythm of crossed legs running across the bottom third of the picture unites the two groups, as does the way in which the leaning-on-the-arm-of-the-chair pose of the artist's elder son, Raphael, mirrors that of his father. But while the picture is divided into two compositional groups, we can divide it into further groups. There is, for example, the generational ages-of-man way of looking at it, which takes us from youth (the West children) to maturity (the artist, his wife and his half-brother) to old age (the artist's father). Most striking perhaps is the division made obvious by the clothing of John and Thomas West, declaring quite clearly their religious identity as members of the Society of Friends, or Quakers, and, a little more subtly, their lower social status. This Quaker identity is made clear not only through their clothes, but also by their practice of wearing hats indoors and even their very poses, with their hands clasped on their laps suggestive of Quaker practice at prayer meetings. What a contrast their plain, homespun clothing, devoid of lapels and even metal buttons, makes with the magnificence of West's fashionable satin banyan and richly embroidered shirt.

The West Family is a conversation piece, if we define such a work as a group of smaller-than-life-size figures in a domestic setting. But it is an atypical one. Desmond Shawe-Taylor observes that in West's group portraits there is 'little place for the high jinks of the conversation piece'.[10] At a time when naughty children, indulgent fathers and spirited familial interaction were becoming the defining characteristic of the genre, *The West Family* stuns us with its solemnity and restraint: no tea is being drunk, no cards are being played, no music is performed. Nor is there the conversation piece's usual delight with materiality. In *The West Family*, worldly goods are remarkable by their absence: only the artist's clothes and the gilded beading on the edge of the door frame hint at luxury.

The newly born Benjamin West junior is a sleeping object of adoration; his elder brother, Raphael, in his London clothes and copycat pose is merely an adult in waiting; Elizabeth West, who had been painted by her husband with such loving vivacity two years earlier, is reduced to a symbol of motherhood, so thinly painted and wanly coloured as to be hardly there. But she is a more solid presence than West, who so marginalizes himself in the picture that he becomes more of an onlooker than a participant. Benjamin and Elizabeth West's bloodlessness serves to underline the prominence – or, rather, dominance – and solidity of John and Thomas West. John West, who died five years after the picture was painted, is sunken-faced, but straight-backed and still projects patriarchal authority. His son Thomas is perhaps the most unusual family member. With a pose and glance that seem to owe something to Holbein's *Thomas Cromwell* (fig. 20), his eye line avoids both mother and children and looks straight out of the window. If this is a nativity, it is an unusual, if not a dysfunctional one.

There is an unsettling ambivalence about this picture, which seems to be as much about separation as connection. This separation makes it a perverse sort of conversation piece, because the conversation piece is essentially about connectedness: connectedness with family and friends, connectedness with the things that represent status and success, connectedness with property. Here there is very little of that connectedness. The centrality of the two Quakers breaks the relationship between West and his wife and their two sons. The disengagement of John and Thomas invites us to question whether they are disapproving or merely bewildered by the worldly success of their son and brother, with his two fine houses, modish family and friendships with the greatest in the land. This is not to suggest that West had anything other than loving familial relationships: all the evidence is that he was an exemplary husband, father, son and brother. However, it does seem to me that in the summer of 1772, West had a rare pause in his race to the top, and *The West Family* is the visual expression of that pause: West's attempt to freeze time and make explicit both his place in the trajectory of which he is in the middle and the speed of his ascent. Within West's body of work, *The West Family* is a rare moment of self-doubt and introspection; a time when the artist seems to be asking whether he is Quaker or Anglican, insider or outsider, material or spiritual.

So commanding are the figures of John and Thomas West that it is tempting to see *The West Family* as a celebration of the artist's Quaker ancestry, although West's attitude towards that ancestry was ambivalent. He was married in a Church of England ceremony at St Martin-in-the-Fields and was buried in St Paul's Cathedral, but he was never christened or confirmed as an Anglican.[11] Contemporaries of West and Quaker historians of subsequent years have agreed that West was not a Quaker and have also seriously doubted the religious status of his parents. The Philadelphian Benjamin Smith Barton wrote in 1789: 'His father was not a Quaker, although he frequented the meetings of the Friends and brought up his children to the same; but neither the father, nor his son, the Historical Painter, were ever received (as the term is) into the Society of the Friends.'[12] John West had arrived in America without a certificate of transfer, which would have testified to his good standing as a Friend.[13] Nonetheless he seems to have lived and worshipped as a Quaker. His second wife – West's mother, Sarah – was altogether more problematic: in February 1718, 'She was disowned from Chester monthly meeting … for disunity.'[14] While West himself seems to have subscribed to a non-committed Anglicanism, he allegedly remarked: 'I was once a Quaker, and have never left their principles.'[15] In terms of outward appearance and behaviour, there appears to be no evidence of this. Perhaps West may have found that his 'Quakerism' added to his attractiveness in a period fascinated by the exotic, but by the time *The West Family* was painted, West was sufficiently well established not to need to display his, anyway dubious, Quaker credentials, and indeed Quakers were no longer felt to be particularly novel.

So, we return to query the prominence of the father and half-brother in the picture. Leslie suggested that *The West Family* was simply an 'original illustration of the oft painted subject, the ages of man', but it may be more of a meditation on the nature of past, present and future, with the artist's father and half-brother representing the past, West and his wife representing the present, and the artist's children the future. The increasing belief in progress and improvement in the eighteenth century – which we shall return to as a defining characteristic of modernity – also encouraged increased speculation about the nature of past, present and future and how they fed one another. James Harris, the philosopher and nephew of the 3rd Earl of Shaftesbury, asserted that 'Knowledge of the Future comes from Knowledge of the Past; as does Knowledge of the Past from Knowledge of the Present, so that their order to us is that of Present, Past and Future.'[16] In *The West Family*, we can see West struggling to work out this relationship between present, past and future in his own family. As Harris further observed, 'the present Now may so far belong to Time of either sort as to be the End of the past and the Beginning of the future'.[17] Here was West poised on another threshold. Considering West's career, his optimism and ambitions, it would seem that he subscribed to a progressive doctrine. *The West Family* is about the interweaving of past and present; where the one stops and the other begins, a pattern as intricate as the rhythm of the sitters' criss-crossed legs. In *The West Family*, the artist is posing a number of questions: Who am I? How did I get to be that man? Where am I going? Through this questioning, West may have been revisiting his youthful study of the artist and theorist Jonathan Richardson, who wrote, 'the man I was yesterday is now no more; if I live till tomorrow, that man is not yet born … What is past we know, but it is vanished as a morning dream; we are moving on; and every step we take is a step in the dark.'[18]

Who was Benjamin West? If you scratched the surface of West the courtier/painter of 1772, would the Pennsylvania Quaker still be there? Does *The West Family* celebrate a young man's escape from a wayside tavern in rural Pennsylvania, or is it a recognition of the importance of ancestral values? Is it perhaps an ex-voto of thanks for worldly success and a statement of the hope that Raphael and his baby brother will fly even higher than their father?

West was born in Springfield, Pennsylvania, on 10 October 1738, the tenth child of the second marriage of John West, an erstwhile English Quaker who had settled in America in 1714. Much altered following a devastating fire in 1874, the West birthplace is a solid, but modest, two-storey stone house, on what was then the main road leading from Philadelphia to the market town of Chester and so an ideal spot from which John West – having previously tried his hand as a cooper and tinsmith – could pursue his new trade as an innkeeper. Today the house stands in the midst of the campus of Swarthmore College, and Springfield is a pleasant commuter suburb of Philadelphia, just 16 kilometres (10 miles) from the city centre. But in 1738 Springfield was not too far from the edge of the British Empire, although it was more a dependency of Philadelphia than a frontier town. A scant hundred miles to the west, European settlement stopped and there was wilderness all the way across the continent to the Pacific. Philadelphia, though, like Boston and New York, faced east and was affected by the relative speed and regularity with which London fashions, manners and, most importantly, ideas flowed to the mercantile cities of the American colonies. So from birth, West was balanced between the primeval and the metropolitan.

The Swedish artist Gustavus Hesselius arrived in Philadelphia in 1712 and two years later sent his mother a vivid account of his new life in America. On the one hand there were the elements of town life that would have been familiar to any European. 'I now live among the English in Philadelphia,' Hesselius reported, 'have thank God my rich livelihood among them. There is no other Portrait

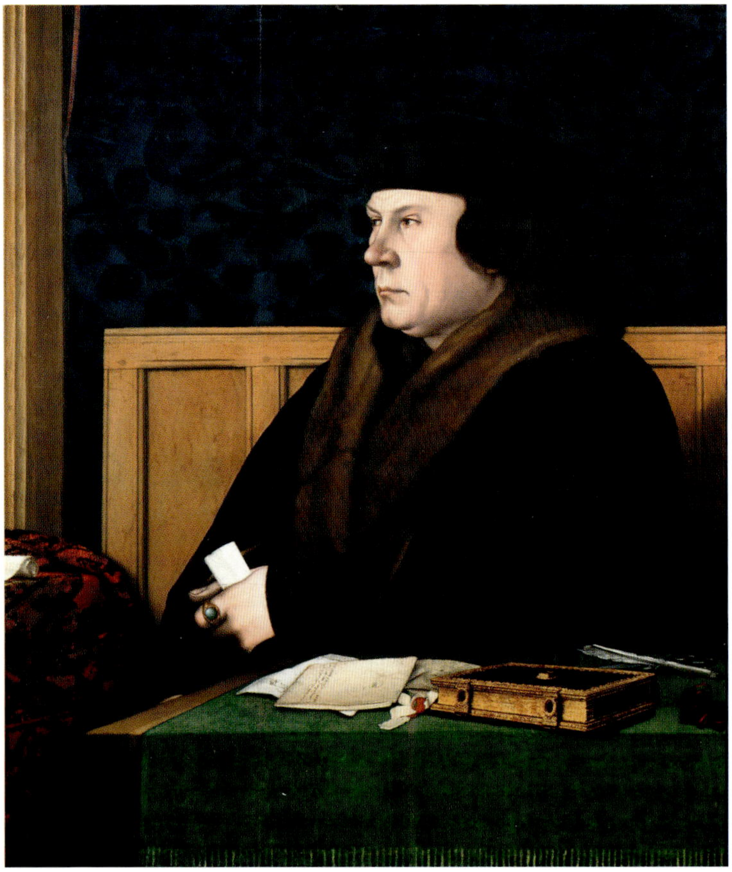

20
Hans Holbein the Younger
(*c.* 1497–1543)
Thomas Cromwell
1532–33
Oil on oak panel
78.4 × 64.5 cm
(30⅞ × 25⅜ in.)
THE FRICK COLLECTION, NEW YORK

Painter here, work I have enough.'[19] So even as early as 1714 – the year in which John West arrived in Pennsylvania – the small but growing town of Philadelphia created enough demand and was sufficiently sophisticated to support a professional portraitist. Philadelphia was also very much a new settlement in a new world. 'Last year', Hesselius told his mother, 'I saw with my own eyes that an Indian killed his own Wife in bright daylight in the street here in Philadelphia, and that bothered him nothing.'[20]

By mid-century, immigration and explosive economic growth had transformed both the colony of Pennsylvania and its capital. As William Smith reported: 'Of all the British Colonies in North America, Pennsylvania is the most flourishing. Its staple is chiefly Provisions of which it produces enough to maintain itself, and a Hundred thousand men besides. From the Port of Philadelphia, at least 400 sail of Vessels clear out annually.'[21]

Pennsylvania grain and flour, beef and pig iron were booming, creating newer and bigger fortunes, and in turn encouraging greater immigration from Europe. By 1760, with a population approaching 20,000, Philadelphia was the biggest city in the colonies and the third or fourth largest in the British Empire. It was also a city that was becoming ever more modern and elegant. Where there had been Native Americans in the streets a few short decades earlier, there was now paving and street lighting (from whale-oil lamps), a substantial library and an abundance of new building exemplified by the Anglican Christ Church, with its Wrenish, 60-metre-high (196 ft) tower and spire, the tallest structure in North America.[22]

What particularly distinguished Philadelphia and Pennsylvania from other colonial settlements was the extremely mixed nature of the population, a consequence of both economic pull and the unique nature of 'the holy experiment' of the colony's founder, William Penn. At a time when the idea of religious tolerance was gaining acceptance among enlightened thinkers in Europe – Voltaire was a prominent advocate – Pennsylvania was not only *not* a confessional colony, but also a positively tolerant one. Penn had founded the colony to provide a safe haven from prosecution for his fellow Quakers, but also as an object lesson in religious toleration, which was spelled out in his *First Frame of Government* (1682), Pennsylvania's earliest constitution. The result was striking to visitors. The Scottish doctor Alexander Hamilton noted in the diary of his visit to Philadelphia in 1744: 'I dined in a tavern with a very mixed company of different nations and religions. There were Scots, English, Dutch, Germans, and Irish; there were Roman Catholicks, Churchmen, Presbyterians, Quakers, Newlightmen, Methodists, Seventh-daymen, Moravians, Anabaptists, and one Jew.'[23]

West very much wanted to be seen as a self-taught artist with God-given genius who, in spite of his modest origins, went on to conquer the world capitals of art. As Galt noted:

> After what has already been mentioned of the state of Society in Pennsylvania, it is needless to say that at the period to which these memoirs refer, there were but few pictures in the British Plantations; indeed, without any other explanation, all that should be contended for by any person who might imagine it necessary to advocate the pretensions of Benjamin West to be placed in the list of original and self-instructed artists, would be readily granted, upon stating the single fact, that he was born in Pennsylvania, and did not leave America till the year 1760.[24]

The case may be precisely the opposite. The conditions of life and society in Pennsylvania superbly equipped West for his triumphant assault on the Old World and enabled him to transform history painting when and as he did. Of course, every time and place of birth is unique and formative, but the conditions of life in Pennsylvania from West's birth until his departure to Italy in 1760 are of paramount importance in trying to understand his mental world, his artistic intentions and his determination and ability to succeed. West was supremely a man of his time and not afraid to be so, and Pennsylvania in the 1730s–50s was seething with change and struggle. The growth of cities, the stirrings of industrialization, the expansion of international trade, the melting pots of belief and ethnicity, the first steps towards representative democracy, these and so many other familiar characteristics of the modern world can all be found in and around the Philadelphia of those years, and they can be seen all the more clearly – and no doubt would have been felt all the more strongly – because of the rapidity with which they happened in the New World.

It is possible, as his biographer Galt claimed, that the six-year-old West first manifested his talent by drawing a portrait of his sleeping baby niece Sally; it is possible that the fur of the family cat, Grimalkin, provided the young West with the bristles of his first paintbrushes; it is possible that the local Indians taught West how to use pigments. No doubt even in his earliest youth West was motivated and resourceful, but all of these possible incidents are used by West and Galt to make the point that

> the means of giving body and effect … are rarely withheld from men of genius. If the circumstances of Fortune are unfavourable, Nature instructs them to draw assistance immediately from herself, by endowing them with the faculty of perceiving a fitness and correspondence in things which no force of reasoning, founded on the experience of others, could enable them to discover. This aptness is, perhaps, the surest indication of the possession of original talent.[25]

It is all reminiscent of, perhaps even consciously copying, Vasari's biography of Giotto, in which the young shepherd boy from the village of Vespignano is, at the age of ten, spotted drawing a sheep on a flat stone by Cimabue, who happens to be passing by. The peasant boy is whisked off to Florence and in spite of being 'born among inept craftsmen, by the gift of God revived that art, which had come to a grievous pass, and brought it to such a form as could be called good'.[26] So too is West, the son of an innkeeper, relocated from the agricultural hinterlands of colonial Pennsylvania to the courts of Europe, where he revives the art of history painting, which had also 'come to a grievous pass', as Vasari would say.

While he repeatedly stressed the unpromising artistic conditions surrounding his birth and youth – 'In the whole Christian world no spot was apparently so unlikely to produce a painter as Pennsylvania'[27] – West both directly and indirectly acknowledged some, but not all, of the many mentors who prepared him for take-off. Those mentors can be arranged in two groups: the usually itinerant, professional artists who may have taught West something about technique and composition, and a larger group of public figures who sometimes educated, sometimes commissioned and always encouraged West to pursue an artistic career.

As we have seen, Philadelphia had a sufficiently rich and socially ambitious population to support the work of a full-time portraitist, Hesselius, as early as 1712–14, a mere thirty years after the city was founded. Unsurprisingly, as Philadelphia grew, it became more attractive to visiting artists. With increasing wealth, the Quaker ethos of the city was eroded. First, because many Quaker families turned to the Church of England, eager for its greater social and political cachet; among them the children of William Penn himself. Secondly, as the economy boomed, the flood of immigrants, whether English, Welsh, Scots-Irish or German, reduced the Quakers to a minority. This had implications for the arts in particular, as Quaker simplicity was indifferent to and sometimes downright hostile towards both the visual and the performing arts. Even those families who remained Quakers were becoming more opulent in dress, furnishing and behaviour, including the commissioning of portraits.[28]

West's first artist mentor was the Bristol-born painter and adventurer William Williams, who met the nine-year-old West in 1747, not long after Williams himself arrived in Philadelphia. West was new to Philadelphia too, staying with his relative Edward Pennington, who had brought him there 'indulging the hope of seeing some pictures in the city'.[29] West was soon taken to see a landscape recently completed by Williams for the Philadelphia merchant Samuel Shoemaker, and 'the blush of joy which overspread my face on the picture first being exposed to view attracted the attention of those present even more than the picture itself … it being the first picture I had seen except the small essays I made in the country'.[30] Even with the benefit of West's enthusiastic description, it is hard to imagine the effect that seeing that newly completed painting must have had on the child artist. West's upbringing would have taken place in a world of visual scarcity: rural Quaker families did not hang their walls with pictures. In Philadelphia, the sight of Williams's painting would have been the first of many such revelations for West, as there were increasing numbers of portraits, landscapes and engravings in the homes of the well off and an abundance of illustrated books, too.

From the time of their first meeting until West left Philadelphia for good in 1760, Williams was a source of inspiration to the young man: 'my attention was directed to every point necessary to accomplish me for the profession of painting; this often brought me to the house of Williams'.[31] Most importantly, Williams – who must have been exceedingly impressed by West to do so – lent his precious copies of Jonathan Richardson's *Essay on the Theory of Painting* (1715) and Charles-Alphonse Du Fresnoy's *Art of Painting* (*De arte graphica*, 1668) to West, who recalled that 'those two books were my companions by day, and under my pillow by night'.[32]

It seems unlikely that a nine-year-old boy with little more than some village schooling could have immediately immersed himself in the somewhat dense and sometimes obscure theoretical writings of Richardson and Du Fresnoy. But the very fact that there were books about painting would have made them objects of inspiration and wonder to a boy who had grown up in a household where the few books would have been sacred, not secular. The works of Du Fresnoy, as a popularizer of French academic theory, and of Richardson, as the English mouthpiece for the same, were influential among artists and connoisseurs, and widely distributed. West's exposure to them was a transformational experience.[33]

From his inspirational opening lines, Du Fresnoy proclaimed painting's high moral purpose: 'Painting and poesy are two Sisters … For both those Arts, that they might advance the sacred Honours of Religion, have raised themselves to Heaven; and, having found a free admission into the Palace of Jove himself, have enjoyed the Sight and Conversation of the Gods'.[34] And painters themselves are no ordinary individuals: 'The Qualities requisite to form an excellent Painter, are, a true discerning Judgment, a Mind which is docible, a noble Heart, a sublime Sense of things, and Fervour of Soul'.[35]

The most talented painters in history enjoyed not just the patronage, but also the friendship and respect of the powerful. Alexander the Great 'had no greater Pleasure, than when he was in the Painting-room of Apelles',[36] and the Holy Roman Emperor Charles V, we are told quoting Titian's biographer Carlo Ridolfi, 'valued himself, not so much in subjecting Kingdoms and Provinces, as that he had been thrice made Immortal by the Hand of Titian'.[37]

Richardson, too, stressed the special qualities of the painter, writing: 'it is not every picture-maker that ought to be called a painter, as every rhymer, or Grub-street tale-writer is not a poet, or historian: a painter ought to be a title of dignity, and understood to imply a person endued with such excellencies of mind, and body, as have ever been the foundations of honour amongst men.'[38]

Richardson went on to declare that 'The great, and chief ends of Painting are to raise, and improve nature; and to communicate ideas; not only those which we may receive otherwise, but such as without this art could not possibly be communicated; whereby mankind is advanced higher in the rational state, and made better; and that in a way, easy, expeditious, and delightful.'[39]

This must have been heady stuff for the boy West, and perhaps helped to endow him with the self-confidence, shading into egotism, that propelled him forward. Almost in a flash, what had been youthful precocity was elevated to a quasi-sacred vocation.

Like Du Fresnoy, Richardson was unequivocal in his defence of the moral purpose of painting:

> Painting relates the histories of past and present times, the fables of the poets, the allegories of moralists, and the good things of religion: and consequently a picture, besides its being a pleasant ornament, is useful to instruct and improve our minds, and to excite proper sentiments and reflections, as a history, a poem, a book of ethics, or divinity.[40]

Throughout his career, West had most definite views about the nobility and worth of painting, and his particular drive to excel at history painting, the most elevated but least commercially promising branch of the profession, can have begun only with his early familiarity with the highfalutin works of Du Fresnoy and Richardson. Otherwise it is hard to explain the young West's single-minded devotion to a genre of painting that was scarcely represented anywhere in British America.

Aside from Williams, West also fell under the influence of another visiting English artist, John Wollaston,[41] as well as the Moravian preacher and painter of religious scenes John Valentine Haidt.[42] So West was no autodidact, but benefited from the attentions of a string of visiting artists of varying but nonetheless helpful talent.[43] Even Haidt, the least proficient of them, had something to offer in terms of his clumsy but ambitious attempts to paint more complex and elevated subjects. However, two men stand out as making the greatest contribution to the early shaping of Benjamin West: his most influential teacher and guide, William Smith, and his first significant patron, William Henry.

21
Benjamin West
The West Family
c. 1772
Oil on canvas
52.1 × 66.7 cm
(20½ × 26¼ in.)
PAUL MELLON COLLECTION, YALE CENTER FOR BRITISH ART, NEW HAVEN, CONNECTICUT

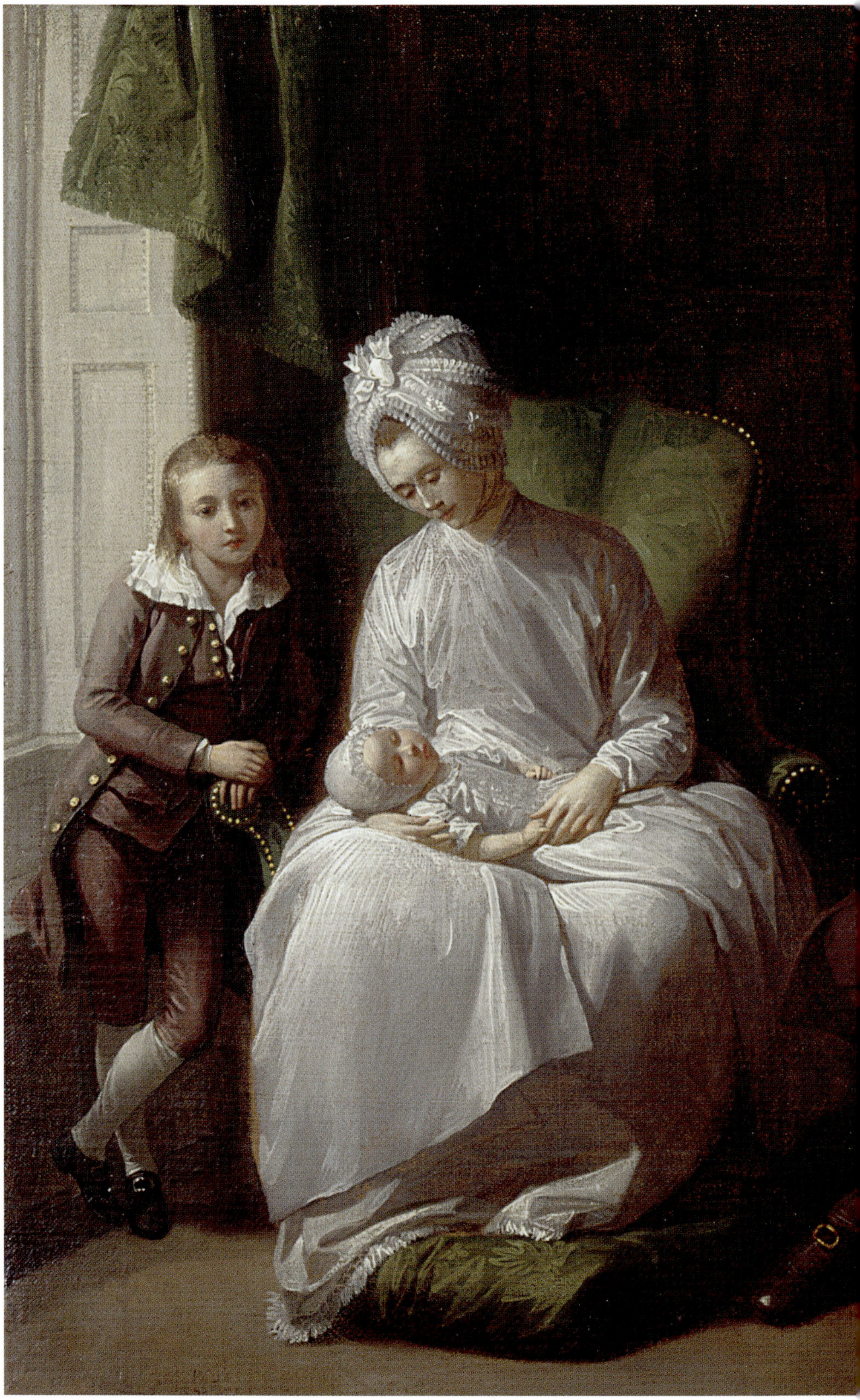

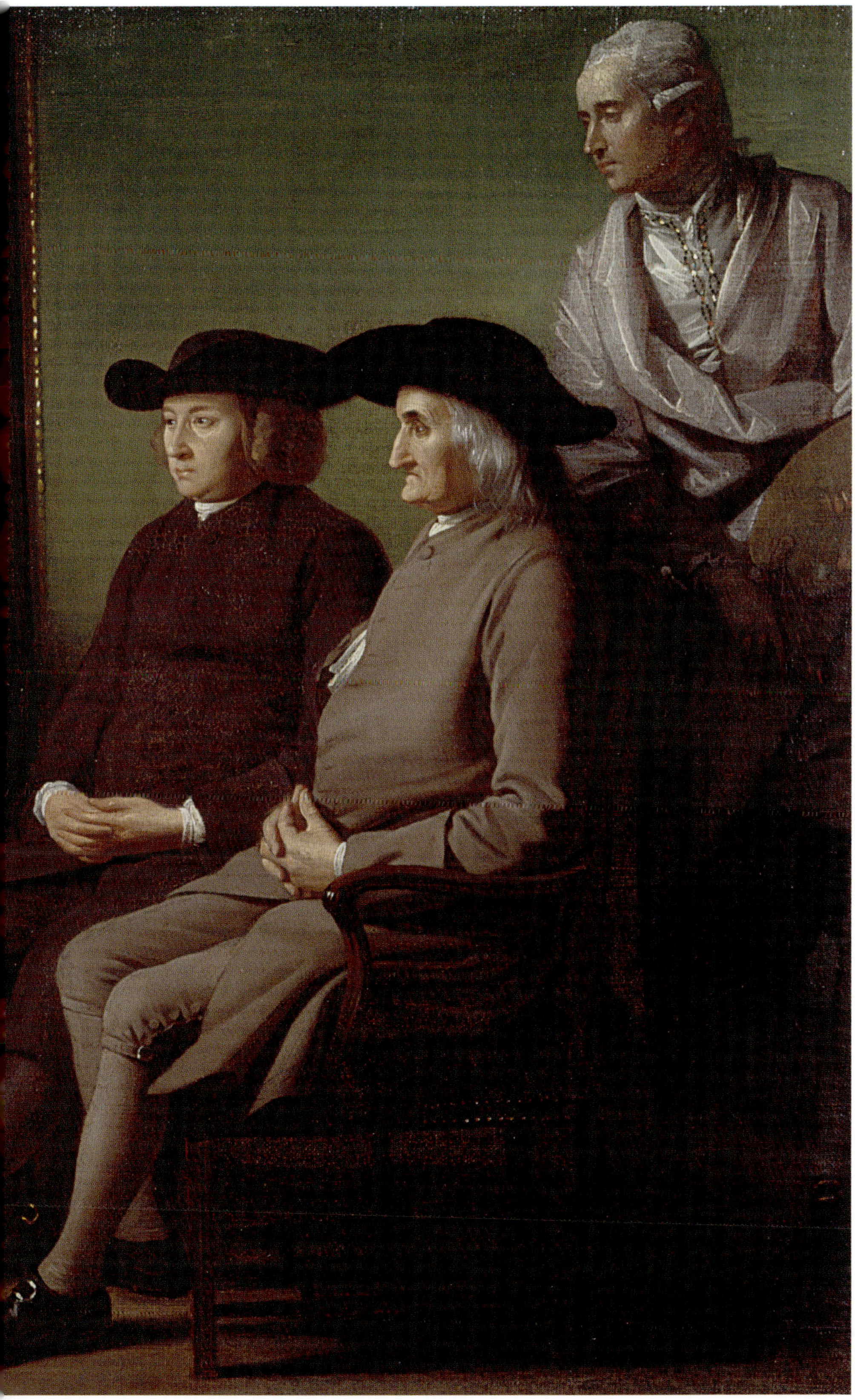

Not every Pennsylvania entrepreneur was either as aspirational or as successful as Henry, but the colony seemed to produce men who were both commercially astute and intellectually ambitious. The pattern was perhaps set by James Logan, the Penn family's man of business in Pennsylvania. Having amassed a fortune in the fur trade, Logan assembled a library of 2500 books (including the first copy of Newton's *Principia* in North America), conducted experiments in crop breeding that were praised by Linnaeus, and undertook the first published translation of a classical work in the colonies. He also gave his considerable patronage to the young Benjamin Franklin.[44]

Henry was an exceptional individual, but also a type; a type best exemplified by Benjamin Franklin, described by Stuart Sherman as 'obviously a product of provincial America – the first great Yankee with all the strong lineaments of the type: hardness, shrewdness, ingenuity, practical sense, frugality, industry, self-reliance'.[45] Sherman goes on to say that Franklin was more than 'a product of the provinces. All Europe has wrought upon and metamorphosed the Yankee printer … With no softening of his patriotic fibre or loss of his Yankee tang, he has acquired all the common culture and most of the master characteristics of the Age of Enlightenment.'[46] This combination of determination, pragmatism and cultural aspiration, common to Franklin, West and Henry, seems to be characteristic of many of the successful British-American colonials, particularly those from Pennsylvania, where the pressing demands of carving a new society out of the wilderness required determined, practical men and women, yet the seeming closeness of London brought constant exposure to a more cosmopolitan way of life. The latest books from London quickly found their way on to Philadelphia bookshelves – those of private individuals, as well as the Library Company of Philadelphia, which Franklin had founded. And Philadelphia interests were broad. The Library Company catalogue of 1741 ranges from history and travel to literature, science, medicine, agriculture, law, politics and linguistics.[47] The proportion of subjects is revealing. As analysed by Thomas Keys, while 60 per cent of the books in New England libraries were theological, in the mid-Atlantic colonies, which include Pennsylvania, the proportion was only 25 per cent, and 'this change is of the utmost importance. It suggests a desire to know more about the affairs of the world – more emphasis on the present world and less on the world to come.'[48]

Henry, like Franklin and West, was a self-made man of modest background. Like Franklin, he had a great deal of mechanical skill and ingenuity and a huge range of intellectual interests. Like West, he had – and this was unusual for Pennsylvania and indeed anywhere in colonial America – a belief in the value of history painting. Henry is often described as a gunsmith, which rather belittles his prominence and achievements. As a fifteen-year-old he was apprenticed to a gunsmith and was in business on his own by 1750. The colonial skirmishes that preceded the Seven Years War and the war itself made Henry a considerable fortune. He visited England in order to meet James Watt; he was elected to the first American Congress after the War of Independence; the transatlantic radical polemicist Thomas Paine was a friend and lodger; and Henry was an early supporter of the young Robert Fulton, future student of West and more prominent as the inventor of the marine torpedo and the father of commercial steam navigation. Henry was a frontier gunsmith, but his home town of Lancaster, Pennsylvania, was the largest inland city in the British colonies, and his friends and associates were international and variously accomplished.

West arrived in Lancaster in 1756, and the bustling but unsophisticated – at least relative to Philadelphia – town would have offered him good opportunities for portrait commissions. He first painted the family of George Ross, a Lancaster lawyer, and 'Such was the success with which he executed this task, that the sphere of his celebrity was greatly enlarged; and so numerous were the applications for portraits, that it was with difficulty he could find time to satisfy the demands of his admirers.'[49] Among the admirers was Henry, who commissioned portraits of his wife and himself and then remarked to West that 'if he [Henry] could paint as well, he would not waste his time on portraits, but would devote himself to historical subjects'.[50]

This was an extraordinary moment in the life of the young artist. Fired with zeal for the highest forms of his art by Du Fresnoy and Richardson, the teenage West must have wondered how he could escape a career as an itinerant face painter, and suddenly in Lancaster he walked into the embrace of an equally high-minded patron. As Scott Paul Gordon observes, Henry might very well have read George Turnbull's *Observations upon Liberal Education* (when Henry helped to establish the local library, a copy of this book was in the collection), with its praise of the value of history paintings that 'represent moral actions and characters'.[51] Henry suggested that West should paint the death of Socrates, and the result was the first secular history painting created in America.

As West recounted it, the source of the work lay in a volume of Plutarch from which Henry read to him;[52] but the more likely source appears to be Charles Rollin's *Ancient History of the Egyptians, Carthaginians, Assyrians, Babylonians, Medes and Persians, Macedonians, and Grecians* (1730–38). Rollin provided a pictorial as well as a literary source to West. Many of the elements of West's *Death of Socrates* (fig. 22) can be found in Jacques Philippe Le Bas's engraving after Hubert-François Gravelot's *Death of Socrates* (fig. 23), which was the frontispiece to the fourth volume of Rollin's work.[53] West never acknowledged his debt to Gravelot – indeed, it would have been highly unusual to do so – but the engraving is unequivocally the source for West's picture. However, West's *Socrates* was no mere copy. In changing Gravelot's composition as he did – moving Socrates to the centre of the action, and placing him between competing crowds of citizens and soldiers – West was following Richardson's advice:

> The painter that can take a hint, or insert a figure, or groups of figures from another man, and mix these with his own, so as to make a good composition, will thereby establish such a reputation to himself, as to be above fearing to suffer by the share those to whom he is beholden will have in it.[54]

The question of why Henry should have commissioned *Socrates* is debatable. Gordon proposes that *Socrates* should be seen as an artefact of the political conditions in the colony on the eve of the Seven Years War, at a time when the needs for colonial defence were colliding with the Quaker commitment to pacifism. Gordon writes, 'The painting is militant: advocating war, it celebrates a moment in which men commit themselves to martial practice. The soldiers reach, in effect, for the patriotism that *Socrates* symbolizes.'[55] He declares *Socrates* to be 'West's first painting about the French and Indian War', which 'celebrates patriotic devotion to a military ideal that the elected assembly had ceased to embody'.[56] *Socrates* should not be divorced from the political milieu in which it was produced, and the picture can certainly be plausibly read as a statement about the increasingly bitter political rifts dividing mid-eighteenth-century Pennsylvania; but *Socrates* was principally a status symbol, advertising Henry's increasing prosperity and importance, his intellectual sophistication and his gentlemanly position. It seems perfectly reasonable to think that Henry wanted the sort of history painting that he thought an intellectual English gentleman would have at home – although, in fact, they mostly did not – and that Socrates, seen by many in the eighteenth century as a *philosophe avant la lettre,* made an ideal subject: recognizable, dramatic and impressive. Commissioning a history painting, even from such a young and unknown artist as West, would still have been a risky venture for both patron and artist. The overarching fact about *Socrates* must be that an eighteen-year-old who had never left his

22
Benjamin West
The Death of Socrates
c. 1756
Oil on canvas
86.4 × 104.1 cm (34 × 41 in.)
PHILADELPHIA HISTORY MUSEUM AT THE ATWATER KENT

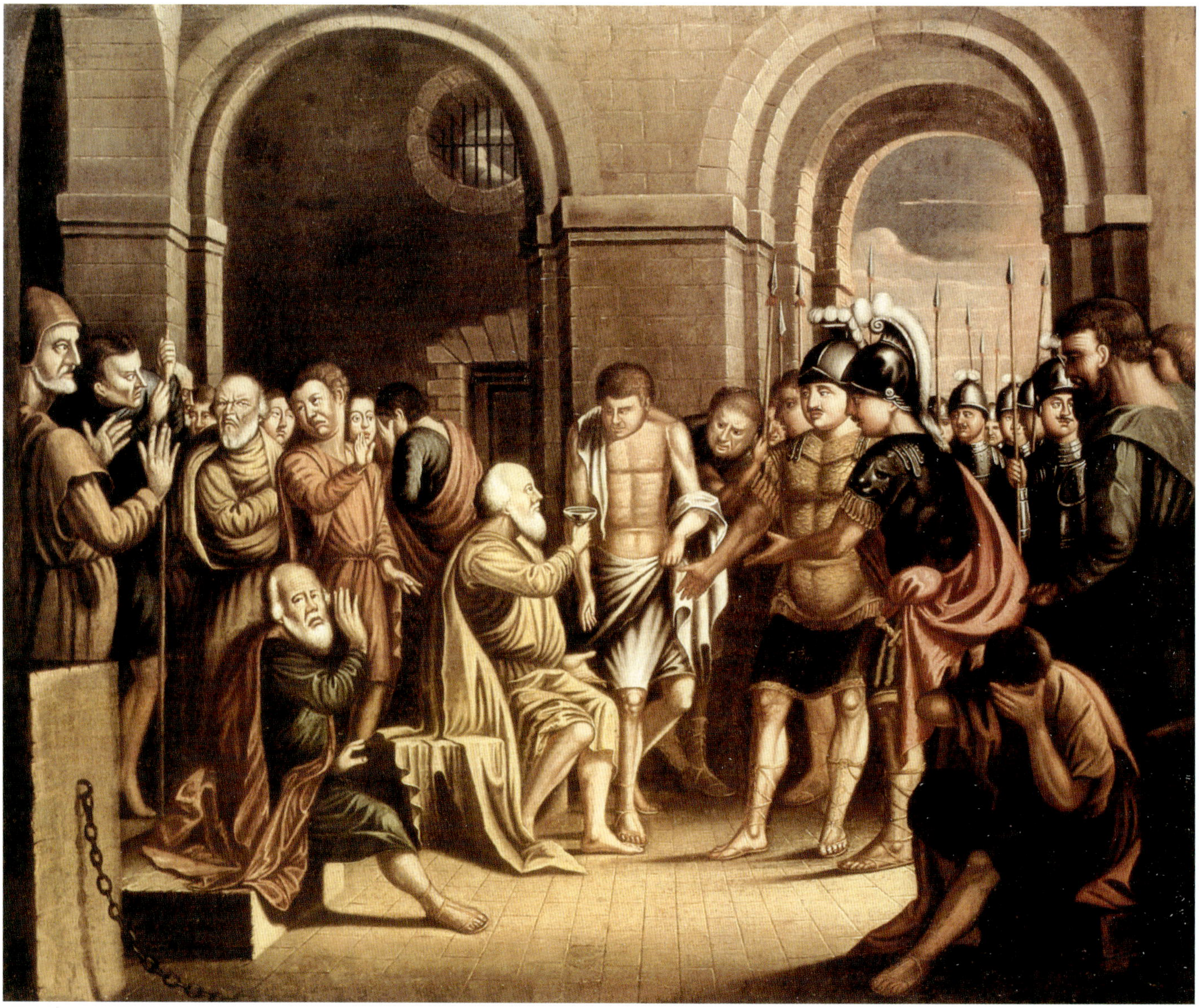

23
Jacques Philippe Le Bas
(1707–1783), after Hubert-
François Gravelot (1699–1773)
The Death of Socrates
c. 1738–40
Etching with some engraving
14.3 × 8.8 cm (5⅝ × 3½ in.)
THE BRITISH MUSEUM, LONDON

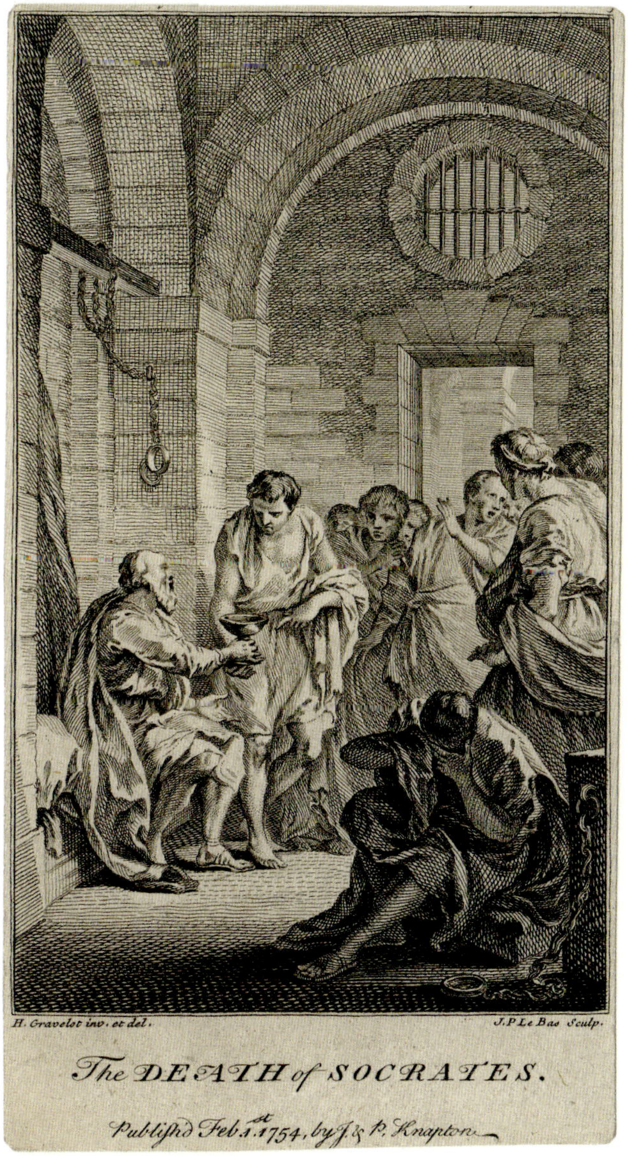

native Pennsylvania had the determination and talent to create a relatively complex, reasonably large-scale example of a genre that he knew only through engravings and theoretical writings.

Although *Socrates* has some of the primitive simplicity of an inn sign, it is for all of that, perhaps because of that, a remarkably powerful and impressive painting. The drapery is clumsy; it is spatially and tonally flat, and quite clearly the work of an artist with little training or experience. But the large number of figures – some two dozen – are cleverly grouped, and if the expressions are pantomimic, West may have been taking Richardson's advice too literally: 'The expression must be proper to the subject, and the characters of the persons; it must be strong, so that the dumb-shew may be perfectly well, and readily understood.'[57] Most unusually, when the picture was cleaned in 1962 two signatures were revealed; those of West and Henry.[58] So while West did not explicitly acknowledge his debt to Gravelot, he certainly paid tribute to Henry as patron and inspiration for the picture.

Henry's *Socrates* must have attracted a great deal of attention in Lancaster: such a newly commissioned painting, hanging in the house of one of the most prominent local citizens, would be the talk of the town. Among those who were impressed by *Socrates* was a visitor from Philadelphia, William Smith, who would turn out to be West's most important teacher, guide and patron.[59]

Scholarly, vitriolic, slovenly, silver-tongued and possibly a drunkard, Smith was one of those gifted but difficult and ambitious men who flared and flourished or sometimes crashed and burned in the dynamic surroundings of the British colonies. While such men as Henry and Franklin had come to the Enlightenment through 'distance learning' as it were, Smith had learned at the source. A product of the Scottish Enlightenment, he was educated at Aberdeen University – which he left without taking his degree – at a time when Scottish universities were among the most progressive in Europe.[60] He emigrated from Scotland to America in the early 1750s in order to work as a tutor to the children of a New York mercantile family – a familiar pattern when Scotland exported brainpower, especially the brainpower of those with little 'interest', as powerful family connections were then called. Smith's mother was a sister of the future Admiral Viscount Duncan, but Adam Duncan was then just a struggling lieutenant, being helped up the ladder by Augustus Keppel, who would be such an important friend and patron of Reynolds.

Smith's energy and enthusiasm established him as a public intellectual in New York, where he was embroiled in the debate raging around the establishment of a new university – King's College, politically contentious because of its robust Anglicanism – intended to rival the well-established New England institutions of Harvard and Yale as well as the College of William and Mary in Virginia.[61] In 1753 Smith published his thoughts on education in *A General Idea of the College of Mirania*, which attracted the attention of Benjamin Franklin, who then invited Smith to join the faculty of the Academy of Philadelphia, of which Franklin was a founder.

Both zealots for self-improvement and civic virtue, Smith and Franklin made a powerful pair. Franklin's political acumen was the perfect complement to Smith's à la mode polemics and dedication to teaching, and they soon transformed the Academy into the College of Philadelphia, forerunner of today's University of Pennsylvania. At the College of Philadelphia, Smith – with the support of Franklin – instituted a new type of curriculum, taught largely in English (rather than Latin), which represented a radical break with the 'New England perpetuation of the scholastic tradition of Oxford and Cambridge'.[62] Writing in 1752, Smith had unambiguously declared that the university was no ivory tower: 'the Knowledge of Languages, Philosophy and Mathematicks, is but a small Part of the Education of such as are designed to be useful in Society: Those ought to know Men and the World.'[63] That phrase, 'to know Men and the World', represents Smith's commitment to an important strand of Enlightenment thinking.

Lawrence Klein, discussing Shaftesbury's influential *Characteristics of Men, Manners, Opinions, Times* (1711), observed that Shaftesbury aimed 'at nothing other than returning philosophy to the world … Shaftesbury thought that philosophy should make people effective participants in the world.'[64] This belief that education should create a group of engaged citizens was perhaps best summed up by Voltaire's statement that 'We live in society; really, therefore, the only things that are good for us are those that are good for society … Virtue among men is an interchange of kindness; he who has no part in this interchange should not be counted.'[65]

Smith's educational mission was to equip his students for success. In his Utopian educational manifesto, *A General Idea of the College of Mirania,* he warned: 'It is dangerous to send raw and unpractis'd Virtue abroad into a World where Right and Wrong are too often confounded; and nothing can obviate this Danger but the giving Youth a previous Acquaintance with the World, and making them behold Virtue and Vice with all their Consequences painted in genuine Colors by the Historian.'[66]

Thanks to Smith, West moved to Philadelphia, where he became part of a small group of unusually gifted young men: Thomas Godfrey, Francis Hopkinson and Jacob Duche. A member of one of Pennsylvania's richest families, the eloquent and spiritual Duche became chaplain to the first two Continental Congresses. Godfrey, who died young, wrote poetry and the first tragedy by a native-born American to be staged professionally. The virtuoso Hopkinson was the first native-born American to compose a secular song, a future signatory of the Declaration of Independence, and one of the designers of the American flag. These were West's companions. Here he was at the age of eighteen, suddenly living in North America's largest city, a protégé of the most innovative educator in the British colonies and the intimate of the most brilliant young men of his time and place.[67] West was well prepared to take advantage of such company, perhaps remembering Richardson's advice that a painter should 'frequent the brightest company, and avoid the rest: Rafaelle was perpetually conversant with the finest geniuses, and the greatest men at Rome; and such as these were his intimate friends.'[68] To the young man from Springfield, Philadelphia was, at least for the time being, Rome.

The evidence is that Smith, for all his faults, cared deeply for his young students. When one of them, William Thomas Martin, died, Smith preached *A Sermon … Occasioned by the Death of a Beloved Pupil* from the pulpit of Christ Church. After reminding the students in his congregation that 'you hold your Lives on a very uncertain Tenure, and that no Period of your Age is exempted from the common Lot of Mortality', Smith went on to praise the late Martin: 'That he truly deserved the Esteem he enjoyed I can vouch from Experience. He grew up under me. With pleasure I marked his gradual Improvement. My highest Hopes were fixed upon him. To me he never was once wanting in Duty or Affection, and I returned him, my warmest Regard.'[69] Because of Smith's conviction of the need 'to Centre every Aim in Common Weal; In public Deeds to spend all private Zeal',[70] his care for his students extended well beyond the classroom.

Determined that those students should have worldly as well as academic success, Smith pushed and promoted them in the public arena. The chief means for doing this was through the *American Magazine*, a monthly that Smith edited in 1757–58. The magazine published an eclectic mix of material ranging from recipes and news reports to poetry and articles on natural history and geometry. It was in the pages of the February 1758 issue of the magazine that Benjamin West took his first small steps towards fame:

> We are glad of the opportunity of making known to the world the name of so extraordinary a genius as Mr. West. He was born in Chester county in this province, and without the assistance of any master,

24
Benjamin West
Mrs William Smith
(Rebecca Moore)
c. 1758
Oil on canvas
117 × 96.5 cm (46 × 38 in.)
PRIVATE COLLECTION

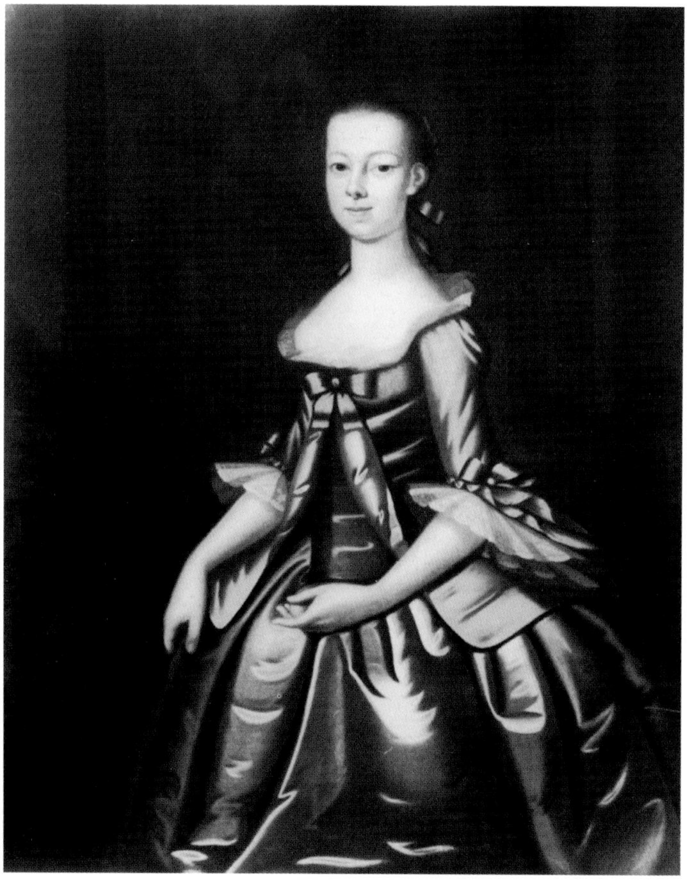

25 OPPOSITE
Benjamin West
Jane Galloway
(Mrs Joseph Shippen)
c. 1757
Oil on canvas
126.5 × 99.5 cm
(49¾ × 39¼ in.)
PHILADELPHIA HISTORY MUSEUM AT THE ATWATER KENT

> has acquired such a delicacy and correctness of expression in his paintings, joined to such a laudable thirst for improvement, that we are persuaded, when he shall have obtained more experience and proper opportunities of viewing the productions of able masters, he will become truly eminent in his profession.[71]

Here was the first hint that West must go to Europe to find those 'proper opportunities of viewing the productions of able masters'.

This piece of puffery was followed by a poem, 'Upon Seeing the Portrait of Miss **-** by Mr. West', in which West's recently completed portrait, which may have been that of either Rebecca Moore (fig. 24) or Jane Galloway (fig. 25), was praised for 'The easy attitude, the graceful dress, The soft expression of the perfect whole.'

Seven months later, the *American Magazine* promoted West even more extravagantly in a poem ostensibly in praise of John Wollaston, written by West's friend Godfrey:

> Nor let the muse forget thy name O West ...
> Loved youth, with virtue as by nature blest!
> If such the radiance of thy early Morn,
> What bright effulgence must thy Noon adorn?
> Hail sacred Genius! May'st thou ever tread,
> The pleasing paths your Wollaston has lead.
> Let his just precepts all your works refine,
> Copy each grace and learn like him to shine.
> So shall some future muse her sweeter lays,
> Swell with your name and give you all his praise.[72]

West was never enrolled as a student at the College of Philadelphia – Smith may have realized that the scantily educated young man would be unable to tackle the more demanding parts of the curriculum – but for nearly two years Smith taught, protected and promoted West, who was most assuredly a key part of Smith's group of bright young men. From Smith, West gained at least a veneer of metropolitan sophistication, some further knowledge of the classics, entrée to the top table of Philadelphia society and some more practical lessons on the value of what we would now call publicity. Furthermore, from Smith, West

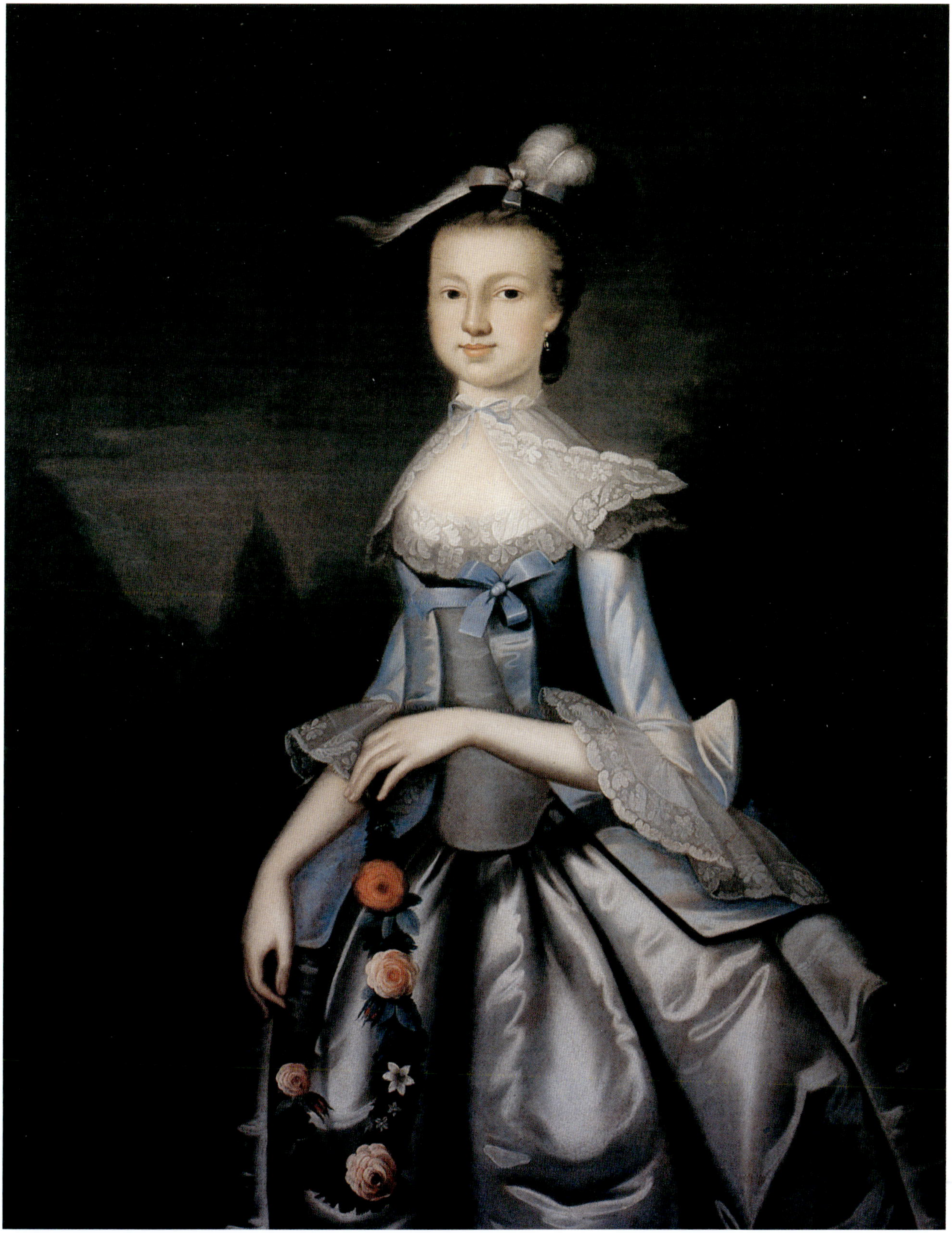

imbibed Enlightenment notions of civic virtue. Smith's young men were being moulded to be public men, useful men, men of the world, and in so being were also fulfilling a historic mission that Smith saw in patterns of the rise and fall of nations. Smith's success in moulding West, Godfrey, Hopkinson, Duche and others would determine, he felt, 'whether our New-World … shall be, the last Retreat / Of Arts, imperial Liberty and Truth'.[73]

West was an ambitious young man, surrounded and tutored by ambitious men: ambitious for status, power and money in a rapidly changing world. Such ambition was a common condition in the eighteenth century, as old social and economic hierarchies were cracking and the rapid expansion of population and commerce created a demand for talent to take its place at the top of what was an ever-broadening pyramid. This was also a time when individual identity was emerging ever more strongly from the collective identities of previous centuries. Indeed, it could be said that the social Darwinism of the nineteenth century was a logical conclusion to the conditions of the eighteenth. Such canonical works of West's time as Bernard Mandeville's *Fable of the Bees* (1714), Adam Ferguson's *Essay on the History of Civil Society* (1767) and Adam Smith's *Inquiry into the Nature and Causes of the Wealth of Nations* (1776) were just a few of the attempts to explore and explain the moral, political and economic implications of individualization. Even in Britain, where powerful individuals used their 'interest' to advance those who were tied to them by blood or marriage, patronage also began to flow towards the ambitious and capable, no matter how modest their origins. In the colonies, with their faster growth and looser social hierarchies, there was even more scope for rising men such as Franklin, Henry, Smith and West.

The necessity of ambition was eloquently summed up by West's contemporary Richard Cumberland, the poet, playwright and biographer of George Romney. Looking back on his own youthful lack of worldliness, Cumberland wrote:

> The happy faculty of noting times and seasons, and a lucky promptitude to avail themselves of moments with address and boldness, are alone such all-sufficient requisites, such marketable stores of worldly knowledge, that although the minds of those, who own them, shall be as to all the liberal sciences a rasa tabula, yet knowing these things needful to be known, let their difficulties and distresses be what they may, though the storm of adversity threaten to overwhelm them, they are in a life-boat, buoyed up by corks, and cannot sink … In a nation like this, where all ranks and degrees are laid open to enterprize, merit or good fortune, it is fit, right and natural that sudden elevations should occur and be encouraged.[74]

West was already imbued with the high status of history painting through his reading of Du Fresnoy and Richardson. Smith's insistence on the usefulness of education would have further convinced him that the successful practice of history painting was, to use Voltaire's words, 'good for society'. West's belief in the moral and educational value of history painting stayed with him for life. While it is sometimes hard to disentangle this belief from West's naturally high opinion of himself, it does appear to be both deeply and honestly held. 'The power of expressing historical events in painting with perspicuity', he declared, 'is one of the most impressive powers that can be given by man to convey useful lessons to others.'[75]

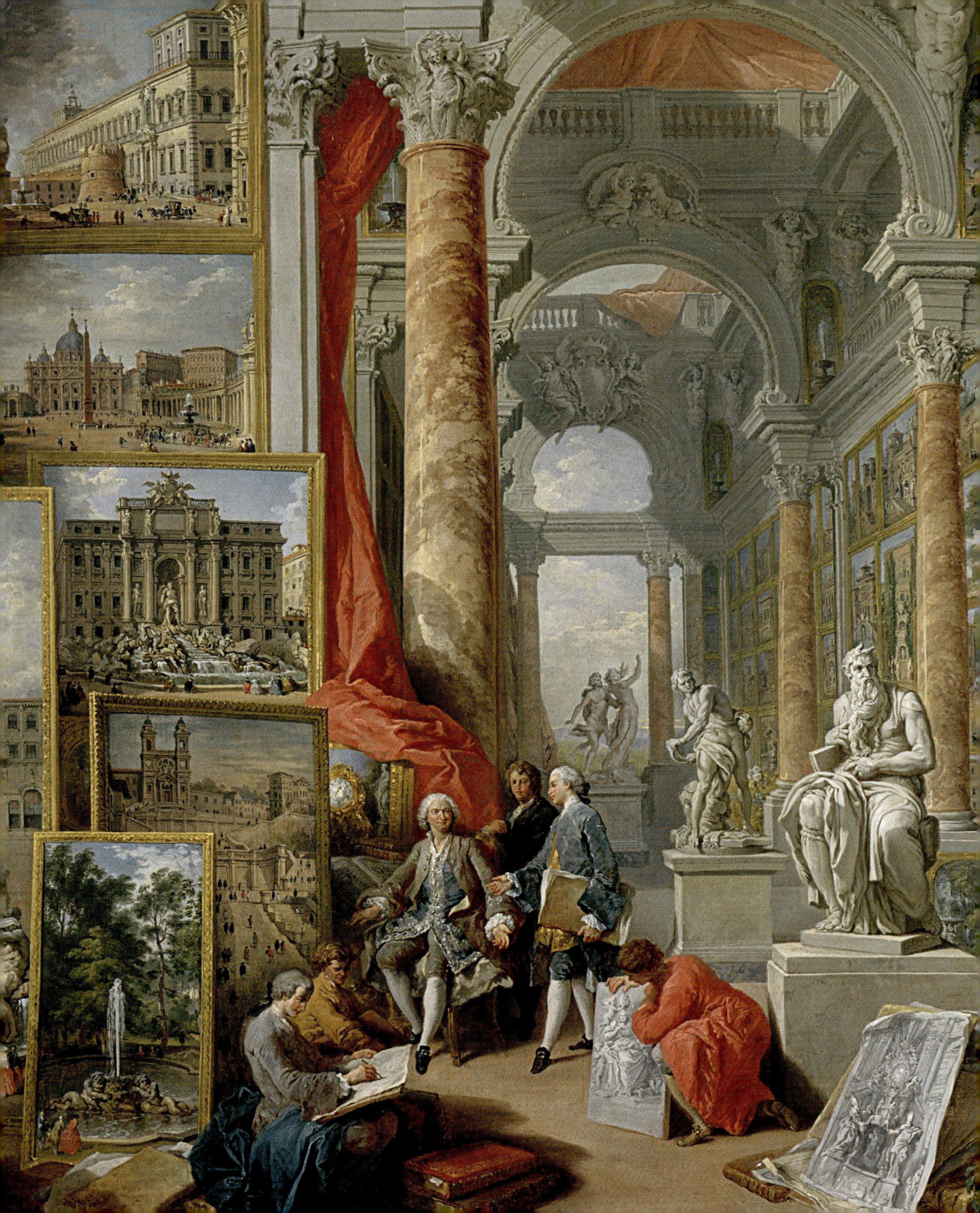

A PENNSYLVANIA YANKEE IN CARDINAL ALBANI'S COURT

Detail of Giovanni Paolo Panini, *Modern Rome*, 1757 (see fig. 27)

Thanks to the support and encouragement of his influential friends in Pennsylvania, West arrived in Rome on 10 July 1760, one of the first Americans – and certainly the first American artist – to make the Grand Tour. By the time of West's arrival in Italy, the Grand Tour had become a well-established formula with an itinerary codified by a number of guidebooks and conducted by professional and semi-professional ciceroni, or bear leaders as they were colloquially known. For the children of Britain's nobility and greater gentry, such trips to Italy were an indispensable part of the training to assume their social and political responsibilities at home, a fashion accelerated by Britain's growing empire, which invited comparisons to its ancient Roman prototype.[1] As the author of *Letters to a Young Nobleman* (1762) advised his readers: 'A man of fortune and rank cannot possibly be an idle spectator of human affairs; one way or other he must do good or harm.'[2] By studying the works of Livy, Sallust and Tacitus, the rising generations of the ruling class would learn to emulate the Romans, who 'by bravery, by temperance, by a warm love of their country, of liberty and of truth, attained to greatness and empire'.[3] Rome also gave an opportunity for 'viewing fine pieces, and of having one's fancy often warmly struck with the charming productions of sculpture and painting, which is not to be met with in Protestant countries, and consequently must afford young people many occasions of feeling the power of their genius, and of discovering their taste for the imitative arts'.[4]

For such ambitious young artists as West, time spent in Italy added mightily to their professional skills and credentials. Nearly thirty years later, the mature West advised the young artist Johann Heinrich Ramberg:

> That City being the great repository of both painting and sculpture has ever been the favourite place where men of eminence in those professions have resortes to, and have of course united to the protection which have been given by her Popes and Princes to men of Genius, brought within her walls, such a prodigious number of celebrated

pictures and statues, that no other city in the universe, containd anything equal to her, in number, and I may say in excellence …[5]

In Rome, a young artist could study the greatest works of antiquity and the Renaissance and, just as importantly, meet future patrons and visit the studios of modish practitioners. Here indeed were what West called 'the sources of true taste'[6] as well as the practical elements of professional success. For so many reasons, West's career and that of the other young artists who descended on Rome 'was as dependent on making it in Rome as the careers of his successors today are dependent on making it in New York or London'.[7]

West entered the city through the sixteenth-century Porta del Popolo (formerly the Porta Flaminia), so his introduction to Rome was the expanse of the Piazza del Popolo. In West's day the piazza was not yet the elegant oval designed by Joseph Valadier, but with its twin churches and Egyptian obelisk, it presented West with a vision far grander than anything he would have seen either in America or thus far in Italy, having spent some months at Leghorn (Livorno) recovering from the rigours of the transatlantic voyage. The Rome of Pope Clement XIII was a complex mix of grandeur and dilapidation, luxury and neglect. Cows and ragged peasants famously roamed the Forum, flocks of goats blocked aristocratic carriages on urban streets, and an air of abandonment hung over large parts of what once had been *Caput Mundi*. But in every sense the sheer scale of Rome would have overwhelmed the young artist. With a population of about 120,000 at the time of West's arrival, Rome was far bigger than Philadelphia; far bigger indeed than even Philadelphia, New York and Boston put together. The multitude of churches and palaces, monuments and ruins, cafes and markets were woven together in a complex urban fabric that made even the largest American cities look mean and unsophisticated.

West was exhilarated and overwhelmed. As he wrote:

That sudden a climax from the cities of America, where he saw no productions in painting, but a few English Poets, and what his own pencil produced, to the City of Rome the seat of arts and taste, had so forceable an impression on his feeling, that he was under the necessity of leaving Rome in a few weeks, by the advice of his Physician and friends, or it would have put a period to his life …[8]

Driven away by sensory overload or perhaps merely by the discomfort and danger of a Roman August, West returned to Leghorn for a brief stay before renewing his assault on Rome. West's was an extreme but not uncommon reaction to 'this galaxy of rarities which dazzles, diverts, confounds and nearly fatigues one'.[9] Such reactions and such extravagant praise of Rome's wonders serve to remind us of the extraordinary prestige and status that Rome had in eighteenth-century minds – a prestige and status perhaps best summed up by Joseph Baretti's description of this 'famous metropolis which it is scarce possible to pass a whole day in any polite part of Europe without hearing mentioned'.[10] Or as Joseph Wilcocks put it, 'from our earliest childhood, we have all been daily hearing or reading something relative to ancient Rome'.[11]

In spite of the cattle grazing amid the ruins of the Forum, Rome was no backward-looking cow town. 'For the British,' as David R. Marshall and Karin Wolfe point out, 'Rome was the present as well as the past, the slippage between them being continuous … the British visitor in the eighteenth century would have been just as interested in the presentness of Rome as in its past'.[12] That 'presentness' existed not only because Rome was a magnet for a pan-European cultural and intellectual elite, but also because the fabric of the city continued to be the subject of bold and progressive urban interventions. Clement XIII, who had been elevated to the throne of St Peter in 1758, two years before West arrived, was not a great builder pope, but even so, the vitality of modern Rome was apparent during his reign. The recent construction of the Spanish Steps had transformed the area around the Piazza di Spagna, where most Grand Tourists congregated, and Clement's inauguration of the Trevi Fountain in 1762 added another contemporary monument to rival the ancients' legacy. The architectural and urban vigour of modern Rome is best represented by the pair of large-scale capricci, *Ancient Rome* (fig. 26) and *Modern Rome* (fig. 27), painted by Giovanni Paolo Panini for the comte de Stainville (later the duc de Choiseul), the departing French ambassador to the Holy See. In these pictures, Stainville, an assiduous collector as well as a diplomat, is dwarfed by a huge gallery of architectural and artistic wonders conveying the clear message that modern Rome is the worthy successor to the capital of the Caesars. It is this constant juxtaposition or 'slippage' between the ancient and modern that helped Rome to maintain its tight grip on eighteenth-century imaginations. Even Goethe, the most subtle and penetrating of Grand Tourists, was both bewildered and exhilarated by 'an entity which has suffered so many drastic changes in the course of two thousand years, yet is still the same soil, the same hill, often even the same column or the same wall'. This constant rubbing up against the past made the observer 'a contemporary of the great decrees of destiny, and this makes it difficult for him to follow the evolution of the city, to grasp not only how Modern Rome follows on Ancient, but also how, within both, one epoch follows upon another'.[13]

If Philadelphia was a geographically liminal city poised between civilization and the wilderness, Rome was a chronologically liminal one on the threshold between past and present. The city itself, and not just Panini's depiction of it, epitomized the Quarrel between the Ancients and the Moderns, a bitter, if sometimes slightly absurd, intellectual war that raged across Europe for half a century before fading away thanks to exhaustion and irresolution. But although there was no clear winner in the contest between those who thought the ancients could be surpassed and those who believed they could not, the struggle, with its contest to weigh the relative merits of the past and the present, coloured European artistic and intellectual life throughout the eighteenth century.

The complex physicality of the city's past meant that in Rome 'one reads [history] quite differently here from anywhere else in the world. Everywhere else one starts from the outside and works inward; here it seems to be the other way around. All history is encamped about us and all history sets forth again from us. This does not apply only to Roman history, but to the history of the whole world.'[14] This sense of being inside history, which Goethe so well identified, had profound implications for West as a history painter. Although West was never able to articulate so distinctly how Italy had affected him, for almost all those who visited, Rome was a life-changing experience. 'No one who has not been here can have any conception of what an education Rome is', Goethe wrote. 'One is, so to speak, reborn and one's former ideas seem like a child's swaddling clothes. Here the most ordinary person becomes somebody, for his mind is enormously enlarged even if his character remains unchanged.'[15]

The depth and complexity of that Roman past would have electrified West and entirely changed his outlook. James Northcote's critique of American literature may be applied to the visual arts as well. 'The fault of American literature', he remarked, 'was that it ran too much into dry, minute, literal description; or if it made an effort to rise above this ground of matter-of-fact, it was forced and exaggerated … [Americans] had no natural imagination. This was likely to be the case in a new country like America, where there were no dim traces of the past – no venerable monuments – no romantic association; where all (except the physical) remained to be created'.[16] In Rome, West's imaginative deficit would be more than filled.

Sprawling Rome was also intimate: 'Each little circle, though they all sit at the feet of the Queen of the world, now and then displays the spirit of a small provincial town.'[17] There may have been fifty or sixty English visitors at any one time on the

26
Giovanni Paolo Panini
(1691–1765)
Ancient Rome
1757
Oil on canvas
172.1 × 229.9 cm
(67¾ × 90½ in.)
THE METROPOLITAN MUSEUM OF ART, NEW YORK

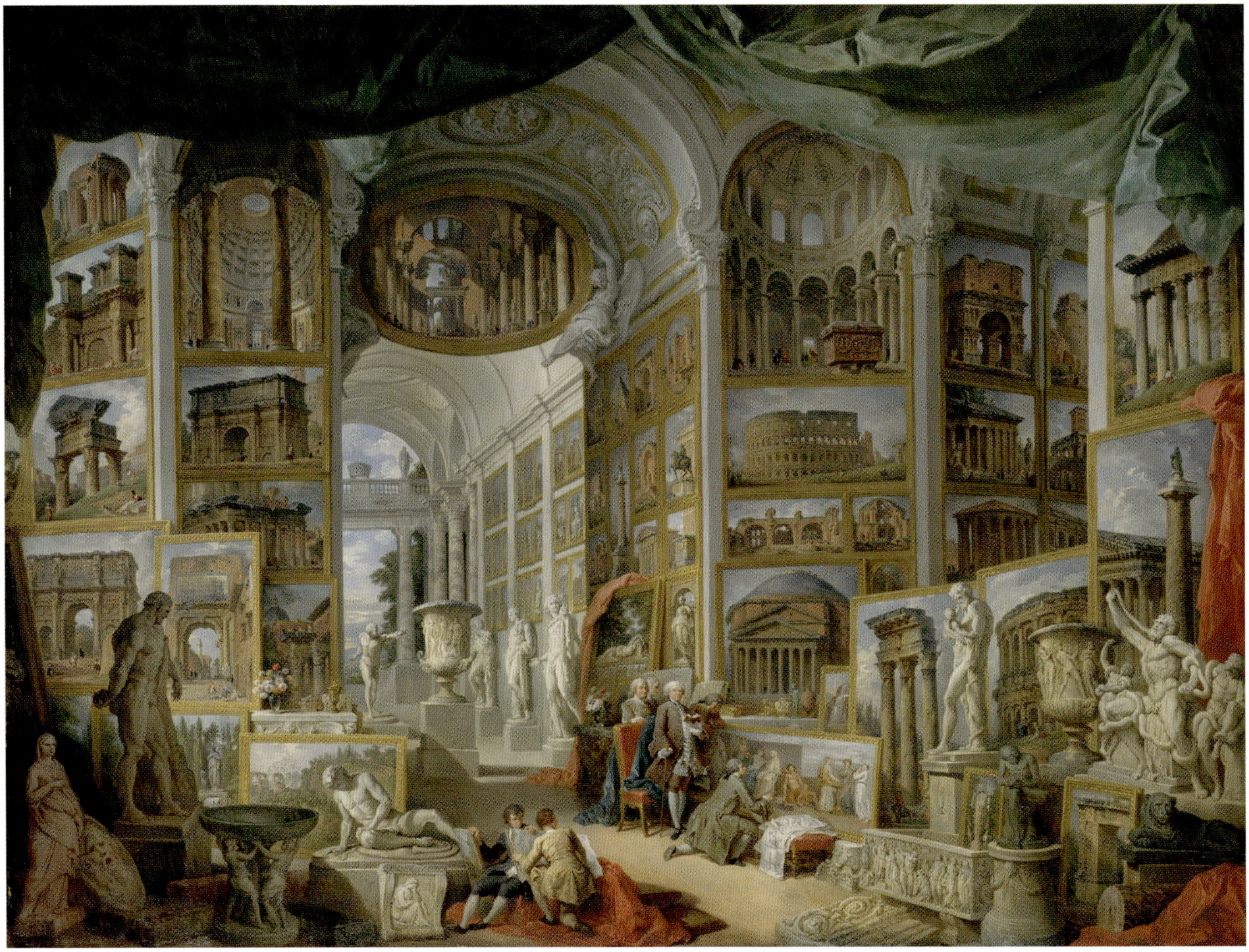

27
Giovanni Paolo Panini
(1691–1765)
Modern Rome
1757
Oil on canvas
172.1 × 233 cm
(67¾ × 91¾ in.)
THE METROPOLITAN MUSEUM OF ART,
NEW YORK

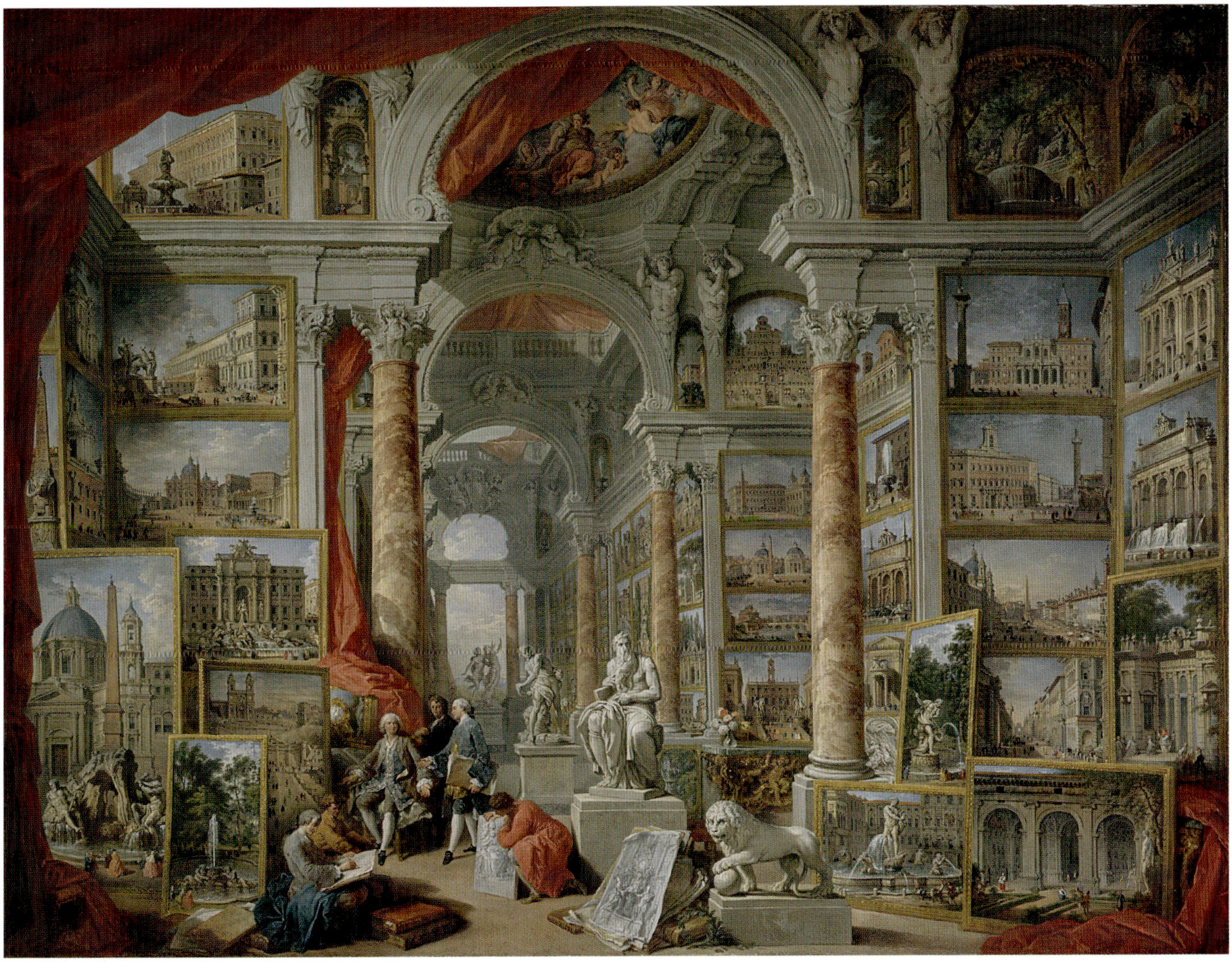

Grand Tour, as well as the resident ciceroni, artists and dealers, and they almost inevitably lodged in the neighbourhood around the Piazza di Spagna, and drank, read newspapers and gossiped in the Caffè degli Inglesi on the corner of the piazza and Via delle Carrozza.[18] As Nathaniel Dance wrote home: 'I am now in such a situation in Rome that I cannot fail of making acquaintance with some of the greatest people in England.'[19] Certainly, artists and patrons mixed more freely in Italy than they would have done at home, but it would be misleading to suggest that all barriers of class and status were broken down in the intimacy of the British colony in Rome. As Wilcocks noted, 'The English at Rome may be generally considered as consisting of two distinct classes, (each of which is frequently assistant to the other) the gentlemen travellers, and the resident artists.'[20] The author of *Letters from a Young Painter* was keenly aware of the gulf that still existed between the artists and the always richer and often aristocratic Grand Tourists, writing that 'on holydays, and at other times, when a recess from my business will permit, I take every opportunity of accompanying gentlemen to see the palaces, etc. for as those grand doors flie open only to the rich, I am glad to follow in their shadow, and to crowd in as one of their attendants'.[21]

'Frequently assistant to the other', as Wilcocks described it, meant that Grand Tourists and artists were interdependent. The Grand Tourists relied on the artists for guidance in the matter of taste, the purchase of archaeological souvenirs and validation of their Grand Tourist status, usually in the form of portraits to bring home. The artists frequently relied on the Grand Tourists for employment in Rome and for future commissions on their return to Britain.

Almost from the moment of his arrival in Italy, West was drawn into the highest artistic and social circles: Cardinal Alessandro Albani, Sir Horace Mann, Pompeo Batoni, Anton Raphael Mengs and Thomas Robinson were all his patrons, friends, promoters or teachers. Just as he had done in Pennsylvania, West demonstrated a clear knack for meeting the right people at the right time. In contrast, Reynolds had had a more difficult time in Rome ten years earlier. Less eager to please by nature than West, Reynolds brought a critical eye to the Grand Tourists and their activities. 'Reynolds painted several caricatures of English gentlemen at their own request,' Joseph Farington wrote, 'in which unworthy employment, however, he was not long occupied, for having made them like, but ridiculous, they did not relish the degradation, and therefore suspended their commissions.'[22] Reynolds's bitter experience still rankled a decade later when he advised James Barry, then in Rome, 'Were I in your place, I would consider myself playing a great game, and never suffer the little malice and envy of my rivals to draw off my attention to the main object, which, if you pursue with a steady eye, it will not be in the power of all the Cicerones of the world to hurt you.'[23] Unlike Reynolds and Barry, when in Rome, West knew how to play the 'great game'. Who knows whether this was a matter of calculation, natural charm or the inevitable consequence of a handsome young man of talent arriving from a far-flung place. Perhaps it was all three.

Soon after meeting West, Cardinal Albani's friends 'became curious to witness the effect which the works of Art in the Belvedere and the Vatican would produce on him'. In the consequent, rather anthropological experiment, 'the principal Roman nobility, and strangers of distinction' took West to view the *Apollo Belvedere* (fig. 28). No incident from West's Italian sojourn better illustrates his mixture of the ingenuous and the calculating than the events supposedly surrounding this visit. For Neoclassicists, the *Apollo Belvedere* was at the summit of artistic achievement. Johann Joachim Winckelmann proclaimed it 'the highest ideal of art amongst all the works of antiquity that have escaped its destruction'.[24] 'My God,' West exclaimed on his first view of *Apollo*, 'how like it is to a young Mohawk warrior.' After their shock and amusement at West's statement, Albani's friends listened attentively to his lengthier explanation and, of course as West recounted, concluded that 'a better criticism had rarely been pronounced on the merits of the statue'. As he would be in his argument with Reynolds over the way to paint *Wolfe*, West was first bold and then conciliatory: he knew how to grab his listeners' attention and then how to beguile them. He was also not averse to using his 'frontier' credentials. 'How like … a young Mohawk warrior' was clearly a manipulative remark. Having grown up among the more peaceful Lenape or Delaware Indians, West most probably had never seen a Mohawk warrior.[25] But he knew that Mohawks were well known to Europeans and did not hesitate to use that fact when faced with the choice between honesty and effect. 'How like … a young Mohawk warrior' was a perceptive remark too, drawing an analogy between the honesty, simplicity and strength of the ancient Greeks and that of the North American Indians.

The ease with which West connected to the important in Italy is also a testament to the web of transatlantic relationships of which his Philadelphia patrons were part. His voyage to Italy had been made possible because his intellectual mentor, William Smith, had commended him to the attention of William Allen, landowner, merchant, long-serving Chief Justice of Pennsylvania and, along with Franklin, a founder of the College of Philadelphia, where Smith was Provost. The Seven Years War had disrupted trade throughout the Mediterranean, and Allen saw an opportunity in 1759 to engage in a risky but potentially highly profitable venture to ship a cargo of £1000 worth of West Indian sugar to Leghorn. Allen's eldest son, John, and his friend Joseph Shippen would accompany the cargo and then tour Italy for their further education. They would be accompanied by 'Mr. West, a young, ingenious painter of this City, who is desirous to improve himself in that Science, by visiting Florence & Rome'.[26] Allen himself had important friends and business partners in Italy. He had read law at Clare Hall, Cambridge, where a fellow student was Horace Mann, who later became the British representative at Florence and a key provider of hospitality, advice and contacts to British visitors to Italy.

Shortly after arriving in Rome, perhaps even on his first evening there, West met Thomas Robinson, a rich and influential Grand Tourist of his own age, and the heir to the fortune, estates and political influence of his father, Sir Thomas Robinson, soon to be created the 1st Baron Grantham. Nathaniel Dance has left us a vivid portrait of Robinson and companions. In *James Grant of Grant, John Mytton, the Hon. Thomas Robinson, and Thomas Wynne* (fig. 29), painted just a few months before West's arrival, four opulently dressed young men and their dogs strike a relaxed pose before a concocted woodland scene featuring the ruined Colosseum as a backdrop and with a massive ancient urn decorated with the *Borghese Dancers* providing a convenient and, at the same time, instructional object against which to lean. Robinson, seated, has been studying a plan of the Temple of Jupiter Stator to show, in spite of the somewhat louche glance he exchanges with Thomas Wynne, that a young gentleman's classical education was a serious affair.

While drink, debauchery and gaming were among the Grand Tourists' activities, it is indeed likely that Robinson and his friends were more restrained than many others, as they were under the guidance of the strait-laced Joseph Wilcocks, antiquarian son of the recently deceased Dean of Westminster. West later recalled that his falling in with Robinson and Wilcocks gave him 'the felicity to visit all that was great in modern elegant art, or worthy of observation in antiquity'.[27] 'The Roman History', Wilcocks wrote, 'is in all places of education the general study of all young men. In reviewing it with his friends here, he [Robinson] earnestly wished that he could in the least degree and in the humblest manner be assistant to them in adapting and directing that study to the best and wisest purposes of a Christian education.'[28] As described by Wilcocks, Robinson was the model of the hard-working, high-minded Grand Tourist, and West became his most constant companion.

28
Apollo Belvedere
c. AD 120–140
Marble
Height 224 cm (88⅛ in.)
VATICAN MUSEUMS, ROME

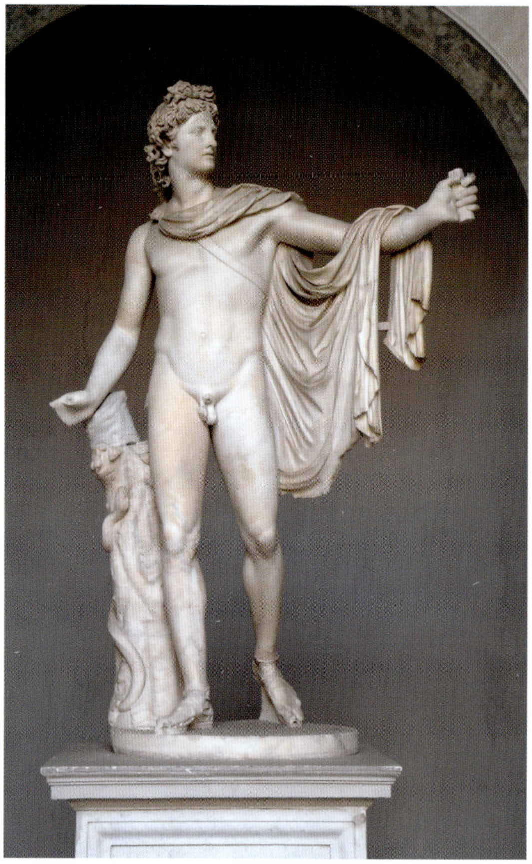

Wilcocks recalled how Robinson 'received great assistance and instruction in his beloved studies from some of these artists. By one of them in particular [West] he was attended almost every afternoon, in examining the sculptures and paintings in the Roman palaces and villas.'[29]

While the quiet contemplation of ancient ruins and the scholarly exegesis of classical texts are a *beau idéal* of the Grand Tour, the atmosphere of the Eternal City was heady, if not fervid. Energetic excavations – as Samuel Powel noted in wonder, '250 years ago there were only Six Antique Statues in Rome, whereas they are now said to be as numerous as the Inhabitants'[30] – fuelled a frenzy of not just digging and dealing, but also copying and collecting. Intoxicated by so much antiquarian and artistic activity, possessed of sometimes large fortunes and most importantly far from home, the Grand Tourists may very well, as Brendan Cassidy suggests, have created a bubble – a bubble in which the commodity being so enthusiastically promoted was Neoclassicism: 'Their enthusiasm for the antique which had found nourishment abroad, was not shared by their families, nor the British public in general. For some the tastes they had developed in Italy did not survive the journey home, or, as Charles Townley put it "our young travellers … generally think little of the virtu after they have passed Dover".'[31]

However, Neoclassicism was more than a passing fancy and not exactly like the cask of Orvieto, which lost most of its freshness and charm by the time it reached British shores. The new movement had a long pedigree of artistic and intellectual substance, and, like an archaeological stratum, rested on older layers of earlier Neo-classicisms, such as Alberti's Renaissance classicism and Poussin's *grand siècle* classicism.

When West arrived in Rome, Mengs and Winckelmann stood at the forefront of Neo-

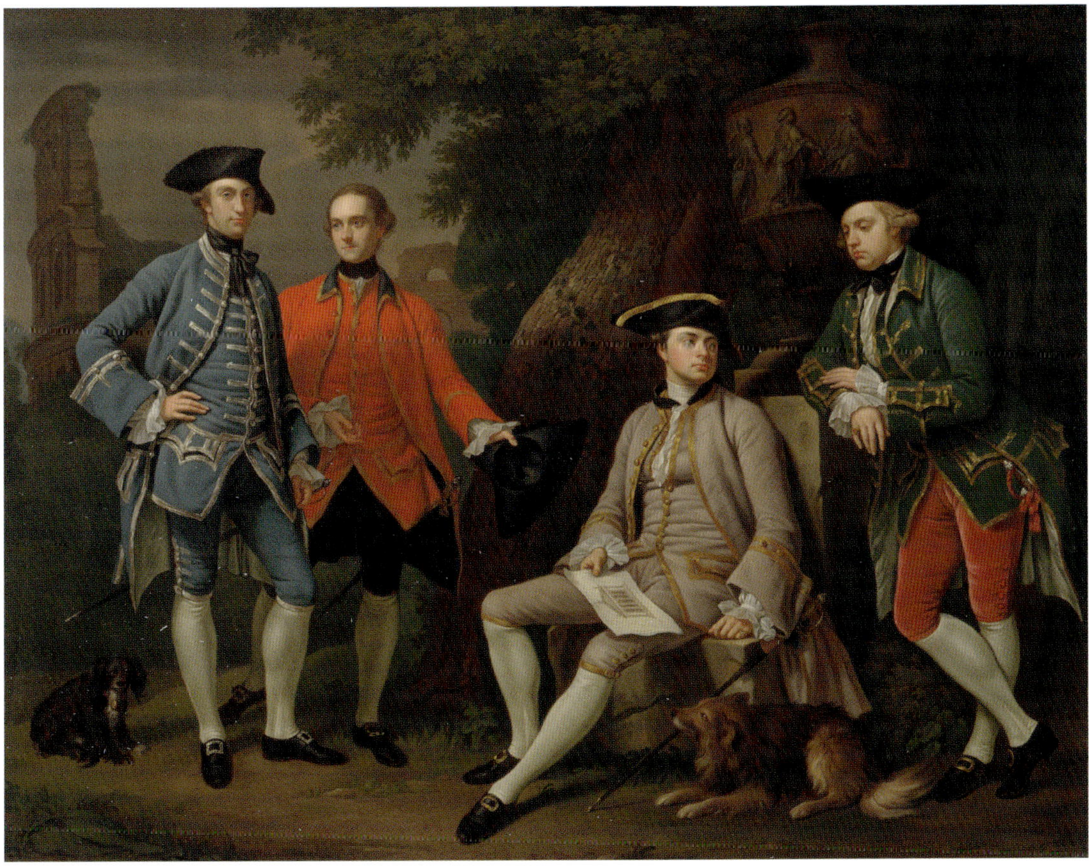

29
Nathaniel Dance (1735–1811)
James Grant of Grant, John Mytton, the Hon. Thomas Robinson, and Thomas Wynne
c. 1760
Oil on canvas
98.1 × 123.8 cm
(38⅝ × 48¾ in.)
PAUL MELLON COLLECTION, YALE CENTER FOR BRITISH ART, NEW HAVEN, CONNECTICUT

classicism as leading practitioner and arch-theorist respectively.[32] Batoni may well have been busier as a painter, but Mengs – thanks in particular to his intimate association with Albani – was on the cutting edge and as such must have dazzled West, to whom he was introduced by either Albani himself or Robinson. Almost certainly West would have shared, or at least recognized the plausibility of, Winckelmann's boast that Mengs, 'the German Raphael in Rome itself', was 'the greatest painter of his time and perhaps of the following age as well'.[33]

Winckelmann was on an upward curve in 1760. The once humble court librarian from Saxony had emerged as the chief theorist of the new movement. His *Essay on Imitation*, published in 1755, had been much discussed, and in 1760 he was nearing the end of writing his *History of the Art of Antiquity*, which established his international reputation. He and Mengs collaborated so closely that it is difficult to tell where the thoughts of one end and those of the other begin. Certainly Winckelmann was the first to condense the qualities of what he found in Greek art as 'a noble simplicity, and a still grandeur',[34] and to promote those as the values that should inform the Neoclassical. Looking at the whole range of works that shelter under that large umbrella, we might join Robert Rosenblum in wondering 'whether Neoclassicism may properly be termed a style at all or whether it should not be termed, to use Giedion's phrase, a "coloration"'. A 'coloration' is perhaps rather too subtle. While recognizing the existence of many sub-genres – Rosenblum, for example, points out the 'Neoclassic Erotic', the 'Neoclassic Horrific', the 'Neoclassic Archaeologic'[35] – such amusing salami-slicing may belittle the vitality of this movement. Neoclassicism was possibly as much a mood and a feeling as a style, but what makes it different from previous classical revivals is its programme, conscious or otherwise, as the visual wing of the Enlightenment.

Winckelmann described how he felt when he stood before the *Apollo Belvedere*: 'In gazing upon this masterpiece of art, I forget all else, and I myself adopt an elevated stance, in order to be worthy of gazing upon it.'[36] In other words, the perfect forms of antiquity could provide the viewer with an experience that was both transcendent and transformational. And it is this latter quality – that the work of art is able to elevate and improve the individual – that fits in so neatly with Enlightenment ideas of progress and perfectibility. Although Winckelmann was no revolutionary, nor were the circles in which he moved especially Enlightened, he recognized the ideological underpinnings of Neoclassicism. Describing what he characterized as the high style of ancient Greek art, Winckelmann wrote, 'at the time when full enlightenment and freedom appeared in Greece, art likewise became freer and more elevated'.[37] This belief that art can reach its highest potential only within the context of enlightened and free societies was essential to the powerful appeal of the Neoclassical. François Hartog has observed how the eighteenth-century Neoclassicists politicized their approach to the ancients. Unlike the Poussin generation, who looked to the ancient world for 'examples of morality, models of heroism and good taste', the eighteenth-century classicists 'prioritized the political dimension, looking for political models'.[38]

Perhaps Hartog has a slight, maybe even more than a slight, tendency to view the Neoclassicism of the 1760s through the lens of David's proto-revolutionary Neoclassicism of the 1780s; but his observation reminds us that, Janus-like, Neoclassicism turned backwards in order to move forwards and that, while it may have looked conservative, it was in fact progressive. Coming at the end of the Quarrel between the Ancients and the Moderns, Neoclassicism tried to harness the past in the service of the present, and largely met with success.

West could never be described as a political animal. Other than a long-term commitment to the maintenance of a Protestant political monarchy, he made few explicit political statements and was even remarkably silent on the subject of the American Revolution, certainly the political event that most directly affected him and his family.[39] Nor was he a theorist. His few theoretical writings lack the fluency and penetration of Reynolds or Fuseli. There is little to indicate that he followed Winckelmann's arguments in detail, and as James Larson has commented, 'Winckelmann, again like many aesthetic theorists of the period, rarely followed a consistent line of reasoning.'[40] In spite of his discursive and sometimes disconnected writing, Winckelmann had the ability to produce such terse and memorable slogans as 'a noble simplicity, and a still grandeur', which Ellis Waterhouse described as 'the golden phrase',[41] to which may be added Winckelmann's dictum that 'The one way for us to become great, and perhaps inimitable, is by imitating the ancients.'[42]

West would have easily grasped and enthusiastically subscribed to Winckelmann's headline thoughts on the primacy of ancient models, the moral and spiritual value of art and the need for the artist to transmute nature into something superior. None of these thoughts is indeed particularly original. Winckelmann himself acknowledges this by quoting Raphael's remark that 'Beauty being so seldom found among the fair, I avail myself of a certain ideal image'[43] – an observation that seems to have given birth to Winckelmann's statement that 'It is not only nature which the votaries of the Greeks find in their works, but still more, something superior to nature; ideal beauties'.[44] So the great works of antiquity represent an 'ideal image', or 'ideal beauties', which the artist must study and then use to inform his own work.

Winckelmann was familiar with, though not impressed by, Jonathan Richardson's *Account of the Statues, Bas-reliefs, Drawings and Pictures in Italy, France, &c.* (1754), at that time the most comprehensive and widely read guidebook to Italian art in the English language. 'Richardson has described the palaces and villas of Rome ...', Winckelmann wrote, 'as if they had appeared to him only in a dream. Because of his short stay in Rome, he did not see many palaces at all'. Nonetheless, 'for all its many deficiencies and errors ... his book is the best we have'.[45] But Richardson's *Account* was more than just a guidebook. In it, Richardson wrote that 'every picture, statue or bas-relief, besides what it was intended to exhibit, leaves upon the mind of him that sees it an idea of its self'.[46] This thought, that a work of art has a 'self' that transcends its physicality, is a powerful perception from Richardson, and suggests that artists and indeed all men and women of taste should get to know the 'selves' of great works, which would then remain with them as a gallery of the mind.

Richardson may not have influenced Winckelmann, but Shaftesbury did, and we can find Shaftesburian foundations beneath Winckelmann's thoughts. Writing half a century before Winckelmann, Shaftesbury advised the artist

> to reject those false Ornaments of affected Graces, exaggerated Passions, hyperbolic and prodigious Forms; which equally with the mere capricious and grotesque, destroy the just Simplicity and Unity, essential in a Piece. And for his Colouring; he would then soon find how much it became him to be reserv'd, severe, and chaste ... nothing is more fatal, either to Painting, Architecture or the other Arts, than this false Relish which is govern'd rather by what immediately strikes the Sense, than by what consequentially and by reflection pleases the Mind and satisfies the Thought and Reason.[47]

This appeal to reason rather than the emotions, this call for personal as well as artistic restraint, this praise of simplicity, this seriousness about the moral purpose of art were all messages that West, too, was ready and willing to hear, as the zeal of the autodidact and the gravity of the child of Pennsylvania Quakers combined to create a mind and a man ready for the Neoclassical.

It has often been the case that Neoclassical earnestness is posited as a reaction against the playfulness, froth and licentiousness of the Rococo. Hugh Honour, for example, writes: 'The intellectual reaction against flippancy, cynicism and all the iniquities summed up by *l'infâme* was paralleled in the arts by a rejection of the Rococo',[48] and he goes on to use such terms as the 'revulsion against the Rococo'.[49] Similarly, when discussing the prevalence of Neoclassical deathbed scenes (to which we shall return), Rosenblum describes them as 'anti-Rococo catharsis' and 'an antidote to the hedonistic pursuits of Rococo art'.[50] It could be argued that viewing Neoclassicism in such a dialectical way – serious Neoclassicism as an inevitable reaction against playful Rococo – fails to explain the magnetic appeal of the new movement. Indeed, the suggestion that styles are reactions to or rejections of what came before them, is not particularly illuminating. Looking at Neoclassicism as a reaction against the Rococo is as unhelpful as looking at Gothic as a reaction against Romanesque or the Beatles as a reaction against Frank Sinatra. It also betrays a misunderstanding of the creative personality. Critics may react 'against' things, artists react 'to' things. West was most definitely not seeking an antidote to any aspect of the Rococo: he was seeking, instead, a prescription for a morally purposeful art.

Newly arrived in Rome, ambitious for success, eager to learn and eager to please, West would have been swept up in the excitement of what was quite clearly the next big thing. Decades later, he clearly recalled 'The collision of minds fraught with learning, in that high state of excitement which the genius of the place produced on the coldest imaginations'.[51] West arrived in Rome at exactly the time when all the elements of the Neoclassical were gelling, many of them centred on the still mysterious figure of Albani: prince of the Church, diplomat, dealer, collector, patron and impresario-in-chief of Neoclassicism.[52]

Albani was perhaps the most important contact a young visitor could make in Rome. His

30
Carlo Marchionni (1702–1786)
Villa Albani, Rome
1751–63

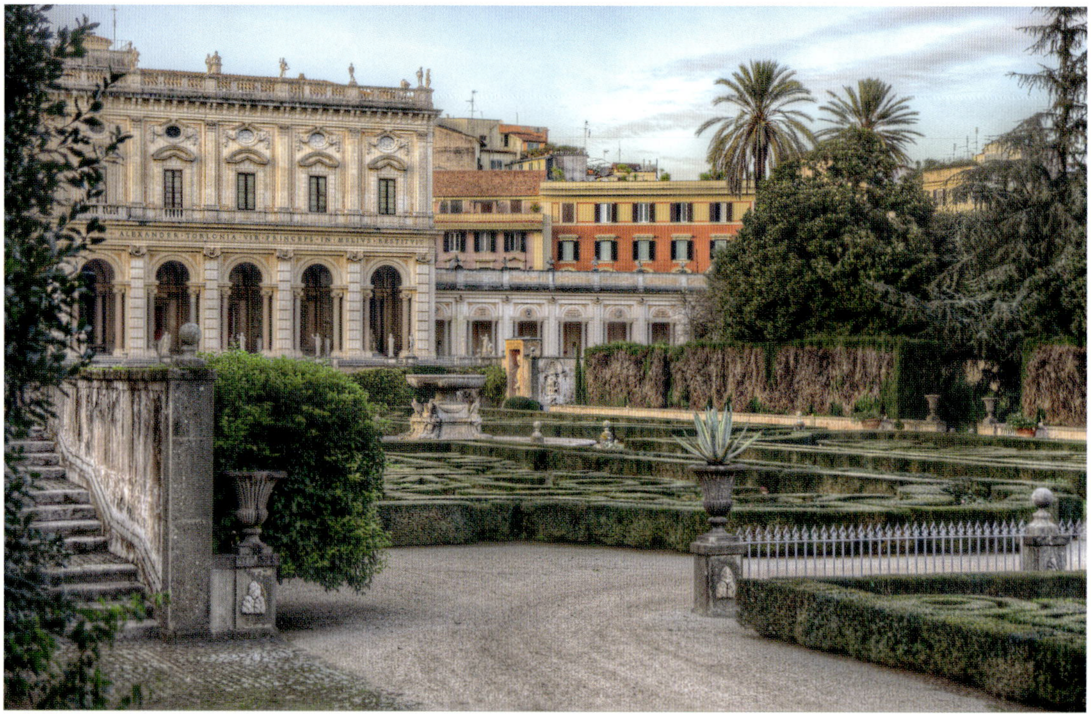

31
Anton Raphael Mengs
(1728–1779)
Parnassus
1761
Fresco
313 × 580 cm
(123¼ × 228⅜ in.)
VILLA ALBANI, ROME

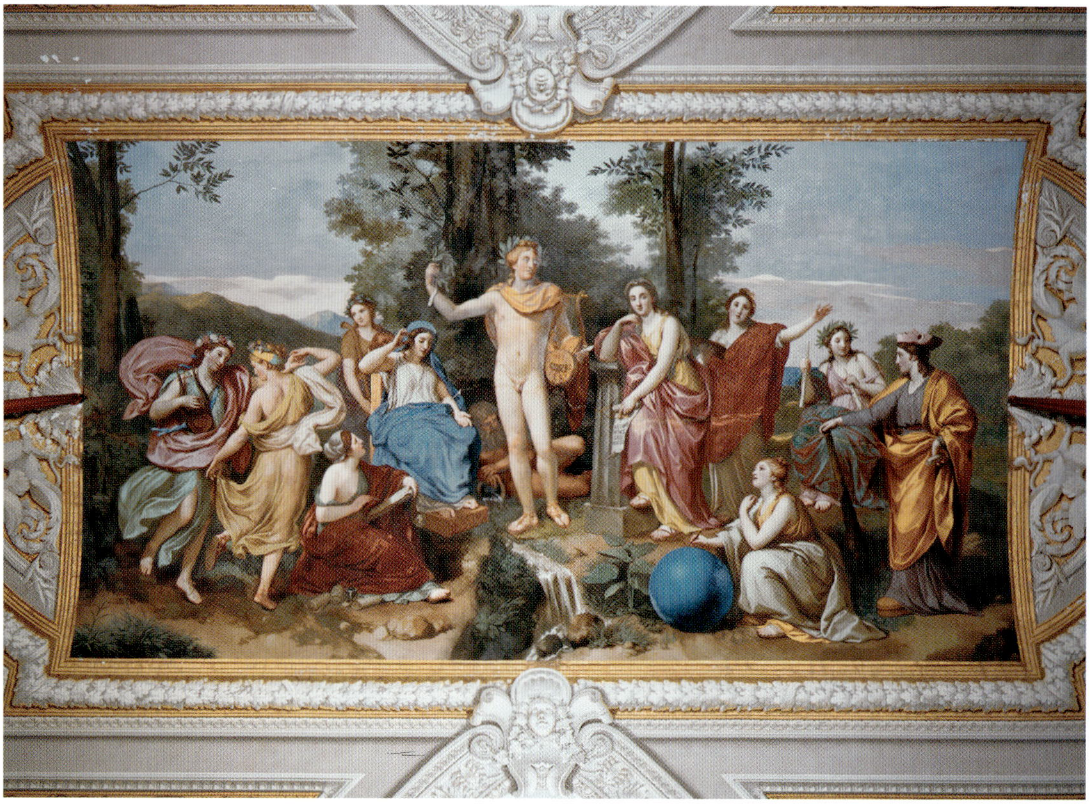

usefulness to the Grand Tourist and perhaps a hint of his possible role as a spy in the service of Britain can be seen in his election as an Honorary Fellow of the Society of Antiquaries of London in May 1761, when it was recorded that Albani, 'from his high rank, distinguished Abilities, & Affection to the British Nation, which has remarkably appeared by his Civilities to British Travellers & Artists at Rome, is certified as likely to prove a most useful & Valuable Member'.[53] With a keen sense of his 'high rank', Albani asked his friend and assistant, Baron Philip von Stosch, to reply to the Antiquaries that 'The Cardinal though you did not give him his title *Eminentissimo Principi* is extremely proud of being a Member of the Academy.'[54]

In the summer of 1760, Albani was much occupied by the building of his great new villa, which was nearing the end of construction. For West, brought up, as he put it, 'amid the sobriety of rural and commercial economy',[55] the Villa Albani (fig. 30) must have been a bemusing wonderland. Far larger than any building West had ever seen in America, it was, more to the point, a building with no overtly practical purpose. Albani's home and court were at the Palazzo Albani, a few miles away and conveniently close to the Quirinal Palace, then the favourite papal residence. Not a place to live in, nor merely a statement of Albani's power and erudition, the Villa Albani was a lavish physical manifesto of the Neoclassical movement, a place of state rooms and arcades, loggias and sunken gardens in which to rest, walk, dine and talk amid the Cardinal's collection of antiquities. Hester Lynch Piozzi described it as 'the most dazzling of any place yet … replete with wonders, and distracting with objects each worthy a whole day's attention'.[56]

We do not know exactly how the great theoretical–practical double act of Neoclassicism, Winckelmann and Mengs, helped to shape the villa, but certainly Mengs's ceiling painting *Parnassus* (fig. 31), on which he was working at the time of West's arrival in Rome, could be described as the villa's rhetorical and intellectual climax.

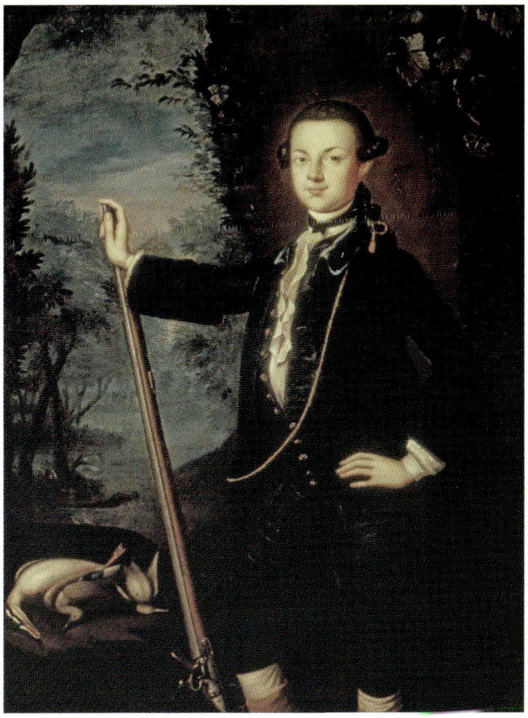

32
Benjamin West
Thomas Mifflin
1758–59
Oil on canvas
131 × 98 cm (51½ × 38½ in.)
HISTORICAL SOCIETY OF PENNSYLVANIA, PHILADELPHIA

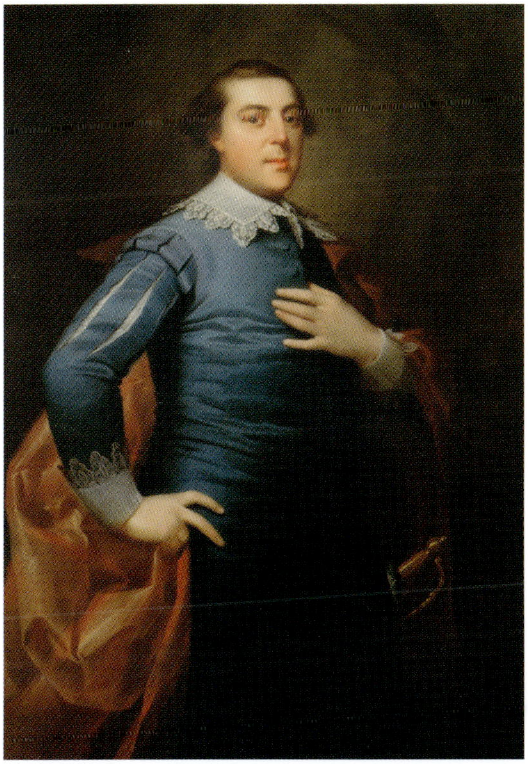

33
Benjamin West
John Allen
1760
Oil on canvas
125 × 99.5 cm
(49⅛ × 39⅛ in.)
PRIVATE COLLECTION

Occupying the central panel of the barrel-vaulted ceiling of the largest and most important room on the villa's *piano nobile*, *Parnassus* portrays Apollo, the god of arts and adorable focus of the Muses' attention, as an obvious analogy to Albani. Aside from celebrating Albani's patronage, *Parnassus* is also an exemplar, perhaps the exemplar, of Neoclassical painting according to the principles largely developed by Mengs and Winckelmann. There is the shallow depth of field, the frieze-like arrangement of figures, the variety of poses derived from classical statuary, the thinly veiled homage to Raphael, the literary and intellectual content, and that most prized Winckelmannian virtue, the sense of calm. Compared to other great Neoclassical works with their solemn didacticism, *Parnassus* has perhaps a suspicious touch of gaiety, with its dancing Muses in the left-hand section. It can even appear a rather silly picture when seen in isolation. It was not, however, intended to be understood as anything other than part of a complex decorative and intellectual scheme that is the *Gesamtkunstwerk* of the Villa Albani.

Amid the wealth of apocrypha surrounding West's stay in Rome, his supposed first encounter with Mengs is worth examining. When West painted a portrait of his new friend Robinson, a 'Mr. Crespigné' displayed the picture to a group of his fellow connoisseurs, who immediately mistook it for a work by Mengs. No, it is not by Mengs, Crespigné announced. Who could have painted such a portrait, his guests asked, 'for there is no other painter now in Rome capable of executing any thing so good?' West was revealed as the artist, the guests congratulated him and acknowledged the new arrival 'as only second in the executive department of the art to the first painter then in Rome'. Shortly afterwards Mengs and West met. 'You have already, sir, the mechanical part of your art', Mengs declared in praise of the young artist.[57]

The question of just how good an artist West was before he left America continues to intrigue, and it is an important one if we want to determine just what Rome did to West. Aside from *Socrates*, the only other attempt at history painting in West's American œuvre may be a large and highly finished drawing in the Morgan Library, *Rebecca at the Well* (fig. 34).[58] While not entirely proficient, it is a relatively complex composition, and displays a more masterful handling of gesture, expression and drapery than anything West had previously attempted. It is clearly inscribed, in what appears to be West's handwriting, *One of the first attempts at historical composition by Benjn West. While in Philadelphia 1757*. It seems to be an impossibly precocious advance over *Socrates*, which had been painted only the year before. Indeed, it is considerably more able than anything West painted or drew before his arrival in Italy. On stylistic grounds it would certainly seem to date from relatively early in West's career, but West may have added the date and inscription sometime later in yet another effort to establish himself as a prodigy with a divinely ordained destiny to be the pre-eminent history painter of his time.[59]

At the time of the Robinson portrait – the summer of 1760 – West was an ambitious and talented but clearly inexperienced artist. His artistic education up to that point consisted of reading Richardson and Du Fresnoy, along with some tuition from two, quite frankly, second-rate itinerant painters, Williams and Wollaston. We can look at the state of West's work as he left America through his portrait of Thomas Mifflin. West's American portraits are formulaic; hardly, if at all, above the norm of contemporary itinerant portraitists in the colonies whose skills West could imitate, even though he could go no further. Their generic facial features, awkward poses and poor handling of space and volume give them a certain primitive charm, and they do contain evidence of raw pictorial talent: von Erffa and Staley declare that *Thomas Mifflin* (fig. 32) is the best of the American portraits,[60] but it is in no way outstanding.

West's portrait of Thomas Robinson, which supposedly so impressed the Roman connoisseurs, is lost, but we can look at another portrait painted early in West's Italian tour. There is a great deal of difference between the *Thomas Mifflin* of 1758–59 and West's portrait of his travelling companion John Allen, painted in Rome in September or October 1760. *John Allen* (fig. 33) is a significantly more sophisticated portrait than anything West had previously done, and even down to its modish use of Vandyke costume, it is in thoroughly up-to-date style. Composition, colouring, modelling and light are all more confidently and coherently handled, and it has an individuality and vivacity that had previously been missing from West's work. If this leap forward was the result of less than two months in Rome, it is a remarkable testament to West's ability as a quick learner. However, even if the lost *Robinson* was of equal quality, it is beyond reasonable belief that the leading virtuosi would have praised West as second only to Mengs, who was then considered to be in the first rank of European artists. Standards in Rome were neither so low, nor West's largely untrained skills so high.[61]

West worked hard in Rome to address that lack of training, and his Italian sketchbooks evince a sense of wonder at almost everything he came across in Italy.[62] They make a sharp contrast with Reynolds's sketchbooks from a decade earlier, when, as Giovanna Perini observes, Reynolds was 'already certain that he would be a portrait painter. In consequence, most of his sketches were meant as mementoes of costumes and attitudes, both of single figures and of small groups (notably mothers and children), taken from the paintings of various Italian masters whose inventions and compositions he thought might prove capable of future exploitation in portrait painting.'[63]

Less visually and professionally sophisticated than Reynolds at the time of his arrival in Italy, West was perhaps more open to experience everything in what to him was a new world. His sketchbooks are an eclectic mix of decorative details (fig. 35), classical friezes, studies of urns and vases, drapery and armour, and some highly worked-up drawings after, for example, Sebastiano Conca's *Saint Cecilia Playing the Harp* (fig. 36), or a composition based on Giovanni Lanfranco's *Triumph of Galatea*, as well as sketches of details from Raphael's *Disputa*. There are also numerous studies ranging from the sketchiest renditions to more carefully rendered observations of some of the canonical works of classical sculpture then on view in Rome: the *Apollo Belvedere*, *Farnese Hercules* (fig. 38) and *Hermes Longhios* among others. In spite of Mengs's alleged remark that West had already mastered 'the mechanical part' of art, the sketchbooks provide evidence – in the form of carefully rendered drawings of limbs and torsos – that West must have been attending classes in life drawing, an activity for which Rome was renowned and which was definitely not available in the American colonies.

The sketchbooks also tell us a certain amount about West the man as well as West the artist. Compared to other surviving eighteenth-century artists' sketchbooks, they are remarkably small and are obviously cheap. Perhaps they are a testimony to the limited allowance that West was being paid by his Pennsylvania patrons. More likely they show the artist's frugality, one of the cardinal virtues promulgated to colonial Americans by Benjamin Franklin through his best-selling *Poor Richard's Almanac*. When Franklin advised 'A small leak will sink a great ship' or 'Buy what thou hast no need of, and e're long thou shalt sell thy necessaries', West and thousands of his fellow colonials behaved accordingly.[64] Certainly West wasted nothing. It appears that he frequently returned to the sketchbooks after he left Italy, not just to refresh his memory, but also to fill in the blank pages. There is, for example, a detail of Raphael's *St Paul Preaching at Athens* (fig. 37), which from the right-facing attitude of the saint shows that it was copied from the cartoons on display in London, visited by West in 1763, rather than from the tapestries he would have seen on his many trips to the Vatican. The sketchbooks also contain studies for much later paintings, such as *The Departure of Regulus from Rome* (fig. 39), which was not commissioned from West until 1768.

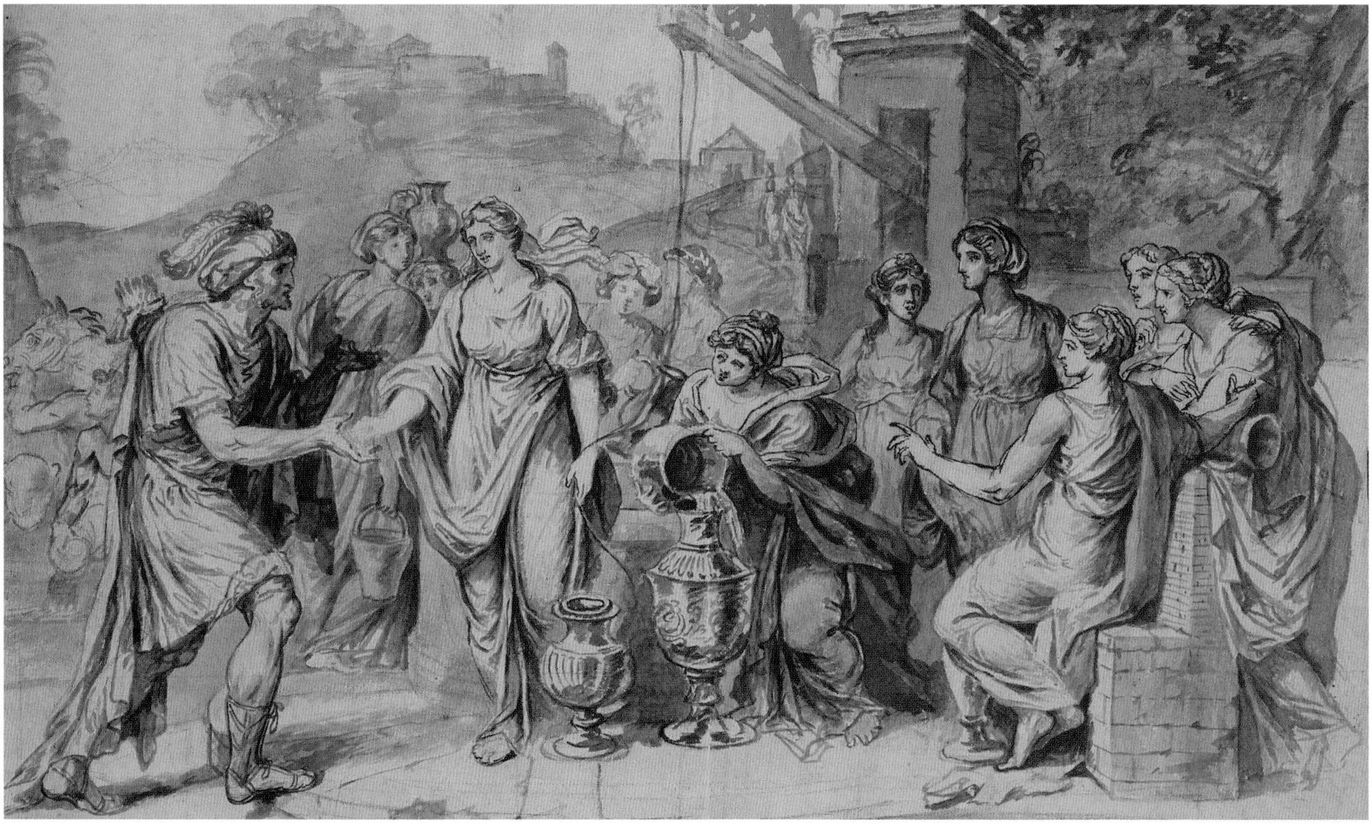

34 ABOVE
Benjamin West
Rebecca at the Well
1757
Brush and black wash over black chalk with pen and ink on paper
33.9 × 52.3 cm (13⅜ × 20⅝ in.)
THE MORGAN LIBRARY AND MUSEUM, NEW YORK

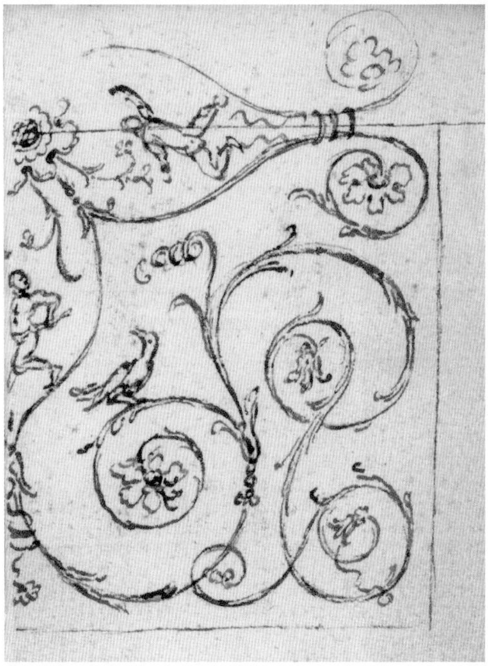

35 RIGHT
Benjamin West
Sketch of foliate design
1760s
Pen and ink on paper
12.2 × 8.3 cm (4¾ × 3¼ in.)
ROYAL ACADEMY OF ARTS, LONDON

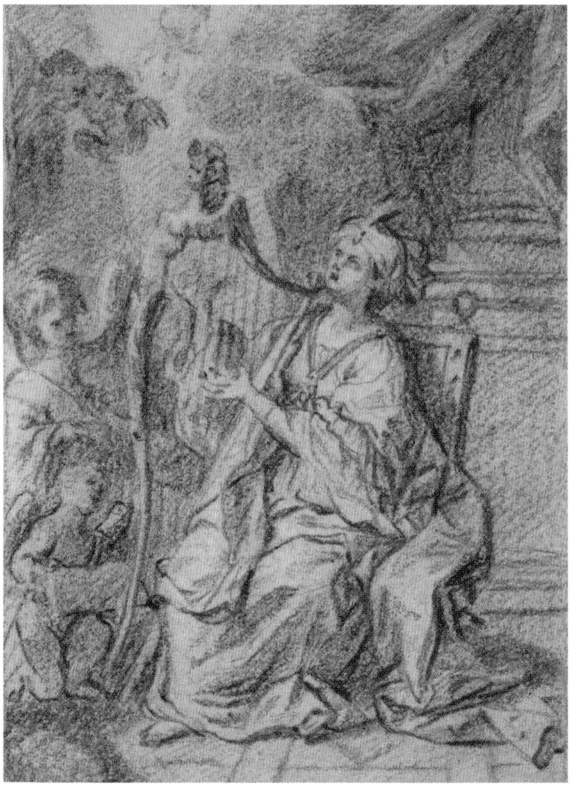

36 FAR RIGHT
Benjamin West, after Sebastiano Conca (1680–1764)
Drawing after a painting of St Celicia
1760s – early 1770s
Pencil on paper
10 × 9.1 cm (4 × 3⅝ in.)
ROYAL ACADEMY OF ARTS, LONDON

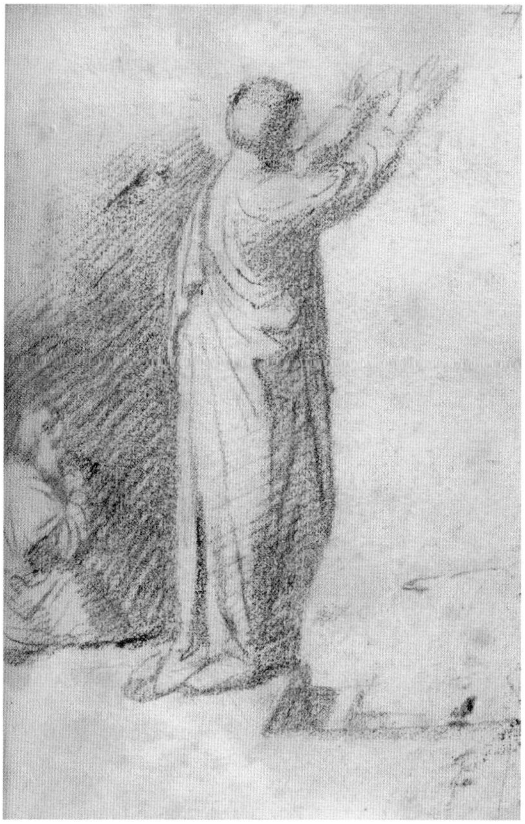

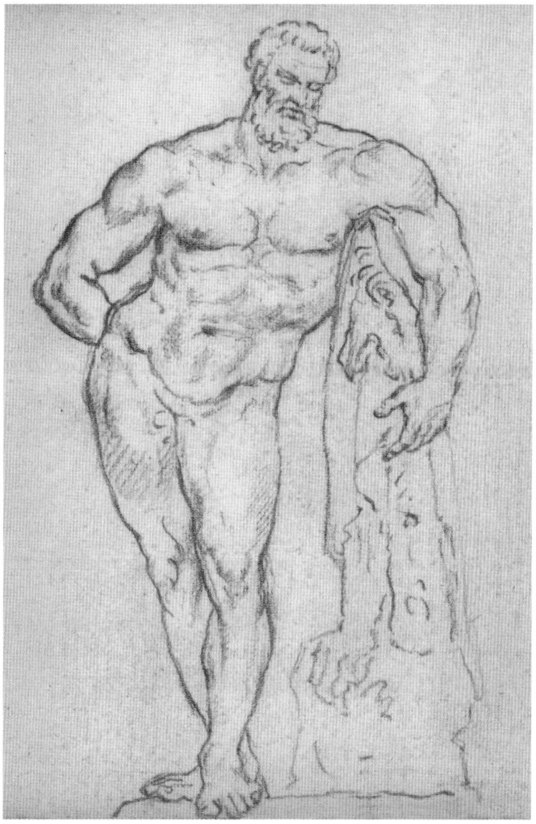

37 FAR LEFT
Benjamin West, after Raphael (1483–1520)
Drawing after Raphael's *St Paul Preaching at Athens*
Probably 1763 or after
Pencil and black chalk on paper
12.3 × 9.1 cm (4⅞ × 3⅝ in.)
ROYAL ACADEMY OF ARTS, LONDON

38 LEFT
Benjamin West
Drawing of the *Farnese Hercules*
1760s
Pencil on paper
12.2 × 8.3 cm (4¾ × 3¼ in.)
ROYAL ACADEMY OF ARTS, LONDON

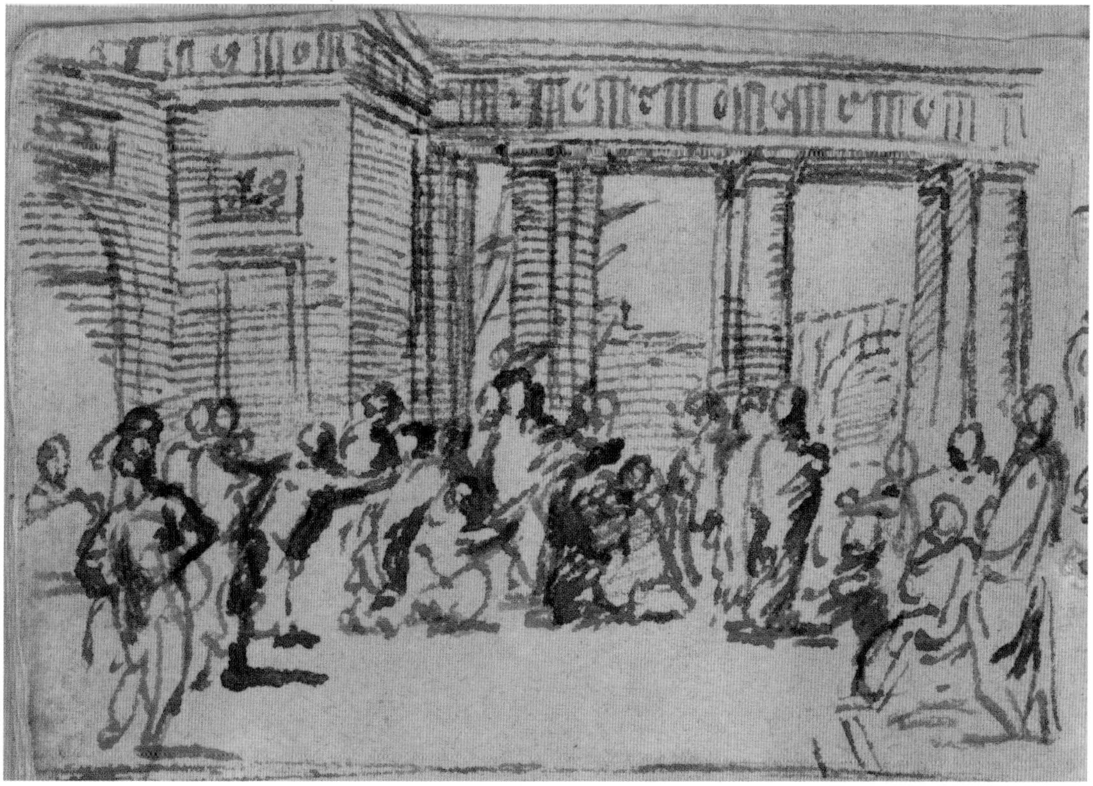

39
Benjamin West
Preparatory sketch for *The Departure of Regulus from Rome*
1760s
Pen and ink on paper
5 × 8.3 cm (2 × 3¼ in.)
ROYAL ACADEMY OF ARTS, LONDON

In Rome, West was transformed from a precocious but modestly talented local portraitist to someone standing near the front rank of international Neoclassicism in the short space of three years. How do we explain the speed of this transformation? Perhaps Neoclassicism provided the artistic direction that West was looking for. It was his way of escaping from the drudgery of portraiture to the higher planes of history painting. West was by background and by education sympathetic to the new ideas, and his artistic practice was sufficiently unformed to enable him to fall in step immediately with the requirements of Neoclassicism. West's lack of finish, his very provincialism, his ability to learn quickly all meant that he was ready to be moulded into a fully fledged *homo neoclassicus*.[65] Ironically West's provincialism may also have helped him to fit into the cosmopolitan artistic scene in Rome: colonial Philadelphia was a polyglot, ethnic stewpot, too.[66]

Intellectually, West was nowhere near Winckelmann, Mengs or the rest of their circle. He had a modest knowledge of the Classics, no Greek or Latin, and a familiarity with Enlightenment language and ideas thanks to William Smith. But he was extraordinarily serious: serious about the high moral purpose of art, and serious about his own destiny. It was a seriousness that had been inspired by his youthful reading of Du Fresnoy's *Art of Painting,* with its emphasis on painterly glory: 'Let not the covetous Design of growing rich, induce you to ruin your Reputation ... let your Thoughts be wholly taken up with acquiring to your self a glorious Name, which can never perish, but with the World; and make that the Recompence of your worthy Labours.'[67] When the serious painter met the earnest movement, it was love at first sight. The visual language of Neoclassicism, with its suppression of the brushstroke, its shallow spaces and planar compositions, played to West's strengths, too: the strengths of an artist brought up on prints.

'Without the example of actual paintings by Titian, Rubens or Van Dyck,' David Rosand notes, 'and knowing European art masters essentially through prints after their work, the colonial artist in America could hardly be expected to understand the ways of the brush.'[68] It is this early education through prints that led West and his fellow American Copley to be frequently criticized for a certain hard linearity in their art. Looking at Copley's portrait of Henry Pelham (fig. 41), Reynolds detected 'a little hardness in the Drawing, Coldness in the Shades, an over minuteness',[69] and Walpole found West 'hard and heavy'.[70]

Another important aspect of West's provincialism is that it allowed him to become Europeanized before he had a chance to be Americanized. In order to explain that, here is the place to say something about what being American meant in the mid-eighteenth century – a time when, as West told Galt, 'the mother country was ... still regarded as the home of her American offspring'.[71] Generations of art historians, beginning with William Dunlap in the nineteenth century, have retrospectively nationalized West in order to strengthen his position as the founding father of American art. Certainly West was American in spite of having left the colonies at the age of twenty-one, never to return. In the mid-eighteenth century, though, being American was not yet a matter of nationality. It is worth remembering that when West was in Rome, George Washington had recently been an officer in the British army and Benjamin Franklin was, in the words of Gordon S. Wood, 'a thoroughgoing imperialist and royalist' who described himself as speaking 'not merely as I am a Colonist, but as I am a Briton'.[72] Franklin's route from imperial subject to patriot to American citizen was a decades-long political process; a process in which neither West nor his fellow American in London, John Singleton Copley, participated.

For the painter-turned-polemicist Allan Ramsay, nationality was purely a matter of political allegiance. Ramsay declared that 'The English nation has hitherto divided the whole human race into two classes only, viz. Foreigners, who are always supposed to be, at bottom, enemies; and Englishmen, who are always supposed to be, at bottom, friends to England',[73] and then went on to describe his American 'brethren' as 'Being descended from an English stock; speaking the English language; holding amongst themselves laws, customs, and religion, somewhat similar to those of England; being in the practice of calling themselves Englishmen'.[74] But they were not, because their 'allegiance to the King of England is of a very weak and ambiguous kind; little more than nominal'.[75]

The case of West, and indeed of Copley, makes it important to distinguish between what we might call 'cultural Americanism' and 'political Americanism'. West certainly had what were commonly identified in his own time as American characteristics. Some of these were the characteristics of the frontier, others were those of the economic, religious and sometimes ideological migrants who settled in the American colonies. These characteristics, together with distance from the metropolis and the reliance on prints to which Rosand has referred, produced the linear, literal look of some early American art. West's time in Italy – especially in Rome – radically transformed his abilities as an artist, but he still retained a certain 'dryness' that would provoke his critics for years to come. Nonetheless, in the cosmopolitan setting of Rome, West became a European artist in style.

It is difficult to tell just how much this Europeanization was due to Mengs, as it is hard to determine just how formal West's relationship with him was. As a young man, West never hesitated to praise Mengs, describing him in a letter of 1763 to one of his patrons, Joseph Shippen, as 'my favorite master'.[76] Steffi Roettgen has written that 'in many respects' West 'can be regarded as Mengs's heir', and goes on to describe their 'artistic interchange' as 'intense'.[77] 'Intense' it must have been, because it was also short-lived. By August 1761, West's second summer in Italy, Rome had become too small for Mengs. Lured by a salary of 7000 scudi a year, lavish travelling expenses, a coach and horses and a grand house, Mengs accepted the post of first painter to King Charles III of Spain, and left for Madrid, never to return.[78]

One can assume that West spent some time in Mengs's studio, as he was quickly able to paint in Mengs's style, producing two accomplished copies of Mengs's work, *A Sibyl* (fig. 40) and *A Holy Family,* in 1761 and 1762 respectively. It is worth noting that among the copies that West produced while in Italy – most, although not all, of which were painted in return for the money that his American patrons had advanced to him – only these two were copies of contemporary works.[79]

Whatever West's exact arrangements with Mengs, he unquestionably followed the older painter's advice

> to see and examine every thing deserving of your attention here [in Rome], and after making a few drawings of about half a dozen of the best statues, go to Florence, and observe what has been done for Art in the collections there. Then proceed to Bologna, and study the works of the Caracci; afterwards visit Parma, and examine, attentively, the pictures of Corregio; and then go to Venice and view the productions of Tintoretti, Titian, and Paul Veronese. When you have made this tour, come back to Rome, and paint an historical composition to be exhibited to the Roman public.[80]

West's residence in Rome during his three-year visit to Italy was punctuated by the need to travel to other cities both to look at works of art and to attend to his often frail health. He was particularly tormented by severe osteomyelitis, which required a series of harrowing, life-threatening operations culminating in that carried out by the Florentine surgeon Angelo Nannoni, whose case notes describe how 'once the cut was made there began a great and prolonged pain in the leg and foot' and how West's wounds were dressed with a caustic mixture of silver nitrate. The Italian surgeon proudly noted that 'Mr. West, triumphant by our surgery … is admired for his great talents as a painter.'[81] After a lengthy convalescence in Florence, West resumed his travels and by the late

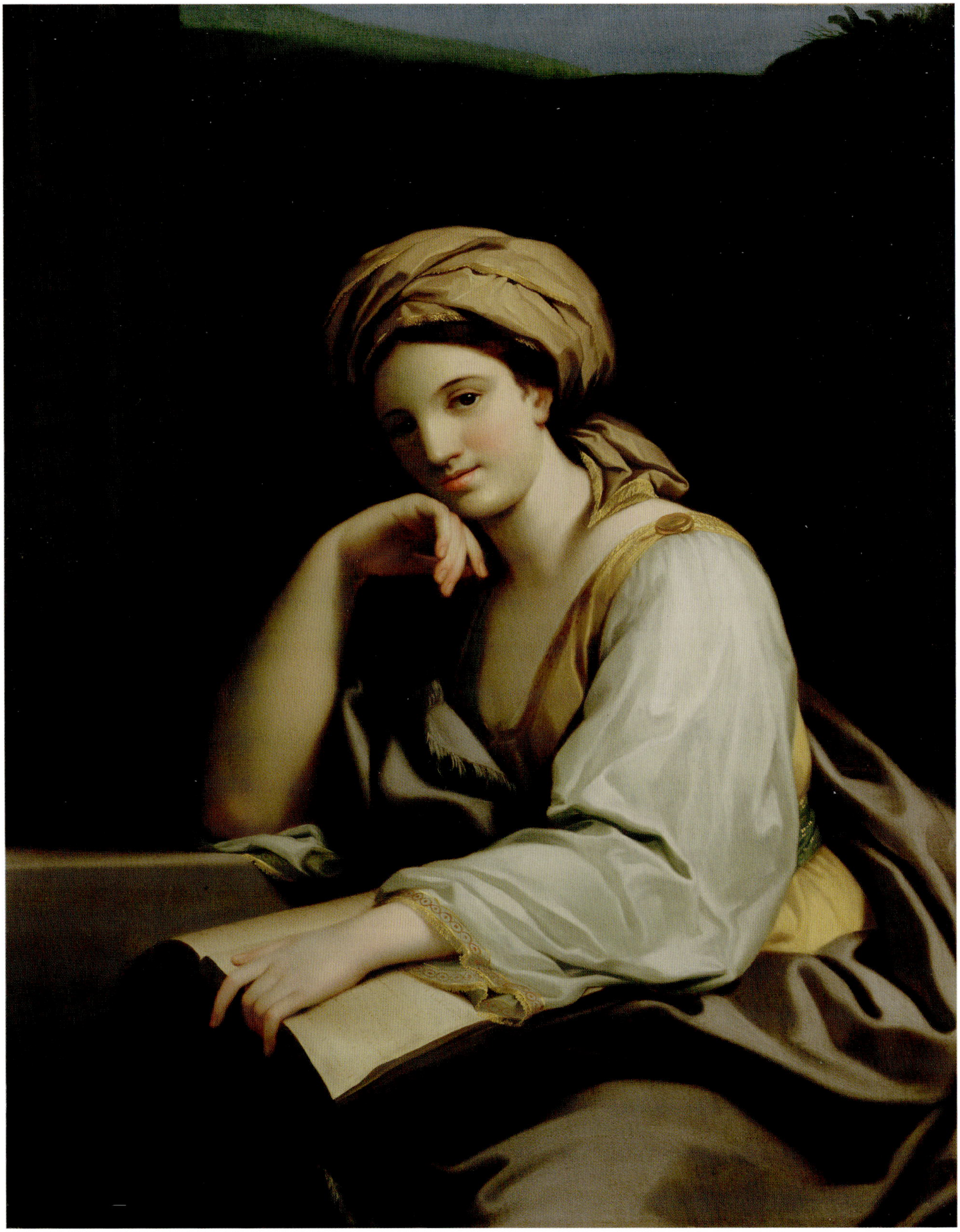

40 OPPOSITE
Benjamin West
Copy after a Sibyl by Mengs
1761
Oil on canvas
118 × 92.7cm (46½ × 36½ in.)
FERENS ART GALLERY, KINGSTON UPON HULL

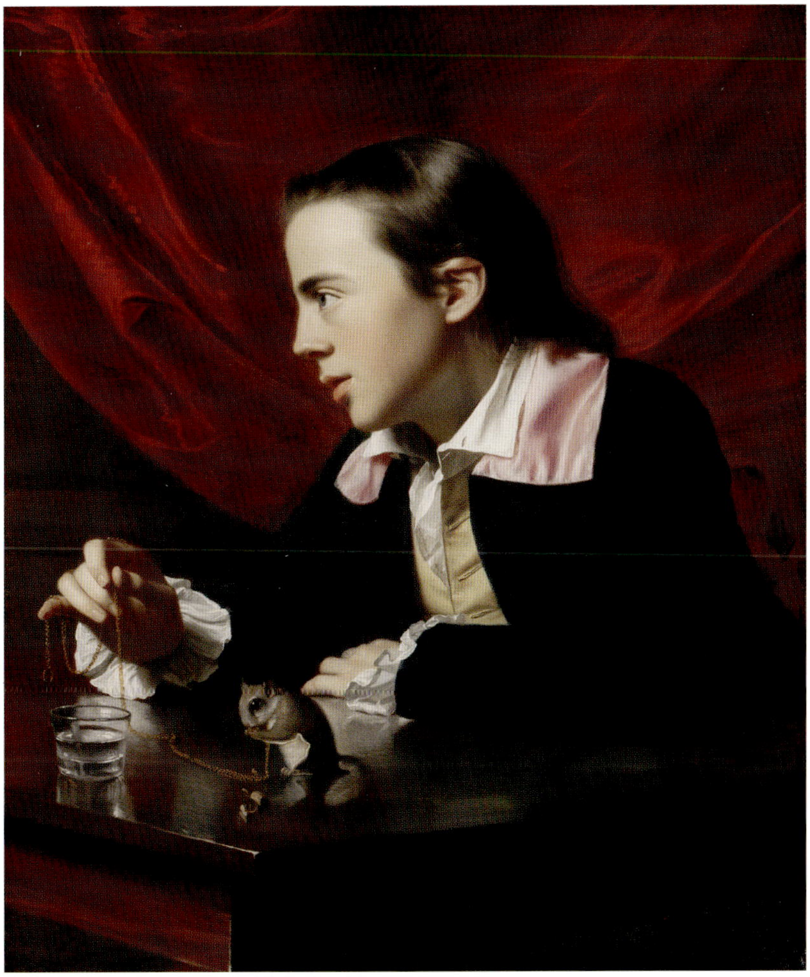

41
John Singleton Copley
(1738–1815)
A Boy with a Flying Squirrel (Henry Pelham)
1765
Oil on canvas
77.2 × 63.8 cm
(30⅜ × 25⅛ in.)
MUSEUM OF FINE ARTS, BOSTON

spring of 1763 was back in Rome for the last time and ready to be judged by 'the Roman public'.

West recalled how,

> after an Absence of more than twelve months from Rome he again visited that City, where he put into practice all that he had acquired in painting since his first arrival in Italy from America by painting two pictures, the subjects were Simon and Ephigenia ... and Angelica and Madoro, as well as composing several other subjects from the Poets and historical facts; all of which were viewed with much complacency by the professors of art, as well as by most ... connoisseurs.[82]

Cymon and Iphigenia has been lost,[83] and we do not know what the 'several other subjects from the Poets and historical facts' were, but *Angelica and Medoro* (fig. 11) shows how far West had travelled during his three years in Italy. The subject, taken from Ariosto's *Orlando Furioso,* is a sweetly romantic one: the young lovers proclaim their love by writing their names on every tree and stone they come across. Von Erffa and Staley think it owes much to what they describe as the 'quasi-Rococo' approach that Batoni had adopted.[84] West never acknowledged learning anything from Batoni, although he declared that when he arrived in Rome, 'the Italian artists of that day thought of nothing, looked at nothing but the works of Pomepio Battoni'.[85] In later years, West mocked Batoni's pomposity, telling Joseph Farington that he had been invited to Batoni's studio to watch the final brushstrokes being applied to his latest picture as the Italian uttered 'tones of delight' before 'He fell back into a chair & cried out, Viva Battoni.'[86] The debt to Mengs and Correggio is greater. While a proficient, engaging and thoroughly attractive work, *Angelica and Medoro* hardly burns with Neoclassical zeal, nor hints at the great power and scope that West was to exhibit over the next decade.

While both West himself and many West scholars declared that Mengs 'had by far the strongest impact on West',[87] it is Gavin Hamilton to whom we must turn when we consider the strength, originality and daring of West's contribution to both Neoclassicism and history painting. At the time of West's visit to Italy, Gavin Hamilton was among the most significant members of Rome's artistic colony. Born into the Scottish landed gentry in 1723, Hamilton received some education at the University of Glasgow, where the economist Adam Smith was among his contemporaries. Having decided to become a painter, Hamilton made the trip to Rome as early as 1743. By the early 1750s he was in London working largely as a portraitist, but returned to Rome in 1756 and stayed there, except for two brief visits to Scotland, for the rest of his life. While Mengs and Winckelmann were defining Neoclassicism, it was Hamilton who first produced the most enduring works. As a painter, Mengs found it hard to escape a certain prettiness that sits uncomfortably with the moral earnestness of Neoclassicism. Hamilton was, from the beginning of the movement, more visionary and less compromising. His decision in the late 1750s to begin a heroic cycle of canvases depicting the great events of the *Iliad* was as defining a moment for Neoclassicism as Winckelmann's emotional reaction to the *Apollo Belvedere*.

Hamilton's attempt to paint Homer was as bold as it was presumptuous. In the mid-eighteenth century the *Iliad* was regarded as the greatest secular literary work and Homer as the poet against whom all other poets were measured. There are a number of ways to explain the popularity, status and influence of Homer in the eighteenth century. As the Enlightenment elite increasingly doubted the authority and indeed even the validity of organized religion, the Homeric canon became a secular analogue to the Bible, providing a rich alternative store of character, drama and moral instruction. In the preface to his best-selling translation of the *Iliad*, Alexander Pope made an explicit comparison that also prefigured Winckelmann's preoccupation with the simplicity and purity of Greek art. 'Simplicity', Pope wrote, 'is the Mean between Ostentation and Rusticity. This pure and noble Simplicity is nowhere in such perfection as in the Scripture and Our Author ... his

Style must of course bear a greater Resemblance to the sacred Books than that of any other Writer.'[88] In a century that was beginning to be dominated by the costly, deadly and ever more global series of wars between England and France and their allies, the epic story of the Trojan War, with its noble deaths, long and hard fighting, and dramatic turns of fate, resonated well with contemporary events.

As Dora Wiebenson has painstakingly pointed out, Homeric subjects can be found in painting as far back as the fifteenth century, but it was in the period between 1750 and 1825 that they became increasingly popular among artists and even emblematic of Neoclassicism. 'It was the intention of the Neoclassical artist ...' she writes, 'to arrive at an unchanging essence of antique life – an essence related as much to the eighteenth century as to antiquity ... [The *Iliad* illustrations] demonstrate the development of subject and style toward a universal ideal – transcending time, place, medium, and the individuality of the artist – an ideal which was, nevertheless rooted in observation of the real world, and focused on man.'[89]

Hamilton's first Homeric painting, *Andromache Lamenting the Death of Hector*, painted for the Earl of Northampton, has been lost. His second in the series, *Achilles Lamenting the Death of Patroclus* (fig. 42) was bought for the large sum of £350 by James Grant of Grant, the travelling companion of West's friend Thomas Robinson. Unlike the works of Mengs and Batoni, with their lingering hints of the Rococo, Hamilton's *Iliad* pictures are something completely different. Hamilton nurtured an intense devotion to his subject matter, telling James Boswell, 'I sleep with Homer under my head.'[90] The *Iliad* pictures reflected the epic scale and significance of their subject matter. Huge in size, they featured big figures brought right up close to the picture plane, minimal detail, archaeological accuracy and powerful though controlled expression of emotions – particularly grief, anger and compassion – and broadcast clear lessons in the Homeric virtues of loyalty, bravery and determination. As Cassidy points out, the *Iliad* paintings presented a particularly tragic view of history, 'intended to provoke terror and pity in a tale of suffering'.[91] The first two paintings in the series would have been in Hamilton's studio during West's time in Rome, and it is inconceivable that West would not have been familiar with them. Certainly Hamilton's muscular, grave, didactic, big-in-size and big-in-subject pictures seem to have provided the model that West followed when he began to create his great Neoclassical pictures of the late 1760s.

Winckelmann lavishly praised Hamilton's work, remarking that 'the composition is good, the figures are intelligently thought out and conceived with taste', but noted that Hamilton's colouring was 'harsh, unpleasant and raw'.[92]

West knew Hamilton – it would have been difficult for any member of the British community in Rome not to – but the nature of their relationship is unclear. It is puzzling that while West extravagantly stated the importance of Batoni and lengthily acknowledged his artistic debt to Mengs,[93] he was remarkably reticent on the subject of Hamilton. There is not a single mention of Hamilton in the autobiographical manuscript, and in Galt, Hamilton is mentioned only in connection with an incident in which he took West to visit 'a coffee-house, the usual resort of the British travellers' soon after West arrived in Rome.[94]

West may have been so silent regarding Gavin Hamilton owing to the fact that, by the time West was reminiscing, Hamilton's star had long faded, and it may be that West, ever mindful of his own success and status, was not inclined to attribute much to an artist who was headed for obscurity and to whose obscurity West himself had been a major contributor.[95]

It is another painting of Hamilton's, however, that may have most significantly contributed to West's future success: *James Dawkins and Robert Wood Discovering the Ruins of Palmyra* (fig. 43). In March 1751 the British travellers Dawkins and Wood reached the ruins of Palmyra, the ancient trading capital of central Syria. Wood's survey of

42
Gavin Hamilton (1723–1798)
Achilles Lamenting the Death of Patroclus
1760–63
Oil on canvas
227.3 × 391.2 cm
(89½ × 154 in.)
NATIONAL GALLERIES OF SCOTLAND, EDINBURGH

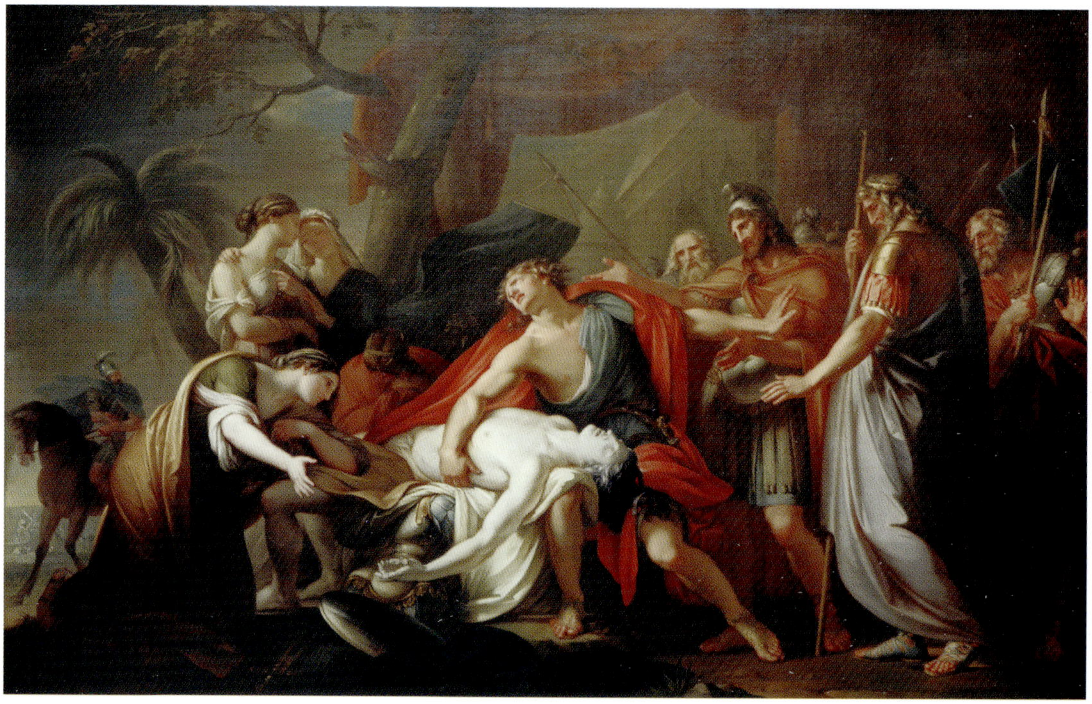

43
Gavin Hamilton (1723–1798)
James Dawkins and Robert Wood Discovering the Ruins of Palmyra
1758
Oil on canvas
309.9 × 388.6 cm
(122 × 153 in.)
NATIONAL GALLERIES OF SCOTLAND, EDINBURGH

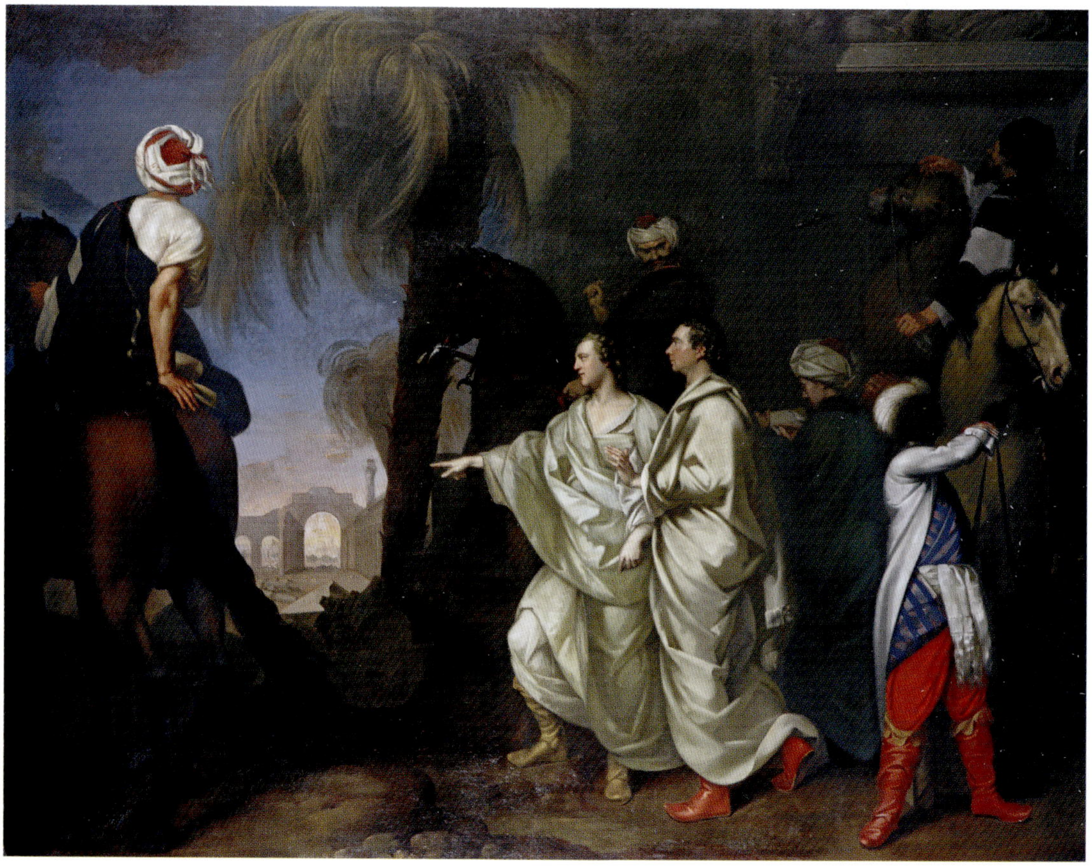

the ruins published in 1753 was, along with Stuart and Revett's *Antiquities of Athens* (1752), a landmark in the eighteenth century's scientific rediscovery of the ancient world.[96] When Dawkins died in September 1757, his brother Henry commissioned Hamilton to memorialize the late antiquarian's achievements. The picture was completed sometime in 1758: fast work for the usually dilatory Hamilton. Even by Hamilton's later standards, the canvas is huge. In subject matter, scale and iconography, *Dawkins and Wood* is some sort of breakthrough; almost the revolution in history painting that West accomplished so definitively with *Wolfe* more than a decade later.

'It is remarkable among renderings of contemporary subjects', Clare Pace writes, 'in showing not a military exploit or heroic naval battle … nor the arrival or apotheosis of a monarch, but two amateur archeologists.'[97] With its hints of Rubens and Van Dyck, *Dawkins and Wood* is less severely Neoclassical than the *Iliad* series, but shows Hamilton's imaginative powers even more forcefully. Like much of Hamilton's work, it combines exceptional intellectual reach with a sometimes poor technical grasp. The profiled heads of the two explorers, for example, are sadly lifeless and comically too small for their bodies.

Using some of the compositional elements to be found in pictures of the Journey of the Magi, Hamilton's painting can, as Brendan Cassidy puts it, 'be seen as celebrating the "new religion" of scholarly discovery that characterized the age of Enlightenment'.[98] But it is considerably more than a tribute to Enlightenment scholarship. In celebrating a contemporary secular event with the grand scale and iconography usually devoted to subjects of universal significance, *Dawkins and Wood* boldly asserts the value of the present. Infuriatingly, we do not know if West ever saw it. There are no records yet found to tell us when the picture left Rome.[99] Perhaps it was still in Hamilton's studio when West arrived in 1760. As Hamilton's most important commission to date, we can probably assume that West would have heard of it and discussed it, even if he had not seen it. It raises the intriguing possibility that the most important lesson that West learned in Rome was from a Scottish artist, who taught him that a contemporary subject could be treated with the awe and grandeur previously reserved for the events of the Bible, classical literature and mythology. After *Dawkins and Wood*, Hamilton returned to the classical world and stayed there. As usual, West was moving on.

HISTORY MEN AND WOMEN

Artists paint with their brains, even artists who, like West, find it hard to articulate what they are thinking. As Michael Baxandall reminds us, 'painters cannot be social idiots: they are not somehow insulated from the conceptual structures of the cultures in which they live'.[1] The intellectual aspect of painting is a constant theme in classical and Neoclassical art theory. In his *Della pittura* of 1435–36, Leon Battista Alberti wrote how the painter had to 'follow with his hand what he has learned with his mind',[2] and when it came to the highest genre of painting, *istoria*, he insisted, 'We will force ourselves to have every part well thought out in our mind from the beginning'.[3] Du Fresnoy echoed Alberti's language and intentions when he advised the artist not to 'give the least touch with your Pencil … till you have present in your Mind a perfect Idea of your Work',[4] and went on to declare: 'let the Labour of the Hand accompany the Study of the Brain; let the former second and support the latter'.[5] Unlike Richardson, Ramsay or Reynolds, West had no apparent intellectual or literary aspirations, but he was nonetheless the product of a tradition that insisted that painting was first and foremost an intellectual activity. The intellectual currents of the time took Benjamin West's paintings to very new worlds, and chief among those currents was a change in the style and intentions of history writing.

In order to understand how and why West created *Wolfe* and why that picture enjoyed such rapid and enduring success, West needs to be situated within the Enlightenment. Generations of art historians, perhaps shocked by West's lack of formal education, have denigrated his intelligence. His terse and rather stilted writing, his lack of self-examination, his wish to be thought of as a prodigy of God-given artistic talent and his – even by eighteenth-century standards – shaky grasp of spelling and grammar have all conspired to divorce him from the intellectual context in which he thought and worked. As we have already seen, West emerged from Pennsylvania as a young man familiar with Enlightenment ideas, and this familiarity was reinforced by the elite artistic and intellectual circles that he joined in Rome.

The Enlightenment was not merely an *affaire des savants*. It kindled the brightest hopes and addressed the most profound fears of a conflicted and turbulent century, but it was no monolith. The sheer wit and panache of the *philosophes* have long encouraged the view that the Enlightenment was a French-driven juggernaut – a view that Jonathan Israel, in particular, has tried to amend with his ambitious segmentation of this complex movement.

Britons were privileged among followers of the Enlightenment. Unlike in France, where Voltaire's exhortation '*écrasez l'infâme*' was still a work in progress culminating in the Revolution, in Britain 'the Enlightenment's principal aims – as formulated by Locke, Newton, Hume, Montesquieu, and Voltaire – empiricism in science, religious toleration, freedom of thought and the press, personal liberty, and security of person, had all been accomplished already'.[6] In spite of the agitation of the Wilkesites and the radical writings of Thomas Paine, Catherine Macaulay and Major John Cartwright, the Enlightenment in Britain was a moderate affair. As Israel observes, the Enlightenment programme was quickly deradicalized in Britain:

> Britain constituted a novel and exciting scenario characterized by a host of innovative new features, among the more unexpected and remarkable of which … was the rise among most of the population of the prestige not just of Parliament, the constitution, navy, army, and English law, but also of the crown, aristocracy, empire, and the British state generally.[7]

To Israel's point – that the Enlightenment in Britain, while 'novel and exciting', also reinforced Establishment values and institutions – could be added Gertrude Himmelfarb's observation on what she calls 'the unique character and historic importance' of the British Enlightenment:

> In the usual litany of traits associated with the Enlightenment – reason, rights, nature, liberty, equality, tolerance, science, progress – reason invariably heads the list. What is conspicuously absent is virtue. Yet it was virtue, rather than reason, that took precedence for the British, not personal virtue but the 'social virtues' – compassion, benevolence, sympathy – which, the British philosophers believed, naturally, instinctively, habitually bound people to each other.[8]

As the depiction of the death of a popular hero by a fashionable young artist, *The Death of General Wolfe* was bound to attract attention. As a bold and striking composition, it was bound to attract acclaim. But the way in which *Wolfe* attached itself so quickly, so strongly and so persistently to such a wide audience can be explained only by its appeal to more profound factors – factors to which West was sensitive and which helped to make *Wolfe* very much the right picture at the right time. Voltaire, with his sparkling mixture of cynicism and subtlety, well knew that timing was, if not everything, a large part of success. 'That is what it means to come into the world at the right moment', he wrote.[9]

To use Israel's terms, *Wolfe* was 'novel and exciting' as well as proclaiming the heightened prestige of 'the constitution, navy, army, and English law … the crown, aristocracy, empire, and the British state'. And to use Himmelfarb's terms, *Wolfe* emphatically paid tribute not just to the virtue of an individual hero, but also to 'the "social virtues" – compassion, benevolence, sympathy'.

There is nothing to suggest that West read the works of Voltaire and David Hume that we are about to consider, but as the friend and protégé of Enlightenment men, West would have been familiar with their ideas and attitudes. It is not too fanciful to say that much of what Voltaire and Hume thought, West painted.

Hume's triumphant assertion of 1770 that 'this is the historical age and this the historical nation'[10] not only celebrated the commercial success of his *History of England*, but also proclaimed that a revolution in history writing, the introduction of 'philosophical history', had taken place. Hume and Voltaire – soon to be joined by William

Robertson and, slightly later, by Edward Gibbon – were the first on the barricades of this revolution: a revolution that changed both the writers and the readers of history. This revolution in history writing – centred on the middle decades of the eighteenth century – came before West's revolution in history painting and helped to create the context in which his innovations could be both understood and welcomed. The revolution in history writing did not somehow cause the revolution in history painting. Instead, both revolutions are best understood as manifestations of a rise in historical consciousness in the eighteenth century: an increase in the sense that history was important to more people than ever before and that what was happening to them now was part of history too. We shall return to consider why this rise in historical consciousness happened when it did. But first we should consider how philosophical history – like the novel, the rise of which has been much studied – became a defining genre of the century.

The Enlightenment narrative, as presented by the philosophical historians, not only provided a hopeful account of the triumph of reason over superstition, but also implied, or perhaps even assumed, the belief that one's own time was the culmination of that story. Enlightenment writers and historians were not reticent when it came to making such claims. The difficulty of reconciling a belief in the value of the present with the veneration of classical models had brought the Quarrel between the Ancients and the Moderns to a stalemate: 'There are … spheres in which the moderns are far superior to the ancients,' Voltaire wrote, 'and others, very few in number, in which we are their inferiors.'[11]

Some of the enlightened could not resist a more triumphalist flourish. James Boswell wrote that while there were always those who affected 'to despise and abhor human nature in general', it was 'surely more agreeable to good notions of Providence, that the world should be in a progressive state of improvement; and I do sincerely think that this age is better than ancient times.'[12] A similar satisfaction was felt by Hume when acknowledging the effects of the Glorious Revolution: 'And it may be justly affirmed without any danger of exaggeration, that we, in this island, have ever since enjoyed, if not the best system of government, at least the most entire system of liberty, that ever was known amongst mankind.'[13]

If Neoclassicism was the visual wing of the Enlightenment, philosophical history can be described as its propaganda machine. When the *Göttingische Anzeigen* reviewed the first volume of Hume's *History* in 1755, its journalist lauded his 'pragmatic writing style' and 'serious observation of customs', and singled out his 'quite rare talent of using this knowledge for the purpose of enlightenment'.[14] The philosophical historians presented a history that told an unfolding story of progress and human advancement; a history that not only recounted, but also – and here is the propaganda element – positively celebrated the change that led mankind into the new republic of reason. For example, here is Robertson discussing early sixteenth-century mentalities in his *History of the Reign of the Emperor Charles V* (1769):

> Mankind seem, at that period, to have recovered the powers of enquiring and of thinking for themselves, faculties of which they had long lost the use; and fond of the acquisition, they exercised them with boldness upon all subjects. They were not now afraid of entering an uncommon path, or of embracing a new opinion. Novelty appears rather to have been a recommendation of a doctrine; and instead of being startled when the daring hand of Luther drew aside, or tore the veil which covered and established errors, the genius of the age applauded and aided the attempt.[15]

However committed to progress the Enlightenment may have been, older cyclical theories of history and biological analogies that suggested that societies, just like individuals, moved from infancy to maturity to old age, continued to be popular and provided not a counter-narrative to the progress story but a memento mori footnote.[16] The sense of rapid change that so many experienced was not without cost, and may have contributed to an elegiac strain that emerged in English thought and literature in the first half of the century and took its most eloquent form in Thomas Gray's *Elegy Written in a Country Church-Yard* (1751). 'The Boast of Heraldry, the Pomp of Power,/ And all that Beauty, all that Wealth e'er gave,/ Awaits alike th' inevitable Hour./ The Paths of Glory lead but to the Grave'[17] refers as cogently to the decline and fall of nations as to the fate of individuals. But decline and death also implied rebirth and revival.

These subjects were much on the mind of West's Philadelphia mentor William Smith in 1752 when he wrote *Some Thoughts on Education,* in which he observed that 'all Governments are subject to Death' but that the American colonies would not 'contentedly suffer ourselves to be laid in the same Grave' with Britain.[18] Smith questioned 'whether our New-World/ (When by the sad Vicissitude of Things/ The Old has sunk in to its pristine Sloth/ And Barbarism) shall be, the last Retreat/ Of Arts, imperial Liberty and Truth'.[19] 'Who knows,' he further asked 'but Empire, Liberty and Arts,/ With their resplendant Train, are doom'd to move/ From East still Westward.'[20] Written on the eve of Britain's rise to greater-than-ever political and commercial pre-eminence, Smith's words show how ideas of rise and fall were deeply embedded in the minds of even the most committed followers of the Enlightenment. However, whether history unfolded in a linear or a cyclical fashion, the philosophical historians viewed human experience as an ascent from barbarism to reason.

Classical theories of history tended to value the discipline as providing a how-to book for the ruling classes, at whom Viscount Bolingbroke aimed his celebrated aphorism that 'history is philosophy teaching by examples how to conduct ourselves in all the situations of private and public life'.[21] In *Of the Art Both of Writing and Judging of History* (1695), the French theorist Pierre Le Moyne defined history as 'a continued Narration of things True, Great and Publick, writ with Spirit, Eloquence and Judgment; for Instruction to Particulars and Princes'.[22]

With the introduction of philosophical history, the scope of what was 'True, Great and Publick' grew; the 'continued Narration of things' was popularized, and 'Instruction' was married to entertainment for an ever-widening audience. In his influential and widely circulated lectures on rhetoric, delivered to the students at the University of Edinburgh from the early 1760s, Hugh Blair praised the revolution in history writing:

> I cannot conclude the subject of history, without taking notice of a very great improvement which has, of late years, begun to be introduced into historical composition; I mean, a more particular attention than was formerly given to laws, customs, commerce, religion, literature, and every other thing that tends to show the spirit and genius of nations. It is now understood to be the business of an able historian to exhibit manners, as well as facts and events; and assuredly, whatever displays the state and life of mankind, in different periods, and illustrates the progress of the human mind, is more useful and interesting than the details of sieges and battles.[23]

Le Moyne and Bolingbroke looked to history to present *exempla virtutum* for the elite. The philosophical historians did not abandon the need to present inspiring examples of virtuous behaviour, but were clear that they would draw examples from a broader range of human activities in order to attain their moral goals. If the chief use of history was to demonstrate progress 'for the purpose of enlightenment', this change of instrumentality went hand in hand with an appeal to a much wider audience, to whom philosophical history could provide a compelling narrative of the maturing of humanity, culminating in a fortunate present. It was a narrative in which all could play a part.

As Louis Halphen describes it, this new way of writing history had an electrifying effect on its audience, 'giving the wondering reader the illusion that after centuries of waiting, history was suddenly revealed to him'.[24] Voltaire set out the philosophical history stall unequivocally with the famous opening sentences of *Le Siècle de Louis XIV* (1751): 'It is not just the life of Louis XIV that one claims to write; one is proposing a greater object ... to depict to posterity not the actions of a single man, but the mind of mankind in the most enlightened century there has yet been.'[25]

Voltaire's mind or spirit of mankind – the hard-to-translate *'l'esprit des hommes'* – Robertson's 'genius of the age' and Hume's 'spirit of the age' were all phrases announcing the broadening both of the subject matter of history and of the historical cast of characters. Gibbon recognized and deplored the tendency of pre-Enlightenment history to concentrate on a few, mostly military leaders such as Alexander the Great and Trajan, writing that 'as long as mankind shall continue to bestow more liberal applause on their destroyers than on their benefactors, the thirst for military glory will ever be the vice of the most exalted characters'.[26] Voltaire had already expressed similar sentiments: 'It is to the man who rules over minds by the power of truth, not to those who enslave men by violence, it is to the man who understands the universe and not to those who disfigure it, that we owe our respect.'[27]

Hume went further. 'The same age which produces great philosophers and politicians, renowned generals and poets, usually abounds with skillful weavers, and ship-carpenters', he wrote.

> We cannot reasonably expect, that a piece of woollen cloth will be wrought to perfection in a nation which is ignorant of astronomy, or where ethics are neglected. The spirit of the age affects all the arts; and the minds of men, being once roused from their lethargy, and put into fermentation, turn themselves on all sides, and carry improvements into every art and science. Profound ignorance is totally banished, and men enjoy the privilege of rational creatures, to think as well as to act, to cultivate the pleasures of the mind as well as those of the body.[28]

While kings, generals and sundry grandees continued to play the leading roles, philosophical history recognized that they were part of a social web. 'The newfound importance of "society" in the narrative of the Enlightenment', Dan Edelstein declares, 'was symptomatic of underlying changes in the philosophical, religious, cultural, and political climates of the age.'[29] Giving 'society' a starring role in the narrative quite clearly struck a sympathetic chord with the growing non-elite audience for history. Before turning to the phenomenon of that audience, there are two other forces to consider that helped to shape philosophical history: the desire to emulate the empirical methods and success of the natural sciences, and the use of history to enhance national prestige.

One of the new factors in historical explanation, Dario Perinetti writes, 'was the impact of the "experimental approach" developed by natural philosophers, particularly in England'.[30] Voltaire and the other philosophical historians were inspired by the advances in the natural sciences, the methods of which they wished to apply to history. Writing in *Nouvelles considérations sur l'histoire* (1744), Voltaire speculated: 'Perhaps we will soon arrive at a way of writing history that we have already reached with physical science. New discoveries are getting rid of old systems. One wants to understand human beings in an interesting detail that will create a basis now for a natural philosophy.'[31] In spite of having such high aspirations to make history a science, the philosophical historians failed to do so, perhaps because of their preoccupation with style rather than method.

The philosophical historians were more successful in creating histories that, while cosmopolitan in context, were nonetheless national manifestos.[32] The centuries-old Anglo-French power struggle was mirrored on cultural and intellectual battlefields. Just as contemporary commentators were much agitated by Britain's lack of a national school of painting to rival the French academy – an agitation that led to the establishment of the Royal Academy – there were perhaps greater worries attached to the lack of an outstanding national historian. If Britain was the new Rome, who would be its Livy or Tacitus? 'In general the country's slowness to develop national schools of arts or letters aggravated a sense of inferiority to France that is a persistent theme of British cultural history', Mark Salber Phillips observes. 'It is worth speculating, however, on the particular anxieties that attach themselves to historical writing, since it is hard to silence the doubt that a nation lacking a great national historian also lacks a great history.'[33]

The rivalry in historiography was more complex than other cultural and intellectual contests. While Voltaire and Hume share the honours as the leading lights of philosophical history, it is unclear who came first. The idea of philosophical history was in the air long before either of them began writing, and may have its roots in French theory. In 1694 Claude-François Ménestrier was already foreshadowing philosophical history when he wrote that the historian needed to understand 'the morals, the religion, the clothes, the strengths, the riches, the cleverness, the government, the wars, the arts, the businesses, the ceremonies, the politics, and the way of behaving' of those he was writing about.[34] The national origins of philosophical history are further complicated by the facts that Voltaire's thinking was transformed during his three-year political exile in England, and Hume wrote his *Treatise of Human Nature* (1739–40) while resident in France.

From the late 1720s, Voltaire was increasingly involved in history writing, but the tentative arrival of philosophical history came only with the publication of the first chapters of his *Essai sur les mœurs* in 1745–46. Hume's interest in history can be dated from his 'Of the Rise and Progress of the Arts and Sciences' of 1742.[35] Karen O'Brien suggests that 'Historians' interest in manners (a people's customs, cultural practices and habits of thought) began with the English translation, published in 1758, of Voltaire's *Essai sur les mœurs*',[36] but Hume was well advanced in the writing and publication of his *History* by then. In 1760 Hume asked a friend if he could borrow 'a Copy of Voltaire's Universal History ... I know that Author cannot be depended on with regard to Facts; but his general Views are sometimes sound, & always entertaining.'[37] Voltaire, as the arch-stylist of the Enlightenment, equally celebrated on both sides of the Channel, may have influenced Hume's style, but it seems that there was 'nothing whatsoever to indicate ... that it was Voltaire's revolutionary approach to history in that work that had induced Hume, among others, to recognize him as a master'.[38]

Key to the enthusiastic reception of philosophical history was the growth of a new, bigger, richer audience of citizen readers of newspapers, books and periodicals, for whom literature provided the lubrication of polite society and for whom a knowledge of history in particular was a qualification for an enhanced engagement in public affairs. Hume's praise of Voltaire as being 'always entertaining' gets straight to one of the most important qualities of philosophical history, a quality that is always implicit, though rarely discussed: the need to attract and keep an audience. As professional writers, Voltaire, Hume and the other philosophical historians were well aware that the public, not a few individual patrons, were their new masters. This implied writing about what they felt the public wanted, as well as writing about it in a way that would please.

Oliver Goldsmith's *History of England*, which began appearing in 1771, typifies the audience-driven approach of the eighteenth-century history writers, and that term 'history writers' includes both historians and the other men of letters, such as Tobias Smollett and Goldsmith, who were attracted to history writing because of rising public demand. Goldsmith's aspirations were not lofty. He hoped that readers would find his *History* 'a plain, unaffected narrative of facts, with just ornament enough to keep attention awake, and with reflection barely sufficient to set the reader upon thinking'. Goldsmith went on to define his readership as 'those who intend to lay a foundation for future study, or desire to refresh their memories upon the old, or who think a moderate share of history sufficient for the purposes of life'.[39] Goldsmith's conception of historical knowledge as a necessary middle-class attribute is a long way from older conceptions of history as a practical guide for the ruling elite.

In the first chapter we considered the somewhat slippery eighteenth-century concept of truth when reviewing the facts of West's life as presented in both his autobiography and Galt's biography. The distinction between 'essential truth' and literal truth also plays a role in philosophical history. Hayden White is of the view that eighteenth-century history writing was principally a literary art 'and its "fictive" nature generally recognized. Although eighteenth-century theorists distinguished … between "fact" and "fancy", they did not on the whole view historiography as a representation of the facts untainted by elements of fancy.' This 'fancy' was the aspect of history writing that served to engage – perhaps, ensnare – the reader in the historical narrative:

> Truth was not equated with fact, but with a combination of fact and the conceptual matrix within which it was appropriately located in the discourse. The imagination no less than the reason had to be engaged in any adequate representation of the truth; and this meant that the techniques of fiction-making were as necessary to the composition of a historical discourse as erudition might be.[40]

The use of 'fictive technique' to get to the essential truth was noted by Mark Akenside in his immensely popular poem of 1754, *The Pleasures of Imagination*: 'Where virtue, rising from the awful depth/ Of truth's mysterious bosom, doth forsake/ The unadorn'd condition of her birth;/ And dress'd by fancy in ten thousand hues,/ Assumes a various feature, to attract,/ With charms responsive to each gazer's eye,/ The hearts of men.'[41] 'Fancy' or 'fictive technique' can then be seen as a legitimate tool with which to engage the audience. In *Northanger Abbey* (1817), Jane Austen's Miss Tilney declares, 'I am fond of history – and am very well contented to take the false with the true.'[42] We shall return to this issue of eighteenth-century truth when we consider the truthfulness, or not, of *Wolfe* in the penultimate chapter.

The rise in the power of the public was endorsed, perhaps over-optimistically, by many writers and artists eager to be freed from the perceived capriciousness of royal and noble patronage. 'The people is far less often mistaken in its choice than the prince', Rousseau proclaimed in *The Social Contract* (1762).[43] The radical philosophical historian Catherine Macaulay, whose works ranked in popularity just behind those of Hume, Gibbon and Robertson, declared that 'Individuals may err, but the public judgement is infallible. They only want a just information of facts, to make proper comment. Labour to attain truth, integrity to set it in its full light are indispensable duties in an historian. I can affirm that I am not wanting in those duties.'[44] As early as 1719 in his *Réflexions critiques sur la poésie et sur la peinture*, translated into English in 1748, Voltaire's colleague Dubos eulogized the public voice: 'The public appraises a work to its full value, and gives it the rank due to its merit, or condemns it to oblivion. Tis never deceived in this decision, because it judges disinterestedly, and likewise by a sensible perception.'[45] To sound a slight note of caution, the eighteenth-century public was a narrowly defined one. Dubos would explain that 'The public therefore here in question, is limited to persons that read, and have a knowledge of theatrical entertainments, who see or hear people talk of pictures, and who have acquired by some means or other, that discernment which is called the Taste of Comparison'.[46]

Even such a narrowly defined public was expanding in size and power throughout the eighteenth century. While the emergence of this public sphere is a truism of eighteenth-century studies, it is worth reminding ourselves that it is not just a piece of elegant a posteriori analysis. Although it was, of course, never identified at the time in such terms, this 'structural transformation of the public sphere', to use Jürgen Habermas's phrase,[47] was keenly observed and strongly felt by West's contemporaries. Among those aspects of life that most distinguished Britain from other European countries, the vigour of its public sphere was immediately apparent to foreign visitors. 'In England as a rule people think', Voltaire wrote admiringly. 'In London there are some eight hundred people with the right to speak in public and uphold the interests of the nation; about five or six thousand aspire to the same honour in their turn, all the rest set themselves up in judgement on these'.[48]

For Hume, as it was for other *philosophes*, the expansion of the public sphere was an unalloyed blessing, improving the knowledge, the reasoning and consequently the behaviour of the public. 'The people', he observed, 'are no such dangerous monster as they have been represented, and that it is in every respect better to guide them like rational creatures, than to lead or drive them as brute beasts.'[49] Such freedom of public discussion reinforced Enlightenment ideas of progress: 'it is to be hoped that men, being every day more accustomed to the free discussion of public affairs, will improve in the judgement of them, and be with greater difficulty seduced by every idle rumour and popular clamour'.[50]

In order to improve 'the people', Hume had to reach them first, and he sought to do this by emotionally connecting with his readers in a way that no historian had yet done. Indeed, his historical writing has been characterized as 'sentimental history':[51] it is certainly history that invites us to feel. The drama, the detail, the emotional power of Hume's history writing is nowhere more obvious than in his description of the execution of Charles I:

> The street before Whitehall was the place destined for the execution: For it was intended by choosing that very place, in sight of his own palace, to display more evidently the triumph of popular justice over royal majesty. When the King came upon the scaffold, he found it so surrounded with soldiers, that he could not expect to be heard by any of the people: He addressed, therefore, his discourse, to the few persons who were about him; particularly Colonel Tomlinson, to whose care he had lately been committed, and upon whom, as upon many others, his amiable deportment had wrought an entire conversion ... Though innocent towards his people, he acknowledged the equity of his execution in the eyes of his Maker; and observed, that an unjust sentence, which he had suffered to take effect, was now punished by an unjust sentence upon himself. He forgave all his enemies, even the chief instruments of his death; but exhorted them and the whole nation to return to the ways of peace, by paying obedience to their lawful sovereign, his son and successor. When he was preparing himself for the block, bishop Juxon called to him: 'There is, sir, but one stage more, which, though turbulent and troublesome is a very short one. Consider, it will soon carry you a great way; it will carry you from earth to heaven; and there you shall find, to your great joy, the prize to which you hasten, a crown of glory.' 'I go,' replied the King, 'from a corruptible to an incorruptible crown; where no disturbance can have place.'
> At one blow was his head severed from his body. A man in a vizor performed the office of executioner: Another, in a like disguise, held up to the spectators the head streaming with blood, and cried aloud, This is the head of a traitor!
> It is impossible to describe the grief, indignation, and astonishment, which took place, not only among the spectators who were overwhelmed with a flood of sorrow, but throughout the whole nation, as soon as the report of this fatal execution was conveyed to them. Never monarch, in the full triumph of success and victory, was more dear to his people, than his misfortunes and magnanimity, his patience and piety had rendered this unhappy Prince.[52]

Compare this with how Paul de Rapin de Thoyras, writing in the 1720s, described the same event: 'The sentence was executed the 30th January, 1648–49 on a scaffold erected in the street at the windows of the Banqueting House at Whitehall. The king suffered death with great constancy and without showing the least signs of weakness or amazement.'[53]

After reading Hume on Charles's death, Robert Adam wrote to his sister Janet, 'I own I suffered inwardly, on the miserable state poor Charles was reduced to, & if I coud have help'd him, Humanity I thought would call on me to do it.'[54]

Hume calculated a delicate balance between historical record and emotional appeal or, in his terms, the need to be both truthful and interesting. 'The first Quality of an Historian is to be true and impartial;' Hume wrote to his friend William Mure in 1754, 'the next to be interesting. If you do not say that I have done both Parties Justice; and if Mrs. Mure be not sorry for poor King Charles, I shall burn all my Papers, and return to Philosophy.'[55] The marquise Du Deffand could not even finish Robertson's *History of Scotland* (1759), such were its emotional demands. 'These last few days, I've been reading Robertson's *History of Scotland'*, she wrote to her friend Horace Walpole in June 1766. 'I've had to give it up because it's giving me the vapours; I'm afraid of everything that makes me sad.'[56] Perhaps it was Robertson's description of the execution of Mary, Queen of Scots, that gave Madame Du Deffand the vapours:

> Mary mounted the steps with alacrity, beheld all this apparatus of death with an unaltered countenance, and signing herself with the cross, she sat down in the chair ... She then prepared for the block, by taking off her veil, and upper garments; and one of the executioners rudely endeavouring to assist, she gently checked him, and said with a smile, that she had not been accustomed to undress before so many spectators, nor to be served by such valets. With calm but undaunted fortitude, she laid her head on the block; and while one executioner held her hands, the other at the second stroke, cut off her head, which falling out of its attire, discovered her hair already grown quite gray, with cares and sorrows.[57]

Thanks partially to such an infusion of drama and sentiment, historians were, as Terry Belanger points out, 'the first writers as a class to make really substantial amounts of money in eighteenth-century England'.[58] William Robertson was paid £3500 for the copyright in his first edition of *The History of the Reign of Charles V*. This was at a time when Samuel Johnson, possibly England's hardest-working man of letters, was earning around £400 a year. For Hume, who had struggled to earn a living as a philosopher, the rewards of being 'true' and 'interesting' were considerable. After the publication of the first volumes of his *History* he was able to declare that 'I was becoming not only independent, but opulent.'[59] When he arrived in France as secretary to the new British Ambassador, Lord Hertford, he was so feted that he wrote to Robertson, only half humorously: 'I eat nothing but ambrosia, drink nothing but nectar, breathe nothing but incense, and tread on nothing but flowers.'[60]

Reporting the frenzied public demand for history, the *Critical Review* in 1771 observed that histories 'have multiplied upon us in great abundance. Compilations of this kind have been repeated in a variety of different forms; and now every stall in London, from Piccadilly to Moorfields, is loaded with this species of literary lumber.'[61]

Hugely popular it was, but the critics of philosophical history compare it unfavourably to the more scientific history of Ranke, Taine, Michelet and Mommsen that followed. For those critics – R.G. Collingwood, for example – philosophical history lacked 'historical mindedness', an interest in history for its own sake rather than as a justification of some present position. As Collingwood wrote, referencing the philosophical historians' disdain for the Middle Ages, 'To think of any phase of history as altogether irrational is to look at it not as an historian but as a publicist, a polemical writer of tracts for the times. Thus the historical outlook of the enlightenment was not genuinely historical; in its main motive it was polemical and anti-historical.'[62]

Philosophical history does have its shortcomings. The philosophical historians did not significantly advance scholarly technique, they had simplistic theories of causation, treated human nature as a constant and, perhaps most fatally, prized only those elements of the past that were a prelude to the enlightened present. As Friedrich Meinecke put it when discussing Robertson, 'the past continued to be worth research ... not for its inherent value, but only as a means of getting to know more about the rise of modern civilisation'.[63] There may be more teleology than history in the approach of the philosophical historians, who were less inclined to investigate the causes of events and more interested in their purpose, especially when that purpose was the replacement of superstition by reason, the headline of Enlightenment thinking. But even the opponents of philosophical history recognized its liberalization of the subject matter, its appeal to a wider public, its cosmopolitan nature and the excellence of its literary style.[64]

As the best-selling works of the philosophical historians show, the market for history grew explosively throughout the high eighteenth century, and it is worth considering whether this growth was driven more by audience demand or by the development of new ways of writing and presenting history.

That the success of philosophical history was driven by demand seems obvious from the huge sales of Paul de Rapin de Thoyras's *History of England,* which predates the innovations of Hume and Voltaire and began to appear in English translation in 1725. Rapin's *History* was such a best-seller that a London newspaper could proclaim 'no Book in our Language ever had more Buyers or Readers'.[65] Eighteen thousand complete sets of this multivolume history of England were sold,[66] and at a time when books remained expensive, Rapin's *History* was also issued as a shilling-per-instalment partwork, bringing history to a far wider audience than any guinea volume could do.

While we should not deny or minimize the internal logics that drove its development, it is evident that philosophical history arrived at a time when there was already an audience hungry for it. Quite clearly in eighteenth-century England, much more so than in France, there was an ever-growing demand for history, and it was that demand that helped to ensure the extraordinary success and influence of *Wolfe*.

Karen O'Brien describes the growth in historical consciousness as 'the growing recognition of the present as a point within a process of change'.[67] The process of change was everywhere apparent in mid-eighteenth-century Britain. Any one of a whole range of quantitative measures attests to the intensity and thoroughness of that change. From population growth to the number of patents issued, everything points to disruptive increases in scale, opulence and social mobility. Between 1721 and 1771 overseas trade more than doubled.[68] In the decade of the 1730s, 56 patents were granted; in the decade of the 1760s, there were 205.[69] In 1741 the population of England and Wales was around six million; by 1771 it was approaching seven and a half million.[70] The growth of London was particularly explosive: the population of the metropolis was around half a million in 1700 and had nearly reached 750,000 by 1750.[71] From 1750 to 1770, coal imports to the city increased by a third.[72] All of this activity created extraordinary opportunities for the getting and spending of money and for social mobility.

This early phase of the Industrial Revolution – what economic historians refer to as the 'take off' – was hardly the first boom in history, but it was significantly different from any previous boom both in its scale and its nature. David Landes captured the unique quality of the times:

> now for the first time in history, both the economy and knowledge were growing fast enough to generate a continuing flow of investment and technological innovation, a flow that lifted beyond Malthus's positive checks. The Industrial Revolution thereby opened a new age of promise. It also transformed the balance of political power, within nations, between nations, and between civilizations; revolutionized the social order; and as much changed man's way of thinking as his way of doing.[73]

Ways of thinking were changing, as were ways of sharing that thinking. 'Anyone can print what he thinks,' Voltaire wrote in admiration of England, 'so the whole nation is obliged to study.'[74] What 'the whole nation' was 'obliged to study' were newspapers and, increasingly, histories, as the tumultuous events of the present blurred the threshold between current events and history. Perhaps it was the hunger for reports of current events that created a news culture in Britain, a culture that subsequently provided the fertile soil in which historical consciousness could grow. After arriving in London in 1729, Montesquieu declared that he was in a country of 'a hundred million little opinions', and was astonished to note that even a skilled labourer such as a roofer 'had a newspaper delivered to him on the roof so that he could read it'.[75] This more than fulfilled Joseph Addison's earlier aspiration: 'I shall be ambitious to have it said of me, that I have brought philosophy out of closets and libraries, schools and colleges, to dwell in clubs and assemblies, at tea-tables and in coffee houses.'[76]

In his essay 'Of the Liberty of the Press' (1742), Hume declared that 'Nothing is more apt to surprise a foreigner than the extreme liberty which we enjoy in this country of communicating whatever we please to the public'.[77] In that essay, Hume went on to analyse the *longue durée* reasons for Britain's free press, concluding that it was a product of Britain's mixed constitution. The proximate cause of Britain's news culture, though, was the lapsing in May 1695 of the Licensing of the Press Act, effectively removing state control over who could publish newspapers. Within a year, it could be observed that 'So many news papers (or so called) are daily published that it would seem needless to trouble the world with more.'[78] Throughout the eighteenth century, the number of titles published and their readership expanded rapidly. Roughly two and a half million newspapers were sold in 1713; by 1780 newspaper sales were around fourteen million. In 1760 London was home to four daily and five tri-weekly newspapers. Ten years later there were five daily, eight tri-weekly and four weekly newspapers published in the city.[79] Even though these newspapers printed between only 2000 and 5000 copies each,[80] circulation and readership were large thanks to the sharing of copies, in coffee houses in particular.

London's emergence as the capital of world trade significantly increased the demand for news. The movement of ships, the announcement of new goods and reports of political events in far-flung places filled newspaper pages and were the lifeblood of the developing global mercantile society. Political events at home, too, stimulated readership. Following the Triennial Act of 1694 there were ten general elections between 1694 and 1716. Even with a relatively restricted franchise, newspapers became powerful weapons in the battle to mobilize public opinion. Bolingbroke's political paper, *The Craftsman*, published between 1726 and 1752, could sell as many as 12,000 copies an issue.[81] Economics and politics fuelled the public desire for regular news, but what really drove sales was the constant, increasingly global struggle for supremacy fought between Britain and France.

In the long century from 1689 to 1815, Britain and France were at war for sixty-three years. There was almost constant warfare – both formal and informal – between 1740 and 1783,[82] and in many senses the Seven Years War, fought from India to the Caribbean to the plains of central Europe, could be described as the first world war. The cost of such wars was, by all previous measures, huge. Britain's final victory was uncertain, perhaps even unlikely. At mid-century, Gerald Newman reminds us, France was three times as populous as Britain, with greater industrial and agricultural output,[83] yet Britain was able to create the world's largest navy and an army that was capable of defeating the French. Such an achievement was a testimony to British tenacity and ingenuity, but also required the transformation of society. John Brewer has described the process by which Britain became a fiscal-military state characterized by 'high taxes, a growing and well-organized civil administration, a standing army and the determination to act as a major European power'.[84] Although by nineteenth-century and later standards the state was very small indeed, its activities intruded into the lives of all Britons in an unprecedented manner: 'Landed gentry, farmers, shopkeepers and traders, labourers in husbandry and industry, merchants and manufacturers: all, in their different ways, were touched by the activities of the fiscal-military state.'[85]

The financial and emotional tolls of war were widespread, and war-weariness became a feature of British life. As early as 1711, Jonathan Swift bemoaned that England was 'sinking under heavy debts of a nature and degree never heard of by us or our ancestors; the bulk of the gentry and people heartily tired of the war'.[86] A full seventy years later Horace Walpole could echo those feelings, writing to the Earl of Strafford that 'though we are engaged in such big and wide wars, they produce no striking events, nor furnish anything but regrets for the lives and millions we fling away to no purpose!'[87] Catherine Macaulay was moved to anger and despair by the seemingly endless wars:

> It has ever been, and, I believe, ever will be the bane of this country … to ruche into unnecessary and expensive wars; to give up all the fruits of very dear-bought conquests in the patching up of hasty treaties of peace; and when the nation is just on the point of emerging out of the poverty which war produces, the paroxysms of Quixote rage return, and we are again, without the plea of necessity, or even rational cause, suddenly thrown into all the horrors and distresses of war.[88]

Those 'horrors and distresses', the bewildering nature of great contemporary events as reported in the newspapers, the sense that unprecedentedly rapid economic change was happening, the rapid growth of cities, all stimulated a public demand for historical explanation. Describing the evolution of historical writing in the nineteenth century, Isaiah Berlin declared that 'Ideas are not born out of ideas by parthenogenesis … the process has its roots in great cultural changes which go back to the Renaissance and Reformation if not beyond. The rise in historical consciousness … responded to the need at once to explain and justify the open struggles of nations and classes in its day.'[89]

To paraphrase Berlin, the rise of historical consciousness in eighteenth-century Britain was the result of the need to 'explain and justify' the rapid, profound, exhilarating and often bewildering political, economic and social changes that were affecting the lives of Britons. This rise in historical consciousness both helped to create and was reinforced by the introduction of philosophical history.

Contemporary observers clearly felt that news was quickly becoming history. Writing about the first three years of the Seven Years War, Nicholas Tindal proclaimed that 'the great events that followed came too thick upon one another … they were glorious for Britain, beyond all parallel that is to be found in history'.[90] What newspapers reported, history, claiming to make sense of the confused present, could explain. Readers of Hume could see how past mistakes led to current troubles. Drawing a lesson from Charles II's failure to help with the Anglo-French peace negotiations of 1677, Hume wrote 'that this was the critical moment, when the King … might with ease have preserved the balance of power in Europe, which it has since cost this island an infinite profusion of blood and treasure to restore'.[91]

There appears to be no evidence that West read history. However, his library did contain historical works. Mrs West's domestic accounts, from later in the artist's career, record the purchase of four volumes of Goldsmith's histories.[92] West's library was perhaps more about his gentlemanly status than his intellectual needs, illustrating that there was an aspirational side to the growing demand for history. Just as manuals devoted to such desirable social skills as deportment, etiquette and conversation were appealing to a rising middle-class audience eager to emulate their social superiors, the reading of history was a form of emulation, not only contributing to the reader's social skills, but also perhaps signalling their intention to play a greater role in public affairs. 'Some knowledge of History is expected from every one who is of a rank above that of the lowest mechanic', the author of *Letters to a Young Nobleman* wrote. Some read history

> to entertain and unbend their minds, after a studious application to the proper business of their various professions; some may do it to amuse themselves, and to acquire such a share of knowledge as may make them entertaining companions, and fit them for the conversation of men of sense and learning … The chief subjects of History, are such events as peculiarly interest the superior part of mankind, and in producing or preventing which, their station obliges them to have some share … A man of fortune and rank cannot possibly be an idle spectator of human affairs; one way or other he must do good or harm.[93]

West was educated and came to maturity in a cultural context that valued history and recognized its increasing sophistication. William Smith, West's most significant intellectual influence, was keenly aware of the role history should play in the lives of his protégés. In his idealized vision of a university published in 1753 as *A General Idea of the College of Mirania*, Smith wrote that students should have 'a pretty full knowledge of the principal events that happened in the world before they were born'. They should then 'review those events in the calm light of philosophy … attended with a deduction of their immediate and remote causes and consequences, in order to make them a lesson in ethics and politics, and a useful rule of conduct and manners throughout life'. As in the case of the philosophical historians, Smith discounted the whole medieval period and proposed that, after studying the ancients, his students should turn to modern history, which he, like many of his contemporaries, dated from the early 1500s. Smith's description of the stuff of modern history reflects the broad and cosmopolitan practice of the philosophical historians: he prescribes a curriculum that includes the study of 'the rise, interests, dependencies and constitutions of the several nations and states, whose histories are interwoven with that of England'.

As a result of such study,

> The youth are thus sent out into the world well acquainted with the History of those Nations they are likely to be most concerned with in Life; and also with the History of Greece and Rome, which may be justly called the History of Heroism, Virtue and Patriotism. This is enough to prepare them for Society, and put them in the Method of studying the History of other Nations they think proper, in a philosophical Manner, whenever their Inclination and Leisure shall prompt them to it.[94]

As a history painter, West did not have as subtle nor as well articulated an intellectual programme as the philosophical historians did. For him, history painting's purpose was 'to instruct the rising generation in honourable and virtuous deeds. They are the good, and great points which the historical pencil has to effect – and that can only be done by placing before them, those bright examples of their predecessors – or contempories, and to transmit their virtues from generation to generation.'[95]

West reiterated the classical need to present *exempla virtutum,* but his rather generalized use of 'the rising generation' is moving away from the specificity of the ruling class. More significantly, his use of 'or contempories' is particularly telling, and shows that he very much intended to bring history up to date, as it were, tying the events of the present to the past and indicating that even the greatest events of history could be equalled by the achievements of the present generation. Like Hume and Voltaire, West was sensitive to what those two great historians called respectively 'the spirit of the age' and *'l'esprit des hommes'*. And like Hume and Voltaire, West too would turn from the universal to the particular, in order to convey what was essentially a message of progress. Hume abandoned philosophy for history, and Voltaire gave up a successful career as a poet and dramatist for that of a historian. West moved from the lofty and remote world of the classical past to the more immediate and no less instructive realm of the contemporary. Or we might say that West moved from history painting to painting history.

For the philosophical historians, history was an inspiring testament to human will. The course of human history is the product of human hands and minds. Human agency rather than divine planning is the motive force of history. The Enlightenment promoted a disenchanted world, and that disenchantment began when Martin Luther nailed his Ninety-Five Theses to the door of the Castle Church in Wittenberg in 1517. Nowhere is this made more clear than in Robertson's description of the consequences of the Reformation in his *History of the Reign of the Emperor Charles V*:

> Men who had the courage to overturn a system supported by everything which can command respect or reverence, were not to be overawed by any authority, how great or venerable soever. After having been accustomed to consider themselves as judges of the most important doctrines in religion, to examine these freely, and to reject, without scruple, what appeared to them erroneous, it was natural for them to turn the same daring and inquisitive eye towards government, and to think of rectifying whatever disorders or imperfections were discovered there.[96]

This testing of authority, this 'courage to overturn a system supported by everything which can command respect or reverence', this subversiveness, which Peter Gay calls 'the lure of heresy',[97] gets built into the DNA of modernity. Wherever we look in the eighteenth century, we find hierarchies of all forms under attack.[98] Even the newspapers displayed this tendency, presenting contemporary events as a busy conjunction of the lordly and the mundane: advertising and politics, gossip and foreign wars all merged into one stream of news. 'This Chaos-heap of News', as the author of *Conversation: A Poem* described it in 1767,[99] certainly complemented, perhaps even influenced, the preoccupation of philosophical history with presenting a more complete picture of society: 'in the public Journals we peruse;/ Where, as if Chance had held the Writer's Hand,/ Contending Opposites together stand ... Things of no Kin are jumbled in a Breath,/ A Kitt'ning coupled with a Monarch's Death'.[100]

Social, political, artistic and intellectual hierarchies remained important – Adam Smith equated 'civilised society' with the establishment of 'the distinction of rank'[101] – but were increasingly scrutinized and challenged. This is a key eighteenth-century dilemma, continuing to confuse even after the French Revolution lit the bonfire of authority. No wonder Kant declared, in some exasperation, that 'nearly everything is paradoxical'.[102]

In the guise of satire – for example, John Gay's *Beggar's Opera* (1728), the picaresque novel with its anti-hero and Hogarth's modern moral subjects – high art forms were being subverted. This liberalization of subject matter leads to high forms of all artistic and intellectual endeavour dealing with content once regarded as low. Dubos asked, 'How shall our attention be engaged by a picture representing a peasant driving a couple of beasts along the highway, if the very action which this picture imitates, has no power of affecting us?'[103] A hundred years later, Baudelaire could declare that 'all subjects are equally good or bad according to the manner in which they are treated':[104] the unity of form and content that had guided artistic and intellectual expression for centuries was collapsing under the onslaught of Enlightenment and post-Enlightenment scrutiny. Benjamin West, an unlikely revolutionary, played a starring role. With *Wolfe,* West took the content of a secular hero's death and cast it in the form of a Lamentation over the dead Christ.

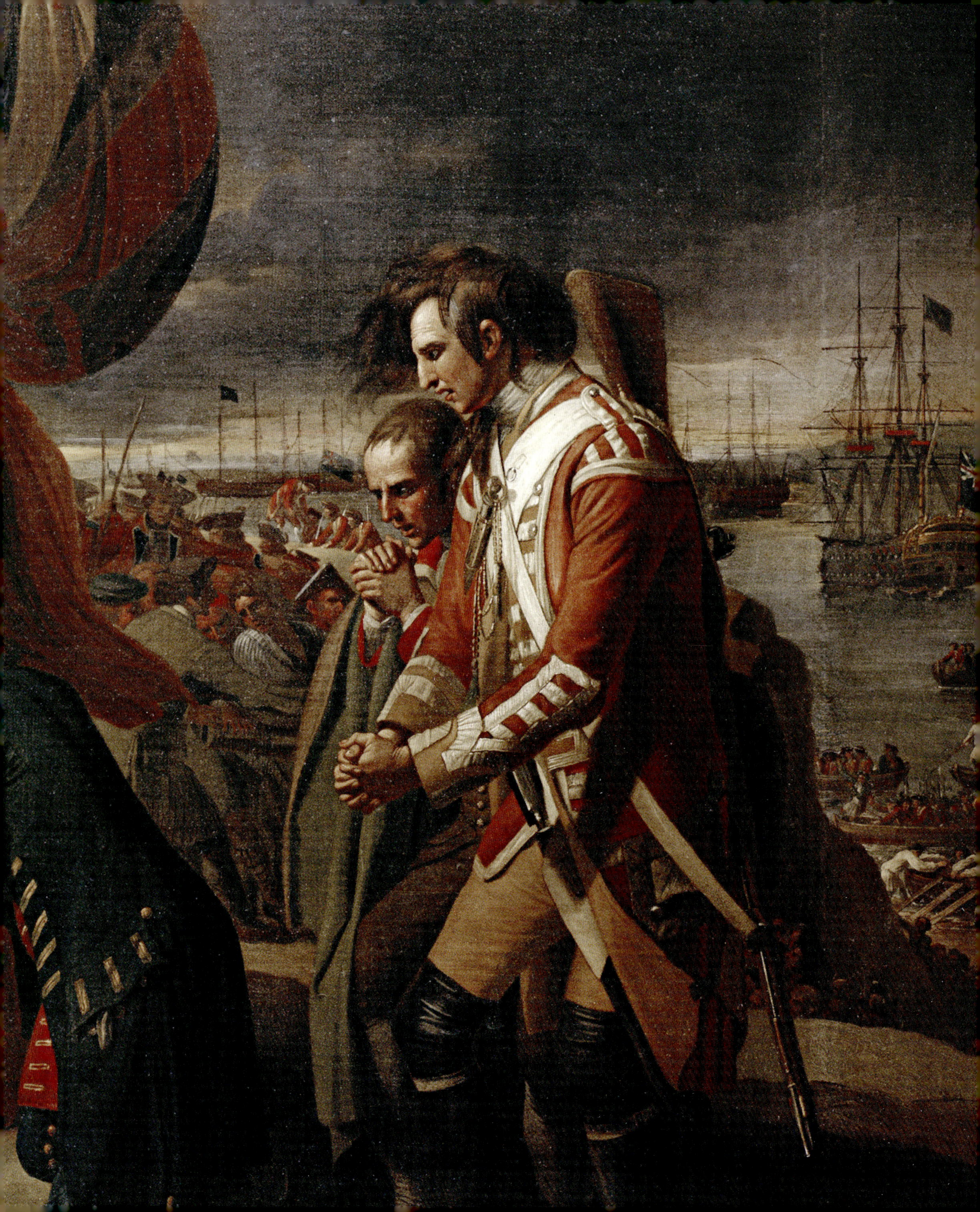

'HOW BEAUTIFUL IS DEATH'

Detail of Benjamin West, *The Death of General Wolfe*, 1771 (see fig. 73)

Formally, West's *Wolfe* is a Lamentation over the dead Christ, a subject well practised by painters, particularly since the mid-fifteenth century. West would have been familiar with many variations on this popular theme, through both engravings and his studies in Italy. In *Wolfe*, the young general stands in for Christ. The flagpole above him echoes the cross, and the billowing Union flag, the winding sheet. The blood dripping from Wolfe's side and his bandaged wrist recall Christ's wounds. The musket and tomahawk in the foreground are the instruments of the Passion and, just as Christ's mourners did, the circle of Wolfe's colleagues display a wide gamut of shocked and grieving emotions. The most prominent of them, the wounded General Monckton, even mimics a swooning Virgin Mary. West may have drawn inspiration from Dürer's *Lamentation for Christ* (fig. 44), Van Dyck's *Lamentation* (fig. 45) or Rembrandt's *Deposition* (fig. 46), as Charles Mitchell speculated.[1] Given the huge variety of sources available to West, such pose-hunting may be a futile exercise. In his only reference to such sources, West himself 'candidly declared in public, that he borrowed the principal figure in the composition from van Dyck's then-famous picture of *Belisarius Receiving Alms*' (fig. 47).[2]

Whatever West's most direct inspirations were, it would seem that any Christian should have immediately recognized *Wolfe* as a secularized Lamentation. Yet no contemporary sources known to me in any way refer to it as such. This raises intriguing questions. Was the Lamentation theme so obvious that no eighteenth-century viewer would have remarked upon it? Or did eighteenth-century viewers not even see it as a Lamentation?[3] Perhaps the latter: in the 1770s, form and content were still so welded together in the viewer's mind that a Lamentation form became a Lamentation only when it featured Christ, the Virgin Mary, Mary Magdalene and the other usual protagonists. Our more modern minds, so used to the independence of form and content, find this hard to grasp. However, whether explicitly recognized or not,

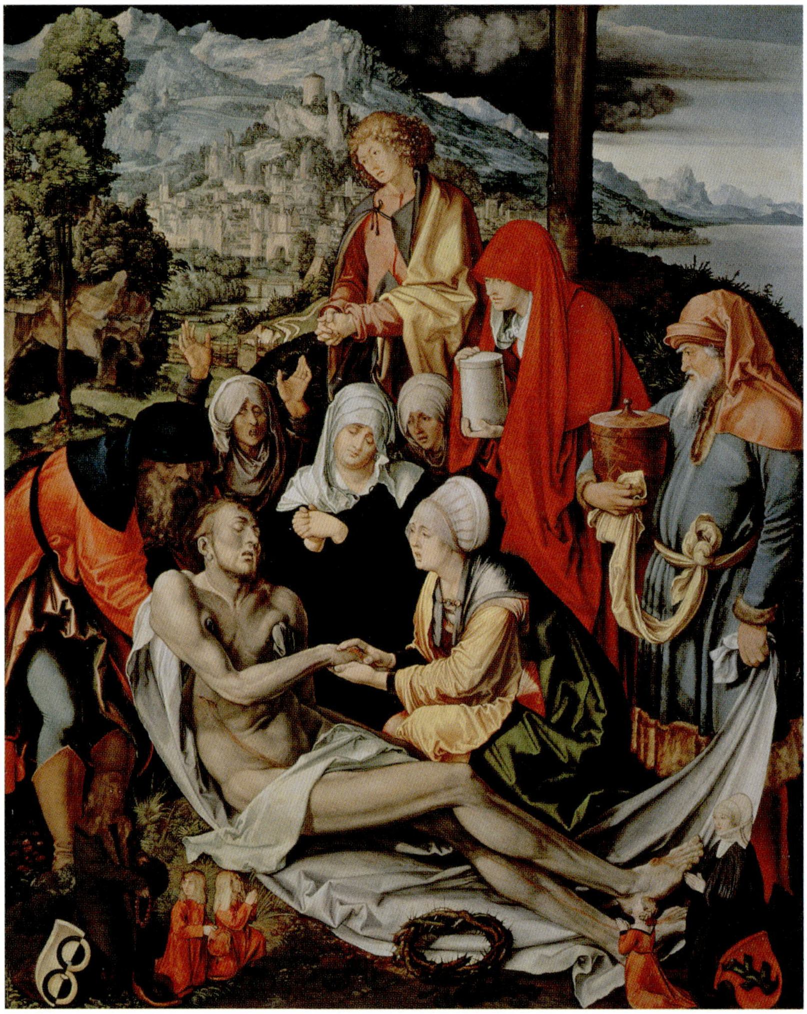

44
Albrecht Dürer (1471–1528)
Lamentation for Christ
c. 1500–03
Oil on panel
151 × 121 cm (59½ × 47⅝ in.)
ALTE PINAKOTHEK, MUNICH

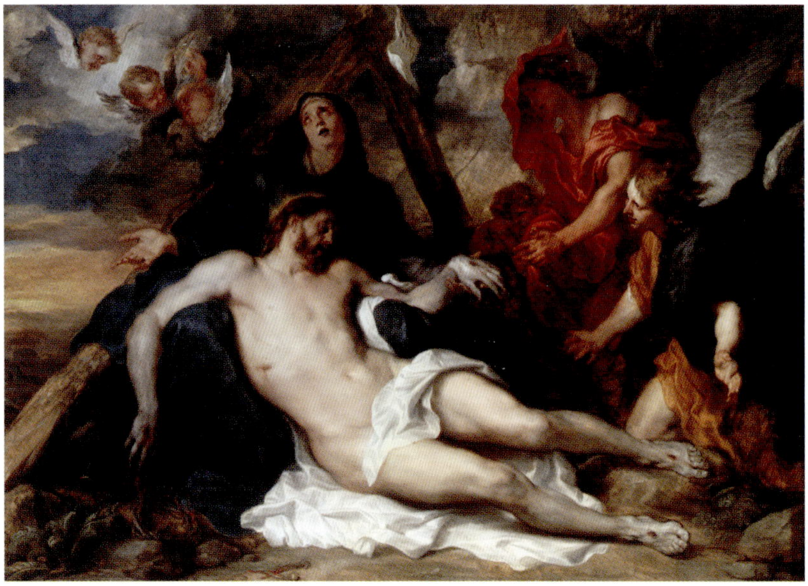

45
Anthony van Dyck
(1599–1641)
The Lamentation
1634
Oil on canvas
109 × 149 cm (42⅞ × 58⅝ in.)
ALTE PINAKOTHEK, MUNICH

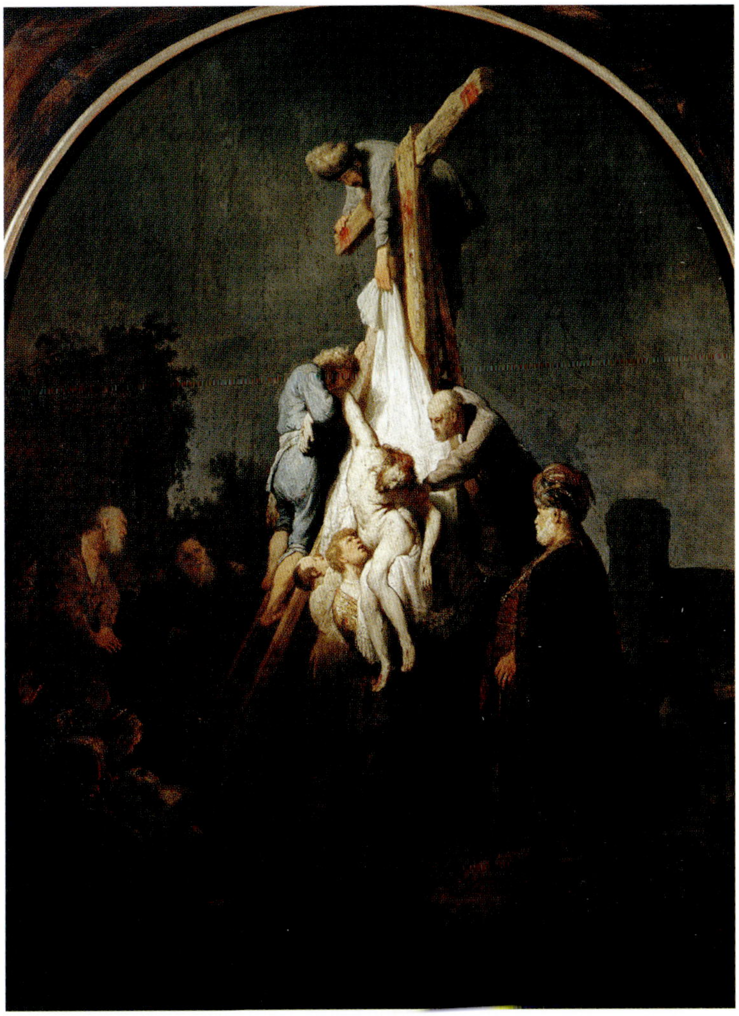

46
Rembrandt Harmensz.
van Rijn (1606–1669)
The Deposition
1633
Oil on panel
89.4 × 65.2 cm
(34¼ × 25⅝ in.)
ALTE PINAKOTHEK, MUNICH

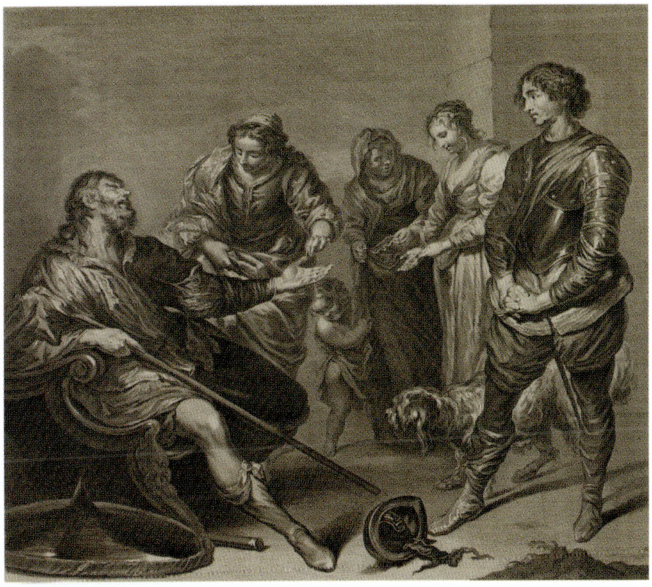

47
Gérard-Jean-Baptiste
Scotin (1698 – after 1755),
after Anthony van Dyck
(1599–1641; attrib.)
Belisarius Receiving Alms
18th century
Engraving
50.3 × 57 cm (19¾ × 22⅜ in.)
VICTORIA AND ALBERT MUSEUM, LONDON

48
Raphael (1483–1520)
Madonna della seggiola (Madonna della sedia)
c. 1513–14
Oil on panel
Diameter 71 cm (28 in.)
GALLERIA PALATINA, PALAZZO PITTI, FLORENCE

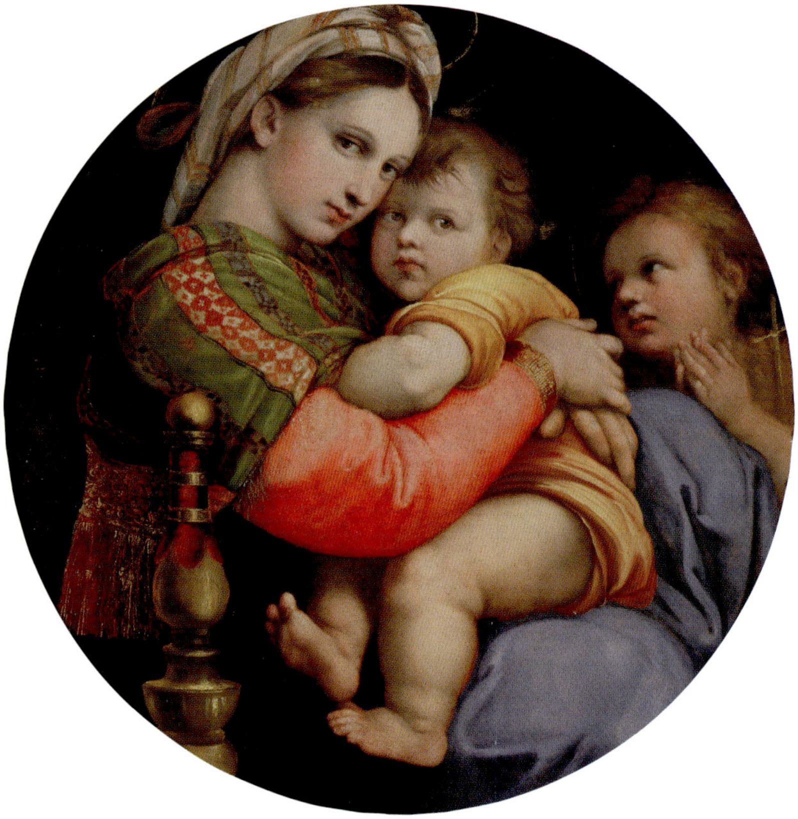

such forms as the Lamentation, which had been sanctioned by centuries of use, must have struck a powerful, if perhaps subconscious, chord with the audience.

It is unsurprising that the image of Britannia mourning her dead son would suggest a Lamentation to West, who had received his real artistic training in Italy, with its abundance of religious imagery, and had, even by the 1760s, developed a leaning towards, if not yet an absolute mastery of, complex, multi-figure compositions.

The secular agenda of the Enlightenment gave artists a licence to use such powerful prototypes, which had previously been restricted to sacred subjects, in new ways. West's *Mrs West with Raphael West* (fig. 49), in which the artist painted his wife and young son in a composition borrowed from Raphael's *Madonna della sedia* (fig. 48), was painted around the same time as *Wolfe*, if not a little earlier, and is a fine example of the use of sacred form to portray a secular subject. As early as 1762, when he painted *Anne, Countess of Northampton, and Her Daughter, Lady Elizabeth Compton* (fig. 50), West had experimented with a similar Renaissance Madonna and Child formula. He was notable but hardly original in this. When West was working on both *Wolfe* and *Mrs West with Raphael West*, Johann Zoffany produced his *Beggars on the Road to Stanmore* (fig. 51), in which a family of unusually handsome beggars are portrayed in the manner of the Holy Family resting on the Flight into Egypt. Joseph Wright of Derby was similarly inclined. 'Probably in the late 1760s',[4] he began to work out his ideas for what became *The Blacksmith's Shop* (fig. 52), exhibited in 1771, in which three heroic blacksmiths forge a horseshoe in a scene reminiscent of representations of both the Nativity and the Adoration of the Magi.[5] As discussed in the third chapter, Gavin Hamilton had already made use of Magi imagery in his *James Dawkins and Robert Wood Discovering the Ruins of Palmyra* as early as 1758.

'The general trend in culture and ideas towards rationalization and secularization'[6] had

49
Benjamin West
Mrs West with Raphael West
c. 1770
Oil on canvas
Diameter 90.2 cm (35½ in.)
UTAH MUSEUM OF FINE ARTS, SALT LAKE CITY

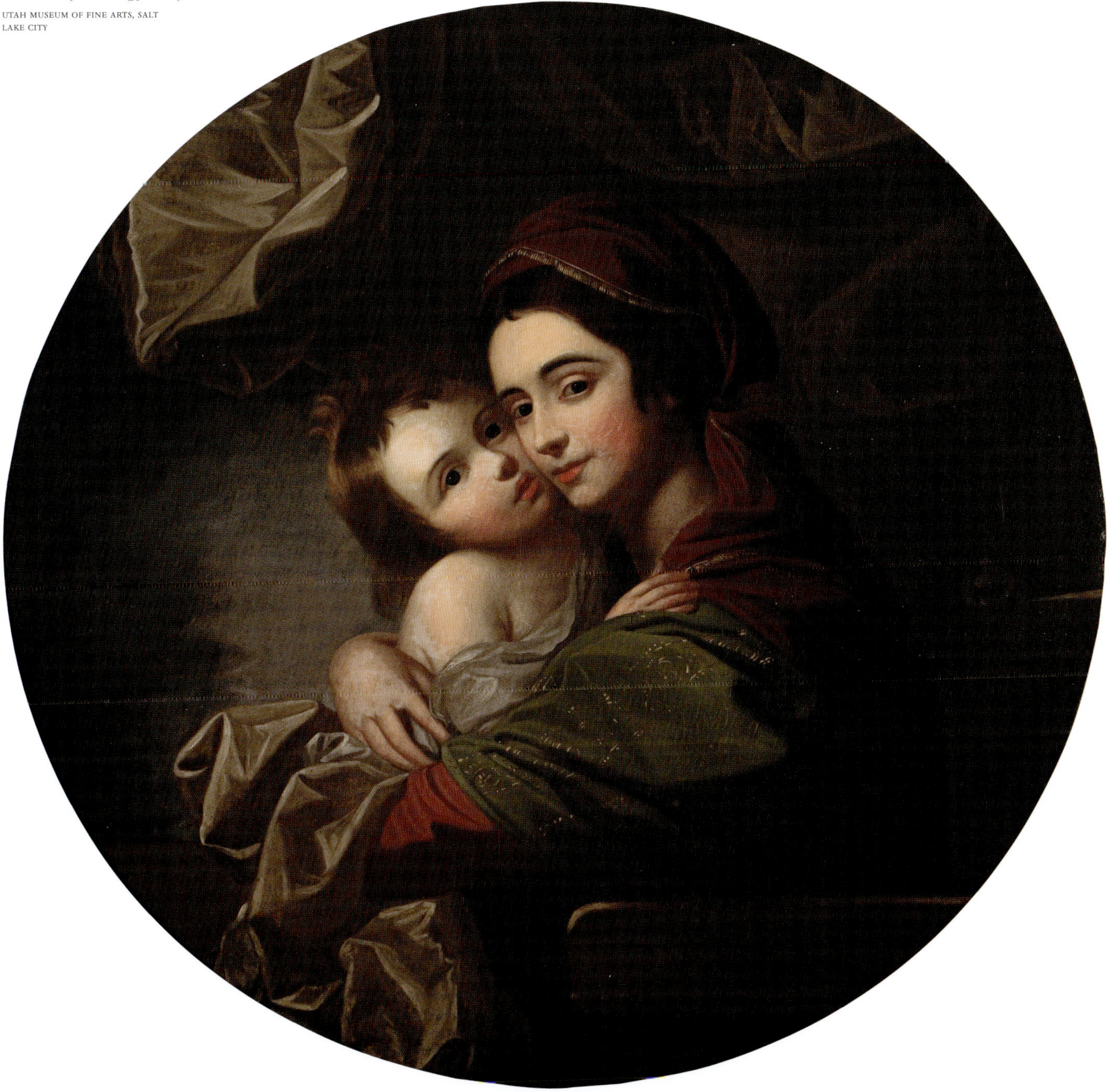

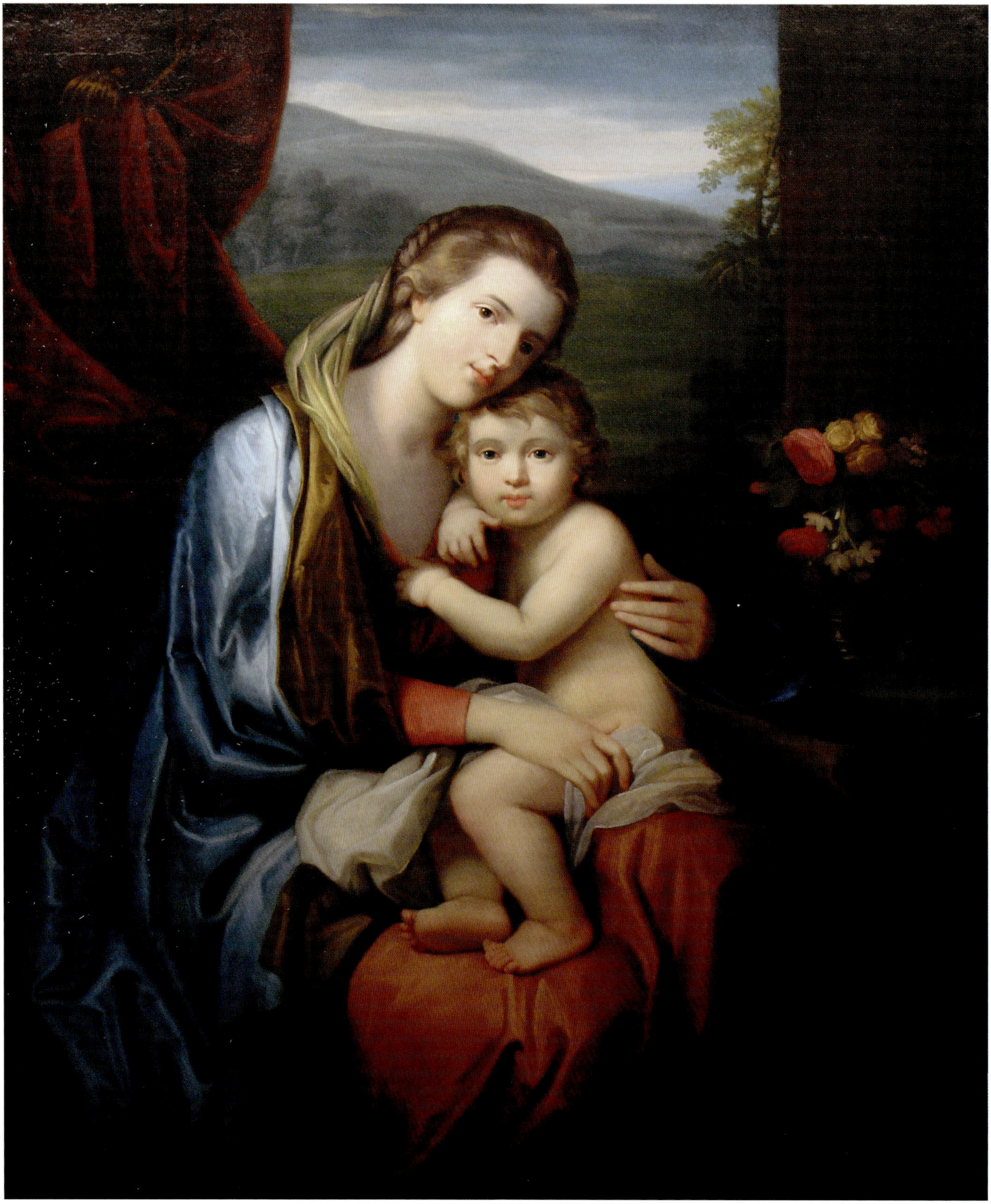

50 OPPOSITE
Benjamin West
Anne, Countess of Northampton, and Her Daughter, Lady Elizabeth Compton
1762
Oil on canvas
130.7 × 105.2 cm
(51½ × 41⅜ in.)
BASS MUSEUM OF ART, MIAMI BEACH, FLORIDA

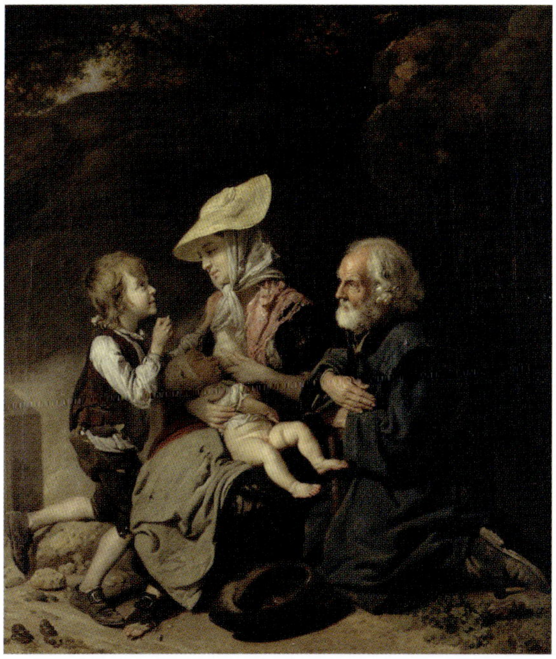

51
Johann Zoffany (1733–1810)
Beggars on the Road to Stanmore
c. 1769–70
Oil on canvas
91.5 × 76 cm (36 × 29⅞ in.)
PRIVATE COLLECTION

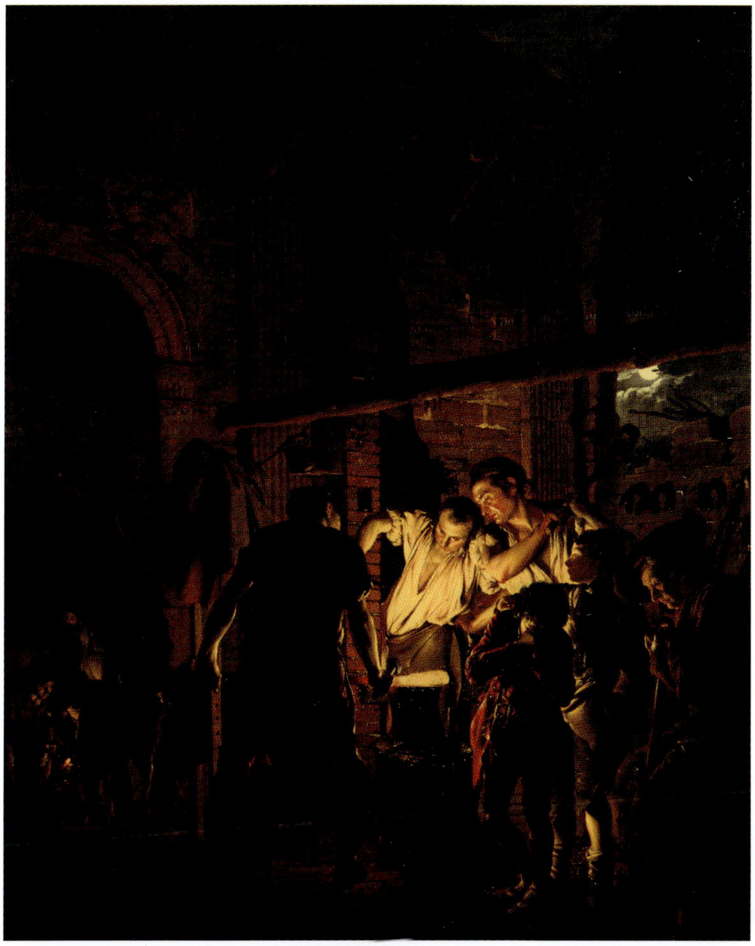

52
Joseph Wright (1734–1797)
The Blacksmith's Shop
1771
Oil on canvas
128.3 × 104.1 cm (50½ × 41 in.)
PAUL MELLON COLLECTION, YALE CENTER FOR BRITISH ART, NEW HAVEN, CONNECTICUT

been gathering strength since at least the mid-seventeenth century, but the Enlightenment put that 'rationalization and secularization' at the top of a reforming agenda that included, in Peter Gay's words, 'secularism, humanity, cosmopolitanism … freedom from arbitrary power, freedom of speech, freedom of trade, freedom to realize one's talents, freedom of aesthetic response'.[7] From Gay's list of freedoms, those of speech, trade and aesthetic response would have a special effect on the artist in terms of both subject matter and commercial practice.

Secularization was liberating, but it was destabilizing, too: 'most people at all levels of society', Jonathan Israel observes, 'were profoundly disquieted by such sweeping intellectual and cultural change'.[8] Pictorial secularization was a manifestation of that 'sweeping intellectual and cultural change'. Partially a product of the Enlightenment's intellectual programme, it was also a practical response to an audience who were quite clearly becoming bored with the limited repertoire of subject matter drawn from the Bible, mythology and ancient history.

We have seen how the exhaustion of such subject matter contributed to the failure of the competition to decorate the Louvre's Galerie d'Apollon, an exhaustion that inspired Diderot's wish that we should 'agree that no more Virgins, nor Saint Johns, nor Josephs, nor Saint Annes, nor Elizabeths, nor Christs, nor Apostles, nor any church paintings should be made', with the result that 'we'd be reduced to historical subjects and public or domestic scenes drawn from life, and perhaps this wouldn't be such a bad thing'.[9] Hogarth had already expressed similar sentiments, wishing that painting might 'be made more entertaining and more useful than the eternal blazonry, and tedious repetition of hackneyed, beaten subjects, either from the Scriptures, or the old ridiculous stories of heathen gods'.[10]

This demand for new subject matter presented a clear challenge as well as a major opportunity for artists. The challenge was to apply the lessons of the grandest style of painting, to which they were urged to aspire, to a whole new range of subject matter drawn increasingly from the everyday world around them. The opportunity was to reach an ever-bigger audience and to benefit from the commercial and reputational rewards this offered.

In order to keep within an Enlightenment context, the appropriation of sacred forms for secular subjects is described here as secularization, but could just as easily be called sacralization, which, perhaps a little more accurately, implies that sacred forms were being used to elevate and dignify subjects that would previously have been the domain of the lesser genres of painting. Viewers may not have explicitly seen *Wolfe* as a Lamentation or *The Blacksmith's Shop* as a Nativity, but when they looked at those pictures, they would have seen figures in modern dress, arranged in heroic attitudes that were previously off limits to all but a small handful of contemporary men and women. This sacralization of the everyday is part of the process previously referred to, of heroizing the present, one of the essential characteristics of modernity.

West, somewhat immodestly, and often, declared that *Wolfe* was a turning point: 'on that occasion and from the date of that picture, we must fix a revolution in the art of painting, not only in England, but in all countries where the art is cultivated'.[11] Eighteenth-century and indeed many later commentators identified the importance of *Wolfe* with the introduction of contemporary dress. Even West himself discussed his innovation in terms that suggested it was the introduction of contemporary dress that constituted the revolution in history painting. It did not. The introduction of contemporary dress signified a revolution; a revolution in which history painting was allowed to proclaim the value of the present.

While praising West as having 'a great deal of true genius', the author of *Observations on the Pictures Now in Exhibition at the Royal Academy* (1771) was disappointed that in *Wolfe*, 'the dresses of the officers give it something of a motley appearance'.[12] But such unease was becoming rare. Henry Fuseli used the example of a hypothetical *Death of Germanicus* to drive home the point about accurate costume, demanding that artists should use 'all the real modifications of time and place, which may serve unequivocally to discriminate that moment of grief from all others'.[13] This need for 'the real modifications of time and place' was becoming important not just in painting but also in the other arts, as anachronism was increasingly unacceptable. The actor Henry Angelo recalled, 'in justice to the ingenious memory of my father … Garrick frequently consulted him on the more important subject of costume, the absurdity of which, from its entire unfitness, and the anachronisms committed … were so obviously burlesque, that the mere endurance of them was a disgrace to the taste of the age'.[14]

Reverend Robert Bromley was clear that the accurate use of contemporary dress was a key part of *Wolfe*'s popularity. 'Had the painter been seduced by a kind of established veneration,' he wrote, 'which in this case would have been most absurd, we might have looked forever without success for a British army.'[15] On the other hand, James Beattie expressed the fear that *Wolfe*'s appeal would be transient:

> An historical picture, like West's *Death of Wolfe*, in which the faces are all portraits of individual heroes, and the dresses according to the present mode, may be more interesting now, than if these had been more picturesque, and those expressive of different modifications of heroism. But in a future age, when the dresses are become unfashionable, and the faces no longer known as portraits, is there not reason to fear, that this excellent piece will lose of its effect?[16]

West felt he knew better, and turned out to be right. He was proud to take credit for ending

> The prejudices which had long prevailed; that modern dresses would not admit of being painted, where Heros, or dignity were the leading characteristics of the subject. Over that prejudice the picture of Wolfe has been triumphant – and the British Heros in that picture, hold their rank with the Greeks, and Romans Heros clad in armour. It is now admitted, that the superiority of the ancient dress in a picture has no influence over the passions of the mind, and no painter is now bold enough to paint a subject out of the dress of the country to which it belongs – as was the case some years past, by making the subjects of all nations, bow to the Greeks, and Roman customs.[17]

The debate about dress, within and without the Academy, was about much more than the appropriate costume for heroes. It has been perhaps tempting to regard the discussion as a quaint, parochial affair, much as the caricature of medieval speculations about angels and pinheads was used to trivialize scholastic philosophy.[18] When Reynolds wrote 'we could no more venture to paint a general officer in a Roman military habit, than we could make a statue in the present uniform',[19] and West declared that after his *Wolfe* there was 'a revolution in the dressing of figures in historical pictures',[20] they and their contemporaries were using the question of dress as a metaphor for much more profound and widespread issues about the relative merits of past and present, and about artistic representation. In effect, they were asking, what should contemporary artists represent, and how should they do it? Or, to put it another way, who should the heroes be, and what should they look like? To borrow a term from Peter Burke, this was a crisis of representation.[21]

In December 1771, in the immediate afterglow of *Wolfe*'s popular success, Reynolds delivered to the students of the Royal Academy his fourth *Discourse*, which may be read as an anti-West or at least an anti-*Wolfe* manifesto. Discussing the grand style, Reynolds reminded his audience that the highest art should be 'either some eminent instance of heroick action, or heroick suffering … in which men are universally concerned, and which powerfully strikes upon the publick sympathy'.[22] Specificity of time and place would only diminish such universal concern as the viewer should not be distracted by 'the minute peculiarities of the dress, furniture, or scene of action'.[23] In his magisterial summing-up, Reynolds declared himself on the side of the universal – or, as he called it, the 'general' – in the contest with the particular:

> On the whole, it seems to me that there is but one presiding principle which regulates, and gives stability to every art. The works, whether of poets, painters, moralists, or historians, which are built upon general nature, live for ever; while those which depend for their existence on particular customs and habits, a partial view of nature, or the fluctuation of fashion, can only be coeval with that which first raised them from obscurity. Present time and future may be considered as rivals, and he who solicits the one must expect to be discountenanced by the other.[24]

Magnificent rhetoric indeed, clearly derived from his friend Johnson's preface to Shakespeare, with its declaration that 'Nothing can please many, and please long, but just representations of general nature.'[25] Such language, though, was beginning to sound hopelessly out of touch with the particularist approach – if I may call it that – being so successfully promoted through the historical works of Hume and Robertson and the fiction of Henry Fielding and Tobias Smollett among many others.

The intellectual arguments in favour of modern – or accurate – costume were being made in the French academy as far back as 1675, when François Blondel, director of the Académie Royale d'Architecture, asked, 'How do we know which clothes should be given those figures which we wish to represent the history of our times?'[26] Blondel unhesitatingly declared, 'I don't know if we have any more reason to dress our figures in the Roman style, than the Romans had to dress theirs in the fashion of the Greeks or Egyptians.'[27] In *The Art of Painting* (1706), Roger de Piles questioned 'Whether Truth in History be Essential in Painting', and invited his readers to 'suppose then, that a painter should imagine Alexander the Great was dressed as we dress this day and should represent the conqueror with a hat and periwig, he would doubtless do a very ridiculous thing and be guilty of an unpardonable error'.[28] In *The Theory of Painting*, Jonathan Richardson, while still broadly in favour of classical dress, made it clear that issues of costume were a matter of choice and appropriateness, noting, for example, that in portraiture, 'What is to be said for the common dress is, that It gives a greater resemblance; and Is historical as to that article.'[29] Richardson promoted French academic theory in Britain, but interpreted it through a pragmatic, English prism.[30]

Around 1720, when Sir James Thornhill considered how to portray the landing of George I at Greenwich (fig. 53) as part of the series of murals that he had been commissioned to paint for the Royal Naval Hospital there, he weighed the appeal of accuracy against the dignity of a classicizing approach. Thornhill considered both a matter-of-fact view of the event and the possibility of presenting it as a full-blown allegory, with the chariot-borne King in Roman dress attended by figures representing commerce, courage and justice.[31] He sketched a realistic version, but in his marginal notes admitted that 'Objections will arise from the plain representation of the King landing as it was in fact', as 'the King's own dress then not graceful, nor enough worthy of him to be transmitted to posterity'. Seeking a compromise, Thornhill wondered if he might 'Make the King's dress as it now is as it should have been then, rather than what it was.'[32] In the end, the Hospital decided to commission an allegorical representation as more in keeping with the existing decorative scheme. It would be another fifty years before heroes in classical dress were on the run.

Reynolds may have attempted to establish an orthodox canon of academic practice, but – very much in the pragmatic spirit of Richardson – he left the door open for innovation. 'Instead of copying the touches of those great masters,' Reynolds advised in his second *Discourse*, 'copy only their conceptions. Instead of treading in their footsteps, endeavour only to keep the same road. Labour to invent on their general principles and

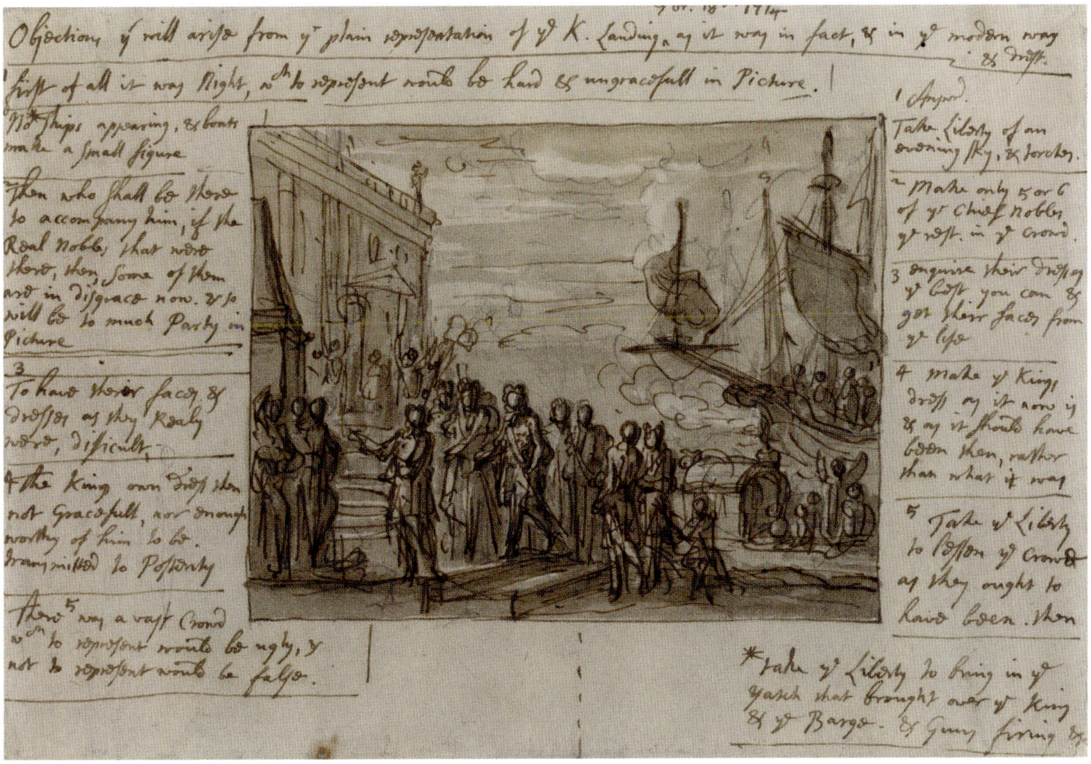

53
Sir James Thornhill
(1675–1734)
Landing of George I
1718–25
Pen and ink with wash over graphite on paper
15.8 × 22.8 cm (6¼ × 9 in.)
THE BRITISH MUSEUM, LONDON

way of thinking.'[33] It is worth reminding ourselves that, contrary to William Blake's vitriolic critique of the *Discourses*, Reynolds, and by extension one can say the Academy, discouraged slavish imitation and indeed positively encouraged artists to respond to changing circumstances. 'The great business of study', according to Reynolds, 'is, to form a *mind,* adapted and adequate to all times and all occasions.'[34]

This emphasis on '*mind*' (the italics are Reynolds's), shows the familiar wish to situate the artist within an intellectual rather than a mechanical tradition. What is also clear is Reynolds's intention that the artist should be trained to be 'adapted and adequate' to succeed in the public sphere with its rapidly shifting demands and expectations. West himself and subsequent writers have liked to portray *Wolfe* as some sort of challenge to the authority of the Academy. Edgar Wind, for example, described *Wolfe* as 'supplying a test case against the academic rules advocated by Reynolds'.[35] It was no such thing. As discussed in the first chapter, West, as a founder of the Academy and a rising star, was highly unlikely to confront either the institution or its president. The Academy was neither a mere talking shop nor a totalitarian regime: the Academy could speak with authority, but that authority had its limits. A wide divergence of views was tolerated within its walls.[36]

Consequently, it would be too simple to portray Reynolds as the chief upholder of academic orthodoxy and West as the leading subversive. The positions of both men were fluid, if not opportunistic. Reynolds famously struggled to reconcile his high-minded principles with his more powerful desire to be commercially successful. In a telling moment of self-criticism in his *Discourse* of 1770, he recognized that 'A man is not weak, though he may not be able to wield the club of Hercules; nor does a man always practise that which he esteems the best; but does that which he can best do.'[37]

Similarly, West was not irrevocably committed to his declaration that 'no painter is now bold enough to paint a subject out of the dress of

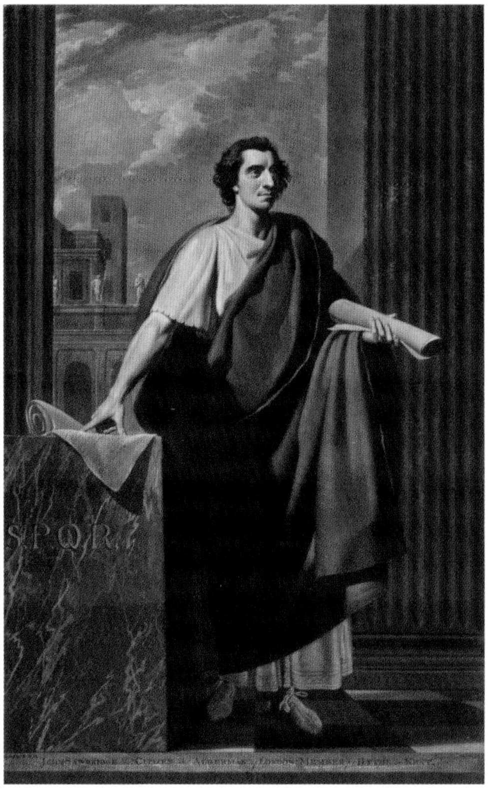

54
Thomas Watson (1750–1781), after Benjamin West
Alderman John Sawbridge
1772
Mezzotint
61.6 × 38 cm (24¼ × 15 in.)
ROYAL ACADEMY OF ARTS, LONDON

the country to which it belongs'. The year after *Wolfe* was exhibited at the Royal Academy, West produced his 'most thoroughly classicizing' portrait,[38] that of Alderman John Sawbridge, in which the togated and sandal-wearing Member of Parliament for Hythe poses alongside a plinth carved with the letters SPQR (fig. 54). Sawbridge's dress and stance, with its unmistakable references to Roman virtues, were appropriate for a politician with his republican tendencies,[39] in spite of West's commitment to what he called 'modern dresses'.

That commitment to 'modern dresses' was hardly unprecedented: even the most cursory survey of Western art reveals a great number of examples of contemporary events depicted in contemporary costume. A short list would include Uccello's *Battle of San Romano* (fig. 55), Leonardo's *Battle of Anghiari* (fig. 56), Velázquez's *Surrender of Breda* (fig. 57) and the battle paintings of Adam Frans van der Meulen (fig. 58). Even closer to West's own time and place were Louis Laguerre's murals for Marlborough House in central London (begun in 1710) and, closer still, Francis Hayman's four scenes from the Seven Years War commissioned for Vauxhall Gardens.

Laguerre's work in Marlborough House, a colossal cycle of wall paintings celebrating the Duke of Marlborough's great victories over the armies of Louis XIV in the War of the Spanish Succession, is now rather overlooked because of limited public access.[40] The Marlborough cycle contains some extraordinarily powerful and well-painted passages, and presents a comprehensive – indeed brutally comprehensive – report of the battles. In the end, Laguerre's talent was overwhelmed by the sheer scale of the project, encompassing a grand saloon and two large staircases, and lapsed into a tiresome glorification of the Duke, a stiff, almost hieratic figure on a white horse (fig. 59). Laguerre's difficulties derived not just from the scale of the project, but also from problems with both content and intent.

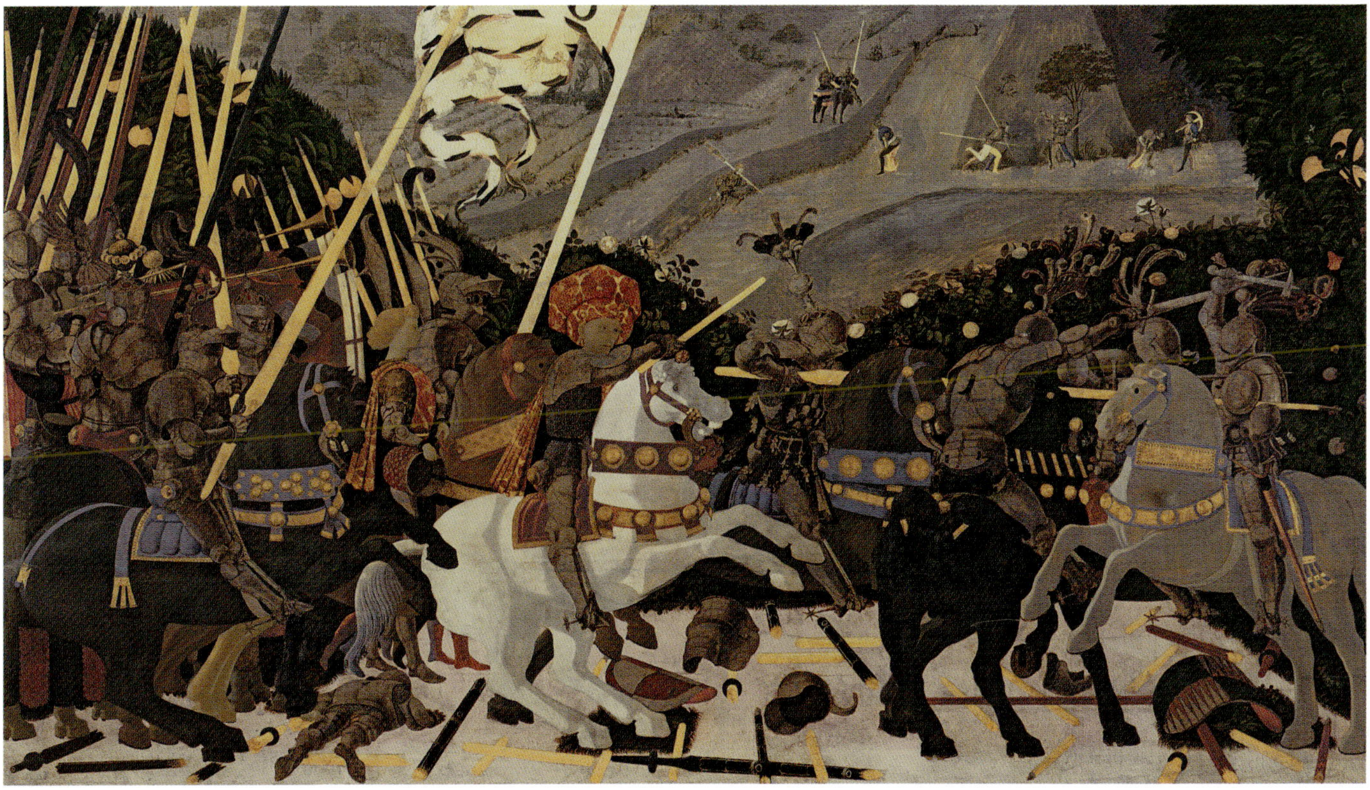

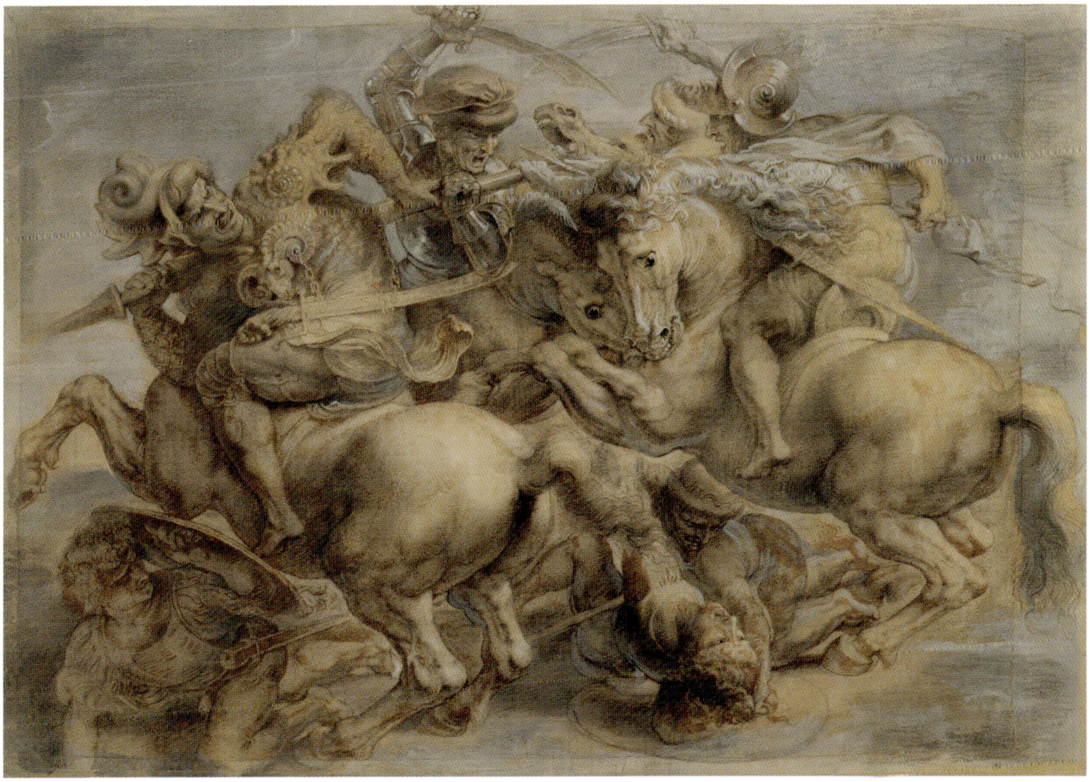

55 ABOVE
Paolo Uccello (*c.* 1397–1475)
The Battle of San Romano
c. 1438–40
Tempera with oil on panel
182 × 320 cm (71⅝ × 126 in.)
THE NATIONAL GALLERY, LONDON

56
Peter Paul Rubens (1577–1640), after Leonardo da Vinci (1452–1519)
Battle of Anghiari
c. 1603
Black chalk with pen and ink, and highlights in grey and white on paper
45.3 × 63.6 cm (17⅞ × 25 in.)
MUSÉE DU LOUVRE, PARIS

57
Diego Velázquez (1599–1660)
The Surrender of Breda
c. 1635
Oil on canvas
307 × 367 cm
(120⅞ × 144½ in.)
MUSEO NACIONAL DEL PRADO, MADRID

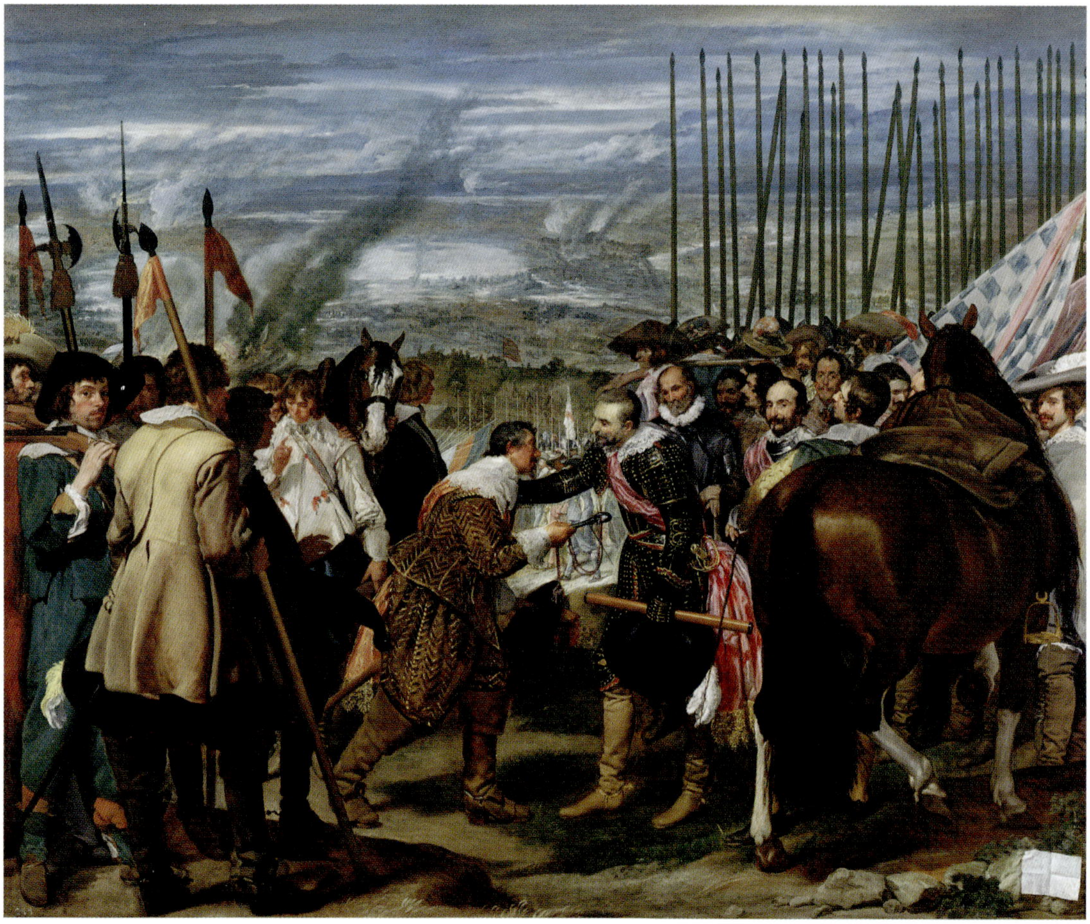

58
Adam Frans van der Meulen
(1632–1690)
Louis XIV Crossing into The Netherlands at Lobith
1672–90
Oil on canvas
103 × 159 cm (40½ × 62⅝ in.)
RIJKSMUSEUM, AMSTERDAM

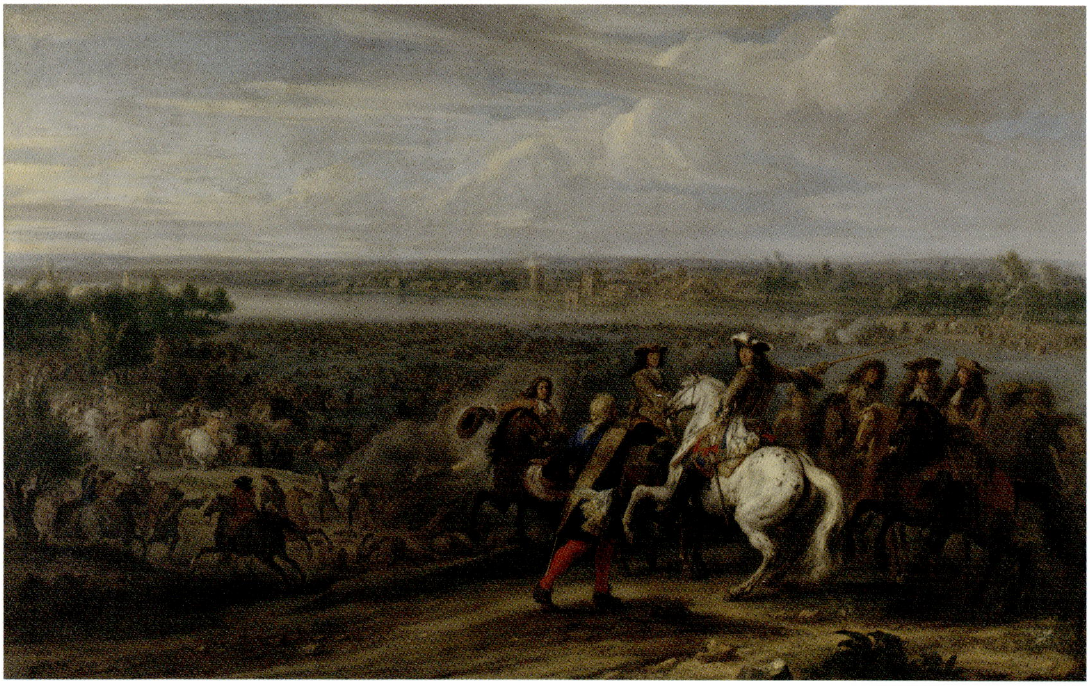

The War of the Spanish Succession (1701–14) was the beginning of a shift away from dynastic wars led by monarch generals, towards the more modern style of national wars led by managerial, professional commanders. The depiction of Marlborough poised between existing and emerging traditions of leadership was a difficult task. Laguerre unsurprisingly and unsatisfactorily compromised, combining realistic portraiture of the hard-bitten self-made soldier with a quasi-regal attitude. In the Marlborough cycle, the Duke, a model of determination and imperturbability, presides over scenes of the stripping of the dead by camp followers (fig. 60) and French soldiers being shot in the back or bludgeoned to death by rifle butt in scenes worthy of Jacques Callot.

Fifty years later, in 1760/61, Jonathan Tyers, the impresario and owner of the pleasure gardens at Vauxhall, commissioned Francis Hayman to create four very large canvases on patriotic themes to decorate the Pillared Saloon, 'the grandest of all the eighteenth-century rooms',[41] at Vauxhall. The four pictures represented the aftermath of two notable British victories – the surrender of Montreal to General Jeffery Amherst in 1760, and the homage of the Nawab of Bengal to Lord Clive, after Clive's victory at Plassey in 1757 – and presented two allegories of Britannia triumphant by land and sea. None of the paintings survives, but we know two of them through modellos and one from an engraving. In terms of their possible influence on West, *The Surrender of Montreal to General Amherst* (fig. 61) and *Robert Clive and Mir Jafar after the Battle of Plassey* (fig. 62) are the most important pictures. Both are naturalistic portrayals, even if *Amherst* depicts a highly idealized, perhaps entirely fictional, incident.

David Coke and Alan Borg cite a contemporary commentary on *Amherst*: 'clemency is the genius of the British nation; and liberty and security the natural fruits of the British government. – One of the most striking scenes in modern story!'[42] Visitors to Vauxhall Gardens responded well to such sentiments. 'Look at it long enough and you will

59 BELOW & 60 BOTTOM
Louis Laguerre (1663–1721)
The Battle of Malplaquet (details)
1710–13
Oil on canvas
MARLBOROUGH HOUSE, LONDON

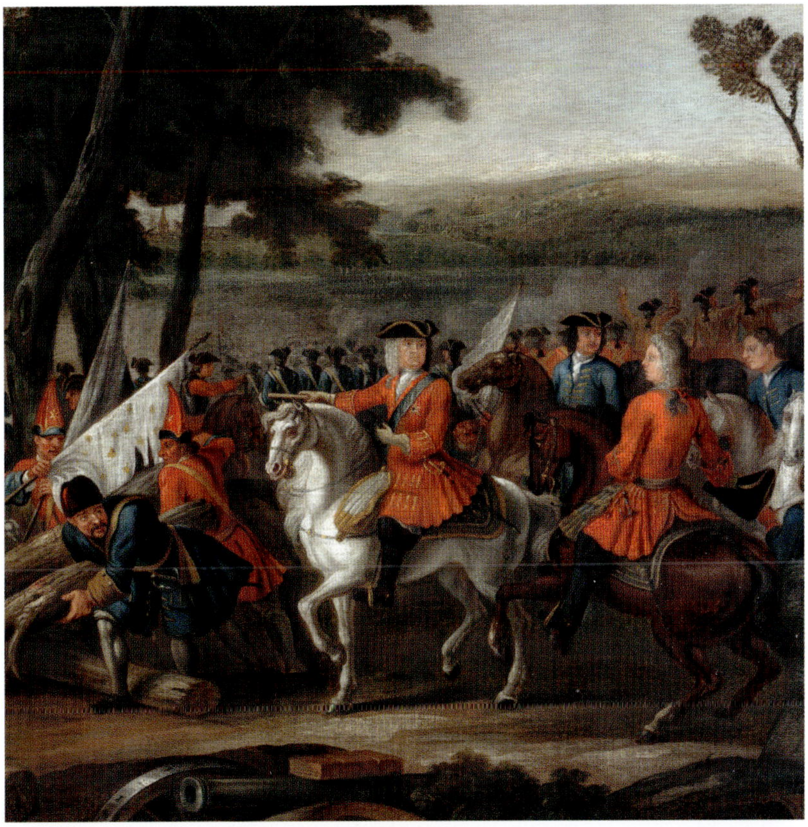

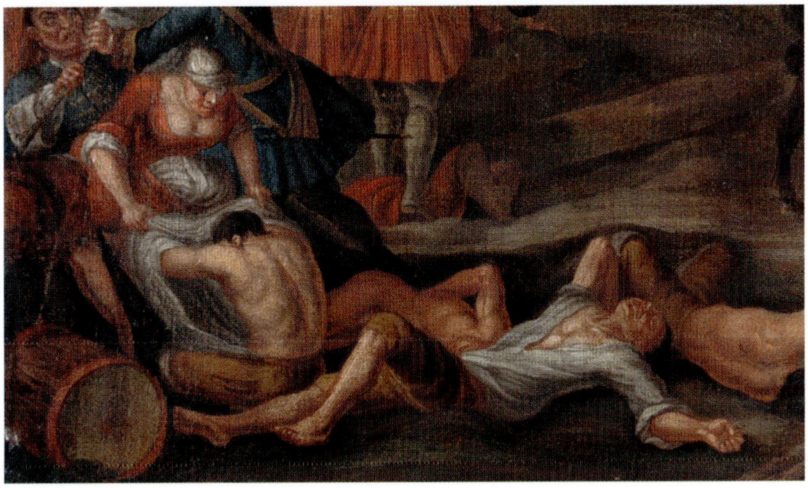

61
Francis Hayman
(*c.* 1708–1776)
Modello for *The Surrender of Montreal to General Amherst*
c. 1760
Oil on canvas
70.8 × 91.4 cm (27⅞ × 36 in.)
BEAVERBROOK ART GALLERY, FREDERICTON, NEW BRUNSWICK

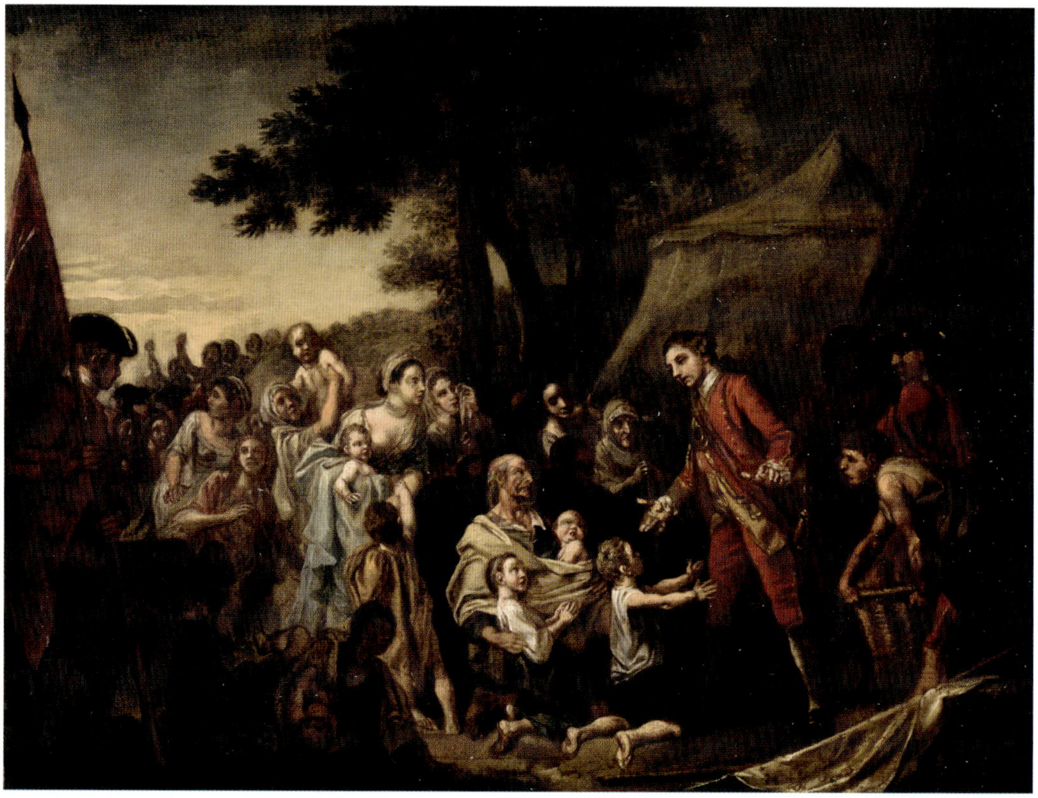

62
Francis Hayman
(*c.* 1708–1776)
Robert Clive and Mir Jafar after the Battle of Plassey, 1757
c. 1760
Oil on canvas
100.3 × 127 cm (39½ × 50 in.)
NATIONAL PORTRAIT GALLERY, LONDON

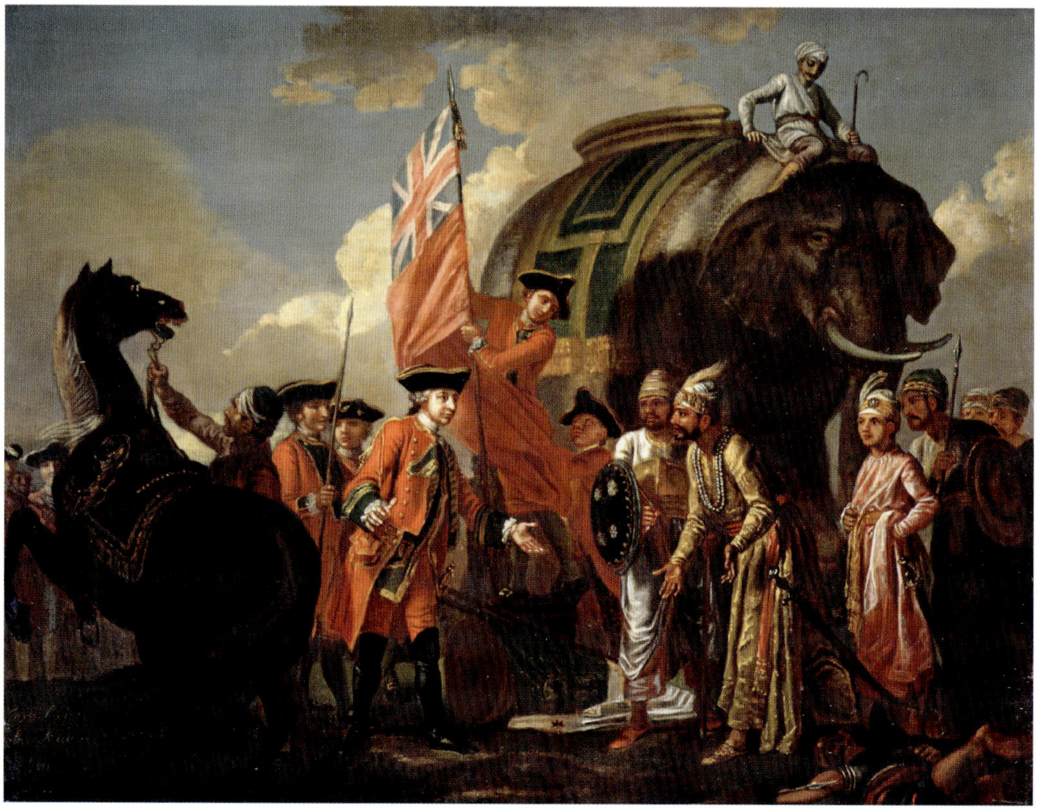

be driven to tears', one such visitor wrote about *Amherst*. 'The impression of distress, bordering on despair, as the beleaguered citizens await in fear the victors' decision regarding their fate, is so lifelike that … you become almost convinced that you are looking at no mere picture.'[43] A French tourist remarked on the 'tender and noble compassion … visible in the countenance and the whole attitude of that general'.[44]

Yet, in spite of their deft tug on the heartstrings, Hayman's history paintings failed to make the profound impact that *Wolfe* did a decade later. First, as far as we can tell from the sketches, which are well worked up, the paintings were visually rather lightweight, on the tail end of Rococo at a time just, only just, before West and Hamilton would bring a new, sparser, more muscular Neoclassical sensibility to British art. Secondly – and perhaps more importantly – there is the issue of context. After the victories of 1759, it was increasingly likely that Britain would emerge triumphant from the Seven Years War, so perhaps a series of pictures celebrating victories was not entirely inconsistent with decorating London's leading centre for mass entertainment. However, even though Hayman's paintings were installed in the most imposing room in Vauxhall Gardens, they were still in the midst of an establishment devoted to recreation of the higher and lower kind. The earlier paintings by Hayman and others that decorated the supper boxes in the Gardens were charming and elegant, depicting scenes of dancing, skating, the theatre and rustic diversions. One has to wonder if paintings created from the 1730s onwards, such as *The Milkmaid's Garland* (fig. 63) or *Blind-Man's Bluff*, would really have set an appropriate tone in which to celebrate hard-won victories, especially in the increasingly serious 1760s.

In the space of the fifty years that separate Laguerre's Marlborough cycle from Hayman's paintings of the Seven Years War, thoughts on both how war should be fought and how war should be portrayed – in art and literature – changed significantly. Laguerre was happy to paint Marlborough – and the Duke must have been happy to be thus painted – in the midst of the horrors of war. Instead of dwelling on the bloody process of killing, as Laguerre did, Hayman's Vauxhall pictures presented a benign and morally uplifting view of the results of modern warfare.

Theodore Rabb has identified an earlier transformation in the depiction of war that may hold some clues to the way British art and literature looked at war in the early eighteenth century. Rabb describes a 'new outlook' in the 1620s and '30s, 'born amidst the brutality of the Thirty Years' War'. For Rabb, 'As the viciousness of the fighting intensified, alternatives to heroism attracted new attention, and antiwar sentiments for the first time became respectable within the European Establishment.'[45] For visual evidence, Rabb turns to *The Surrender of Breda* and its companion piece in the Buen Retiro Palace, Juan Bautista Maíno's *Recapture of Bahía de Todos los Santos* (fig. 64),[46] both of which celebrate the more polite virtues of war, just as Hayman's Seven Years War pictures promoted not so much British force of arms as British generosity and benevolence in victory.

Writing in the midst of the War of the Spanish Succession in his 'Sensus Communis: An Essay on the Freedom of Wit and Humour in a Letter to a Friend' (1709), Shaftesbury mused:

> It is strange to imagine that war, which of all things appears the most savage, should be the passion of the most heroic spirits. But it is in war that the knot of fellowship is closest drawn. It is in war that mutual succour is most given, mutual danger run, and common affection most exerted and employed. For heroism and philanthropy are almost one and the same.[47]

This desire to find goodness in wars, which were being fought on a larger and deadlier scale than ever before, made savagery and civility uncomfortable bedfellows. Wolfe himself is a fine example of the resulting moral confusion, writing that if he failed to capture Quebec,

> I propose to set the Town on fire with Shells, to destroy the Harvest, Houses, & Cattle both

> above and below, to send off as many Canadians as possible to Europe, & to leave famine and desolation behind me: belle resolution & très chretienne! But we must teach these Scoundrels to make war in a more gentlemanlike manner.[48]

This wish 'to make war in a more gentlemanlike manner' was a worthy aspiration that nonetheless paved the road to hell. Like Laguerre, men of letters did not shy away from graphic descriptions of the horrors of the eighteenth-century battlefield. Describing chain shot in his poem *Blenheim* (1705), John Phillips wrote: 'By Chains connex't, and with destructive Sweep/ Behead whole Troops at once; the hairy Scalps/ Are whirl'd aloof, while numerous Trunks bestrow/ Th'ensanguin'd Field.'[49] Blood and guts were no stranger to the novel either, as Tobias Smollett's hero Roderick Random recounted the war at sea in 1748:

> I concealed my agitation as well as I could, till the head of the officer of Marines, who stood near me, being shot off bounced from the deck athwart my face, leaving me well-nigh blinded with brains. – I could contain myself no longer, but began to bellow with all the strength of my lungs; when a drummer coming towards me, asked if I was wounded; and before I could answer received a great shot in his belly which tore out his intrails ...[50]

While novels, a lesser literary genre than poetry, were increasingly able to present war in such anti-heroic and picaresque terms, John Richardson notes that many poets 'seemed to have entertained the double ambition of celebrating victory in heroic forms derived from the ancients and of representing modern battle with a degree of accuracy'. The difficulties around achieving this 'double ambition' led to 'a growing realization that ancient martial models might not fit, or be made to fit modern experience'.[51] In a belligerent century, this crisis of representation was significant and hard to resolve. Writing in 1809, Joel Barlow observed that

> Our heaven and earth are not only shaken and tormented with greater noise, but filled and suffocated with fire and smoke. If Homer, with his Grecian tongue ... had had the battle of Blenheim to describe, the world would have possessed a picture and a piece of music which now it will never possess. The description would have astonished all ages, and enriched every language into which it might have been translated.[52]

But West was poised to do what the poets could not. From the moment he arrived in London, he would have been aware of the bustle of activity as artists rushed to commemorate the dead hero of Quebec: there were paintings by George Romney and Edward Penny, and the Monument to General James Wolfe by Joseph Wilton, a work long in progress from the early 1760s until its public unveiling in Westminster Abbey in 1773. However, this commemorative frenzy came at a time when artists were facing almost unprecedented upheaval on all fronts. The growing power of public opinion, the commodification of artistic production, the rise of historical consciousness, the globalization of trade and warfare, the decline of classical authority, the exaltation of sentiment; all these phenomena came into sharp focus in the 1760s and early 1770s. Small wonder, then, that producing an iconic vision of Britain's greatest contemporary hero would prove to be so problematic.

Romney's *Death of General Wolfe* was shown at the Society of Artists exhibition in May 1763, a few months before West's arrival in London. Three years earlier, the Society for the Encouragement of Arts, Manufactures and Commerce had begun awarding prizes for history paintings with subjects drawn from British history.[53] In 1763 Robert Edge Pine, a previous winner, was awarded the first prize of one hundred guineas for *Canute Reproving His Flattering Courtiers,* and Romney the second prize of fifty guineas for *Wolfe*. In the somewhat confused events that followed, it was decided to revoke Romney's prize and award the fifty guineas instead to John Hamilton Mortimer, another previous winner, for *Edward the Confessor Stripping His Mother of Her Effects*. As a consolation prize, Romney was awarded a bounty of twenty-five guineas. Romney's son – and perhaps the rest of

63 RIGHT
Francis Hayman (*c.* 1708–1776)
The Milkmaid's Garland (Humours of May Day)
1741–42
Oil on canvas
138.5 × 240 cm (54½ × 94½ in.)
VICTORIA AND ALBERT MUSEUM, LONDON

64
Juan Bautista Maíno (1581–1649)
The Recapture of Bahía de Todos los Santos
1634–35
Oil on canvas
309 × 381 cm (121⅝ × 150 in.)
MUSEO NACIONAL DEL PRADO, MADRID

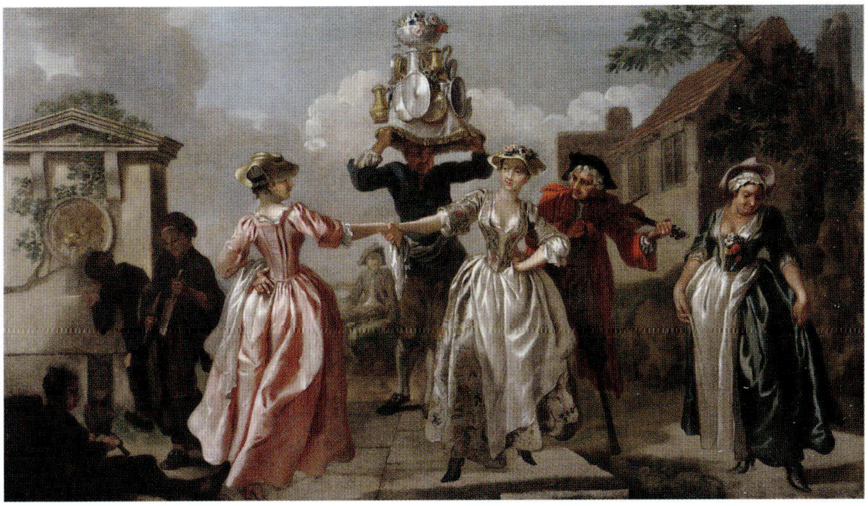

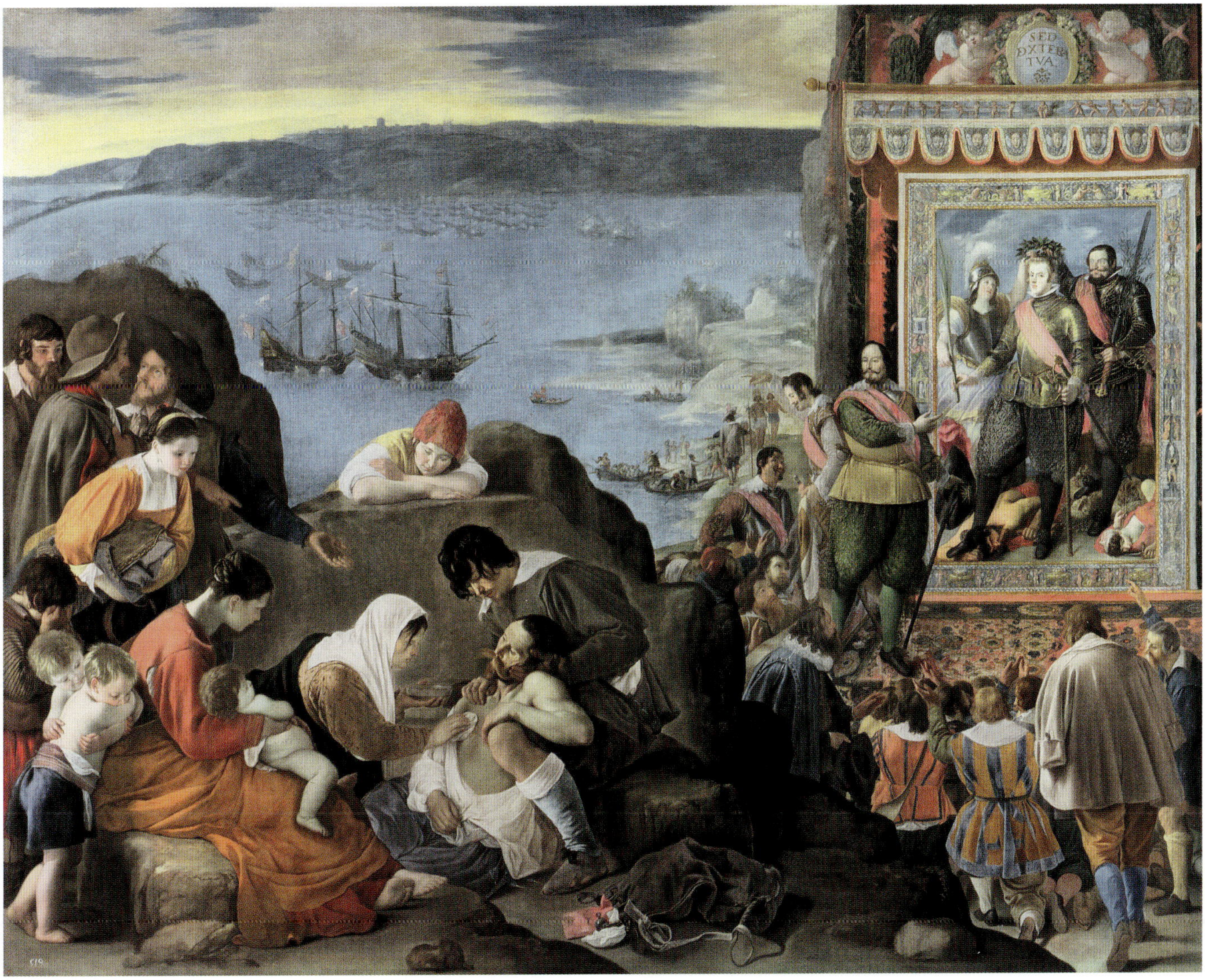

Romney's family and friends – saw malevolence and ignorance behind the plot against the young provincial painter. Romney's picture, 'capable of exciting so strong a feeling of admiration in the public mind', may have been a threat to Reynolds, who was 'too much versed in his profession, and had too shrewd an intellect not to perceive in the author of that picture a future rival'.[54] Or perhaps, more likely, the public was not quite ready for a full-blown history painting in modern dress of so recent an event. Some may have objected

> to the propriety of its being considered as an historical composition, when, in fact, no historian had then recorded the event on which it was founded. Other criticisms even more ridiculously minute and frivolous than the above were offered against it; as that the officers and soldiers were not all in their proper regimentals, that Wolfe himself had on a handsome pair of silk stockings, against the costume of a general on the field of battle; and some objected to the deadly paleness of his countenance … Some, also, by way of reproach have called it a coat and waistcoat subject; an objection which would exclude from the pencil all important events in modern warfare …[55]

Romney's picture was bought by his friend, the banker Rowland Stephenson, for twenty-five guineas[56] and given by him to Harry Verelst, the newly appointed Governor of the Bengal Presidency, who took the picture to India. Once in Calcutta, Verelst installed the picture in the Council Chamber there. Two years later, whether with or without the picture, Verelst returned to England: the whereabouts of Romney's *Wolfe* have remained a mystery ever since. It was never reproduced and the most significant clue to its appearance is a surviving study (fig. 7) showing the pallid young general in red coat and buff waistcoat with his head collapsing towards his left shoulder. Among the few things we know about Romney's *Wolfe* is that it was a big picture. Walpole describes 'figures large as life',[57] which may have caused problems for Romney 'who was obliged to work on his canvas … in a studio so small that he could not step back to survey the overall effect'.[58]

Whatever problems there were with Romney's picture, Walpole was impressed enough to describe it in some detail:

> The Genl. is represented leaning against & supported (by) two Officers who Express great Concern, the Blood appears trickling from the Wound in his Wrist & from that in his Breast agt. which one of the Officers holds his Hand a third Officer is coming to the Genl. (to) inform him the French give way & appears greatly struck with Surprize … the great Fault found with it was the Genl.('s) Countenance which was more like a Dead than a dying Man's.

Walpole declared it to be 'better than Manini's picture of Edward the Black Prince & John of France'.[59] Certainly it was a bold and ambitious move for a young, relatively unknown artist, newly arrived in London from the north. Scarcely four years after the event, Wolfe's death at Quebec was – and was to remain so for many years – a vivid and highly charged subject, and Romney's *Wolfe* was its first significant artistic commemoration.[60]

Romney hoped that his picture would appeal to the Duke of Richmond, a well-known devotee of the Wolfe cult. Perhaps Romney was motivated by 'the simple and cynical idea of attracting the Duke's attention and patronage'[61] – if so, he failed. 'Romney's choice of the subject … and the way he depicted it', Alex Kidson writes, 'perfectly illustrate the compounded opportunism and naivety in his artistic make-up.'[62] It may be harsh to level the charges of opportunism and naivety against a young artist in the highly competitive milieu of mid-eighteenth-century London. If it was opportunistic to choose a popular subject and if it was naive to expect such popularity to attract patronage, then many other artists – a list of whom could include both Reynolds and West – were also naive and opportunistic. In the rough and tumble of exhibitionary culture, choosing the right subject matter was critically important. Portraits of celebrities – Garrick is the prime example – would guarantee public attention, so it is no wonder at all that the death of Britain's greatest military hero should be a popular choice for artists.[63]

West would have been aware of Romney's *Wolfe* and would almost certainly have seen it, but its almost immediate disappearance from the public sphere robbed it of influence.[64] The year after Romney's *Wolfe*, Edward Penny displayed his *Death of General Wolfe* at the Society of Artists exhibition, which opened on 9 April 1764. There are two extant versions, small (50.8 × 74.9 cm/20 × 29½ in.) and large (102 × 127 cm/40⅛ × 50 in.; fig. 6), in private hands and at the Ashmolean respectively. The smaller *Wolfe* would seem to be the one exhibited at Spring Gardens.[65] Described by David Solkin as 'a remarkably modest and prosaic affair that quite closely attends to what was known about the specific circumstances of the last moments in the general's life',[66] it nonetheless, in Solkin's view, 'arguably constitutes a far more radical intervention into the tradition of heroic art than the so called "revolution of history-painting" that has been credited to Benjamin West'.[67] For Solkin, this 'radical intervention' may be seen to reside in the very lack of conventional heroism in Penny's painting: 'Rather than elevating his protagonist to a quasi-divine status, the artist confronts us at close range with the personal tragedy of a death no more or less noble, perhaps than that of any other soldier.'[68]

Penny provides us with a poignant scene of the hero's death. While both versions feature a powerful pyramidal composition of the dying general supported by two grenadiers and attended by a kneeling officer, the smaller version, which lacks the crowded battlefield background of the Ashmolean one, is a much more moving evocation of a lonely death in a corner of a battlefield. Although Penny's *Wolfe* was a timely and forthright expression of the rising sentimental zeitgeist – 'well told' in Horace Walpole's words[69] – it is a picture with many weaknesses. Its self-effacing charm, small scale, dull colours and eccentricities of execution (it is, for example, not an especially good likeness of what was by then a well-known public face) all combine to make it more anecdotal genre and less grand-style history. Admirably empathetic, Penny was an artist of consistent but modest talent, and that modest talent failed to rise to the grandeur of Wolfe's death. While Penny saw the death of Wolfe as an individual disaster, for West it was an epic tragedy. To draw an analogy with Christian art, Penny's *Wolfe* is reminiscent of a private devotional work, while West's is more akin to a full-blown altarpiece.

Shunning triumphalism, Penny chose to demonstrate 'the moral righteousness of the British cause … by telling the tragic story of General Wolfe's success, and eliciting a noble flood of sympathetic tears'.[70] In his vision, Wolfe is no Imperial Caesar, but a slight, almost insubstantial figure, as he was in real life. Penny presents us with a Wolfe who is one of us. There is the suggestion that, Christ-like, Wolfe is dying for us, and we are invited to share his suffering and to shed a tear with him.

This was, indeed, becoming a tearful era, exemplified by Henry Mackenzie's novel of 1771, *The Man of Feeling*, in which the hero, Harley, seldom has a dry eye. Harley's face is often 'bathed in tears';[71] at Harley's death, the narrator finds 'time to weep',[72] and Harley's friend Edwards's breast is 'heaving with the most convulsive throbs'.[73] Amid all this lachrymose melodrama, there is a lesson to be learned. Stricken with a fatal illness, Harley declares that 'To meet death as becomes a man, is a privilege bestowed on few. — I would endeavor to make it mine.'[74]

What one might call sentimental collusion – the emotional identification with the subject of our attention – is something that we have already seen emerging in history writing, most strongly in the work of Hume and Robertson. It was this complicit emotionalism that had, most likely, particularly displeased Pitt when he went to view West's *Wolfe,* as described in the first chapter. The tearful faces of two of the foreground figures in West's *Wolfe* are something that neither Pitt, nor I suspect anyone else, would have seen in such a painting before.

65
Benjamin West
Study for *The Death of General Wolfe*
c. 1769
Pen and ink and oil on paper
43 × 61.4 cm (17 × 24⅛ in.)
NATIONAL GALLERY OF CANADA, OTTAWA

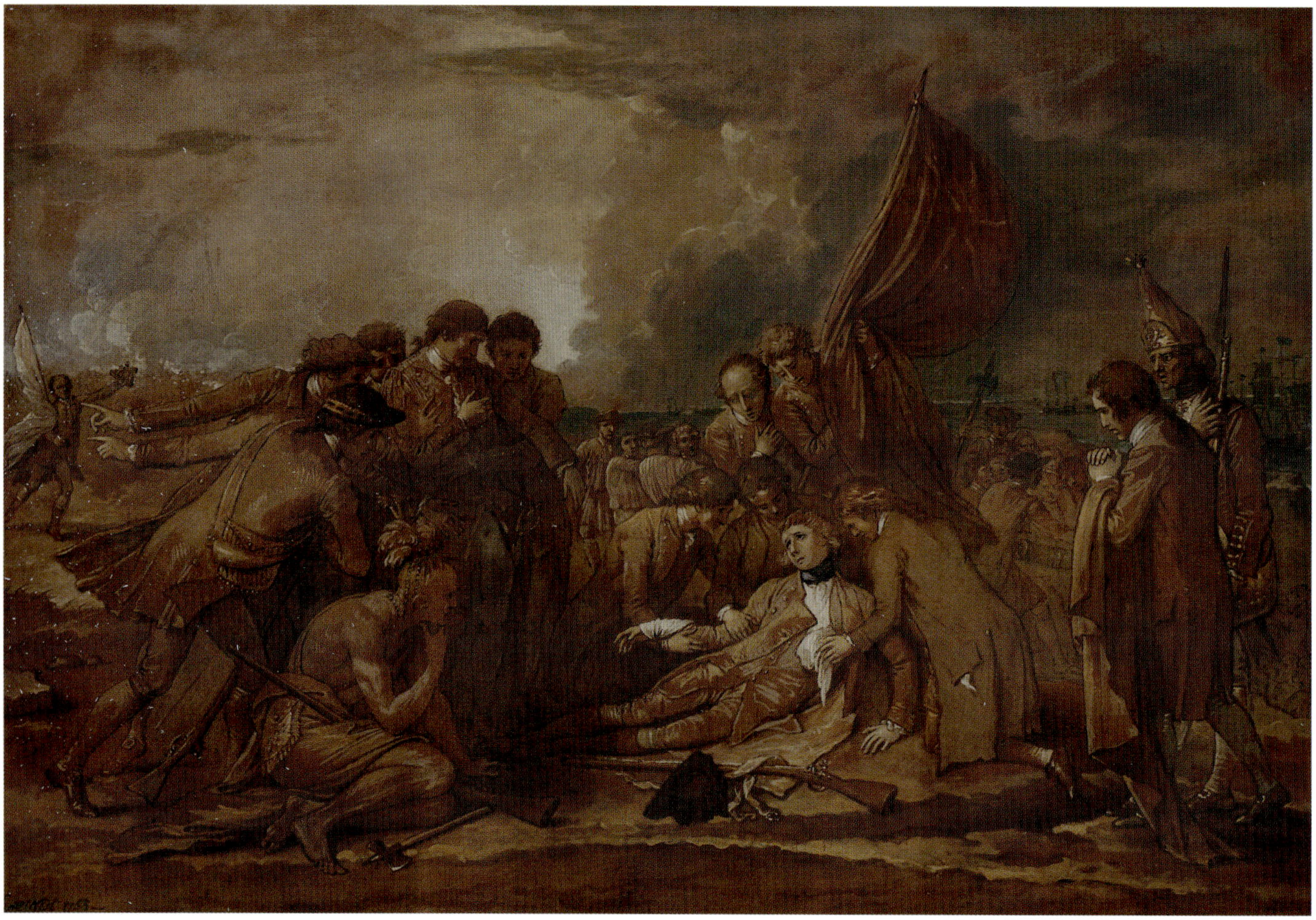

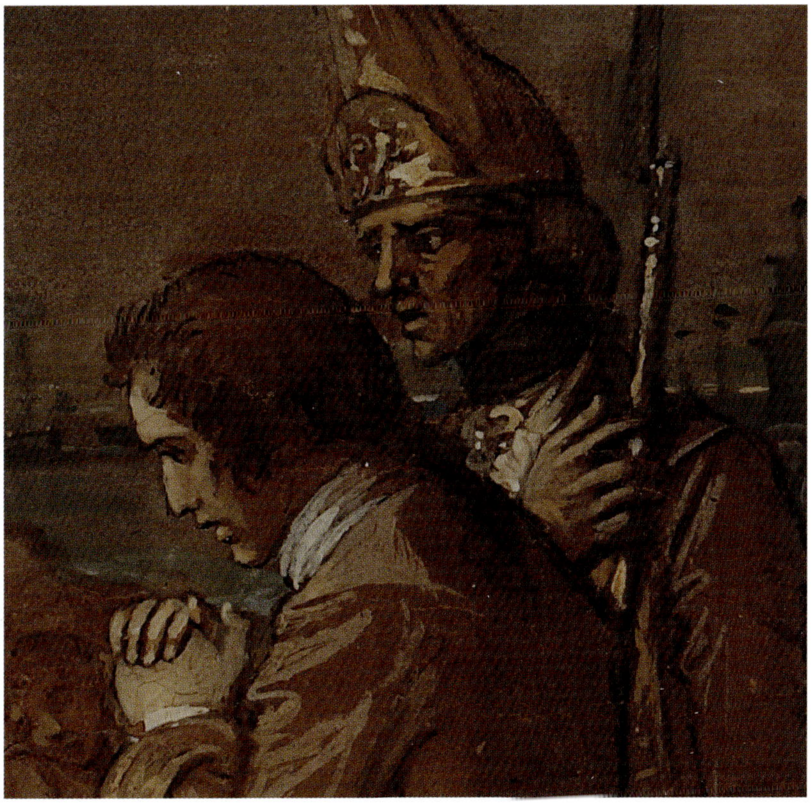

66
Benjamin West
Study for *The Death of General Wolfe* (detail)
c. 1769
Pen and ink and oil on paper
NATIONAL GALLERY OF CANADA, OTTAWA

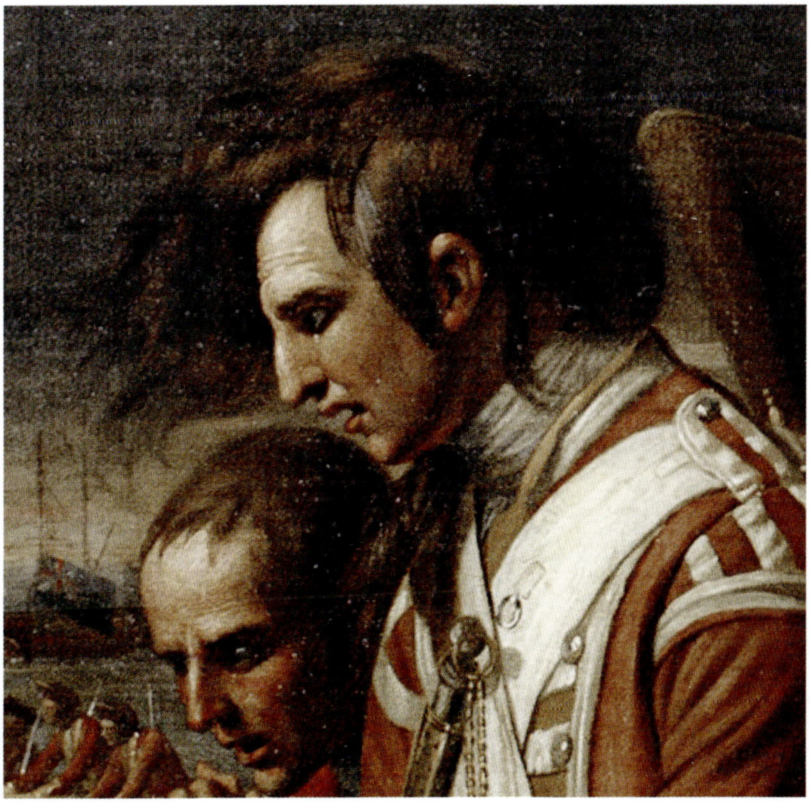

67
Benjamin West
The Death of General Wolfe (detail)
1771
Oil on canvas
ROYAL COLLECTION, LONDON

There is a highly worked-up preparatory study for *Wolfe* in the National Gallery of Canada (fig. 65); a study that is intriguing for a number of reasons. The high degree of finish and detail underlines the care, perhaps even the caution with which West approached what he knew to be a work of potentially great importance. There are some relatively minor but noticeable differences between the sketch and the finished oils – mostly in the detailed placement of the figures, the positions of their arms, the set of their facial expressions – but the sketch is probably 90 per cent like the final version. The biggest change between the study and the painting is in the faces of the soldier/servant and the very tall grenadier. In the study, they look shocked and concerned (fig. 66); in the painting, there are tears in their eyes (fig. 67). These two *pleurants* are private soldiers: the members of the officer class do not weep. Nonetheless, their presence is startling testimony to the impact of the sentimental revolution and West's sensitivity to it.[75]

Romney, and in particular Penny and West, all created a new type of *exemplum virtutis,* perhaps more well aimed at the middling audience than at the magisterial likes of Pitt, and in this new *exemplum virtutis*, virtue rubs off on us through a shared emotional experience rather than by the emulation of the actions of some more elevated hero. In other words, virtue is becoming democratized. In this process, Penny's *Wolfe* is a step forward.

These deaths of Wolfe, whether painted by Romney, Penny or West, need to be viewed within the context of an extraordinary number of deathbed scenes that began to appear shortly after mid-century. As Robert Rosenblum describes it in his *tour d'horizon*, 'examples may well run into the thousands … this somber theme served to evoke a new aura of gravity and seriousness'.[76] Although undoubtedly inspired by Poussin's *Death of Germanicus* (fig. 68), then in the Barberini Palace and an obligatory picture for every Grand Tourist, Gavin Hamilton was once again the pioneer of the formula – just as he had been with large-scale secular history painting. Hamilton painted *Andromache Lamenting the Death of Hector* in 1761, when West was in Rome. Rosenblum describes how 'A distant Homeric world of noble deeds and simple, powerful passions is created by a staid, gravity-bound composition in which the strong horizontal accent of the deathbed, in parallel alignment to the picture plane, is offset by the chorus of standing and seated mourners who demonstrate their grief with academic rhetoric.' Rosenblum also identifies, but maybe understates, that 'Christian associations with the Lamentation and with the expiration of saints are inevitable.'[77] It might be more forcefully contended that the eighteenth-century preoccupation with the deathbed scene is principally the consequence of more than a thousand years of Christian art regularly featuring scenes of death, dying and martyrdom, which provided a large stock of emotionally charged models waiting to be adapted for secular use. This theme of the exemplary death became a familiar eighteenth-century trope. Wolfe himself seems to have had frequent premonitions, writing, for example, to his mother, 'All that I wish for myself is that I may at all times be ready and firm to meet that fate we cannot shun, and to die gracefully and properly when the hour comes.'[78] Such sentiments are not too far from those in Joseph Addison's *Cato* (1713), one of the most frequently performed plays in eighteenth-century Britain, when Cato looks on his dead son and says, 'How beautiful is Death, when earn'd by Virtue!/ Who would not be that Youth? What Pity is it/ That we can die but once to serve our Country!'[79]

The same exhibition that featured Penny's *Wolfe* also marked West's debut on the London exhibition scene with his full-length portrait *General Robert Monckton* (fig. 12). While Monckton was one of the heroes of Quebec – succeeding Wolfe as commander of the British forces – he chose to use his portrait instead to commemorate his victorious invasion of Martinique in 1762, painted in some detail in the background. For the Monckton portrait, West adopted the *Apollo*

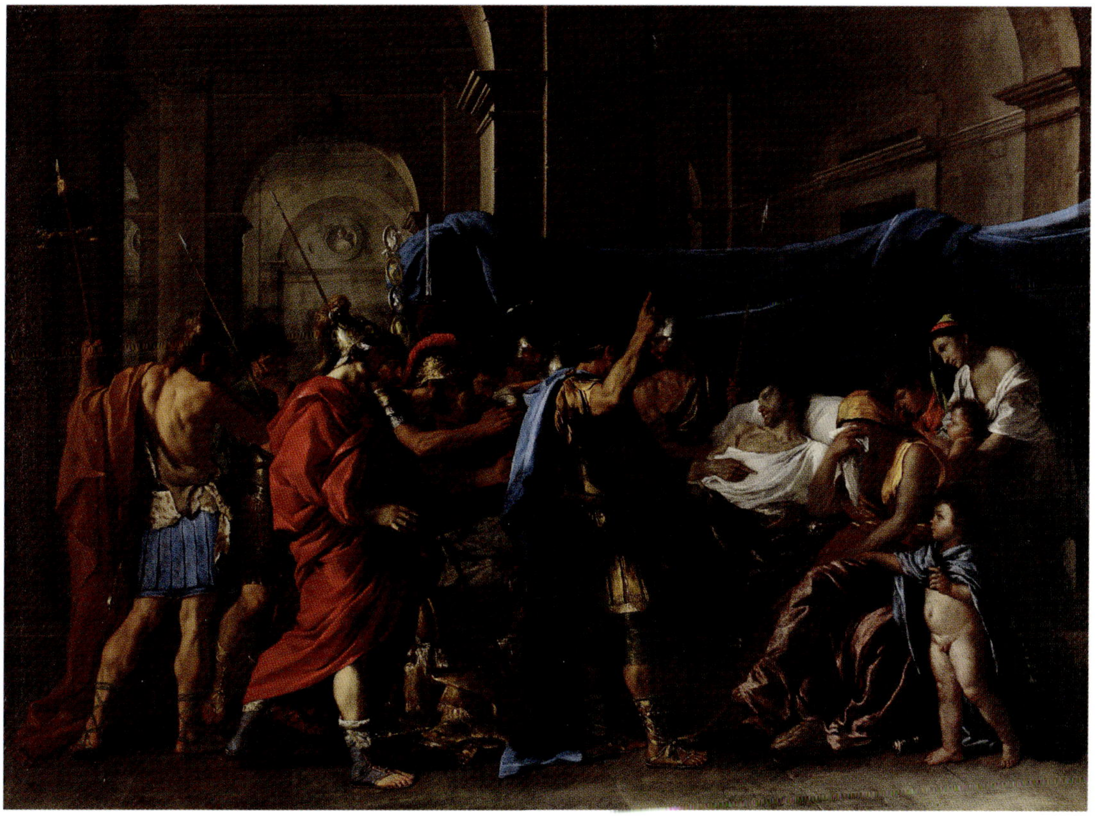

68
Nicolas Poussin (1594–1665)
The Death of Germanicus
1627
Oil on canvas
148 × 198.1 cm (58¼ × 78 in.)
MINNEAPOLIS INSTITUTE OF ARTS

Belvedere pose that Reynolds had popularized in his portrait of Augustus Keppel, but in this case the portrait, while impressive, is unsuccessful. Monckton's stance is awkward, his gaze and expression are dull; the uniform is more convincing than the man. However, it is possible that West's acquaintance with Monckton may have further encouraged him to think about creating his own painting of the death of Wolfe.

While Penny's and Romney's paintings show the public appetite to commemorate Wolfe, it is more likely that two works of sculpture had the greatest influence on how West chose to portray the general. The grandest homage of all to Wolfe was the monument by Joseph Wilton intended for Westminster Abbey (fig. 8), a monument first called for in a speech to the House of Commons by Pitt on 9 November 1759; a monument that was a work in progress when West arrived in London; a monument that was not unveiled in Westminster Abbey until two years after West exhibited his *Wolfe*.

The prolonged gestation of Wilton's monument and the importance of its subject matter made its commissioning and creation a matter of public interest. 'I saw a complete model of it, in the sculptor's work-shop such as it is to be executed in marble', the French antiquary and travel writer Pierre-Jean Grosley recalled in the account of his visit to London in 1765:

> A grenadier is represented supporting him [Wolfe] unarmed, expiring, and reclined upon an antique couch, and, at the same time, shewing him at a distance, Victory, which flies towards him, with a crown of laurel: opposite to this figure, a groupe of military men and Canadians express, by a variety of different attitudes, the most profound sorrow: the drooping hero has, as a carpet under his feet, a great pair of colours, thrown there at random, part of which falls upon the monument: upon these colours are represented three flower-de-luces, in the strongest embroidery.[80]

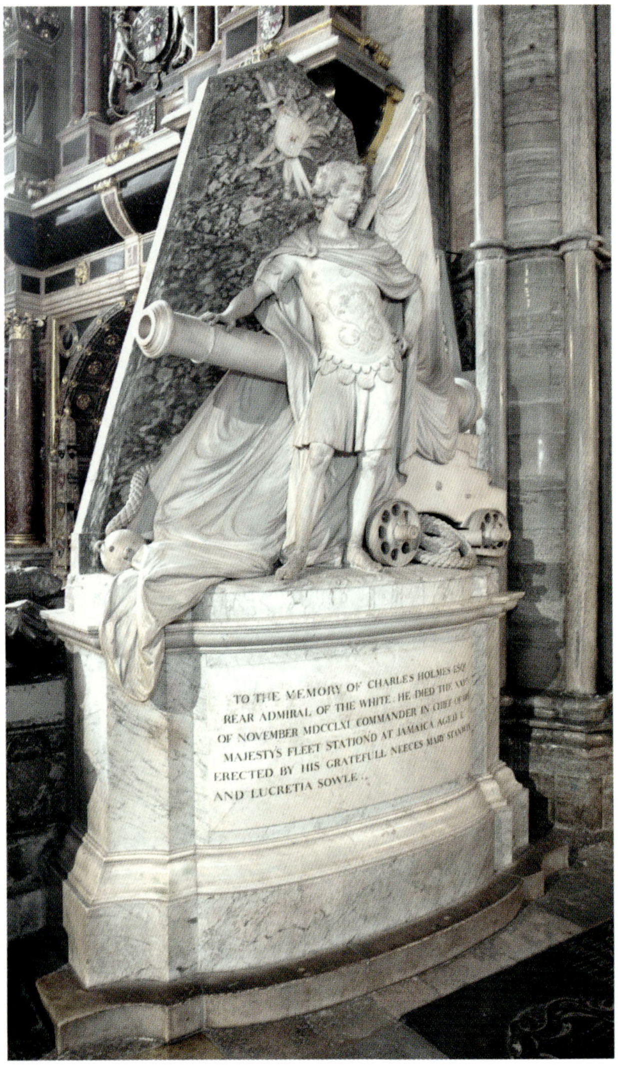

69
Joseph Wilton (1722–1803)
Monument to Rear Admiral Charles Holmes
1764
Marble
WESTMINSTER ABBEY, LONDON

Wilton's Wolfe monument is a retrograde work of art, running counter to the spirit of the times in both execution and intention. Its triumphalism – Wolfe's trampling the French flag – was clearly distasteful to Grosley, who remarked tartly that 'Lewis the Fourteenth is the first modern sovereign, who insulted foreign nations with standing monuments of this kind: but they have since paid him in his own coin … we may say with the Greeks, who when they had subdued the Trojans, lamented their victory … We are all punished for our pride.'[81]

As well as offending the rising ideals that gentlemanly behaviour in war should exemplify civility and compassion, Wilton's *Wolfe* spectacularly failed to resolve the struggle between the veneration of ancient models and the need to commemorate contemporary events in a way that made aesthetic and emotional sense to an audience that was becoming ever less comfortable with classical allusions. Wilton had already portrayed Wolfe, wearing a Roman cuirass, in a magnificent Rococo bust of 1760, but his first major essay in martial glorification was his monument in Westminster Abbey to the memory of Rear Admiral Charles Holmes (fig. 69), in which the sandal-wearing, Roman-armour-clad sailor, in relaxed hand-on-hip pose, leans against a beautifully modelled 18-pound naval cannon ready for action. Even in the early 1760s it must have seemed a blatant, if not downright odd compromise.

Sculpture had its own particular problems. As practitioners of the most permanent and highest form of artistic representation, sculptors were understandably slow to solve the problem of representing the contemporary.[82] With his monument to Wolfe, the biggest and most prominent commission to any sculptor, indeed to any artist, in Britain at the time, Wilton quite clearly struggled to combine the demands for classical dignity with the hunger for accurate representation. The result, centred on a near-naked Wolfe partially veiled in classical drapery, is unhappy. Margaret Whinney judged that 'In combination, however, with the extreme naturalism of the two soldiers and the Baroque allegory of the Victory, it borders on the grotesque, and here more than in any other work, the confusion, and perhaps also the pretentiousness of the artist is apparent.'[83] To add further 'confusion', the plinth of the monument is mounted with a deep relief presenting a highly detailed bird's-eye view of the landing and battle, sculpted and cast in lead by Giovanni Cappezoldi. Cappezoldi's work brings an element of reportage to the monument, but makes Wilton's mix of allegory and naturalism even more uncomfortable.

Matthew Craske feels that 'Wilton's choice to combine historical narrative with allegory' risked identification with what English Protestants would have considered 'the corrupting mythologizing of Roman Catholicism'. Craske goes on to speculate that

> When honouring Wolfe, Wilton seems to have been keen to exploit the visual language that Catholics had employed to convey the suffering and sacrifice of Christ. While it is commonly believed that Wilton borrowed from the iconography of the Deposition to add pathos to his patriotic narrative ... his usage of mixed allegory risked reminding viewers of the types of compositions deployed in Catholic painters' celebrations of Christ's sufferings.[84]

Craske may overstate the risk of such an association with Catholic imagery. As Wilton neared completion of the monument, the Anglican Establishment was engaged in debate about increasing the Protestant use of imagery, much of it centred on the installation in 1757 at St Margaret's, Westminster – significantly, the parish church of the House of Commons – of a window depicting the Crucifixion. Such debate continued into the 1770s, culminating in the ultimately unsuccessful proposal to decorate St Paul's Cathedral with the works of a number of the Royal Academicians.[85] In that light, it would seem that Wilton's greatest risk was not so much with Roman Catholic associations, but with committing the newly perceived sin of anachronism.

70
Robert Adam (1728–1792)
Proposal for Wolfe monument
1759
Pen, pencil and wash on paper
84.8 × 65.7 cm
(33⅜ × 25⅞ in.)
SIR JOHN SOANE'S MUSEUM, LONDON

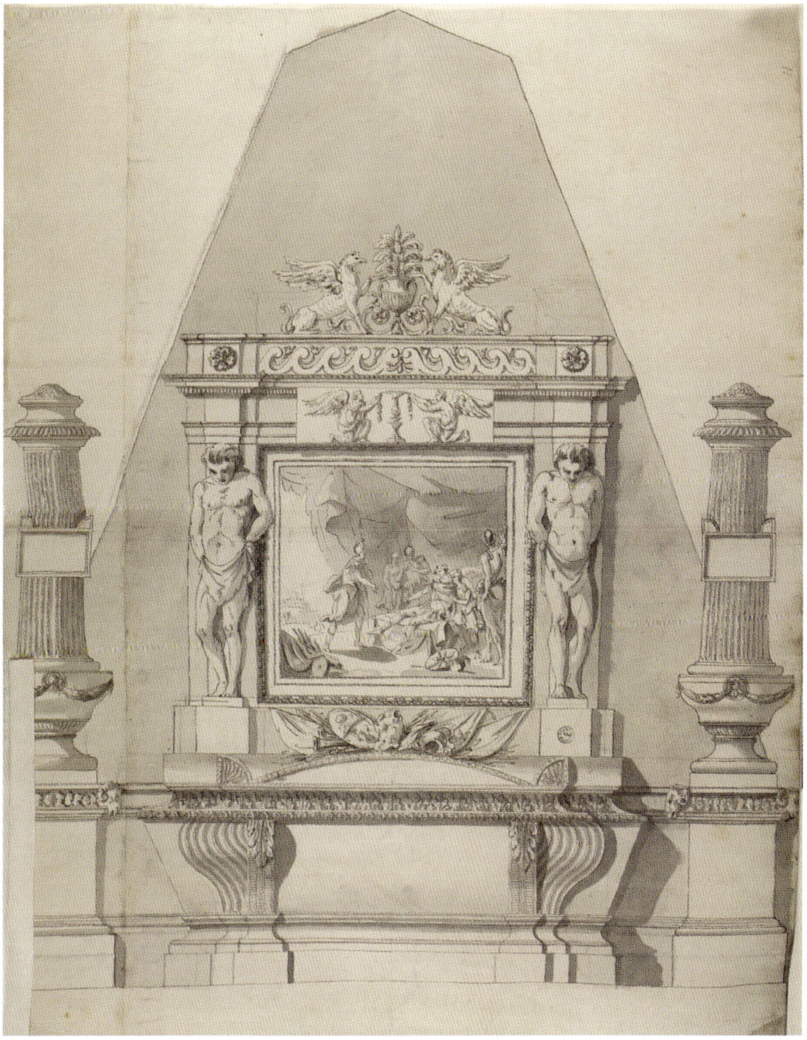

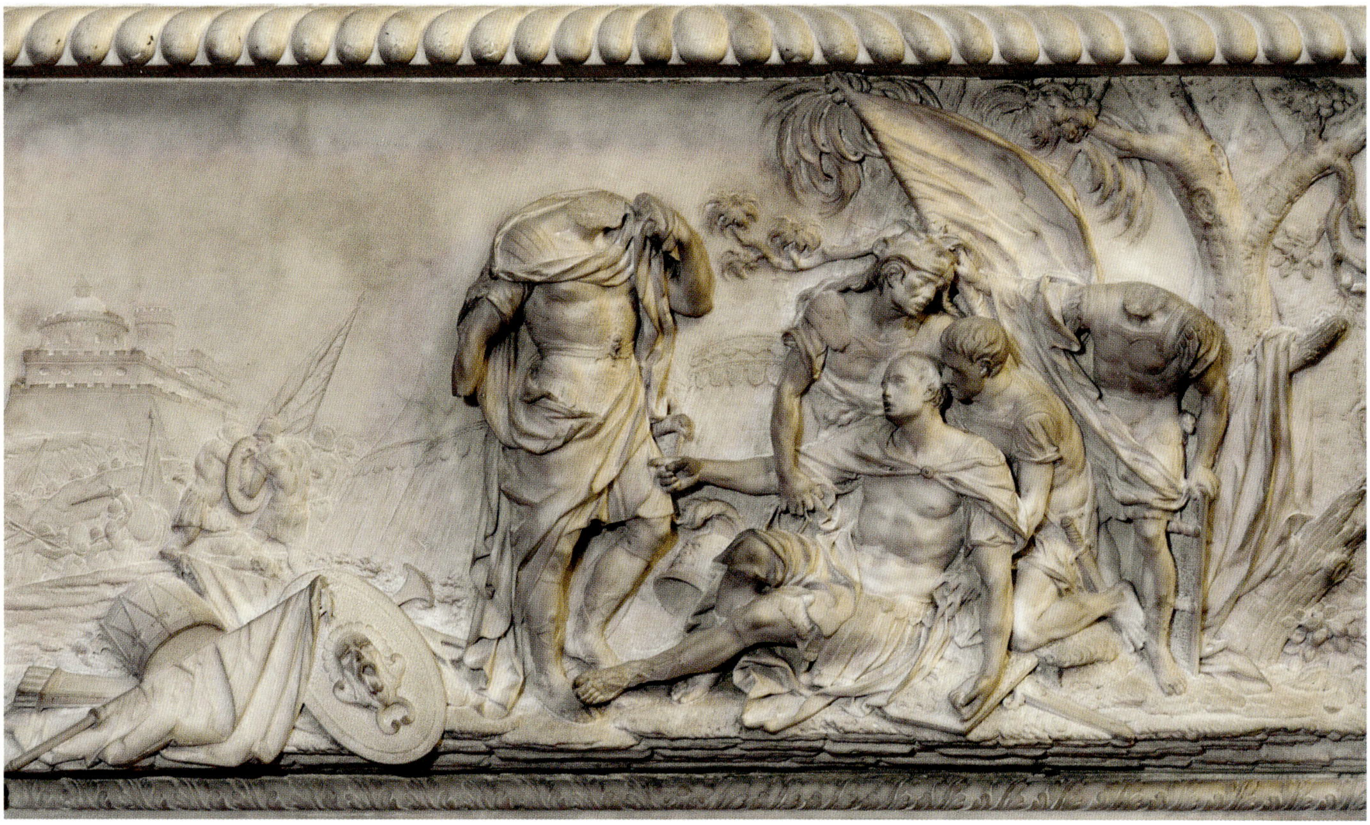

In order to win the commission for the Wolfe monument, Wilton had competed against some of the most established sculptors working in Britain – Louis-François Roubilliac, Peter Scheemakers, Sir Henry Cheere and John Michael Rysbrack – as well as against such younger artists as Robert Chambers, James 'Athenian' Stuart and Robert Adam. One of Adam's unsuccessful designs (fig. 70) consisted of a bas-relief of a classically dressed Wolfe expiring in a tent, surrounded by spear-carrying attendants, with an archaically clad army approaching a fanciful castle in the distance. The relief was to be mounted within an entablature flanked by two loincloth-wearing youths acting as caryatids.

In spite of not winning the Wolfe competition, Adam was commissioned soon after to design another monument in the Abbey; this time to the memory of Lieutenant Colonel Roger Townshend, killed by a cannonball while reconnoitering the French defences at Fort Ticonderoga, New York, two months before Wolfe's death at Quebec. The monument, completed at great speed and installed in the Abbey in November 1761, recycled some elements of Adam's proposed Wolfe monument. The bas-relief, carved by John Eckstein I, was simplified, with the dying Townshend and his mourners dressed in Roman fashion, as Adam proposed Wolfe should have been, but the death scene was moved outdoors and the figures arranged in Lamentation form (fig. 71). A bigger change, though – with implications for West – was the transformation of the two caryatids – now supporting the tomb rather than being flanking figures – from generalized, classical youths to carvings of muscular American Indian warriors, portrayed with a great attention to details of dress, weaponry and hairstyle (fig. 72).[86] Like Wilton's monument to Wolfe, Adam's Townshend monument 'produced a curious stylistic mélange', in John Fleming's words.[87] Nonetheless, the ever-confident Adam pronounced it 'superior to anything in the abbey'.[88]

Neither Wilton's nor Adam's attempt to mediate between the ancient and the modern, the universal and the particular, would suit the growing historical consciousness of their public. Such artistic mixed metaphors – Roman armour and British muskets – had become unconvincing. Soon after the unveiling of the Wolfe Monument, a correspondent wrote that 'The General appears to have been very ill-used, when dying in a cold country, to be stripped quite naked, and exposed to the weather at the outside of his tent, assisted by his soldiers in health, fully cloathed.'[89] What had been worthy in 1763 looked ridiculous in 1773.

The efforts of Romney and Penny, Wilton and Adam epitomized the mid-eighteenth-century crisis of representation: a crisis that West resolved triumphantly with *Wolfe*. When it came to conceiving that picture, West was far more affected by Wilton's and Adam's failures than by either Penny's or Romney's limited success. Daring and cautious by turn; when it came to *Wolfe*, West's intention was not to search for a compromise.

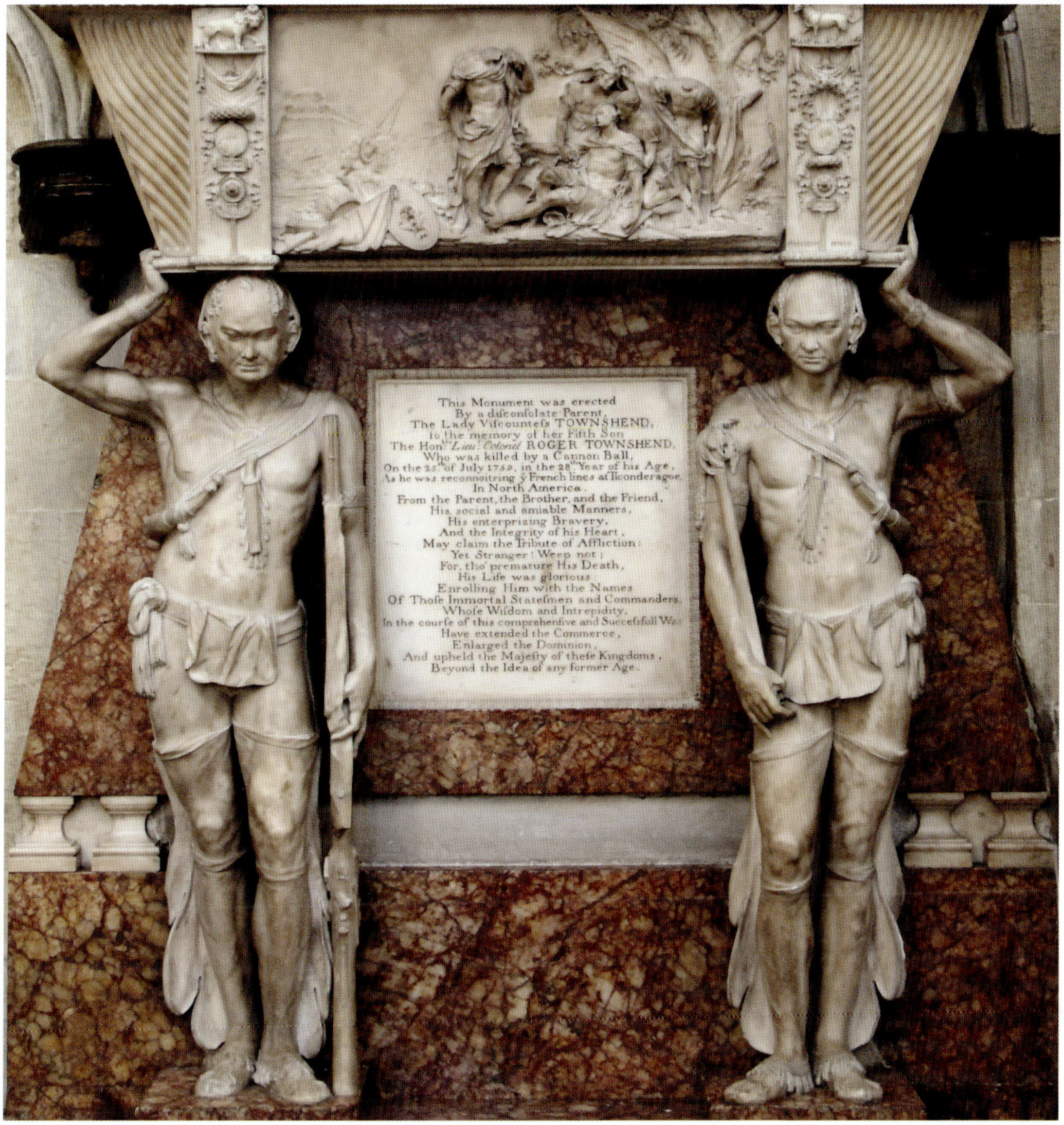

71 OPPOSITE & 72
Robert Adam (1728–1792)
Monument to Lieutenant Colonel Roger Townshend (details)
1760 (unveiled 1761)
Marble
WESTMINSTER ABBEY, LONDON

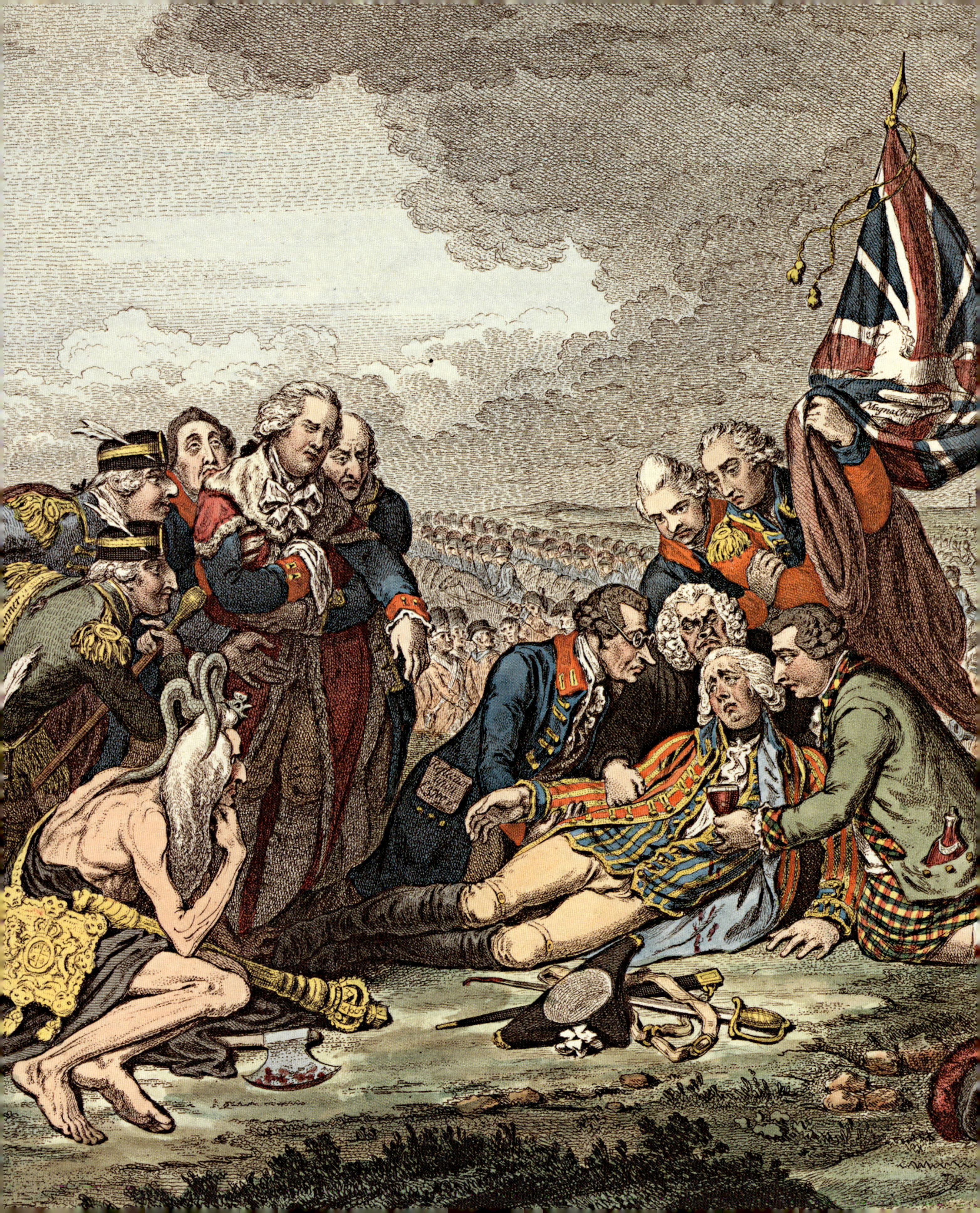
Magna

PALACE AND PRINT SHOP

Detail of James Gillray, *The Death of the Great Wolf*, 1795 (see fig. 88)

Although derided by John Wilkes as 'a late baronet's smoky house at the end of a great smoky town',[1] Buckingham House was bought by George III shortly before his coronation in 1761 and 'with the aid of a royal purse and a great deal of Treasury tolerance ... was transformed between the years 1762 and 1776'[2] to become the royal family's favourite domestic residence in London.

The King put his copy of *Wolfe* (fig. 73) and six other pictures by West in what was known as the Warm Room, part of his suite of ground-floor apartments. A 'warm room' is not found in other English houses of the period and may indeed have been a concept derived from German prototypes,[3] but it appears from Johann Zoffany's portrait *George, Prince of Wales, and Frederick, later Duke of York, at Buckingham House* (fig. 74) that a warm room was a relatively – by royal standards – informal drawing room;[4] both the King and Queen had their own. What is most remarkable is that, with a collection so rich in outstanding Dutch and Italian works, George III chose to devote the Warm Room to the work of West and to make West, along with Van Dyck, one of only two artists in the royal collection who did not have to share wall space with others.

It is not too fanciful to describe the Warm Room pictures as a collaboration between West and the King, who discussed and agreed on the subjects and their display. The seven Warm Room pictures, although developed on an ad hoc basis from 1769 to 1773, make up a pictorial cycle unequalled elsewhere in eighteenth-century Britain.[5]

West first met George III sometime in early 1768 when West's then most important patron, Archbishop Drummond, arranged for the artist to show his just-completed *Agrippina* (fig. 9) to the King. With its archaeological purity – deriving from West's personal knowledge of the Ara Pacis Augustae in Rome and Robert Adam's engravings of 1764 of Diocletian's palace at Split – its gravity and high-toned moralizing about marital fidelity, *Agrippina* appealed powerfully to the serious young King: 'There is another noble Roman subject

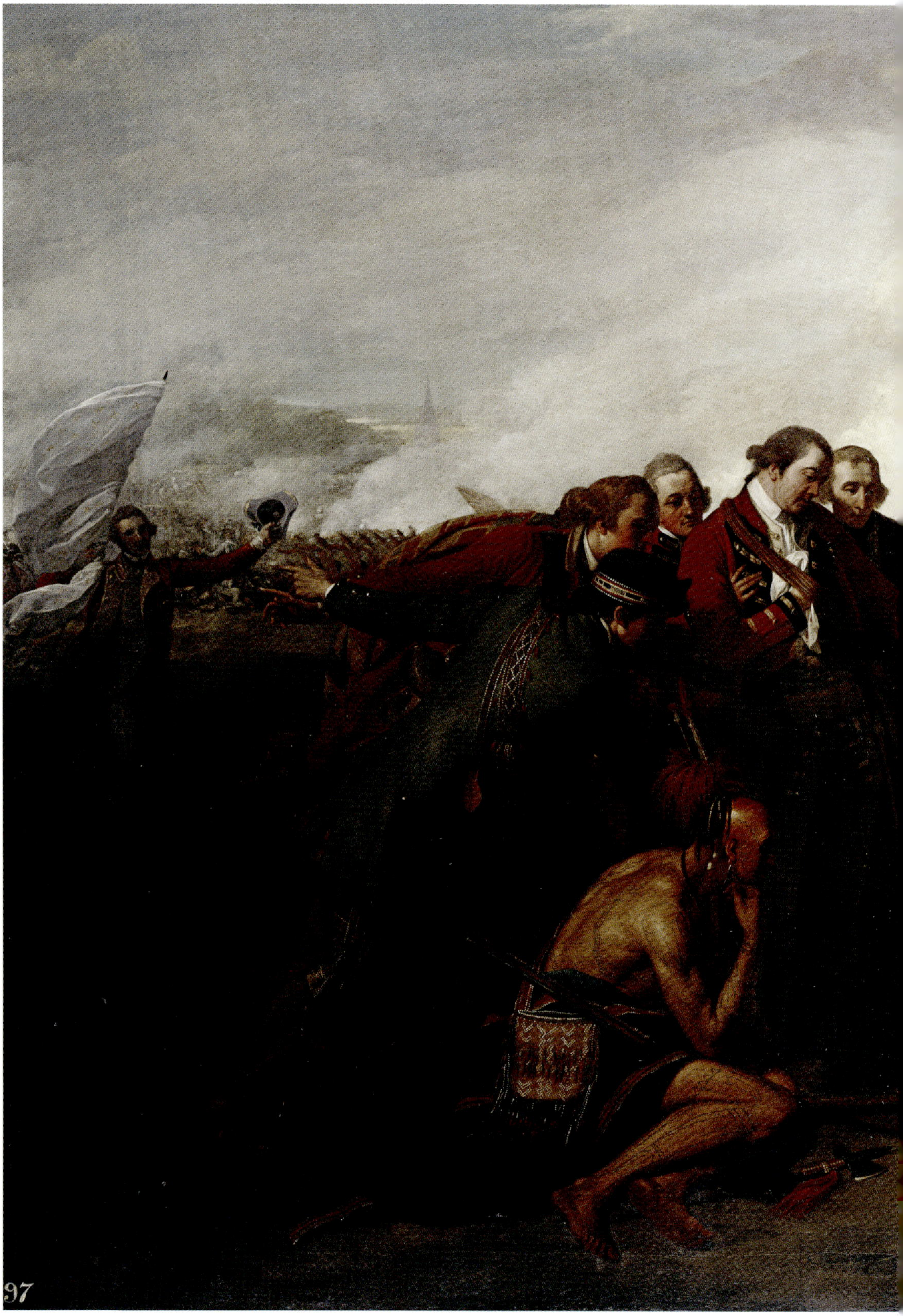

73
Benjamin West
The Death of General Wolfe
1771
Oil on canvas
153.5 × 245.9 cm
(60½ × 96¾ in.)
ROYAL COLLECTION, LONDON

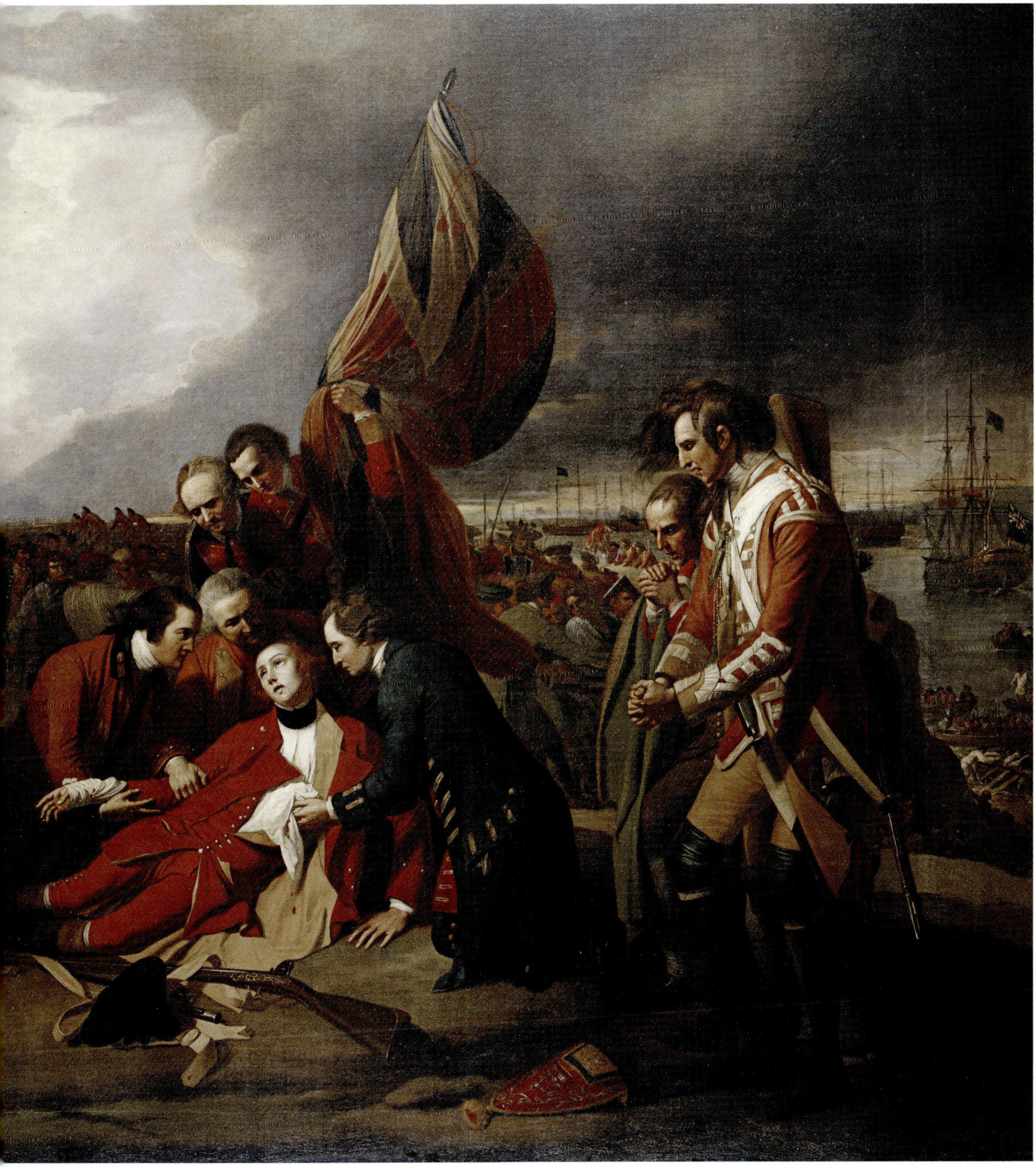

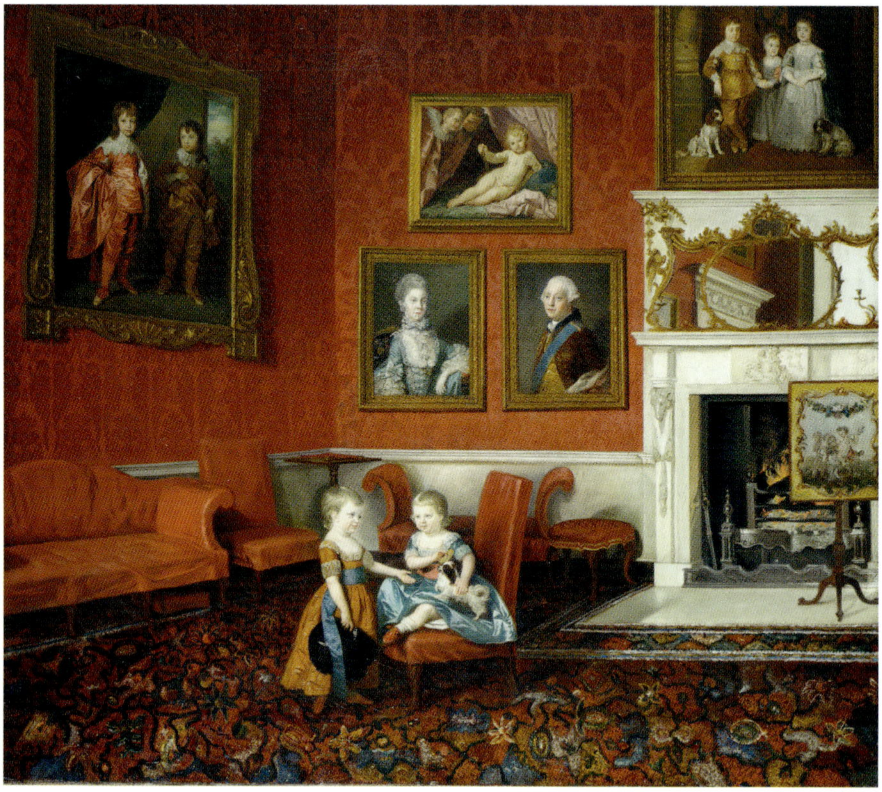

74
Johann Zoffany (1733–1810)
George, Prince of Wales, and Frederick, later Duke of York, at Buckingham House
1765
Oil on canvas
111.9 × 127.9 cm
(44 × 50⅜ in.)
ROYAL COLLECTION, LONDON

which corresponds to this one, and I believe it also has never been well painted; I mean the final departure of Regulus from Rome. Don't you think it would make a fine picture?' the King asked West, before commissioning him on the spot with the command, 'Then you shall paint it for me.' As West recalled, the King then called for the volume of Livy in which the story of Regulus was told, and announced, 'I will read to him myself the subject of my picture.'[6]

The story of Regulus was well known. William Havard's popular play *Regulus* had first been performed at the Theatre Royal in 1744 with Garrick in the title role. The Roman consul Marcus Atilius Regulus was captured by the Carthaginians and then sent back to Rome as an envoy, with the understanding that he would return to Carthage with the Senate's reply to the Carthaginian peace proposals. Regulus urged the Senate to reject the Carthaginian plans, even though he knew that this meant certain death when he delivered the news to his captors. Salvator Rosa chose to paint Regulus' death scene in which the unfortunate consul was rolled inside a barrel spiked with nails, in what may be seen as a pagan prefiguration of the Crucifixion. Following the King's suggestion, West decided to paint the moment when, rejecting the pleas of the Senate and people of Rome to stay, the consul allows himself to be led back to Carthage: a scene of moral choice rather than martyrdom. The high drama of the moment is made even more tense by the way in which West placed his protagonist off centre, creating a powerful void between the doomed consul and the crowd of his bereft countrymen.[7] Regulus' exemplary stoicism and self-sacrifice resonated with the wishes of the young King, who had declared that 'the interest of my country ever shall be my first care, my own inclinations shall ever submit to it. I am born for the happiness or misery of a great nation, and consequently must often act contrary to my own passions.'[8]

Soon after West delivered *Regulus* (fig. 4) in late 1768, he was at work on another large

75 OPPOSITE
Benjamin West
The Death of Epaminondas
1773
Oil on canvas
222.2 × 179.4 cm
(87½ × 70⅝ in.)
ROYAL COLLECTION, LONDON

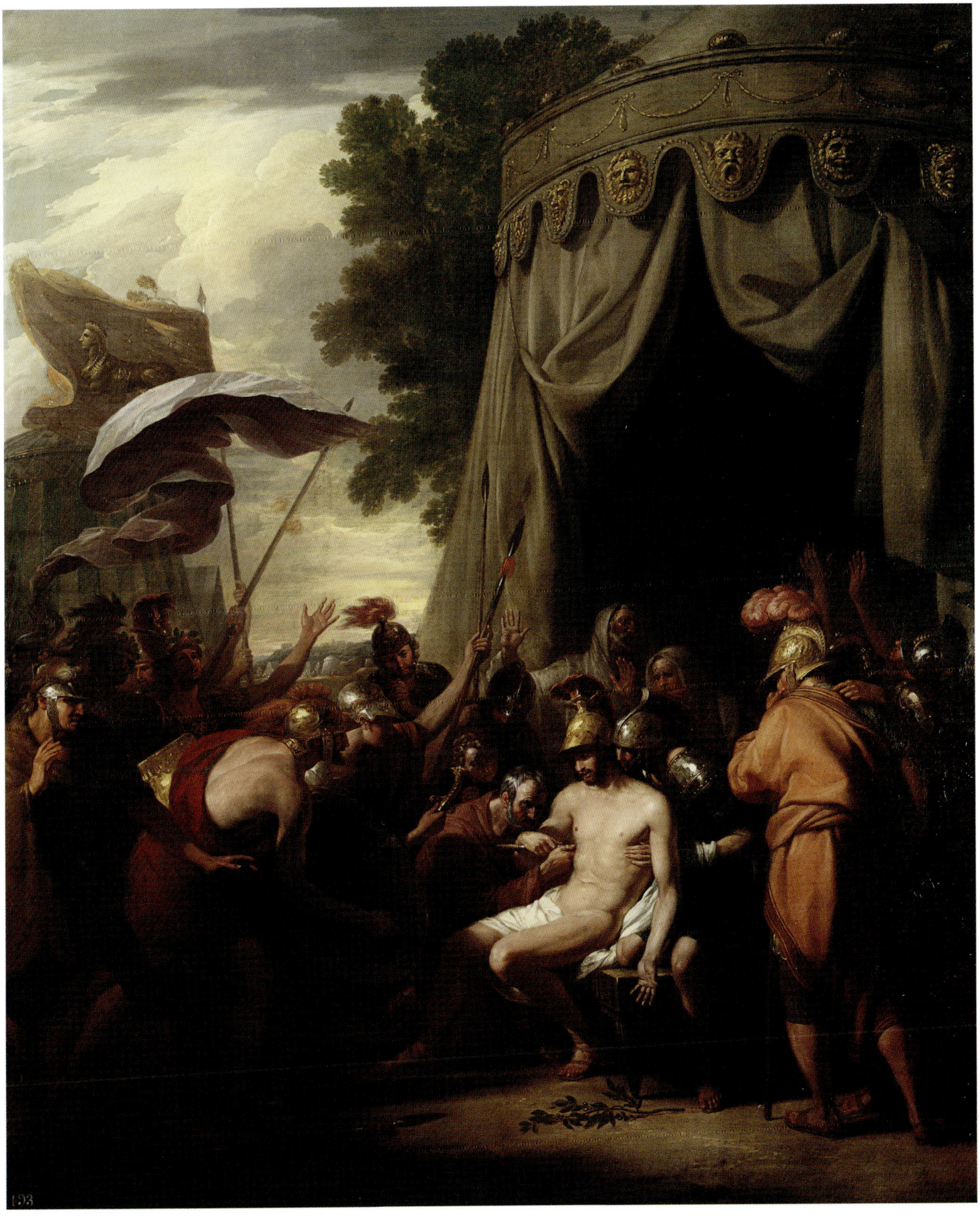

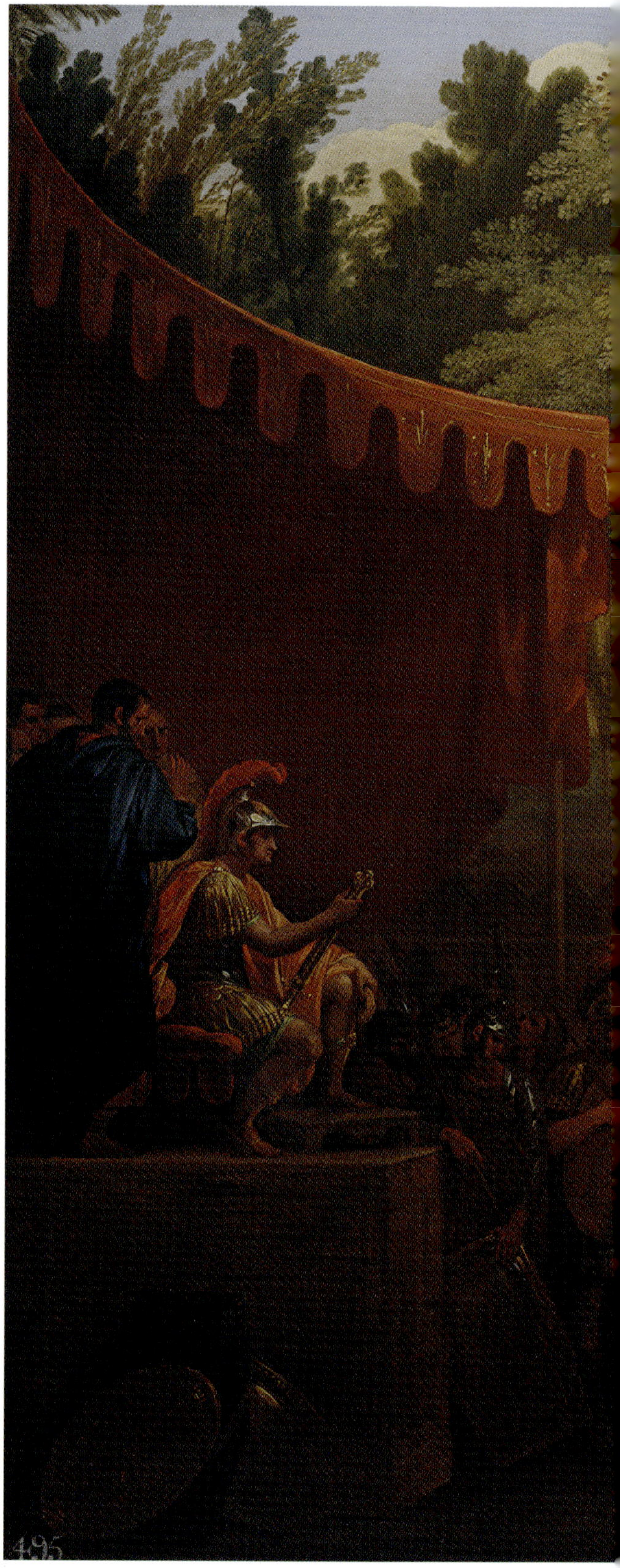

76
Benjamin West
Segestes and His Daughter before Germanicus
1773
Oil on canvas
104.5 × 136.7 cm
(41⅛ × 53⅞ in.)
ROYAL COLLECTION, LONDON

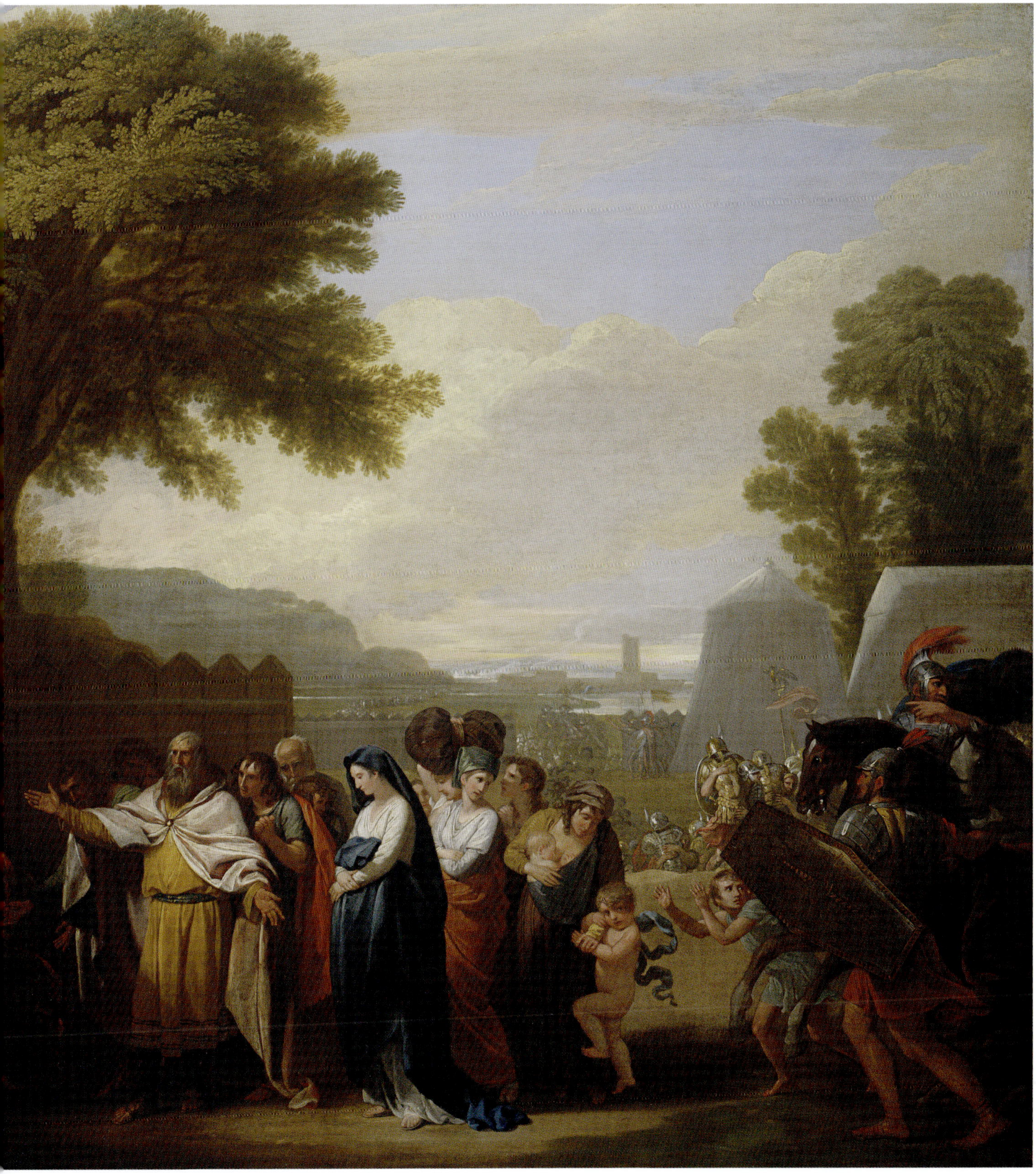

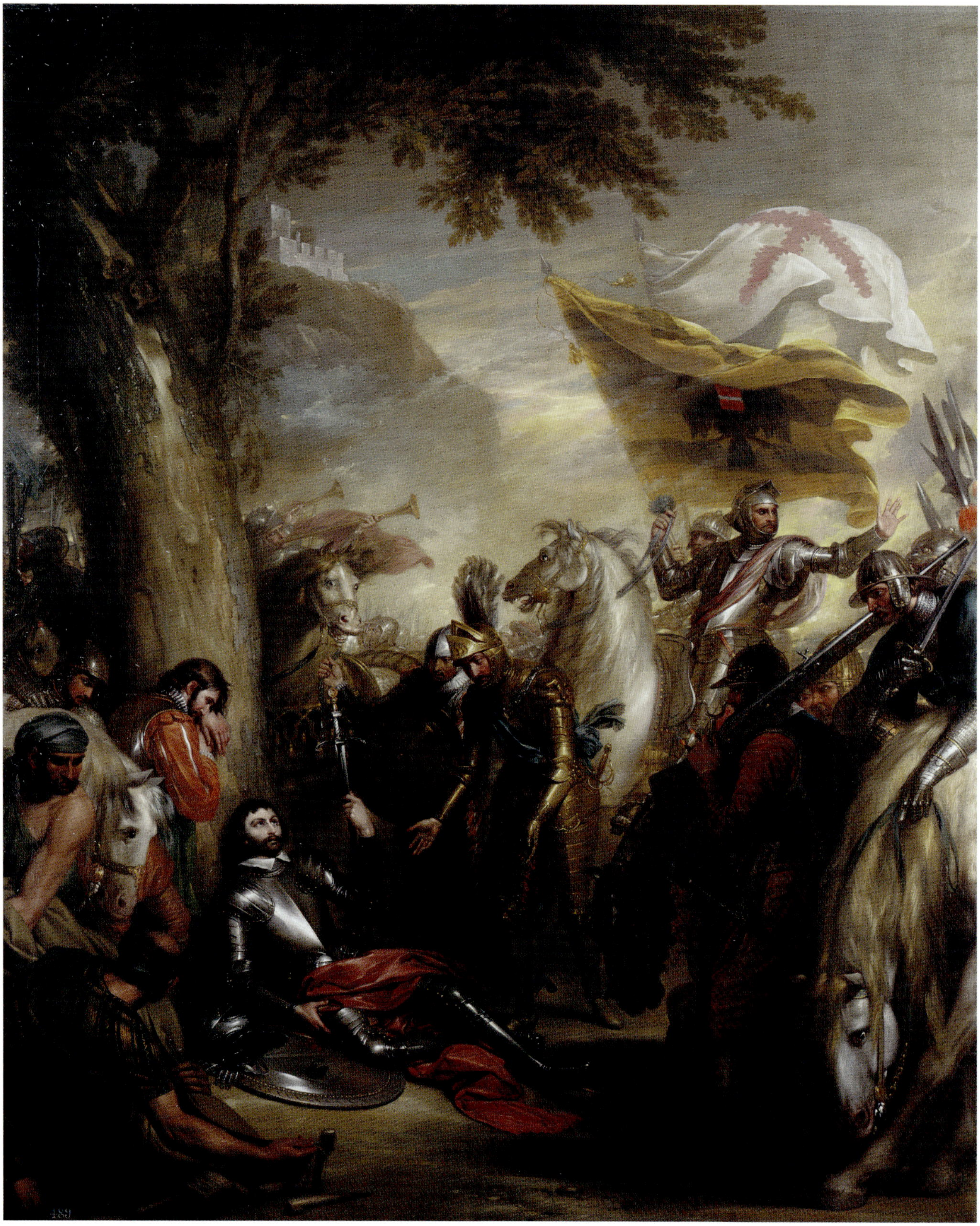

history painting for the King, *The Oath of Hannibal* (fig. 5), depicting the moment when the nine-year-old Hannibal is taken to the temple by his father, the Carthaginian King Hamilcar, to swear an oath of eternal enmity to Rome. Once again, the subject had been previously painted – most recently by the Venetian Giovanni Antonio Pellegrini – and was well known. As Oliver Millar pointed out, in spite of West's reminiscence that the King read the story of Regulus to him from Livy, the more likely source was Silius Italicus' epic *Punica,* which also provides the most vivid source for *Hannibal.*[9] Although neglected today, Silius was a widely read classical author in eighteenth-century Britain. In *Hannibal,* West brilliantly captured the gloom, terror and exoticism of the Carthaginian temple as described by Silius:

> A hundred altars stood here in order, sacred to the gods of heaven and the lord of Erebus ... The earth rumbles in the gloom and breaks forth into awesome hissings; and fire blazes unkindled upon altars ... To this shrine Hannibal was brought by his father's command ... No terrors for him had the Massylian priestess, raving in her frenzy, or the horrid rites of the temple, the blood-bespattered doors, and the flames that mounted at the sound of incantation.[10]

In spite of all its atmosphere and emotion, *Hannibal* is in many ways an unsuccessful picture, marred by shocking errors of execution, particularly the laughable anatomy of Hamilcar. Yet it was, along with *Wolfe*, one of the undoubted hits of the 1771 exhibition[11] and certainly pleased George III, who increased his patronage of West by ordering not only his own version of *Wolfe,* but also four more pictures from West to complete the decoration of the Warm Room. As West told the story, he proposed that two large pictures, *The Death of Epaminondas* (fig. 75) and *The Death of the Chevalier Bayard* (fig. 77) should be painted to flank *Wolfe,* and that two further, smaller pictures – *Segestes and His Daughter before Germanicus* (fig. 76) and *The Family of the King of Armenia before Cyrus* (fig. 78) – would serve as overdoors. These smaller pictures were based on less familiar stories, but share a common theme of clemency and magnanimity in victory. Furthermore, the German princess Thusnelda, from whom the Hanoverians claimed descent, was the daughter of Segestes.

The deaths of Epaminondas and the chevalier Bayard were obvious classical and Renaissance parallels to *Wolfe*. As we have seen, within weeks of his death so factually reported in the newspapers, Wolfe was already being described as either the dead son of a disconsolate Britannia or the eighteenth-century Epaminondas, after the Theban general whose death at the moment of victory was recounted by Xenophon. Both comparisons were so current and so constant that they must have stuck in the minds of both the artist and his public. Samuel Johnson had not only declared that 'Genius is chiefly exerted in historical pictures', but also had gone on to suggest in the same essay published in *The Idler* in 1759 that the death of Epaminondas would make an exemplary picture: 'The mixture of gladness and grief in the face of the messenger who brings his dying general an account of the victory; the various passions of the attendants; the sublimity of composure in the hero ... the faint gleam of satisfaction that diffuses itself over the languor of death'.[12] This is the death of Wolfe, *avant la lettre*, written a short seven months before the actual event.

Bayard (1473/76–1524) was a well-known symbol of knightly bravery, who resolved, even as he lay dying, to remain facing his enemy with the words, 'I am dying and will not in my last moments turn my back to the enemy for the first time in my life.'[13] Biographies of him had been in print since 1525.

The King's involvement with the Warm Room pictures and his decision to give such a large series of commissions to West testify to the almost intimate relationship that existed between painter and sovereign. West's Quaker ancestry and demeanour pleased the King, whose 'dislike of show and a concern to avoid the consequences of overeating and drunkenness contributed, alongside his shyness and parsimony, to a simple lifestyle'.[14]

77
Benjamin West
The Death of the Chevalier Bayard
1772
Oil on canvas
221.6 × 179.1 cm
(87¼ × 70½ in.)
ROYAL COLLECTION, LONDON

78
Benjamin West
The Family of the King of Armenia before Cyrus
1773
Oil on canvas
104.9 × 137.2 cm
(41¼ × 54 in.)
ROYAL COLLECTION, LONDON

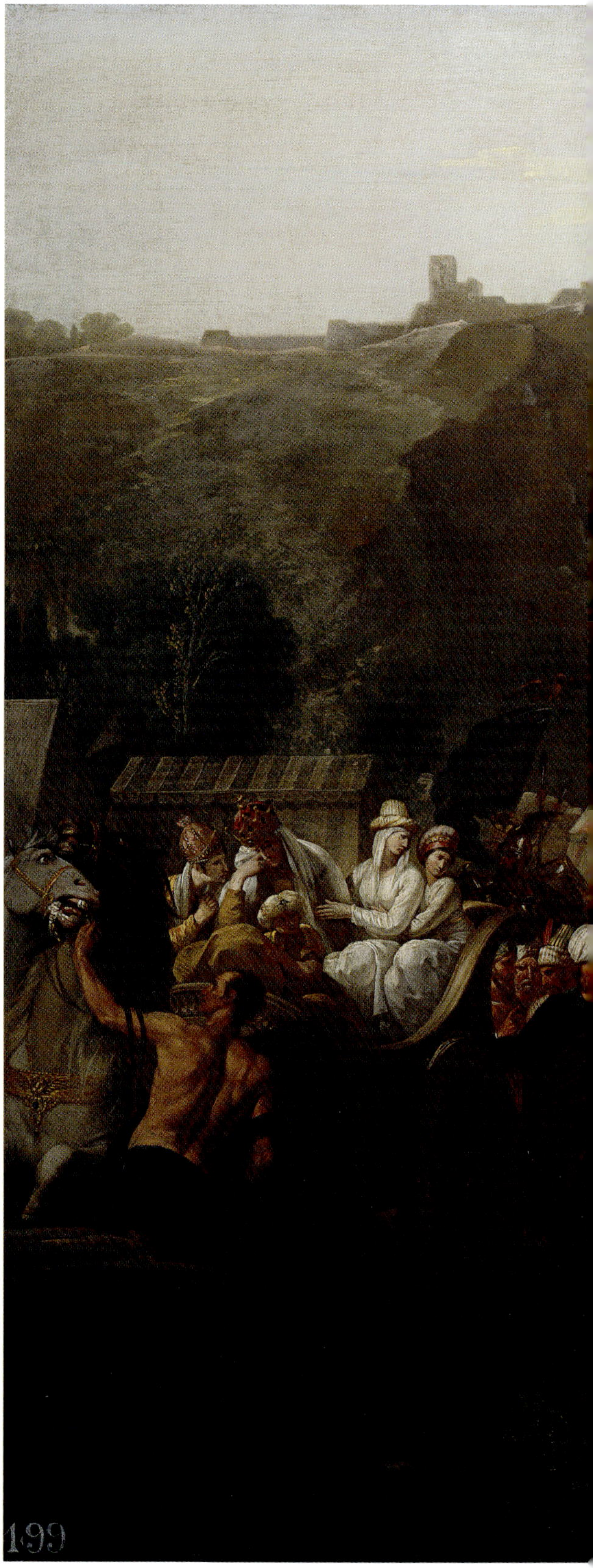

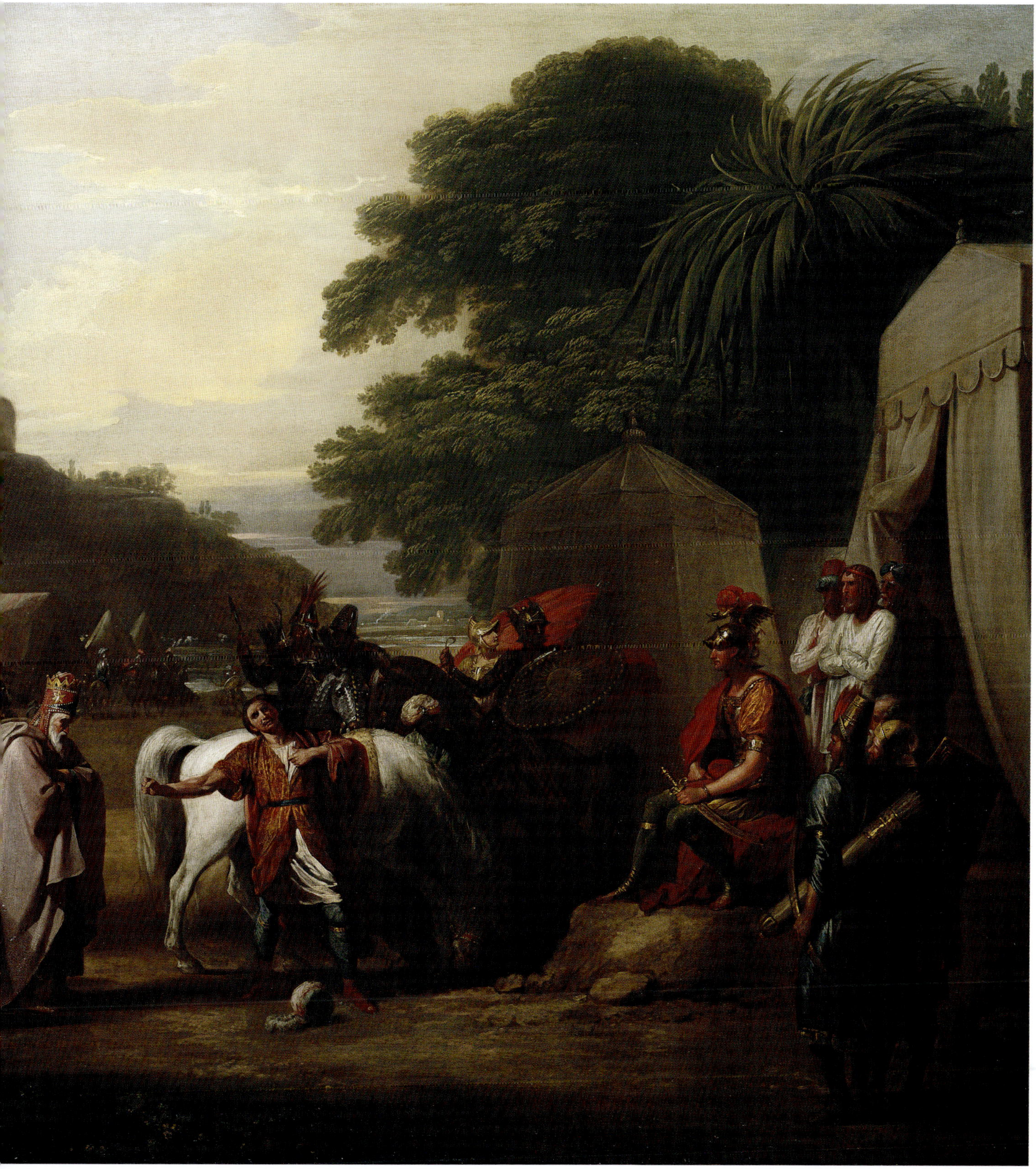

In West – whose wife told Farington that 'in the 40 years she had been married ... she had but once seen him intoxicated; & never saw him in a passion'[15] – George III found a kindred spirit.

So it may be unsurprising that from that first meeting a friendship sprang that lasted nearly forty years, through the vicissitudes of political upheavals and the King's recurring mental illness. When he was told about the King's death, West may well have said, 'I have lost the best friend I ever had in my life',[16] and while the King may not have felt quite so strongly, there certainly was something like genuine friendship between the two. George III was an unusually approachable monarch: 'He was not afraid to engage people in conversation and would often arrive unannounced ... the ease with which the royal family mingled in public is a marked feature of the reign.'[17]

West's friendship with the King also continued what had by then become his established career pattern. This pattern saw him moving from village to town to ever larger cities, engaging ever more important patrons and protectors along the way, from William Henry in Lancaster, Pennsylvania, to William Smith and William Allen in Philadelphia, thence to Rome and Cardinal Albani, and finally to London, the largest city in the Western world, and its most important resident, the King.

Ellis Waterhouse considered that 'West was ... lucky in that the very mediocrity of his mind found a kindred spirit in the mind of George III',[18] a remark that betrays a lack of understanding of either man's abilities. The reassessment of George III's accomplishments, which has been under way since the publication in 1972 of John Brooke's biography of the King,[19] helps us to understand why the relationship between West the artist and George the patron was so close. Focusing on George III's artistic interests, both David Watkin and the contributors to *George III and Queen Charlotte: Patronage, Collecting and Court Taste* are among those who have attempted, mainly successfully, to portray the King as a man who was of an Enlightened mind.[20]

The King's response to West's works was perhaps literary and instrumental rather than aesthetic. In other words, George III appears to have been principally moved by the narrative and didactic qualities of West's paintings. This reminds us that West and the King were living in a world where pictures were valued as much for their purpose and intent as for their appearance. West himself acknowledged this when he told Galt that while the King was

> an accomplished gentleman. For the fine arts he had not, perhaps, any natural taste ... His employment of Mr. West, although altogether in his private capacity, was ... not wholly without a view to the public advantage, and it is the more deserving of applause, as it was rather the result of principle than of personal predilection.[21]

Viewed in that light, the King's patronage of West can be seen as a corollary to his development of the library at Buckingham House, a library intended for the use of scholars and as a national asset. George put considerable resources into the library, buying books abroad 'in addition to the amount ... [he] was spending in England, which from 1768 to 1771 was never less than £1,000 a year on books and binding. By 1769 the library had increased to almost ten thousand volumes.'[22]

At precisely the time that George began to commission West, his other picture-buying was slowing down: the King wrote to his agent in Paris in 1770, declaring, 'I have, at least for the present, given up collecting pictures.'[23] Perhaps after so many purchases, including that of Consul Joseph Smith's great collection, which contained pictures by Canaletto, Sebastiano, Marco Ricci and Vermeer, the King felt that he had bought enough European work. His increasing dislike for Reynolds may account for the King's turning to West, but a more powerful factor may be that the serious King and the idealistic painter from Pennsylvania shared a view about the purpose of art. Unlike many of his predecessors, for whom collecting was about enhancing royal prestige and pleasure, it seems that for George III the buying of pictures was more important for the contribution it made to what he called 'the interest of my country'.[24]

With the encouragement of his most important mentor and future chief minister, Lord Bute, the King had developed a wide range of intellectual pursuits. As Jonathan Marsden writes, 'for him, and for many of his contemporaries, the arts were now part of a broad spectrum of complementary spheres of interest which we now consider quite separate, such as astronomy, meteorology, botany, geography, agriculture and music'.[25] This seamless approach to knowledge and the moral drive to make that knowledge useful were hallmarks of the Enlightenment. When Diderot defined the *Encyclopédie*, he wrote that its aim was

> to collect all the knowledge scattered over the face of the earth, to present its general outlines and structure to the men with whom we live, and to transmit this to those who will come after us, so that the work of past centuries may be useful to the following centuries, that our children, by becoming more educated, may at the same time become more virtuous and happier ...[26]

In the same spirit, West thought that 'painting could do much good if properly directed',[27] and doing 'much good' was an Enlightenment imperative he shared with the King.

When Horace Walpole visited Buckingham House, he was not impressed either by the King's taste or by West's pictures. 'In the Library & in the other rooms are many very fine Pictures, some very bad', he wrote. 'Most were in the Royal Collection before, or purchased by the late Prince, which were all good. A few very fine by the present King & most of the bad. Of the Latter is a whole room by West, of which none have much merit, but the Death of General Wolfe.'[28] Walpole was an aesthete and the King was not. In some ways neither was West.

'There is a real sense in which English painting ... was a branch of literature rather than art', Ronald Paulson wrote, and he suggested that Hogarth's work should be assimilated 'to the literature rather than the art of the period, and so to the methods of literary criticism, in the context of which he does make a great deal of sense and is of primary importance'.[29] West's education was more literary than visual. He frequently acknowledged his debt to Du Fresnoy, Richardson and Plutarch. Other than through the medium of print, he would never have seen a first-rate picture until his trip to Italy. From the time he painted *Socrates* in 1756, West's sources were primarily literary.

Certainly, West's paintings for the Warm Room are narrative and didactic. Certainly, they are difficult to understand without a knowledge of the texts from which they sprang, whether those texts be Xenophon or the newspapers. But for all of that, I would be reluctant to describe West's paintings as merely 'a branch of literature'. West's paintings for the King were not a part of George III's library, but there was a subtle interplay in which the Warm Room pictures both reinforced and were supported by the contents of the library. There was a precedent for this in the work that William Chambers had earlier begun for the King at Kew, in which his variety of architectural styles were related to the botanical collections being developed there, and where 'Chambers's buildings also served an educational role associated with the history of architecture'.[30]

The *Wolfe* that West painted for George III was one of six versions: there are five large and one much smaller one painted on panel. The five large *Wolfes* vary in size. The prime version and one subsequently painted for the Earl of Bristol are nearly identical, at 152.6 × 214.5 cm (60 × 84½ in.) and 152.5 × 216 cm (60 × 85 in.) respectively. The versions painted for the King and the Prince of Waldeck and one that West kept for himself are all in larger format, at 153.5 × 245.9 cm (60½ × 96¾ in.), 153.7 × 244.8 cm (60½ × 96⅜ in.) and 165 × 244.5 cm (65 × 96¼ in.) respectively.

It is not surprising that West should have painted *Wolfe* in larger format for the King and Waldeck. Such royal commissions would certainly have demanded the higher status that larger sizes conferred, and a larger size also allowed

79
Benjamin West
The Battle of La Hogue
c. 1778
Oil on canvas
152.7 × 214 cm
(60⅛ × 84¼ in.)
NATIONAL GALLERY OF ART,
WASHINGTON, D.C.

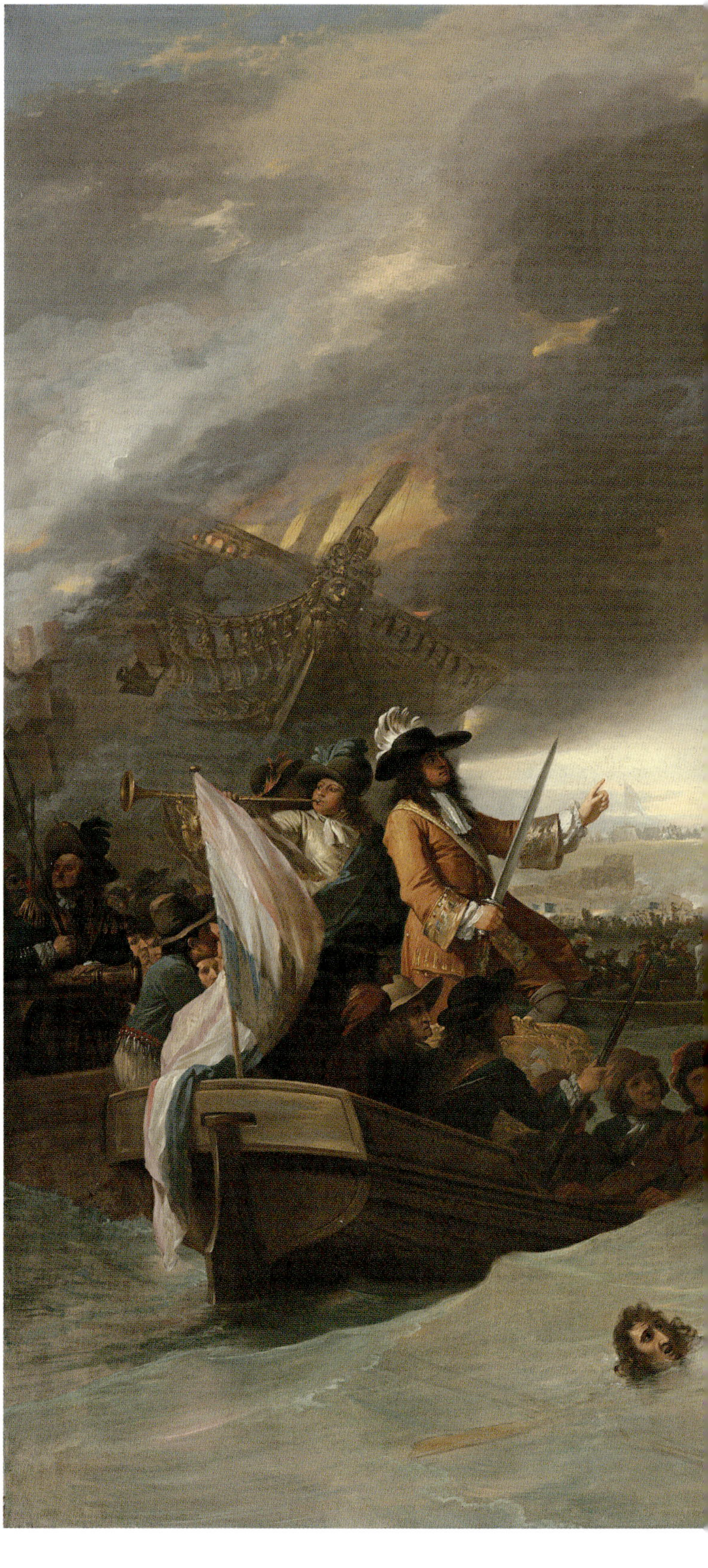

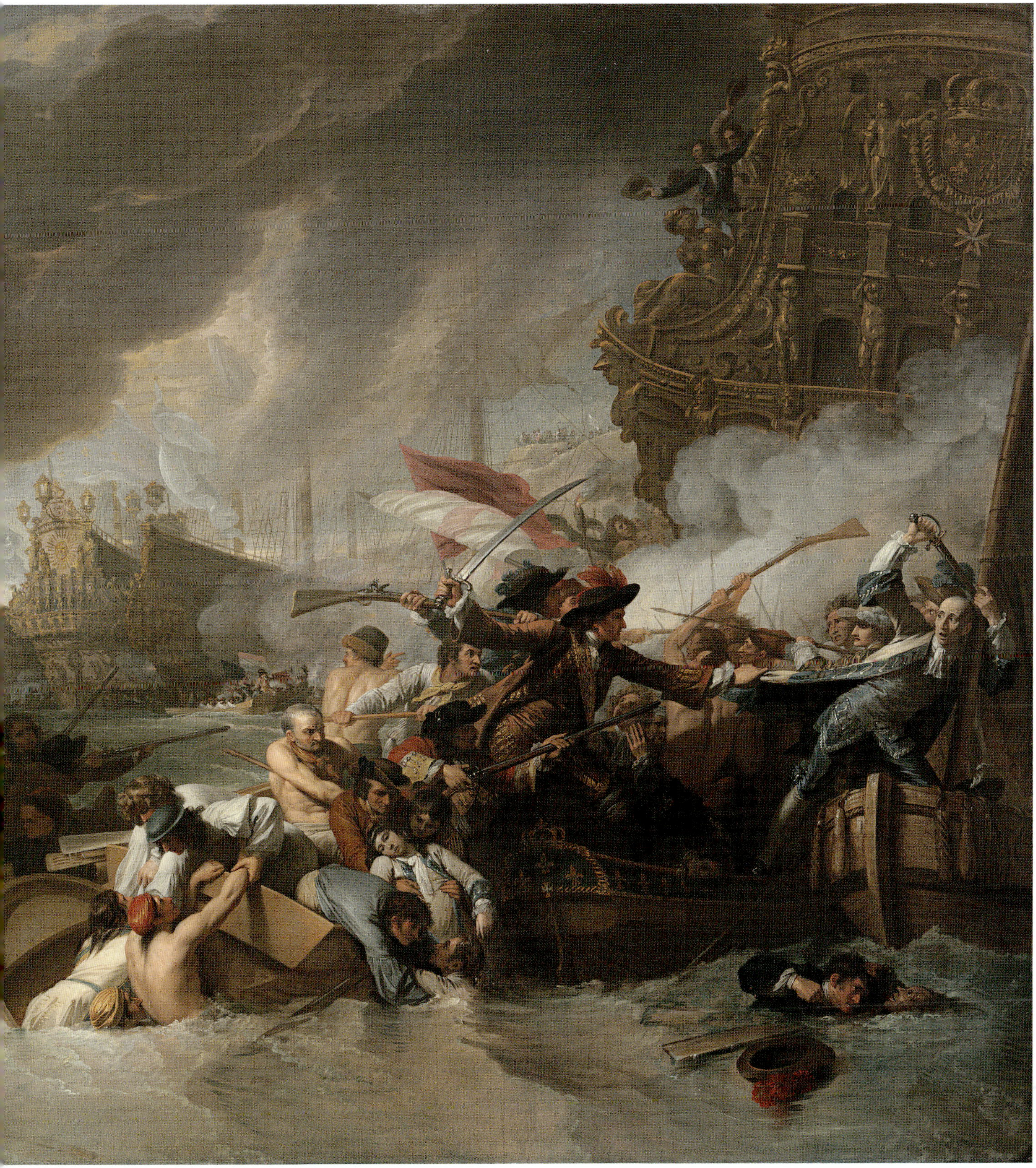

West to create a more panoramic view of the battlefield and to incorporate some refinements in the composition. Moreover, it is unlikely that the King would have settled for a mere copy. Of the six *Wolfes,* the two most significant are Lord Grosvenor's prime copy, from which William Woollett's engraving was taken, and the King's version, which benefited from the most exalted patronage and the most elaborate display.

Grosvenor is variously said to have paid anywhere from £400 to 600 guineas for his *Wolfe*. A considerable landowner, a notorious profligate and a supporter of Pitt the Elder (who rewarded him with a peerage), Grosvenor was likely to have been introduced to West by Richard Dalton, whom he employed as a picture agent and who had first met West in Italy. While Dalton was buying pictures for Grosvenor he was doing the same for George III, for whom he worked as librarian. A further connection with West was Dalton's role in the foundation of the Royal Academy.

Yet another example of the tangled and somewhat incestuous world of the Georgian elite was the discovery in December 1769, at the White Hart Inn at St Albans, of Lady Grosvenor in bed with Prince Henry, Duke of Cumberland, one of George III's younger brothers. This was followed by a spectacularly scandalous trial during the summer of 1770, in which the Duke was found guilty of 'criminal conversation' with Lady Grosvenor and ordered to pay £10,000 in damages to her aggrieved husband. So when West was painting *Wolfe,* relations between the royal family and Grosvenor were strained. This might have added to the King's determination to have his own version of the celebrated picture, and may also have encouraged West to create what may be judged a bigger and better version for the King.

In spite of such royal competition and West's growing friendship with the King, Grosvenor was pleased with *Wolfe*, and went on to commission West to paint four further scenes from British history: *The Battle of La Hogue* (fig. 79), *Oliver Cromwell Dissolving the Long Parliament* (fig. 80), *The Battle of the Boyne* (fig. 81) and *General Monk Receiving Charles II on the Beaches of Dover* (fig. 82).

West finished his series for Grosvenor by 1782 and the paintings were hung together at Grosvenor's London house,[31] where select members of the public were able to view them, as was the practice with most great private collections of the period. Taken together, the Grosvenor series may be said to celebrate a century of triumphant Protestantism, with the victory at Quebec as the latest and greatest example. There are few details of how Grosvenor displayed his pictures, but West appears to have been unhappy with the way in which they were presented. 'I went to Lord Grosvenor's at 4 o'Clock, it being the last day of shewing the House, this season', Farington recorded in July 1808. 'Constable sd. Mr. West had complained of His pictures at Lord Grosvenor's being ill hung, & said "It was a national concern" – particularly meaning His Wolfe & La Hogue.'[32]

We have a much clearer idea of how George III displayed his *Wolfe* and are able to reconstruct with exactness the picture hang at Buckingham House thanks to a series of picture-hanging plans dating from 1774, published in the *Burlington Magazine* by Francis Russell, and also from a detailed plan of Buckingham House dated 23 March 1776. The Warm Room was a substantial near-square of close to 7.6 metres (25 ft) by just over 7.9 metres (26 ft), with a 6-metre-high (20 ft) ceiling and two large, fifteen-light windows, which looked westwards to the Buckingham House gardens. It was perhaps not quite big enough to display five large – of which four were very large – paintings, and indeed the hang on the fireplace wall, where *Wolfe* is squeezed between *Bayard* and *Epaminondas*, seems extremely cramped. But the Warm Room was obviously very personal to the King and well situated on a route that took visitors from the hall, with its Canalettos and Zuccarellis, into the dining room, from there into the dressing room, hung with fourteen seventeenth-century landscapes, and then into the Warm Room, which led to the Passage Room, hung mostly with Van Dycks.[33]

80
Benjamin West
Oliver Cromwell Dissolving the Long Parliament
1782
Oil on canvas
153 × 214.6 cm
(60¼ × 84½ in.)
MONTCLAIR ART MUSEUM, NEW JERSEY

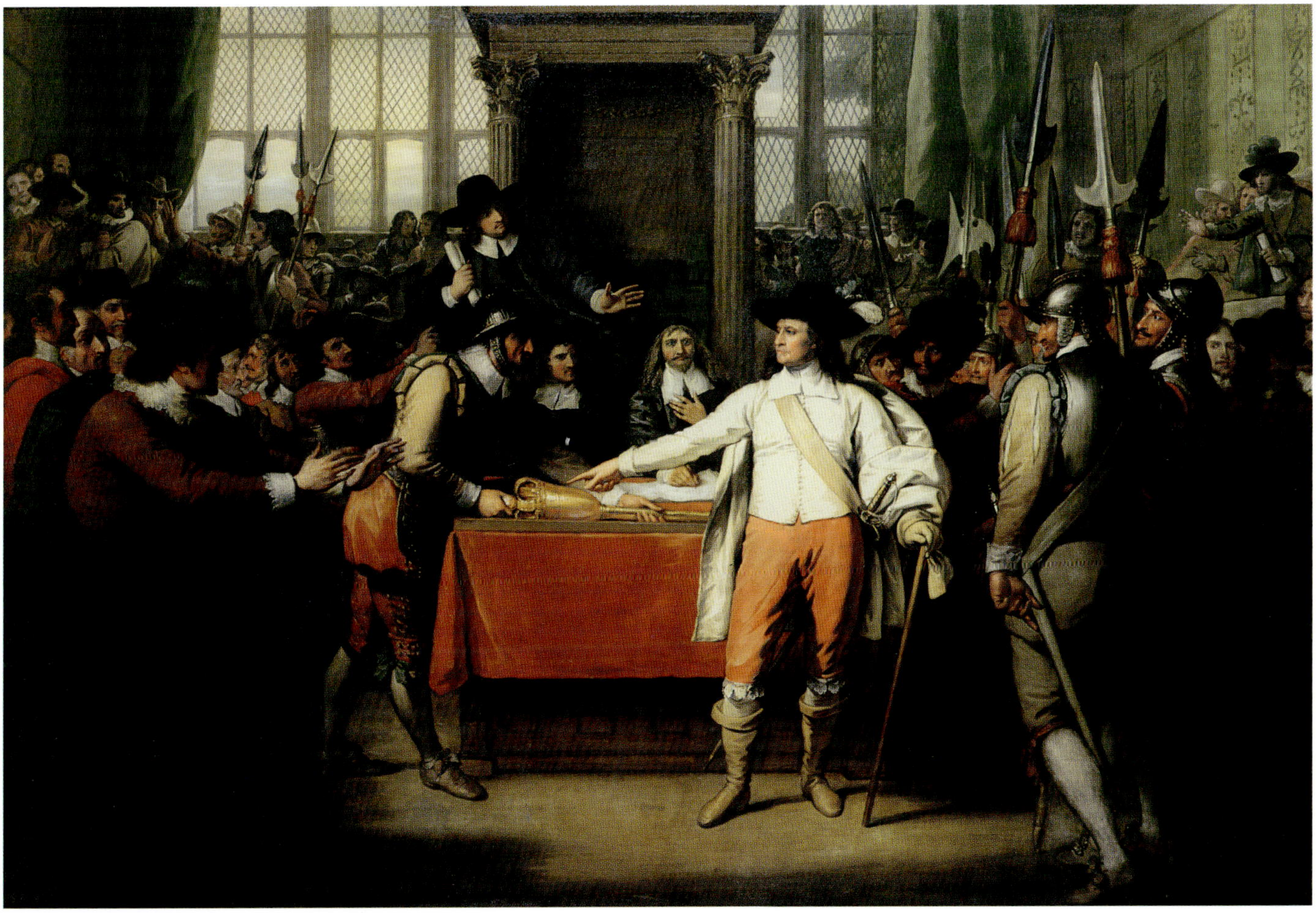

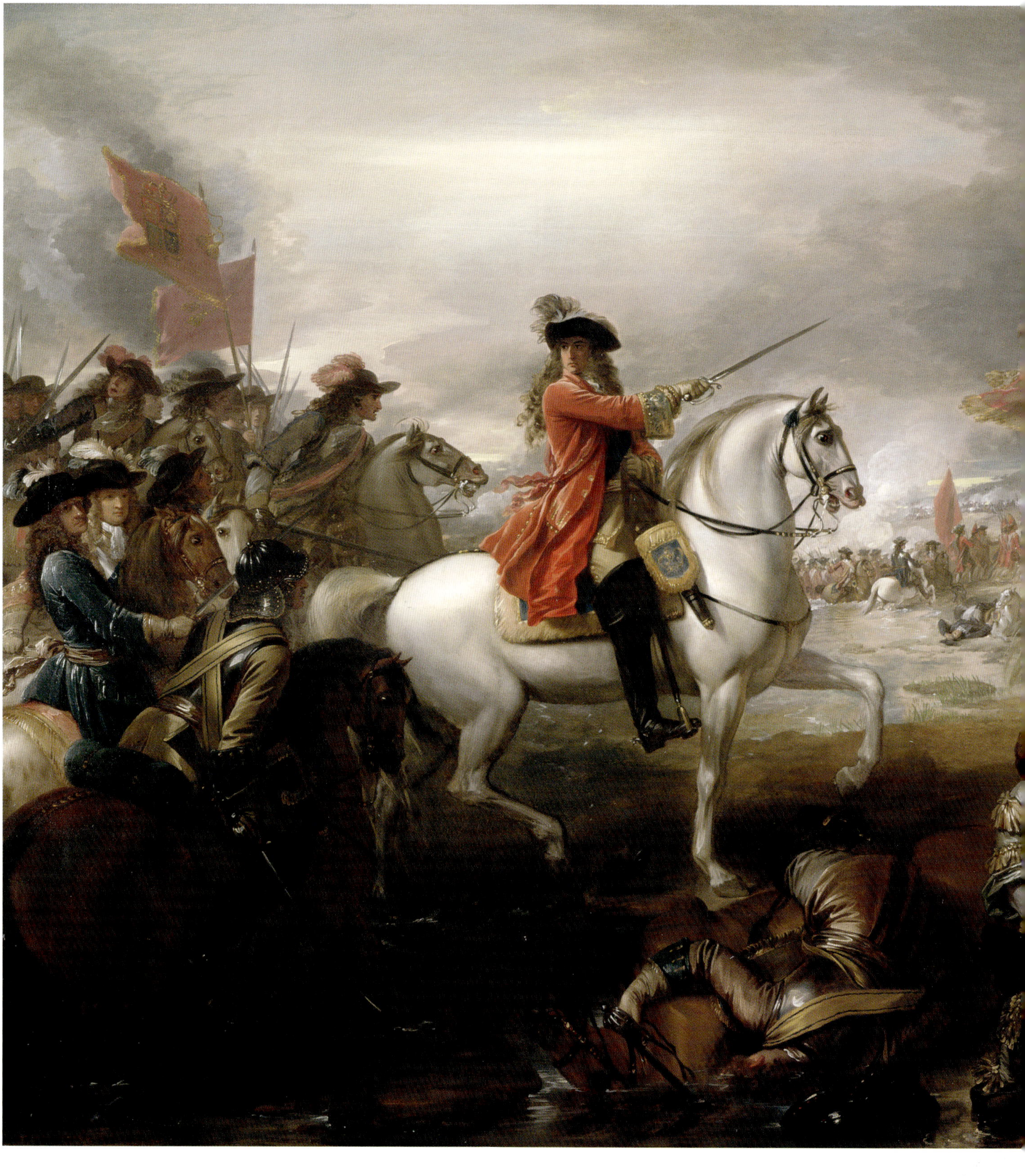

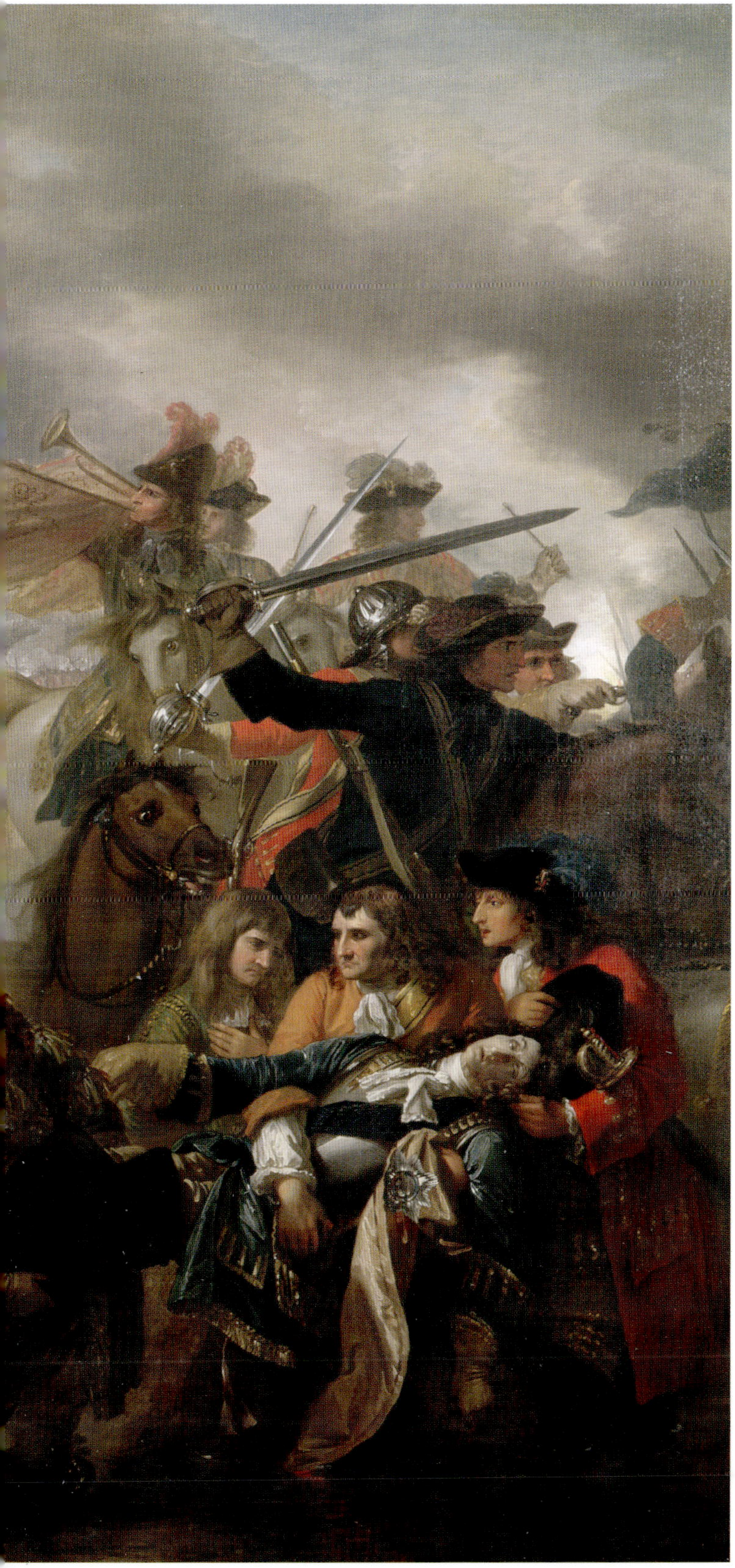

81
Benjamin West
The Battle of the Boyne
1778
Oil on canvas
152.5 × 211 cm (60 × 83 in.)
THE DUKE OF WESTMINSTER

82
Benjamin West
General Monk Receiving Charles II on the Beaches of Dover
1782
Oil on canvas
152.4 × 215.9 cm (60 × 85 in.)
MILWAUKEE ART MUSEUM

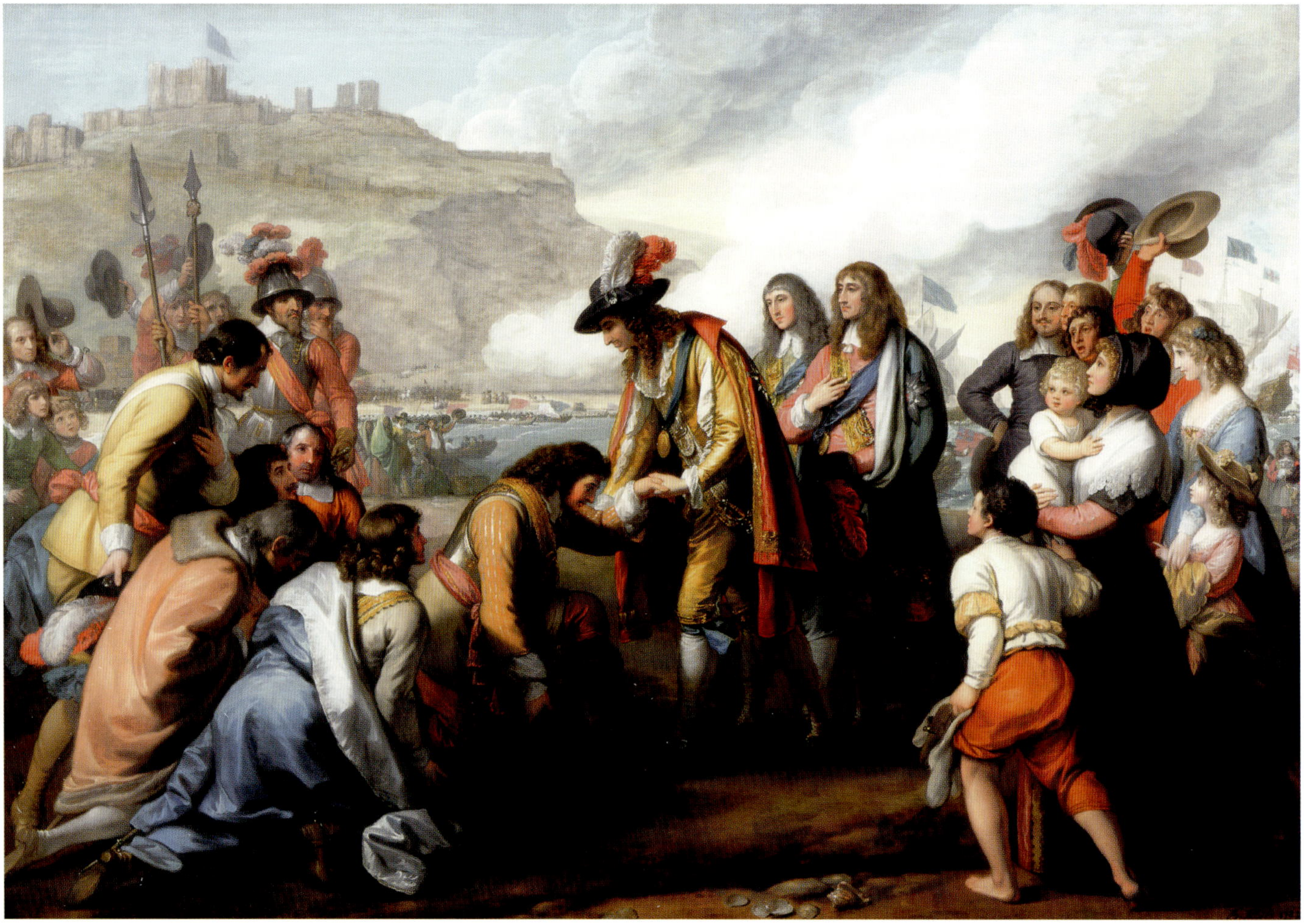

A visitor entering the Warm Room and turning his back to the windows would face *Wolfe* hanging over the fireplace, flanked by the much larger canvases of *Bayard* to the left and *Epaminondas* to the right (fig. 83). *Regulus* hung on the wall to the left of the fireplace (fig. 84), and *Hannibal* on the wall to the right (fig. 85). The smaller pictures of *The Family of the King of Armenia before Cyrus* and *Segestes and His Daughter before Germanicus* were placed over the doors, quite frankly overwhelmed by the size and drama of the other pictures. Their homage to the Hanoverians' ancestry and their themes of regal clemency must have been rather lost. Although handsome and interesting pictures in their own right, they show a surprising carelessness. West was clearly familiar with the Warm Room and knew that the two small pictures were to be used as overdoors, yet they are painted to be seen from normal viewing height: looking at them from below is unsatisfactory. Perhaps, after all the grander commissions that preceded them, West could not help dealing with them in such a perfunctory way.

Self-sacrifice is the overarching theme of the Warm Room pictures, with *Wolfe, Bayard, Epaminondas* and *Regulus* displaying two thousand years of exemplary patriotic behaviour. *Hannibal*'s lesson is slightly different. Such oath pictures were becoming a familiar eighteenth-century theme, broadcasting messages of constancy, loyalty, tenacity and determination.[34] What ties *Hannibal* and *Regulus* together is that both pictures are based on episodes in the Punic Wars. Just as Homeric subjects were increasingly popular throughout the eighteenth century, the Punic Wars, too, would have resonated with the British public. After all, if Britain was the new Rome, France could be seen as the new Carthage.[35] The long and exhausting century of warfare between Rome and Carthage must – just as in the case of the Trojan War – have seemed like an ancient prototype for the eighteenth-century struggle between France and England. There is a distinct subtext of respect for the French in the Warm Room pictures, with *Hannibal* as a warning that the French were a determined and cunning enemy, and *Bayard* paying tribute to French bravery.[36]

'In his hands the pencil was always employed for the noblest purposes, on subjects the moral interest of which outweighs their mechanical execution', Martin Archer Shee wrote when eulogizing West. 'He delighted to commemorate heroic deeds, to illustrate the annals of sacred history, and perpetuate the triumphs of patriotism and public virtue.'[37] Taken all together, the Warm Room pictures are West's greatest statement of 'the triumphs of patriotism and public virtue'. The arrangement of the pictures, with *Wolfe* as the decorative climax, suggests that contemporary Britain not only was the heir to centuries of heroic endeavour, but also stood at the top of the class. The very qualities apotheosized in the Warm Room – doggedness, bravery, loyalty and a touch of magnanimity in victory – were also the very qualities required for political and commercial empire building.

Simon Schama has used the phrase 'The Many Deaths of General Wolfe',[38] but there were also 'The Many Lives of *Wolfe*'. *Wolfe* had three significant, overlapping but distinct iterations: as an exhibition piece, as an elaborately contextualized object in one of the King's most personal rooms, and as a reproductive print that found its place in many households. Thanks to its legendary commercial success and wide circulation, it was as a print (fig. 3) that *Wolfe* was perhaps most important.

On 17 November 1772, a year and a half after *Wolfe*'s triumphant display at the Royal Academy's Third Exhibition, 'Messrs Woollett, Boydell, and Ryland' announced their proposal 'for Publishing by Subscription, a Print, Representing the Death of General Wolfe; from a Capital Picture Painted by Benjamin West, Esq; R.A. Engraving by William Woollett'.[39] Woollett, Boydell and Ryland constituted a formidable team. William Woollett was approaching the height of his powers and fame as an engraver, and had already shown entrepreneurial flair by taking a stake in a number

83, 84 & 85
Digital reconstructions of the Warm Room picture hang

From left to right:
The Death of the Chevalier Bayard; *The Death of General Wolfe*; *The Death of Epaminondas*; *The Family of the King of Armenia before Cyrus*; *The Departure of Regulus from Rome*; *The Oath of Hannibal*; *Segestes and His Daughter before Germanicus*

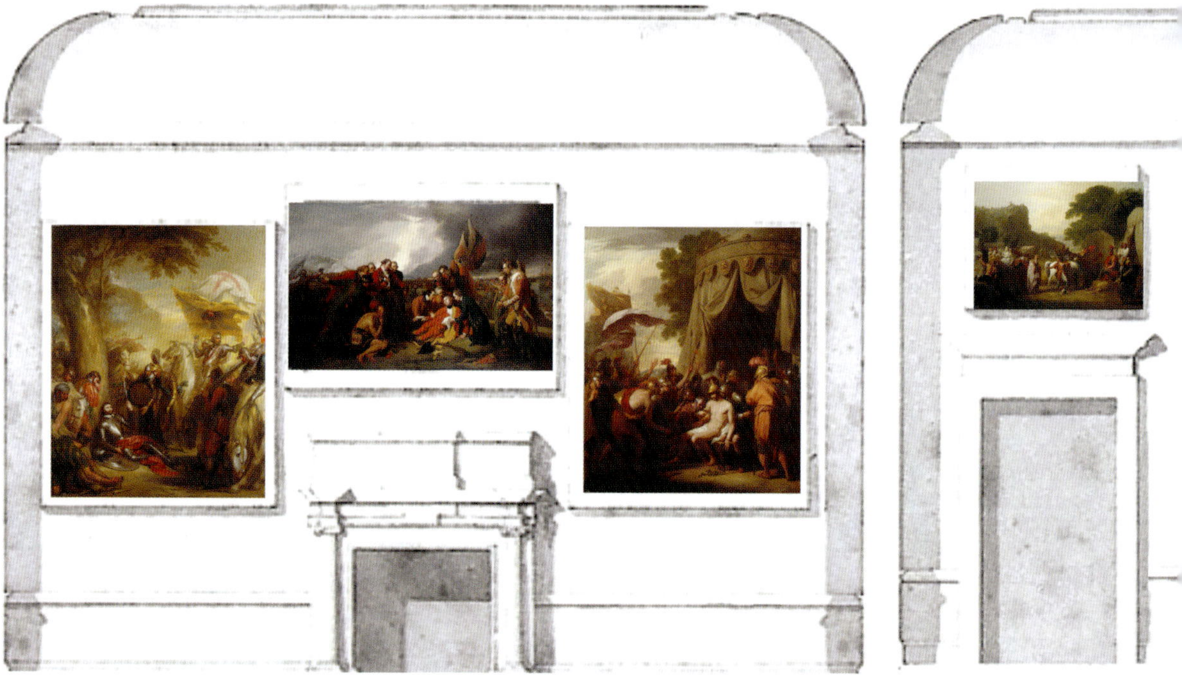

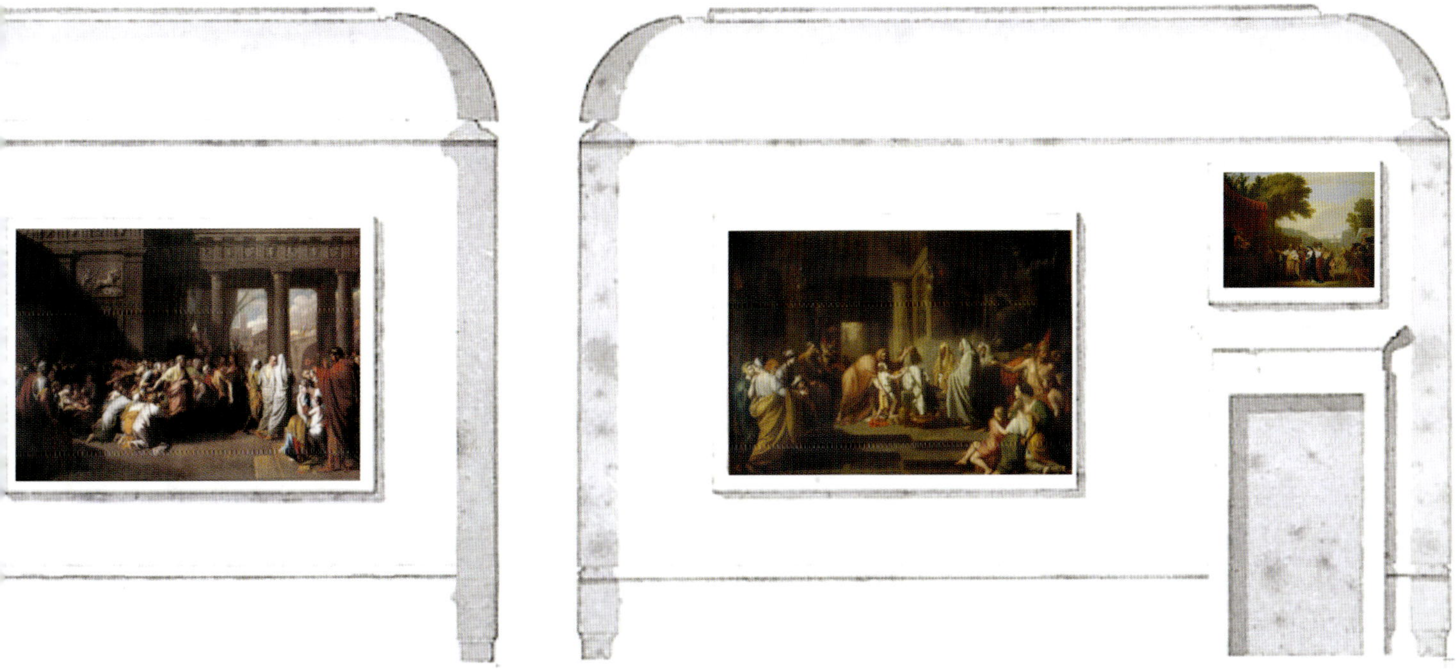

of publishing projects.[40] William Wynne Ryland, a former student of François Boucher, had been Engraver to the King and pursued a successful career as a picture dealer and print seller until a disastrous failure to sell a consignment of pictures in India forced him into bankruptcy in 1771. Nonetheless, he was astute and well connected at court and in fashionable circles: the notably rich Sir Watkin Williams Wynn (3rd baronet and father of the Grand Tourist and collector 4th baronet) may have been his godfather.[41] John Boydell was the most opulent and powerful of the three partners, well into the trajectory – almost as remarkable as West's – that took him from a modest family in rural Shropshire to the Mansion House, where he would serve as Lord Mayor of London in 1790–91. Boydell's combination of business acumen and his mission to promote British art led Edmund Burke to dub him 'the commercial Maecenas'.[42]

The partnership of Woollett, Boydell and Ryland reflected the prestige of the project and the considerable rewards a successful print could offer. Potential subscribers were warned that delivery 'cannot be in less than two years … owing to the great care and attention necessary for the highly finishing the portraits of those gentlemen whose valour so eminently signalized them in the battle where General Wolfe so gloriously fell'.[43]

The enterprise was dogged by delays from the start – delays, foreshadowed in the prospectus, that were due to the great time it would take the already busy Woollett to produce such a complex engraving. Near-disaster occurred when the son of Mrs Hocquet, who had been employed as printer, attacked the plate with a hammer, allegedly shouting, 'General Wolfe is dying and I'll be d----d if I don't kill him quite.'[44] Wolfe's head was badly damaged and needed to be repaired by Woollett. There were further delays caused by the unexpectedly slow take-up of subscriptions. 'Fashion, cabal, prejudice, in short a thousand essential and incidental considerations determine the fortune or misfortune of a work of art even in England', a German print collector wrote.

> You would scarcely believe it, but nonetheless it is absolutely true that West's masterpiece the Death of Captain Wolfe met with the same fate. It was more than a year before it was considered worth the risk of proceeding with the subscription. The value of the work went unrecognized until the stock of impressions was already widely distributed and many had already gone abroad: now everybody wanted the Death of General Wolfe and the initial delay from lack of connoisseurs was made up for by a tenfold increase in the original price.[45]

This combination of technical and commercial issues meant that subscribers did not receive their prints until 1776: seventeen years after the Battle of Quebec and five years after the painting's public exhibition. Sales may have got off to a slow start, but Woollett, Boydell and Ryland soon realized that the long wait and considerable investment would produce significant financial and reputational returns as demand grew steadily both at home and abroad. In July 1777 the print was being advertised for sale in France, and by the end of the decade copies had been published in Nuremberg, Basle, Augsburg and Paris.[46] Woollett 'watched over the reputation this work acquired for him, by superintending the printing of it, and by giving the plate such occasional labour as was necessary to enable it to answer the demand. And thus the sale of the print went on, proofs and impressions commanding progressively increasing prices'.[47]

The exact arrangement among the partners themselves and between the partners and West is unclear. There is no evidence that West retained a share of the ownership and it is legitimate to assume, as Louise Lippincott does, that 'Boydell may have bought the rights from either the artist or the painting's owner'.[48] Boydell is alleged to have earned £15,000 from the sale of *Wolfe* in the years up to 1791; alleged, because although often repeated, there appears to be no source for this figure.[49] In a speech to the House of Lords in 1804, the Earl of Suffolk claimed that Woollett earned 'between £5,000 and £7,000' from the print. Following Woollett's death in 1785, Boydell had sole ownership of the plate,[50] which suggests that the partners may have had a 'tontine' arrangement, not uncommon in the eighteenth century – although most often used to finance building projects – in which surviving investors inherited the shares of their deceased partners.[51] It is possible to reconcile Boydell's and Woollett's supposed incomes of £15,000 and £5000 to £7000 respectively in a way that indicates that the relationship between the partners' incomes is plausible.[52]

What is impossible to determine with any degree of accuracy is just how many copies of the print were sold and at what price, as the original one-guinea price for subscribers seems not to have held for long. We can say with assurance that the engraving generated a great deal of money for the partners, but simple arithmetic shows that the earnings attributed to Woollett and Boydell from the print are as significantly exaggerated as they are frequently repeated. If we put Woollett's and Boydell's alleged earnings together and add another, say, £2000 to £3000 for the time during which Ryland was a partner, it would appear that the owners of the plate earned something like £25,000 between 1776 and 1791, when the worn-out plate needed to be re engraved.[53] For the owners to have made such an income from the sales of *Wolfe* after the costs of printing and distribution, gross sales would have had to be in the order of at least £30,000.[54] Was this possible? Even with Woollett's careful and constant attention, the original plate could not have produced more than three thousand impressions,[55] which would have had to sell for an average price of £10 each to generate the level of income so frequently mentioned over the last two hundred years. There is little evidence that many prints of *Wolfe* sold for anything even approaching that price during the period.

Comparing prices across centuries is hugely difficult and crude multipliers have little use, but some examples may help us to understand just who could afford to buy the engraving of *Wolfe*. Newly arrived in London in 1762 and keen to make a sartorial splash, the young James Boswell 'wanted to have a silver-hilted sword' and visited the shop of Mister Jefferys, 'sword-cutter to his Majesty', where he 'picked out a very handsome one at five guineas'.[56] Such a sword was undoubtedly a luxury item, intended only for the gentry and nobility, and we can compare its five-guinea price with the price of a one-guinea engraving. Does this mean that engravings were expensive or that swords were cheap?

The market for prints in eighteenth century Britain – especially in London – cut across most social classes. With prices starting as low as a few pence, all but the poorest were able to buy prints. Writing in 1755, Jean-André Rouquet observed how, after the introduction of the Engraving Copyright Act of 1735, the number of print sellers in London 'suddenly increased to some hundreds: and if we consider the number and abilities of the engravers who are now in that metropolis, we must allow that of all arts relative to design, that of engraving has made the greatest and quickest progress in England'.[57] Engravings of the size, quality and price of *Wolfe* held a position at the top of the market and, like Boswell's silver-hilted sword, were both luxury items and status symbols. The increased availability of prints and reductions in the cost of glass allowed the more affluent of the middling households to hang their walls with framed glazed prints, but the one-guinea-plus price of *Wolfe* would have put it out of the reach of many such households.

The fashion for prints was such that even the greatest in the land collected them, keeping them in portfolios and scrapbooks and also framing, glazing and hanging them just as more modest households did, as well as sometimes gluing them directly on to walls. The difference in display was that while aristocratic and greater-gentry families decorated the most public spaces of their houses with paintings, prints were for the more private and lesser rooms. An inventory of 1772 of Ditchley House in Oxfordshire, for example, tells us that the Earl of Litchfield's large but private dressing room was hung with portraits of Queen Elizabeth, Lord Le Despencer, Lord North, Lord Ireland and

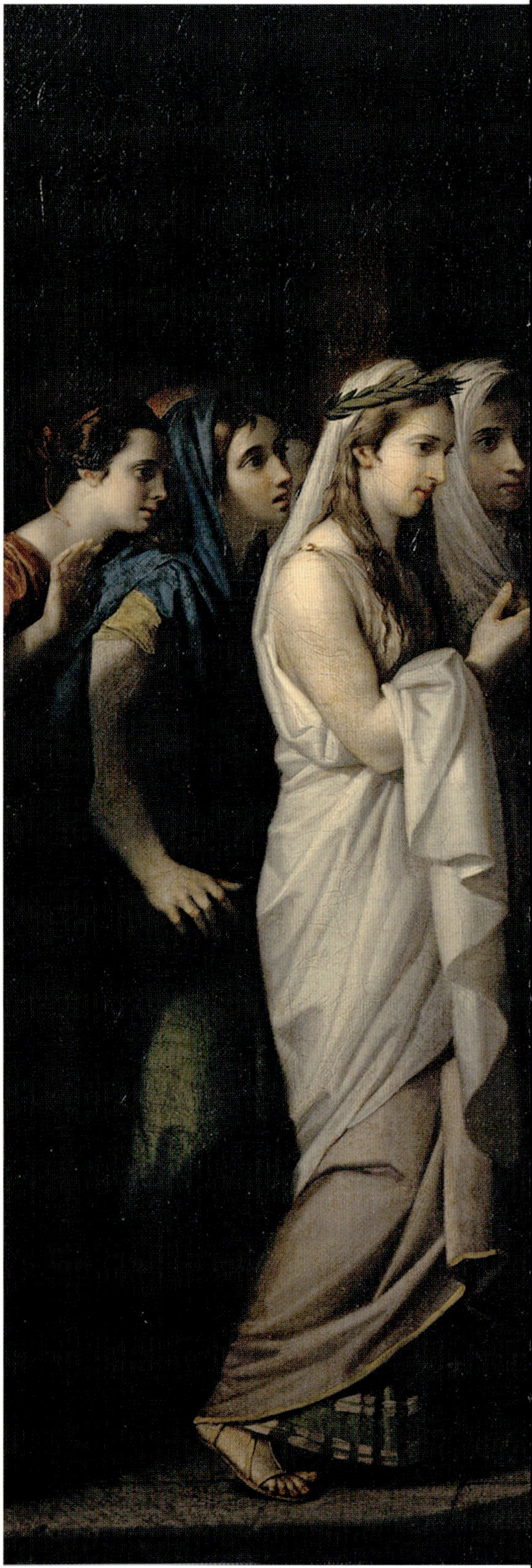

86
Benjamin West
Pylades and Orestes
1766
Oil on canvas
100.3 × 126.4 cm
(39½ × 49¾ in.)
TATE, LONDON

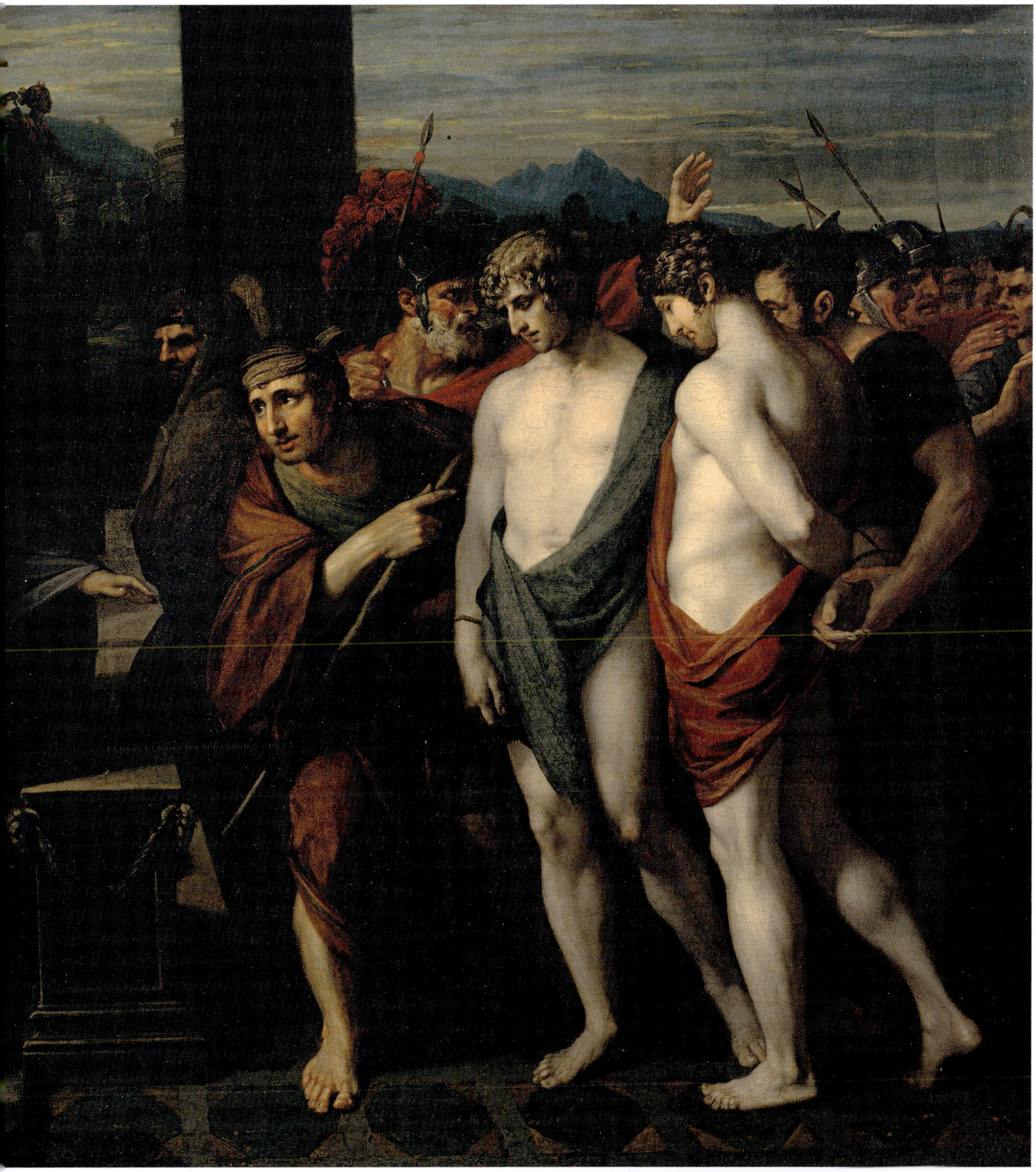

others, as well as '3 Glazed Prints', and a relatively modest bedroom displayed 'A Map, 15 Views of Stow, and 2 Glazed Prints'.[58]

At a time when a working man in London might earn two shillings for a day's labour, a modest but gentlemanly lifestyle could be maintained on around £200 a year, a level that would still make the buying of a one-guinea print a notable expense. When it comes to the market for the finest prints such as *Wolfe*, we have to look to the aristocracy and greater gentry, with annual incomes ranging from £1000 to £5000 and more for the richest. This group would consist of some 4000 to 5000 families who were in London for all or part of the year, and this is the group that would make up the great bulk of the exhibition-going and art-buying public.[59] But were they a market for history painting and, if not, why did they buy Woollett's engraving in such great numbers?

Creating a history painting was time-consuming and expensive, requiring a considerable outlay for the large canvases that the genre demanded and the large studio spaces in which to paint them, as well as needing many models, costumes and artefacts. And all of this without any certainty of a buyer. 'From the point of view of the producer,' Lippincott writes, 'history paintings were enormous gambles.'[60] Infuriatingly for the artists, such pictures attracted a great deal of public attention that rarely translated into sales.

When West displayed *Pylades and Orestes* (fig. 86) in 1766, 'His house was soon filled with visitors from all quarters', according to Northcote, and 'not withstanding all this vast bustle and commendation bestowed upon this justly admired picture, by which Mr. West's servant gained upwards of thirty pounds for showing it, yet no one mortal ever asked the price of the work'. One admirer, when asked why he did not offer to buy it, replied, 'What could I do, if I had it? – you would not surely have me hang up a modern English picture in my house, unless it was a portrait?'[61]

Without either the state patronage of absolutist regimes or the church patronage of Catholic countries, history painting in Britain was at the mercy of the marketplace, which, with few exceptions, would neither commission nor directly pay for history paintings. However, as the successful marketing of history painting by such entrepreneurs as Boydell proved, that same market was willing, even eager, to buy large numbers of often expensive reproductions of the most popular paintings.

Some felt that this created a problem rather than presented a solution. John Barrell describes how those

> who were wedded, in particular, to an account of the hierarchy of genres by which the various kinds of painting were valued in proportion to their tendency to promote public virtue ... were faced with the task of considering how history-painting could be described or redescribed so as to counter the spirit of self-interest they saw prevailing in contemporary Britain.[62]

Barrell goes on to cite Shee's rant on the evils of commercialization and Shee's fear that, in the new world of Adam Smith-elucidated self-interest, 'the arts must ever be the first victims; for they flourish only in the prevalence of feelings which the sordid and selfish passions effectively destroy'.[63] For Lippincott, the business model for history painting that relied on the sale of engravings created an existential crisis for the genre: 'That the highest form of art should be dependent on the grubby speculations of merchants and undertakers aroused the ire of every thinking artist, theorist, and connoisseur of the era. The situation violated the most fundamental tenet of history painting: the ostensibly disinterested motivation of the parties involved in its production and appreciation.'[64]

There are a number of disputable premises in Lippincott's assertion. The ire of 'every thinking artist, theorist, and connoisseur' was not roused. Nor could anyone seriously subscribe to the belief that those who commissioned, painted or viewed history paintings could be economically, ideologically or doctrinally neutral figures of 'disinterested motivation'. Nor is there much substance in Lippincott's further assertion that 'After 1768 history painters faced an unattractive choice between financial disaster or professional ostracism.'[65] Such interpretations overstate the scale of the problem with history painting and confuse the theoretical with the practical.

It is indeed hard to tell just who these 'history painters' were. There was West; the young James Barry, already beginning to show hints of the madness that was to overtake him; Gavin Hamilton, enjoying a comfortable life in Rome; and only a tiny handful of others, including Angelica Kauffmann, who pursued history painting with close to single-mindedness. During the decade that stretched from his time in Rome until the public exhibition of *Wolfe* in 1771, West produced an impressive thirty-five history paintings, yet nonetheless painted some fifty-eight portraits during the same period. Even the most ambitious, well-connected and dedicated history painter – as West was – needed the money generated by portrait painting, until in West's case he secured a stable income thanks to the sale of prints and an annual stipend from the King.

The dilemma faced by the few who wished to be history painters in Britain was how best to reconcile the aspiration to work in the most rarefied genre with the rapidly changing nature and demands of the marketplace. Given the almost complete lack of patronage for history paintings, how could the public be made to pay for them? This problem was solved by such print entrepreneurs as Boydell rather than by the artists themselves, and consequently the entrepreneurs – with a few exceptions, such as the artist/entrepreneur Copley – reaped the greatest rewards, but also assumed the greatest risk.[66] The imperative for the artists themselves was to create pictures that the public wished to view and of which they would subsequently buy reproductions.

In his booklet of 1782 *A Review of the Polite Arts in France*, Valentine Green launched a spirited if muddled and *retardataire* attack on the state of affairs in British art, contrasting its commercial nature unfavourably with the situation in France, where he thought 'Patronage was warm, fervent, and dignified … And the result has been a National Honour.'[67] In his call for a greater degree of sovereign intervention in the commissioning of art, Green failed to recognize that George III, even as Patron of the Royal Academy, was greatly constrained compared to French monarchs: whereas the French king was the state, the British king was merely a metaphor for it. In a most provocative passage, Green questioned how 'it is insisted on, that the most liberal encouragement is given to the English Artists? Is it because a Guinea is subscribed to the purchase of a Print'. Even worse for Green was

> the expedient of challenging attention by offering those Works to public view, and of setting the price of a Shilling on the humiliating Practice? But this Patronage is unique, it belongs only to ourselves; and, in addition to its other merits, is likely to produce this further brilliant effect, namely the making *Marchands d'Estampes* of our first men of Genius, and in reducing the study of their Professions to *Connoisseurship in proof impressions from Engravings*.[68]

Green was probably the greatest British, if not European, mezzotinter of the century, and his scathing attack on the print trade in which he himself flourished can be seen as just another example of eighteenth-century confusion verging on hypocrisy. It was also an expression of Green's aspirations to higher social and intellectual status as an artist rather than as a mere engraver.

West himself frequently complained about the economic difficulties facing the history painter, but was never foolish enough to attack the print trade. His usual target was portrait painting, as the American diplomat Nicholas Biddle reported after a conversation with West in 1807:

> Most English painters are obliged to earn their subsistence so that before they reach the summit of their art they are wholly occupied in portrait painting & pleasing the people, so that they paint chiefly from common nature. He would himself

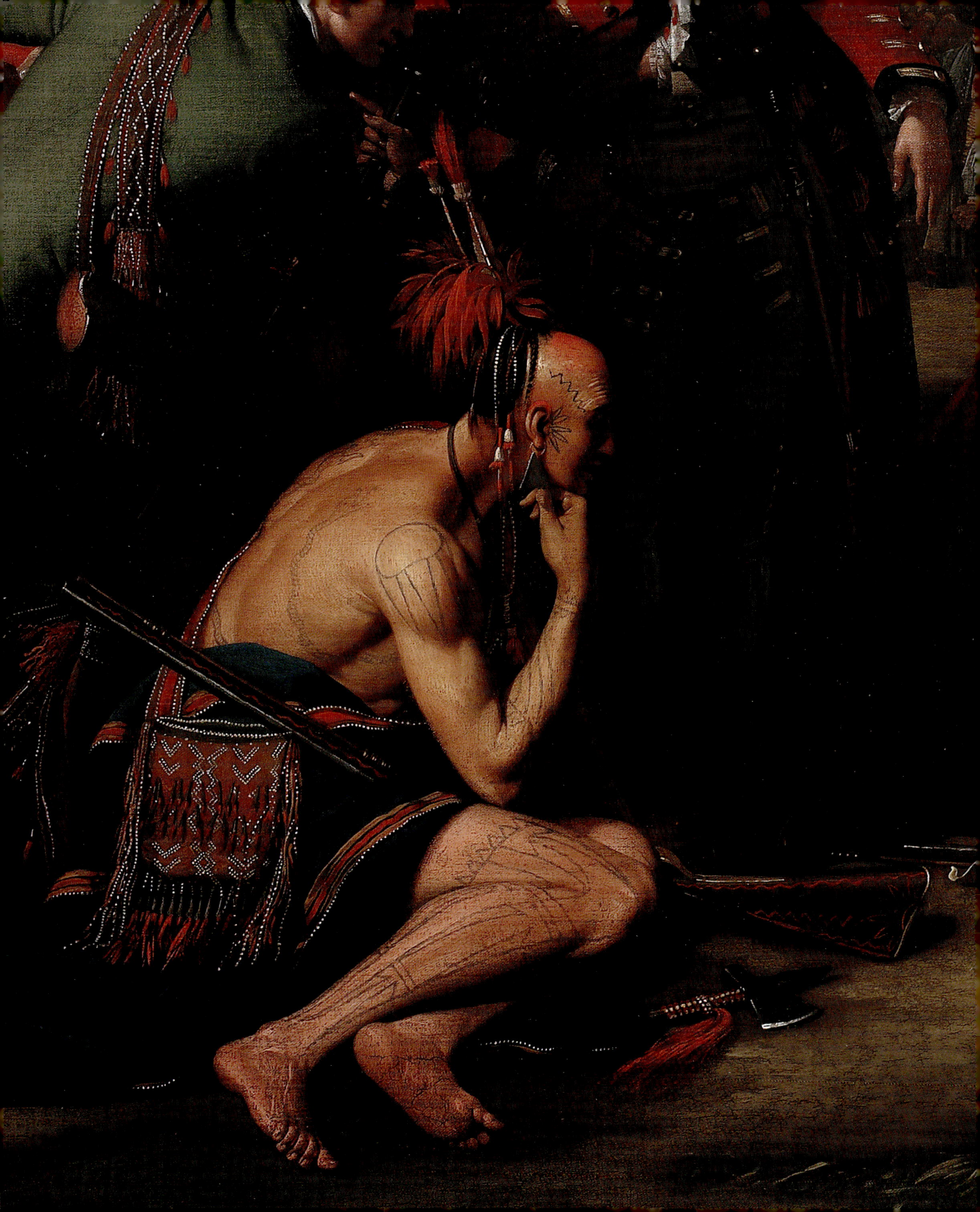

87 OPPOSITE
Benjamin West
The Death of General Wolfe
(detail)
1770
Oil on canvas
NATIONAL GALLERY OF CANADA, OTTAWA

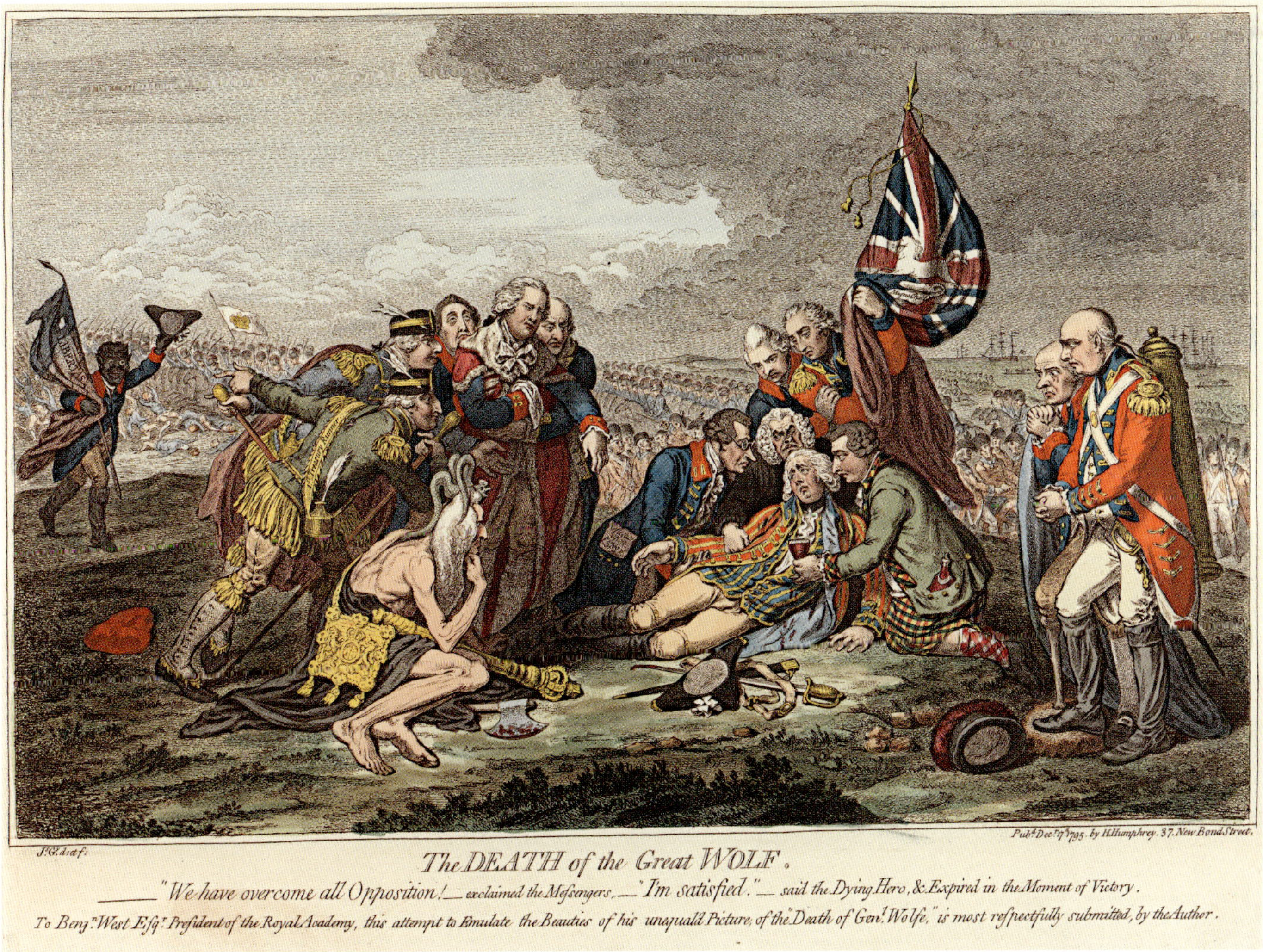

88
James Gillray (1756–1815)
The Death of the Great Wolf
17 December 1795
Hand-coloured etching and
stipple engraving
34 × 44.3 cm (13⅜ × 17⅜ in.)
PAUL MELLON COLLECTION, YALE CENTER FOR BRITISH ART, NEW HAVEN, CONNECTICUT

> have been reduced to the same necessity had it not been for the private patronage of the King, his public profits not being enough.[69]

The dilemma faced by the history painter was not the stark choice between Olympus and the agora. To believe the theoretical and polemical writings that say that it was so, or even to believe the complaints of artists, is to fail to understand what we have come across so often: the manifold contradictions of a society painfully emerging, in this case, into a market economy. For centuries, artists complained about the capriciousness of patrons; now they feared their new masters, the public: *plus ça change*. In truth, while there was a problem in British history painting, it was a problem that affected very few, a scant handful of Academicians. We can say with some assurance that the market supported as much history painting as it wanted.

Although the emergence of the public sphere was an exciting and transformational development in eighteenth-century society in Britain and elsewhere, it is worth reminding ourselves that this public sphere – certainly the core of the public sphere – constituted a small and indeed, in London, almost intimate group, frequently tied together by intermarriage and interlocking commercial arrangements. In the fourth chapter we considered the significance of news culture in eighteenth-century London. While newspapers were widely circulated and read, the actual number of copies of each title sold remained in the low thousands. As Richard Altick reminds us, 'In 1768, the *Public Advertiser*'s average was 2,800 or 2,900 daily, and even when it was making journalistic history by printing the letters of Junius (1769–71) its average circulation was no more than 3,400.'[70] When, with great fanfare, Boydell launched his scheme to publish eight magnificently illustrated volumes of Shakespeare, it attracted 1384 subscribers.[71]

At a time when there were at most only 3000 to 5000 economic decision-makers and opinion-formers in Britain,[72] at least two thousand copies of *Wolfe* were sold on the domestic market – a very conservative estimate – which means that roughly half of the most important people in the country may have owned a copy of the engraving by 1791.[73]

To explain the extraordinary popularity and importance of West's *Wolfe* both in its original and reproduced forms, we have to look well beyond its immediate appeal as a dramatic tribute to a fashionable hero by an equally modish artist. Almost from the time of its first display, the veracity of *Wolfe* was subject to criticism. Did the hero of Quebec really die in such a fashion? Were those painted with him actually there? The answer to both questions is, as was well known at the time, 'no'. In spite of what was known then and now about eighteenth-century notions of artistic truth (which we discussed in the first chapter) – notions that are in many ways more creative and inspiring than a mere commitment to the reporting of fact – this tiresome furrow is still being ploughed. 'As a representation of an historical event,' Colonel C.P. Stacey, Director of the History Department of National Defence in Canada, writes, 'it is among the worst ever produced',[74] echoing many other critiques, such as J. Clarence Webster's description of *Wolfe* as 'an amalgam of historical inaccuracies, which should have furnished the critics with sufficient ammunition to destroy the reputation of the artist and to make the picture the joke of London'.[75]

West frequently and clearly reiterated his simple view that the objects of history painting were moral and didactic: such considerations transcended basic factual accuracy. As Greg Sullivan has documented, there was a well-developed tradition of historical illustration upon which West could have drawn, and did to some extent.[76] But West was attracted to a heightened alternative to the matter-of-fact depiction of great events, and indeed this heightened alternative coexisted in the popular mind alongside more mundane reportage.

One consequence of West's use of a Lamentation model was the availability of a larger cast of characters, perhaps more in keeping with the spirit of the times, which, while not denigrating the importance of individual heroism, nonetheless was becoming accustomed to view the triumphs of modern warfare as something of a collective effort. 'Oh what pleasure is it to every true Briton,' the Sussex shopkeeper Thomas Turner wrote on hearing the news of the victory at Quebec, 'to see with what success it pleases Almighty God to bless His Majesty's arms … in this affair our generals, officers and common men have behaved with uncommon courage and resolution'.[77] Through his appropriation of the Lamentation model West was able to atomize the mourning mother into the constituent parts of the collective effort. Once again we see the universal defeated by the particular, as the Virgin Mary/Britannia is transmuted into Wolfe's brothers-in-arms crossing boundaries of class and ethnicity, as common soldiers, aristocrats, middle-class professionals, Americans and Scots collectively mourn their fallen leader.

Given the detail with which the Battle of Quebec was reported, and considering the prominence of many of the key figures involved, it should be clear that West was not trying to fool anyone with his dramatis personae, hardly any of whom were with Wolfe at the time of the General's death, many of whom did not take part in the battle, and some of whom were not even in Canada at the time. For example, Monckton was badly wounded and being attended elsewhere on the field of battle, and the surgeon Robert Adair, who ministers to Wolfe, was, at the very least, some hundreds of miles away. West carefully assembled his witnesses, attendants and mourners in the construction of what he felt to be the essential truths about Wolfe's death, the course of the battle and most importantly the British triumph over French arms.[78] The collective nature of the group was greater than the sum of the individual parts.

We might, for example, turn to the portrayal of Isaac Barré, the Irish-born soldier and politician, who features prominently (he is the grey-haired man immediately behind Wolfe). Sarah Monks feels that Barré's prominence gave West 'an opportunity to highlight his specifically colonial identity, with the portrayal of Captain Isaac Barre who had gone on to become an outspoken champion of the American colonies' right to legal and fiscal self-determination'.[79] Such an interpretation credits West with a pro-American independence political agenda that he never otherwise articulated. If Barré was so obviously 'an outspoken champion of the American colonies', it begs the question why West would feature him in a painting that he hoped would appeal to the King.

There is a greater deal of sense in Monks's feeling that *Wolfe* addresses the issue of British–American relations 'within an image which gives emblematic form to the concept of mutual interest promoted by colonists in their struggles with George III's ministers'.[80] There may be such a coded message within *Wolfe*, but it seems to me a message that is seen only with considerable hindsight and more in the eye of the beholder than in the mind of the artist. West's political apathy; his growing friendship with George III, from whom not only had he already received two major commissions but also hoped for more; the lack of a distinctive American national identity at the time the picture was painted, all militate in favour of a belief that West's intention was to place the dying Wolfe within the bosom of a happy, if grief-stricken imperial family. As Dennis Montagna put it, 'this work is also a product of the nationalist sentiment of the 1760s that grew up around Wolfe's death and the victory of Quebec'.[81] Even though events in the colonies were moving quickly in the early 1770s, the 'nationalist sentiment' that West expressed in *Wolfe* was clearly British and imperial. It is worth returning to an earlier point, that the sense of American political identity was very slow to develop, even on the eve of the Revolution.[82] I cannot see any value in interpreting *Wolfe* either as a response to pre-Revolutionary events in the colonies or indeed as a pro-American independence manifesto.

Perhaps the most controversial figure in *Wolfe,* and the one subject to the greatest degree of recent attention, is the Indian warrior in the left foreground (fig. 87). That this should be so is

89
Albrecht Dürer (1471–1528)
Melencolia I
1514
Engraving
23.9 × 18.5 cm (9⅜ × 7¼ in.)
THE BRITISH MUSEUM, LONDON

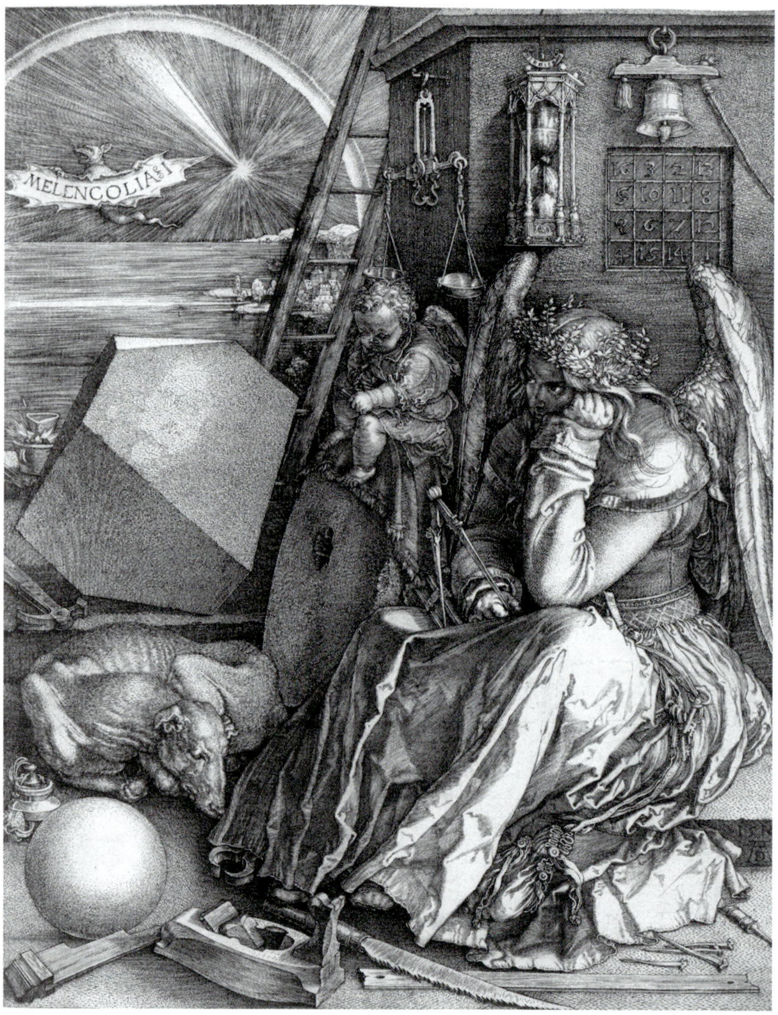

90
Raphael (1483–1520)
The School of Athens (detail)
Fresco
1508–11
STANZA DELLA SEGNATURA, VATICAN PALACE, ROME

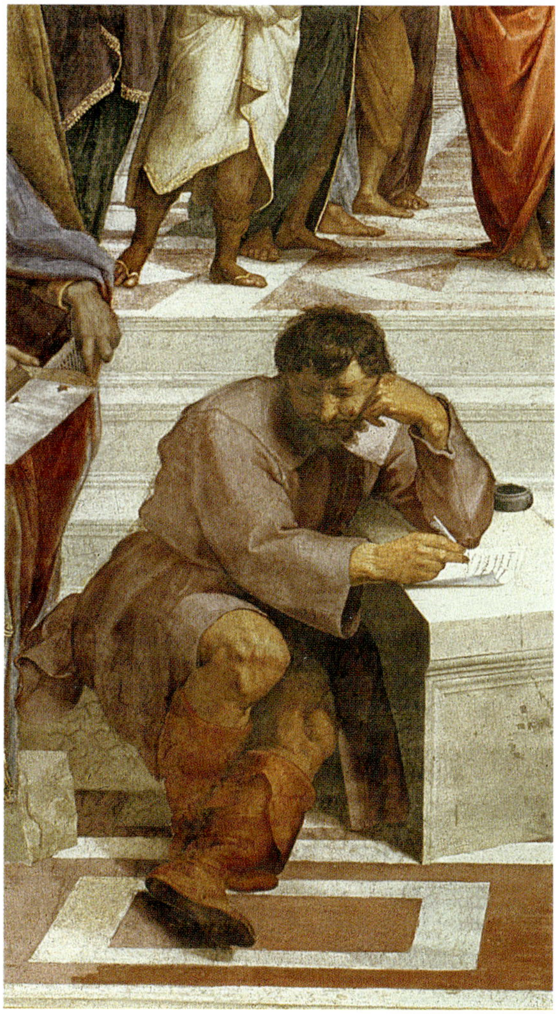

91
Belvedere Torso
1st century BC
Marble
VATICAN MUSEUMS, ROME

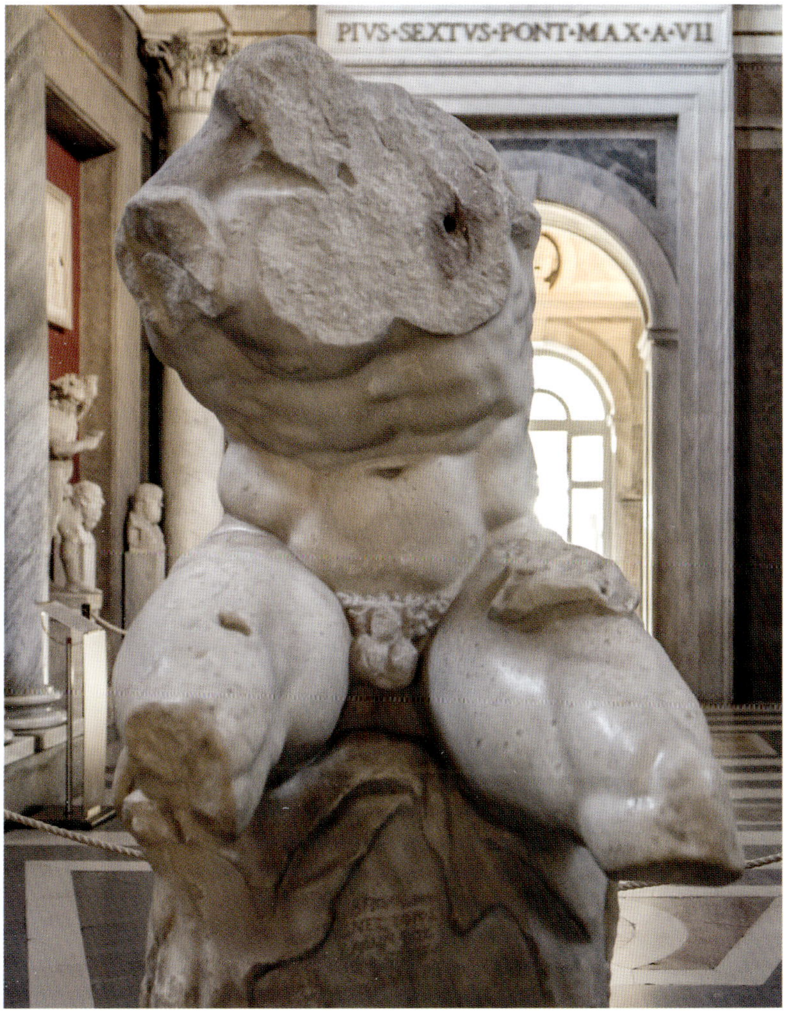

92
Michelangelo (1475–1564)
Lorenzo de' Medici, from the Tomb of Lorenzo de' Medici
1524–31
Marble
630 × 420 cm (248 × 165⅜ in.) overall
MEDICI CHAPEL, SAN LORENZO, FLORENCE

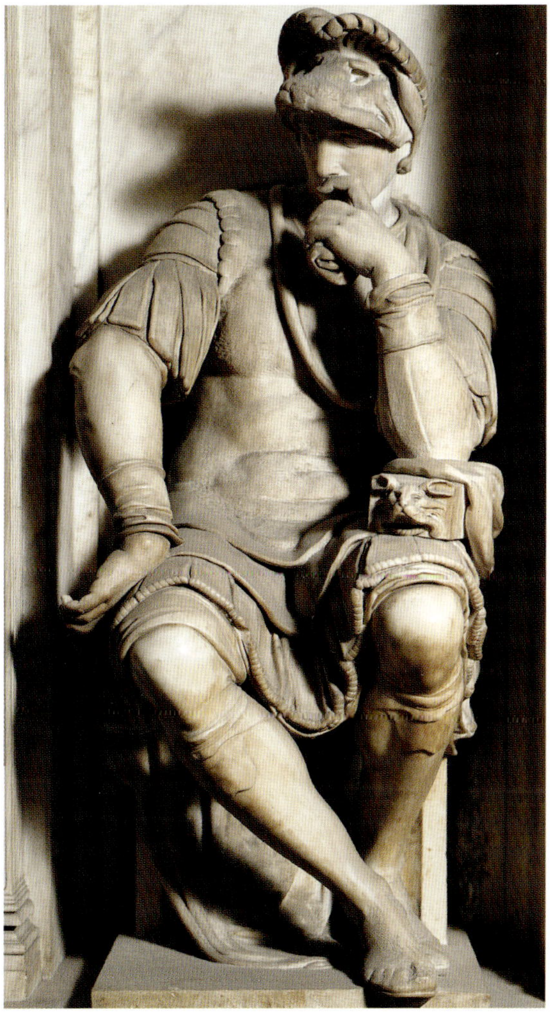

due to the detail, power and flair with which this individual is painted; the ever-growing interest in the portrayal of Native Americans; and the recognition from early in the painting's life that no Native Americans fought with the British forces at Quebec.

Edgar Wind felt that the Indian warrior provided West with a sort of get-out-of-jail card for those hard-line Academicians who were disturbed by West's use of contemporary costume in a history painting. Citing Racine's dictum from the preface to the tragedy *Bajazet* (1672) that 'the respect that one has for the hero grows in proportion as he recedes from us', Wind argues that the Indian by 'leading the imagination into a distant land, effectively offsets the shock of seeing the hero die in a modern uniform'.[83] This elegant explanation of the Indian's purpose rests on the assumption that audiences would otherwise have been 'shocked' by the depiction of Wolfe in modern dress. There is nothing to suggest that they would have reacted that way, and that the Indian somehow provided a 'mitigated realism' (Wind's term) that made West's picture more acceptable. The audience of the 1770s was becoming accustomed to the more-or-less accurate depiction of contemporary events, often in far-off places. Many of the elite who attended the exhibition and who subsequently bought the print would have had first- or second-hand experience of modern warfare: after all, they were the very class that supplied Britain's naval and army officers. Wind's remark that 'distance of country is as conducive to grandeur as distance of time, and that it allows what the classical rules of the grand style had forbidden; the representation of contemporary events without disguise'[84] significantly overstates the authority of 'classical rules', and misses a more important point. There was no need for 'disguise'. Wilton's Wolfe monument, with its ingenious 'disguise', would be met with both lack of interest and ridicule. The public was crying out for a celebration of contemporary events: with *Wolfe*, West took painting to where the press and poetry and drama had already gone.[85]

The use of the Native American was entirely consistent with the belief that truth in painting was about depicting things as they should have been. The Indian clearly situated the action in North America. Since the first half of the sixteenth century, American Indians had appeared on maps of the New World and were subsequently enshrined as the allegorical representation of the Americas in the canon of allegory, Cesare Ripa's *Iconologia* of 1593. All educated people in the eighteenth century would have been familiar with such visual shorthand.[86] 'This scene must be North America,' Bromley wrote in defence of the picture's truthfulness, 'for the savage warrior shews us that the country was his ... And is not that savage warrior every way as just as the crocodile on the Nile?'[87]

With the Indian's pose, West was able to display his familiarity with the highest artistic vocabulary, as there are hints of Dürer's *Melencolia I* (fig. 89), the so-called 'Heraclitus' in Raphael's *School of Athens* (fig. 90) and the *Belvedere Torso* (fig. 91), although perhaps the greatest debt is to Michelangelo's figure of Lorenzo de' Medici (fig. 92). But the attention to the most minute details of costume, weaponry, hairstyle and body decoration – details that contrast with the broader way in which some of the other figures are painted – also showed West's intimate knowledge of North America and, as Stephanie Pratt puts it, 'allowed him to stake a very particular claim for understanding the American situation, giving him a specialism by which to differentiate his practice from others'.[88] Yet in spite of the care with which West painted the Indian, he is an oddly detached figure in both formal and emotional terms. Working admirably as *repoussoir*, the Indian is in the scene, but in some ways not of it. His role is both allegorical and spectatorial, an onlooker like us. This ambiguity has encouraged some to seek out an encoded meaning in this enigmatic figure.

'That Wolfe is oblivious to the warrior gazing intently at him, even though they are both foregrounded, suggests that West intended another, more far reaching prophesy – that of the Vanishing American in the nineteenth century',[89] Vivien Green Fryd writes, going on to describe the Indian as 'an omen of the inevitable destruction of indigenous peoples – represented here by a single, solemn, seated figure contemplating death'.[90] For Pratt, the Indian was less prophetic than a comment on the contemporary balance of power in the colonies: 'the Indian man's subordinate position and contemplative pose place him outside the action of the picture. In one sense, this could be seen as the American Indians' most proper alignment with respect to the whole question of control of North America, for by the time this was painted in 1770, many tribal groups had lost the "middle ground" roles they had played in the preceding decades.'[91] While such interpretations are intriguing, to accept them would be to credit West with a greater degree of foresight or political sophistication than he has shown elsewhere.[92]

Just as the role of the Indian warrior has been subjected to perhaps too much analysis, back-projecting twentieth- and twenty-first-century values into eighteenth-century minds, there has been a tendency to overinterpret the supposedly encoded gender references contained in *Wolfe*. 'In contrast to the activity and purpose demonstrated by the British soldiers,' Fryd writes, 'the Iroquois and Wolfe are inactive and passive, qualities coded as feminine. Wolfe's pale skin, wounded state, and expressive face with upward-looking eyes reinforce this impression.'[93] Even the living Wolfe was known for his pallor, and to suggest that such a complexion, combined with a 'wounded state' and 'upward-looking eyes', was a specifically feminine quality would pervert our understanding of the values conveyed by any number of death-bed scenes.

Rather than searching for such feminine subtexts or even homoerotic ones as Fordham has done,[94] it may be more valuable to consider how *Wolfe* conveyed what Martin Myrone calls 'the refined qualities of a genteel masculinity'. Myrone describes Wolfe as someone 'who combined valour and personal grace, and who had risen to high status by his virtuous action alone'.[95] Although revisionist studies of Wolfe often characterize him as neurotic, lascivious and wantonly cruel, the mythologized Wolfe – the Wolfe that the eighteenth-century public believed in – was embraced by the elite, and also by those who aspired to elite status, as a poster boy for the highest eighteenth-century masculine values, which were in demand for the battlefield, the quarterdeck and the colonies.

Eighteenth-century Britain was both a hierarchical society and a society in flux, thanks to a rapidly transforming economy. Emulation plays an important role in such conditions, as taste and behaviour trickle down from the top of society and 'new' people strive to conform to the patterns set by their established social superiors. Hence the profusion of etiquette manuals, fencing instructors and dancing masters in London and the bigger provincial towns.

Some will have wanted to buy their own copy of *Wolfe* simply in emulation of the King's taste. But given what we know about the economic and social status of those who were able to buy *Wolfe*, it seems that the majority of buyers were validating beliefs and behaviours to which they already subscribed: in Linda Colley's words, *Wolfe* 'encouraged prominent Britons to see themselves as heroes of a national and imperial epic'.[96] It was much more, though, than just a powerfully painted and elegantly conceived piece of propaganda.

With his classical and religious references, his boldness, and the beauty and daring of his composition, West firmly situated current events in the mainstream of history, celebrating the present, and in the words of André Breton, creating a work of art that quivered 'with reflections of the future'.[97] *Wolfe* was a thoroughly modern picture.

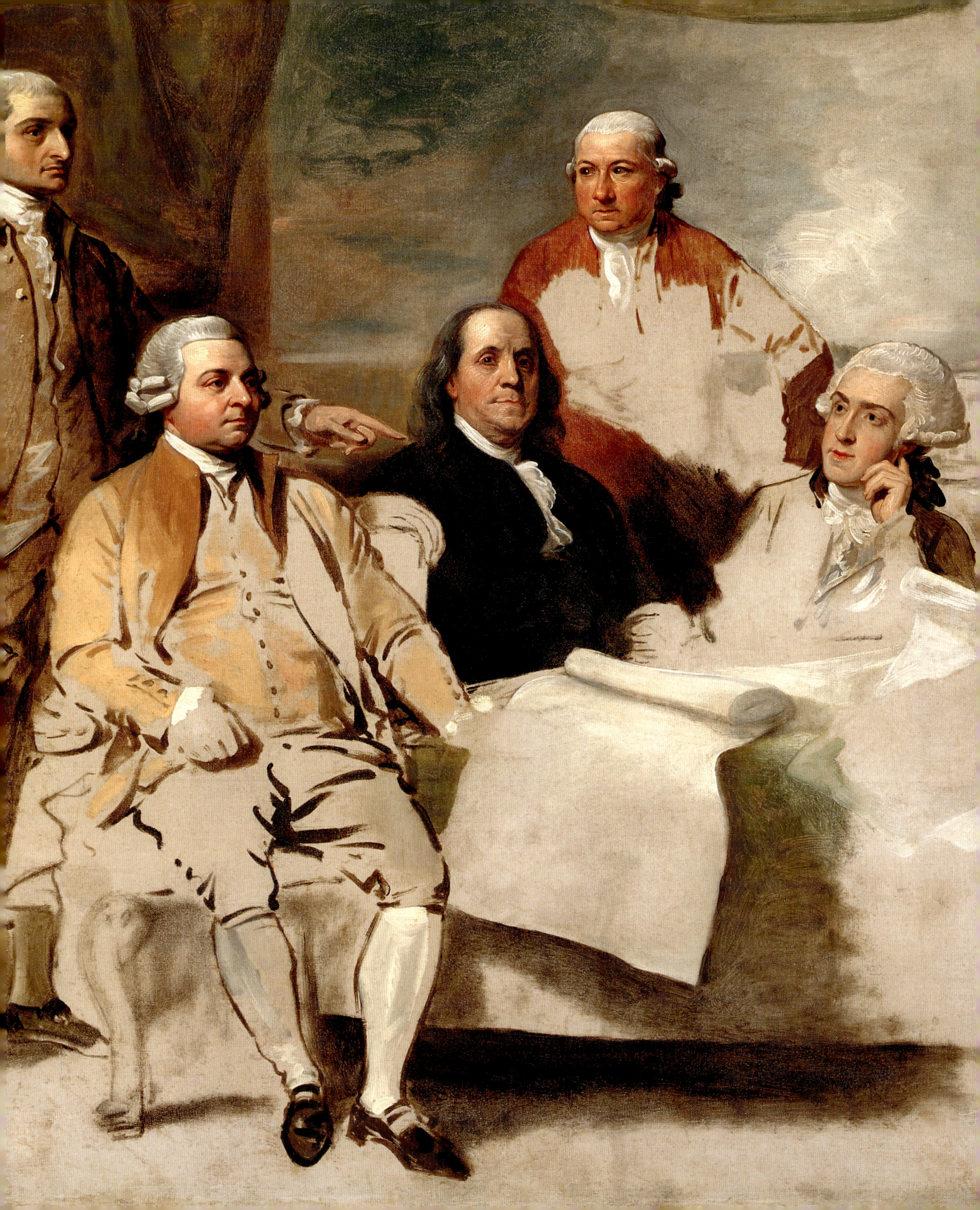

BEING MODERN FROM *WOLFE* TO *WHAAM!*

Detail of Benjamin West, *The Signing of the Preliminary Treaty of Peace in 1782*, begun 1783 (see fig. 96)

'I have this Day, by Special Permission from their Majesties obtained by Mr. West the Painter who with Mr. Copely do so much honour to our Country, Seen the Appartements in the Queens House', John Adams wrote to his wife, Abigail, on 8 November 1783.

> It is a great Curiosity indeed. There is an inestimable Collection of Paintings by the greatest Masters, Raphael, Rubens, Vandyke, and many others. There is one Room which the King calls Mr. Wests, as it is ornamented with a Collection of his Works – the Return of Regulus – The Death of Epaminondas – The Death of Bayard – The Death of General Wolf – and &c.[1]

As one of the first American ambassadors to the courts of Europe, John Adams was both fascinated and repelled by the cultural wealth of the Old World. 'The richness, the magnificence and splendor are beyond all description', he had written to Abigail five years earlier. 'But what is all this to me?' he asked. 'I receive but little pleasure in beholding all these things, because I cannot but consider them as bagatelles, introduced by time and luxury in exchange for the great qualities, and hardy, manly virtues of the human heart. I cannot help suspecting that the more elegance, the less virtue in all times and countries.'[2]

Such puritanical indignation was a time-honoured response to periods of rapid social and economic change – Cato the Elder and Savonarola excoriated the immoral spending of both aristocrats and the nouveau riche – and the old anxiety that luxury subverted virtue was particularly acute in the eighteenth century. In 1739 the pseudonymous author of *The Modern Englishman* complained that 'Virtue's abandon'd, Honesty's disgrac'd;/ Good Sense is scorn'd – what Rivals all is TASTE.'[3]

To such worries about moral decline were added concerns that the arts were being used as repressive and propagandistic tools by authoritarian regimes, absolute monarchs and the Catholic Church. 'The Burin and the Pencil, the Chisel and the Trowell,' Adams cautioned the American artist John Trumbull, 'have in all ages and Countries

… been enlisted on the side of Despotism and Superstition'.[4] On his Grand Tour, West had been appalled by what 'a degraded state painting was brought in Italy, and France, as stimulating bigotry, superstition and lascivious passions', and resolved that he would help painting 'recover its dignity', a dignity that was founded on what West defined as the 'real use' of painting: 'a moral point of view'.[5]

The sternly Calvinist Adams could never quite admit that the arts had such an explicit moral purpose, but nonetheless felt that they must be a hallmark of any mature society. 'I must study politics and war, that my sons may have liberty to study mathematics and philosophy', he wrote in 1780. 'My sons ought to study mathematics and philosophy, geography, natural history and naval architecture, navigation, commerce and agriculture, in order to give their children a right to study painting, poetry, music, architecture, statuary, tapestry and porcelain.'[6]

Adams's remarks were prophetic. During the lifetime of his great-grandson the aesthete and historian Henry Adams, the United States was challenging the European powers for economic and political pre-eminence. By 1896, clearly about to become the world's leading industrial power and on the threshold of its first overseas imperial adventure – the Spanish–American War – the United States Treasury had commissioned, as if in celebration of America's rising status, a new series of so-called 'educational' banknotes, featuring allegorical compositions by the leading artists of the day on the obverse and portraits of the most significant Americans on the reverse.

Perhaps the most remarkable of this series is the $2 bill decorated with Edwin Howland Blashfield's *Science Presenting Steam and Electricity to Commerce and Manufacture*, the reverse of which bears portraits of Robert Fulton and Samuel F.B. Morse (fig. 93). This bill is especially prized by collectors not only for the beauty of its composition and engraving, but also because it is the only American banknote ever to feature neither political figures nor military heroes.[7] Fulton, the father of commercial steam navigation, and Morse, one of the inventors of the telegraph, were among the transformative figures of American history: their innovations in transport and communications were critical tools for the realization of America's expansionist 'Manifest Destiny'. Before their success as inventors and entrepreneurs, Fulton and Morse were practising artists: both students of Benjamin West.

From the very first of those students, Matthew Pratt in 1764, who wrote that West 'rendered me every good & kind office he could bestow on me, as if I was his Father, friend and brother',[8] to the much later, such as Thomas Sully, who recalled that West 'superintended my studies with the solicitude of a parent',[9] those who spent time under West's tutelage were uniform in their praise of him. For over half a century, West's London studios were literally 'The American School' (fig. 94),[10] and while the artists who emerged from it ran the whole gamut of style and skill, what united so many of them was a commitment to, using Walter Benjamin's phrase, 'the here and now',[11] a commitment that emanated from West and the proven success of *Wolfe*.

Like West, Fulton emerged from rural Pennsylvania and was a protégé of West's first patron, William Henry of Lancaster. Fulton was a picaresque figure, attempting at various times to sell canal improvements to the British and invasion plans for Britain to the French. He lacked the application and perhaps the talent to be an artist, confiding to his mother that 'Painting requires more studdy than I at first imagined',[12] but like so many of West's students, Fulton became a grateful and devoted friend.

Unlike Fulton, Morse was sophisticated, Yale-educated and from near the top of New England society; he was the son of Jedidiah Morse, Congregationalist preacher and author, celebrated as the 'father of American Geography'.[13] Morse was the most theoretically doctrinaire of all West's students. Lecturing in the 1820s, Morse reminded his audience that 'The character of the picture is determined from the character of the intention and the importance of the object copied. If it is to copy an apple with exactness, the aim is not very elevated'[14] – words that could have come straight from the pages of French academic theory a century earlier.[15] Yet Morse was a thoroughly modern man, and his role as a creator of practical electronic communications makes him one of the founding fathers of our modern world. But, in West's lifetime, what did it mean to be modern?

Defining 'the modern' involves an extended walk through a definitional minefield. The modern and its corollaries provide particular difficulties for art history, in which 'modern', 'modernity' and 'modernism' all jostle for intellectual space, and confusion reigns between words and ideas that may be describing an outlook, a chronological period or a style. Charles Baudelaire's *Painter of Modern Life,* published in 1863, is often regarded by art historians as the defining document of what it means to be modern. Baudelaire's provocative and scintillating prose coincided with the unmissable emergence of Manet and the first stirrings of Impressionism, and has, unsurprisingly, caused the modern to be described – rather lazily – as a French-driven narrative, the birth of which takes place in a specific *haut bourgeois* context in Second Empire Paris.

'"Modernism"...', T.J. Clark writes, 'is used here in the customary, somewhat muddled way. Something decisive happened in the history of art around Manet which set painting and the other arts upon a new course.'[16] In her more widely informed discussion of modern, modernity, modernist, modernism and modernization, Ludmilla Jordanova gently moves the locus, arguing that modernity long predates Manet:

> significant shifts in 'modern' art have been located earlier in the nineteenth century, while the origins of 'modernity' have also been found in the Enlightenment. Debates about the relative merits of the 'ancients and moderns' took place in the seventeenth century. Hence 'modern' has a long history, and the nature and timing of 'modernity' could hardly be more contested.[17]

Without falling into the bear trap of 'period chauvinism', in which someone studying the eighteenth century feels compelled to prove that everything that happened in the nineteenth century really took place one hundred years earlier, one can assert that 'being modern' was an eighteenth-century possibility that Benjamin West and his followers embraced and to which they gave visual expression.

To return briefly to the Quarrel between the Ancients and the Moderns is to be reminded that the crucible of the modern was the court of Louis XIV rather than the boulevards of Haussmann's Paris. Charles Perrault's poem '*Le Siècle de Louis le Grand*', publicly recited in 1687 to celebrate Louis XIV's recovery from a potentially fatal operation, was the most notable *casus belli* of the quarrel and a rallying cry for the modern. 'I look at the Ancients without bending my knees', Perrault proclaimed. 'They are great, it is true, but men like us;/ And without fear of being unjust, one can compare/ the century of Louis with the beautiful century of Augustus.'[18] Perrault's declaration articulates an important shift in consciousness. It is among the first clear signals that we should abandon the habit of looking back over our shoulders and escape from what had become the stifling influence of the Ancients.

Periodization encourages us to locate the birth of the modern in a particular event or work of art, but being modern was a long and complex process: there was never a moment, whether in the late seventeenth, the mid-eighteenth or indeed the mid-nineteenth century, when suddenly 'we are all modern now.' This is not surprising given that our modern world is such a bundle of different phenomena, including industrialization, the growth of cities, the spread of representative democracy, secularism, improvements in the speed and reliability of transport, and the expansion of the public realm. All these lineaments of the modern world become discernible in the eighteenth century and move in and out of focus for decades. Along with these meta-characteristics

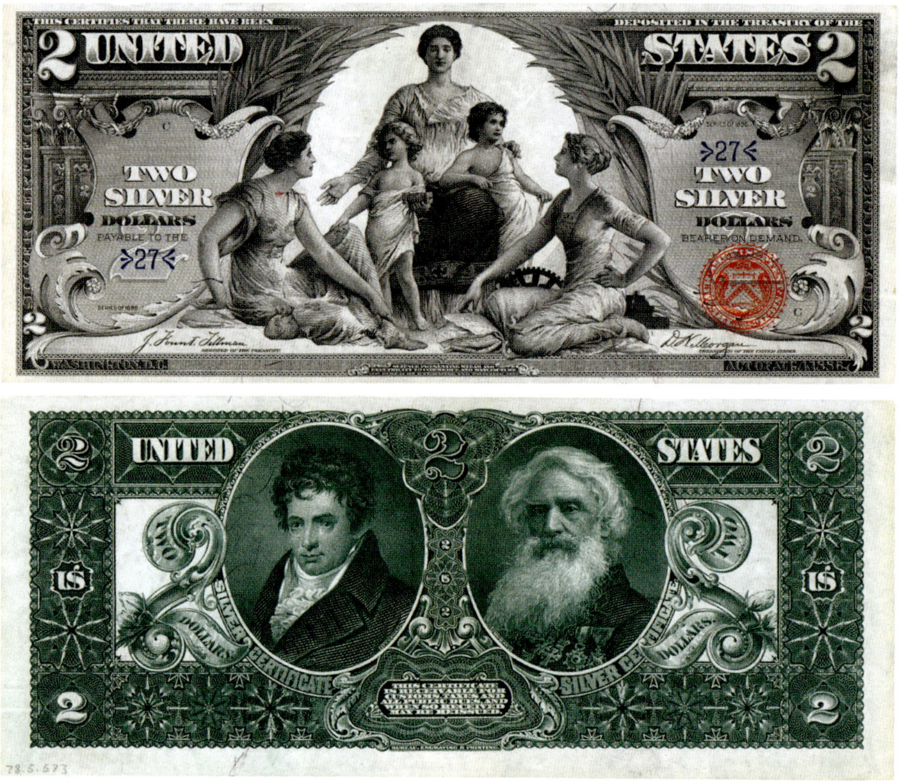

93
US $2 bill, Educational Series
1896

of modernization – identified by such big-picture historians as Eric Hobsbawm – we can enumerate individual behaviours and mindsets that underpinned, reinforced and contributed to the shift into the modern world: such qualities as scepticism towards received authority, the decline of traditional deference, the fetishization of reason, and greater personal and historical self-consciousness.

In his analysis of what he calls 'The Continuing "Riddle of the Modern"', C.A. Bayly recaps how the word has been used 'to denote a clutch of global developments, which combined to create a step-change forward in human organization and experience'.[19] While Bayly defines modernity as a process as well as a period, he also observes that 'an essential part of being modern is thinking you are modern. Modernity is an aspiration to be "up with the times".'[20]

'I wonder whether we may not envisage modernity rather as an attitude than as a period of history', Foucault asks. 'Modernity is the attitude that makes it possible to grasp the "heroic" aspect of the present moment', he continues.[21] I want to be clear about the distinction between what is modern as a style – which is often the default position of art history – and what is modern as an attitude. For example, Christopher Atkins in his consideration of Frans Hals as a proto-modernist writes that 'The multifaceted features of Hals's manner – roughness, sketchiness, liveliness, seeming spontaneity, virtuosity, calligraphic handling, self-referentiality, and materiality – all came to be, at various times, signs of modern painting. In the process, Hals's signature style, as the combination of these elements, came to be designated as modern in its own right.'[22]

All true and illuminating, but considering Hals, should we not instead look to the scale and confidence with which he celebrated the contemporary as a more significant contribution to the agenda of modernism than his brushstrokes? Modernity is more about matter than manner. Even Courbet in his so-called 'Realist Manifesto'

94
Matthew Pratt (1734–1805)
The American School
1765
Oil on canvas
91.4 × 127.6 cm (36 × 50¼ in.)
THE METROPOLITAN MUSEUM OF ART, NEW YORK

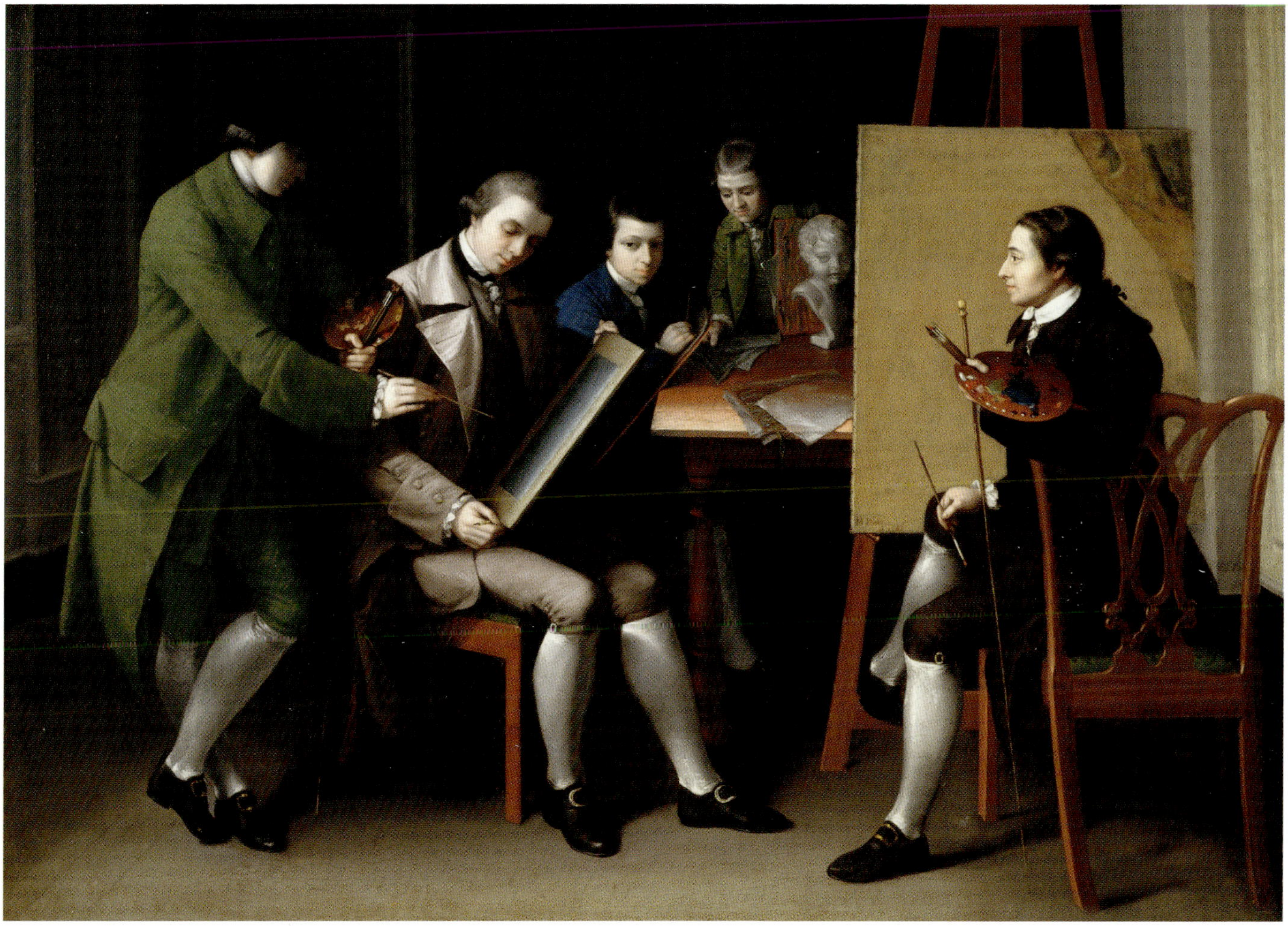

disdained what he called 'the trivial goal of "art for art's sake"', and declared his aspiration 'To be in a position to translate the customs, the ideas, the appearance of my time, according to my own estimation; to be not only a painter, but a man as well; in short, to create living art – this is my goal.'[23] Such a goal, to create a living art that values the present, is consistent with Foucault's observation that 'Modernity is not a phenomenon of sensitivity to the fleeting present; it is the will to "heroize" the present.'[24]

Baudelaire put it slightly differently when he wrote, 'The past is interesting, not only because of the beauty that the artists for whom it was the present were able to extract from it, but also as past, for its historical value.' He then goes on to make this most important point: 'The same applies to the present. The pleasure we derive from the representation of the present is due, not only to the beauty it can be clothed in, but also to its essential quality of being the present.'[25]

This proclamation of the virtues of the modern had been a long time coming and was exercising imaginations a century before Baudelaire so neatly expressed it. Take, for example, Joseph Warton's statement in 1756 that

> We have been too long attached to Grecian and Roman stories. In truth, the DOMESTICA FACTA, are more interesting, as well as more useful: more interesting, because we all think ourselves concerned in the actions and fates of our countrymen; more useful, because the characters and manners bid the fairest to be true and natural, when they are drawn from models with which we are exactly acquainted.[26]

Warton's thoughts had in turn been foreshadowed in 1739 by Joseph Addison, whose popular *Discourse on Ancient and Modern Learning* celebrated the virtues of familiarity and contemporaneity. Addison noted how Virgil or Homer had engaged their own readers

> by choosing their heroes out of their own nation … so that the narration renders [the reader] more intent, the happy events raise a greater pleasure in him, the passionate part more moves him, and in a word the whole poem comes more home, and touches him more nearly, than it would have done, had it been laid in another country, and a foreigner been the subject of it.[27]

Both Warton and Addison were making the point that neither distance of time nor of place were indispensable qualities and, by extension, that the great events of the past had first gained their narrative power because they were once current affairs. The exhortation to apply ourselves to the present was a key driver of the industrial, agricultural and political revolutions. As he toured England and Wales, the polemicist and agricultural reformer Arthur Young urged his readers to 'Get rid of that dronish, sleepy, and stupid indifference, that lazy negligence, which enchains men in the exact paths of their forefathers, without enquiry, without thought, and without ambition'.[28] In a similar vein, Fulton observed, 'if we consider for a moment, how much men are the sons of habit, we shall find, that almost the whole operations of society are the produce of accident, and a combination of events, rendered familiar by custom'. What was important for Fulton was 'a mind active to investigate, and which feels only contented to rest on the basis of reason; for without this, man must ever remain in a fixed point, and improvement will be at an end'.[29]

This urgency to 'improve' in all aspects of human life was an eighteenth-century fever. As J.H. Plumb put it, late eighteenth-century Britain was 'the first society dedicated to ever-expanding consumption based on industrial production'. This consumption 'required men and women to believe in growth, in change, in modernity; to believe that the future was bright, far brighter than the past; to believe, also, that what was new was desirable'.[30] It was a time, as well, when the belief was becoming embedded, 'perhaps not yet profound nor accepted even by the majority of society, that there was virtue in modernity and change'.[31] The quantitative change in eighteenth-century Britain is startling in its scope and rapidity, but it would be misleading to interpret that change as caused solely by what

R.H. Tawney characterized as 'the worship of production and ever greater production – the slavish drudgery of the millionaire and his unhappy servants'.[32] The intellectual transformation of eighteenth-century Britain was after all both cause and effect of the economic changes, so it is important not to discount the unquantifiable but nonetheless significant phenomena, such as the growth of curiosity and optimism.[33]

Such economic and spiritual changes bring impatience with them. 'He cannot wait for the future', Gotthold Lessing wrote about the modern type he described as the '*prophète philosophe*'. 'He wants this future to come more quickly, and he himself wants to accelerate it … for what has he to gain if that which he recognizes as the better is actually not to be realized as the better within his lifetime?'[34] This modern mindset also helps to explain the fierce ambition that motivated West and his followers.[35]

An American recalled how on a trip to London in September 1816, he had visited West and been 'received with great politeness' and invited 'into his painting room'. They talked about Philadelphia, which West had last seen in 1760; West praised the painting of Thomas Sully, Charles Robert Leslie and Gilbert Stuart. Then they turned to the *Apollo Belvedere,* and perhaps West shared the well-rehearsed anecdote about how, as a young man newly arrived from America, he had electrified and seduced the Roman art establishment by comparing that sculpture to a young Mohawk warrior. But the Elgin Marbles, West went on, were 'the finest specimen of sculpture in the world' and the 'production of the most brilliant period of the arts in Greece', and as such they eclipsed the *Apollo Belvedere,* which belonged to a period when the arts had 'begun to decline'. West spoke too about how 'he had been in the habit of meeting Johnson often at Sir Joshua Reynolds's'. And the elderly West also discussed 'the increasing use of steam-boats' with his guest.[36]

Apollo Belvedere and steamboats: the struggle to be modern meant reconciling a mentality that had been trained to venerate the artistic and intellectual achievements of the past with the urge to celebrate the accomplishments of the present. It was not easy to do so, especially when the world was changing so rapidly. Like travellers in a sandstorm, the men and women of the long eighteenth century were trying to find their way, sometimes blindly, in an often unforgiving world. For what he describes as 'the definitive vision of the modern environment', Marshall Berman turns to Marx's observation:

> Constant revolutionizing of production, uninterrupted disturbance of all social relations, everlasting uncertainty and agitation, distinguish the bourgeois epoch from all earlier ones … All fixed, fast-frozen relations, with their train of ancient and venerable prejudices and opinions, are swept away, all new-formed ones become antiquated before they can ossify. All that is solid melts into air, all that is holy is profaned, and men at last are forced to face … the real conditions of their lives and their relations with their fellow men.[37]

Although firmly located in the mid-nineteenth century, Marx's words, so pregnant with foreboding and trauma, further illuminate the fact that while we identify the eighteenth century with the growth of a belief in progress, that progress was red in tooth and claw. Without overdramatization, West's world was one of instability and uncertainty: a modern world, with all that that implies. The inconsistencies, the hypocrisies and the brutalities, the successes and the failures were all part of a long struggle to work out how to live in that modern world. It was not easy for the men and women of the eighteenth century to find stability and meaning in a world in which, as Kant put it, 'nearly everything is paradoxical'.[38]

Many of West's contemporaries were aware that they lived in times of rapid and irreversible change. 'Everything that was seen and described was conceived in terms of change and upheaval', Reinhart Koselleck writes. 'Revolution covered morals, law, religion, economy, countries, states, and portions of the earth – indeed, the entire

95
Benjamin West
William Penn's Treaty with the Indians
1771–72
Oil on canvas
191.8 × 273.7 cm
(75½ × 107¾ in.)
PENNSYLVANIA ACADEMY OF THE FINE ARTS, PHILADELPHIA

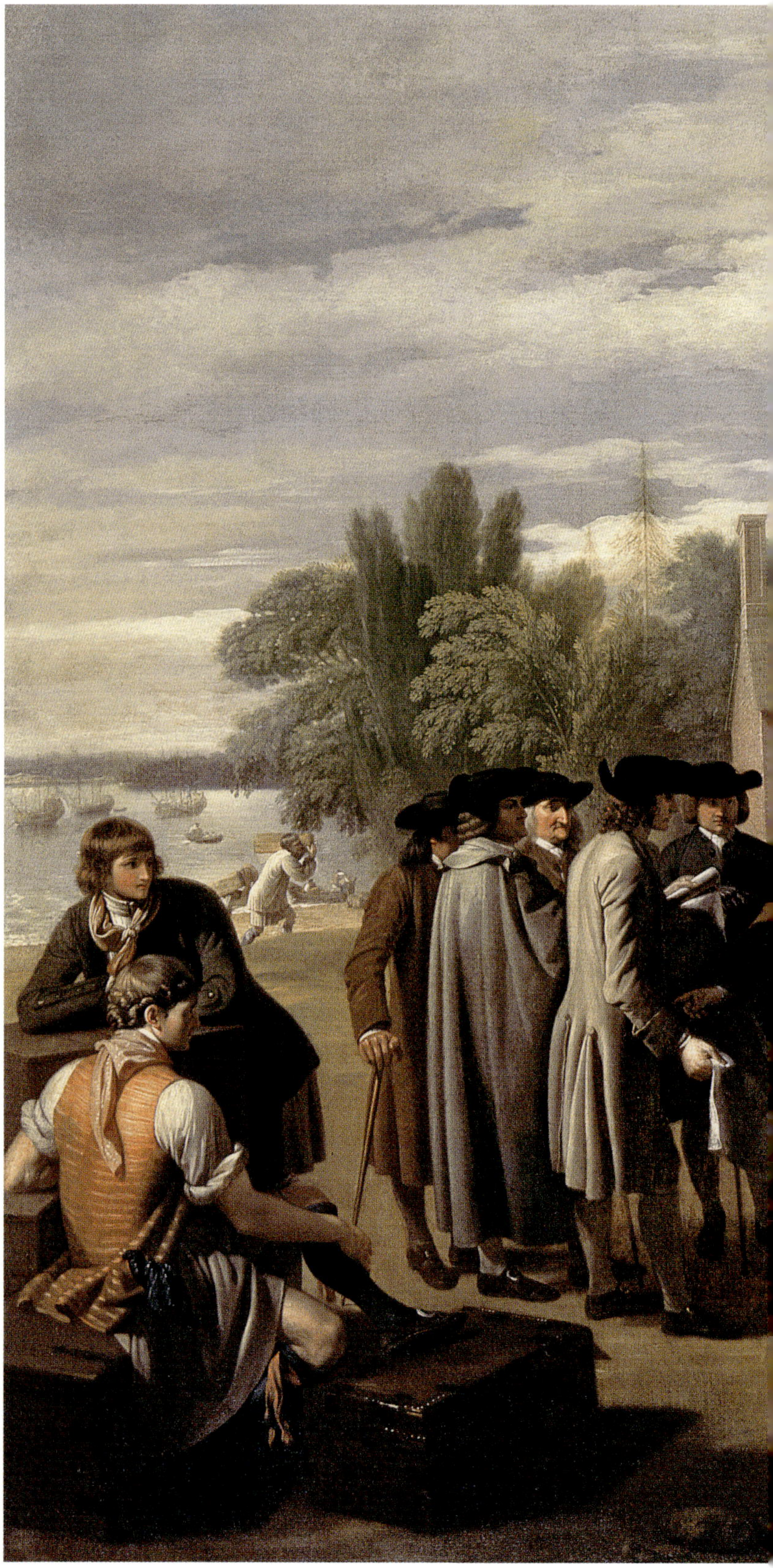

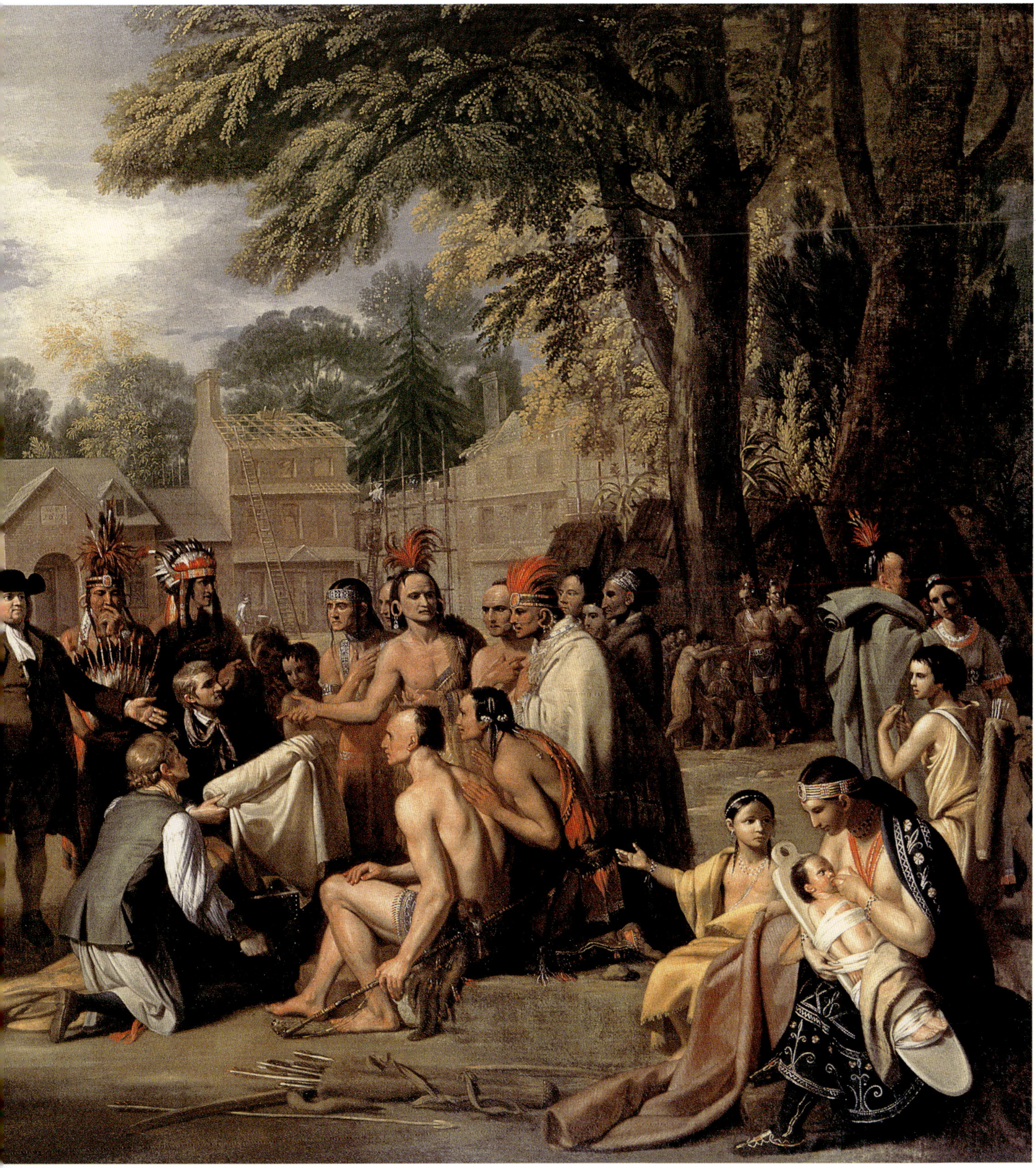

globe. As Louis Sébastien Mercier said in 1772, "*Tout est revolution dans ce monde.*"'[39] All is revolution. Perhaps Mercier was merely paraphrasing Heraclitus' 2000-year-old observation that 'all is flux'; but while Heraclitus was referring to the hidden processes of the universe, Mercier was talking about phenomena observed and experienced by many.

In their discussion of the Industrial Revolution, F.W. Botham and E.H. Hunt warned against 'naïve cataclysmic interpretations' based on notions of 'marked discontinuity'.[40] Indeed, revolutions are long in the making, ragged in the execution and unpredictable in the consequences. And revolutions – even in art – do not always look like revolutions. In his deft account of Louis Napoleon's *coup d'état* of 1851, Marx observed:

> The tradition of all dead generations weighs like a nightmare on the brains of the living. And just as they seem engaged in revolutionizing themselves and things, in creating something that has never yet existed, precisely in such periods of revolutionary crisis they anxiously conjure up the spirits of the past to their service, and borrow from them names, battle-cries, and costumes in order to present the new scene of world history in this time-honoured disguise and this borrowed language.[41]

Marx went on to consider the seeming irony that the French revolutionaries 'performed the task of their time in Roman costume and with Roman phrases'. Importantly for my view of West's revolution, Marx realized that 'the awakening of the dead in those revolutions served the purpose of glorifying the new struggles, not of parodying the old'.[42] With *Wolfe*, West dared to take the Lamentation, a form sanctified by centuries, and use it to glorify the 'new struggles', as Marx might say, or to '"heroize" the present', as Foucault put it.

The year after *Wolfe*'s public debut, West exhibited five pictures at the Fourth Exhibition of the Royal Academy in 1772, four of which were drawn from biblical, mythological or literary sources. The fifth, *William Penn's Treaty with the Indians* (fig. 95) depicted, like *Wolfe*, an event from contemporary or near-contemporary history: the moment in 1682 when the Quaker founder of Pennsylvania purchased land for his colony and signed a treaty of peace with the indigenous Lenape Indians. As West described it:

> In the Penn, we see the legislature with that simplicity and dignity, of a man render justice to others and difusing his bounties in the midst of savage tribes, and disarming their ferocity by his rectitude and benevolence; – while himself and those about him, rest in perfect security by conscious mind, that they are rendering to others what they wish to have rendered to them and by that, conquering the savage, without any weapon to denote any other conquest but that which justice renders.[43]

Penn's Treaty can be viewed as a sanitized version of the foundation myth of Pennsylvania. Like *Wolfe,* it was criticized almost from the start for numerous inaccuracies. Writing in 1789, Benjamin Smith Barton, who was no friend of West, attacked the height of the houses and indeed the height of Penn himself, as well as the picture's lack of likenesses of the participants. 'Chronology and truth are sacrificed,' Barton lamented, 'and yet what beauty or embellishment acquired?'[44] *Penn's Treaty* may be a straightforward piece of propaganda, commissioned by Thomas Penn (son of William) to promote the increasingly shaky claims of the Penn family for the continued political control of what had once been in every sense their colony. But while it was painted to order, it is perhaps most usefully seen as a companion piece to *Wolfe.* Indeed, West discussed *Agrippina*, *Regulus*, *Hannibal*, *Wolfe* and *Penn* collectively, noting proudly that 'The fine prints from those pictures ... were by a commercial intercourse spread throughout the civilized world – and those subjects being real facts founded in history, exhibited to mens view what dignified his nature'. West went on to claim that his pictures

> broke down those licentious abuses of art, as well as those prejudices that had long prevailed, that modern dresses could not be admitted into pictures where Heroism, and dignity were the caracteristics;

96
Benjamin West
The Signing of the Preliminary Treaty of Peace in 1782
Begun 1783
Oil on canvas
72.3 × 92.7 cm
(28½ × 36½ in.)
WINTERTHUR MUSEUM, GARDEN AND LIBRARY, DELAWARE

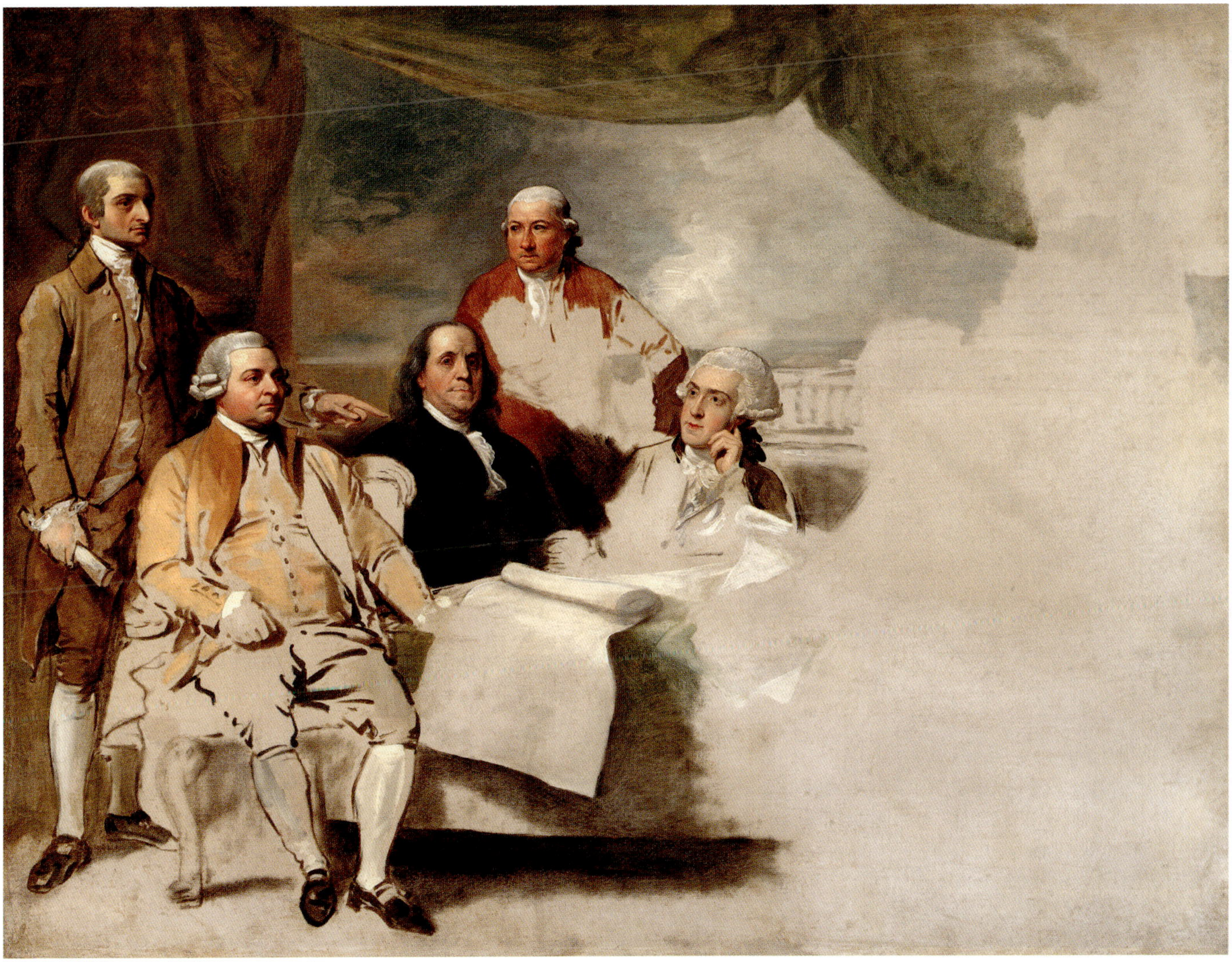

97
John Trumbull (1756–1843)
The Battle of Bunker's Hill, June 17, 1775
1786
Oil on canvas
65.1 × 95.6 cm
(25⅝ × 37⅝ in.)
YALE UNIVERSITY ART GALLERY, NEW HAVEN, CONNECTICUT

98
John Trumbull (1756–1843)
The Death of General Montgomery in the Attack on Quebec, December 31, 1775
1786
Oil on canvas
62.5 × 94 cm (24⅝ × 37 in.)
YALE UNIVERSITY ART GALLERY, NEW HAVEN, CONNECTICUT

> – over those prejudices the two pictures of Wolfe, and Penn have been triumphant; and the British Hero, and Legislature in those pictures stands confused by all with the Greeks, and Romans.[45]

Although they were never intended to be displayed together, *Wolfe* and *Penn's Treaty* are a conceptually rich pair of pictures, representing West's attempt to monumentalize both the power of action – Wolfe's triumph at Quebec – and the power of ideas – Penn's 'Holy Experiment' of religious toleration. Like *Wolfe*, *Penn's Treaty* attained iconic status; unlike *Wolfe*, it did so without recycling long-sanctified pictorial formulas.[46] Such was the popularity of *Penn's Treaty* that 'by the 1850s one could have the peace treaty not only as a framed picture for wall ornamentation, but also on dishes, candle screens, hand-painted trays, bed curtains, window curtains, whisky glasses, bed quilts and iron plates'.[47] A reason for that popularity was that *Penn's Treaty* presented a wishful view of America's westward expansion, in which the 'settling' of the frontier could be seen as a rational, collaborative enterprise rather than the morally dubious and bloody conquest that it was.

Penn's Treaty is considerably bigger than even the 'Royal' version of *Wolfe*, yet it is altogether a more modest and self-effacing work, lacking the panache and emotional punch of the earlier picture. Rather than showing any lessening of West's inventiveness or commitment, the quieter authority with which *Penn's Treaty* is presented grows implicitly from its subject matter. While *Wolfe* exalts British victory by force of arms, *Penn's Treaty* is all about victory through force of reason. It was, in West's words, intended to be a 'demonstration to all nations of a conquest made without sword or dagger'.[48]

After *Wolfe* and *Penn's Treaty*, West did not completely abandon modern history painting, but he was increasingly distracted by the demands of royal patronage and the creation of two large picture cycles for Windsor Castle. Nonetheless, West continued to consider the great events of his time as subject matter. He began, and then gave up on, both a dramatic scene of the Earl of Chatham's fatal stroke on the floor of the House of Lords and a more ambitious idea of creating a picture cycle dedicated to the great events of the American Revolution. 'I mean the arrangement of the subjects most expressive and most pointed,' West wrote to Charles Willson Peale in 1783, 'as for instance – the cause of the Quarel, the commencement of it, the carrying it on, the Battles, alliances &c. &c. &c. – to form one work, to be given in eligent engavings – call'd the American revolution'.[49]

The intended series began inauspiciously. West was unable to finish a group portrait, *The Signing of the Preliminary Treaty of Peace in 1782* (fig. 96).[50] The American delegation – Benjamin Franklin, William Temple Franklin, John Jay, Henry Laurens and John Adams – were happy to be painted by West, but the British commissioner, Richard Oswald, was unavailable. According to Adams's son, John Quincy Adams, Oswald 'was an ugly-looking man, blind in one eye'[51] and consequently would not pose for portraits: it is perhaps more likely that a British envoy would not wish to help commemorate a humiliating peace. On reflection, West himself may have decided that celebrating the success of the American Revolution was inconsistent with his patronage by the King. The planned series was abandoned, and West suggested that the project should be taken up by his student John Trumbull.

Trumbull began his series of history paintings with two spectacular battle scenes – *The Battle of Bunker's Hill, June 17, 1775* (fig. 97) and *The Death of General Montgomery in the Attack on Quebec, December 31, 1775* (fig. 98) – and carried on painting the great events of the revolution for nearly forty years. The early brilliance soon faded, and Trumbull, exhausted by the reluctant patronage of the United States Government, produced increasingly turgid work. When four of Trumbull's history paintings were installed in the rotunda of the United States Capitol in 1826, Senator John Holmes remarked irately that Congress 'had been taken in. Those paintings, which cost thirty-two thousand dollars, were not worth thirty-two cents.'[52]

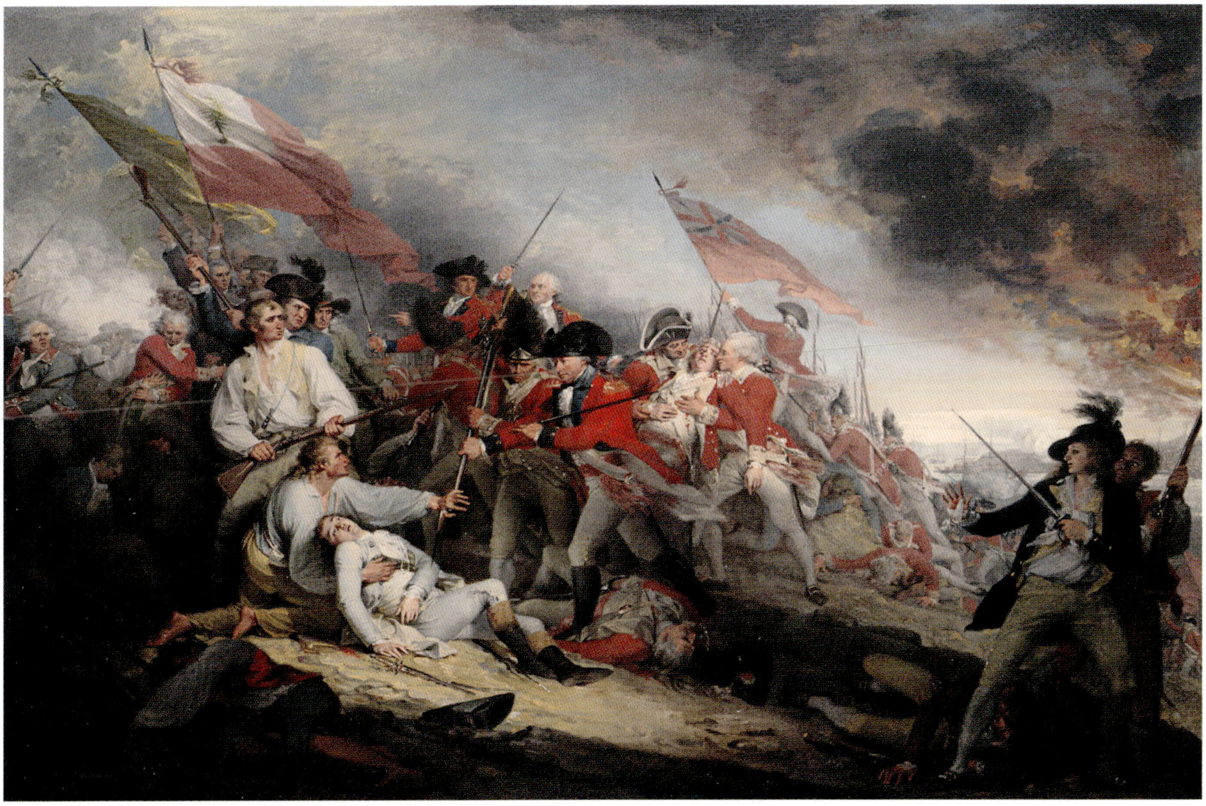

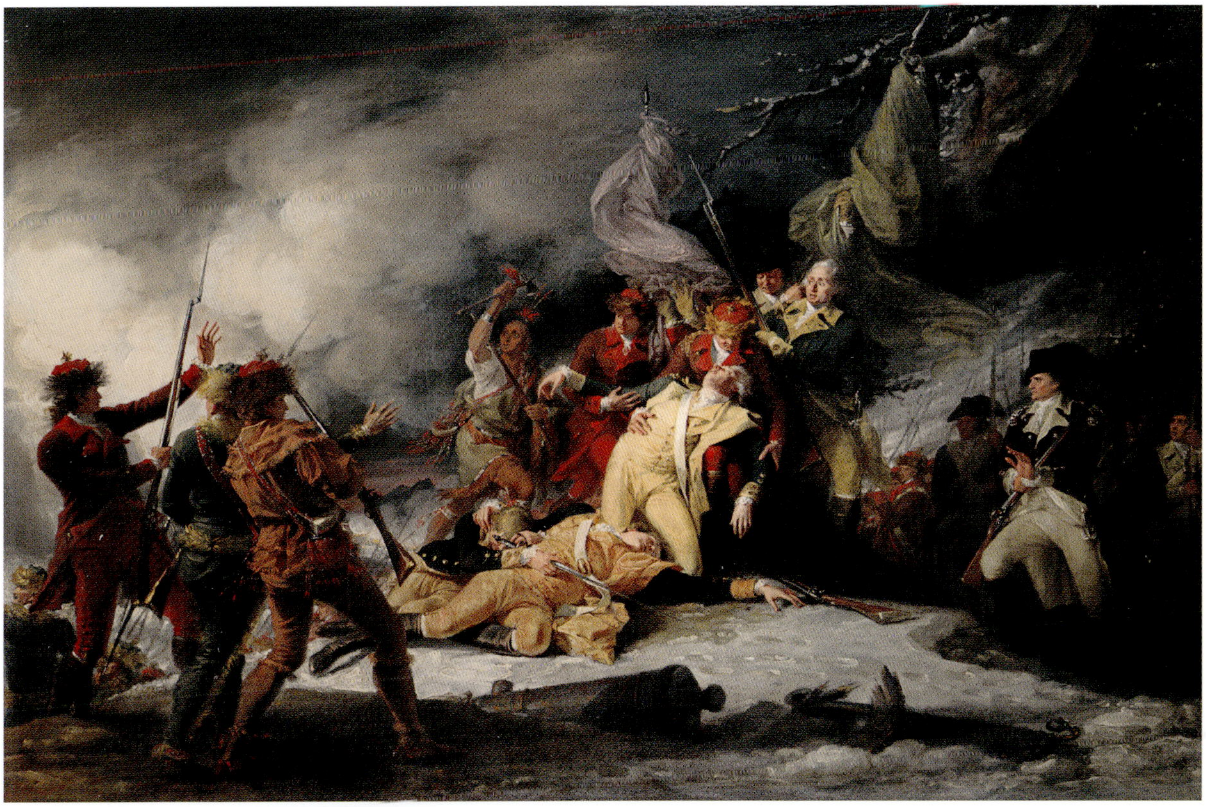

Among the four paintings in the Capitol rotunda is a late copy of Trumbull's most well-known painting, *The Declaration of Independence, July 4th, 1776* (fig. 99), on which he began work as early as 1786.[53] Like *Wolfe*, it attracted criticism on the grounds of inaccuracy: the event pictured took place on 28 June, not 4 July; some of those pictured were not present; the room did not look the way Trumbull saw it. Such carping aside, it seems that the real difficulty with *The Declaration of Independence* was its failure to address convincingly the problem posed by *Penn's Treaty*: how, without the use of allegory, to portray convincingly what is essentially intellectual action?[54] While it rapidly attained status as the definitive vision of a – perhaps the – formative moment in American history, there is something absurd about this picture, teetering on the threshold between history painting and group portraiture. Joseph Rodman Drake went beyond mere satire when he described it in his poem 'The National Paintings':

> Old, young, great, small, the grave, the gay,
> Each man might swear the next his brother,
> And there they stand in dread array,
> To fire their votes at one another.
>
> How bright their buttons shine! How straight
> Their coat-flaps fall in plaited grace!
> How smooth the hair on every pate!
> How vacant each immortal face![55]

Bemused by the neatly arranged breeches and stockings of the legislators in Trumbull's painting, John Randolph remarked in the House of Representatives that the picture 'ought to be called the Shin Piece, for surely never was there before such a collection of legs submitted to the eyes of man'.[56]

Copley's earlier painting in a legislative setting, *The Death of the Earl of Chatham* (fig. 100), had met with similar criticism. 'On first entering the room,' the reporter for the *London Chronicle* wrote, 'I could not help being immediately fascinated by the predominance of drapery in the picture; the whole seemed to me drapery in motion; there seemed to be a war of dress'. *Chatham* portrayed the dramatic moment on 7 April 1778 when the former Prime Minister collapsed in the midst of a fierce debate on British policy towards the rebellious American colonies.[57]

Like Trumbull's *Declaration of Independence*, *Chatham* sits uncomfortably between portraiture and history painting. 'In theory this should have lowered the status of [Copley's] history,' Jules Prown comments, 'since, according to accepted standards, portraiture marked a lesser level of artistic achievement.' Prown goes on to assert that, having 'tilted his lance at this particular doctrine', Copley 'set out to prove that a factually accurate history painting was more meritorious than a work based on imagination alone'.[58] But *Chatham* was no more 'factually accurate' than *Wolfe* (for example, despite being painted as such by Copley, the peers were not wearing robes at the time of Chatham's seizure), nor, by eighteenth-century standards, did it need to be. As previously discussed, the boundary between fact and imagination was a blurred and shifting one in the eighteenth century: to set them in opposition creates a false dichotomy.

Furthermore, there is no reason to believe that West or Copley or any of the other painters of contemporary history were primarily concerned with challenging academic theory. First, there was no monolithic theory to challenge: there were numerous, sometimes competing academic voices. Secondly, while theory loomed large in the education and discourse of artists, their careers were inevitably dominated by practical matters: how to earn a living, get commissions, acquire praise, attract an audience. This only intensified as the art world became increasingly marketized throughout the second half of the eighteenth century. Having painted *Chatham* speculatively, Copley exhibited it successfully to a large paying public and subsequently arranged for it to be engraved, hoping to emulate the commercial success of *Wolfe*.[59]

It is exaggerated to claim, as Holger Hoock has done, that while West revolutionized history painting, with *Chatham* 'Copley took this a step

99
John Trumbull (1756–1843)
The Declaration of Independence
1818
Oil on canvas
365.8 × 548.6 cm
(144 × 216 in.)
UNITED STATES CAPITOL, WASHINGTON, D.C.

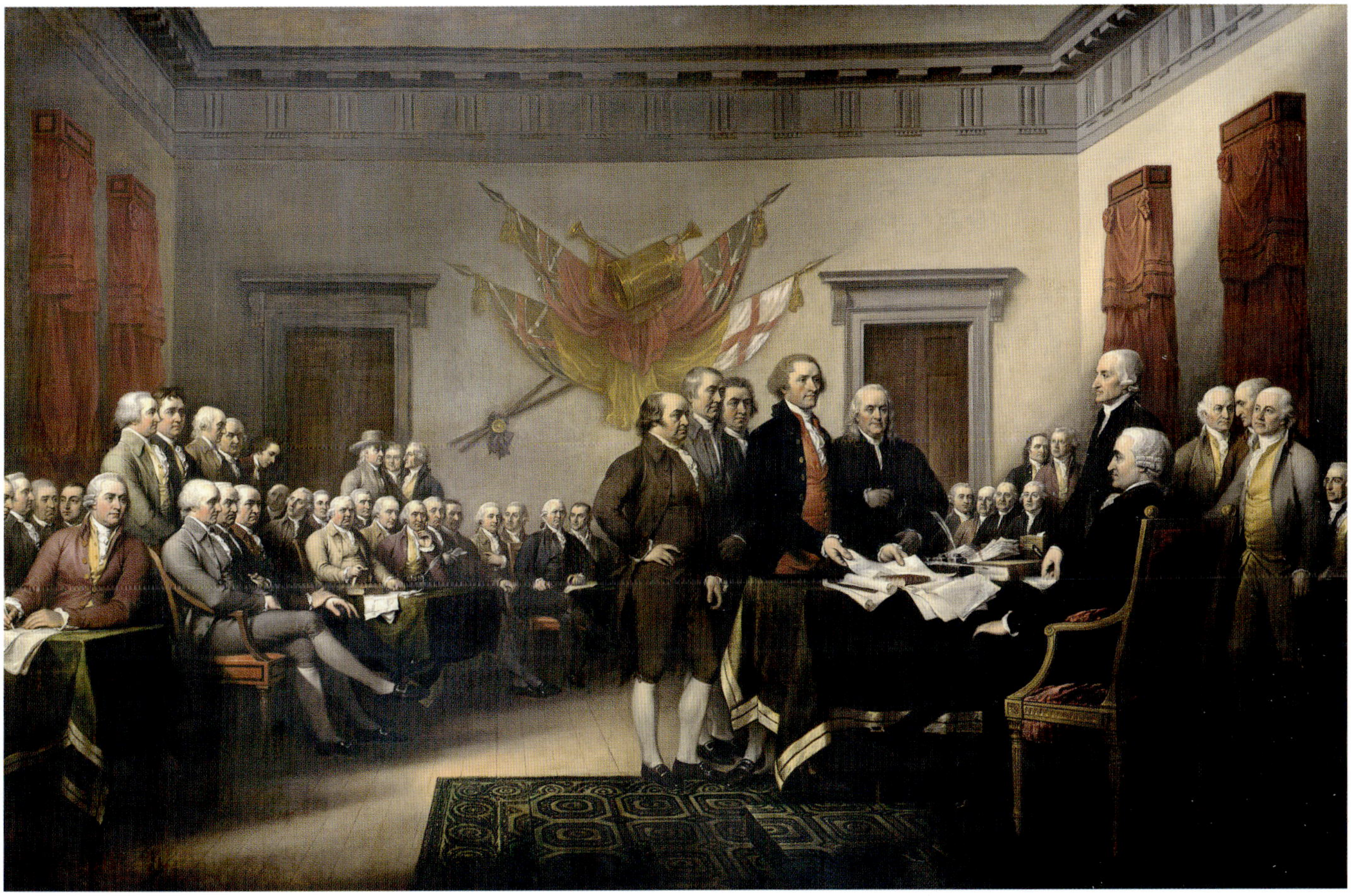

100
John Singleton Copley
(1738–1815)
The Death of the Earl of Chatham
1779–81
Oil on canvas
228.6 × 307.3 cm (90 × 121 in.)
NATIONAL PORTRAIT GALLERY, LONDON

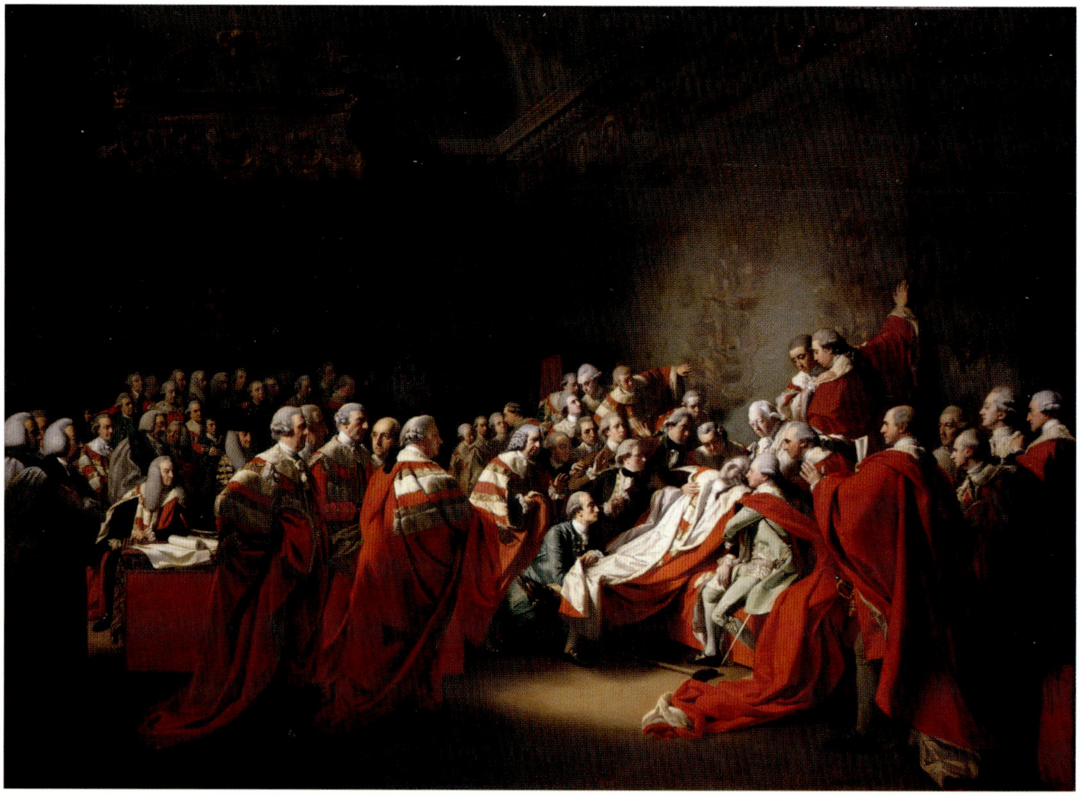

101
William Hogarth (1697–1764)
The Gaols Committee of the House of Commons
c. 1729
Oil on canvas
51.9 × 68.8 cm
(20⅜ × 27⅛ in.)
NATIONAL PORTRAIT GALLERY, LONDON

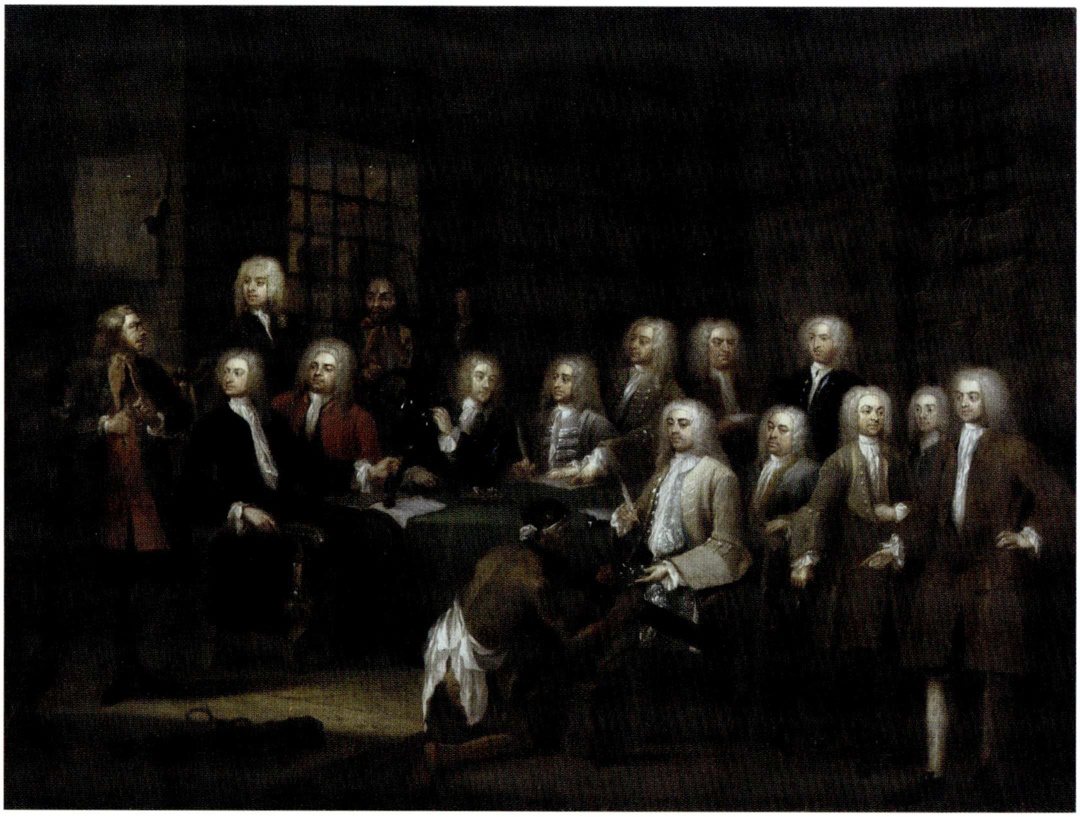

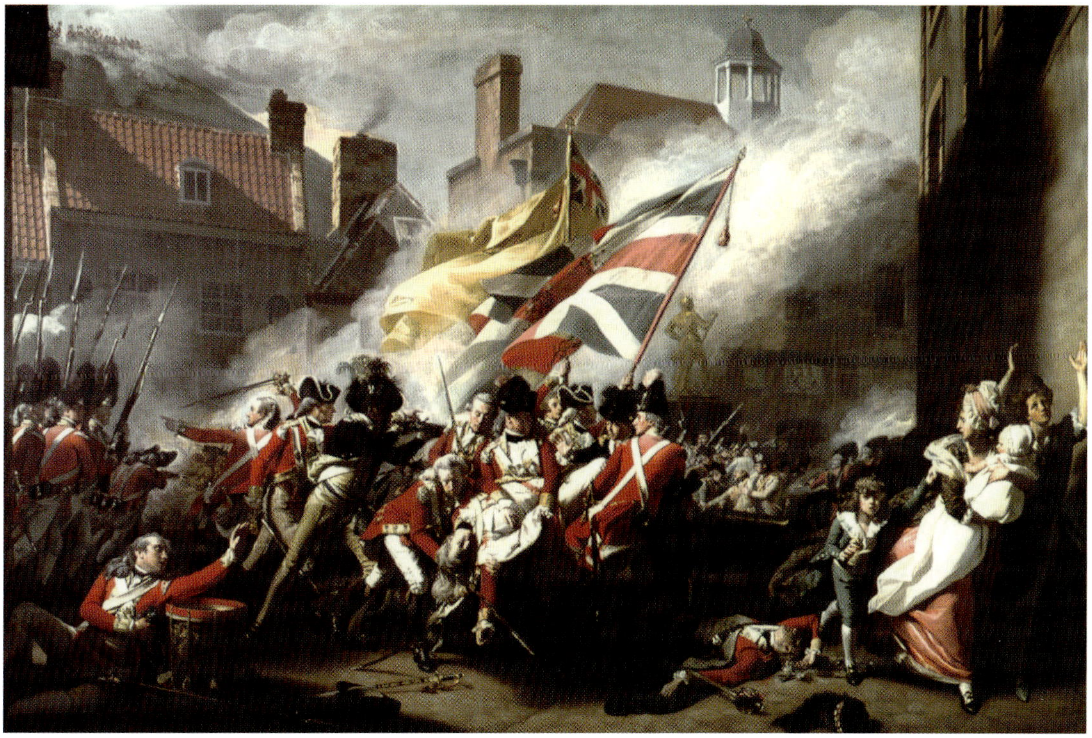

102
John Singleton Copley
(1738–1815)
The Death of Major Peirson, 6 January 1781
1783
Oil on canvas
251.5 × 365.8 cm (99 × 144 in.)
TATE, LONDON

further and depicted a contemporary political rather than military event … Copley elevated portraiture … by introducing it into a patriotic historical painting. He was thus adapting the genre of history painting to combine historical reportage with political journalism'.[60]

Having proved the possibility and the popularity of modern history painting with *Wolfe*, it was West himself, with *Penn's Treaty*, who took his own innovation 'a step further' to explore the heroization of modern civil subjects. Both the reporter from the *London Chronicle* and the poet Drake used military metaphors – 'a war of dress', 'fire their votes at one another' – to describe civil pictures, which suggests that the move to heroize the contemporary had to progress slowly and needed to remain focused on acts of individual heroism and drama. After *Chatham*, Copley turned to military subjects, reaching the height of his success with *The Death of Major Peirson, 6 January 1781* (fig. 102). The debating chamber would always lack the drama of the battlefield.

It was Copley's earlier work *A boy attacked by a shark, and rescued by some seamen in a boat; founded on a fact which happened in the harbor of the Havannah,* which we now know as *Watson and the Shark* (fig. 103), that had far more implications than *Chatham* and represented a further development of the potential set out by West in *Wolfe* and *Penn's Treaty* for a new type of history painting. Copley chose to capture the moment in 1749 when the then fourteen-year-old Brook Watson, serving as a cabin boy, was rescued from a near-fatal shark attack while swimming in Havana harbour.[61] Watson went on to a great career as a City merchant and public official, including service as an MP, a director of the Bank of England and Lord Mayor of London. Copley might have met Watson through his brother-in-law, Jonathan Clarke, an erstwhile business associate of Watson: among their ventures was a shipment of tea to Boston that was destroyed in the Boston Tea Party. Whether the idea of commemorating Watson's foolhardy swim was Copley's or Watson's continues to intrigue.

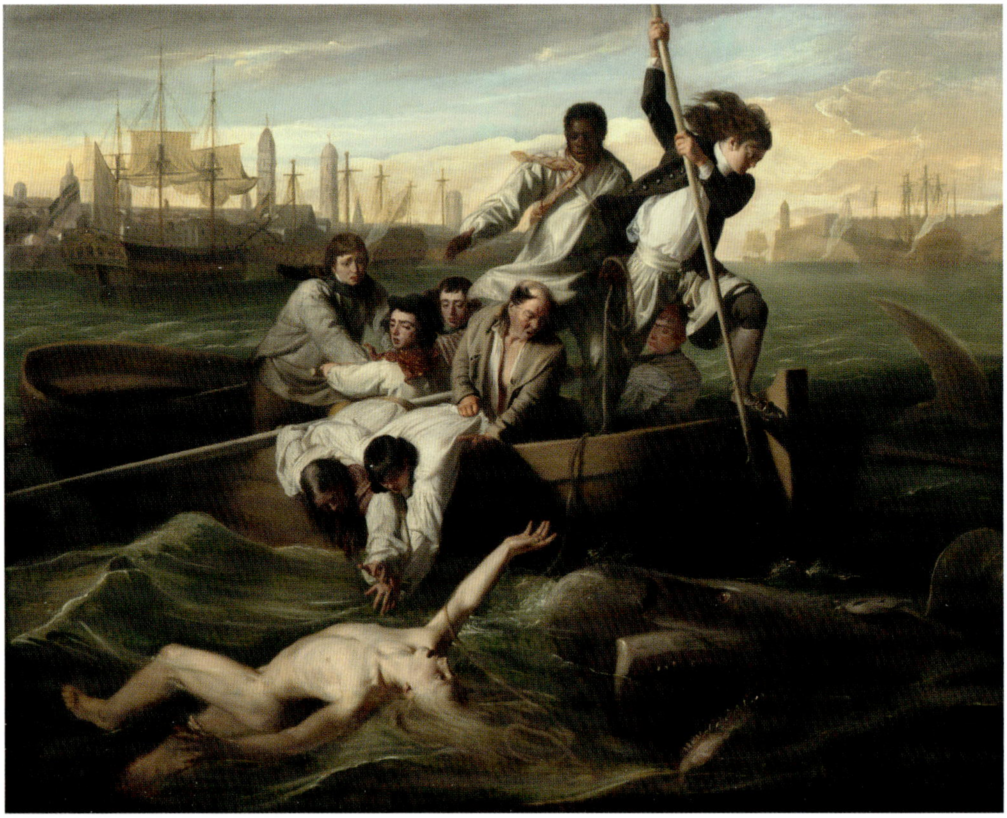

103
John Singleton Copley
(1738–1815)
Watson and the Shark
1778
Oil on canvas
182.1 × 229.7 cm
(71¾ × 90½ in.)
NATIONAL GALLERY OF ART, WASHINGTON, D.C.

Highly dramatic, powerfully composed and attractively exotic, *Watson* was the sensation of the Royal Academy Exhibition of 1778. The *Morning Post and Daily Advertiser* declared that *Watson* 'may fairly be estimated among the first performances of this exhibition'.[62] The reporter of the *St James's Chronicle* was even more enthusiastic:

> The Drawing of the Figures is correct and firm; their various Actions, and every one of their Features, such as the Terror of the Situation requires, and they are expressed in so excellent and masterly a Manner, and the Whole is so well coloured, that we heartily congratulate our Countrymen on a Genius, who bids fair to rival the great Masters of the ancient Italian Schools.[63]

Just as West had done with *Wolfe*, Copley used sophisticated academic rhetoric to narrate a contemporary event and consequently elevate it to an epic level. For example, the boatload of sailors is a clear reference to Raphael's *Miraculous Draught of Fishes* (fig. 104), then among the most admired works of art in Britain; the harpoonist recalls both Guido Reni's *Archangel Michael* and Raphael's *St Michael Vanquishing Satan* (figs. 105 and 106), and Rubens's *Lion Hunt* (fig. 107); and the pose of Watson himself 'is a mirror image of *The Gladiator* in the Villa Borghese' (fig. 108).[64] What makes *Watson* so influential, though, is its further democratization of subject matter.[65] Wolfe may have been a middle-class Englishman, but he was nonetheless an imperial martyr. Watson, on the other hand, was 'merely' a successful London businessman who wished to commemorate his own triumph over the adversity of physical disability, and had the wherewithal to commission Copley to do so.

Watson believed that his life could be an example to others, and bequeathed the picture to a public school, Christ's Hospital, with the hope that it would be 'hung up in the Hall of their Hospital as holding out a most usefull Lesson to Youth'.[66] In spite of Watson's explicit understanding of

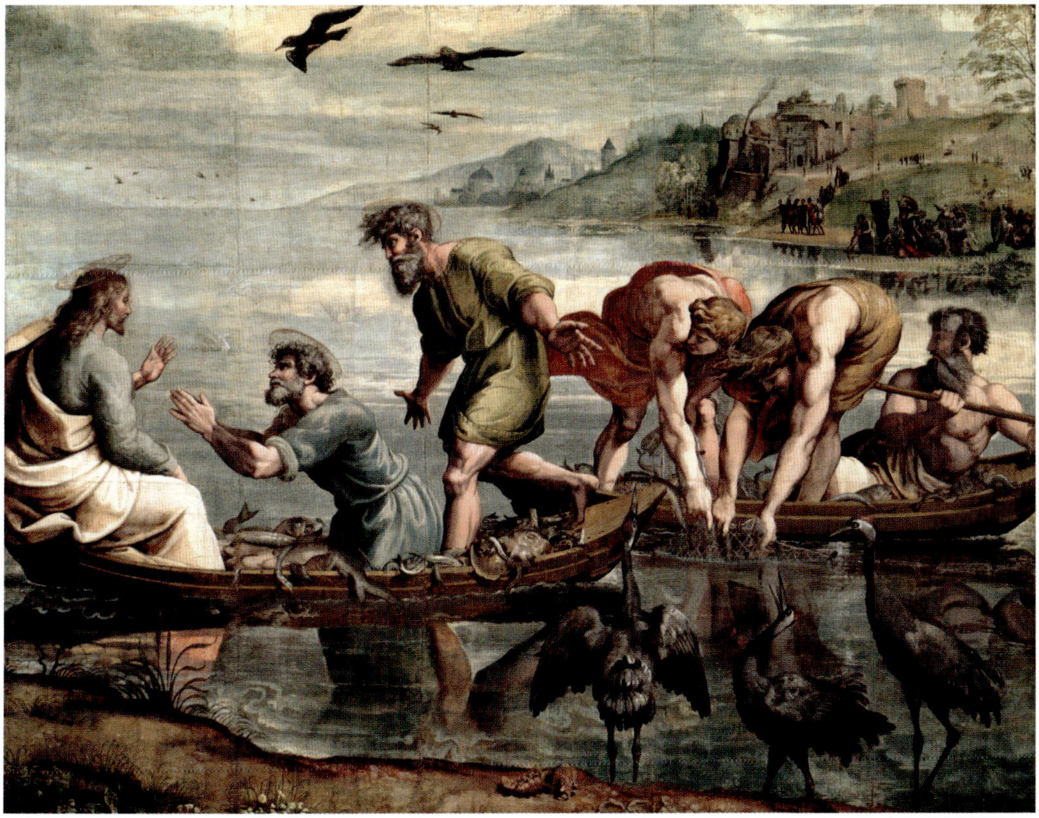

104
Raphael (1483–1520)
The Miraculous Draught of Fishes
c. 1515–16
Bodycolour on paper laid on to canvas
320 × 390 cm (126 × 153½ in.)
VICTORIA AND ALBERT MUSEUM, LONDON

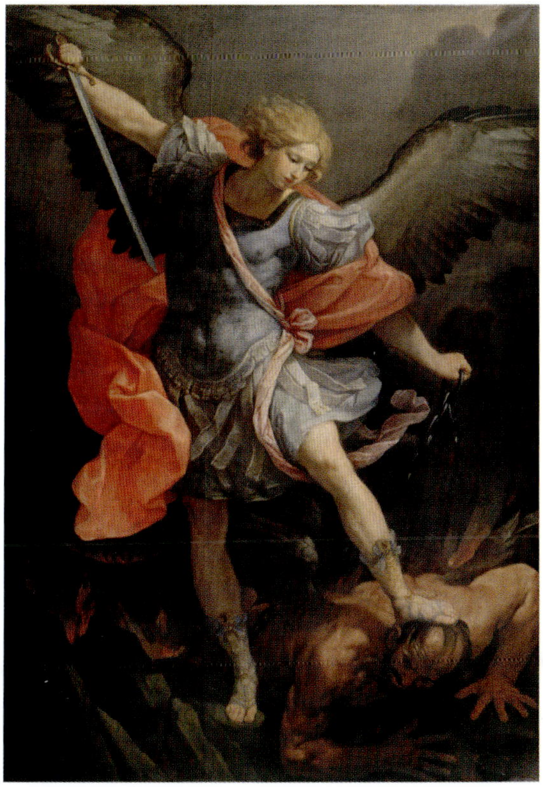

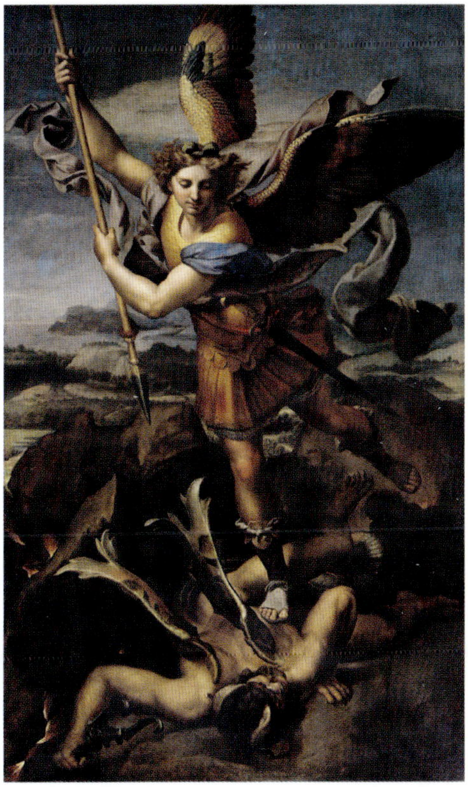

105 FAR LEFT
Guido Reni (1575–1642)
Archangel Michael
c. 1636
Oil on canvas
293 × 202 cm
(115⅜ × 79½ in.)
SANTA MARIA DELLA CONCEZIONE, ROME

106 LEFT
Raphael (1483–1520)
St Michael Vanquishing Satan
1518
Oil transferred from wood to canvas
268 × 160 cm (105½ × 63 in.)
MUSÉE DU LOUVRE, PARIS

107
Peter Paul Rubens
(1577–1640)
Lion Hunt
c. 1621
Oil on canvas
248.7 × 377.3 cm
(97⅞ × 148½ in.)
ALTE PINAKOTHEK, MUNICH

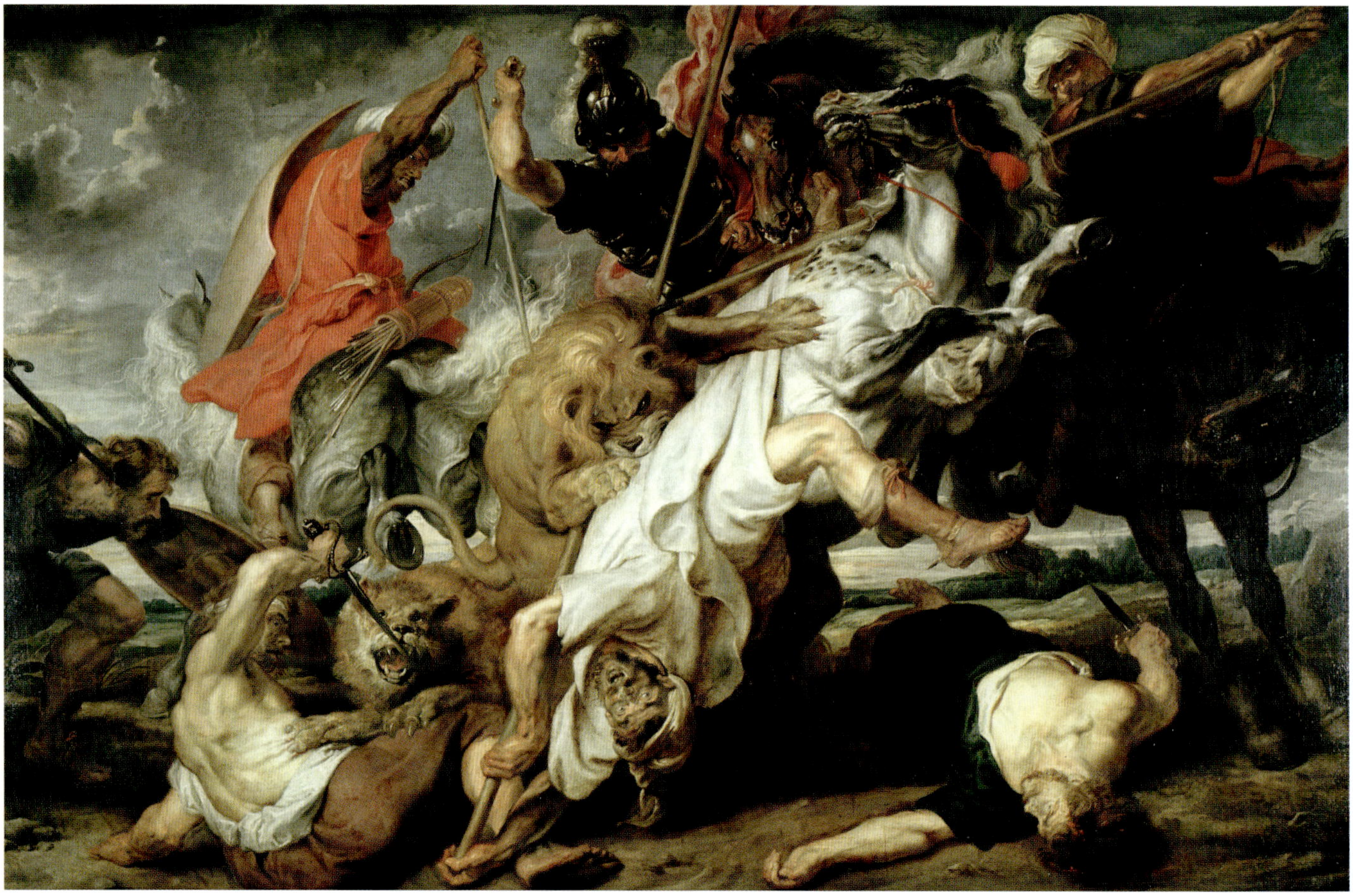

the meaning of his picture, it has been subject to numerous interpretations seeking to find within it coded references to the American Revolution or the abolition of the slave trade.[67] Its significance need not rest on such intricate if fanciful analysis.

The relationship between West and Copley was a complicated one, beginning in friendship, with West's efforts to help Copley establish himself in London, and ending in rancour as Copley plotted to oust West from the presidency of the Royal Academy. Perhaps it was simple envy: Copley could never be Britain's greatest history painter while West was recognized as such. Copley had money troubles, too. We are not sure exactly when the major rupture between the two happened, but its intensity is best explained by what Freud called 'the narcissism of small differences'[68] – the fact that the more alike people are, the more vicious the falling out between them will be. Both born in 1738 in America, both intensely ambitious, both living in London, both seeking to be at the top of the artistic tree; how could it not have ended in disaster?

The difficult relationship between the two makes it impossible to tell just how influenced Copley was by West and, more to the point, how *Wolfe* and *Watson* were related. But *Wolfe*'s instant success clearly established that there was an appetite for history painting with a contemporary theme. It is hard to imagine any artist of the time in London who was neither aware of West's success nor somehow influenced by him.[69] Many of them must have felt as Fuseli did some years later when he wrote:

> 'There are,' says Mr. West, 'but two ways of working successfully, that is, lastingly, in this country for an artist – the one is, to paint for the king; the other, to meditate a scheme of your own.' The first he has monopolized; in the second he is not idle: … In imitation of so great a man, I am determined to lay, hatch, and crack an egg for myself too … [70]

As we have seen, West explicitly intended that his revolution in history painting should

108
Borghese Gladiator
c. 100 BC
Marble
Height 199 cm (78⅜ in.)
MUSÉE DU LOUVRE, PARIS

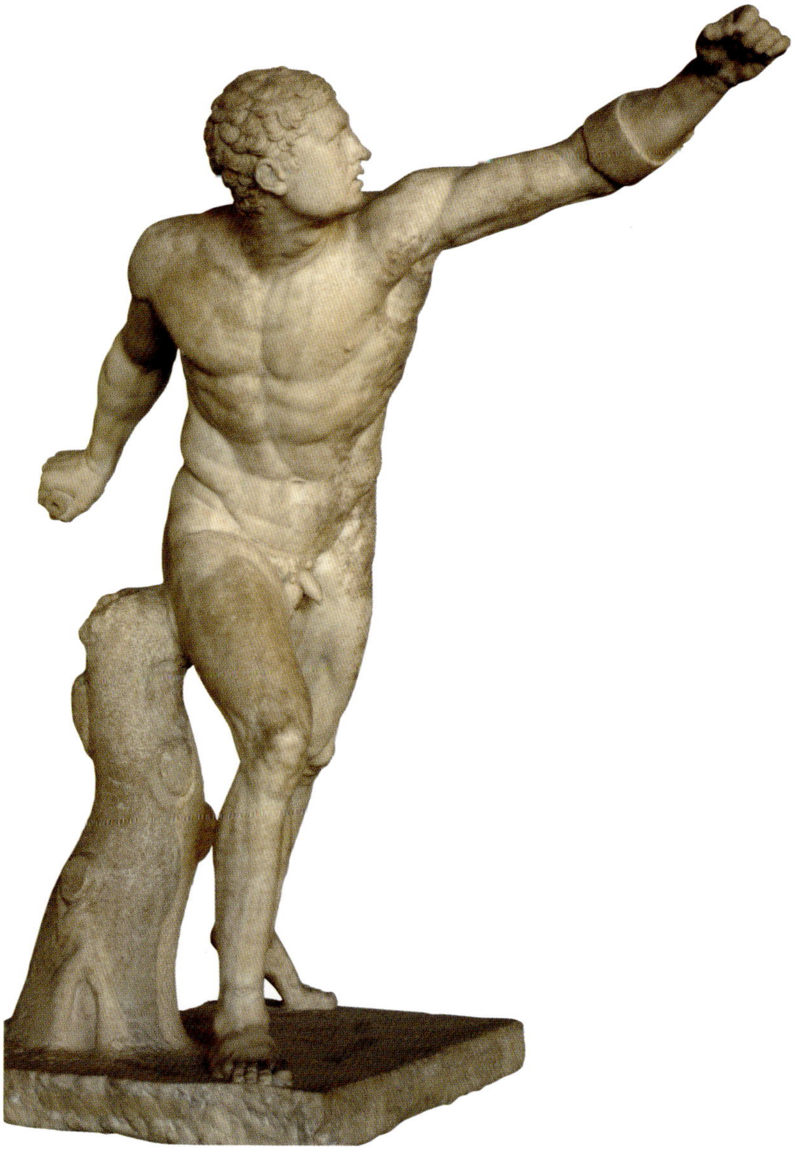

apply to both civil and military events, or, as he characterized them, 'the British Hero, and Legislature'.[71] With *Wolfe,* West solved the problem of how to historicize a contemporary event, but was perhaps immediately overtaken by another problem: a change in the very nature of great events. The new challenge for artists was how to make heroic art out of those aspects of modern life that were increasingly collective, bureaucratic, process-driven and middle class.

Two of West's former students – Morse and Peale – addressed the challenge boldly, but with mixed success. Peale had been one of West's first students, studying under him in London from 1767 to 1769, before commencing an extraordinarily varied career as a soldier, politician, prolific portraitist and cultural entrepreneur. Peale's natural history museum in Philadelphia was the first in America organized along scientific lines, and in order to add a spectacular new exhibit to that museum, Peale led an expedition to upstate New York in 1801 in search of mastodon skeletons. In a broadside promoting his museum, Peale announced that he was 'in possession of a SKELETON of this ANTIQUE WONDER of North America; after a long, laborious and uncertain enterprize'.[72]

To commemorate the successful digging-up of the skeleton, Peale began work in 1806 on his first history painting. Writing to West the following year, the 66-year-old Peale proudly remarked, 'I often say that the aged ought not to be discouraged from undertaking works of improvement.'[73] *The Exhumation of the Mastodon* (fig. 110) is an affirmation of Enlightenment values, celebrating the spirit of rational enquiry – in this case, the discovery and explanation of another link in what at the time was referred to as 'the chain of being'. Although Peale and his family are specifically featured, it is – and this is certainly to its artistic detriment, as it lacks focus – a statement about the virtues of collective enterprise in which savants and labourers, machinery and landscape play equally important roles. It is a cleverly constructed picture, and David Brigham has described well how Peale's 'Repetition of the shapes established by the machine [which dominates the central space of the canvas] develops a sense of the people and the machinery as a collective unit, working in concert to achieve the excavation.'[74]

The Exhumation certainly fulfils West's injunction that painting should have a high moral purpose, and as Lillian Miller points out, Peale intended that the picture should convey 'courage in the face of overwhelming odds, perseverance in a task with a socially useful purpose, and a concern for … the future generations who would benefit from the enlightenment his work would bring'. Above all, 'the courage it honored was called forth by civilian rather than military goals. Not civil strife, but civil harmony was the inevitable result of understanding God's great design for the universe'.[75] So far, so good. But pictorially it is a magnificent failure. In spite of borrowing some compositional elements from West – the frieze-like arrangement of the Peale family, for example – Peale lacked the skill and experience to compose an epic, multi-figured scene. The scale, proportions and poses of many of the figures are awkward and unreal. *The Exhumation* is laudable in intention and charming in execution, but it has all the heroism of a doll's house. Nonetheless it remains among the bravest attempts to render homage to one of the mainsprings of the modern world, the spirit of scientific enquiry.[76]

Peale's son Rembrandt Peale also studied with West, and between 1820 and 1822 his vast, melodramatic potboiler *The Court of Death* (fig. 111) toured the United States, attracting 30,000 paying viewers and earning $9000 for the artist. *The Court of Death*'s success, along with that of Trumbull's *Declaration of Independence* also on tour, seems to have galvanized Morse into creating his own large history painting. His daring choice was to heroize representative democracy through a view of the workings of the American Congress. Morse began work on *The House of Representatives* (fig. 113) in late 1821 and finished it in January 1823.

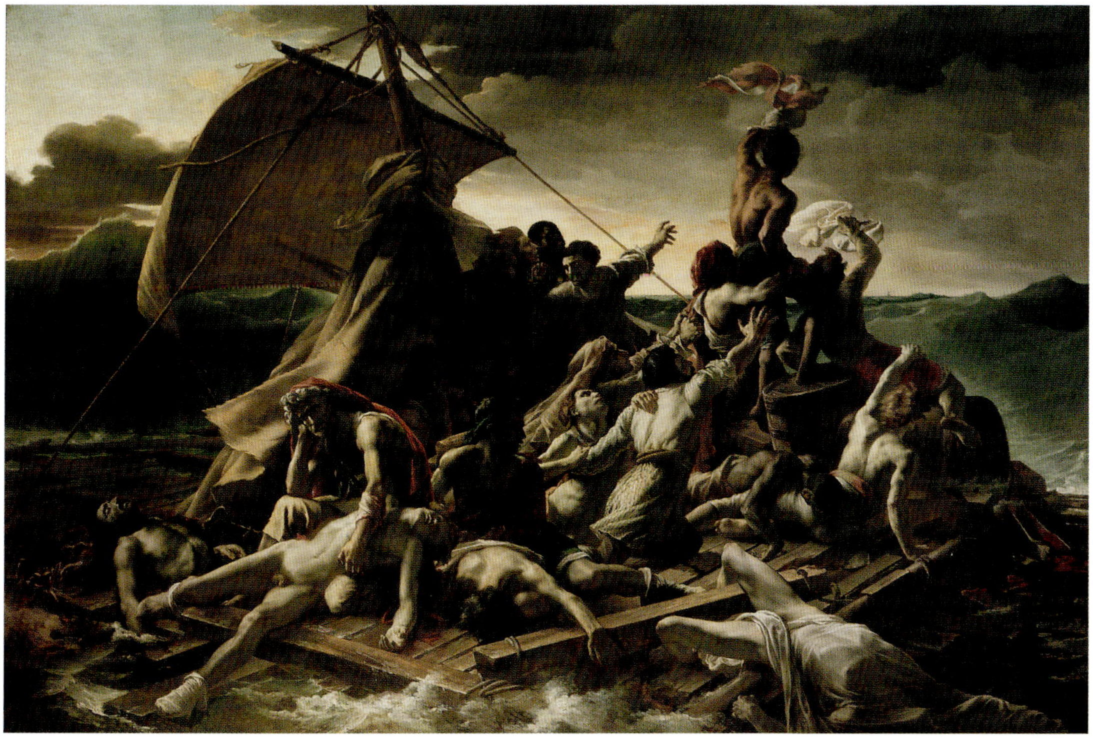

109
Théodore Géricault
(1791–1824)
The Raft of the Medusa
1819
Oil on canvas
491 × 716 cm
(193¼ × 281⅞ in.)
MUSÉE DU LOUVRE, PARIS

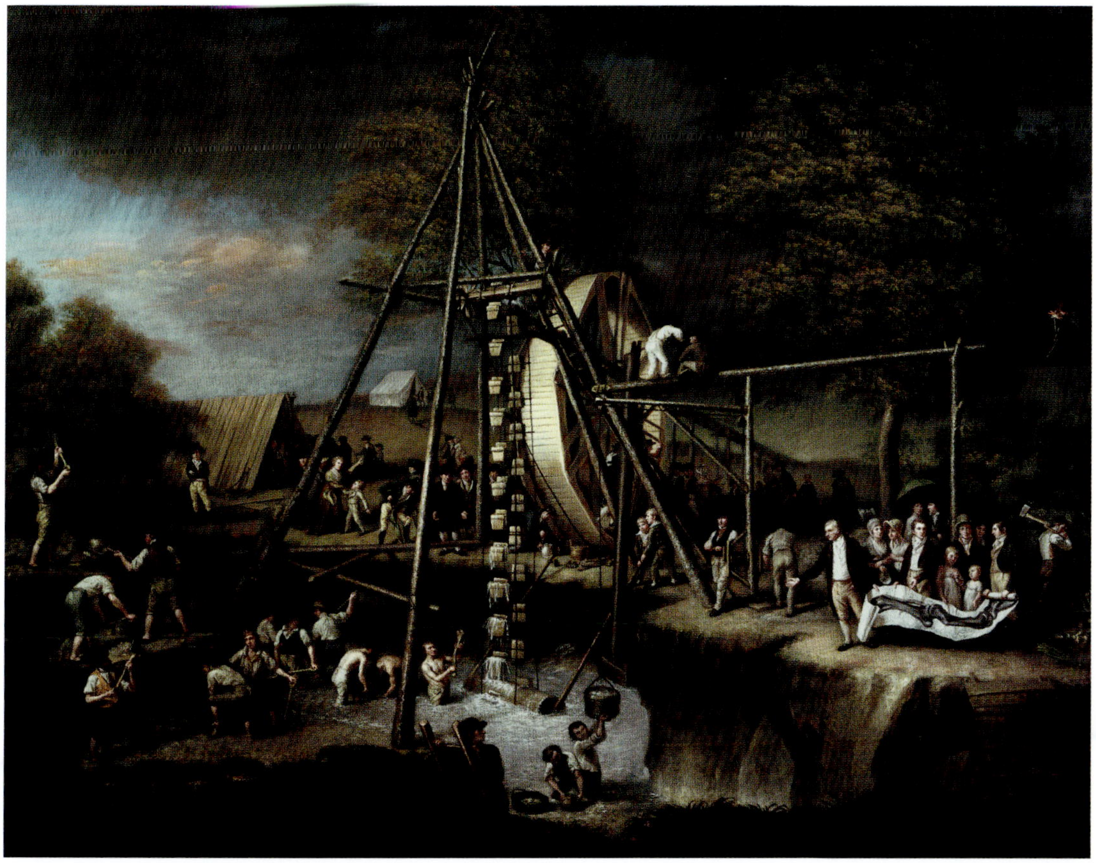

110
Charles Willson Peale
(1741–1827)
The Exhumation of the Mastodon
1806–08
Oil on canvas
127 × 158.8 cm (50 × 62½ in.)
MARYLAND HISTORICAL SOCIETY, BALTIMORE

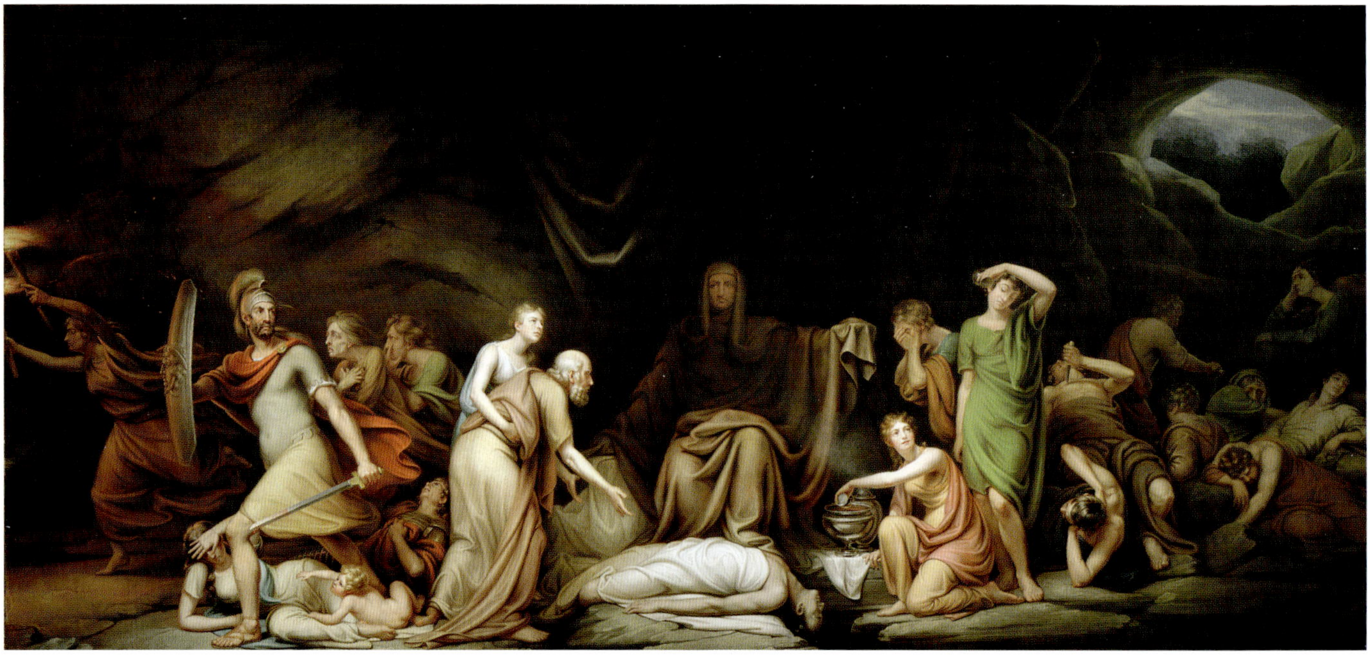

111
Rembrandt Peale (1778–1860)
The Court of Death
1820
Oil on canvas
350.5 × 713.7 cm (138 × 281 in.)
DETROIT INSTITUTE OF ARTS

112 OPPOSITE
Benjamin West
Benjamin Franklin
c. 1816
Oil on slate
34 × 25.6 cm (13⅜ × 10 in.)
PHILADELPHIA MUSEUM OF ART

His struggles to complete the picture are a reminder of the extreme technical and financial challenges that continued to be presented by history painting, as well as the sheer endurance required. 'I have had a great deal of difficulty in the perspective of my picture, but by hard study and perseverance I have conquered thus far', Morse wrote to his wife, adding, 'I can give you no certain time when I shall be with you again my dearest wife.' There were constant difficulties. 'After having drawn in the greater part three times ... I have as many times rubbed it all out again', he wrote in exasperation. 'I have several times been a whole day from day-light until 11 o'clock at night solving a single problem.'[77]

The finished picture is impressive and bizarre in the extreme, featuring the portraits of ninety-four individuals overwhelmed by the vast room in which the Representatives sat, pictured at the moment when the large central chandelier is being lit in preparation for an evening's session. 'The painting is of a class somewhat novel ...', the *Charleston Courier* judged, 'in many respects it is similar to Copley's celebrated death of Chatham ... in which however the *figures* are *principal*; in Mr. Morse's picture, the *room* is *principal*'.[78] This seems almost to have been Morse's intention, as he explained:

> The primary design of the present picture is not so much to give a highly finished likeness of the individuals introduced, as to exhibit to the public a faithful representation of the National Hall, with its furniture and business during the session of Congress. If the individuals are simply recognized by their acquaintance as likenesses, the whole design of the painter will be answered.[79]

It is an excellent portrait of a room and a fine likeness of a chandelier, but it completely lacks the narrative core that is necessary for a history painting. Morse may have been the principal evangelist of academic theory in early nineteenth-century America,[80] but with *The House of Representatives*, he violated what might be considered the one inviolable rule of history

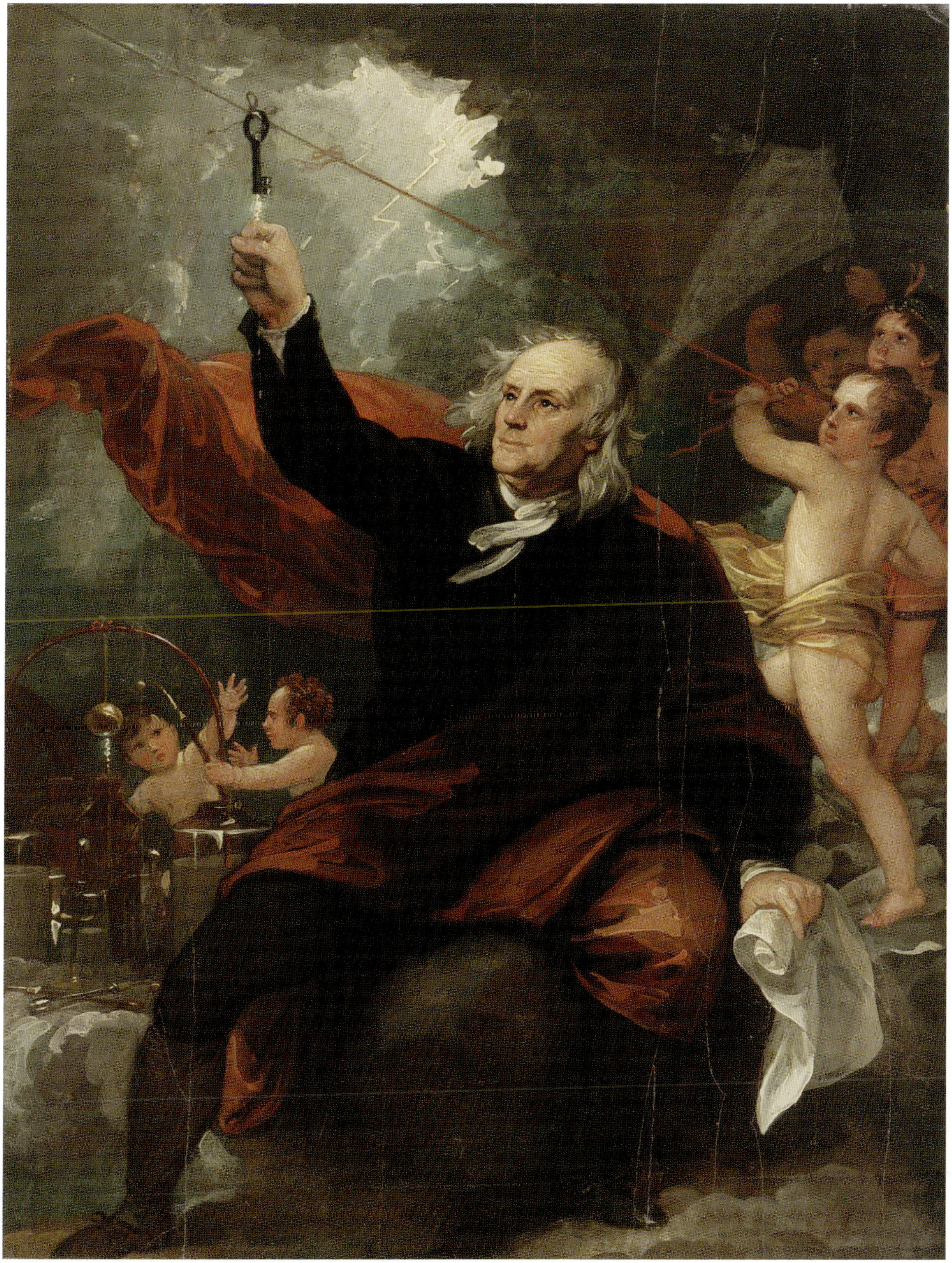

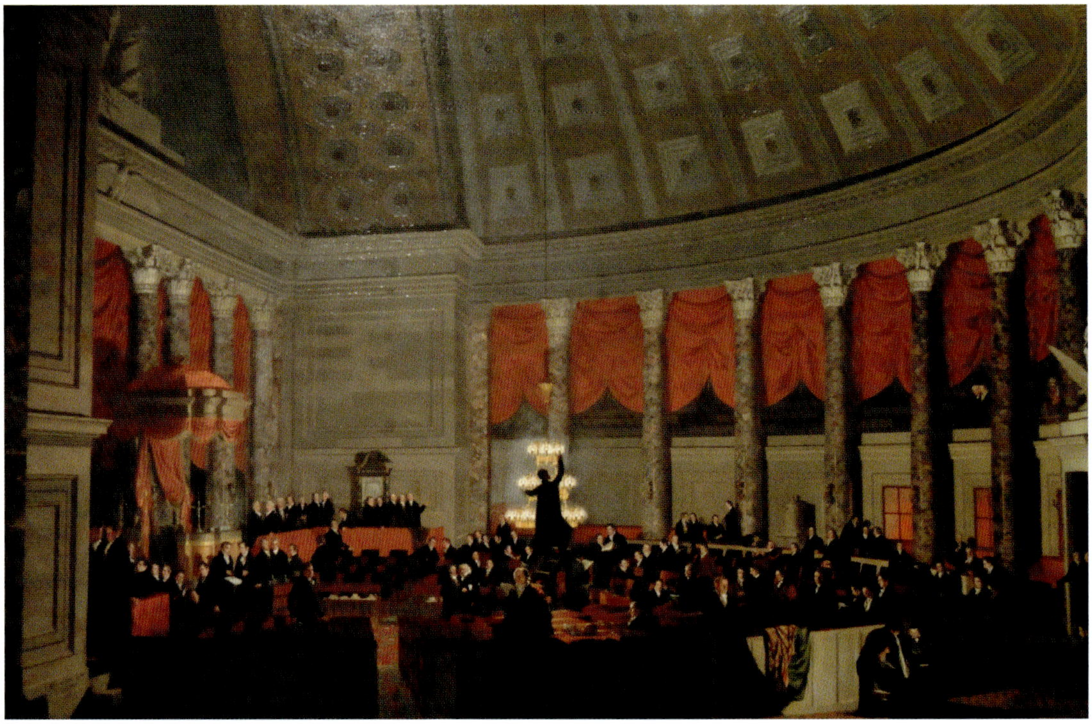

113
Samuel F.B. Morse
(1791–1872)
The House of Representatives
1822 (reworked 1823)
Oil on canvas
220.7 × 331.8 cm
(86⅞ × 130⅝ in.)
CORCORAN COLLECTION, NATIONAL GALLERY OF ART, WASHINGTON, D.C.

painting: that something important must be happening. As Du Fresnoy instructed, 'imitate the Sister of Painting, Tragedy: which employs the whole Forces of her Art in the main Action'.[81] But it was an extraordinarily ambitious effort to create a new type of history painting. 'Unlike Copley's *Death of the Earl of Chatham*, to which it bears a strong resemblance in composition, space, and motifs, the *House of Representatives* decenters itself', Paul Staiti writes. 'It tends to scatter attention, and even when a viewer locates potentially significant moments in the picture ... these moments tend to be narratively hollow.'[82] In Staiti's analysis, with which I agree, the very lack of action is essential to Morse's aspirations. Morse's 'decision not to depict debate, vote, or dissent is in itself a political statement, as is the collective propriety, monumental space, even handling, and avoidance of narrative. In his unusual choices, which produce a rhetoric of peace and unity, lay Morse's vision of an ideal legislative body radiant with Calvinist ethics and republican political theory.'[83]

Lack of public interest – in Boston on 6 March 1823 the day's takings 'were less than a dollar'[84] – cut short the proposed tour of *The House of Representatives.* For Morse, the painting was a financial catastrophe, and part of the process of embitterment with the public that drove him out of art and fuelled his political extremism.[85] Four years later, in May 1827, Morse lectured in New York and gloomily described the fate of the American artist who had been educated abroad and who, like Morse himself, 'returns to practice his profession at home. Unless he possesses great firmness of nerve, great self-denial, and a share of public spirit that belongs to few individuals in any class of society, he will scarcely be saved from misanthropic seclusion and despair.' Burning with indignation at his own failure to engage the public, Morse concluded, 'No! the artist may go abroad, but he must not return.'[86]

The shipwreck of Morse's ambitions marked the end of a fascinating phase in the history of history painting: fifty years of restless artistic innovation,

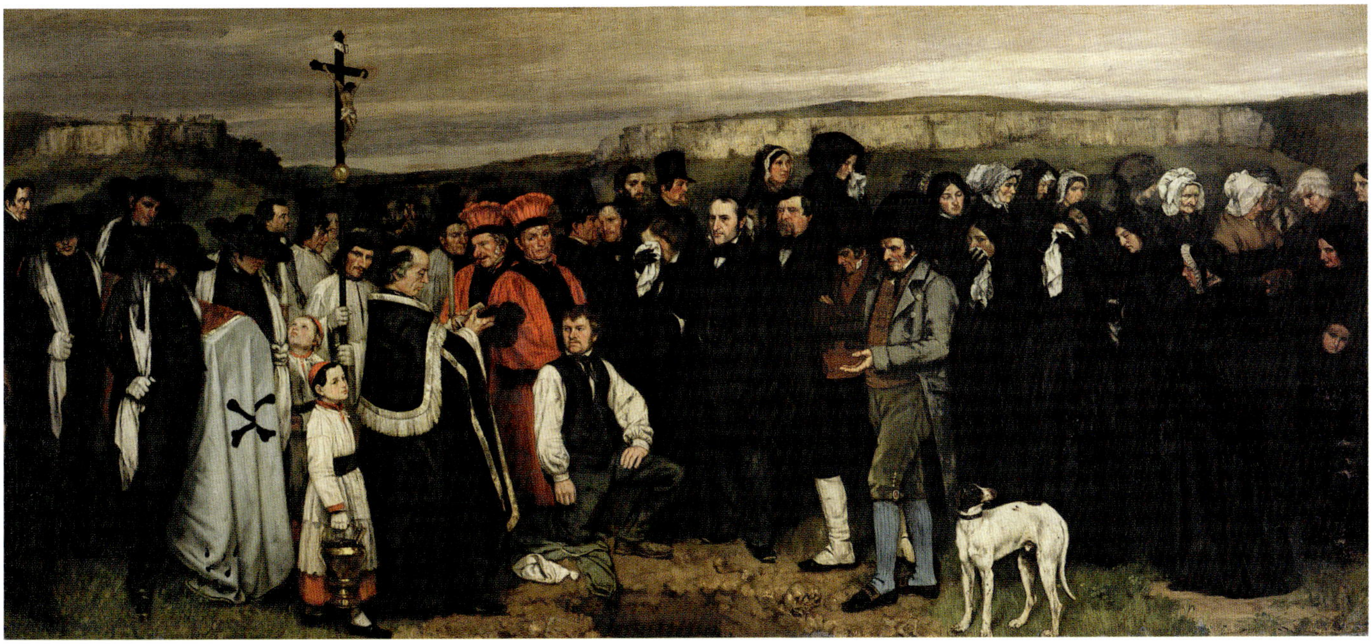

intellectual excitement and public acclaim. Fifty years during which the aims and aspirations of the history painters were in harmony with the spirit of the times, the spirit of modernity. Then history painting, as a genre, turned in on itself; a direction that led to the melodrama of Delaroche, the meticulously rendered jingoism of Meissonier and the smug banality of Frank O. Salisbury.

Of course, it was not only grand-style history painters who were giving visual expression to the modern. As David Solkin has shown, David Wilkie, Edward Bird, William Collins and others were turning their attention to painting what Francis Ludlow Holt identified in 1809 as 'the EPIC of common life'.[87] These and other 'artists committed to the portrayal of everyday modernity', as Solkin describes them,[88] were masters of deftly expressed sentiment and acute observation, and may be said to have presented a modernism that was both complementary to and narratively competitive with that of the grand-style artists: a more demotic vision of the modern from below.

I am reluctant to endorse a simple causal chain in which a succession of masterpieces is somehow seen to move art forward. However, there are game-changing pictures: I believe that *Wolfe* was one of those, as was *Watson*. The game-changing picture is not just an expression of creative genius; it also requires the perfect synchronization of intention and execution on the part of the artist, as well as expectation and demand from the audience. Such pictures bring about a paradigm shift in the way that artists do things, and perhaps more importantly represent a paradigm shift occurring in society at large. I cannot say that without *Wolfe* there would have been no *Watson*, and that without *Watson* there would have been no *Raft of the Medusa*, and consequently that the whole history of modern art would have been a different one. Certainly, the success of *Wolfe* showed Copley that *Watson* was possible, just as, I believe, Hamilton's *Dawkins and Wood* may have alerted West to the potential of creating a modern epic painting. The revolution in history painting and all its ramifications would

114
Gustave Courbet (1819–1877)
A Burial at Ornans
1849–50
Oil on canvas
315 × 668 cm (124 × 263 in.)
MUSÉE D'ORSAY, PARIS

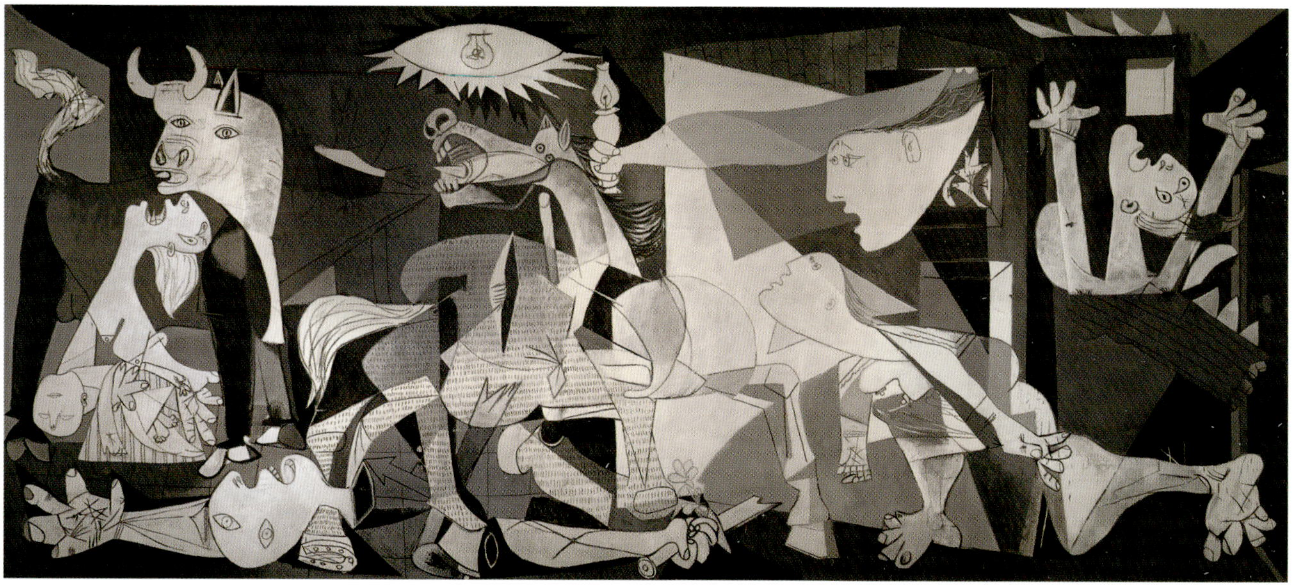

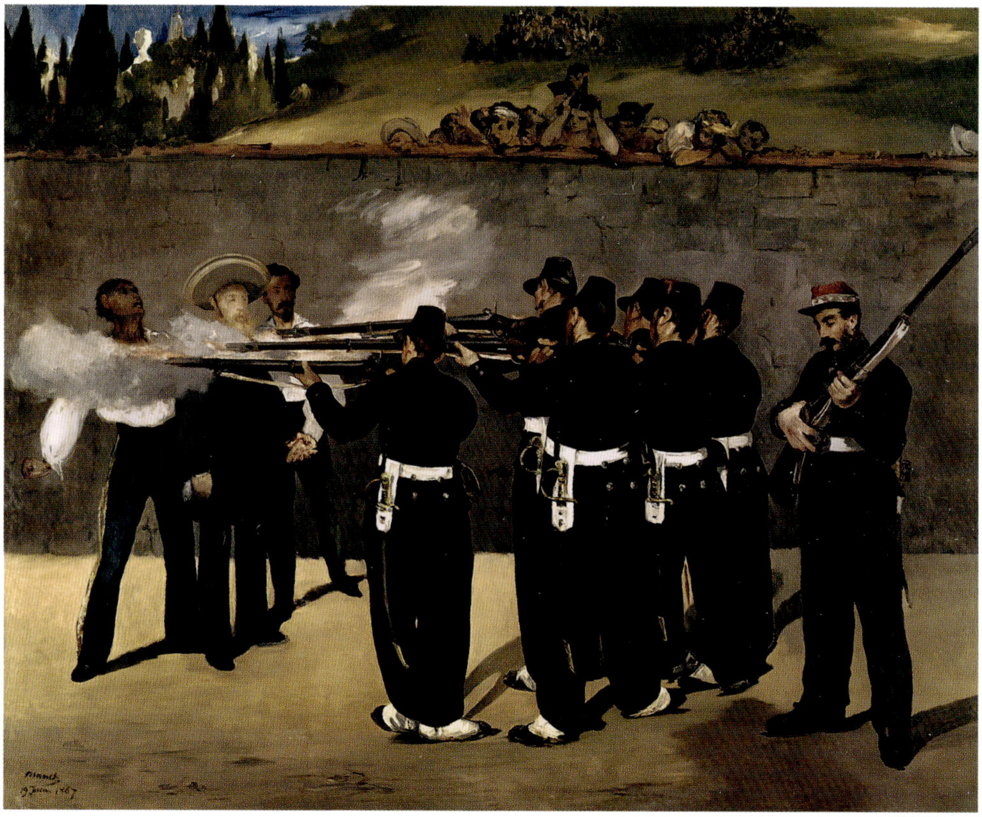

115 ABOVE
Pablo Picasso (1881–1973)
Guernica
1937
Oil on canvas
349.3 × 776.6 cm
(137½ × 305¾ in.)
MUSEO NACIONAL CENTRO DE ARTE REINA SOFÍA, MADRID

116
Édouard Manet (1832–1883)
The Execution of Emperor Maximilian
1868–69
Oil on canvas
252 × 302 cm
(99¼ × 118⅞ in.)
KUNSTHALLE MANNHEIM

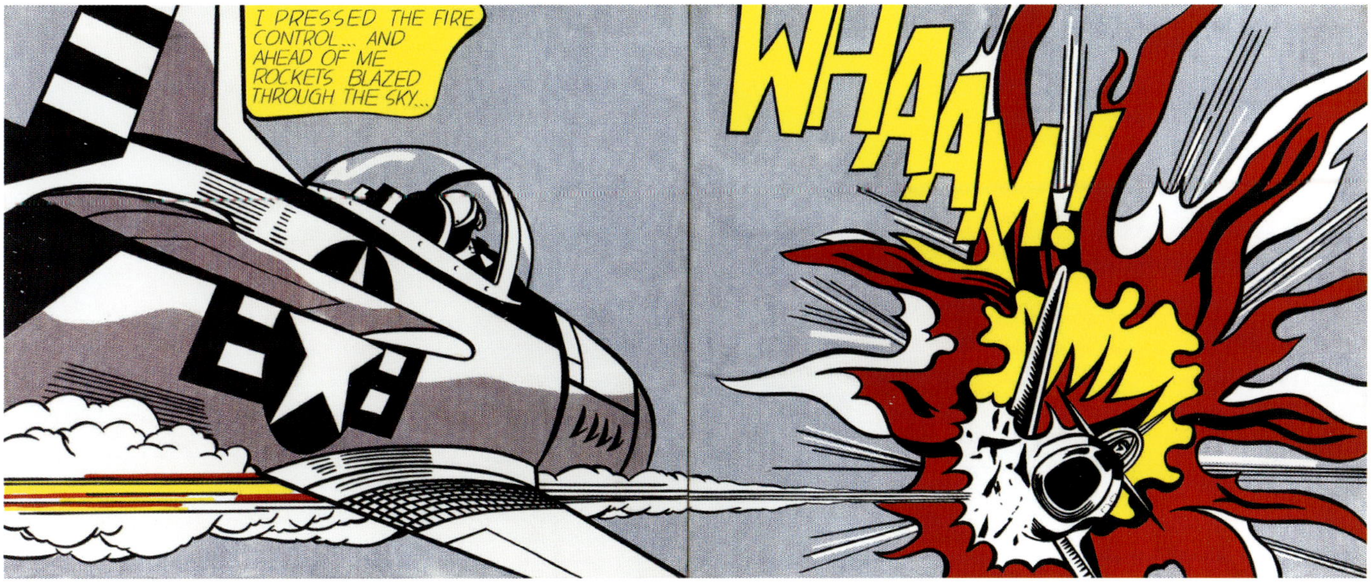

have happened with or without West – indeed, was happening. But someone had to lead. West, with his acute sense of the intellectual and social currents swirling around him, knew when it was time to leap on to the barricades.

But even as the old artistic hierarchies ceased to have any meaning, it can be seen that West had put something vital and persistent into the bloodstream of art. Courbet's *Burial at Ornans* (fig. 114), Manet's *Execution of Emperor Maximilian* (fig. 116), Picasso's *Guernica* (fig. 115) and Lichtenstein's *Whaam!* (fig. 117) are all history paintings; all the children of West; all combining an insistence on the importance of the present with the need to satisfy the immemorial human demand for epic narrative.

117
Roy Lichtenstein (1923–1997)
Whaam!
1963
Acrylic and oil on canvas
172.7 × 406.4 cm (68 × 160 in.)
TATE, LONDON

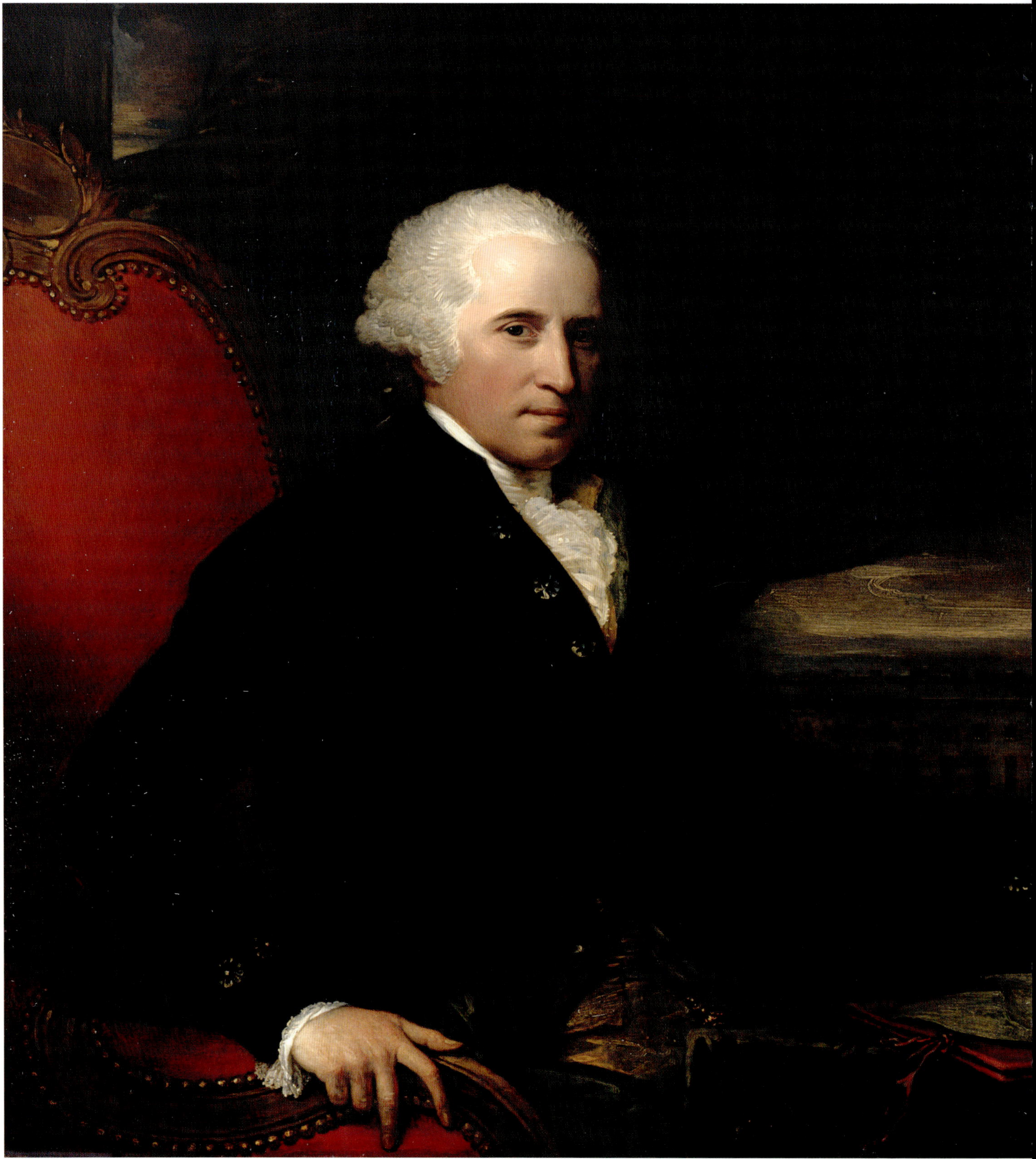

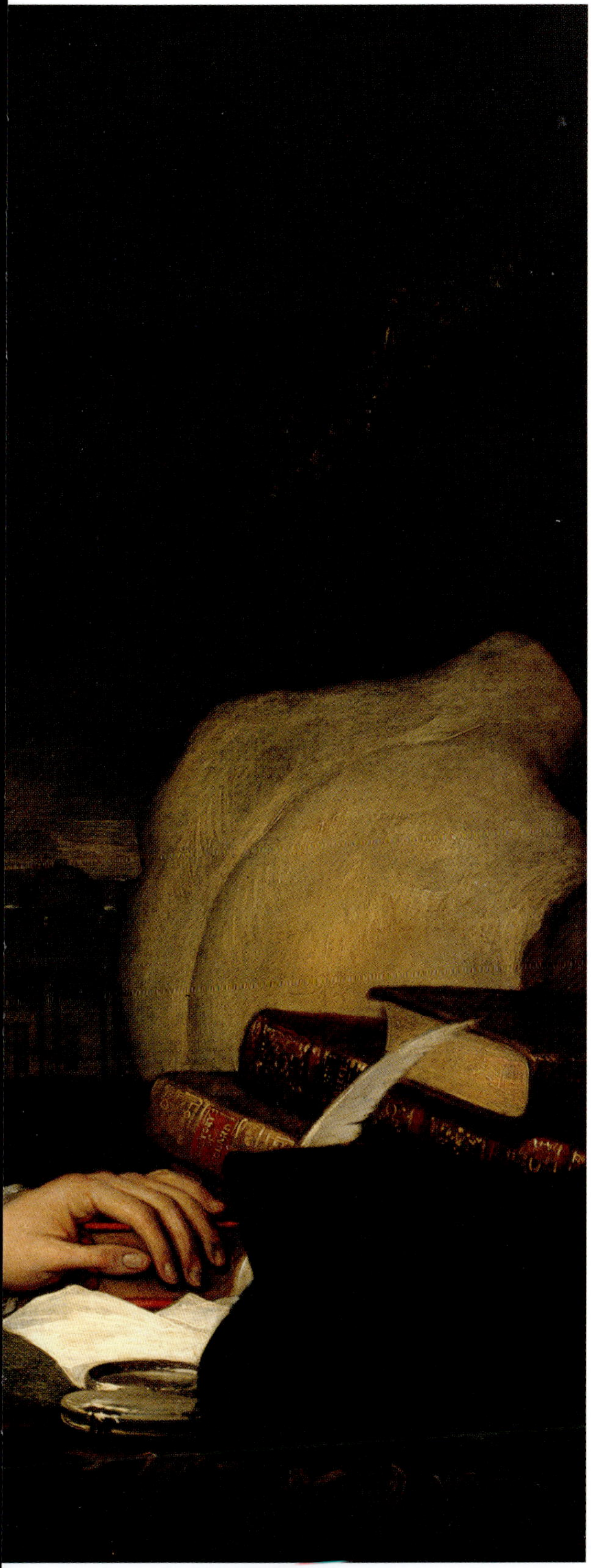

118
Benjamin West
Self-Portrait
1793
Oil on panel
101.5 × 132 cm (40 × 52 in.)
ROYAL ACADEMY OF ARTS, LONDON

NOTES

PREFACE

1 William Holden Hutton, *Hampton Court*, London, 1897, 203.

A COSTUME DRAMA

1 George Washington, *The Writings of George Washington*, ed. Jared Sparks, Boston, 1835, vol. 9, 185–86.

2 The titles of all paintings by West are as given by Helmut von Erffa and Allen Staley, *The Paintings of Benjamin West*, New Haven, Conn., and London, 1986. With West's pictures and others, I have given their full title on first mention and subsequently a short title.

3 Michel Foucault, 'What is Enlightenment?', in *The Foucault Reader*, ed. Paul Rabinow, London, 1991, 40.

4 Joel Barlow, *Life and Letters of Joel Barlow: Poet, Statesman, Philosopher*, ed. Charles Burr Todd, New York and London, 1886, 193.

5 West cited the incorrect year for Wolfe's death; it was 1759, not 1758.

6 Quoted in John Galt, *The Life, Studies and Works of Benjamin West, Esq.*, London, 1820, part 2, 46–50. Part 1, which is included in this edition and deals with West's life prior to his arrival in England, was originally published in 1816.

7 *The Progress of Genius, or Authentic Memoirs of the Early Life of Benjamin West: Abridged for the use of young persons by a Lady*, Boston, 1831.

8 Quoted in William Hazlitt, *The Collected Works of William Hazlitt*, ed. A.R. Waller and Arnold Glover, London, 1903, vol. 6, 509.

9 William Dunlap, *A History of the Rise and Progress of the Arts of Design in the United States* [1834], Boston, 1918, vol. 1, 33.

10 In particular, see Susan Rather, 'Benjamin West, John Galt, and the Biography of 1816', *Art Bulletin*, 86:2, June 2004, in which Rather describes the Galt biography as 'a public relations effort of enormous consequence for the history of American and, arguably, also of British Art' (p. 341).

11 Quoted in Galt, part 2, 48.

12 There are few biographical details of Bromley, the Oxford- and Cambridge-educated son of a lawyer from Wigan. See J.A. Venn, *Alumni Cantabrigiensis*, Nendeln, Liechtenstein, 1978, part 2, vol. 1, 392.

13 Robert Anthony Bromley, *A Philosophical and Critical History of the Fine Arts*, London, 1793, vol. 1, 45–46. There is some resonance here with Reynolds's view, expressed in *Discourse XIII* and elsewhere, that painting 'is, and ought to be … no imitation at all of external nature' and should be 'far removed from the vulgar idea of imitation'. Sir Joshua Reynolds, *Discourses on Art*, ed. Robert R. Wark, New Haven, Conn., and London, 1975, 232–33.

14 Begun in the 1710s, but not published until 1782. Jean-Jacques Rousseau, *Confessions* [1782], ed. P.N. Furbank, New York, 1992, 3.

15 Paul Barolsky, *A Brief History of the Artist from God to Picasso*, University Park, Pa., 2010, 66–67.

16 James Boswell, *Boswell's London Journal, 1762–1763*, ed. Frederick A. Pottle, London, 1950, 47.

17 Philadelphia, Historical Society of Pennsylvania, Ferdinand J. Dreer Autograph Collection, vol. 5: Painters and Engravers.

18 Charles Willson Peale, *The Autobiography of Charles Willson Peale*, ed. Lillian B. Miller and Sidney Hart, New Haven, Conn., and London, 2000, 38.

19 Quoted in Douglas Fordham, *British Art and the Seven Years' War: Allegiance and Autonomy*, Philadelphia and Oxford, 2010, 234.

20 *Ibid.*, 235.

21 Copley's blockbuster of 1784, *The Death of Major Peirson, 6 January 1781* (fig. 102), was heavily influenced by Pelham's and Revere's engravings.

22 Quoted in *General Evening Post*, 21–24 April 1770.

23 London, Royal Academy of Arts, Library and Archive, Minutes of the Council of the Royal Academy, vol. 1, 77, RAA/PC/1/1.

24 Horace Walpole, *The Yale Edition of Horace Walpole's Correspondence*,

ed. W.S. Lewis, New Haven, Conn., and London, 1937–83, vol. 23, 209–11.

25 New York, Fordham University Library, Charles Allen Munn Collection, Benjamin West, Manuscript Autobiography, 3, Part 2, Box 7, Item 45. Hereafter cited as West. Internal evidence dates the Manuscript Autobiography to 1805. It is a heavily amended, repetitious and often clumsily phrased work, and clearly the source for a number of contemporary profiles of West, such as 'Benjamin West Esq. President of the Royal Academy', published in four issues of *La Belle Assemblée; or, Bell's Court and Fashionable Magazine* in early 1808.

26 West, 5.

27 *Ibid.*, 6.

28 *The Exhibition of the Royal Academy MDCCLXIX*, London, 1769; *The Exhibition of the Royal Academy MDCCLXX*, London, 1770; *The Exhibition of the Royal Academy MDCCLXXI*, London, 1771.

29 Charles Robert Leslie and Tom Taylor, *Life and Times of Sir Joshua Reynolds*, London, 1865, vol. 1, 323.

30 West to Peale, 21 June 1770. Historical Society of Pennsylvania, Dreer Collection, vol. 5: Painters and Engravers.

31 William Carey, *Critical Description and Analytical Review of 'Death on the Pale Horse', Painted by Benjamin West P.R.A.*, London, 1817, 11–12.

32 Quoted in Nicholas B. Wainwright, 'Conversations with Benjamin West', *Pennsylvania Magazine of History and Biography*, 102:1, January 1978, 109.

33 Royal Academy, Library and Archive, Accounts of the Exhibitions at the Royal Academy 1769–1772, RAA/TRE/13/1.

34 *Public Advertiser*, 25 April 1771.

35 Royal Academy, Library and Archive, Royal Academy Critiques 1769–1793, 37.

36 *The Exhibition of Painting: A Poem Addressed to the Ladies*, London, 1775, 21. The copy I consulted in the Historical Society of Pennsylvania belonged to West himself.

37 *Middlesex Journal or Chronicle of Liberty*, 23–25 April 1771.

38 Quoted *ibid.*, 7–10 September 1771.

39 Quoted in Samuel Foote, *The Works of Samuel Foote, Esq.*, London, 1830, 58.

40 William T. Whitley, *Artists and Their Friends in England, 1700–1799*, London and Boston, 1928, vol. 1, 282.

41 *The Gazetteer*, 20 May 1771.

42 Reynolds, *Discourses*, 89–90.

43 Oliver Goldsmith, *The Citizen of the World; or, Letters from a Chinese philosopher, residing in London, to his friends in the East* [1762], London, 1969, 115.

44 *Horace Walpole's Correspondence*, vol. 23, 211.

45 William Sandby, *The History of the Royal Academy of Arts*, London, 1862, vol. 1, 34.

46 *Middlesex Journal*, 23–25 April 1771.

47 *Ibid.*, 20–23 April 1771.

48 David H. Solkin, 'The British and the Modern', in *Towards a Modern Art World*, ed. Brian Allen, New Haven, Conn., and London, 1995, 1.

49 C.S. Matheson, '"A Shilling Well Laid Out": The Royal Academy's Early Public', in *Art on the Line: The Royal Academy Exhibitions at Somerset House, 1780–1836*, ed. David H. Solkin, New Haven, Conn., and London, 2001, 40.

50 Francis Parkman, *Montcalm and Wolfe* [1884], London, 1964, 481.

51 David H. Solkin, *Painting for Money: The Visual Arts and the Public Sphere in Eighteenth-Century England*, New Haven, Conn., and London, 1993, 208–209.

52 Among many accounts of the Battle of Quebec: Fred Anderson, *Crucible of War: The Seven Years' War and the Fate of Empire in British North America, 1754–1766*, London, 2000; Stephen Brumwell, *Paths of Glory: The Life and Death of General James Wolfe*, London, 2006; Frank McLynn, *1759: The Year Britain Became Master of the World*, London, 2004; Stephen Manning, *Quebec: The Story of Three Sieges*, London, 2009; Stuart Reid, *Wolfe: The Career of General James Wolfe from Culloden to Quebec*, Staplehurst, 2000.

53 Quoted in *London Gazette*, 17 October 1759.

54 *Whitehall Evening Post or London Intelligencer*, 20 October 1759.

55 *New York Gazette*, New York, 15 October 1759.
56 *Ibid.*, 22 October 1759.
57 Judah Champion, *Two Sermons Delivered at Litchfield on the General Fast, April 18, 1770*, Hartford, 1770, 27–28.
58 John Pringle, *The Life of General James Wolfe, the Conqueror of Canada*, London, 1760, 2–3.
59 George Cockings, *The Conquest of Canada; or, the Siege of Quebec*, London, 1773, 75.
60 Rev. Mr Blacklock, *A Collection of Original Poems*, Edinburgh, 1760, 73.
61 Myles Cooper, *Poems on Several Occasions*, Oxford, 1761, 70–72.
62 Anthony Pasquin, *Memoirs of the Royal Academicians; Being an Attempt to Improve the National Taste*, London, 1796, 73–74.
63 Carey, *'Death on the Pale Horse'*, 145–46.
64 *Horace Walpole's Correspondence*, vol. 38, 128. Historian of the rise of Rome and the Punic Wars, Polybius was highly regarded in the eighteenth century.
65 Quoted in Thomas E. Crow, *Painters and Public Life in Eighteenth-Century Paris*, New Haven, Conn., and London, 1985, 12.
66 Denis Diderot, *Diderot on Art*, ed. / trans. John Goodman, New Haven, Conn., and London, 1995, vol. 1, 41.
67 Abbé [Jean-Baptiste] Dubos, *Critical Reflections on Poetry, Painting and Music*, trans. Thomas Nugent, London, 1748, vol. 1, 43.

'THE MAN I WAS YESTERDAY'

1 The other is *The Cricketers*, *c.* 1763.
2 *Morning Chronicle and London Advertiser*, 26 April 1777.
3 *Ibid.*, 25 April 1777.
4 London, Victoria and Albert Museum, National Art Library, *General Advertiser*, Press Cuttings from English Newspapers on Matters of Artistic Interest, 1686–1835, vol. 1.
5 *Ibid.*
6 Kate Retford, *The Art of Domestic Life: Family Portraiture in Eighteenth-Century England*, New Haven, Conn., and London, 2006, 125.
7 Charles Robert Leslie, *A Handbook for Young Painters*, London, 1855, 292–93.
8 Jules David Prown, 'Benjamin West's Family Picture: A Nativity in Hammersmith', in *Essays in Honor of Paul Mellon, Collector and Benefactor*, ed. John Wilmerding, Washington, D.C., 1986, 277–78.
9 *Ibid.*, 272.
10 Desmond Shawe-Taylor, *The Conversation Piece: Scenes of Fashionable Life*, London, 2009, 140.
11 Robert C. Alberts, *Benjamin West: A Biography*, Boston, 1978, 65, 385–86.
12 Historical Society of Pennsylvania, Commonplace Book while travelling from Gravesend to Philadelphia, 1789, Benjamin Smith Barton Papers, 0034.
13 Charles Henry Hart, 'Benjamin West's Family: The American President of the Royal Academy of Arts Not a Quaker', *Pennsylvania Magazine of History and Biography*, 32:1, 1908, 2.
14 Swarthmore, Pennsylvania, Friends Historical Library, Sussana Morikawa to the Friends Historical Library, 6 May 1998, Biographical and Genealogical Documents, PG7.
15 *Ibid.*, 'EH' to *The Friend*, fifth month 3 1923, PG7.
16 James Harris, *Hermes; or, A Philosophical Inquiry Concerning Universal Grammar*, London, 1765, 113.
17 *Ibid.*, 115.
18 Jonathan Richardson, *The Works of Jonathan Richardson*, London, 1792, 235.
19 Quoted in Roland E. Fleischer, Carin K. Arnborg and Gustavus Hesselius, '"With God's Blessing on Both Land and Sea": Gustavus Hesselius Describes the New World to the Old in a Letter from Philadelphia in 1714', *American Art Journal*, 21:3, 1989, 9.
20 Quoted *ibid.*
21 William Smith, *A Brief State of the Province of Pennsylvania*, London, 1755, 4.
22 For the transformation of Philadelphia, see Edwin B. Bronner, 'Village into Town, 1701–1746' and Theodore Thayer, 'Town into City, 1746–1765', in *Philadelphia: A 300 Year History*, ed. Russell F. Weigley, New York, 1982.
23 Alexander Hamilton, *Hamilton's Itinerarium; being a narrative of a journey from Annapolis, Maryland, through Delaware, Pennsylvania, New York, New Jersey, Connecticut, Rhode Island, Massachusetts and New Hampshire, from May to September, 1744, by Doctor Alexander Hamilton*, ed. Albert Bushnell Hart, Early Americas Digital Archive, mith.umd.edu/eada/html/display.php?docs=hamilton_itinerarium.xml&action=show, 66 (accessed December 2014).
24 Galt, part 1, 70.
25 *Ibid.*, 20.
26 Giorgio Vasari, *Lives of the Painters, Sculptors and Architects* [1568], trans. Gaston du C. de Vere, London, 1996, 96.
27 Galt, part 1, 16.
28 David Sox, *Quakers and the Arts: 'Plain and Fancy' – An Anglo-American Perspective*, York, 2000, 11–15.

29 Quoted in David H. Dickason, 'Benjamin West on William Williams: A Previously Unpublished Letter', *Winterthur Portfolio*, 6, 1970, 130.

30 Quoted *ibid.*, 130–31.

31 Quoted *ibid.*, 131.

32 Quoted *ibid.*

33 Richardson was a major influence on the young Reynolds as well, 'the book which, as he used to tell his friends, fired him in first youth to become a painter'. George Watson, 'Joshua Reynolds's Copy of Richardson', *Review of English Studies*, New Series, 42:167, August 1991, 425.

34 Charles-Alphonse Du Fresnoy, *The Art of Painting*, trans. John Dryden, London, 1716, 5.

35 *Ibid.*, 69.

36 *Ibid.*, 87.

37 *Ibid.*, 89.

38 *Works of Jonathan Richardson*, 11.

39 *Ibid.*, 176.

40 *Ibid.*, 9.

41 Wayne Craven, 'John Wollaston: His Career in England and New York City', *American Art Journal*, 7:2, November 1975, 19–31.

42 For Haidt's possible influence on West, see Ann Uhry Abrams, *The Valiant Hero: Benjamin West and Grand-Style History Painting*, Washington, D.C., 1985, 52–54.

43 Ann Uhry Abrams, 'A New Light on Benjamin West's Pennsylvania Instruction', *Winterthur Portfolio*, 17:4, Winter 1982.

44 Jeffrey B. Webb, 'James Logan', *American National Biography Online*, anb.org/articles/01/01-00529.html (accessed December 2014; subscription required); E. Gordon Alderfer, 'James Logan: The Political Career of a Colonial Scholar', *Pennsylvania History*, 24:1, January 1957.

45 Stuart P. Sherman, 'Franklin and the Age of Enlightenment', in *Benjamin Franklin and the American Character*, ed. Charles L. Sanford, Boston, 1955, 74.

46 *Ibid.*, 75.

47 *A Catalogue of Books Belonging to the Library Company of Philadelphia*, Philadelphia, 1741.

48 Quoted in Edwin Wolf II, *The Book Culture of a Colonial American City: Philadelphia Books, Bookmen, and Booksellers*, Oxford, 1988, 79.

49 Galt, part 1, 35.

50 *Ibid.*, 36.

51 Scott Paul Gordon, 'Martial Art: Benjamin West's *The Death of Socrates*, Colonial Politics, and the Puzzles of Patronage', *William and Mary Quarterly*, Third Series, 65:1, January 2008, 98.

52 Galt, part 1, 36. According to Meyer Reinhold, 'no other classical author was as popular in seventeenth and eighteenth-century America'. Quoted in Wolf, 89.

53 Gordon, 83–89.

54 *Works of Jonathan Richardson*, 38.

55 Gordon, 96.

56 *Ibid.*

57 *Works of Jonathan Richardson*, 112.

58 I have examined the picture (then in storage), which belongs to the Philadelphia History Museum at the Atwater Kent.

59 West himself seems to have regarded *Socrates* and his other American pictures as juvenilia: none figures in 'The List of pictures painted by Benjn. West President of the Royal Academy London' appended to the Manuscript Autobiography.

60 For some examples of Aberdeen's importance, see Ronnie Young, 'James Beattie and the Progress of Genius in the Aberdeen Enlightenment', *Journal for Eighteenth-Century Studies*, 36:2, June 2013.

61 King's College became the foundation of Columbia University.

62 Theodore Hornberger, 'A Note on the Probable Source of Provost Smith's Famous Curriculum for the College of Philadelphia', *Pennsylvania Magazine of History and Biography*, 58:4, October 1934, 372.

63 William Smith, *Some Thoughts on Education*, New York, 1752, 9.

64 Anthony Ashley Cooper, 3rd Earl of Shaftesbury, *Characteristics of Men, Manners, Opinions, Times* [1711], ed. Lawrence E. Klein, Cambridge, 1999, viii.

65 Voltaire, *Philosophical Dictionary* [1764], trans. H.I. Woolf, Mineola, NY, 2010, 311.

66 William Smith, *A General Idea of the College of Mirania*, New York, 1753, 27.

67 'Under the guidance of a great teacher, the group was unique for the birth within it of American drama, painting, and music.' Albert F. Gegenheimer, *William Smith: Educator and Churchman, 1727–1803*, Philadelphia, 1943, 121.

68 *Works of Jonathan Richardson*, 85.

69 William Smith, *A Sermon, Preach'd on Sunday Sept. 1, 1754, in Christ-Church, Philadelphia; Occasioned by the Death of a Beloved Pupil*, Philadelphia, 1754, iii–iv.

70 William Smith, *A Poem on Visiting the Academy of Philadelphia, June 1753*, Philadelphia, 1753.

71 *American Magazine and Monthly Chronicle for the British Colonies*, Philadelphia, 1:5, February 1758, 237.

72 *American Magazine*, 1:12, September 1758, 608.

73 Smith, *Some Thoughts on Education*, 19.

74 Richard Cumberland, *Memoirs of Richard Cumberland*, London, 1806, 112–13.

75 West, 7.

A PENNSYLVANIA YANKEE IN CARDINAL ALBANI'S COURT

1 See, for example, Christopher M.S. Johns, 'Visual Culture and the Triumph of Cosmopolitanism in Eighteenth-Century Rome', in *Roma Britannica: Art Patronage and Cultural Exchange in Eighteenth-Century Rome*, ed. David R. Marshall, Susan Russell and Karin Wolfe, London, 2011, 14.

2 *Letters to a Young Nobleman*, London, 1762, 14.

3 *Ibid.*, 36.

4 *Ibid.*, 220.

5 Quoted in Franziska Forster-Hahn, 'The Sources of True Taste: Benjamin West's Instructions to a Young Painter for His Studies in Italy', *Journal of the Warburg and Courtauld Institutes*, 30, 1967, 376–77.

6 Quoted *ibid.*, 377.

7 David R. Marshall and Karin Wolfe, 'Roma Britannica', in Marshall, Russell and Wolfe, 5.

8 West, 2. Perhaps this is an early example of what later became known as Stendhal's syndrome, after the French novelist's account in 1817 of his exhausting and neurotic reaction to the art treasures of Florence.

9 Hester Lynch Piozzi, *Observations and Reflections Made in the Course of a Journey Through France, Italy and Germany*, London, 1789, vol. 1, 379.

10 Joseph Baretti, *An Account of the Manners and Customs of Italy*, London, 1769, vol. 2, 160.

11 Joseph Wilcocks, *Roman Conversations; or, A Short Description of the Antiquities of Rome*, London, 1797, vol. 1, v.

12 Marshall and Wolfe, 5.

13 J.W. von Goethe, *Italian Journey* [1816–17], trans. W.H. Auden and Elizabeth Mayer, in *Selected Works*, London, 1999, 507.

14 *Ibid.*, 530.

15 *Ibid.*, 525.

16 E. Gosse, ed., *Conversations of James Northcote R.A.*, London, 1894, 109.

17 Goethe, 529.

18 John Ingamells, *A Dictionary of British and Irish Travellers in Italy, 1701–1800*, New Haven, Conn., and London, 1997.

19 Quoted in *Nathaniel Dance, 1735–1811*, exhib. cat., intro. David Goodreau, London, Kenwood House, 1977, unpaginated.

20 Wilcocks, vol. 1, 467.

21 *Letters from a Young Painter Abroad to His Friends in England*, London, 1750, vol. 1, 75–76.

22 Joseph Farington, 'Memoirs of the Life of Sir Joshua Reynolds', in Sir Joshua Reynolds, *The Literary Works of Sir Joshua Reynolds*, London, 1819, cliii.

23 *Ibid.*, ccxcvi.

24 Johann Joachim Winckelmann, *History of the Art of Antiquity* [1764], trans. Harry Francis Mallgrave, Los Angeles, 2006, 333. All other quotations in this paragraph are from Galt, part 1, 104–106.

25 Rather, 'Benjamin West, John Galt, and the Biography of 1816', 325. I am also grateful to David Haugaard, Director of Research Services, Historical Society of Pennsylvania, for his information on the eighteenth-century Indian population of Eastern Pennsylvania.

26 Letter from William Allen to Messrs Jackson and Rutherford, 5 April 1760, quoted in E.P. Richardson, 'West's Voyage to Italy, 1760, and William Allen', *Pennsylvania Magazine of History and Biography*, 102:1, January 1978, 10. Allen's statement that West was 'desirous' to visit Italy implies that West was actively seeking passage to Europe rather than being the beneficiary of mere happenstance.

27 Quoted in Wilcocks, vol. 1, xl.

28 *Ibid.*, 64.

29 *Ibid.*, vol. 2, 112. West also studied the works of Michelangelo, Raphael and Poussin. West, 4.

30 The Grand Tourist had a crowded itinerary. West's fellow Pennsylvanian Samuel Powel, who visited Rome in 1764, described a whirlwind of visits guided by the antiquary Joseph Byers, in whose company Powel and friends viewed the antiquities of the Vatican Museums, the palaces and collections of the great Roman families ranging from the Farnese and the Borghese to the Barberini, the Rospigliosi and the Spadas, and the works of artists dead, such as the Carracci, and living, such as Mengs. Philadelphia, American Philosophical Society, Samuel Powel, Short Notes on a course of Antiquities at Rome, in Company with Messrs. Apthorp, Morgan & Palmer, 1764, Hare Papers, BH22.

31 Brendan Cassidy, *The Life & Letters of Gavin Hamilton (1723–1798): Artist & Dealer in Eighteenth-Century Rome*, London and Turnhout, 2011, vol. 1, 90.

32 West eventually became disenchanted with Winckelmann, as Nicholas Biddle recorded in 1807: 'Of Winkelman, West now thinks less than he used to do. I asked him if he believed to be true what was often said, that the best part of Winkelman's book was made by Mengs. He believed it was. Winkelman used to stick very close to Mengs.' Quoted in Wainwright, 112.

33 Winckelmann, 213.

34 *Ibid.*, 8.

35 Robert Rosenblum, *Transformations in Late Eighteenth Century Art*, Princeton, NJ, 1974, 11–24.

36 Winckelmann, 333–34.

37 *Ibid.*, 232.

38 '*... des exemples de morale, des modèles d'héroïsme et de bon goût ... s'attache, en priorité, à la dimension politique, voir trouve des modèles politiques*'. François Hartog, *Anciens, modernes, sauvages*, Paris, 2005, 98.

39 An exception to West's lack of interest in politics was his vehement attack on the state of affairs in Italy: 'the general theocratical despotism which overspread the whole country, like an unwholesome vapour ... those minute subdivisions of territory, in which political tyranny exercised its baleful influence'. Galt, part 1, 146. Ingamells regards these remarks as evidence that 'West was not impressed with Italy' (p. 992).

40 James L. Larson, 'Winckelmann's Essay on Imitation', *Eighteenth-Century Studies*, 9:3, Spring 1976, 391.

41 Ellis Waterhouse, 'The British Contribution to the Neo-Classical Style in Painting', *Proceedings of the British Academy*, 40, 1954, 58.

42 Quoted in Larson, 392.

43 Quoted *ibid.*, 396.

44 Quoted *ibid.*

45 Winckelmann, 73.

46 Jonathan Richardson, *An Account of the Statues, Bas-reliefs, Drawings and Pictures in Italy, France, &c.*, London, 1754, A6.

47 Anthony Ashley Cooper, 3rd Earl of Shaftesbury, *An Essay on Painting: Being a Notion of the Historical Draught or Tablature of the Judgment of Hercules*, London, 1714, 46.

48 Hugh Honour, *Neo-classicism*, London, 1977, 18.

49 *Ibid.*

50 Rosenblum, 28.

51 Galt, part 1, 97.

52 There is surprisingly little written in English on Albani's career and influence other than Lesley Lewis, *Connoisseurs and Secret Agents in Eighteenth Century Rome*, London, 1961, although he is mentioned in many other works: for example, Ilaria Bignamini and Clare Hornsby, *Digging and Dealing in Eighteenth-Century Rome*, New Haven, Conn., and London, 2010.

53 London, Society of Antiquaries of London, Library, Minute Book of the Society of Antiquaries of London, vol. 8, 336.

54 *Ibid.*, 411. In 1721 Stosch was put on an annual salary of £400 by the British government to report on the doings of the Stuart court in exile in Rome. Lewis, *Connoisseurs and Secret Agents*, 61–62.

55 Galt, part 1, 99.

56 Piozzi, vol. 2, 125.

57 Quoted in Galt, part 1, 121–22.

58 New York, The Morgan Library and Museum, Department of Drawings and Prints, Benjamin West drawings, 1970.11:1.

59 Ruth S. Kraemer accepts *Rebecca at the Well* as a 1757 work (Ruth S. Kraemer, *Drawings by Benjamin West and His Son Raphael Lamar West*, New York, 1975), as does, to a slightly lesser extent, Abrams, who writes, 'If West created *Rebecca at the Well* at age nineteen as the inscription indicates, the drawing remains as convincing testimony that the young artist had developed a skillful hand and practiced eye before ever leaving America.' Abrams, *Valiant Hero*, 66. In an email correspondence, Allen Staley told me that, while he had not closely examined *Rebecca,* he was sceptical.

60 Von Erffa and Staley, 13.

61 West's pupil William Dunlap wrote in the early 1830s: 'We have been obliged to search diligently for any specimen of West's portrait painting before he left America, and when we have found it, it has hardly been worth the search.' Dunlap, vol. 1, 51.

62 Royal Academy, Library and Archive, Benjamin West Sketchbooks, 07/5053, 07/5054, 07/5055.

63 Giovanna Perini, 'Sir Joshua Reynolds and Italian Art and Literature: A Study of the Sketchbooks in the British Museum and in Sir John Soane's Museum', *Journal of the Warburg and Courtauld Institutes*, 51, 1988, 144–45.

64 Benjamin Franklin, *The Way to Wealth; as clearly shewn in the preface of an old Pensylvania almanack, intitled, Poor Richard improved*, London, 1774, 9–10.

65 Few have noted how beneficial West's provincialism was. An exception is Joseph Allard, who wrote: 'What marked West out from his contemporaries, though and allowed for his freedom from academic constraints and his later innovations, was precisely that he had absorbed his classical influence in America through reading ... His sense of mission allowed him to adopt whatever stance seemed most likely to lead to his desired ends – the edification of his fellow man and his own elevation.' Joseph Allard, 'West, Copley, and Eighteenth-Century American Provincialism', *Journal of American Studies*, 17:3, December 1983, 397.

66 The portraits of the academicians in the Accademia di San Luca in Rome present a vivid picture of international Neoclassicism, with French, German, Austrian, British and Italian artists rubbing shoulders.

67 Du Fresnoy, 69.

68 David Rosand, *The Invention of Painting in America*, New York, 2004, 54.

69 Quoted *ibid.*, 48.

70 *Horace Walpole's Correspondence*, vol. 23, 211.

71 Galt, part 1, 143.

72 Gordon S. Wood, *The Americanization of Benjamin Franklin*, New York, 2004, 91.

73 Allan Ramsay, *Letters on the Present Disturbances in Great Britain and Her American Provinces*, London, 1777, 17.

74 *Ibid.*, 20.

75 *Ibid.*, 21.

76 Quoted in Steffi Roettgen, *Anton Raphael Mengs, 1728–1779*, Munich, 1999–2003, vol. 2, 503.

77 Steffi Roettgen, *Anton Raphael Mengs, 1728–1779, and His British*

Patrons, trans. Eileen Martin, London, 1993, 18.

78 Thomas Pelzel, *Anton Raphael Mengs and Neoclassicism*, New York and London, 1979, 127.

79 Von Erffa and Staley, 445.

80 Quoted in Galt, part 1, 122. West followed Mengs's advice as well as the itinerary suggested to him by Richardson's *Account*, and that advice informed the directions that West himself later gave to Copley, Ramberg and others regarding their own trips to Italy.

81 Quoted in Adrian W. Zorgniotti, 'Benjamin West's Osteomyelitis: A Translation', *Bulletin of the New York Medical Academy*, 49:8, August 1973, 702–707.

82 West, 4.

83 There is a later version of about 1766 in the Yale Center for British Art.

84 Von Erffa and Staley, 33–36.

85 Quoted in Joseph Farington, *The Diary of Joseph Farington*, ed. Kenneth Garlick and Angus Macintyre, New Haven, Conn., and London, 1978–98, vol. 13, 4600.

86 *Ibid.*, vol. 2, 449.

87 Von Erffa and Staley, 14.

88 Alexander Pope, 'Preface to *The Iliad of Homer*' [1715], in *The Prose Works of Alexander Pope*, ed. Norman Ault and Rosemary Cowler, Oxford, 1936–86, vol. 1, 246.

89 Dora Wiebenson, 'Subjects from Homer's Iliad in Neoclassical Art', *Art Bulletin*, 46:1, March 1964, 37.

90 Quoted in Cassidy, vol. 1, 192.

91 *Ibid.*, 71.

92 Quoted in Julia Lloyd Williams, *Gavin Hamilton, 1723–1798*, Edinburgh, 1994, 9–10. Williams notes that *Andromache* was 'one of the very few modern paintings mentioned' by Winckelmann.

93 Mengs failed to return the compliment. 'Mengs, the German painter who was in great repute at Rome, said that He never met with but 2 English Artists of superior genius, they were R. Wilson, – and Athenian Stuart.' *Diary of Joseph Farington*, vol. 5, 1554.

94 Galt, part 1, 114–18. This refers to the *Caffè degli Inglesi*.

95 As Ellis Waterhouse observes, Hamilton continued to plough a furrow that West had abandoned with *Wolfe*: 'he boldly persisted in the old classical tradition after the innovations of West and Copley in the modern heroic manner had won the day'. Ellis Waterhouse, *Painting in Britain, 1530–1790*, New Haven, Conn., and London, 1994, 273.

96 Thanks to his family's 10,200-hectare (25,000-acre) plantation in Jamaica, Dawkins was able to finance not only his own trip to the Middle East, but also to help fund Stuart and Revett.

97 Clare Pace, 'Gavin Hamilton's *Wood and Dawkins Discovering Palmyra*: The Dilettante as Hero', *Art History*, 4:3, September 1981, 271.

98 Cassidy, vol. 1, 68.

99 I am grateful to Helen Smailes, Senior Curator of British Art, National Galleries of Scotland, for this information.

HISTORY MEN AND WOMEN

1 Michael Baxandall, *Patterns of Intention: On the Historical Explanation of Pictures*, New Haven, Conn., and London, 1985, 75.

2 Leon Battista Alberti, *On Painting* [1435–36], trans. John R. Spencer, London, 1956, 59.

3 *Ibid.*, 96.

4 Du Fresnoy, 63.

5 *Ibid.*, 66–67.

6 Jonathan Israel, *Democratic Enlightenment: Philosophy, Revolution, and Human Rights, 1750–1790*, Oxford, 2011, 223.

7 *Ibid.*, 222.

8 Gertrude Himmelfarb, *The Roads to Modernity: The British, French, and American Enlightenments*, New York, 2004, 5–6.

9 Voltaire, *Letters on England* [1733], trans. Leonard Tancock, London, 2005, 43.

10 Quoted in David Wootton, 'David Hume: "The Historian"', in *The Cambridge Companion to Hume*, ed. David Fate Norton and Jacqueline Taylor, Cambridge, 2009, 447.

11 Voltaire, *Philosophical Dictionary*, 20.

12 James Boswell, *Boswell's Column*, ed. Margery Bailey, London, 1951, 266–67. Writing as 'The Hypochondriack', Boswell contributed to the *London Magazine* from 1777 to 1783.

13 Quoted in Israel, *Democratic Enlightenment*, 221.

14 Quoted in James Fieser, ed., *Early Responses to Hume's History of England*, Bristol, 2005, vol. 1, 22–23.

15 William Robertson, *The History of the Reign of the Emperor Charles V* [1769], in *The Works of William Robertson, D.D.*, London, 1852, 467.

16 For a discussion of such theories, see David Spadafora, *The Idea of Progress in Eighteenth-Century Britain*,

New Haven, Conn., and London, 1990.

17 Thomas Gray, *An Elegy Written in a Country Church-Yard*, London, 1751, 7. Wolfe is alleged to have recited Gray's *Elegy* before his attack on Quebec, remarking, 'I would rather have written those lines than take Quebec.' Parkman, 550. 'Impossibly romantic as it seems, in essence the anecdote is likely to be authentic', according to Brumwell, 272.

18 Smith, *Some Thoughts on Education*, vii.

19 *Ibid.*, 19.

20 *Ibid.*, 23.

21 Henry St John, Viscount Bolingbroke, *Letters on the Study and Use of History*, London, 1752, 48.

22 Quoted in Philip Hicks, *Neoclassical History and English Culture: From Clarendon to Hume*, Basingstoke, 1996, 8.

23 Hugh Blair, *Lectures on Rhetoric and Belles Lettres* [1783], London, 1817, vol. 3, 52.

24 '*… donnent au lecteur émerveillé l'illusion qu'après des siècles d'attente l'histoire vient tout à coup de se dévoiler à lui*'. Quoted in Voltaire, *Oeuvres historiques*, ed. René Pomeau, Paris, 1957, 7.

25 '*Ce n'est pas seulement la vie de Louis XIV qu'on prétend écrire; on se propose un plus grand objet … de peindre a la postérité, non les actions d'un seul homme, mais l'esprit des hommes dans le siècle le plus éclairé qui fut jamais.*' Voltaire, *Le Siècle de Louis XIV* [1751], in *Oeuvres historiques*, 616.

26 Edward Gibbon, *The Decline and Fall of the Roman Empire* [1776–88], London, 1993–94, vol. 1, 9.

27 Voltaire, *Letters on England*, 57.

28 David Hume, 'Of Refinement in the Arts' [1752], in *Selected Essays*, ed. Stephen Copley and Andrew Edgar, Oxford, 2008, 169.

29 Dan Edelstein, *The Enlightenment: A Genealogy*, Chicago and London, 2010, 33.

30 Dario Perinetti, 'Philosophical Reflection on History', in *The Cambridge History of Eighteenth-Century Philosophy*, ed. Knud Haakonssen, Cambridge, 2006, vol. 2, 1117.

31 '*Peut-être arrivera-t-il bientôt dans la manière d'écrire l'histoire ce qui est arrivé dans la physique. Les nouvelles découvertes ont fait proscrire les anciens systèmes. On voudra connaître le genre humain dans ce détail intéressant qui fait aujourd'hui la base de la philosophie naturelle.*' Voltaire, *Nouvelles considérations sur l'histoire* [1744], in *Oeuvres historiques*, 46.

32 Writing in 1769, the French Jesuit historian Claude-François-Xavier Millot noted approvingly of Hume that 'as a subject of Great Britain, he is attached to the principles of his own country … he is not unjust to other nations … and his countrymen would applaud him, as well as less prejudiced foreigners'. Quoted in Fieser, vol. 2, 400.

33 Mark Salber Phillips, *Society and Sentiment: Genres of Historical Writing in Britain, 1740–1820*, Princeton, NJ, 2000, 39.

34 '*… les mœurs, la religion, les habits, les forces, les richesses, l'adresse, le gouvernement, les guerres, les arts, les entreprises, les cérémonies, la politique et les manières d'agir*'. Quoted in Myrtille Méricam-Bourdet, *Voltaire et l'écriture de l'histoire: un enjeu politique*, Oxford, 2012, 131.

35 Victor G. Wexler, 'David Hume's Discovery of a New Scene of Historical Thought,' *Eighteenth-Century Studies*, 10:2, Winter 1976–77, 186.

36 Karen O'Brien, 'History and the Novel in Eighteenth-Century Britain', *Huntington Library Quarterly*, 68:1–2, March 2005, 407.

37 Quoted in Paul H. Meyer, 'Voltaire and Hume as Historians: A Comparative Study of the *Essai sur les mœurs* and the *History of England*', *PMLA*, 73:1, March 1958, 51.

38 *Ibid.*, 52.

39 Oliver Goldsmith, *The History of England: From the Earliest Times to the Death of George the Second* [1771], London, 1794, vol. 1, v.

40 Hayden White, *Tropics of Discourse: Essays in Cultural Criticism*, Baltimore and London, 1978, 123.

41 Mark Akenside, *The Pleasures of Imagination*, London, 1754, 45–46.

42 Quoted in Fieser, vol. 2, 403.

43 Jean-Jacques Rousseau, *The Social Contract* [1762], in *The Social Contract and the Discourses*, trans. G.D.H. Cole, New York and London, 1993, 243.

44 Catherine Macaulay, *The History of England from the Accession of James I to the Elevation of the House of Hanover*, London, 1769, vol. 1, x.

45 Dubos, vol. 2, 236.

46 *Ibid.*, 245.

47 Jürgen Habermas, *The Structural Transformation of the Public Sphere: An Inquiry into a Category of Bourgeois Society*, Cambridge, 1989.

48 Voltaire, *Letters on England*, 101.

49 David Hume, 'Of the Liberty of the Press' [1742, revised 1777], in *Theory of Politics*, ed. Frederick Watkins, London, 1951, 133.

50 *Ibid.*, 134

51 J.C. Hilson, 'Hume: The Historian as Man of Feeling', in *Augustan Worlds*, ed. J.C. Hilson, M.M.B. Jones and J.R. Warson, Leicester, 1978, 209.

52 David Hume, *The History of England from the Invasion of Julius Caesar to the Revolution in 1688*, London, 1767, vol. 7, 147–48.

53 Paul de Rapin de Thoyras, *The History of England*, trans. Nicholas Tindal, London, 1760, vol. 10, 537–38.

54 Quoted in Hilson, 220.

55 Quoted *ibid.*, 210.

56 '*Je lisais ces jours passés l'Histoire d'Écosse du Robertson; je l'ai quitté parce qu'elle me donnait des vapeurs; je crains tout ce qui m'attriste.*' *Horace Walpole's Correspondence*, vol. 3, 64.

57 William Robertson, *The History of Scotland During the Reigns of Queen Mary and of King James VI*, London, 1761, vol. 2, 173–74.

58 Terry Belanger, 'Publishers and Writers in Eighteenth-Century England', in *Books and Their Readers in Eighteenth-Century England*, ed. Isabel Rivers, Leicester, 1982, 22. As the reactions of Mrs Mure and Madame du Deffand show us, part of the success of the philosophical historians was the ability to compete with novelists for the attention of the growing audience of female readers.

59 Hume, *History of England*, vol. 1, xii.

60 Quoted in Hicks, 204.

61 Quoted in Fieser, vol. 1, xiv.

62 R.G. Collingwood, *The Idea of History*, Oxford, 2005, 77.

63 Friedrich Meinecke, *Historism: The Rise of a New Historical Outlook*, trans. J.E. Anderson, London, 1972, 196.

64 R.N. Stromberg, 'History in the Eighteenth Century', *Journal of the History of Ideas*, 12:2, April 1951, 295–304, presents a well-balanced account of the philosophic historians: 'They were victims of their philosophical limitations.' For a more current assessment of their strengths, see Karen O'Brien, *Narratives of Enlightenment: Cosmopolitan History from Voltaire to Gibbon*, Cambridge, 2005.

65 *Daily Gazeteer*, quoted in Hicks, 148.

66 O'Brien, 'History and the Novel', 401.

67 *Ibid.*, 397.

68 B.R. Mitchell and Phyllis Deane, *Abstract of British Historical Statistics*, Cambridge, 1971, 279–80.

69 *Ibid.*, 268; Spadafora, 60.

70 Mitchell and Deane, 5.

71 Jerry White, *London in the Eighteenth Century: A Great and Monstrous Thing*, London, 2012, 3.

72 Mitchell and Deane, 112.

73 David S. Landes, *The Unbound Prometheus: Technological Change and Industrial Development in Western Europe from 1750 to the Present*, Cambridge, 1969, 41.

74 Voltaire, *Letters on England*, 101.

75 Charles-Louis de Secondat, baron de La Brède et de Montesquieu, 'Montesquieu in England: His "Notes on England"', trans. Iain Stewart, Oxford University Comparative Law Forum 6, 2002, ouclf.iuscomp.org/articles/montesquieu.shtml (accessed January 2015).

76 Quoted in Himmelfarb, 10.

77 Hume, 'Of the Liberty of the Press', 129.

78 Quoted in Jeremy Black, *The English Press in the Eighteenth Century*, London, 1987, 13.

79 Jeremy Black, *The English Press, 1621–1861*, Stroud, 2001, 73–74.

80 Hannah Barker, *Newspapers, Politics and English Society, 1695–1855*, Harlow, 2000, 32.

81 James van Horn Melton, *The Rise of the Public in Enlightenment Europe*, Cambridge, 2001, 27.

82 'Between 1739 and 1783, twenty-four years were spent at war, twenty at peace. During peacetime itself war seemed all too close.' Paul Langford, *A Polite and Commercial People: England, 1727–1783*, Oxford, 1989, 622.

83 Gerald Newman, *The Rise of English Nationalism: A Cultural History, 1740–1830*, London, 1997, 11.

84 John Brewer, *The Sinews of Power: War, Money and the English State, 1688–1783*, Cambridge, Mass., 1990, 137.

85 *Ibid.*, 250.

86 Jonathan Swift, *The Conduct of the Allies* … [1711], in *Major Works*, ed. Angus Ross and David Woolley, Oxford, 2003, 288.

87 *Horace Walpole's Correspondence*, vol. 35, 360.

88 Catherine Macaulay, *The History of England from the Revolution to the Present Time in a Series of Letters to a Friend*, Bath, 1778, vol. 1, 315.

89 Quoted in Meinecke, ix.

90 Nicholas Tindal, *The Continuation of Mr. Rapin's History of England*, London, 1759, vol. 21, 548.

91 Quoted in O'Brien, *Narratives of Enlightenment*, 69.

92 Friends Historical Library, Mrs. Benjamin West, Household Account Book, 1785–1789, Mss001/057.

93 *Letters to a Young Nobleman*, 13–14.

94 Smith, *General Idea of the College of Mirania*, 30.

95 West, 10.

96 Robertson, *History of the Reign of the Emperor Charles V*, 508.

97 As in the subtitle of Peter Gay, *Modernism: The Lure of Heresy from Baudelaire to Beckett and Beyond*, London, 2009.

98 Pope somewhat mischievously laid this at the door of the ancients, writing that 'the ancient poets are in one respect like many modern ladies; let an action be never so trivial in itself, they always make it appear of the utmost importance'. Alexander Pope, *The Rape of the Lock* [1712], in *The Major Works*, ed. Pat Rogers, Oxford, 2006, 77–78.

99 Evan Lloyd, *Conversation: A Poem*, London, 1767, 24.

100 *Ibid.*

101 Adam Smith, *An Inquiry into the Nature and Causes of the Wealth of Nations*, London, 1790, 2044.

102 Immanuel Kant, *An Answer to the Question: 'What is Enlightenment?'* [1784], trans. H.B. Nisbet, London, 2009, 10.

103 Dubos, vol. 1, 44.

104 Quoted in Gay, *Modernism*, 40.

'HOW BEAUTIFUL IS DEATH'

1 Charles Mitchell, 'Benjamin West's "Death of General Wolfe" and the Popular History Piece', *Journal of the Warburg and Courtauld Institutes,* 7, 1944, 31.

2 Pasquin, 73. Van Dyck's *Belisarius* was one of the masterpieces displayed at Chiswick House when West arrived in London, and the subject of a popular engraving by Gérard-Jean-Baptiste Scotin. Reattributed to Luciano Borzone, the painting now hangs at Chatsworth House in Derbyshire.

3 This question was raised in conversation by Allen Staley.

4 *Wright of Derby*, exhib. cat. by Judy Egerton, London, Paris and New York, 1990, 98. See also David H. Solkin, 'Joseph Wright of Derby and the Sublime Art of Labor', *Representations,* 83:1, Summer 2003, in which Solkin identifies a number of *vanitas* elements. More testimony perhaps to the elegiac strain in mid-eighteenth-century Britain?

5 Wright's later, 1773 version of the theme, *An Iron Forge Viewed from Without*, now in the Hermitage, is even more obviously a Nativity. Elizaveta Renne, *State Hermitage Museum Catalogue: Sixteenth- to Nineteenth-Century British Painting*, New Haven, Conn., and London, 2011, 249. See also Celina Fox, *The Arts of Industry in the Age of Enlightenment*, New Haven, Conn., and London, 2009, 428–33. There may be religious symbolism in Wright's *Experiment on a Bird in the Air Pump* (1768), with the white cockatoo representing the Holy Ghost, according to Laura Baudot, 'An Air of History: Joseph Wright's and Robert Boyle's Air Pump Narratives', *Eighteenth-Century Studies*, 46:1, Fall 2012, 21–22.

6 Jonathan Israel, *Radical Enlightenment: Philosophy and the Making of Modernity, 1650–1750*, Oxford, 2001, 7.

7 Peter Gay, *The Enlightenment: An Interpretation. Volume 1: The Rise of Modern Paganism*, New York, 1966, 3.

8 Israel, *Radical Enlightenment*, 4.

9 Diderot, vol. 1, 41.

10 William Hogarth, *Anecdotes of William Hogarth, Written by Himself*, London, 1833, 12.

11 Quoted in an untitled, undated, anonymous document that may be a contemporaneous note by Galt of one of his conversations with West. Historical Society of Pennsylvania, *The Life, Studies and Works of Benjamin West Esq.*, by John Galt in extra-illustrated form, 3239.

12 *Observations on the Pictures Now in Exhibition at the Royal Academy*, London, 1771, 15.

13 Henry Fuseli, *Lectures on Painting: Delivered at the Royal Academy March 1801*, London, 1801, 143.

14 Henry Angelo, *Reminiscences of Henry Angelo*, London, 1830, vol. 1, 15.

15 Bromley, vol. 1, 57.

16 James Beattie, *Essays on the Nature and Immutability of TRUTH, in Opposition to Sophistry and Scepticism*, Edinburgh, 1776, 432.

17 Historical Society of Pennsylvania, Galt extra-illustrated, 3239.

18 Even in the twentieth century some corners of the cultural Establishment stubbornly clung to the supposedly elevating values of archaic dress. In 1923 Sir Barry Jackson's production of Shakespeare's *Cymbeline* in modern costume shocked audiences.

19 Reynolds, *Discourses*, 138.

20 West, 10.

21 In Burke's study of the imagery of Louis XIV, he identifies a 'crisis of representations', which he divides into two parts, 'the decline of antiquity and the decline of correspondences'. As we have discussed, the decline of antiquity was highlighted by the Quarrel between the Ancients and the Moderns. Burke's 'decline of correspondences' is a sort of meta-metaphor: 'If a ruler ... was represented as (say) Hercules, this was much more than a metaphor saying that he is strong ... The ruler was in some important sense of the term identified with Hercules, as if the aura of the demigod rubbed off on him.' Peter Burke, *The Fabrication of Louis XIV*, New Haven, Conn., and London, 1992, 126–27.

22 Reynolds, *Discourses*, 57.

23 *Ibid.*, 58.

24 *Ibid.*, 73.

25 Samuel Johnson, ed., *The Plays of William Shakespeare*, London, 1765, vol. 1, 2.

26 *'Quels habillements il faut donner aux figures dont nous voulons représenter les Histoires de notre temps?'* François Blondel, *Cours d'architecture*, Paris, 1675, part 2, 167.

27 *'Et je ne sais si nous aurions plus de raison maintenant d'Habiller nos Figures à la Romaine, que les Romains n'en ont eue dans leur temps d'Habiller les leurs à la Grecque ou à l'Égyptienne.' Ibid.*, 171.

28 Roger de Piles, *The Art of Painting and the Lives of the Painters*, London, 1706, 23.

29 *Works of Jonathan Richardson*, 83.

30 See Carol Gibson-Wood, *Jonathan Richardson: Art Theorist of the English Enlightenment*, New Haven, Conn., and London, 2000, 143–78.

31 London, British Museum, Department of Prints and Drawings, 1865-6-10-1353 L.B. 24 (b).

32 British Museum, Department of Prints and Drawings, 1865-6-10-1327 L.B. 23. For Richardson's possible influence on Thornhill, see Gibson-Wood, 157–59. Thornhill's dilemma is discussed in some detail in Edgar Wind, 'The Revolution of History Painting', *Journal of the Warburg Institute*, 2:2, October 1938, 122–24.

33 Reynolds, *Discourses*, 30.

34 *Ibid.*, 204.

35 Edgar Wind, 'Penny, West, and the "Death of Wolfe"', *Journal of the Warburg and Courtauld Institutes*, 10, 1947, 160.

36 As Thomas Crow tells us, the much more powerful Académie in France had its inconsistencies too: 'our received picture of the Academy as a monolithic, exclusionary body has been largely a myth'. Crow, *Painters and Public Life*, 134.

37 Reynolds, *Discourses*, 52. There is also Reynolds's valedictory remark that, having failed to live up to the ideals of Michelangelo, 'I have taken another course, one more suited to my abilities, and to the taste of the times in which I live' (p. 282).

38 Von Erffa and Staley, 551.

39 The Sawbridge portrait owes a great deal to the 1768 portrait of William Pitt by West's student Charles Willson Peale. Sawbridge was the brother of the fashionable radical historian Catherine Macaulay, which raises the intriguing possibility that West might have come in contact with her. Writing in 1770, John Adams praised Macaulay's *History of England* as 'calculated to strip off the Gilding and false Lustre from worthless Princes and Nobles, and to bestow the Reward of Virtue, Praise upon the generous and worthy only'. John Adams, *Revolutionary Writings. Volume 1: 1755–1775*, ed. Gordon Wood, New York, 2011, 186.

40 The French-born Laguerre, 'ironically, was a godson of King Louis XIV', according to John Brooks, *Marlborough House: Royal Palace and International Headquarters of the Commonwealth*, Norwich, 2002, 4. Because Marlborough House is the working headquarters of the Commonwealth Secretariat, visits are restricted. 'These are interesting as contemporary military documents,' Edward Croft-Murray wrote rather dismissively about the murals, 'but apart from that they have little merit.' Edward Croft-Murray, *Decorative Painting in England, 1537–1837*, London, 1962, vol. 1, 64.

41 David Coke and Alan Borg, *Vauxhall Gardens: A History*, New Haven, Conn., and London, 2011, 126.

42 Quoted *ibid.*, 131.

43 Quoted *ibid.*, 135.

44 Pierre-Jean Grosley, *A Tour to London; or, New Observations on England, and Its Inhabitants*, trans. Thomas Nugent, London, 1772, vol. 1, 103.

45 Theodore Rabb, *The Last Days of the Renaissance: & the March to Modernity*, New York, 2006, 162–63.

46 Hinting at the formula West used for *Wolfe*, the foreground of the *Recapture of Bahia* is dominated by a family group around a wounded man arranged in the form of a Lamentation.

47 Shaftesbury, *Characteristics*, 52.

48 Quoted in Reid, 180–81.

49 Quoted in John Richardson, 'Modern Warfare in Early Eighteenth-Century Poetry', *Studies in English Literature, 1500–1900*, 45:3, Summer 2005, 561.

50 Tobias Smollett, *The Adventures of Roderick Random* [1748], Oxford, 1979, 167–68. See also David McNeil, *The Grotesque Depiction of War and the Military in Eighteenth-Century English Fiction*, Newark, Del., 1990.

51 Richardson, 'Modern Warfare', 557.

52 Joel Barlow, *The Columbiad: A Poem*, London, 1809, xii.

53 Matthew Greg Sullivan, 'Historiography and Visual Culture in Britain, 1660–1783', PhD thesis, University of Leeds, 1998, 170.

54 John Romney, *Memoirs of the Life and Works of George Romney*, London, 1830, 47. Recent studies of Romney absolve Reynolds. See *George Romney, 1734–1802*, exhib. cat. by Alex Kidson, Liverpool, London and San Marino, Calif., 2002, 14, and David A. Cross, *A Striking Likeness: The Life of George Romney*, Aldershot, 2000, 78.

55 Romney, 46.

56 William Hayley, *The Life of George Romney, Esq.*, London, 1809, 40.

57 Horace Walpole, 'Notes by Horace Walpole, Fourth Earl of Orford, on the Exhibitions of the Society of Artists, 1760–1791', ed. Hugh Gatty, *Walpole Society*, 27, 1938–39, 77.

58 *George Romney*, 13.

59 Walpole, 'Notes by Horace Walpole', 77. The Italian Gaetano Manini, who enjoyed some vogue during his years in London, did not perhaps set the highest standard against which to be judged.

60 An awkward, full-length portrait of Wolfe in profile by J.S.C. Schaak, now in the National Army Museum, had been exhibited at the Society of Artists show in 1762.

61 *George Romney*, 13.

62 *Ibid.*

63 John Romney observed that his father's *Wolfe* had attracted great public interest, even though the wish to see portraits of the famous 'had been so recently gratified (1762) by the exhibition of Sir Joshua's admirable picture of Garrick between Tragedy and Comedy' (p. 47). See also *Joshua Reynolds: The Creation of Celebrity*, exhib. cat., ed. Martin Postle, Ferrara and London, 2005.

64 I am not sure on what basis Kidson states 'there is little doubt that it made a powerful influence on Romney's contemporaries and was a work of seminal importance'. *George Romney*, 13.

65 Solkin, *Painting for Money*, 207.

66 *Ibid.*

67 *Ibid.*, 209.

68 *Ibid.*, 208.

69 Walpole, 'Notes by Horace Walpole', 74.

70 Solkin, *Painting for Money*, 208.

71 Henry Mackenzie, *The Man of Feeling*, London, 1771, 181.

72 *Ibid.*, 265.

73 *Ibid.*, 266.

74 *Ibid.*, 262.

75 The issue of manly tears was on the Enlightenment agenda nearly a century before *Wolfe*. 'One may give way to one's feelings thus unrestrainedly without detriment to the strength of mind which should mark our sex;' the seventeenth-century French philosopher Pierre Bayle wrote, 'and since the mightiest heroes and the greatest saints have shed them, tears should not be looked on as a womanish display of weakness.' Quoted in Paul Hazard, *The Crisis of the European Mind, 1680–1715*, trans. J. Lewis May, New York, 2013, 375.

76 Rosenblum, 28.

77 *Ibid.*, 29.

78 Quoted in Parkman, 483.

79 Joseph Addison, *Cato: A Tragedy*, London, 1713, 53. George III's father, Frederick, Prince of Wales, was fond of amateur theatricals, and as a boy the future King had played the title role in *Cato*.

80 Grosley, vol. 1, 102–103. The Canadians to which Grosley refers were subsequently dropped from the design.

81 *Ibid.*, 103–104.

82 A prominent example of this time lag between painting and sculpture is Sir Richard Westmacott's statue of a toga-wearing Charles James Fox, erected in Bloomsbury Square in 1816.

83 Margaret Whinney, *Sculpture in Britain, 1530–1830*, rev. John Physick, London, 1988, 266.

84 Matthew Craske, *The Silent Rhetoric of the Body: A History of Monumental Sculpture and Commemorative Art in England, 1720–1770*, New Haven, Conn., and London, 2007, 183.

85 See, for example, John Dillenberger, *Benjamin West: The Context of His Life's Work, with Particular Attention to Paintings with Religious Subject Matter*, San Antonio, 1977, 36–44.

86 'These sculptures were taken from life, modeled on a Choctaw boy who had been captured by the British'. Stephanie Pratt, *American Indians in British Art, 1700–1840*, Norman, Okla., 2005, 46.

87 John Fleming, 'Robert Adam, Luc-François Breton and the Townshend Monument in Westminster Abbey,' *The Connoisseur*, 150, May–August 1962, 170.

88 Quoted *ibid.*, 169.

89 *Morning Post and Daily Advertiser*, 15 December 1773.

PALACE AND PRINT SHOP

1 Quoted in Jonathan G.W. Conlin, 'High Art and Low Politics: A New Perspective on John Wilkes', *Huntington Library Quarterly*, 64:3/4, 2001, 370.

2 John Harris, Geoffrey de Bellaigue and Oliver Millar, *Buckingham Palace*, London, 1968, 24.

3 I am grateful to Dr John Goodall, Architectural Editor of *Country Life*, for this information.

4 Mary Webster, *Johan Zoffany, 1733–1810*, New Haven, Conn., and London, 2011, 133–34.

5 Douglas Fordham speculates that *Wolfe* and *Agrippina* were planned at the same time – 1767 – by West, revealing 'a significant unity of purpose in the depiction of ancient and contemporary events'. It is an intriguing suggestion, for which I find no evidence. Fordham, 220.

6 Quoted in Galt, part 2, 25–26.

7 This innovation has created a deal of scholarly debate about which figure is actually Regulus: the departing man to the right, which would satisfy the demands of the narrative, or the bearded figure in the centre, whose prominence would accord with academic practice. In his autobiography, Charles Willson Peale wrote that 'he stood for Mr. West to paint the figure of Regulus'. Peale, 200. There is debate around which figure looks most like Peale. Von Erffa and Staley (p. 168) believe it is the central figure; I am convinced it is the man on the right.

8 Quoted in Christopher Lloyd, 'King, Queen and Family', in *George III and Queen Charlotte: Patronage, Collecting and Court Taste*, exhib. cat., ed. Jane Roberts, London, Queen's Gallery, 2004–05, 12.

9 Oliver Millar, *The Later Georgian Pictures in the Collection of Her Majesty the Queen*, London, 1969, text vol., 131. Millar attributes Livy's

Ab urbe condita as the source for *Hannibal* when it is more obviously *Punica*.

10 Silius Italicus, *Punica*, trans. J.D. Duff, London, 1961, vol. 1, book 1, 9–13.

11 'Perhaps may be reckoned among the best pictures in the world', according to *Observations on the Pictures Now in Exhibition at the Royal Academy*, 14.

12 Samuel Johnson, *The Yale Edition of the Works of Samuel Johnson. Volume 2: The Idler and The Adventurer*, ed. W.J. Bate, John M. Bullitt and L.F. Powell, New Haven, Conn, and London, 1963, 142.

13 *'Je suis mort, & ne veut pas dans mes derniers moments tourner le dos à l'ennemi pour la première fois de ma vie.'* M. Guyard de Berville, *Histoire de Pierre Terrail, dit le Chevalier Bayard, sans peur & sans reproche*, Paris, 1765, 432.

14 Jeremy Black, *George III: America's Last King*, New Haven, Conn., and London, 2006, 122.

15 *Diary of Joseph Farington*, vol. 6, 2480.

16 Quoted in William T. Whitley, *Art in England, 1800–1820*, Cambridge, 1928, 309.

17 Lloyd, 'King, Queen and Family', 16–17.

18 Waterhouse, *Painting in Britain*, 276.

19 John Brooke, *King George III*, New York, 1972.

20 David Watkin, *The Architect King: George III and the Culture of the Enlightenment*, London, 2004; *George III and Queen Charlotte: Patronage, Collecting and Court Taste*, exhib. cat., ed. Jane Roberts, London, Queen's Gallery, 2004–05.

21 Galt, part 2, 32–33.

22 John Brooke, 'The Library of King George III', *Yale University Library Gazette*, 52:1, July 1977, 38.

23 Quoted in Whitley, *Artists and Their Friends*, vol. 1, 260.

24 See note 8 above.

25 Jonathan Marsden, 'Patronage and Collecting', in *George III and Queen Charlotte*, 155.

26 Quoted in Peter Gay, ed., *The Enlightenment: A Comprehensive Anthology*, New York, 1973, 288.

27 West, 7.

28 Horace Walpole, 'Horace Walpole's Journals of Visits to Country Seats, &c.', ed. Paget Toynbee, *Walpole Society*, 16, 1927–28, 79.

29 Ronald Paulson, *Book and Painting: Shakespeare, Milton and the Bible: Literary Texts and the Emergence of English Painting*, Knoxville, Tenn., 1982, 3.

30 Watkin, 60.

31 Von Erffa and Staley, 206.

32 *Diary of Joseph Farington*, vol. 9, 3307.

33 Francis Russell, 'King George III's Picture Hang at Buckingham House', *Burlington Magazine*, 129:1013, August 1987, 525. I have digitally reconstructed the hang using the previously mislabelled measured plan of the Warm Room now in the Westminster City Archives.

34 Rosenblum, 68–70.

35 Conversely, the French thought of themselves as Romans and of the British as Carthaginians, perhaps most notably stated in the Abbé Seran de la Tour's *Parallèle de la conduite des Carthaginois, a l'égard des Romains, dans la seconde guerre punique, avec la conduite de l'Angleterre a l'égard de la France, dans la guerre déclarée par ces deux puissances, en 1756*, published in 1757. Nicholas Rowe, 'Romans and Carthaginians in the Eighteenth Century: Imperial Ideology and National Identity in Britain and France During the Seven Years' War', PhD thesis, Boston College, 1997.

36 This combination of fear and admiration is typical of the complex mix of emotions the British elite felt towards France. George III was the last British sovereign to be styled 'King of France'.

37 Quoted in Dunlap, vol. 1, 108.

38 Simon Schama, *Dead Certainties: Unwarranted Speculations*, New York, 1991.

39 'Proposals by Messrs Woollett, Boydell, and Ryland, for Publishing by Subscription, a Print, Representing the Death of General Wolfe', London, 1772.

40 Timothy Clayton, 'William Woollett', in *Oxford Dictionary of National Biography*, ed. H.C.G. Matthew and Brian Harrison, Oxford, 2004, vol. 60, 271.

41 Timothy Clayton, 'William Wynne Ryland', in *Oxford Dictionary of National Biography*, vol. 48, 474.

42 Quoted in Vivienne Painting, *John Boydell*, London, 2005, 8.

43 'Proposals'.

44 Quoted in Louis Fagan, *A Catalogue Raisonné of the Engraved Works of William Woollett*, London, 1885, xi.

45 Quoted in Timothy Clayton, *The English Print, 1688–1802*, New Haven, Conn., and London, 1997, 238–40.

46 *Ibid.*, 240.

47 Fagan, xi.

48 Louise Lippincott, 'Expanding on Portraiture: The Market, the Public, and the Hierarchy of Genres in Eighteenth-Century Britain', in *The Consumption of Culture, 1600–1800: Image, Object, Text*, ed. Ann Bermingham and John Brewer, London and New York, 1995, 79.

49 See, for example, Painting, 8; Lippincott, 79; Sven H.A. Bruntjen, *John Boydell, 1719–1804: A Study of Art Patronage and Publishing in Georgian London*, New York and London, 1985, 36.

50 Painting, 8.

51 Clayton in *The English Print* states that Boydell bought Ryland's share, but shows no evidence to support this (p. 240).

52 I have attempted to reflect Boydell's ever-increasing share with the formula $\frac{7}{3}x + \frac{3}{3}x + 6x = £15{,}000$, where x is Boydell's average

annual earning from the print. For Woollett, the similar formula is $\frac{7}{3}x + x = £6000$.

53 This re-engraving was highly controversial as Boydell kept Woollett's name on the newly engraved and inferior plate. In a letter written from 'the Banks of the Stygian Lake', a writer pretending to be the late Woollett admonished Boydell, 'who, by cruelly defacing the print of "The Death of General Wolfe," has destroyed forever the only monument desired by the injured'. Fagan, xii.

54 This figure is based on assuming an almost impossible-to-achieve profit margin of 83 per cent. A more realistic margin would further drive up the average price at which each print needed to be sold.

55 Clayton, *The English Print*, 14; Antony Griffiths, *Prints and Printmaking: An Introduction to the History and Techniques*, London, 1996, 38–39. Even this figure may be an overestimation. James Heath, an engraver of great skill if not quite equal to Woollett (although his *Death of Major Peirson*, after Copley, is one of the greatest British engravings of the century), told West that his plate of the *Death of Nelson* would be good for 1500 impressions. *Diary of Joseph Farington*, vol. 8, 2802.

56 *Boswell's London Journal*, 59–60.

57 André Rouquet, *The Present State of the Arts in England* [1755], London, 1970, 28.

58 'An Inventory of the Furniture, Paintings, Linnen, China, and Books of the Late George Henry Earl of Litchfield …', in *Noble Households: Eighteenth-Century Inventories of Great English Houses*, ed. Tessa Murdoch, Cambridge, 2006, 154–56.

59 Various attempts have been made to quantify this group, always hampered by lack of statistics. Most agree that we are dealing with the top 2–3 per cent of the metropolitan population. See, for example, Maxine Berg, *Luxury and Pleasure in Eighteenth-Century Britain*, Oxford, 2005, 207, and L.D. Schwarz, 'Income Distribution and Social Structure in London in the Late Eighteenth Century', *Economic History Review*, 32:2, May 1979, 250–59.

60 Lippincott, 77.

61 James Northcote, *The Life of Sir Joshua Reynolds*, London, 1819, vol. 1, 142–43.

62 John Barrell, *The Political Theory of Painting from Reynolds to Hazlitt: 'The Body of the Public'*, New Haven, Conn., and London, 1986, 50.

63 Quoted *ibid.*, 51.

64 Lippincott, 80.

65 *Ibid.*, 84.

66 Boydell went bankrupt, Valentine Green went bankrupt, Ryland went bankrupt and after a subsequent trial for forgery in 1783 became the last man to be hanged at Tyburn.

67 Valentine Green, *A Review of the Polite Arts in France, at the Time of Their Establishment under Louis the XIVth, Compared with Their Present State in England*, London, 1782, 65.

68 *Ibid.*, 50–51.

69 Quoted in Wainwright, 113.

70 Richard D. Altick, *The English Common Reader: A Social History of the Mass Reading Public, 1800–1900*, Chicago, 1957, 48.

71 Winifred H. Friedman, 'Some Commercial Aspects of the Boydell Shakespeare Gallery', *Journal of the Warburg and Courtauld Institutes*, 36, 1973, 397–98.

72 'The size of the audience must not be exaggerated', we are reminded by J.H. Plumb, 'The Commercialization of Leisure', in *The Birth of a Consumer Society: The Commercialization of Eighteenth-Century England*, ed. Neil McKendrick, John Brewer and J.H. Plumb, London, 1982, 270.

73 A further testimony to *Wolfe*'s popularity was the ease with which it was parodied. See, for example, James Gillray's *Death of the Great Wolf* (fig. 88).

74 C.P. Stacey, 'Benjamin West and "The Death of Wolfe"', *National Gallery of Canada Bulletin* 7, 4:1, 1966.

75 J. Clarence Webster, *Wolfe and the Artists: A Study of His Portraiture*, Toronto, 1930, 67.

76 I would fundamentally disagree with Sullivan's desire 'not to focus on West's innovations, but on his derivations' (p. 307).

77 Thomas Turner, *The Diary of Thomas Turner, 1754–1765*, ed. David Vaisey, Oxford and New York, 1984, 191.

78 It was sometimes rumoured that West included portraits only of those who had paid for the privilege: 'Doughty in his *Siege of Quebec* … states that John Hale, of the 47th Regiment, was asked to pay West £100 … but that he declined, with the result that he was omitted.' Webster, *Wolfe and the Artists*, 69. There seems to be only the scantiest evidence for this allegation.

79 Sarah Monks, 'The Wolfe Man: Benjamin West's Anglo-American Accent', *Art History*, 34:4, September 2011, 655–56.

80 *Ibid.*, 656.

81 Dennis Montagna, 'Benjamin West's *The Death of General Wolfe*: A Nationalist Narrative', *American Art Journal*, 13:2, Spring 1981, 88.

82 In July 1774, less than a year before the outbreak of hostilities, the leading Boston revolutionary Joseph Warren declared, 'Nothing is more foreign from our hearts than a spirit of rebellion. Would to God they all, even our enemies, knew the warm attachment we have for Great Britain.' Quoted in Nathaniel Philbrick, *Bunker Hill: A City, a Siege, a Revolution*, London, 2013, 55.

83 Wind, 'Revolution of History Painting', 117.

84 *Ibid.*, 118.

85 Indeed where marine painting – not a highly respected genre – had long gone, as successful naval officers fuelled demands for portrayals of their glorious and profitable victories. See Alan Russett, *Dominic Serres R.A., 1719–1793: War Artist to the Navy*, Woodbridge, 2001, and Nicholas Tracy, *Britannia's Palette: The Arts of Naval Victory*, Montreal and Kingston, 2007.

86 The allegorical depiction of the continents was 'an eighteenth-century trope, one of the images one most expected to see in any picture gallery or on the walls of a grand house or palace'. Dorinda Outram, *Panorama of the Enlightenment*, London, 2006, 142.

87 Bromley, vol. 1, 57.

88 Pratt, 74.

89 Vivien Green Fryd, 'Rereading the Indian in Benjamin West's "Death of General Wolfe"', *American Art*, 9:1, Spring 1995, 82.

90 *Ibid.*, 84.

91 Pratt, 87.

92 In the 1770s the 'inevitable destruction' of Native Americans was by no means obvious. The Indians remained a considerable military force for some decades: 'During the 1780s and 1790s, and again in the first decade of the nineteenth century, multi-tribal coalitions stalled American advance into the West and mounted formidable opposition to American expansion'. Colin G. Calloway, *The Scratch of a Pen: 1763 and the Transformation of North America*, New York, 2006, 169.

93 Fryd, 84.

94 'At the same time, the enforced separation between modern warriors leaves Monckton unable to cry out and cradle his fallen friend. Eighteenth-century decorum, at least in the suppression of same-sex love, made West's scene all the more heart wrenching.' Fordham, 221–23.

95 Martin Myrone, *Bodybuilding: Reforming Masculinities in British Art, 1750–1810*, New Haven, Conn., and London, 2005, 119.

96 Linda Colley, *Britons: Forging the Nation, 1707–1837*, New Haven, Conn., and London, 2005, 178.

97 Quoted in Walter Benjamin, *The Work of Art in the Age of Mechanical Reproduction* [1936], trans. J.A. Underwood, London, 2008, 48.

BEING MODERN FROM *WOLFE* TO *WHAAM!*

1 Adams, *Revolutionary Writings. Volume 2: 1775–1783*, 596.

2 Quoted in Wendell D. Garrett, 'John Adams and the Limited Role of the Fine Arts', *Winterthur Portfolio*, 1, 1964, 244.

3 A.P., *The Modern Englishman: A Satire*, London, 1739, 1.

4 Quoted in Garrett, 251.

5 West, 8.

6 Quoted in Garrett, 255.

7 Fulton and Morse also figure among the names of the twenty-three most important people in American history on the obverse of the 1896 $1 bill, with its engraving of Will Low's allegory *History Instructing Youth*.

8 Quoted in Charles Henry Hart, 'Autobiographical Notes of Matthew Pratt, Painter', *Pennsylvania Magazine of History and Biography*, 19:4, 1895, 462.

9 Thomas Sully, *Memoirs of the Professional Life of Thomas Sully*, Philadelphia, 1851, 5.

10 For collective discussion of West's students, see James Thomas Flexner, 'The American School in London', *Metropolitan Museum of Art Bulletin*, New Series, 7:2, October 1948, or the more substantial and well-considered *Benjamin West and His American Students*, exhib. cat. by Dorinda Evans, Washington, D.C., and Philadelphia, 1980–81.

11 Benjamin, 5.

12 Quoted in Alberts, 263.

13 The elder Morse was the author of a series of best-selling geographies, beginning with *Geography Made Easy* in 1784.

14 Samuel F.B. Morse, *Lectures on the Affinity of Painting with the Other Fine Arts* [1826–32], ed. Nicolai Cikovsky Jr, Columbia, Mo., and London, 1983, 60.

15 'How shall our attention be engaged by a picture representing a peasant

driving a couple of beasts along the highway, if the very action which this picture imitates, has no power of affecting us?' Dubos, vol. 1, 44.

16 T.J. Clark, *The Painting of Modern Life: Paris in the Art of Manet and His Followers*, London, 1990, 10. In the same spirit are Guy Cogeval, 'Manet: The Return', in *Manet, the Man Who Invented Modernity*, exhib. cat., ed. Stéphane Guégan, Paris, Musée d'Orsay, 2011, and Stéphane Guégan, 'Théophile Gautier, Militant of Modernity', in *Manet: Portraying Life*, exhib. cat., Toledo and London, 2012–13.

17 Ludmilla Jordanova, *The Look of the Past: Visual and Material Evidence in Historical Practice*, Cambridge, 2012, 114–15.

18 '*Je vois les Anciens sans ployer les genoux/ Ils sont grands, il est vrai, mais hommes comme nous;/ Et l'on peut comparer sans crainte d'être injuste/ Le siècle de Louis au beau siècle d'Auguste*.' Quoted in Hélène Tronc, 'Vie littéraire: la naissance du conte de fées littéraire', in Charles Perrault, *Contes de ma Mère l'Oye*, Paris, 2006, 183.

19 C.A. Bayly, *The Birth of the Modern World, 1780–1914*, Oxford, 2004, 9.

20 *Ibid.*, 10

21 Foucault, 'What is Enlightenment?', 39.

22 Christopher D.M. Atkins, *The Signature Style of Frans Hals: Painting, Subjectivity, and the Market in Early Modernity*, Amsterdam, 2012, 195.

23 What came to be known as the 'Realist Manifesto' was Courbet's introduction to the catalogue of his solo exhibition of 1855. Quoted in 'Courbet Speaks', musée-orsay.fr/en/collections/courbet-dossier/courbet-speaks.html (accessed January 2015).

24 Foucault, 'What is Enlightenment?', 40.

25 Charles Baudelaire, *The Painter of Modern Life* [1863], trans. P.E. Charvet, London, 2010, 2.

26 Joseph Warton, *An Essay on the Writings and Genius of Pope*, London, 1756, 276–77.

27 Joseph Addison, *A Discourse on Ancient and Modern Learning*, Glasgow, 1759, 15.

28 Arthur Young, *Annals of Agriculture, and Other Useful Arts*, Bury St Edmunds, 1791, vol. 16, 546.

29 Robert Fulton, *A Treatise on the Improvement of Canal Navigation*, London, 1796, ix.

30 J.H. Plumb, 'The Acceptance of Modernity', in *Birth of a Consumer Society*, 316.

31 *Ibid.*, 328.

32 R.H. Tawney, *Religion and the Rise of Capitalism: A Historical Study*, London, 1926, 430.

33 See, for example, Richard Holmes, *The Age of Wonder: How the Romantic Generation Discovered the Beauty and Terror of Science*, London, 2008.

34 Quoted in Reinhart Koselleck, *Futures Past: On the Semantics of Historical Time*, trans. Keith Tribe, New York, 2004, 22.

35 With the notable exception of that master procrastinator Gilbert Stuart.

36 'Memorandum of a Conversation with the Late Benjamin West, Esq.', *Morning Chronicle*, 19 September 1821.

37 Marshall Berman, *All That is Solid Melts into Air: The Experience of Modernity*, London and New York, 2010, 21.

38 Kant, 10.

39 Koselleck, 48.

40 F.W. Botham and E.H. Hunt, 'Wages in Britain During the Industrial Revolution', *Economic History Review*, 40:3, August 1987, 380.

41 Karl Marx, *The Eighteenth Brumaire of Louis Bonaparte* [1852], in *Karl Marx: Selected Writings*, ed. David McLellan, Oxford 2000, 329.

42 *Ibid.*, 330.

43 West, 7.

44 Philadelphia, Pennsylvania Academy of the Fine Arts, Archives, Object file, *William Penn's Treaty with the Indians*.

45 West, 9.

46 Shunning the near-baroque dynamism of *Wolfe*, *Penn's Treaty* defers to Neoclassical calm with references to both the Ara Pacis and Mengs's *Parnassus*.

47 Ellen Starr Brinton, 'Benjamin West's Painting of Penn's Treaty with the Indians', *Bulletin of Friends' Historical Association*, 30:2, Autumn 1941, 99–100.

48 West to W. Darton, 2 February 1805. Historical Society of Pennsylvania, Galt extra-illustrated, 3239.

49 Quoted in Jules David Prown, 'John Trumbull as History Painter', in *John Trumbull: The Hand and Spirit of a Painter*, exhib. cat., ed. Helen A. Cooper, New Haven, Conn., Yale University Art Gallery, 1982–83, 29.

50 These negotiations prepared the ground for the 1783 Treaty of Paris, which formally ended the American Revolution.

51 Quoted in von Erffa and Staley, 219.

52 Quoted in Allen Guttmann, 'Copley, Peale, Trumbull: A Note on Loyalty', *American Quarterly*, 11:2: part 1, Summer 1959, 180.

53 *John Trumbull*, 76–78.

54 This problem had engaged Leonardo some three centuries earlier: 'Leonardo distinguished between two kinds of subject matter: on the one hand, facts or actions (*fatti*); and on the other, words and mental activity (*parole, operationi della mente*).' Sixten Ringbom, 'Action and Report: The Problem of Indirect Narration in the Academic Theory of Painting', *Journal of the Warburg and Courtauld Institutes*, 52, 1989, 34.

55 Joseph Rodman Drake, 'The National Paintings: Colonel

Trumbull's "The Declaration of Independence"' [1819], bartleby.com/248/69.html (accessed January 2015).

56 Quoted in Guttmann, 180.

57 In spite of the picture's title, Chatham did not die in the House of Lords, but at home on 11 May, a month after his 'death' as painted by Copley.

58 Jules David Prown, *John Singleton Copley: In England, 1774–1815*, Cambridge, Mass., 1966, 279.

59 In its issue of 8 June 1781, *The Morning Chronicle and London Advertiser* reported that Copley's exhibition of *Chatham* 'has been visited already by nearly twenty thousand persons'. The engraving had a troubled history and was not published until 1791. *Ibid*., 284, 289–91.

60 Holger Hoock, *Empires of the Imagination: Politics, War, and the Arts in the British World, 1750–1850*, London, 2010, 93. If we are looking for earlier examples of the marriage of 'historical reportage with political journalism', we can find a splendid one in Hogarth's *Gaols Committee of the House of Commons* (fig. 101).

61 While his life was saved, Watson lost his lower right leg in the attack. The severed limb is depicted on his coat of arms.

62 *Morning Post and Daily Advertiser*, 25 April 1778.

63 *St James's Chronicle or the British Evening Post*, 25 April 1778.

64 Prown, *John Singleton Copley*, 273. See also Irma B. Jaffe, 'John Singleton Copley's "Watson and the Shark"', *American Art Journal*, 9:1, May 1977, 15–25. Martin Kemp suggests that Watson's pose is derived from Titian's woodcut of 1549 *The Submersion of Pharoah's Army in the Red Sea*. Martin Kemp, letter to the Editor, *Art Bulletin*, 62:4, December 1980, 647.

65 *Watson*'s influence on Géricault's *Raft of the Medusa* (fig. 109) is perhaps underappreciated. There are too many conceptual and compositional similarities to be coincidental, and Valentine Green's engraving of *Watson* was well distributed on the Continent. Waterhouse (*Painting in Britain*, p. 279) was a strong advocate of Copley's influence on Géricault; Lorenz Eitner (*Géricault's Raft of the Medusa*, London, 1972, 47) was not.

66 Quoted in Ellen G. Miles, *American Paintings of the Eighteenth Century*, Washington, D.C., 1995, 58.

67 For example, Albert Boime writes in 'Blacks in Shark-Infested Waters: Visual Encodings of Racism in Copley and Homer', *Smithsonian Studies in American Art*, 3:1, Winter 1989, 34, 'The colonies are shown metaphorically as shark-infested waters – dangerous breeding ground for revolutionary ideas that threaten the youth of the New World.' It is to me an unusually weak metaphor that can be understood only two hundred years after the fact: no contemporaries remarked on the political message of *Watson*. Geoff Quilley has rounded up a number of interpretations of *Watson* in 'Questions of Loyalty: The Representation of the British West Indian Colonies During the American Revolutionary War', in *Conflicting Visions: War and Visual Culture in Britain and France, c. 1700–1830*, ed. John Bonehill and Geoff Quilley, Aldershot, 2005. See also *John Singleton Copley in England*, exhib. cat. by Emily Ballew Neff, Washington, D.C., and Houston, Tex., 1995–96, 104.

68 Sigmund Freud, *Civilization and Its Discontents* [1930], trans. David McLintock, London, 2002, 50–51.

69 Prown suggests that possibly 'the influence was not at least mutual'. Prown, *John Singleton Copley*, 274.

70 Quoted in Oskar Bätschmann, *The Artist in the Modern World: The Conflict Between Market and Self-Expression*, Cologne, 1997, 9.

71 West, 9.

72 'Skeleton of the Mammoth is Now to be Seen', American Philosophical Society, Collection of Broadsides, 973.C683.

73 Peale to West, 16 December 1807, Historical Society of Pennsylvania, Dreer Collection, vol. 5: Painters and Engravers.

74 David R. Brigham, *Public Culture in the Early Republic: Peale's Museum and Its Audience*, Washington, D.C., and London, 1995, 38.

75 Lillian B. Miller, 'Charles Willson Peale as History Painter: *The Exhumation of the Mastadon*', in *New Perspectives on Charles Willson Peale: A 250th Anniversary Celebration*, ed. Lillian B. Miller and David C. Ward, Pittsburgh, 1991, 151.

76 West also tried, and failed, to do so with his allegorical portrait *Benjamin Franklin* (fig. 112), featuring Franklin's experiment of 1752 that proved the electrical nature of lightning. The heroic effect is somewhat marred by West's decision to have Franklin attended by a retinue of putti playing with electrical apparatus.

77 Morse to Lucretia Walker Morse, 23 December 1821, Washington, D.C., Library of Congress, Samuel F.B. Morse Papers, General Correspondence and Related Documents, Bound Volume, 24 January 1821 – 8 December 1823, memory.loc.gov/ammem/sfbmhtml, Image 123 (accessed January 2015).

78 Quoted in Paul J. Staiti, *Samuel F.B. Morse*, Cambridge, 1989, 89.

79 Quoted in William Kloss, *Samuel F.B. Morse*, New York, 1988, 72.

80 'But in Morse's case, in the America of the 1820s and 1830s, the distance between theory and practice was so great and signified

a misalignment of the artist with his times so profound and so irresolvable that it finally drove him from art to science', writes Nicolai Cikovsky Jr in his introduction to Morse, *Lectures on the Affinity of Painting*, 29.

81 Du Fresnoy, 15.

82 Staiti, 90.

83 *Ibid.*, 91.

84 *Ibid.*, 95.

85 In 1836 Morse campaigned unsuccessfully to be Mayor of New York as the candidate of the anti-Catholic, anti-immigrant Native American party.

86 Samuel F.B. Morse, *Academies of Arts: A Discourse, Delivered on Thursday, May 3, 1827*, New York, 1827, 24–25.

87 Quoted in David H. Solkin, *Painting Out of the Ordinary: Modernity and the Art of Everyday Life in Early Nineteenth-Century Britain*, New Haven, Conn., and London, 2008, 37.

88 *Ibid.*, 241.

BIBLIOGRAPHY

MANUSCRIPT SOURCES AND UNPUBLISHED MATERIALS

LONDON, BRITISH MUSEUM, DEPARTMENT OF PRINTS AND DRAWINGS

1865-6-10-1327 L.B. 23.

1865-6-10-1353 L.B. 24 (b).

LONDON, ROYAL ACADEMY OF ARTS, LIBRARY AND ARCHIVE

Accounts of the Exhibitions at the Royal Academy 1769–1772, RAA/TRE/13/1.

Benjamin West Sketchbooks, 07/5053, 07/5054, 07/5055.

Minutes of the Council of the Royal Academy, vol. 1. RAA/PC/1/1.

Royal Academy Critiques 1769–1793.

LONDON, ROYAL COLLECTION TRUST, ARCHIVES

Painters file in the Surveyor's Office, Benjamin West, *The Death of General Wolfe.*

LONDON, SOCIETY OF ANTIQUARIES OF LONDON, LIBRARY

Minute Book of the Society of Antiquaries of London, vol. 8.

LONDON, VICTORIA AND ALBERT MUSEUM, NATIONAL ART LIBRARY

Press Cuttings from English Newspapers on Matters of Artistic Interest, 1686–1835, vol. 1.

LONDON, WESTMINSTER CITY ARCHIVES

Gardner Collection, Box 39.

NEW HAVEN, CONNECTICUT, YALE UNIVERSITY LIBRARY, MANUSCRIPTS AND ARCHIVES

John Trumbull papers, MS 506.

NEW YORK, FORDHAM UNIVERSITY LIBRARY

Charles Allen Munn Collection, Benjamin West, Manuscript Autobiography, Part 2, Box 7, Item 45.

NEW YORK, THE MORGAN LIBRARY AND MUSEUM, DEPARTMENT OF DRAWINGS AND PRINTS

Benjamin West drawings.

OTTAWA, NATIONAL GALLERY OF CANADA, LIBRARY AND ARCHIVES

Curatorial file, *The Death of General Wolfe.*

PHILADELPHIA, AMERICAN PHILOSOPHICAL SOCIETY

Collection of Broadsides, 973.C683.

Hare Papers, BH22.

PHILADELPHIA, HISTORICAL SOCIETY OF PENNSYLVANIA

Benjamin Smith Barton Papers, 0034.

Ferdinand J. Dreer Autograph Collection, vol. 5: Painters and Engravers.

The Life, Studies and Works of Benjamin West Esq., by John Galt in extra-illustrated form, 3239.

Titian Ramsay Peale collection of papers related to the Columbianum and the Pennsylvania Academy of Fine Arts 1794–1808, Am. 351.

PHILADELPHIA, PENNSYLVANIA ACADEMY OF THE FINE ARTS, ARCHIVES

Object file, *William Penn's Treaty with the Indians.*

SWARTHMORE, PENNSYLVANIA, FRIENDS HISTORICAL LIBRARY

Biographical and Genealogical Documents, PG7.

Mrs. Benjamin West, Household Account Book, 1785–1789, Mss001/057.

WASHINGTON, D.C., LIBRARY OF CONGRESS

Samuel F.B. Morse Papers, General Correspondence and Related Documents, Bound Volume, 24 January 1821 – 8 December 1823, memory.loc.gov/ammem/sfbmhtml, Image 123 (accessed January 2015).

NEWSPAPERS

The Gazetteer

General Advertiser

General Evening Post

London Gazette

Middlesex Journal or Chronicle of Liberty

Morning Chronicle and London Advertiser

Morning Post and Daily Advertiser

New York Gazette

Public Advertiser

St James's Chronicle or the British Evening Post

Whitehall Evening Post or London Intelligencer

BOOKS, CATALOGUES, PAMPHLETS, PERIODICALS AND OTHER PRINTED SOURCES

A.P. *The Modern Englishman: A Satire*, London, 1739.

Abrams, Ann Uhry. 'A New Light on Benjamin West's Pennsylvania Instruction', *Winterthur Portfolio*, 17:4, Winter 1982.

——. *The Valiant Hero: Benjamin West and Grand-Style History Painting*, Washington, D.C., 1985.

Adams, Henry. *The Education of Henry Adams* [1918], ed. Ira B. Nadel, Oxford, 1999.

Adams, John. *Revolutionary Writings*, ed. Gordon Wood, New York, 2011.

Addison, Joseph. *Cato: A Tragedy*, London, 1713.

——. *A Discourse on Ancient and Modern Learning*, Glasgow, 1759.

The Age of Neo-Classicism, exhib. cat., London, Royal Academy of Arts, and Victoria and Albert Museum, 1972.

Akenside, Mark. *The Pleasures of Imagination*, London, 1754.

Alberti, Leon Battista. *On Painting* [1435–36], trans. John R. Spencer, London, 1956.

Alberts, Robert C. *Benjamin West: A Biography*, Boston, 1978.

Alderfer, E. Gordon. 'James Logan: The Political Career of a Colonial Scholar', *Pennsylvania History*, 24:1, January 1957.

Allard, Joseph. 'West, Copley, and Eighteenth-Century American Provincialism', *Journal of American Studies*, 17:3, December 1983.

Altick, Richard D. *The English Common Reader: A Social History of the Mass Reading Public, 1800–1900*, Chicago, 1957.

American Art, 1750–1800: Towards Independence, exhib. cat., ed. Charles F. Montgomery and Patricia E. Kane, New Haven, Conn., and London, 1976.

American Magazine and Monthly Chronicle for the British Colonies, Philadelphia, 1758.

American Stories: Paintings of Everyday Life, 1765–1915, exhib. cat., ed. H. Barbara Weinberg and Carrie Rebora Barratt, New York and Los Angeles, 2009–10.

Anderson, Fred. *Crucible of War: The Seven Years' War and the Fate of Empire in British North America, 1754–1766*, London, 2000.

Andrews, William D. 'William Smith and the Rising Glory of America', *Early American Literature*, 8:1, Spring 1973.

Angelo, Henry. *Reminiscences of Henry Angelo*, London, 1830.

Art in Rome in the Eighteenth Century, exhib. cat., ed. Edgar Peters Bowron and Joseph J. Rishel, Philadelphia and Houston, Tex., 2000.

Atkins, Christopher D.M. *The Signature Style of Frans Hals: Painting, Subjectivity, and the Market in Early Modernity*, Amsterdam, 2012.

Auerbach, Erich. 'Vico and Aesthetic Historism', *Journal of Aesthetics and Art Criticism*, 8:2, December 1949.

Baretti, Joseph. *An Account of the Manners and Customs of Italy*, London, 1769.

Barker, Hannah. *Newspapers, Politics and English Society, 1695–1855*, Harlow, 2000.

Barker, Virgil. *American Painting: History and Interpretation*, New York, 1951.

Barlow, Joel. *The Columbiad: A Poem*, London, 1809.

——. *Life and Letters of Joel Barlow: Poet, Statesman, Philosopher*, ed. Charles Burr Todd, New York and London, 1886.

Barolsky, Paul. *A Brief History of the Artist from God to Picasso*, University Park, Pa., 2010.

Barone, Dennis. 'An Introduction to William Smith and Rhetoric at the College of Philadelphia', *Proceedings of the American Philosophical Society*, 134:2, June 1990.

Barrell, John. *The Political Theory of Painting from Reynolds to Hazlitt: 'The Body of the Public'*, New Haven, Conn., and London, 1986.

James Barry, 1741–1806: The Great Historical Painter, exhib. cat., ed. Tom Dunne, Cork, Crawford Art Gallery, 2005–06.

Bassett, Edward L. 'Silius Italicus in England', *Classical Philology*, 48:3, July 1953.

Bate, Walter Jackson. *From Classic to Romantic: Premises of Taste in Eighteenth-Century England*, Cambridge, Mass., 1946.

Bätschmann, Oskar. *The Artist in the Modern World: The Conflict Between Market and Self-Expression*, Cologne, 1997.

Baudelaire, Charles. *The Painter of Modern Life* [1863], trans. P.E. Charvet, London, 2010.

Baudot, Laura. 'An Air of History: Joseph Wright's and Robert Boyle's Air Pump Narratives', *Eighteenth-Century Studies*, 46:1, Fall 2012.

Baxandall, Michael. *Patterns of Intention: On the Historical Explanation of Pictures*, New Haven, Conn., and London, 1985.

——. *Words for Pictures: Seven Papers on Renaissance Art and Criticism*, New Haven, Conn., and London, 2003.

Bayly, C.A. *The Birth of the Modern World, 1780–1914*, Oxford, 2004.

Beattie, James. *Essays on the Nature and Immutability of* TRUTH, *in Opposition to Sophistry and Scepticism*, Edinburgh, 1776.

Belanger, Terry. 'Publishers and Writers in Eighteenth-Century England', in *Books and Their Readers in Eighteenth-Century England*, ed. Isabel Rivers, Leicester, 1982.

Belting, Hans. *The Invisible Masterpiece*, trans. Helen Atkins, London, 2001.

Benjamin, Walter. *The Work of Art in the Age of Mechanical Reproduction* [1936], trans. J.A. Underwood, London, 2008.

'Benjamin West Esq. President of the Royal Academy', *La Belle Assemblée; or, Bell's Court and Fashionable Magazine*, 27, January 1808; 28, February 1808; 30, April 1808; 31, May 1808.

Berg, Maxine. *Luxury and Pleasure in Eighteenth-Century Britain*, Oxford, 2005.

Berman, Marshall. *All That is Solid Melts into Air: The Experience of Modernity*, London and New York, 2010.

Berry, Helen. 'Polite Consumption: Shopping in Eighteenth-Century England', *Transactions of the Royal Historical Society*, Sixth Series, 12, 2002.

Bickham, Troy O. 'Sympathizing with Sedition? George Washington, the British Press, and British Attitudes During the American War of Independence', *William and Mary Quarterly*, Third Series, 59:1, January 2002.

Bignamini, Ilaria, and Clare Hornsby. *Digging and Dealing in Eighteenth-Century Rome*, New Haven, Conn., and London, 2010.

Bindman, David, and Malcolm Baker. *Roubiliac and the Eighteenth-Century Monument: Sculpture as Theatre*, New Haven, Conn., and London, 1995.

'Biographical Sketch of William Henry, of Lancaster County, Pennsylvania', *Pennsylvania Magazine of History and Biography*, 27:1, 1903.

Black, Jeremy. *The English Press, 1621–1861*, Stroud, 2001.

——. *The English Press in the Eighteenth Century*, London, 1987.

——. *George III: America's Last King*, New Haven, Conn., and London, 2006.

Blacklock, Rev. Mr. *A Collection of Original Poems*, Edinburgh, 1760.

Blair, Hugh. *Lectures on Rhetoric and Belles Lettres* [1783], London, 1817.

Blanning, T.C.W. *The Culture of Power and the Power of Culture: Old Regime Europe, 1660–1789*, Oxford, 2002.

——. *The Romantic Revolution*, London, 2010.

Blondel, François. *Cours d'architecture*, Paris, 1675.

Boime, Albert. 'Blacks in Shark-Infested Waters: Visual Encodings of Racism in Copley and Homer', *Smithsonian Studies in American Art*, 3:1, Winter 1989.

Bolingbroke, Henry St John, Viscount. *Letters on the Study and Use of History*, London, 1752.

Bordes, Philippe. 'Jacques-Louis David's Anglophilia on the Eve of the French Revolution', *Burlington Magazine*, 134:1073, August 1992.

Boswell, James. *Boswell's Column*, ed. Margery Bailey, London, 1951.

——. *Boswell's London Journal, 1762–1763*, ed. Frederick A. Pottle, London, 1950.

Botham, F.W., and E.H. Hunt. 'Wages in Britain During the Industrial Revolution', *Economic History Review*, 40:3, August 1987.

Brewer, John. *The Pleasures of the Imagination: English Culture in the Eighteenth Century*, London, 1997.

——. *The Sinews of Power: War, Money and the English State, 1688–1783*, Cambridge, Mass., 1990.

Brigham, David R. *Public Culture in the Early Republic: Peale's Museum and Its Audience*, Washington, D.C., and London, 1995.

Brinton, Ellen Starr. 'Benjamin West's Painting of Penn's Treaty with the Indians', *Bulletin of Friends' Historical Association*, 30:2, Autumn 1941.

British Drawings from the National Gallery of Canada, exhib. cat. by Douglas E. Schoenherr, Ottawa and travelling, 2005–08.

Bromley, Robert Anthony. *A Philosophical and Critical History of the Fine Arts*, London, 1793–95.

Brooke, John. *King George III*, New York, 1972.

——. 'The Library of King George III', *Yale University Library Gazette*, 52:1, July 1977.

Brooks, John. *Marlborough House: Royal Palace and International Headquarters of the Commonwealth*, Norwich, 2002.

Brown, Roy Howard. 'The Formation of Delacroix's Hero Between 1822 and 1831', *Art Bulletin*, 66:2, June 1984.

Brownell, Morris R. *Samuel Johnson's Attitude to the Arts*, Oxford, 1989.

Brumwell, Stephen. *Paths of Glory: The Life and Death of General James Wolfe*, London, 2006.

Bruntjen, Sven H.A. *John Boydell, 1719–1804: A Study of Art Patronage and Publishing in Georgian London*, New York and London, 1985.

Burke, Peter. *The Fabrication of Louis XIV*, New Haven, Conn., and London, 1992.

Burrow, John. *A History of Histories: Epics, Chronicles, Romances and Inquiries from Herodotus and Thucydides to the Twentieth Century*, London, 2007.

Caffey, Stephen Mark. 'An Heroics of Empire: Benjamin West and Anglophone History Painting, 1764–1774', PhD thesis, University of Texas at Austin, 2008.

Caldwell, John, and Oswaldo Rodriguez Roque. *American Paintings in the Metropolitan Museum of Art. Volume 1: A Catalogue of Works by Artists Born by 1815*, New York, 1994.

Calloway, Colin G. *The Scratch of a Pen: 1763 and the Transformation of North America*, New York, 2006.

Carey, William. *Brief Remarks on the Anti-British Effect of Inconsiderate Criticism on Modern Art and the Exhibitions of the Living British Artists*, London, 1831.

——. *Critical Description and Analytical Review of 'Death on the Pale Horse', Painted by Benjamin West P.R.A.*, London, 1817.

Carlton, Charles. *The Seat of Mars: War and the British Isles, 1485–1746*, New Haven, Conn., and London, 2011.

Cassidy, Brendan. *The Life & Letters of Gavin Hamilton (1723–1798): Artist & Dealer in Eighteenth-Century Rome*, London and Turnhout, 2011.

A Catalogue of Books Belonging to the Library Company of Philadelphia, Philadelphia, 1741.

Catalogue of the Last Part of the Superb Collection of Drawings, Prints and Books of Prints Formed by the Late Benjamin West, London, 1820.

Champion, Judah. *Two Sermons Delivered at Litchfield on the General Fast, April 18, 1770*, Hartford, 1770.

Charlton, John. *Marlborough House*, London, 1962.

Clark, Anthony M. 'The Development of the Collections and Museums of 18th Century Rome', *Art Journal*, 26:2, Winter 1966–67.

——. *Pompeo Batoni: A Complete Catalogue of His Works with an Introductory Text*, ed. Edgar Peters Bowron, Oxford, 1985.

Clark, T.J. 'Gross David with the Swoln Cheek: An Essay on Self-Portraiture', in *Rediscovering History: Culture, Politics, and the Psyche*, ed. Michael S. Roth, Stanford, Calif., 1994.

——. *The Painting of Modern Life: Paris in the Art of Manet and His Followers*, London, 1990.

Clayton, Timothy. *The English Print, 1688–1802*, New Haven, Conn., and London, 1997.

——. 'William Woollett', in *Oxford Dictionary of National Biography*, ed. H.C.G. Matthew and Brian Harrison, vol. 60, Oxford, 2004.

——. 'William Wynne Ryland', in *Oxford Dictionary of National Biography*, ed. H.C.G. Matthew and Brian Harrison, vol. 48, Oxford, 2004.

Cockings, George. *The Conquest of Canada; or, the Siege of Quebec*, London, 1773.

Cogeval, Guy. 'Manet: The Return', in *Manet, the Man Who Invented Modernity*, exhib. cat., ed. Stéphane Guégan, Paris, Musée d'Orsay, 2011.

Coke, David, and Alan Borg. *Vauxhall Gardens: A History*, New Haven, Conn., and London, 2011.

Colley, Linda. *Britons: Forging the Nation, 1707–1837*, New Haven, Conn., and London, 2005.

Collingwood, R.G. *The Idea of History*, Oxford, 2005.

Coltman, Viccy. *Fabricating the Antique: Neoclassicism in Britain, 1760–1800*, Chicago and London, 2006.

Conlin, Jonathan G.W. 'High Art and Low Politics: A New Perspective on John Wilkes', *Huntington Library Quarterly*, 64:3/4, 2001.

Constable to Delacroix: British Art and the French Romantics, exhib. cat. by Patrick Noon, London, Minneapolis and New York, 2002–03.

Conway, Stephen. 'From Fellow-Nationals to Foreigners: British Perceptions of the Americans, circa 1739–1783', *William and Mary Quarterly*, Third Series, 59:1, January 2002.

Cooper, Myles. *Poems on Several Occasions*, Oxford, 1761.

John Singleton Copley in England, exhib. cat. by Emily Ballew Neff, Washington, D.C., and Houston, Tex., 1995–96.

Courbet, Gustave. 'Courbet Speaks', musée-orsay.fr/en/collections/courbet-dossier/courbet-speaks.html (accessed January 2015).

Coutu, Joan. *Persuasion and Propaganda: Monuments and the Eighteenth-Century British Empire*, Montreal and Kingston, 2006.

Couturier, Sonia. *French Drawings from the National Gallery of Canada*, Ottawa, 2004.

Cowie, Alexander. 'John Trumbull as Revolutionist', *American Literature*, 3:3, November 1931.

Craske, Matthew. *Art in Europe, 1700–1830: A History of the Visual Arts in an Era of Unprecedented Urban Economic Growth*, Oxford, 1997.

——. *The Silent Rhetoric of the Body: A History of Monumental Sculpture and Commemorative Art in England, 1720–1770*, New Haven, Conn., and London, 2007.

Craven, Wayne. 'The Grand Manner in Early Nineteenth-Century American Painting: Borrowings from Antiquity, the Renaissance, and the Baroque', *American Art Journal*, 11:2, April 1979.

——. 'John Wollaston: His Career in England and New York City', *American Art Journal*, 7:2, November 1975.

Croft-Murray, Edward. *Decorative Painting in England, 1537–1837*, London, 1962.

Cross, David A. *A Striking Likeness: The Life of George Romney*, Aldershot, 2000.

Crow, Thomas E. *Emulation: David, Drouais, and Girodet in the Art of Revolutionary France*, New Haven, Conn., and London, 2006.

——. *Painters and Public Life in Eighteenth-Century Paris*, New Haven, Conn., and London, 1985.

Crowley, John E. *Imperial Landscapes: Britain's Global Visual Culture, 1745–1820*, New Haven, Conn., and London, 2011.

Cumberland, Richard. *Memoirs of Richard Cumberland*, London, 1806.

Nathaniel Dance, 1735–1811, exhib. cat., intro David Goodreau, London, Kenwood House, 1977.

Davis, John. 'The End of the American Century: Current Scholarship on the Art of the United States', *Art Bulletin*, 85:3, September 2003.

De Lancey, Edward F. 'Chief Justice William Allen', *Pennsylvania Magazine of History and Biography*, 1:2, 1877.

De Marly, Diana. 'The Establishment of Roman Dress in Seventeenth-Century Portraiture', *Burlington Magazine*, 117:868, July 1975.

De Vries, Jan. *The Industrious Revolution: Consumer Behavior and the Household Economy, 1650 to the Present*, Cambridge, 2008.

DeLorme, Eleanor Pearson. 'Gilbert Stuart: Portrait of an Artist', *Winterthur Portfolio*, 14:4, Winter 1979.

Dickason, David H. 'Benjamin West on William Williams: A Previously Unpublished Letter', *Winterthur Portfolio*, 6, 1970.

Dickson, Harold E. 'Artists as Showmen', *American Art Journal*, 5:1, May 1973.

Diderot, Denis. *Diderot on Art*, ed. / trans. John Goodman, New Haven, Conn., and London, 1995.

Dillenberger, John. *Benjamin West: The Context of His Life's Work, with Particular Attention to Paintings with Religious Subject Matter*, San Antonio, 1977.

Douglass, William. *A Summary, Historical and Political, of the First Planting, Progressive Improvements, and Present State of the British Settlements in North-America*, Boston, 1750.

Drake, Joseph Rodman. 'The National Paintings: Colonel Trumbull's "The Declaration of Independence"' [1819], bartleby.com / 248 / 69.html (accessed January 2015).

Du Fresnoy, Charles-Alphonse. *The Art of Painting*, trans. John Dryden, London, 1716.

Dubos, Abbé [Jean-Baptiste]. *Critical Reflections on Poetry, Painting and Music*, trans. Thomas Nugent, London, 1748.

Duffy, Michael H. 'West's *Agrippina, Wolfe* and the Expression of Restraint', *Zeitschrift für Kunstgeschichte*, 58:2, 1995.

Dunlap, William. *A History of the Rise and Progress of the Arts of Design in the United States* [1834], Boston, 1918.

L'École de la liberté: être artiste à Paris, 1648–1817, exhib. cat. by Anne-Marie Garcia and Emmanuel Schwartz, Paris, École National Supérieure des Beaux-Arts, 2009–10.

Edelstein, Dan. *The Enlightenment: A Genealogy*, Chicago and London, 2010.

Eitner, Lorenz. *Géricault's Raft of the Medusa*, London, 1972.

——, ed. *Neoclassicism and Romanticism, 1750–1850: An Anthology of Sources and Documents*, New York, 1989.

The English Prize: The Capture of the Westmorland, an Episode of the Grand Tour, exhib. cat., ed. María Dolores Sánchez-Jáuregui and Scott Wilcox, Oxford and New Haven, Conn., 2012–13.

Evans, Dorinda. *The Genius of Gilbert Stuart*, Princeton, NJ, 1999.

Evans, Grose. *Benjamin West and the Taste of His Times*, Carbondale, Ill., 1959.

The Exhibition of Painting: A Poem Addressed to the Ladies, London, 1775.

The Exhibition of the Royal Academy MDCCLXIX, London, 1769.

The Exhibition of the Royal Academy MDCCLXX, London, 1770.

The Exhibition of the Royal Academy MDCCLXXI, London, 1771.

Fagan, Louis. *A Catalogue Raisonné of the Engraved Works of William Woollett*, London, 1885.

Farington, Joseph. *The Diary of Joseph Farington*, ed. Kenneth Garlick and Angus Macintyre, New Haven, Conn., and London, 1978–98.

Farnham, Fern. 'Achilles' Shield: Some Observations on Pope's *Iliad*', *PMLA*, 84:6, October 1969.

Fieser, James, ed. *Early Responses to Hume's History of England*, Bristol, 2005.

Flavell, Julie. *When London Was Capital of America*, New Haven, Conn., and London, 2010.

Fleischer, Roland E., Carin K. Arnborg and Gustavus Hesselius. '"With God's Blessing on Both Land and Sea": Gustavus Hesselius Describes the New World to the Old in a Letter from Philadelphia in 1714', *American Art Journal*, 21:3, 1989.

Fleming, John. 'Robert Adam, Luc-François Breton and the Townshend Monument in Westminster Abbey', *The Connoisseur*, 150, May–August 1962.

Fletcher, Charlotte Goldsborough. *Cato's Mirania: A Life of Provost Smith*, Lanham, Md., 2002.

Flexner, James Thomas. 'The American School in London', *Metropolitan Museum of Art Bulletin*, New Series, 7:2, October 1948.

Foote, Samuel. *The Works of Samuel Foote, Esq.*, London, 1830.

Ford, Brinsley. 'James Byres: Principal Antiquarian for the English Visitors to Rome', *Apollo*, 99, June 1974.

——. 'A Portrait Group by Gavin Hamilton: With Some Notes on Portraits of Englishmen in Rome', *Burlington Magazine*, 97:633, December 1955.

Fordham, Douglas. *British Art and the Seven Years' War: Allegiance and Autonomy*, Philadelphia and Oxford, 2010.

Forster-Hahn, Franziska. 'The Sources of True Taste: Benjamin West's Instructions to a Young Painter for His Studies in Italy', *Journal of the Warburg and Courtauld Institutes*, 30, 1967.

Foucault, Michel. *Manet and the Object of Painting*, trans. Matthew Barr, London, 2009.

——. 'What is Enlightenment?', in *The Foucault Reader*, ed. Paul Rabinow, London, 1991.

Fox, Celina. *The Arts of Industry in the Age of Enlightenment*, New Haven, Conn., and London, 2009.

Franklin, Benjamin. 'Information to Those Who Would Remove to America' [1782], in *The Autobiography and Other Writings on Politics, Economics, and Virtue*, ed. Alan Houston, Cambridge, 2004.

——. *The Way to Wealth; as clearly shewn in the preface of an old Pensylvania almanack, intitled, Poor Richard improved*, London, 1774.

Frascina, Francis, *et al. Modernity and Modernism: French Painting in the Nineteenth Century*, New Haven, Conn., and London, 1993.

Freud, Sigmund. *Civilization and Its Discontents* [1930], trans. David McLintock, London, 2002.

Friedman, Winifred H. *Boydell's Shakespeare Gallery*, New York and London, 1976.

——. 'Some Commercial Aspects of the Boydell Shakespeare Gallery', *Journal of the Warburg and Courtauld Institutes*, 36, 1973.

Fryd, Vivien Green. 'Rereading the Indian in Benjamin West's "Death of General Wolfe"', *American Art*, 9:1, Spring 1995.

Fubini, Riccardo. *Humanism and Secularization: From Petrarch to Valla*, trans. Martha King, Durham, NC, and London, 2003.

Fulton, Robert. *A Treatise on the Improvement of Canal Navigation*, London, 1796.

Fuseli, Henry. *Lectures on Painting: Delivered at the Royal Academy March 1801*, London, 1801.

Gaehtgens, Thomas W., and Heinz Ickstadt, eds. *American Icons: Transatlantic Perspectives on Eighteenth- and Nineteenth Century American Art*, Santa Monica, Calif., 1992.

The Gallery of Pictures Painted by Benjamin West Esqr, Historical Painter to His Majesty, and President of the Royal Academy, Engraved in Outline by Henry Moses, London, 1811.

Galt, John. *The Life, Studies and Works of Benjamin West, Esq.*, London, 1820.

Gardiner, Patrick, ed. *Theories of History*, New York, 1967.

Garraty, John A., and Mark C. Carnes, eds. *American National Biography*, New York and Oxford, 1999.

Garrett, Wendell D. 'John Adams and the Limited Role of the Fine Arts', *Winterthur Portfolio*, 1, 1964.

Gay, Peter, ed. *The Enlightenment: A Comprehensive Anthology*, New York, 1973.

——. *The Enlightenment: An Interpretation. Volume 1: The Rise of Modern Paganism*, New York, 1966.

——. *Modernism: The Lure of Heresy from Baudelaire to Beckett and Beyond*, London, 2009.

Gegenheimer, Albert F. 'Artist in Exile: The Story of Thomas Spence Duche', *Pennsylvania Magazine of History and Biography*, 79:1, January 1955.

——. *William Smith: Educator and Churchman, 1727–1803*, Philadelphia, 1943.

Gelber, Michael Werth. 'John Dryden and the Battle of the Books', *Huntington Library Quarterly*, 63:1/2, 2000.

George, M. Dorothy. *Hogarth to Cruikshank: Social Change in Graphic Satire*, London, 1967.

George III and Queen Charlotte: Patronage, Collecting and Court Taste, exhib. cat., ed. Jane Roberts, London, Queen's Gallery, 2004–05.

Gerdts, William H. 'The American "Discourses": A Survey of Lectures and Writings on American Art, 1770–1858', *American Art Journal*, 15:3, Summer 1983.

Gibbon, Edward. *The Decline and Fall of the Roman Empire* [1776–78], London, 1993–94.

——. *The English Essays of Edward Gibbon*, ed. Patricia B. Craddock, Oxford, 1972.

——. *The Letters of Edward Gibbon*, ed. J.E. Norton, London, 1956.

Gibson-Wood, Carol. *Jonathan Richardson: Art Theorist of the English Enlightenment*, New Haven, Conn., and London, 2000.

Gidal, Eric. 'Civic Melancholy: English Gloom and French Enlightenment', *Eighteenth-Century Studies*, 37:1, Fall 2003.

Goethe, J.W. von, *Selected Works*, London, 1999.

Goldsmith, Oliver. *The Citizen of the World; or, Letters from a Chinese philosopher, residing in London, to his friends in the East* [1762], London, 1969.

——. *The History of England: From the Earliest Times to the Death of George the Second* [1771], London, 1794.

Gordon, Scott Paul. 'Martial Art: Benjamin West's *The Death of Socrates*, Colonial Politics, and the Puzzles of Patronage', *William and Mary Quarterly*, Third Series, 65:1, January 2008.

Gosse, E., ed. *Conversations of James Northcote R.A.*, London, 1894.

Gray, Thomas. *An Elegy Written in a Country Church-Yard*, London, 1751.

Green, Valentine. *A Review of the Polite Arts in France, at the Time of Their Establishment under Louis the XIVth, Compared with Their Present State in England*, London, 1782.

Griffiths, Antony. *Prints and Printmaking: An Introduction to the History and Techniques*, London, 1996.

Grosley, Pierre-Jean. *A Tour to London; or, New Observations on England, and Its Inhabitants*, trans. Thomas Nugent, London, 1772.

Guégan, Stéphane. 'Théophile Gautier, Militant of Modernity', in *Manet: Portraying Life*, exhib. cat., Toledo and London, 2012–13.

Guttmann, Allen. 'Copley, Peale, Trumbull: A Note on Loyalty', *American Quarterly*, 11:2: part 1, Summer 1959.

Guyard de Berville, M. *Histoire de Pierre Terrail, dit le Chevalier Bayard, sans peur & sans reproche*, Paris, 1765.

Habermas, Jürgen. *The Structural Transformation of the Public Sphere: An Inquiry into a Category of Bourgeois Society*, Cambridge, 1989.

Hamilton, Alexander. *Hamilton's Itinerarium; being a narrative of a journey from Annapolis, Maryland, through Delaware, Pennsylvania, New York, New Jersey, Connecticut, Rhode Island, Massachusetts and New Hampshire, from May to September, 1744, by Doctor Alexander Hamilton*, ed. Albert Bushnell Hart, Early Americas Digital Archive, mith.umd.edu / eada / html / display.php?docs=hamilton_itinerarium.xml&action=show, 66 (accessed December 2014).

Hargraves, Matthew. *Candidates for Fame: The Society of Artists of Great Britain, 1760–1791*, New Haven, Conn., and London, 2005.

Harris, James. *Hermes; or, A Philosophical Inquiry Concerning Universal Grammar*, London, 1765.

Harris, John, Geoffrey de Bellaigue and Oliver Millar. *Buckingham Palace*, London, 1968.

Hart, Charles Henry. 'Autobiographical Notes of Matthew Pratt, Painter', *Pennsylvania Magazine of History and Biography*, 19:4, 1895.

——. 'Benjamin West's Family: The American President of the Royal Academy of Arts Not a Quaker', *Pennsylvania Magazine of History and Biography*, 32:1, 1908.

Hartog, François. *Anciens, modernes, sauvages*, Paris, 2005.

Haskell, Francis. *History and Its Images: Art and the Interpretation of the Past*, New Haven, Conn., and London, 1995.

Hayley, William. *The Life of George Romney, Esq.*, London, 1809.

Francis Hayman, exhib. cat. by Brian Allen, New Haven, Conn., and London, 1987.

Hazard, Paul. *The Crisis of the European Mind, 1680–1715*, trans. J. Lewis May, New York, 2013.

Hazlitt, William. *The Collected Works of William Hazlitt*, ed. A.R. Waller and Arnold Glover, London, 1903.

Headrick, Daniel R. *When Information Came of Age: Technologies of Knowledge in the Age of Reason and Revolution, 1700–1850*, Oxford, 2000.

Hemingway, Andrew. 'The "Sociology" of Taste in the Scottish Enlightenment', *Oxford Art Journal*, 12:2, 1989.

Herbert, Robert L. *David, Voltaire, Brutus and the French Revolution: An Essay in Art and Politics*, London, 1972.

Hicks, Philip. *Neoclassical History and English Culture: From Clarendon to Hume*, Basingstoke, 1996.

Hilson, J.C. 'Hume: The Historian as Man of Feeling', in *Augustan Worlds*, ed. J.C. Hilson, M.M.B. Jones and J.R. Watson, Leicester, 1978.

Himmelfarb, Gertrude. *The Roads to Modernity: The British, French, and American Enlightenments*, New York, 2004.

Hogarth, William. *Anecdotes of William Hogarth, Written by Himself*, London, 1833.

Holmes, Richard. *The Age of Wonder: How the Romantic Generation Discovered the Beauty and Terror of Science*, London, 2008.

Honour, Hugh. *Neo-classicism*, London, 1977.

Hoock, Holger. *Empires of the Imagination: Politics, War, and the Arts in the British World, 1750–1850*, London, 2010.

——. *The King's Artists: The Royal Academy of Arts and the Politics of British Culture, 1760–1840*, Oxford, 2003.

Hornberger, Theodore. 'A Note on the Probable Source of Provost Smith's Famous Curriculum for the College of Philadelphia', *Pennsylvania Magazine of History and Biography*, 58:4, October 1934.

Howard, Hugh. *The Painter's Chair: George Washington and the Making of American Art*, New York, 2009.

Hume, David. *The History of England from the Invasion of Julius Caesar to the Revolution in 1688*, London, 1767.

——. 'Of the Liberty of the Press' [1742, revised 1777], in *Theory of Politics*, ed. Frederick Watkins, London, 1951.

——. 'Of Refinement in the Arts' [1752], in *Selected Essays*, ed. Stephen Copley and Andrew Edgar, Oxford, 2008.

Hurd, Richard. *Dialogues on the Uses of Foreign Travel; Considered as a Part of an English Gentleman's Education: Between Lord Shaftesbury and Mr Locke*, London, 1764.

Hutton, William Holden. *Hampton Court*, London, 1897.

Ingamells, John. *A Dictionary of British and Irish Travellers in Italy, 1701–1800*, New Haven, Conn., and London, 1997.

Irwin, David. *English Neoclassical Art: Studies in Inspiration and Taste*, London, 1966.

——. 'Gavin Hamilton: Archaeologist, Painter, and Dealer', *Art Bulletin*, 44:2, June 1962.

——. 'James Barry, and the Death of Wolfe in 1759', *Art Bulletin*, 41:4, December 1959.

——. *Neoclassicism*, London, 1997.

Iscrupe, William L., and Shirley G.M. Iscrupe. *Pennsylvania Line: A Research Guide to Pennsylvania Genealogy and Local History*, Laughlintown, Pa., 1990.

Israel, Jonathan. *Democratic Enlightenment: Philosophy, Revolution, and Human Rights, 1750–1790*, Oxford, 2011.

——. *Radical Enlightenment: Philosophy and the Making of Modernity, 1650–1750*, Oxford, 2001.

Jaffe, Irma B. 'John Singleton Copley's "Watson and the Shark"', *American Art Journal*, 9:1, May 1977.

Jaffee, David. *A New Nation of Goods: The Material Culture of Early America*, Philadelphia, 2010.

Jasanoff, Maya. *Liberty's Exiles: American Loyalists in the Revolutionary World*, New York, 2011.

——. 'The Other Side of Revolution: Loyalists in the British Empire', *William and Mary Quarterly*, Third Series, 65:2, April 2008.

Johns, Christopher M.S. 'Visual Culture and the Triumph of Cosmopolitanism in Eighteenth-Century Rome', in *Roma Britannica: Art Patronage and Cultural Exchange in Eighteenth-Century Rome*, ed. David R. Marshall, Susan Russell and Karin Wolfe, London 2011.

Johns, Elizabeth. *American Genre Painting: The Politics of Everyday Life*, New Haven, Conn., and London, 1991.

Johnson, Samuel, ed. *The Plays of William Shakespeare*, London, 1765.

——. *The Yale Edition of the Works of Samuel Johnson. Volume 2: The Idler and The Adventurer*, ed. W.J. Bate, John M. Bullitt and L.F. Powell, New Haven, Conn., and London, 1963.

Jones, Colin, and Dror Wahrman, eds. *The Age of Cultural Revolutions: Britain and France, 1750–1820*, Berkeley, Calif., and London, 2002.

Jones, Richard Foster. *Ancients and Moderns: A Study of the Background of the Battle of the Books*, St Louis, 1936.

Jordanova, Ludmilla. *The Look of the Past: Visual and Material Evidence in Historical Practice*, Cambridge, 2012.

Kant, Immanuel. *An Answer to the Question: 'What is Enlightenment?'* [1784], trans. H.B. Nisbet, London, 2009.

Kelley, Donald R., and David Harris Sacks, eds. *The Historical Imagination in Early Modern Britain: History, Rhetoric, and Fiction, 1500–1800*, Cambridge, 1997.

Kelly, Jason M. *The Society of Dilettanti: Archaeology and Identity in the British Enlightenment*, New Haven, Conn., and London, 2009.

Kemp, Martin. Letter to the Editor, *Art Bulletin*, 62:4, December 1980.

Ketcham, Ralph L. 'Benjamin Franklin and William Smith: New Light on an Old Philadelphia Quarrel', *Pennsylvania Magazine of History and Biography*, 88:2, April 1964.

Kloss, William. *Samuel F.B. Morse*, New York, 1988.

Koselleck, Reinhart. *Futures Past: On the Semantics of Historical Time*, trans. Keith Tribe, New York, 2004.

Kraemer, Ruth S. *Drawings by Benjamin West and His Son Raphael Lamar West*, New York, 1975.

Kramnick, Jonathan Brody. *Making the English Canon: Print-Capitalism and the Cultural Past, 1700–1770*, Cambridge, 1998.

Kristeller, Paul Oskar. *Renaissance Thought and the Arts: Collected Essays*, Princeton, NJ, 1990.

Lajer-Burcharth, Ewa. *Necklines: The Art of Jacques-Louis David after the Terror*, New Haven, Conn., and London, 1989.

Landes, David S. *The Unbound Prometheus: Technological Change and Industrial Development in Western Europe from 1750 to the Present*, Cambridge, 1969.

Landis, Hon. Charles I. 'The Juliana Library Company in Lancaster', *Pennsylvania Magazine of History and Biography*, 43:1, January 1919.

Langford, Paul. *A Polite and Commercial People: England, 1727–1783*, Oxford, 1989.

Larson, James L. 'Winckelmann's Essay on Imitation', *Eighteenth-Century Studies*, 9:3, Spring 1976.

Laslett, Peter. *The World We Have Lost: Further Explored*, London, 2005.

Lemay, J.A. Leo. *The Life of Benjamin Franklin. Volume 3: Soldier, Scientist, and Politician, 1748–1757*, Philadelphia, 2009.

Leslie, Charles Robert. *A Handbook for Young Painters*, London, 1855.

——, and Tom Taylor. *Life and Times of Sir Joshua Reynolds*, London, 1865.

Letters from a Young Painter Abroad to His Friends in England, London, 1750.

Letters to a Young Nobleman, London, 1762.

Levey, Michael. *Painting and Sculpture in France, 1700–1789*, New Haven, Conn., and London, 1993.

——. *Rococo to Revolution: Major Trends in Eighteenth-Century Painting*, London, 1985.

Levine, Joseph M. 'Ancients and Moderns Reconsidered', *Eighteenth-Century Studies*, 15:1, Autumn 1981.

——. *The Autonomy of History: Truth and Method from Erasmus to Gibbon*, Chicago and London, 1999.

——. *The Battle of the Books: History and Literature in the Augustan Age*, Ithaca, NY, and London, 1991.

——. *Humanism and History: Origins of Modern English Historiography*, Ithaca, NY, and London, 1987.

Lewis, Lesley. *Connoisseurs and Secret Agents in Eighteenth Century Rome*, London, 1961.

Lewis, Philip. 'Writing to the King: Charles Perrault's Dedicatory Epistle for the Dictionnaire de l'Académie', *MLN*, 107:4, September 1992.

Lieberman, Ilene D. 'Sir Francis Chantrey's Monument to George Washington: Sculpture and Patronage in Post-Revolutionary America', *Art Bulletin*, 71:2, June 1989.

Lipking, Lawrence. *The Ordering of the Arts in Eighteenth-Century England*, Princeton, NJ, 1970.

——. 'The Shifting Nature of Authority in Versions of *De arte graphica*', *Journal of Aesthetics and Art Criticism*, 23:4, Summer 1965.

Lippincott, Louise. 'Expanding on Portraiture: The Market, the Public, and the Hierarchy of Genres in Eighteenth-Century Britain', in *The Consumption of Culture, 1600–1800: Image, Object, Text*, ed. Ann Bermingham and John Brewer, London and New York, 1995.

Lloyd, Christopher. 'King, Queen and Family', in *George III and Queen Charlotte: Patronage, Collecting and Court Taste*, exhib. cat., ed. Jane Roberts, London, Queen's Gallery, 2004–05.

Lloyd, Evan. *Conversation: A Poem*, London, 1767.

Locquin, Jean. *La Peinture d'histoire en France de 1747 à 1785*, Paris, 1978.

Lubin, David M. *Picturing a Nation: Art and Social Change in Nineteenth-Century America*, New Haven, Conn., and London, 1994.

Macaulay, Catherine. *The History of England from the Accession of James I to the Elevation of the House of Hanover*, London, 1769.

——. *The History of England from the Revolution to the Present Time in a Series of Letters to a Friend*, Bath, 1778.

——. *Observations on a Pamphlet, Entitled, Thoughts on the Cause of the Present Discontents*, Dublin, 1770.

Mackenzie, Henry. *The Man of Feeling*, London, 1771.

McLynn, Frank. *1759: The Year Britain Became Master of the World*, London, 2004.

McNairn, Alan. *Behold the Hero: General Wolfe and the Arts in the Eighteenth Century*, Liverpool, 1997.

McNeil, David. *The Grotesque Depiction of War and the Military in Eighteenth-Century English Fiction*, Newark, Del., 1990.

Mandeville, Bernard. *The Fable of the Bees; or, Private Vices, Publick Benefits* [1714], Indianapolis, 1988.

Manners & Morals: Hogarth and British Painting, 1700–1760, exhib. cat. by Elizabeth Einberg, London, Tate Gallery, 1987–88.

Manning, Stephen. *Quebec: The Story of Three Sieges*, London, 2009.

Mannings, David. 'Reynolds, Garrick and the Choice of Hercules', *Eighteenth-Century Studies*, 17:3, Spring 1984.

——. *Sir Joshua Reynolds: A Complete Catalogue of His Paintings*, New Haven, Conn., and London, 2000.

Marks, Arthur S. 'Angelica Kauffmann and Some Americans on the Grand Tour', *American Art Journal*, 12:2, Spring 1980.

——. 'An Eighteenth-Century American Landscape Painter Rediscovered: John Taylor of Bath', *American Art Journal*, 10:2, November 1978.

Marsden, Jonathan. 'Patronage and Collecting', in *George III and Queen Charlotte: Patronage, Collecting and Court Taste*, exhib. cat., ed. Jane Roberts, London, Queen's Gallery, 2004–05.

Marshall, David R., and Karin Wolfe. 'Roma Britannica', in *Roma Britannica: Art Patronage and Cultural Exchange in Eighteenth-Century Rome*, ed. David R. Marshall, Susan Russell and Karin Wolfe, London, 2011.

Martyn, Thomas. *The Gentleman's Guide in His Tour Through Italy*, London, 1787.

Marx, Karl. *The Eighteenth Brumaire of Louis Bonaparte* [1852], in *Karl Marx: Selected Writings*, ed. David McLellan, Oxford, 2000.

Matheson, C.S. '"A Shilling Well Laid Out": The Royal Academy's Early Public', in *Art on the Line: The Royal Academy Exhibitions at Somerset House, 1780–1836*, ed. David H. Solkin, New Haven, Conn., and London, 2001.

Matthew, H.C.G., and Brian Harrison, eds. *Oxford Dictionary of National Biography*, Oxford, 2004.

Meinecke, Friedrich. *Historism: The Rise of a New Historical Outlook*, trans. J.E. Anderson, London, 1972.

Melton, James van Horn. *The Rise of the Public in Enlightenment Europe*, Cambridge, 2001.

Mengs, Anton Raphael. *Pensées sur la beauté et sur le goût dans la peinture* [1762], Paris, 2000.

Méricam-Bourdet, Myrtille. *Voltaire et l'écriture de l'histoire: un enjeu politique*, Oxford, 2012.

Meyer, Paul H. 'Voltaire and Hume as Historians: A Comparative Study of the *Essai sur les mœurs* and the *History of England*', *PMLA*, 73:1, March 1958.

Middleton, Richard, ed. *Amherst and the Conquest of Canada*, Stroud, 2003.

Miles, Ellen G. *American Paintings of the Eighteenth Century*, Washington, D.C., 1995.

Miles, Jonathan. *The Wreck of the Medusa: The Most Famous Sea Disaster of the Nineteenth Century*, New York, 2007.

Millar, Oliver. *The Later Georgian Pictures in the Collection of Her Majesty the Queen*, London, 1969.

Miller, Jacquelyn C. 'An "Uncommon Tranquility of Mind": Emotional Self-Control and the Construction of a Middle-Class Identity in Eighteenth-Century Philadelphia', *Journal of Social History*, 30:1, Autumn 1996.

Miller, Lillian B. 'Charles Willson Peale as History Painter: *The Exhumation of the Mastadon*', in *New Perspectives on Charles Willson Peale: A 250th Anniversary Celebration*, ed. Lillian B. Miller and David C. Ward, Pittsburgh, 1991.

——. 'In the Shadow of His Father: Rembrandt Peale, Charles Willson Peale, and the American Portrait Tradition', *Pennsylvania Magazine of History and Biography*, 110:1, January 1986.

Miller, Stephen. 'The Death of Hume', *Wilson Quarterly*, 19:3, Summer 1995.

Minor, Heather Hyde. '"Amore regolato": Papal Nephews and Their Palaces in Eighteenth-Century Rome', *Journal of the Society of Architectural Historians*, 65:1, March 2006.

Mitchell, B.R., and Phyllis Deane. *Abstract of British Historical Statistics*, Cambridge, 1971.

Mitchell, Charles. 'Benjamin West's "Death of Wolfe" and the Popular History Piece', *Journal of the Warburg and Courtauld Institutes*, 7, 1944.

——. 'Zoffany's Death of Captain Cook', *Burlington Magazine*, 84:492, March 1944.

Monks, Sarah. 'The Wolfe Man: Benjamin West's Anglo-American Accent', *Art History*, 34:4, September 2011.

Montagna, Dennis. 'Benjamin West's *The Death of General Wolfe*: A Nationalist Narrative', *American Art Journal*, 13:2, Spring 1981.

Montesquieu, Charles-Louis de Secondat, baron de La Brède et de. 'Montesquieu in England: His "Notes on England"', trans. Iain Stewart, Oxford University Comparative Law Forum 6, 2002, ouclf.iuscomp.org/articles/montesquieu.shtml (accessed January 2015).

Moore, John. *A View of Society and Manners in Italy*, Dublin, 1781.

Morse, Samuel F.B. *Academies of Arts: A Discourse, Delivered on Thursday, May 3, 1827*, New York, 1827.

——. *Lectures on the Affinity of Painting with the Other Fine Arts* [1826–32], ed. Nicolai Cikovsky Jr, Columbia, Mo., and London, 1983.

Moyles, R.G. 'Those Paths of Glory: General Wolfe and the Romantic School of British Imperial History', *The Beaver*, 69:4, August/September 1989.

Murdoch, Tessa, ed. *Noble Households: Eighteenth-Century Inventories of Great English Houses*, Cambridge, 2006.

Myrone, Martin. *Bodybuilding: Reforming Masculinities in British Art, 1750–1810*, New Haven, Conn., and London, 2005.

Naginski, Erika. *Sculpture and Enlightenment*, Los Angeles, 2009.

Nash, Gary B. *First City: Philadelphia and the Forging of Historical Memory*, Philadelphia, 2006.

Newman, Gerald. *The Rise of English Nationalism: A Cultural History, 1740–1830*, London, 1997.

Northcote, James. *The Life of Sir Joshua Reynolds*, London, 1819.

Novak, Barbara. *American Painting of the Nineteenth Century: Realism, Idealism, and the American Experience*, Oxford, 2007.

Oaks, Robert F. 'Philadelphians in Exile: The Problem of Loyalty During the American Revolution', *Pennsylvania Magazine of History and Biography*, 96:3, July 1972.

O'Brien, Karen. 'History and the Novel in Eighteenth-Century Britain', *Huntington Library Quarterly*, 68:1–2, March 2005.

——. *Narratives of Enlightenment: Cosmopolitan History from Voltaire to Gibbon*, Cambridge, 2005.

——. *Women and Enlightenment in Eighteenth-Century Britain*, Cambridge, 2009.

Observations on the Pictures Now in Exhibition at the Royal Academy, London, 1771.

O'Gorman, Frank. *The Long Eighteenth Century: British Political and Social History, 1688–1832*, London, 1997.

O'Keeffe, Paul. *A Genius for Failure: The Life of Benjamin Robert Haydon*, London, 2009.

Outram, Dorinda. *Panorama of the Enlightenment*, London, 2006.

Pace, Clare. 'Gavin Hamilton's *Wood and Dawkins Discovering Palmyra*: The Dilettante as Hero', *Art History*, 4:3, September 1981.

Painting, Vivienne. *John Boydell*, London, 2005.

Painting History: Delaroche and Lady Jane Grey, exhib. cat. by Stephen Bann and Linda Whiteley, London, The National Gallery, 2010.

Parkman, Francis. *Montcalm and Wolfe* [1884], London, 1964.

Parrinder, Patrick. *Nation and Novel: The English Novel from Its Origins to the Present Day*, Oxford, 2006.

Pasquin, Anthony. *Memoirs of the Royal Academicians; Being an Attempt to Improve the National Taste*, London, 1796.

Paulson, Ronald. *Book and Painting: Shakespeare, Milton and the Bible: Literary Texts and the Emergence of English Painting*, Knoxville, Tenn., 1982.

——. *Breaking and Remaking: Aesthetic Practice in England, 1700–1820*, New Brunswick, NJ, and London, 1989.

——. *Emblem and Expression: Meaning in English Art of the Eighteenth Century*, London, 1975.

Payne, Christina, and William Vaughan, eds. *English Accents: Interactions with British Art, c. 1776–1855*, Aldershot, 2004.

Peale, Charles Willson. *The Autobiography of Charles Willson Peale*, ed. Lillian B. Miller and Sidney Hart, New Haven, Conn., and London, 2000.

Charles Willson Peale and His World, exhib. cat. by Edgar P. Richardson, Brooke Hindle and Lillian B. Miller, Washington, D.C., Fort Worth, Tex., and New York, 1982–83.

Pears, Iain. *The Discovery of Painting: The Growth of Interest in the Arts in England, 1680–1768*, New Haven, Conn., and London, 1988.

Pelzel, Thomas. 'Anton Raphael Mengs and His British Critics', *Studies in Romanticism*, 15:3, Summer 1976.

——. *Anton Raphael Mengs and Neoclassicism*, New York and London, 1979.

Perinetti, Dario. 'Philosophical Reflection on History', in *The Cambridge History of Eighteenth-Century Philosophy*, ed. Knud Haakonssen, Cambridge, 2006.

Perini, Giovanna. 'Sir Joshua Reynolds and Italian Art and Literature: A Study of the Sketchbooks in the British Museum and in Sir John Soane's Museum', *Journal of the Warburg and Courtauld Institutes*, 51, 1988.

Philadelphia: Three Centuries of American Art, exhib. cat., Philadelphia Museum of Art, 1976.

Philbrick, Nathaniel. *Bunker Hill: A City, a Siege, a Revolution*, London, 2013.

Phillips, Mark Salber. *Society and Sentiment: Genres of Historical Writing in Britain, 1740–1820*, Princeton, NJ, 2000.

Piles, Roger de. *The Art of Painting and the Lives of the Painters*, London, 1706.

Piozzi, Hester Lynch. *Observations and Reflections Made in the Course of a Journey Through France, Italy and Germany*, London, 1789.

Plumb, J.H. 'The Acceptance of Modernity', in *The Birth of a Consumer Society: The Commercialization of Eighteenth-Century England*, ed. Neil McKendrick, John Brewer and J.H. Plumb, London, 1982.

——. 'The Commercialization of Leisure', in *The Birth of a Consumer Society: The Commercialization of Eighteenth-Century England*, ed. Neil McKendrick, John Brewer and J.H. Plumb, London, 1982.

Pointon, Marcia. *Hanging the Head: Portraiture and Social Formation in Eighteenth-Century England*, New Haven, Conn., and London, 1993.

Pollack, John H., ed. *'The Good Education of Youth': Worlds of Learning in the Age of Franklin*, New Castle, Del., and Philadelphia, 2009.

Pope, Alexander. 'Preface to *The Iliad of Homer*' [1715], in *The Prose Works of Alexander Pope*, ed. Norman Ault and Rosemary Cowler, Oxford, 1936–86.

——. *The Rape of the Lock* [1712], in *The Major Works*, ed. Pat Rogers, Oxford, 2006.

Porter, Roy. *English Society in the Eighteenth Century*, London, 1991.

Posner, Donald. 'Concerning the "Mechanical" Parts of Painting and the Artistic Culture of Seventeenth-Century France', *Art Bulletin*, 75:4, December 1993.

Postle, Martin. *Sir Joshua Reynolds: The Subject Pictures*, Cambridge, 1995.

Potts, Alex. *Flesh and the Ideal: Winckelmann and the Origins of Art History*, New Haven, Conn., and London, 1994.

Pratt, Stephanie. *American Indians in British Art, 1700–1840*, Norman, Okla., 2005.

Pressly, William L. *The French Revolution as Blasphemy: Johan Zoffany's Paintings of the Massacre at Paris, August 10, 1792*, Berkeley, Calif., and London, 1999.

——. *The Life and Art of James Barry*, New Haven, Conn., and London, 1981.

Pringle, John. *The Life of General James Wolfe, the Conqueror of Canada*, London, 1760.

The Progress of Genius, or Authentic Memoirs of the Early Life of Benjamin West: Abridged for the use of young persons by a Lady, Boston, 1831.

'Proposals by Messrs Woollett, Boydell, and Ryland, for Publishing by Subscription a Print, Representing the Death of General Wolfe', London, 1772.

Prown, Jules David. 'Benjamin West and the Use of Antiquity', *American Art*, 10:2, Summer 1996.

——. 'Benjamin West's Family Picture: A Nativity in Hammersmith', in *Essays in Honor of Paul Mellon, Collector and Benefactor*, ed. John Wilmerding, Washington, D.C., 1986.

——. 'A Course of Antiquities at Rome, 1764', *Eighteenth-Century Studies*, 31:1, Fall 1997.

——. *John Singleton Copley: In England, 1774–1815*, Cambridge, Mass., 1966.

——. 'John Trumbull as History Painter', in *John Trumbull: The Hand and Spirit of a Painter*, exhib. cat., ed. Helen A. Cooper, New Haven, Conn., Yale University Art Gallery, 1982–83.

Pyne, W.H. *The History of the Royal Residences of Windsor Castle, St James's Palace, Carlton House, Kensington Palace, Hampton Court, Buckingham House, and Frogmore*, London, 1819.

Quilley, Geoff. *Empire to Nation: Art, History and the Visualization of Maritime Britain, 1768–1829*, New Haven, Conn., and London, 2011.

——. 'Questions of Loyalty: The Representation of the British West Indian Colonies During the American Revolutionary War', in *Conflicting Visions: War and Visual Culture in Britain and France, c. 1700–1830*, ed. John Bonehill and Geoff Quilley, Aldershot, 2005.

Rabb, Theodore. *The Last Days of the Renaissance: & the March to Modernity*, New York, 2006.

Ramsay, Allan. *Letters on the Present Disturbances in Great Britain and Her American Provinces*, London, 1777.

Rapin de Thoyras, Paul de. *The History of England*, trans. Nicholas Tindal, vol. 10, London, 1760.

Rather, Susan. 'Benjamin West, John Galt, and the Biography of 1816', *Art Bulletin*, 86:2, June 2004.

——. 'Carpenter, Tailor, Shoemaker, Artist: Copley and Portrait Painting around 1770', *Art Bulletin*, 79:2, June 1997.

——. 'A Painter's Progress: Matthew Pratt and *The American School*', *Metropolitan Museum Journal*, 28, 1993.

Rauser, Amelia. 'Death or Liberty: British Political Prints and the Struggle for Symbols in the American Revolution', *Oxford Art Journal*, 21:2, 1998.

Raven, James. *The Business of Books: Booksellers and the English Book Trade*, New Haven, Conn., and London, 2007.

——. 'New Reading Histories, Print Culture and the Identification of Change: The Case of Eighteenth-Century England', *Social History*, 23:3, October 1998.

Rebora, Carrie. 'Robert Fulton's Art Collection', *American Art Journal*, 22:3, Autumn 1990.

——, *et al. John Singleton Copley in America*, New York, 1995.

Reichardt, Rolf, and Hubertus Kohle. *Visualizing the Revolution: Politics and Pictorial Arts in Late Eighteenth-Century France*, London, 2008.

Reid, Stuart. *Wolfe: The Career of General James Wolfe from Culloden to Quebec*, Staplehurst, 2000.

Reitlinger, Gerald. *The Economics of Taste: The Rise and Fall of Picture Prices, 1760–1960*, London, 1961.

Renne, Elizaveta. *State Hermitage Museum Catalogue: Sixteenth- to Nineteenth-Century British Painting*, New Haven, Conn., and London, 2011.

Retford, Kate. *The Art of Domestic Life: Family Portraiture in Eighteenth-Century England*, New Haven, Conn., and London, 2006.

——. 'From the Interior to Interiority: The Conversation Piece in Georgian England', *Journal of Design History*, 20:4, Winter 2007.

Reynolds, Sir Joshua. *Discourses on Art*, ed. Robert R. Wark, New Haven, Conn., and London, 1975.

——. *The Literary Works of Sir Joshua Reynolds*, London, 1819.

Reynolds, exhib. cat., ed. Nicholas Penny, London, Royal Academy of Arts, 1986.

Joshua Reynolds: The Creation of Celebrity, exhib. cat., ed. Martin Postle, Ferrara and London, 2005.

Richardson, E.P. 'West's Voyage to Italy, 1760, and William Allen', *Pennsylvania Magazine of History and Biography*, 102:1, January 1978.

Richardson, John. 'Modern Warfare in Early Eighteenth-Century Poetry', *Studies in English Literature, 1500–1900*, 45:3, Summer 2005.

Richardson, Jonathan. *An Account of the Statues, Bas-reliefs, Drawings and Pictures in Italy, France, &c.*, London, 1754.

——. *The Works of Jonathan Richardson*, London, 1792.

Ringbom, Sixten. 'Action and Report: The Problem of Indirect Narration in the Academic Theory of Painting', *Journal of the Warburg and Courtauld Institutes*, 52, 1989.

Roberts, Warren. *Jacques-Louis David and Jean-Louis Prieur, Revolutionary Artists: The Public, the Populace, and Images of the French Revolution*, Albany, NY, 2000.

Robertson, William. *The History of the Reign of the Emperor Charles V* [1769], in *The Works of William Robertson, D.D.*, London, 1852.

——. *The History of Scotland During the Reigns of Queen Mary and of King James VI*, London, 1761.

Roettgen, Steffi. *Anton Raphael Mengs, 1728–1779*, Munich, 1999–2003.

——. *Anton Raphael Mengs, 1728–1779, and His British Patrons*, trans. Eileen Martin, London, 1993.

George Romney, 1734–1802, exhib. cat. by Alex Kidson, Liverpool, London and San Marino, Calif., 2002.

Romney, John. *Memoirs of the Life and Works of George Romney*, London, 1830.

Salvator Rosa, exhib. cat. by Helen Langdon with Xavier F. Salomon and Caterina Volpi, London and Fort Worth, Tex., 2010–11.

Rosand, David. *The Invention of Painting in America*, New York, 2004.

Roscoe, Ingrid, Emma Hardy and M.G. Sullivan, eds. *A Biographical Dictionary of Sculptors in Britain, 1660–1851*, New Haven, Conn., and London, 2009.

Rosenblum, Robert. *Transformations in Late Eighteenth Century Art*, Princeton, NJ, 1974.

Rosenthal, Angela. *Angelica Kauffman: Art and Sensibility*, New Haven, Conn., and London, 2006.

Rosenthal, Jerome. 'Voltaire's Philosophy of History', *Journal of the History of Ideas*, 16:2, April 1955.

Rossini, Orietta. *Ara Pacis*, Milan, 2009.

Rouquet, André. *The Present State of the Arts in England* [1755], London, 1970.

Rousseau, Jean-Jacques. *Confessions* [1782], ed. P.N. Furbank, New York, 1992.

——. *The Social Contract* [1762], in *The Social Contract and the Discourses*, trans. G.D.H. Cole, New York and London, 1993.

Rowe, Nicholas. 'Romans and Carthaginians in the Eighteenth Century: Imperial Ideology and National Identity in Britain and France During the Seven Years' War', PhD thesis, Boston College, 1997.

Rubin, James Henry. 'Roger de Piles and Antiquity', *Journal of Aesthetics and Art Criticism*, 34:2, Winter 1975.

Russell, Francis. 'King George III's Picture Hang at Buckingham House', *Burlington Magazine*, 129:1013, August 1987.

Russett, Alan. *Dominic Serres R.A., 1719–1793: War Artist to the Navy*, Woodbridge, 2001.

Rykwert, Joseph. *The First Moderns: The Architects of the Eighteenth Century*, Cambridge, Mass., and London, 1980.

St Clair, William. *The Reading Nation in the Romantic Period*, Cambridge, 2004.

Sandby, William. *The History of the Royal Academy of Arts*, London, 1862.

Saumarez Smith, Charles. *The Company of Artists: The Origin of the Royal Academy of Arts in London*, London, 2012.

Saunders, Richard H. 'Genius and Glory: John Singleton Copley's "The Death of Major Peirson"', *American Art Journal*, 22:3, Autumn 1990.

Sawitzky, William. 'The American Work of Benjamin West', *Pennsylvania Magazine of History and Biography*, 62:4, October 1938.

Schama, Simon. *Dead Certainties: Unwarranted Speculations*, New York, 1991.

Schiff, Stacy. *A Great Improvisation: Franklin, France, and the Birth of America*, New York, 2005.

Schueller, Herbert M. 'The Quarrel of the Ancients and the Moderns', *Music & Letters*, 41:4, October 1960.

Schwarz, L.D. 'Income Distribution and Social Structure in London in the Late Eighteenth Century', *Economic History Review*, 32:2, May 1979.

Scott, Jonathan. *The Pleasures of Antiquity: British Collectors of Greece and Rome*, New Haven, Conn., and London, 2003.

Sellers, Charles Coleman. 'Rembrandt Peale, "Instigator"', *Pennsylvania Magazine of History and Biography*, 79:3, July 1955.

Sellers, Horace Wells. 'Engravings by Charles Willson Peale, Limner', *Pennsylvania Magazine of History and Biography*, 57:2, April 1933.

Shaftesbury, 3rd Earl of, Anthony Ashley Cooper. *Characteristics of Men, Manners, Opinions, Times* [1711], ed. Lawrence E. Klein, Cambridge, 1999.

——. *An Essay on Painting: Being a Notion of the Historical Draught or Tablature of the Judgment of Hercules*, London, 1714.

Shawe-Taylor, Desmond. *The Conversation Piece: Scenes of Fashionable Life*, London, 2009.

——. *The Georgians: Eighteenth-Century Portraiture and Society*, London, 1990.

Sher, Richard B. *The Enlightenment and the Book: Scottish Authors and Their Publishers in Eighteenth-Century Britain, Ireland, and America*, Chicago and London, 2010.

Sherman, Stuart P. 'Franklin and the Age of Enlightenment', in *Benjamin Franklin and the American Character*, ed. Charles L. Sanford, Boston, 1955.

Shovlin, John. *The Political Economy of Virtue: Luxury, Patriotism, and the Origins of the French Revolution*, Ithaca, NY, and London, 2006.

Silius Italicus. *Punica*, trans. J.D. Duff, London, 1961.

Simon, Robin. *Hogarth, France and British Art: The Rise of the Arts in 18th-Century Britain*, London, 2007.

Smart, Alastair. *Allan Ramsay: Painter, Essayist and Man of the Enlightenment*, New Haven, Conn., and London, 1992.

Smith, Adam. *An Inquiry into the Nature and Causes of the Wealth of Nations*, London, 1790.

Smith, William. *A Brief State of the Province of Pennsylvania*, London, 1755.

——. *A General Idea of the College of Mirania*, New York, 1753.

——. *A Poem on Visiting the Academy of Philadelphia, June 1753*, Philadelphia, 1753.

——. *A Sermon, Preach'd on Sunday Sept. 1, 1754, in Christ-Church, Philadelphia; Occasioned by the Death of a Beloved Pupil*, Philadelphia, 1754.

——. *Some Thoughts on Education*, New York, 1752.

Smollett, Tobias. *The Adventures of Roderick Random* [1748], Oxford, 1979.

Solkin, David H. 'The British and the Modern', in *Towards a Modern Art World*, ed. Brian Allen, New Haven, Conn., and London, 1995.

——. 'Joseph Wright of Derby and the Sublime Art of Labor', *Representations*, 83:1, Summer 2003.

——. *Painting for Money: The Visual Arts and the Public Sphere in Eighteenth-Century England*, New Haven, Conn., and London, 1993.

——. *Painting Out of the Ordinary: Modernity and the Art of Everyday Life in Early Nineteenth-Century Britain*, New Haven, Conn., and London, 2008.

Sox, David. *Quakers and the Arts: 'Plain and Fancy' – An Anglo-American Perspective*, York, 2000.

Spadafora, David. *The Idea of Progress in Eighteenth-Century Britain*, New Haven, Conn., and London, 1990.

Stacey, C.P. 'Benjamin West and "The Death of Wolfe"', *National Gallery of Canada Bulletin* 7, 4:1, 1966.

Stafford, Barbara Maria. 'The Eighteenth-Century: Towards an Interdisciplinary Model', *Art Bulletin*, 70:1, March 1988.

Staiti, Paul J. *Samuel F.B. Morse*, Cambridge, 1989.

Stromberg, R.N. 'History in the Eighteenth Century', *Journal of the History of Ideas*, 12:2, April 1951.

Strong, Roy. *And When Did You Last See Your Father? The Victorian Painter and British History*, London, 1978.

Gilbert Stuart, exhib. cat. by Carrie Rebora Barratt and Ellen G. Miles, New York and Washington, D.C., 2004–05.

Sugrue, Thomas J. 'The Peopling and Depeopling of Early Pennsylvania: Indians and Colonists, 1680–1720', *Pennsylvania Magazine of History and Biography*, 116:1, January 1992.

Sullivan, Matthew Greg. 'Historiography and Visual Culture in Britain, 1660–1783', PhD thesis, University of Leeds, 1998.

Sully, Thomas. *Memoirs of the Professional Life of Thomas Sully*, Philadelphia, 1851.

Sunderland, John. 'John Hamilton Mortimer: His Life and Works', *Walpole Society*, 52, 1986.

Swift, Jonathan. *The Conduct of the Allies* ... [1711], in *Major Works*, ed. Angus Ross and David Woolley, Oxford, 2003.

Tawney, R.H. *Religion and the Rise of Capitalism: A Historical Study*, London, 1926.

Taylor, Charles. *A Secular Age*, Cambridge, Mass., and London, 2007.

Tindal, Nicholas. *The Continuation of Mr. Rapin's History of England*, vol. 21, London, 1759.

Tolles, Frederick B. 'The Culture of Early Pennsylvania', *Pennsylvania Magazine of History and Biography*, 81:2, April 1957.

Tracy, Nicholas. *Britannia's Palette: The Arts of Naval Victory*, Montreal and Kingston, 2007.

The Tragic Muse: Art and Emotion, 1700–1900, exhib. cat. by Anne Leonard *et al.*, Chicago, Smart Museum of Art, 2011.

Tronc, Hélène. 'Vie littéraire: la naissance du conte de fées littéraire', in Charles Perrault, *Contes de ma Mere l'Oye*, Paris, 2006.

John Trumbull: The Hand and Spirit of a Painter, exhib. cat., ed. Helen A. Cooper, New Haven, Conn., Yale University Art Gallery, 1982–83.

Turnbull, George. *A Treatise on Ancient Painting*, London, 1740.

Turner, Thomas. *The Diary of Thomas Turner, 1754–1765*, ed. David Vaisey, Oxford and New York, 1984.

Valentine, Helen. 'High Art: Reynolds and History Painting, 1780–1815', Royal Academy, London, 2009.

Vance, William L. *America's Rome. Volume 1: Classical Rome*, New Haven, Conn., and London, 1989.

Vasari, Giorgio. *Lives of the Painters, Sculptors and Architects* [1568], trans. Gaston du C. de Vere, London, 1996.

Venn, J.A. *Alumni Cantabrigiensis*, Nendeln, Liechtenstein, 1974–78.

Voltaire. *Letters on England* [1733], trans. Leonard Tancock, London, 2005.

——. *Nouvelles considérations sur l'histoire* [1744], in *Oeuvres historiques*, ed. René Pomeau, Paris, 1957.

——. *Philosophical Dictionary* [1764], trans. H.I. Woolf, Mineola, NY, 2010.

——. *Le Siècle de Louis XIV* [1751], in *Oeuvres historiques*, ed. René Pomeau, Paris, 1957.

von Erffa, Helmut, and Allen Staley. *The Paintings of Benjamin West*, New Haven, Conn., and London, 1986.

Wahrman, Dror. *The Making of the Modern Self: Identity and Culture in Eighteenth-Century England*, New Haven, Conn., and London, 2004.

Wainwright, Nicholas B. 'Conversations with Benjamin West', *Pennsylvania Magazine of History and Biography*, 102:1, January 1978.

Walpole, Horace. 'Horace Walpole's Journals of Visits to Country Seats, &c.', ed. Paget Toynbee, *Walpole Society*, 16, 1927–28.

——. *Memoirs of the Reign of King George the Third* [1766–72], London, 1894.

——. 'Notes by Horace Walpole, Fourth Earl of Orford, on the Exhibitions of the Society of Artists, 1760–1791', ed. Hugh Gatty, *Walpole Society*, 27, 1938–39.

——. *The Yale Edition of Horace Walpole's Correspondence*, ed. W.S. Lewis, New Haven, Conn., and London, 1937–83.

Warcupp, Edmund, trans. *Italy in Its Original Glory, Ruine and Revival*, London, 1660.

Ward, David C. *Charles Willson Peale: Art and Selfhood in the Early Republic*, Berkeley, Calif., and London, 2004.

Wark, Robert R. 'A Note on James Barry and Edmund Burke', *Journal of the Warburg and Courtauld Institutes*, 17:3/4, 1954.

——. *The Revolution in Eighteenth-Century Art: Ten British Pictures 1740–1840*, San Marino, 2001.

Warton, Joseph. *An Essay on the Writings and Genius of Pope*, London, 1756.

Washington, George. *The Writings of George Washington*, ed. Jared Sparks, vol. 9, Boston, 1835.

Waterhouse, Ellis. 'The British Contribution to the Neo-Classical Style in Painting', *Proceedings of the British Academy*, 40, 1954.

——. *Painting in Britain, 1530–1790*, New Haven, Conn., and London, 1994.

——. 'Painting in Rome in the Eighteenth Century', *Art Institute of Chicago Museum Studies*, 6, 1971.

Watkin, David. *The Architect King: George III and the Culture of the Enlightenment*, London, 2004.

Watson, George. 'Joshua Reynolds's Copy of Richardson', *Review of English Studies*, New Series, 42:167, August 1991.

Webb, Daniel. *An Inquiry into the Beauties of Painting; and into the Merits of the Most Celebrated Painters Ancient and Modern*, London, 1760.

Webb, Jeffrey B. 'James Logan', *American National Biography Online*, anb.org/articles/01/01-00529.html (accessed December 2014; subscription required).

Webster, J. Clarence. *Wolfe and the Artists: A Study of His Portraiture*, Toronto, 1930.

Webster, Mary. *Johan Zoffany, 1733–1810*, New Haven, Conn., and London, 2011.

Weigley, Russell F., ed. *Philadelphia: A 300 Year History*, New York, 1982.

Weinbrot, Howard D. 'Gray's Elegy: A Poem of Moral Choice and Resolution', *Studies in English Literature, 1500–1900*, 18:3, Summer 1978.

Wells, Robert V. 'The Population of England's Colonies in America: Old English or New Americans?', *Population Studies*, 46:1, March 1992.

Wendorf, Richard. 'Jonathan Richardson: The Painter as Biographer', *New Literary History*, 15:3, Spring 1984.

Benjamin West: General Wolfe and the Art of Empire, exhib. cat. by Carole McNamara, Ann Arbor, University of Michigan Art Museum, 2012–13.

Benjamin West and His American Students, exhib. cat. by Dorinda Evans, Washington, D.C., and Philadelphia, 1980–81.

Wexler, Victor G. 'David Hume's Discovery of a New Scene of Historical Thought', *Eighteenth-Century Studies*, 10:2, Winter 1976–77.

Whinney, Margaret. *Sculpture in Britain, 1530–1830*, rev. John Physick, London, 1988.

White, Hayden. *Tropics of Discourse: Essays in Cultural Criticism*, Baltimore and London, 1978.

White, Jerry. *London in the Eighteenth Century: A Great and Monstrous Thing*, London, 2012.

Whitley, William T. *Art in England, 1800–1820*, Cambridge, 1928.

——. *Artists and Their Friends in England, 1700–1799*, London and Boston, 1928.

Whitman, Alfred. *Valentine Green*, London, 1902.

Wiebenson, Dora. 'Subjects from Homer's Iliad in Neoclassical Art', *Art Bulletin*, 46:1, March 1964.

Wilcocks, Joseph. *Roman Conversations; or, A Short Description of the Antiquities of Rome*, London, 1797.

Williams, Julia Lloyd. *Gavin Hamilton, 1723–1798*, Edinburgh, 1994.

Wilson, Kathleen. *The Sense of the People: Politics, Culture and Imperialism in England, 1715–1785*, Cambridge, 1998.

Winckelmann, Johann Joachim. *History of the Art of Antiquity* [1764], trans. Henry Francis Mallgrave, Los Angeles, 2006.

Wind, Edgar. 'Penny, West, and the "Death of Wolfe"', *Journal of the Warburg and Courtauld Institutes*, 10, 1947.

——. 'The Revolution of History Painting', *Journal of the Warburg Institute*, 2:2, October 1938.

Winterer, Caroline. 'Model Empire, Lost City: Ancient Carthage and the Science of Politics in Revolutionary America', *William and Mary Quarterly*, Third Series, 67:1, January 2010.

Wolf II, Edwin. *The Book Culture of a Colonial American City: Philadelphia Books, Bookmen, and Booksellers*, Oxford, 1988.

Wood, Gordon S. *The Americanization of Benjamin Franklin*, New York, 2004.

——. *The Idea of America: Reflections on the Birth of the United States*, New York, 2011.

Woolf, D.R. 'A Feminine Past? Gender, Genre, and Historical Knowledge in England, 1500–1800', *American Historical Review*, 102:3, June 1997.

Wootton, David. 'David Hume: "The Historian"', in *The Cambridge Companion to Hume*, ed. David Fate Norton and Jacqueline Taylor, Cambridge, 2009.

Wright of Derby, exhib. cat. by Judy Egerton, London, Paris and New York, 1990.

Joseph Wright of Derby in Liverpool, exhib. cat. by Elizabeth E. Barker and Alex Kidson, New Haven, Conn., and Liverpool, 2007–08.

Young, Arthur. *Annals of Agriculture, and Other Useful Arts*, vol. 16, Bury St Edmunds, 1791.

Young, Ronnie. 'James Beattie and the Progress of Genius in the Aberdeen Enlightenment', *Journal for Eighteenth-Century Studies*, 36:2, June 2013.

Johan Zoffany RA: Society Observed, exhib. cat., ed. Martin Postle, New Haven, Conn., and London, 2011–12.

Zorgniotti, Adrian W. 'Benjamin West's Osteomyelitis: A Translation', *Bulletin of the New York Medical Academy*, 49:8, August 1973.

ACKNOWLEDGEMENTS

I begin with thanks to Joseph Rykwert, who first demonstrated – to me, at any rate – that it was possible to be modern in the eighteenth century. I am grateful to the staffs of the British Library, the London Library, the Society of Antiquaries of London, the Department of History of Art at the University of Cambridge, the Morgan Library and Museum, the Yale Center for British Art, the National Gallery of Canada, the New-York Historical Society, the British School at Rome, the Paul Mellon Centre for Studies in British Art, the Winterthur Library, the Boston Athenæum, the American Philosophical Society, the Library Company of Philadelphia, the Pennsylvania Academy of the Fine Arts, the Friends Historical Library at Swarthmore College, the New York Public Library, the Sterling Memorial Library at Yale University, and the Westminster City Archives. Particular thanks go to those who work at the Royal Academy of Arts Library and Archive, the Royal Collection Trust and the National Art Library at the Victoria and Albert Museum. The Philadelphia History Museum at the Atwater Kent made special arrangements to allow me to see West's *Death of Socrates* while it was in storage. The staff at Fordham University Library generously made available their manuscript autobiography of Benjamin West in both original and photocopied form. The staff and collections of the Historical Society of Pennsylvania are a remarkable and helpful resource for anyone studying eighteenth-century America.

Desmond Shawe-Taylor and Jonathan Marsden enabled me to have access to a number of important works by West in the Royal Collection and to the Laguerre murals at Marlborough House. Jane Rick cheerfully provided help – and a ladder – to view the Wests now hanging in Spencer House. No one knows more about West than Allen Staley, who was always most generous with his time on my many visits to New York. I was also privileged to discuss some of my ideas about West with Jules Prown. Karen O'Brien provided a most rigorous sounding board when it came to my thoughts on historiography. I am also grateful to Tim Clayton, Greg Sullivan, Frank Salmon, Eamon Duffy, Colin Jones, Michael Kauffmann, Richard Wendorf, Adam Waterton, Kim Sajet, Mark Pomeroy, Nick Savage, Jane Wellesley and Michael Fitzroy. I have benefited from discussions with Melanie Hall and was delighted to exchange ideas with American scholars at a seminar she organized at Boston University. It was also valuable to present to the annual conference of the British Society for Eighteenth-Century Studies and to discuss West with a number of 'straight historians' at seminars at Queens' College and Pembroke College, Cambridge. Jane Kamensky has kept me up to date with her work on John Singleton Copley. I am indebted to the Master and Fellows of Magdalene College, Cambridge, and especially to Duncan Robinson, who was an enthusiastic, assiduous and thoroughly supportive PhD supervisor. My assistant, Camilla Eadie, has been long-serving, long-suffering and close to omnicompetent: I thank her especially for her digital reconstruction of the West pictures in the King's Warm Room. My friend and agent Gillon Aitken has been a constant source of good advice and inspiration, and I would accomplish little without the acuity and dedication of my manager, Peter Schnabl. The team at Merrell Publishers – Hugh Merrell, Claire Chandler, Nicola Bailey and Nick Wheldon – have been exemplary in their patience, professionalism and attention to detail. I have doubtless ignored a great deal of the expert advice so generously given to me, and consequently any errors, obfuscations and inanities are most definitely my own.

PICTURE CREDITS

Abbot Hall Art Gallery, Kendal, Cumbria, UK / Bridgeman Images: fig. 7; akg-images / Erich Lessing: fig. 56; akg-images / Mondadori Portfolio / Sergio Anelli: fig. 31; Alte Pinakothek, Munich, Germany / Bridgeman Images: figs. 44, 46, 107; © 2015 The Art Institute of Chicago: fig. 14; Ashmolean Museum, University of Oxford, UK / Bridgeman Images: fig. 6; The Baltimore Museum of Art: Gift of Dr Morton K. Blaustein, Barbara B. Hirschhorn, and Elizabeth B. Roswell, in Memory of Jacob and Hilda K. Blaustein, BMA 1981.73. Photography by Mitro Hood: front jacket, fig. 1; Collection of the Bass Museum of Art, Gift of John and Johanna Bass: fig. 50; Gift of The Beaverbrook Foundation. The Beaverbrook Art Gallery. Fredericton, NB, Canada: fig. 61; Binghamton University Art Museum: fig. 11; © Riccardo Bonelli: fig. 30; © The Trustees of the British Museum: figs. 23, 53; Capitol Collection, Washington, USA / Bridgeman Images: fig. 99; © Corbis: fig. 20; De Agostini Picture Library / Bridgeman Images: fig. 45; © 2015 De Agostini Picture Library / Scala, Florence: fig. 92; Detroit Institute of Arts, USA / Gift of George H. Scripps / Bridgeman Images: fig. 111; Emiliovillegas24 CC BY-SA 3.0: fig. 91; © Ferens Art Gallery, Hull Museums, UK / Bridgeman Images: fig. 40; Courtesy Loyd Grossman: fig. 33; Hermitage, St Petersburg, Russia / Bridgeman Images: fig. 18; Library of Congress Prints and Photographs Division Washington, D.C.: fig. 10; © Estate of Roy Lichtenstein / DACS 2015. Photo © Tate, London 2015: fig. 117; CC BY-SA 4.0 Livioandronico2013: fig. 28; Louvre, Paris, France / Bridgeman Images: figs. 106, 109; The Metropolitan Museum of Art / Art Resource / Scala, Florence: p. 64, figs. 26, 27, 94; Layton Art Collection, Inc., at the Milwaukee Art Museum, L1964.6, Photographer: John R. Glembin: fig. 82; Minneapolis Institute of Arts, Minnesota, USA / The William Hood Dunwoody Fund / Bridgeman Images: fig. 68; Montclair Art Museum, New Jersey, USA / Bridgeman Images: fig. 80; Musée d'Orsay, Paris, France / Bridgeman Images: fig. 114; © Museum of Fine Arts, Boston, Massachusetts, USA / Gift of the artist's great-granddaughter / Bridgeman Images: fig. 41; Courtesy of the Council, National Army Museum, London: fig. 12; National Army Museum, London, UK / Bridgeman Images: figs. 59, 60; National Gallery, London, UK / Bridgeman Images: fig. 55; Courtesy National Gallery of Art, Washington: figs. 19, 79, 103; Courtesy National Gallery of Art, Washington, Corcoran Collection: fig. 113; Photo © National Gallery of Canada: figs. 65, 66; Photo © National Gallery of Canada. Transfer from the Canadian War Memorials, 1921 (Gift of the 2nd Duke of Westminster, England, 1918): back jacket, frontispiece, p. 10, figs. 2, 87; © National Portrait Gallery, London: figs. 62, 101; Photography by Marie-Lan Nguyen, public domain image: fig. 108; Palazzo Pitti, Florence, Italy / Bridgeman Images: fig. 48; Peale Museum, Philadelphia, Pennsylvania, USA / Bridgeman Images: fig. 110; Pennsylvania Academy of the Fine Arts, Philadelphia, USA / Bridgeman Images: fig. 95; Courtesy of the Philadelphia History Museum at the Atwater Kent, The Historical Society of Pennsylvania Collection: figs. 22, 32; © Philadelphia History Museum at the Atwater Kent / Courtesy of Historical Society of Pennsylvania Collection / Bridgeman Images: fig. 25; Philadelphia Museum of Art, Pennsylvania, USA / Bridgeman Images: fig. 112; © 2014. Photo Art Media / Heritage Images / Scala, Florence: fig. 102; © Succession Picasso / DACS, London 2015. Photo: Museo Nacional Centro de Arte Reina Sofía, Madrid, Spain / Bridgeman Images: fig. 115; © The Pierpont Morgan Library, New York. 1970.11:1. Purchased as the gift of Mrs Robert H. Charles: fig. 34; Prado, Madrid, Spain / Bridgeman Images: figs. 57, 64; private collection: fig. 24; private collection / Bridgeman Images: figs. 51, 81; Rijksmuseum, Amsterdam: fig. 58; © Royal Academy of Arts, London: figs. 35, 36, 37, 38, 39; © Royal Academy of Arts, London; Photographer: Prudence Cuming Associates Limited: fig. 54; © Royal Academy of Arts, London; Photographer: John Hammond: fig. 118; Royal Collection Trust © Her Majesty Queen Elizabeth II, 2015 / Bridgeman Images: p. 104, figs. 4, 5, 67, 73, 74, 75, 76, 77, 78, 83, 84, 85; Santa Maria della Concezione, Rome, Italy / Alinari / Bridgeman Images: fig. 105; © Scottish National Gallery: figs. 42, 43; National Numismatic Collection at the Smithsonian Institution, public domain image: fig. 93; The Snite Museum of Art, University of Notre Dame: fig. 13; By Courtesy of the Trustees of Sir John Soane's

Museum. Photo: Ardon Bar-Hama: fig. 70; Städtische Kunsthalle, Mannheim, Germany / Bridgeman Images: fig. 116; Stratford-upon-Avon Town Council: fig. 15; © Tate, London 2015: fig. 86; © Tate 2015, on loan to the National Portrait Gallery, London: fig. 100; Utah Museum of Fine Arts. Purchased with funds from the Marriner S. Eccles Foundation for the Marriner S. Eccles Collection of Masterworks, from the Permanent Collection of the Utah Museum of Fine Arts: fig. 49; Vatican Museums and Galleries, Vatican City / Bridgeman Images: fig. 90; © Victoria and Albert Museum, London: figs. 47, 63; Victoria and Albert Museum, London, UK / Bridgeman Images: fig. 104; Wellcome Library, London. CC BY 4.0: fig. 89; © Dean and Chapter of Westminster: figs. 8, 69, 71, 72; White Images / Scala, Florence: fig. 17; Courtesy, Winterthur Museum, Gift of Henry Francis du Pont, 1957.856. Photo: Herb Crossan: p. 172, fig. 96; Yale Center for British Art, Paul Mellon Collection: pp. 42, 134, figs. 3, 16, 21, 29, 52, 88; Yale University Art Gallery: figs. 9, 97, 98

The publisher has made every effort to trace and contact copyright holders of the illustrations reproduced in this book; it shall be happy to correct in subsequent editions any errors or omissions that are brought to its attention.

INDEX

Page numbers in *italic* refer to the illustrations.

H

X

Y

Z

First published 2015 by Merrell Publishers,
London and New York

Merrell Publishers Limited
70 Cowcross Street
London EC1M 6EJ

merrellpublishers.com

British Library Cataloguing in Publication Data.
A catalogue record for this book is available from the British Library.

ISBN 978-1-8589-4641-2

Produced by Merrell Publishers Limited
Designed by Nicola Bailey
Project-managed by Claire Chandler
Picture research by Nick Wheldon
Indexed by Hilary Bird

Printed and bound in China

FRONTISPIECE: Detail of Benjamin West, *The Death of General Wolfe*, 1770 (see fig. 2)

JACKET, FRONT: Detail of Benjamin West, *Self-Portrait*, 1770–76 (see fig. 1)

JACKET, BACK: Benjamin West, *The Death of General Wolfe*, 1770 (see fig. 2)